Fodor's

BEST WEEKEND
ROAD TRIPS

D0951840

Welcome to the Road

Americans didn't invent the road trip—that honor goes to Germany's adventurous Bertha Benz, whose husband patented the first gas-powered carriage in 1886—but they did perfect it. They opened the first gas station (in Pittsburgh in 1905), paved the first modern highway (in New York in 1911), and pioneered a new kind of lodging called the "motor hotel" (in California's San Luis Obispo in 1925). Although today you might be searching for different amenities, such as a place to plug in your car, the lure of the open road still draws tens of millions of travelers every year.

TOP REASONS TO GO

★ **Iconic Drives:** From the Blue Ridge Parkway to the Pacific Coast Highway.

★ **Roadside Attractions:** The perfect places to stretch your legs along the way.

★ **Favorites Eats:** Eat at foodie destinations and diners only the locals know about.

★ **Getting There:** Take the fastest route or meander along the road less traveled.

★ **Where to Sleep:** Discover the best national park lodges or beachfront getaways.

★ **Shop Therapy:** Sample local delicacies and uncover one-of-a-kind artworks.

Weekend Getaways

Contents

MAPS

Chapter 1

WEST COAST

WELCOME TO
WEST COAST

TOP REASONS
TO GO

★ **Wide Open Spaces:**
Nature lovers flock
to the snow-capped
mountains of Olympic
National Park.

★ **Vast Vineyards:** Don't
miss the wonderful
wines of Walla Walla
and the Yakima Valley.

★ **Hit the Trail:** Mount
Rainier's 260 miles of
hiking trails lead through
old-growth forests.

★ **Island Hopping:** Ferries
shuttle you across Puget
Sound to the gorgeous
San Juan Islands.

★ **Leavenworth:** It's
always Oktoberfest in
this charming Bavarian-
themed village.

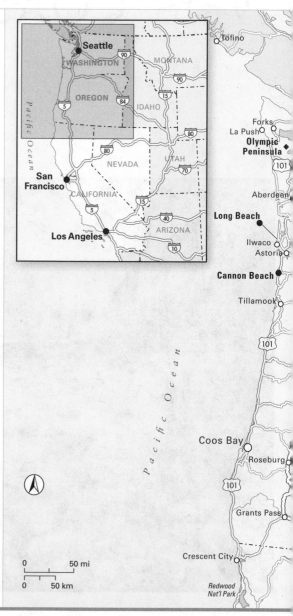

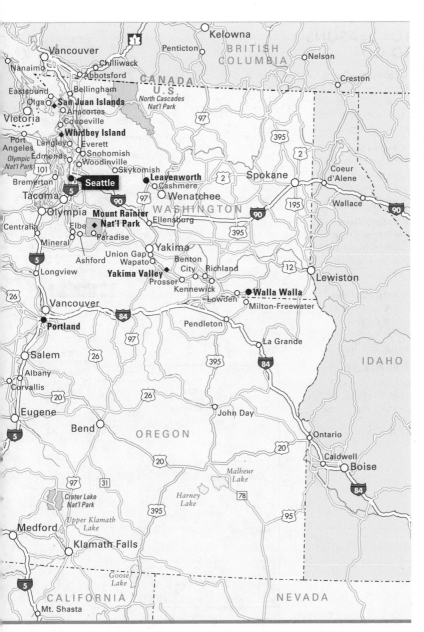

WELCOME TO WEST COAST

TOP REASONS TO GO

★ **Land of the Giants:** There are many places, some off the beaten path, to experience towering redwoods.

★ **Raise a Glass:** Napa and Sonoma are the most famous, but this region is full of wonderful wine routes.

★ **Endless Views:** The Pacific Coast Highway may be the country's most beautiful coastal drive.

★ **Nature Up Close:** The national parks are legendary: Yosemite, Sequioia, and Joshua Tree.

★ **Hit the Beach:** Here you have your pick, from wide swaths of sand to rocky shorelines.

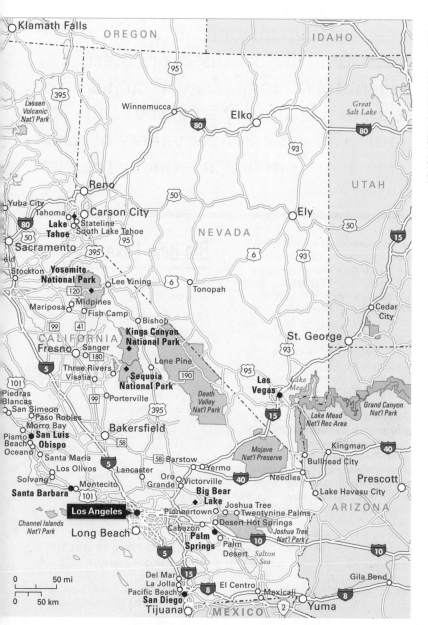

Klamath Falls   OREGON   IDAHO

95

Lassen
Volcanic
Nat'l Park

395

Winnemucca   Elko   80

80   Great
Salt Lake   80

93

Reno   50

Yuba City   Carson City   UTAH
Tahoma   Stateline   Ely
Lake   South Lake Tahoe   NEVADA
Tahoe   95

50   80   95   50   15

Sacramento   50
ald
Stockton   395
Yosemite
National Park   Lee Vining   6   Tonopah   93
120   93

Mariposa   Midpines   Cedar
Fish Camp   City
99   41   Bishop
CALIFORNIA   Kings Canyon
National Park   St. George
Fresno   Sanger   93
180   Lone Pine
Three Rivers   95   Las
Visalia   190   Vegas   Lake
101   Sequoia   Mead
5   National Park   Grand Canyon
99   Porterville   Death   Nat'l Park
Piedras   Valley   Lake Mead
Blancas   395   Nat'l Park   Nat'l Rec Area
San Simeon
Paso Robles   Bakersfield   Kingman   40
Morro Bay   58
Pismo   San Luis   Mojave
Beach   Obispo   Nat'l Preserve   Bullhead City
Oceano   58   Barstow
Santa Maria   Yermo   Needles   Prescott
Los Olivos   5   Lancaster   Oro   Victorville   40
Solvang   Montecito   Grande   Big Bear   Lake Havasu City
Santa Barbara   101   Lake   Joshua Tree   ARIZONA
Los Angeles   Pioneertown   Twentynine Palms
Channel Islands   Desert Hot Springs   Joshua Tree
Nat'l Park   Long Beach   Cabazon   Nat'l Park
5   Palm   Palm   10
Springs   Desert   Salton   10
Del Mar   15   Sea   Gila Bend
La Jolla   El Centro
Pacific Beach   8   8
San Diego   Mexicali   Yuma
Tijuana   MEXICO   2

0   50 mi
0   50 km

No matter what you're looking for—drives along gently curving coastlines overlooking an endless expanse of ocean, treks through misty forests where the trees stand like sentinels, or desert adventures among rocky monoliths that seem to rise directly from the sand—it's hard to imagine a wider variety of road trips than from the cities along the West Coast.

San Francisco comes to mind immediately when you think of road trips, since the popular Napa and Sonoma wine regions are so close at hand (as are the less traveled but equally as impressive vineyards around Mendocino), but it's also the starting point for the glittering waters of Lake Tahoe, the dramatic beaches around Monterey Bay, and natural wonders like Yosemite National Park. You can reach the towering redwoods of Sequoia National Park from either San Francisco or **Los Angeles,** but the latter city is your best starting point for unforgettable journeys into the desert (Palm Springs, gateway to the stunning Joshua Tree National Park) and along the coast (Santa Monica, Santa Barbara, and San Luis Obispo). **Seattle** combines the best of these cities with trips to its own vineyard-covered valleys and meandering shorelines, but adds one-of-a-kind destinations like spectacular Mount Rainier. It's a great starting point for outdoors lovers, as it's an easy drive from the San Juan Islands and the Olympic Peninsula, home to Olympia National Park.

Big Bear Lake, CA

97 miles (approx. 2 hours) from Los Angeles.

While Los Angeles is incredibly appealing with its sunny weather, popular beaches, and eclectic neighborhoods, it's only a matter of time before nature comes calling. Thankfully, Big Bear Lake is just a hop, skip, and jump away from the City of Angels and it's a year-round kind of destination. Whether you're picnicking on a boat with friends, ingesting that crisp mountain air on an early-morning hike, or cozying up in a lodge with hot chocolate for a few days, here's a weekend itinerary for Big Bear Lake we think you might enjoy quite a bit.

Planning

GETTING THERE AND BACK
From Los Angeles, take CA 210 to CA 330 and CA 18. If you're traveling in the winter months, you'll need a four-wheel vehicle or tire chains for the roads around

Big Bear Lake. The number of scenic stops on The Rim of the World (CA 18) may make your head spin. Feel free to pull over, take a selfie, and drink in the views.

PIT STOPS

If you're in need of a quick bite along the way, head to the **First Original McDonald's Museum,** just off CA 210 in San Bernardino. A stop here is also helpful as you'll find a few Arco stations nearby—you're just over halfway to Big Bear, so why not gas up?

WHEN TO GO

While there's never a bad time to enjoy Big Bear Lake, plan your trip between early July and Labor Day for summer activities or mid-December to mid-February, when ski season (and other winter sports) is in full swing.

WHERE TO STAY

The quaint **Hillcrest Lodge** is convenient and utterly charming. Another family-owned option is the **Grey Squirrel Resort,** where 19 rustic cabins make for a beguiling stay. The lakefront **Lagonita Lodge** offers a bevy of on-site amenities, including a popular sundeck.

Day 1

If you're leaving Los Angeles at 10 am on Friday morning, expect to arrive at Big Bear Lake around noon. Stop for a hearty lunch at the old-fashioned **Grind and Grill Café** or the offbeat mom-and-pop eatery **Grizzly Manor.** There's no shortage of shops you can pop into, including **Artisans Etc, The Bath Workshop,** and **Gems of the West.** Depending on the month, include **A Christmas Store 'N' More** on that list. If you're a nature lover, don't miss **Chirp Nature Center** or **Bear Essentials.**

Cool off with a libation at **Big Bear Lake Brewing Company** (which has a few notable cocktails in addition to a wide variety of brews). If you choose not to stay for dinner, get dolled up and head to

The Pines Lakefront for excellent cuisine, fine wines, and sweeping views of the marina.

Day 2

Start your morning with a cup of coffee at the relaxed **Stillwells Restaurant** or at the diner-style **Alpine Country Coffee Shop.** Both open early, which means in the summer months you can beat the crowds to Alpine Hills or the Alpine Pedal Path, two of the best options for hikers in the area. In the winter months, skiers and snowboarders (beginner, or otherwise) should check out **Big Bear Mountain Resort.** Book ahead and you can save hundreds on rentals, lessons, and season passes. For lunch, the resort has a variety of dining options—including **Clubhouse Grill** and **Skyline Taphouse**—but if you're looking to venture out, cozy **Nottinghams Restaurant** offers steaks, seafood, and more.

After you've wrapped up lunch, head to **Big Bear Marina**—if the weather's warm enough—and hire a boat to catch some rays and hang out on for a couple of hours. Alternately, the **Bowling Barn** (complete with arcade games) is fun for the whole family.

It's been a long day, and you deserve a nice meal. **Peppercorn Grille's** offerings—we're talking pastas, chicken, and lamb—will warm your tummy, while its elegant atmosphere will make you feel like you're truly treating yourself. Another treat you may want to consider is the family-owned **Sweet Basil Bistro,** whose Italian dishes are a favorite in the local community.

Day 3

For a hearty breakfast, put your trust in **Mountain Munchies,** which has been serving customers since 1980—we're talking waffles, biscuits and gravy, and other

Accessible all year, California's Big Bear Lake is within easy reach of Los Angeles.

favorites. Another reliable eatery to start your third day off right is **BLT's Restaurant,** which has quite a few specialty omelets on the menu. Today you'll be barrelling down bobsledding tracks at the **Alpine Slide at Magic Mountain,** which also has ziplining and other diversions throughout the warmer months. In the winter, this destination is famous for its snow tubing hill. Lunch is brought to you by way of **Tropicali,** a Hawaiian eatery whose poke bowls and sushi are a hit with customers. **Teddy Bear**—established in 1944—is another solid lunchtime pick whose family-style dining includes homemade mashed potatoes and chicken pot pie. If you have the time, try to fit in a stop at the **Big Bear Alpine Zoo,** home to everything from owls and eagles to foxes and wolves.

Before your trip back, stop at the **Captain's Anchorage**—a lodgelike steak house—or, the casual (but equally delicious) **Maggio's Pizza.**

Recommendations

Sights

Alpine Slide at Magic Mountain. ✉ *800 Wildrose La., Big Bear Lake, CA* ☏ *909/866–4626* ⊕ *www.alpineslidebigbear.com* 🔖 *$7.*

Big Bear Alpine Zoo. ✉ *43285 Goldmine Dr., Big Bear Lake, CA* ☏ *909/584–1299* ⊕ *www.bigbearzoo.org* 🔖 *$12.*

Big Bear Marina. ✉ *500 Paine Ct., Big Bear Lake, CA* ☏ *909/866–3218* ⊕ *www.bigbearmarina.com* 🔖 *$15.*

Big Bear Mountain Resort. ✉ *880 Summit Blvd., Big Bear Lake, CA* ☏ *844/462–2327* ⊕ *www.bigbearmountainresort.com* 🔖 *Lift ticket from $20.*

Bowling Barn. ✉ *40625 Big Bear Blvd., Big Bear Lake, CA* ☏ *909/878–2695* ⊕ *www.bowlingbarn.com* 🔖 *$13.*

ⓦ Restaurants

BLT's Restaurant. $ *Average main: $13* ✉ *41799 Big Bear Blvd., Big Bear Lake, CA* ☎ *909/866–6659* ⊕ *www.bltsrestaurant.com.*

Captain's Anchorage. $ *Average main: $28* ✉ *42148 Moonridge Way, Big Bear Lake, CA* ☎ *909/866–3997* ⊕ *www.captainsanchorage.com.*

Clubhouse Grill. $ *Average main: $12* ✉ *43102 Goldmine Dr., Big Bear Lake, CA* ☎ *909/939–7161* ⊕ *www.bigbearmountainresort.com*

First Original McDonald's Museum. $ *Average main: $5* ✉ *1398 N.E. St., San Bernardino, CA* ☎ *909/885–6324* ⊗ *Closed Mon.*

Grind and Grill Café. $ *Average main: $14* ✉ *42011 Big Bear Blvd., Big Bear Lake, CA* ☎ *909/866–5219* ⊕ *www.grindandgrill.com.*

Grizzly Manor. $ *Average main: $12* ✉ *41268 Big Bear Blvd., Big Bear City, CA* ☎ *909/866–6226* ⊕ *www.grizzlymanorcafe.com.*

Maggio's Pizza. $ *Average main: $26* ✉ *42160 Big Bear Blvd,.Big Bear Lake, CA* ☎ *909/866–8815* ⊕ *www.maggiospizza.com.*

Mountain Munchies. $ *Average main: $11* ✉ *42171 Big Bear Blvd., Big Bear Lake, CA* ☎ *909/866–7767* ⊕ *www.mtmunchies.com.*

Nottinghams Restaurant. $ *Average main: $26* ✉ *40797 Big Bear Blvd., Big Bear Lake, CA* ☎ *909/866–4644* ⊕ *www.nottinghamstavern.com.*

Peppercorn Grille. $ *Average main: $29* ✉ *553 Pine Knot Ave., Big Bear Lake, CA* ☎ *909/866–5405* ⊕ *www.peppercorngrille.com.*

The Pines Lakefront. $ *Average main: $25* ✉ *350 Alden Rd., Big Bear Lake, CA* ☎ *909/866–5400* ⊕ *www.thepineslakefront.com* ⊗ *Closed Mon. and Tues.*

Skyline Taphouse. $ *Average main: $10* ✉ *880 Summit Blvd., Big Bear Lake, CA* ☎ *909/866–5766* ⊕ *www.bigbearmountainresort.com.*

Stillwells Restaurant. $ *Average main: $15* ✉ *40650 Village Dr., Big Bear Lake, CA* ☎ *909/866–3121* ⊕ *www.stillwellsrestaurant.com.*

Sweet Basil Bistro. $ *Average main: $15* ✉ *40629 Big Bear Blvd., Big Bear Lake, CA* ☎ *909/866–9212* ⊕ *www.sweetbasilbistro.net* ⊗ *Closed Mon. and Tues.*

Teddy Bear. $ *Average main: $14* ✉ *Pine Knot Blvd., Big Bear Lake, CA* ☎ *909/866–5415* ⊕ *www.teddybearrestaurant.com.*

Tropicali. $ *Average main: $13* ✉ *40616 Village Dr., Big Bear Lake, CA* ☎ *909/878–0499* ⊕ *www.osotropicali.com* ⊗ *Closed Tues. and Wed.*

🛏 Hotels

Grey Squirrel Resort. $ *Rooms from: $144* ✉ *39372 Big Bear Blvd., Big Bear Lake, CA* ☎ *800/381–5569* ⊕ *www.greysquirrel.com* ⦿ *No meals.*

Hillcrest Lodge. $ *Rooms from: $99* ✉ *40241 Big Bear Blvd., Big Bear Lake, CA* ☎ *909/866–7330* ⊕ *www.hillcrestlodge.com* ⦿ *No meals.*

Lagonita Lodge. $ *Rooms from: $139* ✉ *183 Lagunita Ln., Big Bear Lake, CA* ☎ *909/866–6531* ⊕ *www.lagonitalodge.com* ⦿ *No meals.*

🍸 Nightlife

Big Bear Lake Brewing Company. ✉ *40827 Stone Rd., Big Bear Lake, CA* ☎ *909/878–0283* ⊕ *www.bblbc.com.*

🛍 Shopping

Artisans, Etc. ✉ *646 Pine Knot Ave., Big Bear Lake, CA* ☎ *909/878–0088* ⊕ *www. artisansetc.com.*

The Bath Workshop. ✉ *40729 Village Dr., Big Bear Lake, CA* ☎ *909/366–0143* ⊕ *www.thebathworkshop.com.*

Bear Essentials. ✉ *663 Pine Knot Ave., Big Bear Lake, CA* ☎ *909/866–3957.*

Chirp Nature Center. ✉ *40850 Village Dr., Big Bear Lake, CA* ☎ *888/412–4477* ⊕ *www.chirpforbirds.com.*

A Christmas Store 'N' More. ✉ *620 Pine Knot Ave., Big Bear Lake, CA* ☎ *909/878–0114.*

Gems of the West. ✉ *40847 Big Bear Blvd., Big Bear Lake, CA* ☎ *909/878–0415* ⊕ *www.gemsofthewest.co.*

Humboldt County, CA

270 miles (approx 5 hours) from San Francisco.

Humboldt County pays glorious tribute to the coastal redwoods, where forests of these towering giants, thousands of years old and the earth's tallest trees, create mystical awe. Consider this fact: these trees are so tall, some higher than 300 feet, that there are creatures at the top—flying squirrels and marbled murrelets—that never touch the ground. The short of it is, you will be blown away.

This tucked-away corner in northern California, near the Oregon border, also harbors spirited Victorian villages (built from the redwood forests), breweries, stunning coastline, wild beaches, and the state's freshest oysters. Come here to hike, admire architecture, kayak, backpack, bird-watch, and remember what it's like to be in solitude with nature. Eureka provides the perfect base, within easy reach of the redwood kingdom and the untamed Lost Coast, with plenty of enchanting surprises along the way.

Planning

GETTING THERE AND BACK

Eureka is 270 miles north of San Francisco via U.S. 101, about a five-hour drive. From there, U.S. 101 continues farther north through the national and state parks. There's no quick way to get here, alas, but that's the beauty of it.

WHEN TO GO

Summer is the most popular time to visit the redwood forests, when the main roads may become clogged with cars; coastal fog may hinder the views (and driving visibility). Spring is beautiful with blooming rhododendrons, while fall brings the changing colors of trees. Winter is cool, but crowd free. Expect the possibility of heavy rains October through April.

WHERE TO STAY

The North Coast has all kinds of fun, funky accommodations, many housed in historic Victorians. There aren't tons of budget accommodations, but campers have the luck of sleeping beneath lofty redwoods at both national and state parks. For everyone else, the best hub is Eureka, where **Carter House Inns** offers rooms in a selection of Victorian houses on the same street, just blocks from Humboldt Bay. Trinity is also a favorite place to stay, where the charming **Trinidad Bay Bed & Breakfast Hotel** has expansive ocean views.

Day 1

On the first day, make the 5½-hour drive to Eureka, taking your time to follow the slow, sinuous curves of U.S. 101 (well, you don't really have a choice!).

Near Weott you'll hit the **Avenue of the Giants,** a 31-mile stretch of historic U.S. 101 (parallel to the modern highway)

Misty groves of the world's tallest trees are on display at Redwood National Park and State Parks.

that offers an excellent spot to stretch your legs beneath giant redwoods. Pick up picnic supplies in a number of sleepy towns along the way, including Pepperwood, Redcrest, Myers Flat, and Miranda (or, if you want premade, **Avenue Café** in Miranda has soups, salads, sandwiches, and pasta); take a hike along its multitude of trails; or simply stare up at these magnificent sky-high trees. Interesting stops include the Dyerville Giant, which toppled to the ground and can be seen along a trail at Founders Grove; Rockefeller Forest, a 10,000-acre stand of virgin redwoods; and the Shrine Drive-Thru Tree.

Sitting on stunning Humboldt Bay, Eureka's historic downtown offers ornate 19th-century Victorian houses filled with boutiques, restaurants, and art galleries (the town has more artists per capita than anywhere else in the state). Spend the afternoon soaking in the North Coast vibe, perhaps taking a self-guided architectural tour of the lacy buildings or strolling the 6-mile pedestrian trail along

the waterfront. You could also get out on the water, via kayak, canoe, sail—or take the **Humboldt Bay Oyster Tour,** a boat tour to a nearby oyster farm that includes an oyster tasting.

In the late afternoon, pick up a bottle of local Zin in one of the town's shops and take a sunset stroll along Samoa Beach, a seemingly infinite stretch on Samoa Peninsula, just across the bridge over the bay from Eureka. After, a fresh seafood dinner is in order—with the best to be found at **Sea Grill,** housed in a lovely Victorian in old town. Get ready for amazingly fresh, simply prepared wild Alaskan halibut, wild king salmon, and Dungeness crab. If you happen to not like fish, that's okay—there are plenty of land-based dishes as well. Do not leave without ordering a slice of Key lime pie.

Day 2

Start off today in the Victorian town of Arcata, about 8 miles north of Eureka, who comes by its nickname "Sixties by the Sea" honestly. Just check out some of the shop names: **Moonrise Herbs** and **Isis Osiris Healing Arts,** for starters. In the quaint downtown, filled with Victorian houses, you'll find organic restaurants (**Café Brio,** with its outdoor patio overlooking historic Arcata Plaza, is great for breakfast), ecologically-oriented craft shops, and art galleries. Grab a self-guided walking or driving tour map at the Arcata Chamber of Commerce or stretch your legs at **Arcata Marsh & Wildlife Sanctuary** among flocks of water birds.

Continue north about 40 miles to **Redwood National Park and State Parks,** a magical kingdom of age-old trees, up to 3,000 years old. "Ambassadors from another time," is how John Steinbeck described them in *Travels with Charley*. Once these behemoths flourished across the Northern Hemisphere, until climate changes over time reduced the lush, wet growing conditions to a narrow strip running from southern Oregon to central California. After logging started in the 1800s, they would have disappeared completely if not for the forward-thinking intervention of conservationists. Today, even the most jaded urbanite will be awed by the unworldly beauty of these gigantic living beings—and there's no place on earth where you will find more.

U.S. 101 bisects this composite of parks (comprising Redwood National Park and **Prairie Creek Redwoods State Park, Del Norte Coast Redwoods State Park,** and **Jedediah Smith Redwoods State Park**), making it easy to zoom right through. But take your time to explore misty canyons, sunbeam-filtered groves, and fern-covered glades. Start off at the Kuchel Visitor Center to gather information. Then find Lady Bird Johnson Grove, which has a sublime 2-mile hiking loop. Farther north, in Prairie Creek Redwoods State Park, the short hike up Fern Canyon, a prehistoric grove in Prairie Creek Redwoods, offers an excellent chance to spot resident Roosevelt elk foraging in

the meadows. And Coastal Drive Loop, a 9-mile, partially unpaved out and back, takes you through a remote gathering of the majestic trees, with views of the Klamath River and the glistening Pacific tossed in for good measure.

As you backtrack on U.S. 101, Trinidad is the perfect place to wind down over dinner. This tiny fishing hamlet perched atop dramatic seaside bluffs offers stunning beaches, a fun little harbor complete with fishing pier, and scenic trails in the heart of the redwoods. It is the epicenter of the North Coast's salmon and Dungeness crab—meaning, you know what's for dinner. Trinidad Head is a great sunset spot, then check out **Trinidad Bay Eatery and Gallery** for locally caught seafood. The clam chowder is especially memorable.

Day 3

Before heading back home to San Francisco, strike out for the Lost Coast, a fitting name for this fog-swathed, wildly rugged, little-traveled bulge of land sticking out into the Pacific between Shelter Cove in the south and Ferndale in the north. First stop: charming Ferndale, often lauded as California's most quintessential Victorian village. Tucked away near the banks of the Eel River surrounding dairy lands, this little fairytale hamlet feels frozen in time, and yet it's alive with artists (check out Artisan Alley), old-fashioned mercantiles, and antique and specialty shops. Find breakfast at **Poppa Joe's,** a diner with 19th-century ambiance serving up generous servings of eggs, bacon, hash browns—be sure to ask about the daily special.

Then head out on Mattole Road for the Lost Coast, plunging into a pristine realm of forests and ranchlands. You'll pass through tiny farming towns, admire striking sweeps of ocean, take in sky-high mountain peaks, and meander through stands of old-growth redwoods. The road touches the ocean at Cape Mendocino, following the shore for 6 miles. Stop at striking **Black Sands Beach** near Shelter Cove. It's too rough for swimming, but there's good beachcombing here, plus plenty of tide pools to peek into. If you're hungry, Shelter Cove has a couple restaurants, including **Delgada Pizza and Bakery.** West of Petrolia, named for the oil wells pumping oil here, take a 5-mile detour on Lighthouse Road to the shore, where a 3.5-mile trail meanders to an old lighthouse. From here, the road heads back to U.S. 101 through Humboldt Redwoods State Park. The entire 65-mile drive should take about four hours—or longer, depending on how much you linger. Remember, you have a four-hour drive back to San Francisco.

Recommendations

Sights

Arcata Marsh & Wildlife Sanctuary. ✉ *569 S G St., Arcata, CA* ☎ *707/826–2359* 🌐 *www.arcatamarshfriends.org* 🎟 *Free.*

Avenue of the Giants. ✉ *7119 Ave. of the Giants, Weott, CA* ☎ *707/946–2263* 🌐 *www.parks.ca.gov* 🎟 *Free.*

Black Sands Beach. ✉ *856 Beach Rd., Whitethorn, CA* ☎ *707/986–5400* 🌐 *www.blm.gov* 🎟 *Free.*

Del Norte Coast Redwoods State Park. ✉ *Rte. 101, Crescent City, CA* ☎ *707/464–6101* 🌐 *www.parks.ca.gov* 🎟 *Free.*

Jedediah Smith Redwoods State Park. ✉ *1440 Hwy. 199, Crescent City, CA* ☎ *707/465–7335* 🌐 *www.parks.ca.gov* 🎟 *Free.*

Prairie Creek Redwoods State Park. ✉ *Prairie Creek Rd., Orick, CA* ☎ *707/488–2039* 🌐 *www.parks.ca.gov* 🎟 *Free.*

Redwood National and State Parks. ✉ *Crescent City Information Center, 1111 2nd St., Crescent City, CA* ☎ *707/464–6101* 🌐 *www.nps.gov* 🎟 *Free.*

Samoa Beach. ✉ *New Navy Base Rd., Samoa, CA* ☎ *No phone* 🌐 *www.californiabeaches.com* 🎟 *Free.*

Restaurants

Avenue Café. [$] *Average main: $11* ✉ *6743 Ave. of the Giants, Miranda, CA* ☎ *707/943–9945* 🌐 *www.avenuecafe.biz.*

Café Brio. [$] *Average main: $15* ✉ *791 G St., Arcata, CA* ☎ *707/822–5922* 🌐 *www.cafebrioarcata.com.*

Delgada Pizza and Bakery. [$] *Average main: $16* ✉ *205 Wave Dr., Shelter Cove, Ca* ☎ *707/986–7672* 🌐 *www.innofthelostcoast.com.*

Poppa Joe's. [$] *Average main: $10* ✉ *409 Main St., Ferndale, CA* ☎ *707/786–4180.*

Sea Grill. [$] *Average main: $25* ✉ *316 E St., Eureka, CA* ☎ *707/443–7187* 🌐 *www.seagrilleureka.com.*

Trinidad Bay Eatery and Gallery. [$] *Average main: $16* ✉ *607 Parker St., Trinidad, CA* ☎ *707/677–3777* 🌐 *www.trinidadeatery.com.*

Hotels

Carter House Inns. [$] *Rooms from: $195* ✉ *301 L St., Eureka, CA* ☎ *800/404–1390* 🌐 *www.carterhouse.com* 🍴 *Free breakfast.*

Trinidad Bay Bed & Breakfast Hotel. [$] *Rooms from: $325* ✉ *560 Edwards St., Trinidad, CA* ☎ *707/677–0840* 🌐 *www.trinidadbaybnb.com* 🍴 *Free breakfast.*

Shopping

Isis Osiris Healing Arts. ✉ *44 Sunnybrae Centre, Arcata, CA* ☎ *707/825–8300* 🌐 *www.wholisticheartbeat.com.*

Moonrise Herbs. ✉ *826 G St., Arcata, CA* ☎ *707/822–5296* 🌐 *www.moonriseherbs.com.*

🏃 Activities

Humboldt Bay Oyster Tour. ✉ 205 G St., Eureka, CA ☎ 707/836–3168 ⊕ www. humboldtbayoystertours.com ✉ $75 per person.

Lake Tahoe, CA and NV

188 miles (3½ to 4 hours) from San Francisco.

With more than 70 miles of shoreline, Lake Tahoe is the largest alpine lake in North America and one of the world's deepest and clearest bodies of water. Summertime brings watery fun like scuba trails and stand-up paddleboarding, while winter sees powder hounds flock to the area's more than 20 ski resorts.

Straddling two states, the region is so big that Tahoe North and Tahoe South are considered two separate destinations, each with a handful of communities. Tahoe South is larger and has more of the traditional tourism infrastructure and entertainment options, while Tahoe North is more of a sleepy lake getaway. Whichever portion you choose to visit, rest assured knowing there's never a wrong place to go or a bad time to visit this magical mountain oasis.

Planning

GETTING THERE AND BACK

A three-and-a-half- to four-hour drive from San Francisco, the route is an easy and straightforward jaunt on I–80 east. If you have time and want to avoid the freeway, there are several more scenic routes out of town. U.S. 50 is the prettiest drive and takes you through a handful of mountain passes but essentially doubles your driving time.

If you'd rather bypass traffic completely, in winter, Tahoe Ski Trips runs the Bay Area Ski Bus, which is an easy way to get to the slopes. Amtrak's Zephyr line can also get you close with a stop in Truckee. From there, you can connect to the local bus system or Uber to town.

PIT STOPS

One fun stop along the way is the **Jelly Belly Factory** in Fairfield. You can tour (self-guided or guided) the sweet emporium and pick up some snacks for the road.

WHEN TO GO

Tahoe doesn't have an off-season, but depending on your interests it may appeal to you at different times of year. Ski season runs from November to April, while June to August sees major summer crowds. If you're looking to save some money and avoid the throngs of tourists, consider spring of fall, which are equally lovely by the lake.

WHERE TO STAY

For serenity in the Sierras, the lakefront **Edgewood Tahoe Resort** is the only five-star property in the area. For a more approachable escape, check out **Hotel Azure,** which is also right on the shore and just minutes from Heavenly Resort.

Day 1

If you leave in the morning, you should arrive by lunchtime, just in time to fuel up and make the most of your day. Settle in at the **Oyster Bar** in the Hard Rock Hotel, Lake Tahoe's only raw bar. Hearty chowders, succulent oysters, and steamed mussels promise some of the best slurpable seafood in town. If you're feeling lucky, try your hand at the slots or leave a few bucks on the table before heading out to take in the views of **Emerald Bay State Park.**

Both a National Natural Landmark and one of California's only protected underwater parks, Emerald Bay is Tahoe's crown jewel, with the overlook at Inspiration Point one of the area's most coveted photo ops. For a better view, the

The largest alpine lake in North America, glittering Lake Tahoe extends across two different states.

4½-mile Rubicon Trail provides a stunning vantage point of the rocky outcrops and sandy coves.

When you're ready to hit the town, the lakefront **Riva Grill** has one of the best happy hours around. Their famous Woodies (super-strong frozen cocktails) will transport you to island time in no time. Once you've watched the boats roll in, get a closer look on a sunset dinner cruise at **Zephyr Cove Resort.** You'll enjoy dinner and dancing under the stars as you cruise the lake on an old-fashioned paddle wheeler.

Day 2

Carb up at **Driftwood Cafe** before the morning's festivities. A town favorite for the fluffy pancake towers and omelet creations, the cozy café has been around for more than 50 years.

Clear kayaks make for unbelievable views under the water and amazing photo ops from above. You can rent them by the

hour or take a guided tour of the shore to scout wildlife and marine life. **Clearly Tahoe** also has LED-illuminated night tours for a unique after-dark adventure. If you'd prefer to embark on your own paddling excursion, kayak to the ruins of the tea house on **Fannette Island** near **Vikingsholm Castle.** A Scandinavian palace hidden in Emerald Bay State Park; it was one of the first summer homes built in Lake Tahoe. The island is only accessible by boat.

Head back to town to grab lunch at **Sprouts Café.** With healthy, mostly organic sandwiches, salads, juices, and smoothies, it's the perfect place to refuel. Once you've dried off, it's time to explore the area on two feet—or four hooves. Horseback riding is a leisurely way to get another view of the lake from the back of a saddle on a guided trail ride. In winter, you can try skiing or snowboarding, snowshoeing, snowmobiling, or taking a scenic sleigh ride.

After an afternoon of adventure, **Azul Latin Kitchen** boasts some of the tastiest

Mexican food in town. Splurge on nachos, loaded potato wedges, and Thai curry and sweet potato tacos washed down with a flight of tequila or frozen margarita.

Tahoe is as famous for its nightlife as it is for daytime pursuits, so before you retire for the evening, unwind with some music under the stars. The **Lake Tahoe Outdoor Arena at Harvey's** boasts major headliners all summer long, while **The Shops at Heavenly Village** hosts free concerts every Friday and Saturday evening Memorial Day weekend through Labor Day.

Day 3

Ease into the morning with brunch at **Heidi's Pancake House.** The iconic Swiss chalet has been serving up hearty breakfast fare like French toast melts and crepes since the 1960s. It'll be hard, but pace yourself because you're about to put your bikini back on to enjoy your last day on the water.

You can try a stand-up paddleboard, rent Jet Skis, charter a sailboat, or simply spend a lazy day at the beach. Sometimes the best thing to do on vacation is nothing at all. Lounge around with a good book, don a wide-brimmed sun hat, and watch the waves.

Once your skin is sufficiently bronzed, it's time to make one lasting memory. Since you've seen Tahoe from land and water, it's time to see it from the sky. To get a bird's eye view of the beaches and bays, try parasailing, flightseeing, or go on a helicopter tour. If that's too extreme, you can also just head up the **Heavenly Mountain Gondola** for one last parting view before returning to the hustle and bustle of city life.

Recommendations

Sights

Emerald Bay State Park. ⊠ *138 Emerald Bay Rd., South Lake Tahoe, CA* ☎ *530/541–3030* ⊕ *www.parks.ca.gov /?page_id=506* 🅿 *Parking $10.*

Fannette Island. ⊠ *Lake Tahoe, CA* ☎ *530/541–3030* ⊕ *www.parks.ca.gov /?page_id=1159* 🅿 *Free.*

Jelly Belly Factory. ⊠ *1 Jelly Belly La., Fairfield, CA* ☎ *707/399–2390* ⊕ *www. jellybelly.com/california-factory* 🅿 *Free.*

Vikingsholm Castle. ⊠ *CA 89, Tahoma, CA* ☎ *530/525–9530* ⊕ *www.vikingsholm. com* 🅿 *$15.*

🍴 Restaurants

Azul Latin Kitchen. $ *Average main: $18* ⊠ *1001 Heavenly Village Way, South Lake Tahoe, CA* ☎ *530/541–2985* ⊕ *www. azullatinkitchen.com.*

Driftwood Cafe. $ *Average main: $12* ⊠ *1001 Heavenly Village Way, South Lake Tahoe, CA* ☎ *530/544–6545* ⊕ *www. driftwoodtahoe.com* ⊗ *No Dinner.*

Heidi's Pancake House. $ *Average main: $15* ⊠ *3485 Lake Tahoe Blvd., South Lake Tahoe, CA* ☎ *530/544–8113* ⊕ *www. heidislaketahoe.com* ⊗ *No Dinner.*

Oyster Bar. $ *Average main: $25* ⊠ *Hard Rock Hotel & Casino Lake Tahoe, 50 U.S. 50, Stateline, NV* ☎ *844/588–7625* ⊕ *www.hardrockcasinolaketahoe.com/ dining-restaurants/the-oyster-bar.*

Sprouts Café. $ *Average main: $11* ⊠ *3123 Harrison Ave., South Lake Tahoe, CA* ☎ *530/541–6969* ⊕ *www.sprouts-cafetahoe.com.*

🛏️ Hotels

Edgewood Tahoe Resort. $ *Rooms from: $329* ✉ *180 Lake Pkwy., Stateline, NV* ☎ *855/681–0119* ⊕ *www.edgewoodtahoe.com* ⦿ *No meals.*

Hotel Azure. $ *Rooms from: $152* ✉ *3300 Lake Tahoe Blvd., South Lake Tahoe, CA* ☎ *800/877–1466* ⊕ *www.hotelazuretahoe.com* ⦿ *No meals.*

🎭 Performing Arts

Lake Tahoe Outdoor Arena at Harvey's. ✉ *Hwy. 50 Stateline Ave., Stateline, NV* ☎ *800/342–7724* ⊕ *www.caesars.com/harveys-tahoe.*

👜 Shopping

The Shops at Heavenly Village. ✉ *1001 Heavenly Village Way, South Lake Tahoe, CA* ☎ *775/265–2087* ⊕ *www.theshopsatheavenly.com.*

🏃 Activities

Clearly Tahoe. ✉ *Tahoe Keys Marina, 2435 Venice Dr. E., South Lake Tahoe, CA* ☎ *530/554–4664* ⊕ *www.clearlytahoe.com* 🚤 *Tours from $69.*

Heavenly Mountain Gondola. ✉ *1001 Heavenly Village Way, South Lake Tahoe, CA* ☎ *775/586–7000* ⊕ *www.skiheavenly.com* 🚠 *$50.*

Zephyr Cove Resort. ✉ *760 U.S. 50, Zephyr Cove, NV* ☎ *775/589–4906* ⊕ *www.zephyrcove.com* 🚤 *Cruises from $68.*

Las Vegas, NV

270 miles (approx. 4 hours) from Los Angeles.

You need a break, but not just any break—that's why you're headed to Vegas, baby. But you're probably not 25 any longer, so you're looking for a weekend with a little pampering, some great meals, and yes, a couple of cocktails. Just make sure you stay hydrated, and maybe find time for a few naps.

Planning

GETTING THERE AND BACK

From Los Angeles, it's a four-hour drive to Las Vegas via I–15 N, or a more leisurely five-hour drive via CA 14 N and I–15 N. For a scenic route, we recommend detouring onto iconic Route 66 from Victorville to Barstow. It will add about a half hour to your drive (plus whatever time you take to duck into old diners and antique shops).

INSPIRATION

It may be time to stream or pop in some Rat Pack tunes and listen to a little Sinatra, Deano, or even Sammy to get you in the mood. Frankie's *Nothing But the Best* will get you through this drive, as will *The Rat Pack: Live at the Sands.* Those with more contemporary tastes might prefer a newer legend—Celine Dion.

PIT STOPS

Along Route 66, the town of Oro Grande is home to the **Elmer's Bottle Tree Ranch,** a funky art project in the middle of the desert. **Calico Ghost Town,** in San Bernardino County, is a former silver-mining town founded in 1881. This quaint spot in the Calico Mountains is well worth an hour or two of exploring.

WHEN TO GO

The best time to visit is September through November, with lighter crowds and cheaper rates. Spring and summer are better for lounging around the pool, but expect lots of people and desert heat (although it does cool off at night). Avoid July and August unless you want to be walking around drunk and miserable.

WHERE TO STAY

Our Strip hotel of choice is the **Cosmopolitan,** followed closely by the **Aria** and the **Vdara.** At any of these you'll have quick

The Neon Museum of Las Vegas shows off the city's showstopping signage.

access to the main attractions, a classy room or suite, and rates that aren't too intense. If you want even more luxury, the **Wynn Las Vegas** or the **Waldorf Astoria Las Vegas** are the fanciest options, but you'll be spending some serious dough.

Day 1

To make the most of your weekend, get an early start. If you drive straight through you arrive by mid-afternoon. But who needs a clock? It's always party time in Vegas, my friend. After checking into your accommodations, head out to happy hour at the **Golden Tiki**, one of Vegas's best tiki bars, a few minutes from the Strip. (Another option is **Frankie's Tiki Room**, located downtown and run by the same folks.) Either way your drink will definitely come with huge wedges of fruit and just might be on fire.

By this point you're probably hungry, so make your way to **Battista's Hole in the Wall** for authentic Italian fare in an eclectic yet relaxed atmosphere (a big plus is

the free house wine with every meal). After dinner, head to **J Karaoke Bar** for karaoke followed by drinks at **Commonwealth** (and look for the bar's speakeasy, The Laundry Room). If you'd rather head back to the Strip, head to **Rhumbar** at the Mirage for a cocktail on the terrace overlooking the Strip before heading to the Cosmopolitan for a libation at the glittering **Chandelier Bar.** End the evening with late-night eats at **The Henry** or a nightcap at the Mexico-themed **Ghost Donkey,** both at the Cosmopolitan.

Day 2

If you're feeling worse for the wear, there's no better place for a hangover breakfast than Vegas. We're leaving the Strip again (for the last time this trip), and heading over to the candy-color **Peppermill's Restaurant and Fireside Lounge** for an incredible breakfast menu. Don't feel like leaving the Strip? Proceed directly to **Eggslut** for sandwiches sure to soak up last night's drinks. After breakfast, head to the outlets at **Fashion Show Mall** for some early-afternoon shopping, followed by tacos and tableside guacamole at the nearby **El Segundo Sol.**

After lunch, head to the **Neon Museum of Las Vegas**—affectionately called the Neon Boneyard—to take in 200 gorgeous signs from the city's glory days. Afterward there's a chance you can squeeze in some time at your hotel pool, but make it brief because it's happy hour. Get over to **Canonita,** a stylish eatery at the Venetian, for margaritas. It's a prime spot for people-watching and the perfect place for a light dinner and drinks before you begin your Saturday night festivities.

Head over to the Bellagio for the early evening performance of O, Cirque du Soleil's surreal celebration of "the concept of infinity and the elegance of water." You'll watch swimmers and acrobats do things with their bodies that make your brain fold in half. After the show, head across the street to **Beer Park,** a glassed-in rooftop bar at Paris Las Vegas with more than 100 beers on tap and a perfect view of the dancing waters of the Bellagio Fountains. For a change of scenery there's **Born and Raised Craft Pub** at Bally's for interesting brews or **Bird Bar** at Margaritaville for the kitschy atmosphere (bird cages hanging everywhere) and creative cocktails (the Pink Flamingo blends rosé, peach vodka, and soda). If you're in more of a clubby kind of mood, there's **Chateau** at the Paris Las Vegas or **Voodoo Rooftop Nightclub** at Rio, 51 stories above the city.

Day 3

Oof. How are you feeling? Good? Today we're gonna keep it light, go easy on the alcohol, and get you back on the road at a decent hour. Start the day at the Wynn Hotel, where **Terrace Point Cafe** is a lively spot for breakfast (or brunch), with sweeping views of the gorgeous pool and gardens. (Patio seating is

available, weather permitting.) Choose from brioche toast, chicken and waffles, and other staples. Keep in mind that the dress code is resort casual. We're keepin' it real classy this morning. If you want to go all out, Tableau (also at the Wynn) serves market-fresh breakfast options in a luxe atmosphere.

After breakfast, it's time to get pampered. Proceed to the **Sahra Spa, Salon & Hammam** at the Cosmopolitan (make a reservation beforehand) for a soothing facial, massage, or body treatment, followed by a soak in one of their baths. Continue indulging yourself at the **Grand Lux Cafe,** an upscale eatery with a wide-ranging American menu.

Recommendations

Sights

Calico Ghost Town. ✉ *36600 Ghost Town Rd., Yermo, CA* ☎ *760/254–1123* ⊕ *www.parks.sbcounty.gov/park/calico-ghost-town-regional-park* ✉ *$8.*

Elmer's Bottle Tree Ranch. ✉ *24266 National Trails Hwy., Oro Grande, CA* ☎ *No phone.* ✉ *Free.*

Neon Museum of Las Vegas. ✉ *770 S. Las Vegas Blvd., Las Vegas, NV* ☎ *702/387–6366* ⊕ *www.neonmuseum.org* ✉ *$20.*

🍴 Restaurants

Battista's Hole in the Wall. 🟢 *Average main: $35* ✉ *4041 Linq La., Las Vegas, NV* ☎ *702/732–1424* ⊕ *www.battistaslasvegas.com* 🕙 *No lunch.*

Canonita 🟢 *Average main: $25* ✉ *The Venetian, 3377 S. Las Vegas Blvd., Las Vegas, NV* ☎ *702/414–3773* ⊕ *www.canonita.com.*

Eggslut. 🟢 *Average main: $10* ✉ *The Cosmopolitan, 3708 S. Las Vegas Blvd., NV* ☎ *702/698–7000* ⊕ *www.*

cosmopolitanlasvegas.com/restaurants/eggslut ⏲ *No dinner.*

El Segundo Sol. $ *Average main: $18* ✉ *3200 S. Las Vegas Blvd., Las Vegas, NV* ☎ *702/258–1211* 🌐 *www.elsegundo-sol.com.*

Grand Lux Café. $ *Average main: $16* ✉ *The Venetian, 3327 S. Las Vegas Blvd., Las Vegas, NV* ☎ *702/733–7411* 🌐 *www.grandluxcafe.com.*

The Henry. $ *Average main: $24* ✉ *The Cosmopolitan, 3708 S. Las Vegas Blvd., Las Vegas, NV* ☎ *877/893–2001* 🌐 *www.cosmopolitanlasvegas.com/restaurants/the-henry* ⏲ *No lunch weekends.*

Tableau. $ *Average main: $30* ✉ *Wynn Las Vegas, S. Las Vegas Blvd., Las Vegas, NV* ☎ *702/770–3330* 🌐 *www.wynnlasvegas.com/dining/fine-dining/tableau.*

Terrace Point Café. $ *Average main: $20* ✉ *Wynn Las Vegas, 3131 S. Las Vegas Blvd., Las Vegas, NV* ☎ *702/770–3360* 🌐 *www.wynnlasvegas.com/dining/casual-dining/terrace-pointe-cafe.*

Hotels

Aria Resort & Casino. $ *Rooms from: $179* ✉ *3730 S. Las Vegas Blvd., Las Vegas, NV* ☎ *702/590–7111* 🌐 *www.aria.mgmresorts.com/en.html* 🍴 *No meals.*

Cosmopolitan. $ *Rooms from: $130* ✉ *3708 S. Las Vegas Blvd., Las Vegas, NV* ☎ *702/698–7000* 🌐 *www.cosmopolitanlasvegas.com* 🍴 *No meals.*

Vdara Hotel & Spa. $ *Rooms from: $159* ✉ *2600 W. Harmon Ave., Las Vegas, NV* ☎ *866/745–7767* 🌐 *www.vdara.mgmresorts.com/en.htm* 🍴 *No meals.*

Waldorf Astoria Las Vegas. $ *Rooms from: $140* ✉ *3752 S. Las Vegas Blvd., Las Vegas, NV* ☎ *702/590–8888* 🌐 *www.hilton.com/en/hotels/laswdwa-waldorf-astoria-las-vegas* 🍴 *No meals.*

Wynn Las Vegas. $ *Rooms from: $169* ✉ *3131 S. Las Vegas Blvd., Las Vegas, NV* ☎ *702/770–7000* 🌐 *www.wynnlasvegas.com* 🍴 *No meals.*

Nightlife

Beer Park. ✉ *Paris, 3655 S. Las Vegas Blvd., Las Vegas, NV* ☎ *702/444–4500* 🌐 *www.beerpark.com.*

Bird Bar. ✉ *Flamingo Las Vegas, 3555 S. Las Vegas Blvd., Las Vegas, NV* ☎ *702/733–3111* 🌐 *www.caesars.com/flamingo-las-vegas/things-to-do/bird-bar.*

Born and Raised Craft Pub. ✉ *Grand Bazaar Shops, 3641 S. Las Vegas Blvd., Las Vegas, NV* ☎ *702/818–5794* 🌐 *www.bornandraisedlv.com.*

Chandelier Bar. ✉ *Cosmopolitan, 3708 S. Las Vegas Blvd., Las Vegas* ☎ *702/698–7979* 🌐 *www.cosmopolitanlasvegas.com/lounges-bars/the-chandelier.*

Chateau Nightclub. ✉ *Paris, 3655 S. Las Vegas Blvd., Las Vegas, NV* ☎ *702/776–7777* 🌐 *www.chateaunights.com.*

Commonwealth. ✉ *525 Fremont St., Las Vegas, NV* ☎ *702/445–6400* 🌐 *www.commonwealthlv.com.*

Frankie's Tiki Room. ✉ *1712 W. Charleston Blvd., Las Vegas, NV* ☎ *702/385–3110* 🌐 *www.frankiestikiroom.com.*

Ghost Donkey. ✉ *The Cosmopolitan, 3708 S. Las Vegas Blvd., Las Vegas, NV* ☎ *702/698–7000* 🌐 *www.cosmopolitanlasvegas.com/restaurants/ghost-donkey.*

Golden Tiki. ✉ *3939 Spring Mountain Rd., Las Vegas, NV* ☎ *702/222–3196* 🌐 *www.thegoldentiki.com.*

J Karaoke Bar. ✉ *3899 Spring Mountain Rd., Las Vegas, NV* ☎ *702/586–1142* 🌐 *www.jkaraoke.multiscreensite.com.*

Peppermill's Fireside Lounge. ✉ *2985 S. Las Vegas Blvd., Las Vegas, NV* ☎ *702/735–4177* 🌐 *www.peppermilllasvegas.com.*

Rhumbar. ✉ *The Mirage, 3400 S. Las Vegas Blvd, Las Vegas, NV*

☎ 702/792–7416 ⊕ www.mirage.mgmre-sorts.com/en/nightlife/rhumbar.html.

Voodoo Rooftop Nightclub. ⊠ Rio All-Suites Hotel and Casino, 3700 W. Flamingo Rd., Las Vegas, NV ☎ 702/777–7800 ⊕ caesars.com/rio-las-vegas/restaurants/voodoo-steak-and-rooftop-nightclub.

Shopping

Fashion Show Mall. ⊠ 3200 S. Las Vegas Blvd., Las Vegas, NV ☎ 702/784–7000 ⊕ www.thefashionshow.com/en.html.

Sahra Spa, Salon & Hamman. ⊠ The Cosmopolitan, 3708 S. Las Vegas Blvd., Las Vegas ☎ 702/698–7180 ⊕ www.cosmo-politanlasvegas.com/resort/spa.

Leavenworth, WA

117 miles (approx. 1¼ hours) from Seattle.

Though best known as a Bavarian village, the faux-German façades, steins of beer, and plump pretzels are only part of Leavenworth's draw. The snow-covered peaks and chilly Wenatchee River flowing by, the wide range of outdoor activities, and the eclectic assortment of artisans who've made their home here create the kind of retreat from the city that makes a weekend away as relaxing and rejuvenating as possible. Leavenworth serves as the outdoor escape for urbanites, whether they like their fresh alpine air inhaled during hardcore adventures, sighed out in a steamy spa, or perfumed with the smell of sausage.

Planning

GETTING THERE AND BACK

The drive to and from Leavenworth should, theoretically, take only a bit over two hours, but seasoned locals know that the summer or winter traffic coming down Stevens Pass can easily double

or triple that on a Sunday afternoon or evening. Check the weather and try to avoid travel in late afternoon. Alternatively, Amtrak makes the trip by train, but only once a day. It takes more than three hours and is often plagued by delays.

WHEN TO GO

Naturally, the biggest weekend of the year for the Bavarian-theme village is Oktoberfest, but the crowds pour in during Christmas season as well—if you like the festive nature and don't mind the crowds, it's a great time to visit. Otherwise, the hot summer season makes the chilly river refreshing and the pristine snows of winter keep the peaks looking their best.

WHERE TO STAY

A weekend at the **Posthotel** includes access to their pools, making it an appealing option for a relaxing, upscale vacation. For those on a stricter budget, tiny houses at the **Leavenworth Tiny House Village** from Petite Retreats make for an adorable, comfortable experience halfway between camping and a hotel. The outdoor adventure–focused **Loge** also offers bunks and cabins, along with free bikes—perfect if you're taking the train to town. Finally, among the glut of overly cutesy Bavarian-themed bed and breakfasts, the adults-only **Haus Hanika,** right on the river, shines.

Day 1

Grab a cinnamon roll the size of your head at the **Maltby Café** as you make your way over Stevens Pass and on to Leavenworth. Park the car and immediately walk down to **Waterfront Park** to get your bearings and take in the river and the mountains that make this spot so special. When you walk back to town, head to **Argonaut Kitchen,** where they have the requisite nod to the town's heritage in the form of schnitzel, but also a world of sandwiches like pork belly banh mi and buttermilk fried chicken with garlic aioli.

Washington's Wenatchee River winds its way through spectacular scenery near Leavenworth.

After lunch, embrace the eccentricities and head out to the **Leavenworth Reindeer Farm.** Learn about the animals leading Santa's sled (the big man himself usually hangs around in November and December, too), and then actually get to meet them—the animals eat out your hand, pose for selfies, and welcome gentle pets. In spring, there's sometimes even baby reindeer. Wind down your afternoon on the outdoor patio at **Icicle Brewing Company,** sampling the beers made from the waters flowing through nearby Icicle Creek.

You don't need to dress up much to fit in here, but you'll want to at least shower the reindeer fur off before sitting down to dinnr at **Mana,** a restaurant and yoga studio that serves eight-course vegan tasting menus over the course of three hours on Friday and Saturday.

Day 2

Stop in for a quick bite to eat from the **Bavarian Bakery**—pretzels, strudels, or any of the other classics the name implies—before getting on your way to the morning's activity. Leavenworth, for all its invented Bavarian-ness (it was designed to entice travelers) truly shines because of its setting, and the only way to fully take in the clear waters and high peaks is by spending a few hours out among them. If it's winter, grab a set of snowshoes from **Der Sportsmann** or book a snowshoe tour with **Blue Sky Outfitters.** In summer, head out with Blue Sky for a rafting trip or book a stand-up paddleboard adventure down Icicle Creek. Keeping with the region's theme, head to lunch at the **Leavenworth Sausage Garten,** which takes the classic brats and beer up a notch with their various house-made wursts.

After the morning's adventuring, spend the afternoon relaxing. If you haven't snagged a spot at **Scenic Hot Springs**—the privately owned natural springs about 45-minutes away—you'll want to head out there, but if not, the **Spa at Posthotel** has you covered with their variety of saltwater hydrotherapy pools, steam rooms, dry saunas, cool plunge pools, and lounge areas (the pools are free to guests of the hotel).

When you're rested and rejuvenated, keep the good feelings going with dinner at the polished **Watershed Café,** which transforms local ingredients into such dishes as clams in tomato, saffron, and fennel broth; teriyaki roasted wild king salmon over udon noodles; and slow-roasted Kurobuta pork chops with turnip salad and potato croquettes. Finish the evening with a nightcap at **Pika Provisions,** where you'll find a wealth of unusual spirits and a surprising variety of mezcals, all whipped into expertly made cocktails.

Day 3

Start your day with a 15-minute drive to the east, into the fruit-centric town of Cashmere. There, in an old fruit warehouse, the **Anjou Bakery** turns out velvety espresso drinks and flaky pastries. The laminated doughs—croissants and almandines—are the draw, but it's worth grabbing a loaf of bread or even a whole pie to bring home.

April to December, check out the factory tour of **Liberty Orchards**—the maker of Washington's famous Aplets and Cotlets. Founded by Armenian immigrants from Turkey in 1920, the hundred-year-old confectioner still makes the same Turkish delights using local fruit. If the factory is closed (as it does on weekends for three months of the year), head to **Apple Annie's Antique Gallery** and browse through the 70,000 square feet of all sorts of random stuff you never knew you needed.

Peruse your purchases with a "hot mama" pizza at **Blewett Brewing**—with

bacon, arugula, and Mama Lil's peppers. Then wander through town and pick up a few souvenirs—the gift shop of the **Nutcracker Museum** has many treasures. Before you head back down to the city, grab dinner for the road at the half-century-old **Heidle Burger Drive-In.**

Recommendations

◉ Sights

Leavenworth Reindeer Farm. ☒ *10395 Chumstick Hwy., Leavenworth, WA* ☎ *509/885–3021* ⊕ *www.leavenworthreindeer.com* ☷ *$20* ☉ *Closed Tues.–Thurs.*

Liberty Orchards. ☒ *117 Mission Ave., Cashmere, WA* ☎ *800/888–5696* ⊕ *www.libertyorchards.com* ☷ *Free* ☉ *Closed Jan.–Mar.*

Nutcracker Museum. ☒ *735 Front St., Leavenworth, WA* ☎ *509/548–4573* ⊕ *www.nutcrackermuseum.com* ☷ *$5.*

Scenic Hot Springs. ☒ *Skykomish, WA* ☎ *No phone* ⊕ *www.scenichotsprings. blogspot.com* ☷ *$10.*

Waterfront Park. ☒ *Main St., Leavenworth, WA* ☎ *509/548–5807* ⊕ *www.leavenworth.org/trail/waterfront-park-2* ☷ *Free.*

🍴 Restaurants

Argonaut Kitchen. $ *Average main: $12* ☒ *220 9th St., Leavenworth, WA* ☎ *509/888–5470* ⊕ *www.argonautkitchen.com* ☉ *Closed weekends. No dinner.*

Heidle Burger Drive-In. $ *Average main: $8* ☒ *12708 U.S. 2, Leavenworth, WA* ☎ *509/548–5471* ⊕ *www.heidleburger. com.*

Leavenworth Sausage Garten. $ *Average main: $8* ☒ *636 Front St., Leavenworth, WA* ☎ *509/888–4959* ⊕ *www.viscontis. com/sausage-garten* ☉ *No dinner.*

Maltby Café. $ *Average main: $15* ✉ *8809 Maltby Rd., Snohomish, WA* ☎ *425/483–3123* ⊕ *www.maltbycafe.com* ⊖ *No dinner.*

Mana. $ *Average main: $85 prix fixe* ✉ *1033 Commercial St., Leavenworth, WA* ☎ *509/548–1662* ⊕ *www.manamountain.com* ⊖ *Closed Mon.–Thurs. No lunch.*

Watershed Café. $ *Average main: $32* ✉ *221 8th St., Leavenworth, WA* ☎ *509/888–0214* ⊕ *www.watershedpnw.com* ⊖ *Closed Tues. and Wed. No lunch.*

☕ Coffee and Quick Bites

Anjou Bakery. $ *Average main: $5* ✉ *3898 Old Monitor Rd., Cashmere, WA* ☎ *509/782–4360* ⊕ *www.anjoubakery.com* ⊖ *Closed Mon.–Wed. No dinner.*

Bavarian Bakery. $ *Average main: $5* ✉ *1330 U.S. 2, Leavenworth, WA* ☎ *509/548–2244* ⊖ *Closed Tues. and Wed.*

🛏 Hotels

Haus Hanika. $ *Rooms from: $189* ✉ *8775 Icicle Rd., Leavenworth, WA* ☎ *509/741–0919* ⊕ *www.haushanika.com* ❍ *Free breakfast.*

Leavenworth Tiny House Village. $ *Rooms from: $149* ✉ *20752 Chiwawa Loop Rd., Leavenworth, WA* ☎ *888/229–5445* ⊕ *www.leavenworthtinyhouse.com* ❍ *No meals.*

Loge Leavenworth. $ *Rooms from: $115* ✉ *11798 U.S. 2, Leavenworth, WA* ☎ *509/690–4106* ⊕ *www.logecamps.com/leavenworth-wa* ❍ *No meals.*

Posthotel Leavenworth. $ *Rooms from: $415* ✉ *309 8th St., Leavenworth, WA* ☎ *509/548–7678* ⊕ *www.posthotelleavenworth.com* ❍ *Free breakfast.*

🍸 Nightlife

Icicle Brewing Company. ✉ *935 Front St., Leavenworth, WA* ☎ *509/548–2739* ⊕ *iciclebrewing.com.*

Pika Provisions. ✉ *217 9th St., Leavenworth, WA* ☎ *509/888–0746* ⊕ *pikaprovisions.com.*

🛍 Shopping

Apple Annie's Antique Gallery. ✉ *100 Apple Annie Ave., Cashmere, WA* ☎ *509/782–4004* ⊕ *www.appleannieantiques.com.*

🏃 Activities

Blue Sky Outfitters ✉ *900 Front St. B, Leavenworth, WA* ☎ *800/228–7238* ⊕ *www.blueskyoutfitters.com* 🎫 *Rafting from $15.*

Der Sportsmann. ✉ *837 Front St., Leavenworth, WA* ☎ *509/548–5623* ⊕ *www.dersportsmann.com* 🎫 *Equipment rental from $12.*

Spa at Posthotel. ✉ *309 8th St., Leavenworth, WA* ☎ *509/548–7678* ⊕ *www.posthotelleavenworth.com* 🎫 *Treatments from $140.*

Long Beach, WA to Cannon Beach, OR

171 miles (approx. 3 hours) from Seattle.

The stretch of beach towns from the southwestern corner of Washington down into Oregon, spanning the mouth of the Columbia River, lures visitors in search of sand, storms, and seafood. But while trying to catch crabs or open oysters, coastal visitors often stumble into so many other offerings, from movie landmarks and cold-water surfing to cranberry bogs and Bosnian food. And, in the grand tradition of seaside towns around the country, the ice cream is excellent.

Handsome North Head Lighthouse is a major draw in Washington's Cape Disappointment.

Planning

GETTING THERE AND BACK
The drive to Long Beach takes more than three hours, and much longer with Seattle's storied traffic, but there aren't really any other options. From Long Beach to Astoria is another half-hour, and Cannon Beach another 40 minutes beyond that.

PIT STOPS
The only music option for this drive is the hometown stars of nearby Aberdeen, Washington: Nirvana—you won't quite hit the river, but put on "From the Muddy Banks of the Whiskah" anyway. If you're a big fan, make a pit stop at the **Kurt Cobain Memorial Park.**

WHEN TO GO
Choose between the sunshine of summer and the shellfish of winter. While many might mistake beaches as synonymous with warm weather, this cool coast keeps visitors engaged with storms throughout the year. If you have your pick, though, look to make it for a weekend when the beach is open for razor clamming, a classic local activity.

WHERE TO STAY
Above the Pickled Fish in Long Beach, the **Adrift Hotel** nails the balance between modern amenities like the sauna and pool and classic, breezy, beach-town feel. Meanwhile, The **Atomic Motel** in Astoria brings back midcentury modern style in a big way, right in the center of town. For a higher end feel, head to the **Cannery Pier Hotel,** where you get your own private balcony over the river, along with a free wine hour, bikes, and access to the hot tub and Finnish sauna.

Day 1

The drive to Long Beach is a long one, without much to recommend it until the final scenic hour from Raymond south, but that more than makes up for the rest. And if you aim to arrive by lunch, you'll have forgotten the slog through Seattle's southern suburbs before the two pounds of steamer clams in amber ale hit the table on the enclosed patio at **The Lost Roo.** Revived, you'll be ready to head to the **Skookum Surf Co.** and don a wetsuit to try your hand at hanging a very chilly ten, because whatever the Pacific loses in temperature here, it makes up in consistent, uncrowded waves.

But if you prefer to stay on dry land, the 8.5-mile Discovery Trail winds along the peninsula, including around **Cape Disappointment,** where the crashing waters will mesmerize you. For a shorter jaunt, the **Long Beach Boardwalk** offers a classic beach stroll along the dunes.

Pop off the boardwalk at the **Pickled Fish** and savor the namesake appetizer, along with local seafood like Dungeness in crab cake, mac and cheese, or with brie in sandwich form, smoked sablefish salad, or buttermilk fried rockfish, as well as a little live music as you eat your dinner.

Day 2

Join the locals in line at the **Cottage Bakery** to pick up one of the oversized maple doughnuts first thing in the morning—they will tide you over through your fishing adventure. Depending on the season, you could just walk onto the beach to dig for razor clams. Or, if you plan to spend the whole day in Long Beach, book yourself a voyage with **Coho Charters,** who will help you help you catch all the crab you legally can over the course of a day—and still leave you enough time in the afternoon to visit the **Cranberry Museum** and demonstration bogs.

Alternatively, head south across the river to Astoria, Oregon, where you can work up an appetite by climbing the 164 steps up the **Astoria Column,** a 1926 monument to the settlement of the West. Take in the view of the river and fly a glider (available for purchase at the nearby gift shop) off the top before you head down toward the water for lunch at **Bowpicker Fish and Chips.** It might be a cliché lunch

in a seaside town, but the beer battered freshly caught local albacore tuna steaks served out of this converted gill-netting boat blow any other version of the dish you've had before out of the (pun intended) water.

Spend the afternoon wandering the town. On the western edge, stroll by old canneries, take a ride on the **Astoria Riverfront Trolley,** a restored 1913 streetcar affectionately known as "Old 300," and walk along the riverside. End at the **Fort George Brewery** to sample their beers, particularly their annual "3-Way" collaborative IPA made with two other breweries to kick off each summer.

Finish the evening with a surprisingly unseafood-y dinner: Bosnian food at **Drina Daisy.** Dig into the meaty menu, enjoying traditional stews, sausages, and even whole roasted lamb.

Day 3

Enjoy breakfast at the **Blue Scorcher,** which uses organic artisan bread from their bakery to make big breakfasts such as their breakfast sandwich with chipotle mayonnaise and Scorcher French Toast made from baguette. Then head south to Cannon Beach to visit the iconic Haystack Rock and frolic in the sand—or, depending on the time of year, the fog. Either way, the 235-foot tall lava-formed rock is one of Oregon's most recognizable landmarks, and looking down is just as interesting as looking up: low tide shows off sea stars and fascinating creatures in the tidepools, spring and summer bring in the local tufted puffins, along with tons of year-round seabirds.

Pop into **Ecola Seafood Market** for one last chowder meal before beginning the long drive back up the coast—but leave plenty of time to stop into **Frite and Scoop** in Astoria on the way home for house-made ice cream in innovative flavors like Earl Grey with lemon curd, raspberry with rosewater custard, and malted sweet cream with caramel sauce and blackberry curd.

Recommendations

Sights

Astoria Column. ✉ *16th St. S, Astoria, OR* ☎ *503/325–2963* 🌐 *www.astoriacolumn.org* 🎟 *$2 per car.*

Astoria Riverfront Trolley. ✉ *480 Industry St., Astoria, OR* ☎ *503-325–6311* 🌐 *www.old300.org* 🎟 *$1.*

Cape Disappointment. ✉ *244 Robert Gray Dr., Ilwaco WA* ☎ *360/642–3078* 🌐 *parks.state.wa.us/486/cape-disappointment* 🎟 *$5.*

Cranberry Museum. ✉ *2907 Pioneer Rd., Long Beach, WA* ☎ *360/642–5553* 🌐 *www.cranberrymuseum.com* 🎟 *Free.*

Kurt Cobain Memorial Park. ✉ *Young St., Aberdeen, WA* ☎ *No phone* 🎟 *Free.*

Long Beach Boardwalk. ✉ *Long Beach, WA* ☎ *No phone* 🌐 *www.funbeach.com* 🎟 *Free.*

Restaurants

Blue Scorcher. [$] *Average main: $8* ✉ *1493 Duane St., Astoria, OR* ☎ *503/338–7473* 🌐 *www.bluescorcher.coop.*

Bowpicker Fish and Chips. [$] *Average main: $11* ✉ *1634 Duane St., Astoria OR* ☎ *503/791–2942* 🌐 *www.bowpicker.com* 🕒 *Closed Sun.–Tues. No dinner.*

Cottage Bakery. [$] *Average main: $5* ✉ *118 Pacific Ave. S, Long Beach WA* ☎ *503/642–4441.*

Drina Daisy. [$] *Average main: $19* ✉ *915 Commercial St., Astoria OR* ☎ *503/338–2912* 🌐 *www.drinadaisy.com* 🕒 *Closed Mon. and Tues.*

Ecola Seafood Market. [$] *Average main: $18* ✉ *208 N. Spruce St., Cannon Beach, OR* ☎ *503/436–9130* 🌐 *www.ecolaseafoods.com.*

The Lost Roo. [$] *Average main: $16* ✉ *1700 Pacific Ave. S, Long Beach, WA* ☎ *503/642–4329* 🌐 *www.lostroo.com.*

Pickled Fish. [$] *Average main: $18* ✉ *Adrift Hotel, 409 Sid Snyder Dr., Long Beach, WA* ☎ *503/642–2344* 🌐 *www.pickledfishrestaurant.com.*

Coffee and Quick Bites

Frite and Scoop. [$] *Average main: $4* ✉ *175 14th St., Astoria, OR* ☎ *503/468–0416* 🌐 *www.friteandscoop.com* 🕒 *Closed Mon.–Thurs.*

Hotels

Adrift Hotel. [$] *Rooms from: $104* ✉ *131 W. Marine Dr., Astoria, OR* ☎ *503/325–4051* 🌐 *www.astoriamotel.com* 🍴 *No meals.*

Atomic Motel. [$] *Rooms from: $65* ✉ *131 W. Marine Dr., Astoria, OR* ☎ *503/325–4051* 🌐 *www.astoriamotel.com* 🍴 *Free breakfast.*

Cannery Pier Hotel. [$] *Rooms from: $209* ✉ *10 Basin St., Astoria, OR* ☎ *503/325–4996* 🌐 *www.cannerypierhotel.com* 🍴 *Free breakfast.*

Nightlife

Fort George Brewery. ✉ *1483 Duane St., Astoria, OR* ☎ *503/325–7468* 🌐 *fortgeorgebrewery.com.*

Activities

Coho Charters. ✉ *237 Howerton Ave SE, Ilwaco, WA* ☎ *360/642–3333* 🌐 *www.cohocharters.com* 🎟 *Trips from $120.*

Skookum Surf Co. ✉ *1216 48th St., Long Beach, WA* ☎ *360/358–7873* 🌐 *www.skookumsurf.com* 🎟 *Lessons from $99.*

Mendocino County, CA

Ukiah is 115 miles (approx. 2 hours) from San Francisco.

While not as well-known as the wine hubs of Sonoma and Napa, Mendocino County is quintessential Northern California. In Mendocino, you can drive through verdant golden valleys to discover small towns that feel like a blast from the past. It's also one of the most picturesque sections of California's famous Pacific Coast Highway, where waves crash onto rocky shores and salt air fills your lungs. Mendocino has everything you need to enjoy the best of Northern California, from gorgeous wineries to windswept beaches to mountain trails that take you through the redwoods. It's also one of the best places in the state to get to know California's burgeoning marijuana tourism industry—and pick up some souvenirs.

Planning

GETTING THERE AND BACK

From San Francisco, Ukiah is about a two-hour drive (with no traffic) straight up the 101. From Ukiah, it's an easy (and scenic) drive to Boonville.

PIT STOPS

Make a stop in the town of Cloverdale to stretch your legs and take a peek at the adorable **Gould-Shaw House Museum,** an authentic 1870s Gothic Revival cottage.

WHEN TO GO

There's never a bad time to visit Northern California, but there's something magical about visiting in the fall during harvest season. The grapes are ripe, the weather is beautiful, and everyone's in a great mood.

WHERE TO STAY

Boonville is by far the cutest town in Mendocino County and a great base for your weekend getaway. The hip **Boonville Hotel,** which calls itself "a modern roadhouse," is a vintage-inspired boutique hotel right in the middle of town. If you'd rather spend the night in Ukiah, **Vichy Springs Resort** is a quirky spa hotel with natural thermal baths. In the town of Mendocino, the historic **MacCallum House B&B** is your best bet.

Day 1

Any visit to Medocino County should start with a stop at **Emerald Pharms** in Hopland for the ultimate cannabis dispensary experience. If you're coming from a state where weed isn't legal, you'll feel like a kid in a candy shop. The solar-powered estate is like Willy Wonka's factory for people who like weed, with lush gardens, wacky art, and a dizzying array of smokeables, edibles, oils, sprays, balms, and all the marijuana-related products you can possibly imagine. For the full cannabis experience, it's worth taking the 5-mile detour to **Flow Kana,** where you can take a tour to learn about how cannabis is grown and harvested. Weed tourism still has a way to go until it can compete with wine, but it's a fascinating look into this budding industry.

From Hopland, continue north to the town of Ukiah, where you can explore the **City of Ten Thousand Buddhas,** a psychiatric hospital that's been turned into Buddhist temple and education center. Visitors can stroll the incredible grounds (and gaze at the plentiful Buddha sculptures) before grabbing a bite to eat at the on-site vegetarian restaurant. If you'd like to indulge in something a little less pious for lunch, settle in for a cocktail-fueled meal at **Patrona** in downtown Ukiah, where you can feast on a fancy burger washed down with a cucumber gimlet.

From Ukiah, head to the adorable town of Boonville, tucked away in the hills on Highway 128. Make a reservation at the restaurant at the **Boonville Hotel** for

The dreamlike City of Ten Thousand Buddhas is an unexpected sight in the town of Ukiah, California.

quintessential California cooking—farm fresh ingredients, expertly prepared.

Day 2

Start your day with a coffee and a pastry at the **Boonville General Store** and pick up a few picnic provisions. From there, make a stop at **Pennyroyal Farm** to pick up some cheese and wine. They make all their cheese on site and you can take a tour to look at their adorable goats.

Once you have everything you need for a decadent picnic, drive to **Hendy Woods State Park** to find a nice shady spot to enjoy your feast. There are trails that take you through the old-growth redwoods and the "hermit huts," the former home of a Russian man known as the Hendy Hermit who lived in the park for 18 years. (There are also campsites here for those who have their own gear and want to experience their own hermit vibes.)

Once you've had your fill of peace and quiet in the redwoods, it's time to explore California's other great natural resource: wine. The Anderson Valley, though little-known, produces some of California's best wines. There are vineyards, wineries, and tasting rooms all along Highway 128, but don't miss out on **Scharffenberger** for some excellent (and affordable) Champagne-style sparkling wine and **Goldeneye** for unbeatable Pinot Noir. If beer's more your thing, the **Anderson Valley Brewing Company** is not-to-be-missed, especially when there's live music.

After a long day of hiking and drinking, it's time for burgers. Old-timey **Redwood Drive-In** is a blast from the past, serving milk shakes, burgers, and tacos. If you still have any energy left after dinner, make your way over to **Disco Ranch** to toast the day with one final glass at this casual wine bar.

Day 3

Fuel up for a scenic drive at **Mosswood Market** before leaving Boonville to head for the coast. The road from Boonville to the coast is a gorgeous (but extremely curvy) drive that will take you through redwood forests until you reach the Pacific Coast Highway.

Once you hit the coast, you'll want to head north to the seaside village of Mendocino. The historic **MacCallum House B&B** is a great place to stop for a boozy brunch. If you want to get some beach time in, visit the beach at Big River, where you can rent a canoe and paddle upriver—the ocean is beautiful here, but not ideal for swimming.

When it's time to call it a day and head home, you can try and squeeze in one last great meal at **Cafe Beaujolais** for steaks, risotto, or burgers. After dinner, it's time to cruise home along the PCH, reveling in the scenery at sunset.

Recommendations

Sights

City of Ten Thousand Buddhas. ✉ *4951 Bodhi Way, Ukiah, CA* ☎ *707/462–0939* 🌐 *www.cttbusa.org* 🎟 *Free.*

Emerald Pharms. ✉ *13771 S. U.S. 101, Hopland, CA* ☎ *707/669–4819* 🌐 *www.emeraldpharms.com* 🎟 *Free.*

Flow Kana. ✉ *Solar Living Center, 13771 S. Hwy. 101 Hopland, CA* ☎ *888/850–2999* 🌐 *www.flowkana.com* 🎟 *Free.*

Goldeneye. ✉ *9200 Hwy. 128, Philo, CA* ☎ *866/367–9945* 🌐 *www.goldeneyewinery.com* 🎟 *Tastings $15.*

Gould-Shaw House Museum. ✉ *215 N. Cloverdale Blvd., Cloverdale, CA* ☎ *707/894–2067* 🌐 *www.cloverdalehistoricalsociety.org* 🎟 *Free* 🕒 *Closed Mon. and Tues.*

Hendy Woods State Park. ✉ *18599 Philo Greenwood Rd., Philo, CA* ☎ *707/937–5804* 🌐 *www.parks.ca.gov* 🎟 *Free.*

Pennyroyal Farm. ✉ *14930 Hwy. 128, Boonville, CA* ☎ *707/895–2410* 🌐 *www.pennyroyalfarm.com* 🎟 *$20.*

Scharffenberger. ✉ *8501 Hwy. 128, Philo, CA* ☎ *707/895–2957* 🌐 *www.scharffenbergercellars.com* 🎟 *Tastings $10.*

Restaurants

Cafe Beaujolais. [$] *Average main: $15* ✉ *961 Ukiah St., Mendocino, CA* ☎ *707/937–5614* 🌐 *www.cafebeaujolais.com.*

Mosswood Market. [$] *Average main: $10* ✉ *14111 Hwy., 128 Boonville, CA* ☎ *707/895–3635.*

Patrona. [$] *Average main: $13* ✉ *130 W. Standley St., Ukiah, CA* ☎ *707/462–9181* 🌐 *www.patronarestaurant.com.*

Redwood Drive-In. [$] *Average main: $8* ✉ *13980 CA 128, Boonville, CA* ☎ *707/895–3441.*

Coffee and Quick Bites

Boonville General Store. [$] *Average main: $11* ✉ *14077 Hwy. 128, Boonville, CA* ☎ *707/895–9477* 🌐 *www.boonvillegeneralstore.com.*

Hotels

Boonville Hotel. [$] *Rooms from: $225* ✉ *14050 Hwy. 128, Boonville, CA* ☎ *707/895–2210* 🌐 *www.boonvillehotel.com* 🍴 *Free breakfast.*

MacCallum House B&B. [$] *Rooms from: $179* ✉ *45020 Albion St., Mendocino, CA* ☎ *707/937–0289* 🌐 *www.maccallumhouse.com* 🍴 *Free breakfast.*

Vichy Springs Resort. [$] *Rooms from: $265* ✉ *2605 Vichy Springs Rd., Ukiah, CA* ☎ *707/462–9515* 🌐 *www.vichysprings.com* 🍴 *No meals.*

ⓨ Nightlife

Anderson Valley Brewing Company. ✉ 17700 CA 253, Boonville, CA ☎ 707/895–2337 ⊕ www.avbc.com.

Disco Ranch. ✉ 14025 Hwy. 128, Boonville, CA ☎ 707/901–5002 ⊕ www.discoranch.com.

Monterey Bay, CA

119 miles (approx. 2 hours) from San Francisco, 315 miles (approx. 5¼ hours) from Los Angeles.

So many of California's best destinations are coastal cities or towns—and yet, even among that most esteemed company, there's something particularly special about Monterey. The water here teems with a staggering diversity of marine life. The land is lush with pine trees and knotted with wind-bent cypresses. The once capital of Alta California is the perfect place for anyone who wants to spend their weekend eating good food, sampling local wine, and contemplating the wondrous mysteries of the ocean (like how do sea otters get so cute?).

Planning

GETTING THERE AND BACK

From San Francisco, Monterey is about a two-hour drive via the 101 South. To go via train, take Amtrak from Emeryville to Salinas (3–4 hours) and then take a bus transfer to Monterey (about an hour).

From Los Angeles, the fastest way is to take I–5 N and then around Lost Hills start heading west until you can hop on the 101 North around Paso Robles. From there you'll stay on the 101 North the rest of the way. This will take about five hours. It takes a little longer to take the 101 North from the start, but it is much more scenic and there are more options

if you need to stop for a quick bite or a cup of coffee.

INSPIRATION

As you cross over the iconic Bixby Bridge, hit play on Beach House's album *Bloom*. Let the sounds of gauzy indie-pop wash over you as you gaze down at the crashing waves or up at the marine layer as it rolls in like a sky-bound weighted blanket. This album is the aural equivalent of floating just below the waters' surface and feeling the warm, dappled sunlight gently shimmering across your face—perfect for a dreamy, misty weekend in Monterey.

WHEN TO GO

There's nothing like strolling along the water during Monterey's mild springs and summers—the only downside is that this is when it tends to be busier, so expect crowds, especially around popular attractions like Cannery Row. Because it is so literally centered on the water, it can get quite damp and chilly (by California standards) in the fall and winter. But the fog and mist just adds to the peninsula's dramatic vistas during the days and make it perfect for cozying up with a hot toddy at night.

WHERE TO STAY

For a romantic, intimate atmosphere where you'll be surrounded by verdant gardens, find your way to **Old Monterey Inn.** You'll be farther away from the heart of Monterey but that just adds to luxe, hideaway atmosphere. For a cozy stay that is also easy walking distance to downtown, check in at the **Casa Munras Garden Hotel & Spa.** The rooms here have an old-world, Spanish-inspired style and some feature a fireplace—perfect for those nippier nights. If you prefer to be in the heart of Cannery Row and close to the water, make the **Spindrift Inn** your base of operations. Even if you don't nab one of their bay view rooms, you can take advantage of their rooftop garden for some gorgeous vistas.

One of the most photographed spots along the coast, Bixby Bridge has amazing views of Big Sur.

Day 1

After driving along the coast and finally reaching the Monterey Peninsula, stop for lunch at **Alvarado Street Brewery & Grill** for some gastropub-style food and beer and a rotating selection of their latest craft brew creations. If you'd like to enjoy your Duane's World IPA ale among the fresh air, opt for their beer garden where, if you're lucky, you can nab a spot next to one of the fire pits. For seafood, try **Monterey's Fish House.**

After lunch, take a little time to get the lay of the land at Cannery Row. The eponymous canneries closed decades ago and have been converted into a collection of restaurants and shops. If nothing else, it's worth taking a stroll for the bay views and finding your way to **Coast Guard Pier,** where you're almost guaranteed to see sea lions sunning on the rocks or sea otters frolicking in the water.

Now it's time to really get up close and personal with that bay you've heard so much about. Explore the water via kayak. Go out on your own or book a tour with a company like **Adventures by the Sea** for a chance to see sea otters, harbor seals, and sea lions in their natural habitat. For marine mammals of a larger scale, book a whale watching tour in the winter and early spring to see gray and killer whales or late spring through fall for a chance to see humpback, blue, and killer whales.

Celebrate all the new friendships you've made among the denizens of the sea at **A Taste of Monterey.** This wine shop and tasting room showcases wines from Monterey County. Red, white, sparkling, rose—whatever strikes your fancy, you can sample a curated flight of local vintages all while enjoying a spectacular view of the bay. Another good choice is the **Carmel Ridge Winery Tasting Room.**

For a dinner that does not skip a beat, head to **Montrio Bistro.** Located in a converted historic firehouse, the atmosphere is romantic. The New American menu is as creative as it is delicious. The wine list is spot on. And not only is the food organic and sustainably sourced, they're environmentally friendly behind the scenes, implementing such practices as near-zero waste, full recycling, composting, and in-house reusables.

Day 2

Stop by **Café Lumiere** for a cup of something caffeinated and a quick, satisfying breakfast. But don't let the relaxed atmosphere fool you, every sip or bite you take has been brought to you thanks to an immense degree of consideration. The beans are locally roasted, they work solely with purveyors located in Central and Northern California, and almost everything—from the pastries to the sauces—is prepared in-house. Or grab one of the tiny tables scattered outside at the **Wild Plum Cafe.**

It's time to hop back in the car and gear up for this morning's activity: driving. Specifically, the **17-Mile Drive,** which takes you down the coast from Monterey through Pebble Beach and concludes in Carmel-by-the-Sea. Along the way you'll take in such sights as Point Joe, Bird Rock, and the famous **Lone Cypress.** Because the drive goes through Pebble Beach Resorts there is a per-vehicle entrance fee. But even in an area full of jaw-dropping vistas, it's worth the $11 to take this most scenic of routes. And, hey, it's about the journey not the destination, right? Although the destination isn't too shabby either.

At the end of the 17-Mile Drive you'll find yourself in Carmel-by-the-Sea (or, just simply, Carmel), which has the look of an exquisitely quaint village and the spirit of a high-end resort town. For the dining equivalent of the city's quintessential charm-meets-sophistication vibe, check out **Le Bicyclette.** This bistro serves classic French cuisine in an atmosphere that's suffused in cozy, old-world charm. You could also stop at the **Tuck Box,** in a

1927 cottage that looks like something from *The Hobbit.*

Yesterday was about exploring the region's "surf," now it's time for Central California's equally awe-inspiring "turf." Continue south toward Big Sur (your route will also take you across Bixby Bridge, which you may recognize from the opening credits of *Big Little Lies*) where you'll find yourself in a nature lover's paradise. There are a number of state parks and hiking trails to choose from—some offer ocean views, some allow you to lose yourself in what feels like an enchanted redwood forest, but they all make for an incredible experience in the (truly) great outdoors.

Dinner is at **Passionfish** back up north in Pacific Grove. Sustainability is a vitally important element to this restaurant's mission, which means guests will always be served fish that's incredibly fresh, local, and creatively prepared. All of that, plus the wine list highlights unique vintages from wineries dedicated to sustainable production all at a price that foregoes the usual, over-the-top restaurant markup.

Close out your night with a beer flight at **Dust Bowl Brewing Co. Tap Depot.** Whether you're an IPA devotee (try the Hops of Wrath) or looking for something light and smooth (check out the Taco Truck lager), this taproom makes for the perfect spot to enjoy a relaxed, laid back evening. Plus, if the weather's nice, you can enjoy a friendly game or two of cornhole out on their patio (or if it's on the cooler side, you can still enjoy your brews outdoors cozied up next to one of their fire pits).

Day 3

Start your day at **Wave Street Café,** which has everything you could want in a breakfast spot: cute-as-a-button patio, a view of the bay from said patio, friendly service, and a menu full of generously portioned breakfast favorites. **Rosine's Restaurant** is another good breakfast spot.

You've spent nearly this whole weekend looking out at the bay, hearing about its incredible biodiversity, but the best way to experience everything this incredible ecosystem entails is with a visit to the world-renowned **Monterey Bay Aquarium.** The exhibits here re-create what it might feel like to be immersed in the depths alongside these creatures. Glittering sardines swirl overhead in one room while a variety of ethereal and strange jellyfish flank you on either side of a darkened corridor. When you enter the Kelp Forest exhibit, you're at eye level with mighty sharks and humble hermit crabs alike. And you can watch the sea otters from above the water and below so you don't miss a moment of their playful antics.

By the time you exit the aquarium, you're likely to have clocked quite a few steps on your pedometer, so stop for a quick bite at nearby **El Cantaro** for some delicious vegan Mexican food—try the cactus huarache. For one more taste of the sea, consider **Vivolo's Chowder House.**

Before you head out, take a few moments to stop by **Asilomar State Beach.** With its dunes and tidal pools, it's an idyllic place to have a final, personal moment with the nature and draw your weekend to a close.

Recommendations

Sights

Asilomar State Beach. ✉ *Sunset Dr. and Asilomar Ave., Pacific Grove, CA* ☎ *831/646–6440* 🌐 *www.parks.ca.gov* 🎫 *Free.*

Coast Guard Pier. ✉ *100 Lighthouse Ave., Monterey, CA* ☎ *831/647–7300* 🌐 *www.monterey.org* 🎫 *Free.*

Monterey Bay Aquarium. ✉ *886 Cannery Row, Monterey, CA* ☎ *831/648–4800* 🌐 *www.montereybayaquarium.org* 🎫 *$50.*

17-Mile Drive. ✉ *17-Mile Dr., Pebble Beach, CA* ☎ *No phone.* 🌐 *www.pebblebeach.com/17-mile-drive* 🎫 *$11 per car.*

Restaurants

Alvarado Street Brewery & Grill. [$] *Average main: $16* ✉ *426 Alvarado St., Monterey, CA* ☎ *831/655–2337* 🌐 *www.alvaradostreetbrewery.com.*

Café Lumiere. [$] *Average main: $12* ✉ *365 Calle Principal, Monterey, CA* ☎ *831/920–2451* 🌐 *www.cafelumieremonterey.com.*

El Cantaro. [$] *Average main: $11* ✉ *791 Foam St., Monterey, CA* ☎ *831/646–5465* 🌐 *www.elcantaro.us* 🕒 *Closed Sat.*

Le Bicyclette. [$] *Average main: $18* ✉ *Dolores St. and 7th Ave., Carmel-By-The-Sea, CA* ☎ *831/622–9899* 🌐 *www.labicycletterestaurant.com* 🕒 *Closed Mon. and Tues.*

Monterey's Fish House. [$] *Average main: $20* ✉ *2114 Del Monte Ave., Monterey, CA* ☎ *831/373–4647* 🌐 *www.montereyfishhouse.com.*

Montrio Bistro. [$] *Average main: $15* ✉ *414 Calle Principal, Monterey, CA* ☎ *831/648–8880* 🌐 *www.montrio.com.*

Passionfish. [$] *Average main: $25* ✉ *701 Lighthouse Ave., Pacific Grove, CA* ☎ *831/655–3311* 🌐 *www.passionfish.net.*

Rosine's Restaurant. [$] *Average main: $14* ✉ *434 Alvarado St., Monterey, CA* ☎ *831/375–1400* 🌐 *www.rosinesmonterey.com.*

Tuck Box. [$] *Average main: $11* ✉ *Dolores St., between Ocean St. and 7th Ave., Carmel-By-The Sea, CA* ☎ *831/624–6365* 🌐 *www.tuckbox.com.*

Vivolo's Chowder House. [$] *Average main: $15* ✉ *127 Central Ave., Pacific Grove, CA* ☎ *831/372–5414* 🌐 *www.vivoloschowderhouse.com.*

Wave Street Café. $ *Average main: $15* ⊠ *550 Wave St., Lower Level, Monterey, CA* ☎ *831/718–8171* ⊕ *www.wavestreetcafe.com.*

Wild Plum Café. $ *Average main: $35* ⊠ *731 Munras Ave., Monterey, CA* ☎ *831/646–3109* ⊕ *www.thewildplumcafe.com.*

Hotels

Casa Munras Garden Hotel & Spa. $ *Rooms from: $161* ⊠ *700 Munras Ave., Monterey, CA* ☎ *831/375–2411* ⊕ *www.hotelcasamunras.com* ❑ *No meals.*

Old Monterey Inn. $ *Rooms from: $299* ⊠ *500 Martin St., Monterey, CA* ☎ *831/375–8284* ⊕ *www.oldmontereyinn.com* ❑ *Free breakfast.*

Spindrift Inn. $ *Rooms from: $144* ⊠ *652 Cannery Row, Monterey, CA* ☎ *831/646–8900* ⊕ *www.spindriftinn.com* ❑ *Free breakfast.*

Nightlife

Dust Bowl Brewing Co. Tap Depot. ⊠ *290 Figueroa St., Monterey, CA* ☎ *831/641–7002* ⊕ *www.dustbowlbrewing.com.*

Shopping

Carmel Ridge Winery Tasting Room. ⊠ *700 Cannery Row, Monterey, CA* ☎ *831/324–0035* ⊕ *www.carmelridgewinery.com.*

A Taste of Monterey. ⊠ *700 Cannery Row, Monterey, CA* ☎ *831/646–5446* ⊕ *www.atasteofmonterey.com.*

Activities

Adventures by the Sea. ⊠ *299 Cannery Row, Monterey, CA* ☎ *831/372–1807* ⊕ *www.adventuresbythesea.com* ❑ *$10 per person.*

Mount Rainier and the Yakima Valley, WA

70 miles (approx. 2 hours) from Seattle.

Living just a few hours from both one of the most impressive mountains in the country and an incredible wine country ranks high among the reasons to move to Seattle. In a single weekend, travelers who like both an outdoor adventure and the finer things in life can swoop into Mount Rainier National Park and admire the breathtaking scenery, hike through old-growth forests, and play in the snow year-round, then exit the far side of the park into Washington's dry side, where the sun produces world-class wines.

Planning

GETTING THERE AND BACK
This one is a genuine road trip, with multiple locations, so you'll want to be in a car to make your way across the state. The weaving paths that go from Seattle down to Mt. Rainier and across to Yakima and wine country open and close with the seasons, so make sure you're looking not just at your GPS as you make this drive. Check that everything is open on the Washington Department of Transportation website.

WHEN TO GO
While Mount Rainier National Park is open year-round, and you can visit Yakima and wine country any time, the only way you can combine the two is in the warmer months, as the roads out of the park to the east close seasonally.

WHERE TO STAY
For the peak (pun intended) of the Mt. Rainier experience, book a room at the **Paradise Inn** in Mount Rainier National Park. Just outside the park are a series of glamping-style spots, like **Stormking Cabins and Spa,** where each of the cozy accommodations has its own hot tub. In

Even on the hottest days of summer, the peak of Mount Rainier still glistens with snow.

wine country, **Desert Wind Winery** rents rooms and **Alexandria Nicole Cellars** offers tiny house rentals in the vineyard. On the more affordable end of the spectrum, **The Lodge at Columbia Point** has a great spot overlooking the river.

Day 1

Begin your journey after breakfast, with the drive to **Mineral Lake.** Dip your pole in for a little trout-fishing or cool off by dipping in a toe (but it's chilly, so not too much more). Then beat the heat in an even better way: with a stop at **Scaleburgers** in Elbe, where the roadside shack serves up old-school burgers and a mean malted shake, best eaten at the green picnic tables out front.

From there, head into **Mount Rainier National Park** through the Nisqually entrance, and in less than half-an-hour you'll be at Longmire. Hop out and hike around the Trail of the Shadows to get a sense of the history of the area. Then continue driving another few miles into

the park to Christine Falls for a photo-op before continuing on to Paradise. From Paradise, you can finish up the afternoon with any number of the hikes from the visitor's center, which range from short and paved to longer than you can do before sunset, and maybe a quick snowball fight.

Come dinner time, retrace your steps to just outside of the park entrance, where a former Everest Sherpa and world-record holding mountain climber runs a Nepalese restaurant called **Wildberry** with his family.

Day 2

Grab a coffee from your hotel and get an early start on the day so you can pause at Reflection Lakes before the crowds arrive. They are deservedly named for the mirror-like surface that reflects the vivid colors of the sky and trees. Take a quick walk around the three-mile loop before you make your way through the park and on to the Yakima Valley.

By the time you arrive you'll probably be hungry, to plan on a stop at **Los Hernández Tamales** in Union Gap. The asparagus tamales here bring people from miles around to sample the James Beard Award winner's specialty, which are made from the region's famous crop and masa ground in-house every day. Get back on the road for an afternoon of wine tasting: the Yakima Valley has more than 120 wineries in a few small clusters that make it easy to taste your way through a wide variety without having to go too far. The loamy volcanic soil and high, dry climate combine to make the vines yield abundantly. The same hot days and cool nights that make this a prime fruit-growing area—hit the brakes anytime you see a farm stand—bring the exact conditions that winemakers want.

Red Mountain bursts with high-quality reds from the area's warmest hills: stop into **Fidelitas Wines, Frichette Winery, Col Solare Winery,** or **Hedges Family Estate.** Alternatively, stick a little closer to the town of Prosser and taste your way through **Owen Roe, Airfield Estates Winery, Maryhill Winery,** and **Martinez & Martinez Winery.**

Wind your way back into town for Mexican food at **Xochimilco,** which specializes in the complex and labor-intensive moles from eastern Oaxaca. Or you can stay in wine country, where the food will be less impressive and more expensive, but the wine will likely be much better.

Day 3

Depending on when you wake up, either enjoy a few minutes wandering around the stands at **Yakima Farmers Market** or pop into **Essencia Artisan Bakery** for a quick bite and a few of their chocolates for the road. When you've had your fill, head out to the **Cowiche Canyon Trail** for a hike. It's 3 miles each way that wind along a creek lined with wildflowers and backed with high basalt cliffs. Listen for the birds as you walk along the level gravel path. There are plenty of connecting trails if you find this so lovely you don't want to leave.

Start your brewery crawl at **Bale Breaker Brewing Company,** where a food truck will likely be posted and ready to serve you a picnic lunch. The Yakima Valley is one of the world's biggest growers of hops, and the owners of Bale Breaker makes their beer from those grown on their own farm. Once you're rested and ready to get back on the hops path, make your way through Yakima's beloved beer scene: **Single Hill Brewing Company, Hop Capital Brewing, Hop Nation Brewing Company,** and **Wandering Hop Brewery.** Then grab one final meal at **Miner's Drive-In** for a Big Miner, the kind of giant hamburger that will power you all the way through the drive home.

Recommendations

Sights

Airfield Estates Winery. ✉ *14450 Redmond-Woodinville Rd. NE, Woodinville, WA* ☎ *425/877–1274* ⊕ *www.airfieldwines.com* 🍷 *Tastings from $10.*

Col Solare Winery. ✉ *50207 Antinori Rd., Benton City, WA* ☎ *509/588–6806* ⊕ *www.colsolare.com* 🍷 *Tastings from $20.*

Cowiche Canyon Trail. ✉ *8006 Cowiche Canyon Rd., Yakima, WA* ☎ *509/248–5065* ⊕ *www.cowichecanyon.org* 🍷 *Free.*

Fidelitas Wines. ✉ *14467 Redmond-Woodinville Rd. NE, Woodinville, WA* ☎ *425/558–9001* ⊕ *www.fidelitaswines.com* 🍷 *Tastings $15.*

Frichette Winery. ✉ *39412 N. Sunset Rd., Benton City, WA* ☎ *509/426–3227* ⊕ *www.frichettewinery.com* 🍷 *Tastings $15.*

Hedges Family Estate. ✉ *53511 N. Sunset Rd., Benton City, WA* ☎ *509/588–3155*

⊕ www.hedgesfamilyestate.com 🍷 Tastings $15.

Martinez & Martinez Winery. ⊠ 357 Port Ave., Prosser, WA ☎ 509/786–2392 ⊕ www.martinezwine.com 🍷 Tastings $5.

Maryhill Winery. ⊠ Hollywood Schoolhouse, 14810 N.E. 145th St., Woodinville, WA ☎ 425/481–7925 ⊕ www.maryhillwinery.com 🍷 Tastings $20.

Mineral Lake. ⊠ Mineral Hill Rd., Mineral, WA ☎ No phone ⊕ www.minerallake.com 🍷 Free.

Mount Rainier National Park. ⊠ Mount Rainier National Park Education Center, 55210 238th Ave. E, Ashford, WA ☎ 360/569–2211 ⊕ www.www.nps.gov/mora 🍷 Free.

Owen Roe. ⊠ 309 Gangl Rd., Wapato, WA ☎ 509/877–7717 ⊕ www.owenroe.com 🍷 Tastings $10.

🍴 Restaurants

Miner's Drive-In. $ Average main: $7 ⊠ 2415 S 1st St., Yakima, WA ☎ 509/457–8194.

Wildberry Restaurant. $ Average main: $12 ⊠ 37718 WA 706 E, Ashford, WA ☎ 360/569–2277 ⊕ www.rainierwildberry.com.

Xochimilco Mexican Restaurant. $ Average main: $10 ⊠ 2304 W. Nob Hill Blvd., Yakima, WA ☎ 509/453–3096 ⊕ www.xochimilcoyakima.com.

☕ Coffee and Quick Bites

Essencia Artisan Bakery. $ Average main: $10 ⊠ 4 N. 3rd St., Yakima, WA ☎ 509/575–5570 🕐 Closed Sun. and Mon.

🛏 Hotels

Alexandria Nicole Cellars Rooms. $ Rooms from: $200 ⊠ 158422 W. Sonova Rd., Prosser, WA ☎ 509/832–3877 ⊕ www.anctinyhouses.com ⦿ No meals.

Desert Wind Winery. $ Rooms from: $245 ⊠ 2258 Wine Country Rd., Prosser, WA ☎ 509/786–7277 ⊕ www.desertwindwinery.com ⦿ No meals.

The Lodge at Columbia Point. $ Rooms from: $199 ⊠ 530 Columbia Point Dr., Richland, WA ☎ 509/713–7423 ⊕ www.lodgeatcolumbiapoint.com ⦿ Free breakfast.

Paradise Inn. $ Rooms from: $138 ⊠ Mount Rainier National Park, Paradise Rd. E, Paradise, WA ☎ 360/569–2275 ⊕ mtrainierguestservices.com/accommodations/paradise-inn ⦿ No meals.

Stormking Cabins and Spa. $ Rooms from: $240 ⊠ 37311 WA 706, Ashford, WA ☎ 360/569–2964 ⊕ www.stormkingspa.com ⦿ No meals.

🍸 Nightlife

Bale Breaker Brewing Company. ⊠ 1801 Birchfield Rd., Yakima, WA ☎ 509/424–4000 ⊕ www.balebreaker.com.

Hop Capital Brewing. ⊠ 2920 River Rd., Yakima, WA ☎ 509/654–7357.

Hop Nation Brewing Company. ⊠ 31 N. 1st Ave., Yakima, WA ☎ 509/367–6552 ⊕ www.hopnationbrew.com.

Single Hill Brewing Company. ⊠ 102 N. Naches Ave., Yakima, WA ☎ 509/367–6756 ⊕ www.singlehillbrewing.com.

Wandering Hop Brewery. ⊠ 508 N. 20th Ave., Yakima, WA ☎ 509/426–2739 ⊕ www.wanderinghop.com.

Shopping

Yakima Farmers Market. ✉ *22 S. 3rd Ave., Yakima, WA* ☎ *509/961–2055* ⊕ *www.downtownyakimafarmersmarket.com.*

Napa Valley, CA

50 miles (approx. 1 hour) from San Francisco.

In 1976, the foremost names in French gastronomy gathered for a blind taste test that pitted top quality California and French wines against each other. It was assumed that the French wines would dominate. Instead, the top rated vintages hailed from California's Napa Valley.

The Judgment of Paris didn't just revolutionize the wine industry in California, or even in the United States. It shattered the illusion that great wines could only be made in France, showing winemakers all over the globe that they too could go toe-to-toe with the world's premiere wine regions.

Whether you have the palate of a sommelier or a novice, a visit to Napa Valley is essential for any wine lover. Here you can spend your weekend tasting wine from the industry's biggest names and its most exciting boutiques, sample food from some of the best chefs in the world, indulge in some world class pampering, and generally enjoy the finer things in life against the stunning backdrop of miles and miles of rolling, vineyard-clad hills.

Planning

GETTING THERE AND BACK
It's about 1½ hours of driving from San Francisco. If you're starting from the east side take the Bay Bridge for I–80 E and follow that to CA 29 N. If you're starting from the west side (or looking to optimize your scenery) take the Golden Gate Bridge and take the 101 N toward CA 37 E.

PIT STOPS
As road trips go, San Francisco to Napa Valley is a relatively short drive. But if you're not in a hurry take a detour to the staggeringly beautiful **Muir Woods National Monument** (if you're taking the western route) or stop at **Artís Coffee** in Berkeley for a caffeine boost (if you're taking the eastern route).

WHEN TO GO
There is truly never a bad time to visit Napa Valley. The weather is always fairly mild and the wineries stay open year-round. August through October is the all-important harvest season. Spring and summer bring particularly beautiful weather. Even winter is great timing for your getaway because you may luck out and find some lower rates, plus wintertime means annual events like Napa Valley Restaurant Week and the Napa Truffle Festival.

WHERE TO STAY
If you can't bear to ever be more than a few minutes' walking distance from Michelin-starred dining, check in to **Meadowood,** where the main on-site restaurant has received three coveted stars. For a still elegant but more relaxed experience there's **Solage** in Calistoga, where you can also pamper yourself with a mud treatment and some time enjoying their geothermal pools. For a more low-key base of operations, head to the **Napa River Inn** where you'll be within easy walking distance of the various gems downtown Napa has to offer.

Day 1

To ensure that you're not tasting on an empty stomach, stop by **Oxbow Public Market.** Here, you'll find a range of vendors serving up everything from Mexican food and pizza to oysters and charcuterie. A good backup is **Bistro Don Giovanni.**

Once you're sufficiently sated, make your way to **Domaine Carneros** to kick off your weekend with a sparkling wine tasting. You can head straight for the terrace and pair your tasting with some beautiful views of the vineyard below or arrange to take a tour of the estate and learn about the méthode traditionnelle—the magical process responsible for creating all those wonderful bubbles.

It's time to leave behind the sundrenched grandeur of Domaine Carneros for the intimate, quintessentially Californian atmosphere at **Sequoia Grove.** The tasting room at this winery, acclaimed for their Cabernet Sauvignon, is located inside a renovated barn surrounded by the eponymous conifers.

Dinner is at **Napa Valley Bistro** in downtown Napa where the menu features a wide range of comfort food that's made with high-quality ingredients and a slight twist. When you settle on the burger, it's made with lamb instead of beef. Straightforward classics here are executed with careful consideration for a dining experience that's in perfect, delicious harmony. Another good choice is **Tarla Mediterranean Grill.**

Day 2

Start your day with breakfast at **Boon Fly Café.** Though the menu here could be described as "hearty" and "rustic," make no mistake, this is no rusty food. Benedicts, chicken and waffles, and pancakes are prepared with a modern panache in a lively, airy setting. Even if you're not a sweets-for-breakfast sort, you'd be remiss to not sample their donuts, which arrive in a small pail and are accompanied by chocolate dipping sauce. Locals also swear by **Grace's Table.**

Head north up the valley to Calistoga for your appointment at the **MoonAcre Spa and Baths** at the Calistoga Motor

Lodge and Spa. Guests relax with classic massages and mud soaks or go the only-in-California route and opt for a treatment where guests are exfoliated with a scrub made from crushed grape seeds or a CBD facial. For an additional fee, spa day guests can have extra time by the geothermal mineral pools.

Before diving back into wine tasting, stop to pick up a quick nosh at the **Oakville Grocery,** a wine country institution dating back to the late 19th century. Its shelves are stocked with gourmet groceries, prepared food, and—of course—wine. If you're craving something more substantial, you can order one of their artisan sandwiches or brick oven pizzas. Take your food on the road or grab a spot on their patio for a high-end picnic. If classic French is more up your alley, head to Yountville's **Bistro Jeanty.**

The influence of Robert Mondavi on Napa Valley is twofold: his focus on crafting fine wines helped California's industry gain prominence on the world stage and consciously making his winery a destination in and of itself, something just about every winery now strives to do. So a visit to Napa truly isn't complete without stopping at **Robert Mondavi Winery.** There are a couple of different tour and tasting options, including the Signature Tour (which takes you through the vineyards and cellars) and the Caviar and Fumé Blanc Pairing (if you're looking for an especially luxe experience).

In an area full of impressive estates, **Domaine Chandon** manages to stand out with its sprawling, verdant grounds and the elegantly designed architecture that sits at the heart of the property. Chandon applies French winemaking techniques to the fruit produced by the region's unique terroir. While they also produce still wines, the main draw here is their sparkling wine. You can experience them in the indoor tasting room or take

The sprawling terrace of Domaine Carneros winery has some of the most spectacular views in the Napa Valley.

advantage of the outdoor parts of the property and sample your bubbly picnicking on the lawn or lounging in a cabana during the summer.

For dinner, you know exactly where you're going because you did the work to secure your reservation months in advance. Rest assured, your due diligence is about to pay off, as Chef Thomas Keller's legendary restaurant, **French Laundry,** is a once-in-a-lifetime dining experience worthy of centering your visit to Napa around. Guests have their choice of two set, multicourse menus (the Chef's Tasting Menu and the Tasting of Vegetables), both of which combine classic French cooking techniques, the freshest ingredients, and innovative dishes for a dining experience that's rightfully reputed as one of the best in the entire world. For something with more of an Italian accent, head to **Bottega Napa Valley.**

Day 3

Grab a cup of coffee or a latte from **Napa Valley Coffee Roasting Company** for a little morning pick me up before taking a scenic, winding drive to **The Hess Collection.** And while Hess is known for the Cabernet Sauvignons, something that makes this property particularly special is its unparalleled art collection. What started as Donald Hess' personal art collection has become a carefully selected showcase of 20 living artists. You can view the art at your own pace or you can reserve a docent-led museum walk.

We've all had that moment of regret when our dining companion's order arrives and we think, *Dang, I should've ordered that!* **Farm at Carneros** handily solves that problem with its family-style ordering during brunch, which allows you to order four menu items and share them among your party—which is perfect because you won't want to miss out on the lobster roll or brioche French toast or crispy duck confit hash. Another great spot is **Evangeline.**

Cap off your weekend with one last wine tasting at **Artesa Vineyards.** Established by Spain's oldest winemaking family in 1991, the design of the property is sophisticated yet minimalist so as to not take away from the beauty of the surrounding landscape. Enjoy tasting wine crafted with an artisan's consideration while enjoying the incredible views of the valley.

Recommendations

Sights

Artesa Vineyards. ✉ *1345 Henry Rd., Napa, CA* ☎ *707/224–1668* 🌐 *www.artesawinery.com* 🎫 *Tastings $35.*

Domaine Carneros. ✉ *1240 Duhig Rd., Napa, CA* ☎ *707/257–0101* 🌐 *www.domainecarneros.com* 🎫 *Tastings $40.*

Domaine Chandon. ✉ *1 California Dr., Yountville, CA* ☎ *888/242–6366* 🌐 *www.chandon.com* 🎫 *Tastings $25.*

The Hess Collection. ✉ *4411 Redwood Rd., Napa, CA* ☎ *707/255–1144* 🌐 *www.hesscollection.com* 🎫 *Tastings $35.*

Muir Woods National Monument. ✉ *1 Muir Woods Rd., Mill Valley, CA* ☎ *415/561–2850* 🌐 *www.nps.gov/muwo/index.htm* 🎫 *$15.*

Robert Mondavi Winery. ✉ *7801 St. Helena Hwy., Oakville, CA* ☎ *888/766–6328* 🌐 *www.robertmondaviwinery.com* 🎫 *$50.*

Sequoia Grove Winery. ✉ *8338 St. Helena Hwy., Napa, CA* ☎ *707/944–2945* 🌐 *www.sequoiagrove.com* 🎫 *Tastings $35.*

Restaurants

Bistro Don Giovanni. [$] *Average main: $26* ✉ *4110 Howard La., Napa, CA* ☎ *707/224–3300* 🌐 *www.bistrodongiovanni.com.*

Bistro Jeanty. [$] *Average main: $30* ✉ *6510 Washington St., Yountville, CA* ☎ *707/944–0103* 🌐 *www.bistrojeanty.com.*

Boon Fly Cafe. [$] *Average main: $36* ✉ *Carneros Resort and Spa, 4048 Sonoma Hwy., Napa, CA* ☎ *707/299–4870* 🌐 *www.boonflycafe.com.*

Bottega Napa Valley. [$] *Average main: $32* ✉ *6525 Washington St., Yountville, CA* ☎ *707/ 945–1050* 🌐 *www.bottegnapavalley.com* 🕒 *No lunch Mon.*

Evangeline. [$] *Average main: $28* ✉ *1226 Washington St., Calistoga, CA* ☎ *707/341–3131* 🌐 *www.evangelinenapa.com.*

Farm at Carneros. [$] *Average main: $26* ✉ *Caneros Resort and Spa, 4048 Sonoma Hwy., Napa, CA* ☎ *707/299–4880* 🌐 *www.carnerosresort.com/napa-ca-dining* 🕒 *No lunch Mon.–Sat.*

French Laundry. [$] *Average main: $325 tasting menu.* ✉ *6640 Washington St., Yountville, CA* ☎ *707/944–2380* 🌐 *www.thomaskeller.com/tfl/menu* 🕒 *No lunch Mon.–Thurs.*

Grace's Table. [$] *Average main: $22* ✉ *1400 2nd St., Napa, CA* ☎ *707/226–6200* 🌐 *www.gracestable.net.*

Napa Valley Bistro. [$] *Average main: $32* ✉ *975 Clinton St., Napa, CA* ☎ *707/666–2383* 🌐 *www.napavalleybistro.com* 🕒 *Closed Mon.*

Tarla Mediterranean Bistro. [$] *Average main: $16* ✉ *1480 1st St., Napa, CA* ☎ *707/255–5599* 🌐 *www.tarlagrill.com.*

☕ Coffee and Quick Bites

Artís Coffee. $ *Average main: $5* ✉ *1717 4th St., Berkeley, CA* ☎ *510/898–1104* ⊕ *shop.artiscoffee.com* ☽ *No dinner.*

Napa Valley Coffee Roasting Company. $ *Average main: $5* ✉ *1400 Oak Ave., St. Helena, CA* ☎ *707/963–4491* ⊕ *www. napavalleycoffee.com* ☽ *No dinner.*

🛏 Hotels

Meadowood. $ *Rooms from: $800* ✉ *900 Meadowood La., St. Helena, CA* ☎ *707/531–4788* ⊕ *www.meadowood. com* ❙❍❙ *No meals.*

Napa River Inn. $ *Rooms from: $284* ✉ *500 Main St., Napa, CA* ☎ *707/251– 850* ⊕ *www.napariverinn.com* ❙❍❙ *No meals.*

Solage. $ *Rooms from: $589* ✉ *755 Silverado Trail N, Calistoga, CA* ☎ *866/942– 7442* ⊕ *aubergeresorts.com/solage* ❙❍❙ *No meals.*

🛍 Shopping

MoonAcre Spa and Baths. ✉ *Calistoga Motor Lodge, 1880 Lincoln Ave., Calistoga, CA* ☎ *707/942–0992* ⊕ *calistogamotorlodgeandspa.com/spa.*

Oakville Grocery. ✉ *7856 St. Helena Hwy., Oakville, CA* ☎ *707/944–8802* ⊕ *www. oakvillegrocery.com.*

Oxbow Public Market. ✉ *610 1st St., Napa, CA* ☎ *707/226–6529* ⊕ *oxbowpublicmarket.com.*

Olympic Peninsula, WA

82 miles (approx. 2½ hours, including ferry trip) from Seattle.

In the Pacific Northwest, you can get to nature in no time flat. Even its most populous city, Seattle, is surrounded by so many evergreen trees it's been nicknamed "the Emerald City." Within just a few hours, you can be completely immersed in moss-blanketed rain forests, quiet beaches, and fog-enveloped mountains—and see relatively few people along the way. There's no better place for that than the lush Olympic National Park, a haven for outdoorsy types who crave a weekend of hiking, camping, and lots of sweet, sweet open spaces. Whether you're packing a cooler and camping or staying in mountain lodges, this beautiful (and car-friendly) PNW trip is a breath of fresh air.

Planning

GETTING THERE AND BACK
The Washington State Ferry is the quickest way to get to Olympic National Park. From Seattle, take the Seattle–Bainbridge Island Ferry from Pier 52 (30 to 40 minutes), or, if you're leaving from Seattle's northern suburbs take the 9:35 am Edmonds–Kingston ferry from 199 Sunset Ave. South (30 to 40 minutes). If you miss it, no biggie—a ferry departs every 45 minutes. Regardless of which ferry you take, you will drive to Port Angeles, the gateway to Olympic National Park (1½ hours). The last ferry headed back to Seattle leaves at midnight. If you prefer to drive, take I–5 S and then Highway 101 to Hoh Rain Forest. The trip takes about three hours.

PIT STOPS
You may run into traffic, but you can also make a pit stop in Tacoma to see **Point Defiance Park** or in capital city Olympia to see **Nisqually National Wildlife Refuge.**

WHEN TO GO
Summer through early fall is optimal for camping and hiking, with most campgrounds opening in May and closing around Labor Day. Some lodges, such as Sol Duc Hot Springs Resort, close around mid-October. Crowds peak in July and August, when the campgrounds can be busy. Make sure to pack warm

Hoh Rain Forest's lush Hall of Mosses is worth the trip to Olympia National Park.

clothes for cold nights—the high in July and August is a cool 62 degrees and the average low is a chilly (or rejuvenating) 42 degrees.

WHERE TO STAY

Stay in the rustic cabins at **Sol Duc Hot Springs Resort** on Day 1. Another option is **Lake Crescent Lodge,** a good base that gives you front-and-center access to the lake. If you don't stay put at Lake Crescent, move on to the coast for Day 2. Check into **Manitou Lodge,** a homey mountain lodge with rooms or cabins outfitted with driftwood headboards and quilted bedspreads. Breakfast is included. Camping is a popular option in the Olympic National Park, but be sure to obtain a wilderness camping permit from the Port Angeles Wilderness Information Center.

Day 1

To reach **Olympic National Park** from Seattle, hit the ground running Friday at 8 am. Pick up your favorite coffee and breakfast in town (may we suggest **Slate Coffee Bar** in Ballard or **Milstead & Co.** in Fremont?) before driving onto the 9:35 am **Seattle–Bainbridge Island Ferry** at Pier 52. (If you're leaving from a northern suburb, drive onto the **Edmonds–Kingston Ferry** at Sunset Avenue South.) The ride is about 30 minutes; pop up to the top deck if you can for spectacular views.

Once you depart the ferry, make the 1½-hour drive north to Port Angeles, the park's charming waterside gateway town, where you'll either pick up last minute camping supplies or stop for a noon lunch. Choose a local favorite like **Toga's Soup House,** serving deli sandwiches with a side of Olympic Mountain views, or **Next Door Gastropub** with burgers, tacos, and beer (for your trusty shot-gun seat companions).

After lunch, make the easy drive to Hurricane Hill and hike Hurricane Ridge for dramatic views of the snow-capped Olympic Mountains. Afterward you'll drive deep into the lush evergreens of Hoh Rain Forest to Sol Duc Hot Springs

Resort, where you can opt to camp or check into a cabin. Once you're settled, explore the mineral baths on the grounds, or make a hiking trek to the three-chute waterfalls at Sol Duc Falls, and marvel at the moss covering the forest like a blanket. Nothing has ever been so green!

For dinner, show off your camping prowess by roasting marshmallows over an old-fashioned campfire, or grab a bite at Sol Duc Hot Springs' casual eatery, **Springs Restaurant.** Another option is to drive out to **Granny's Café** on Highway 101 for burgers and a slice of pie—it's a classic in these parts. Nightlife is nonexistent, unless you count campfire s'mores and ghost stories. Drift off to sleep under towering spruce trees with visions of toasted marshmallows dancing in your head.

Day 2

Wake up early on Saturday for a day of driving and hiking in the park. Eat a granola bar or grab breakfast at the **Springs Restaurant** before you head out. Drive an hour to Second Beach, swapping forest views for beach ones.

Your first order of business is to hike the easy Second Beach Trail, meandering through the rainforest. When you reach the end of the forest trail, the view will take your breath away: the Pacific Ocean as far as the eye can see, with sea stacks covered in evergreens, and a beautiful stretch of beach. Dip your toes in the chilly water and breathe in the salty air, keeping an eye out for bald eagles and whales.

For lunch, treat yourself to water views and seafood at the Quileute Nation's **River's Edge Restaurant** in nearby La Push. A great afternoon detour is Rialto Beach, strewn with driftwood and sea stacks.

In the evening your agenda is blissfully free. Relax, recharge, reconnect with

nature. Drive back to the Hoh Rainforest if you like to hike the short **Hall of Mosses** trail with—you guessed it—more moss-covered fairy-tale trees; take a long stroll along Third Beach, or explore the small town of Forks. Whatever you do, make sure to watch sunset on Second Beach.

For dinner, if you're truly sick of your camping snacks, you can drive to **Blakeslees Bar and Grill** in Forks for tacos, beer, and live music, or to **Pacific Pizza** for a cheesy slice before curling up for a night under the stars—with actual ocean sounds to lull you to sleep.

Day 3

Take one last beach walk early Sunday morning, then drive to your final stop before heading back to Port Angeles: **Lake Crescent.** The glacier-carved lake, surrounded by towering mountains, makes a refreshing end to a perfect weekend. En route, grab breakfast in Forks at **A Shot in the Dark,** a tiny cabin with to-go breakfast sandwiches and iced mochas. **In Place** is another solid choice if you'd like to sit down for hearty breakfast food.

The drive to Lake Crescent takes about 45 minutes, by which time you should be ready to go kayaking over the glassy water. Lake Crescent Lodge offers guided kayak tours and kayak, canoe, and paddleboard rentals. When you're out there soaking up all the fresh mountain air, you'll wonder how the lake could possibly appear so blue. In reality it's due to the lake's clarity and reflection, but we like to think it's a little magic, too.

For lunch you can grab a bite of "farm-to-fork" Pacific Northwest cuisine at **Lake Crescent Lodge Dining Room** or casual sandwiches and ice cream from **Fairholme Store,** which is also the spot to buy souvenirs. If you prefer a sit-down restaurant, take a short drive to **Blackberry**

Café for diner-fare like burgers and turkey clubs.

After you take in your last vistas, it's time to grab dinner in Port Angeles before heading home. If you have little time and need a quick on-the-go meal, grab a burrito from **Little Devil's Lunchbox** before hitting the road. If you have some time for a sit-down meal, head to **C'est Si Bon** for an elaborate French dining experience under oil paintings and chandeliers. It's a great spot to cozy up with a bottle of wine and flip through all your new breathtaking nature photos.

Recommendations

Sights

Edmunds–Kingston Ferry. ⊠ *199 Sunset Ave. S, Edmonds, WA* ☎ *206/464–6400* ⊕ *www.wsdot.com/ferries* 🎫 *$9.*

Hall of Mosses. ⊠ *Hoh Valley Rd., Forks, WA* ☎ *360/565–2985* ⊕ *www.nps.gov/ olym/planyourvisit/visiting-the-hoh.htm* 🎫 *$15.*

Nisqually National Wildlife Refuge. ⊠ *100 Brown Farm Rd. NE, Olympia, WA* ☎ *360/753–9467* ⊕ *www.fws.gov/refuge/ billy_frank_jr_nisqually* 🎫 *$3.*

Olympic National Park. ⊠ *Hurricane Ridge Visitor Center, 3002 Mt. Angeles Rd., Port Angeles, WA* ☎ *360/565–3130* ⊕ *www.nps.gov/olym/index.htm* 🎫 *$15.*

Point Defiance Park. ⊠ *5400 N Pearl St., Tacoma, WA* ☎ *253/305–1088* ⊕ *www. metroparkstacoma.org/place/point-defiance-park* 🎫 *Free.*

Seattle–Bainbridge Island Ferry. ⊠ *801 Alaskan Way, Pier 52, Seattle, WA* ☎ *206/464–6400* ⊕ *www.wsdot.wa.gov/ ferries* 🎫 *$9.*

🍴 Restaurants

Blackberry Café. $ *Average main: $14* ⊠ *50530 WA 112, Port Angeles, WA* ☎ *360/928–0141.*

Blakeslees Bar and Grill. $ *Average main: $12* ⊠ *1222 S. Forks Ave., Forks, WA* ☎ *360/374–5003.*

C'est Si Bon. $ *Average main: $35* ⊠ *23 Cedar Park Dr., Port Angeles, WA* ☎ *360/452–8888* ⊕ *www.cestsib-on-frenchcuisine.com* ⊘ *Closed Mon. and Tues. No lunch.*

Granny's Café. $ *Average main: $14* ⊠ *235471 U.S. 101, Port Angeles, WA* ☎ *360/928–3266* ⊕ *www.grannyscafe.net* ⊘ *Closed Tues. and Wed.*

In Place. $ *Average main: $15* ⊠ *320 S. Forks Ave., Forks, WA* ☎ *360/374–4004.*

Lake Crescent Lodge Dining Room. $ *Average main: $40* ⊠ *416 Lake Crescent Rd., Port Angeles, WA* ☎ *360/928–3211* ⊕ *www.olympicnationalparks.com/dining/ lake-crescent-lodge.* ·

Little Devil's Lunchbox. $ *Average main: $10* ⊠ *315 E. 1st St., Port Angeles, WA* ☎ *360/504–2959* ⊕ *www.devilslunch. com* ⊘ *Closed Sun.*

Next Door Gastropub. $ *Average main: $15* ⊠ *113 W. 1st St., Port Angeles, WA* ☎ *360/504–2613* ⊕ *www.nextdoorgastro-pub.com.*

Pacific Pizza. $ *Average main: $15* ⊠ *870 S. Forks Ave., Forks, WA* ☎ *360/374–2626.*

River's Edge Restaurant. $ *Average main: $10* ⊠ *41 Main St., La Push, WA* ☎ *360/374–077.*

Springs Restaurant. $ *Average main: $12* ⊠ *12076 Sol Duc Rd., Port Angeles, WA* ☎ *360/327–3583* ⊕ *www.olympicnation-alparks.com/dining/sol-duc-hot-springs-resort* ⊘ *Closed Nov.–late Mar.*

Toga's Soup House. $ *Average main: $15* ✉ *122 W. Lauridsen Blvd., Port Angeles, WA* ☎ *360/452–1952* ⊕ *www.togas-souphouse.com.*

 Coffee and Quick Bites

Milstead & Co. $ *Average main: $5* ✉ *754 N. 34th St., Seattle, WA* ☎ *206/659–4814* ⊕ *www.milsteadandco.com* ⊘ *Closed Mon.*

A Shot in the Dark. $ *Average main: $4* ✉ *131 N. Forks Ave., Forks, WA* ☎ *360/374–3388.*

Slate Coffee Bar. $ *Average main: $5* ✉ *5413 6th Ave. NW, Seattle, WA* ☎ *No phone* ⊕ *www.slatecoffee.com.*

🛏 **Hotels**

Lake Crescent Lodge. $ *Rooms from: $139* ✉ *Lake Crescent Rd., Port Angeles, WA* ☎ *888/896–3818* ⊕ *www.olympicnationalparks.com/lodging/lake-crescent-lodge* ❣️ *Free breakfast.*

Manitou Lodge. $ *Rooms from: $198* ✉ *813 Kilmer Rd., Forks, WA* ☎ *360/374–6295* ⊕ *www.manitoulodge.com* ❣️ *Free breakfast.*

Sol Duc Hot Springs Resort. $ *Rooms from: $210* ✉ *12076 Sol Duc-Hot Springs Rd., Port Angeles, WA* ☎ *888/896–3818* ⊕ *www.olympicnationalparks.com/lodging/sol-duc-hot-springs-resort* ❣️ *Free breakfast.*

 Shopping

Fairholme Store. ✉ *Olympic National Park, 221121 U.S. 101, Port Angeles, WA* ☎ *360/928–3020* ⊕ *www.olympicnationalparks.com/things-to-do/shopping/fairholme-store.*

Palm Springs, CA

107 miles (approx. 2 hours) from Los Angeles.

The easiest, most foolproof way to get out of the City of Angels for a weekend getaway filled with sunshine, luxury, and decadence is to get in your car and drive the miniscule two-hour trek to Palm Springs. This desert oasis has long been known for being a celebrity hotspot filled with fancy resorts, upscale eateries, and steamy hot springs (and spas and pools) to get your soak on. It's also for lovers of great architecture and gorgeous scenery. Here's how to spend a perfect weekend in the desert.

Planning

GETTING THERE AND BACK

It's a straight shot from Los Angeles to Palm Springs via I–10 E, with a drive time of 1 hour and 55 minutes. Via CA 60 E, the journey is just 10 minutes longer.

PIT STOPS

After driving about 1½ hours from Los Angeles, take the exit to Cabazon for a brief pit stop at **Cabazon Dinosaurs.** It's a scenic desert area where you can stretch your legs and the kids can sit on the legs of some huge dinosaur statues. If you are so inclined, you could also stop by the **Cabazon Outlets** for some low-priced designer duds.

WHEN TO GO

Honestly, there's really not a bad time to go to Palm Springs. There's actually not even a "kind of bad" time to go—it's always a good time. That said, the best time to visit, if you are a true perfectionist, is from January through April, when the weather is literally perfect rather than "fine" or "hot." The temperatures hit triple digits toward the end of the summer, but then again, that's why pools exist.

The otherworldly fauna of Joshua Tree National Park makes it a favorite of photographers.

WHERE TO STAY

The **Parker Palm Springs** and the **Colony Palms Hotel** are two of the city's fancier options. Looking for something a little cheaper? That makes sense. The **Ace Hotel & Swim Club** is a good midrange option, while also being a hipster hot spot and general fun place to be. **Hotel California** is a cute boutique hotel with comfy, stylish rooms and a fire pit where you can sit and enjoy a cocktail.

Day 1

Just because the drive's not long doesn't mean you can sleep in—it means you get more time there to do fun things, and that's why we're hitting the road as early as possible. Try to get on the road around 9 (no later than 10) to make the most of your Friday. Once you arrive in Palm Springs, head to **Workshop Kitchen + Bar** for lunch. This place is a historic movie theater from the 1920s transformed into a spacious eatery with plush booths and small plates that are perfect for sharing.

After lunch you can get the lay of the land by hopping aboard the **Palm Springs Aerial Tramway,** which travels to the 8,516-foot peak of Mt. San Jacinto, from which you can see almost the entirety of the Coachella Valley spread at your feet. Short hiking trails meander along the top of the mountain, and more adventurous types can hike back down to the bottom.

Animal lovers should make a beeline to the 1,800-acre **Living Desert,** an important rescue and breeding center for a wide variety of desert-dwelling wildlife from around the world. At this Palm Desert preserve you can enjoy the singularly weird-but-adorable experience of feeding carrot sticks to the resident giraffes. It's also crisscrossed by trails that reveal a different side of the valley.

After all this activity, you deserve a break. Relax at the **Tonga Hut Restaurant & Tiki Bar,** the perfect place for happy hour drinks and dinner. Chances are you will want to stay awhile, but for a change of scenery keeping with the tropical theme, head over to **Toucan's Tiki Lounge**

& Cabaret for more drinks, drag queen performances, and other live entertainment, long into the night.

Day 2

Get up early, because if you want to get a seat at **Cheeky's** for breakfast (and you do), you should get there when it opens. Here you'll find a lively brunch menu, including a world-famous bacon flight with five different kinds of bacon and something called Custard Cheesy Scrambled Eggs, which, as you can probably tell by the name alone, is one of the most important things ever created. (Cheeky's too packed for your liking? Head to **King's Highway**, the Ace Hotel's diner.)

After breakfast, it's time to sit in some extremely hot water. Use the rest of your morning to have a soak in one of Palm Springs' hot springs, which are located in nearby Desert Hot Springs (a 19-minute drive away). A notable and famed option is **Two Bunch Palms,** an adults-only resort with day packages for hot springs available. Another more intimate option in Desert Hot Springs is **The Good House,** where you can arrange for a day pass if you are not staying at the hotel. Perhaps the most lavish option, however, would be to book a day pass at **El Morocco Inn & Spa,** a lush and exotic hotel in Desert Hot Springs.

After a few hours of soaking, it's time to get back out there into nature. We're headed to **Joshua Tree National Park** (about a 50-minute drive) for a few hours of walking around in nature. First, stop at **Joshua Tree Saloon** for barbeque steaks and burgers (and maybe a quick game of darts) in an actual saloon with major Old West vibes. A similar option is **Crossroads Cafe,** which still boasts the Old West vibe but is slightly more modern (and has vegan options). After you're good and full, you're ready to do some trekking about the desert in Joshua Tree. Park

your car and have a stroll around one of the nature trails.

Once you've got your fill of the desert, head to **Pappy & Harriet's** for dinner and live music (and drinks in mason jars) Note: you will want to make a reservation two to three weeks before to reserve your dinner table. If live music isn't your thing or you'd like to head back to Palm Springs before getting your nightlife on, head back, change out of your day clothes, and hit up **Hair of the Dog,** a laid-back, English-theme pub with more than 50 beers, a jukebox, and bar fare.

Day 3

Rise and shine, precious. It's Sunday, and that means it's brunch time. Head on over to **Norma's** at the Parker Hotel, get a seat preferably on the pretty patio and immediately order some doughnuts to share (followed by, say, eggs Benedict). After, get a game of bocce ball or two in (also at the Parker Palm Springs) and order a vodka lemonade from the lemonade stand followed by heading out to **Cod Street Fair** at the northwest corner of the College of the Desert campus. This street fair is popular among locals and tourists alike, and it's massive, with items for sale for all ages and all budgets.

Once you've gotten your fill, check out some art at the Art Galleries at Backstreet Art District, a community of artists' studios and galleries including paintings, ceramics, jewelry, photography and more. Palm Springs has several excellent vintage stores, including **Iconic Atomic, Gypsyland, Mitchell's,** and **Revivals.** For antiques and collectibles, check out Sunny Dune's Vintage Row, which has a number of shops like **Little Shop of Treasures.** And if these stores didn't satiate your shopping needs, head to Old Town La Quinta (nonchain stores) or to Downtown Palm Springs (mostly chain stores), depending on what you prefer.

Hit up **Rooster and the Pig** for some delicious Vietnamese food, or, if you're feeling super fancy, go to **The Purple Palm** for a glamorous, old Hollywood vibe and new American cuisine. And, would you look at that, it's time to head back to Los Angeles.

Recommendations

Sights

Cabazon Dinosaurs. ⊠ 50770 Seminole Dr., Cabazon, CA ☎ 951/922–8700 ⊕ www. cabazondinosaurs.com 🎫 $13.

Joshua Tree National Park. ⊠ 74485 National Park Dr., Twentynine Palms, CA ☎ 760/367–5500 ⊕ www.nps.gov 🎫 $30 per vehicle.

Living Desert. ⊠ 47900 Portola Ave., Palm Desert, CA ☎ 760/346–5694 ⊕ www. livingdesert.org 🎫 $25.

Palm Springs Aerial Tramway. ⊠ 1 Tramway Rd., Palm Springs, CA ☎ 888/515–8726 ⊕ www.pstramway.com 🎫 $27 round-trip.

🍴 Restaurants

Cheeky's. Ⓢ Average main: $10 ⊠ 622 N. Palm Canyon Dr., Palm Springs, CA ☎ 760/327–7595 ⊕ www.cheekysps. com.

Crossroads Cafe. Ⓢ Average main: $12 ⊠ 61715 Twentynine Palms Hwy., Joshua Tree, CA ☎ 760/366–5414 ⊕ www.cross- roadscafejtree.com.

Joshua Tree Saloon. Ⓢ Average main: $12 ⊠ 61835 Twentynine Palms Hwy., Joshua Tree, CA ☎ 760/366–2250 ⊕ www.josh- uatreesaloon.com.

King's Highway. Ⓢ Average main: $15 ⊠ 1701 E. Palm Canyon Dr., Palm Springs, CA ☎ 760/969–5777 ⊕ www. kingshighwaydiner.com.

Norma's. Ⓢ Average main: $28 ⊠ 4200 E. Palm Canyon Dr., Palm Springs, CA ☎ 760/770–5000 ⊕ www.parkerpalm- springs.com.

Pappy & Harriet's. Ⓢ Average main: $14 ⊠ 53688 Pioneertown Rd., Pioneertown, CA ☎ 760/365–5956 ⊕ www.pappyand- harriets.com ⊘ Closed Tues. and Wed.

The Purple Palm. Ⓢ Average main: $29 ⊠ 572 N. Indian Canyon Dr., Palm Springs, CA ☎ 760/969–1818 ⊕ www. purplepalmrestaurant.com.

Rooster and the Pig. Ⓢ Average main: $14 ⊠ 356 S. Indian Canyon Dr., Palm Springs, CA ☎ 760/832–6691 ⊕ www. roosterandthepig.com ⊘ Closed Tues.

Tonga Hut Restaurant & Tiki Bar. Ⓢ Average main: $18 ⊠ 254 N. Palm Canyon Dr., Palm Springs, CA ☎ 760/322–4449 ⊕ www.tongahut.com ⊘ Closed Mon.

Workshop Kitchen + Bar. Ⓢ Average main: $34 ⊠ 800 N. Palm Canyon Dr., Palm Springs, CA ☎ 760/459–3451 ⊕ www. workshoppalmsprings.com.

Hotels

Ace Hotel & Swim Club. Ⓢ Rooms from: $181 ⊠ 701 E. Palm Canyon Dr., Palm Springs, CA ☎ 760/325–9900 ⊕ www. acehotel.com ❙❍❙ No meals.

Colony Palms Hotel. Ⓢ Rooms from: $135 ⊠ 572 N. Indian Canyon Dr., Palm Springs, CA ☎ 760/969–1800 ⊕ www. colonypalmshotel.com ❙❍❙ No meals.

Hotel California. Ⓢ Rooms from: $145 ⊠ 424 E. Palm Canyon Dr., Palm Springs, CA ☎ 760/322–8855 ⊕ www.palmspring- shotelcalifornia.com ❙❍❙ No meals.

Parker Palm Springs. Ⓢ Rooms from: $319 ⊠ 4200 E. Palm Canyon Dr., Palm Springs, CA ☎ 760/770–5000 ⊕ www. parkerpalmsprings.com ❙❍❙ No meals.

Nightlife

Hair of the Dog. ✉ *555 S. Palm Canyon Dr., Palm Springs, CA* ☎ *760/323–9890.*

Toucan's Tiki Lounge & Cabaret. ✉ *2100 N. Palm Canyon Dr., Palm Springs, CA* ☎ *760/416–7584* ⊕ *www.toucanstikilounge.com.*

Shopping

Cabazon Outlets. ✉ *48750 Seminole Dr., Cabazon, CA* ☎ *951/922–3000* ⊕ *www.cabazonoutlets.com*

Cod Street Fair. ✉ *43-500 Monterey Ave., Palm Desert, CA* ☎ *760/636–7957* ⊕ *www.codaastreetfair.com.*

El Morocco Inn & Spa. ✉ *66810 4th St., Desert Hot Springs, CA* ☎ *760/288–2527* ⊕ *www.elmoroccoinn.com*

The Good House. ✉ *12885 Eliseo Rd., Desert Hot Springs, CA* ☎ *760/251–2885* ⊕ *www.welcometothegoodhouse.com.*

Gypsyland. ✉ *66169 Pierson Blvd., Desert Hot Springs, CA* ☎ *760/251–0588.*

Iconic Atomic. ✉ *1103 N. Palm Canyon Dr., Palm Springs, CA* ☎ *760/322–0777* ⊕ *www.iconicatomic.com.*

Little Shop of Treasures. ✉ *616 E. Sunny Dunes Rd., Palm Springs, CA* ☎ *760/778–4300.*

Mitchell's. ✉ *106 S. Indian Canyon, Palm Springs, CA* ☎ *760/864–1515* ⊕ *www.mitchellspalmsprings.com.*

Revivals. ✉ *611 S. Palm Canyon Dr., Palm Springs, CA* ☎ *760/318–6491* ⊕ *www.revivalsstores.com.*

Two Bunch Palms. ✉ *67425 Two Bunch Palms Tr., Desert Hot Springs, CA* ☎ *760/676–5000* ⊕ *www.twobunchpalms.com.*

Portland, OR

175 miles (approx. 3 hours) from Seattle.

Farther south, more compact, and with none of the sales taxes, Portland tempts Seattleites down the I–5 corridor for visits full of boutique lodgings, interesting shops, and superior (and somehow still cheaper) food scene. Portland's efficient public transportation, flat and bikeable streets, and packed urban core mean no car is necessary—a rarity for the spread-out Pacific Northwest. The city's size and personality provide ample opportunity for up-and-comers of all kinds—musicians, authors, artists, chefs—to find the space and audience to showcase their talents.

Planning

GETTING THERE AND BACK

If there's a mode of transportation, it connects Seattle and Portland. The Sunday afternoon traffic coming north makes driving less than ideal, but it can be more pleasant (and cheaper) when taken in from the back of the ultra-affordable buses that connect the two cities. Flying can be costly, but quick, the train costs and serves up a view, but keeps you beholden to a schedule.

WHEN TO GO

The weather is the only thing that might differ from one season to the next, so if you're okay with walking in a drizzle (and the very occasional snow storm) the cheaper winter lodging prices might appeal. Mostly, the mild climate makes it an always-appealing destination.

WHERE TO STAY

Music lovers might head to **Jupiter Next** to be near the Doug Fir Lounge, but the reality is Portland's boutique hotel boom, including **The Nines,** offers a stunning array of cool rooms and unique amenities at every price level.

Day 1

Leaving Seattle after breakfast gets you into Portland just in time for lunch at **Eem,** the Thai barbecue spot that takes the idea behind musical supergroups into restaurant form. A collaboration between the city's star Thai food chef and a renowned Texas-style pitmaster, it results in dishes like brisket boudain with fried egg salad.

After lunch, make your way through Portland's legendary beer scene. Seattle and Portland battle for IPA supremacy, but everyone actually wins with the overwhelming selection of intriguing, refreshing beers at spots such as **Hair of the Dog, Laurelwood, Hopworks, Base Camp, Breakside,** and **Gigantic.** Break up the brew fest by popping into a different kind of drinking establishment: take the Friday afternoon factory tour and tasting of **Steven Smith Teamaker** and learn about how they source, blend, and produce their high-end teas.

Then head to Bonnie Morales's ode to Russian food, **Kachka,** where you can keep drinking with horseradish vodka, but also dig into the dishes that changed the city—and country's—image of Russian cuisine, like the rainbow-layered salad herring under a fur coat and Siberian dumplings before heading out to hear local or national acts play in small settings at places like the **Doug Fir Lounge, Revolution Hall,** the **Alberta Rose Theatre,** or the **Wonder Ballroom.**

Day 2

Everything about the **Portland Farmers Market** represents the city at its most quintessential self: the connection of people to their food, the spirit of individuality in entrepreneurship, and lots of slow-paced mingling. Wander the nearly 30-year-old market as locals buy products ranging from staples like fruit and vegetables to specialty products like saffron and kefir.

Grab breakfast as you shop from the city's most famous biscuits at **Pine State** or try a few nibbles from stands with less of a line like the giant tater tots from **Obon Shokudo** or the canelé from **Mio's Delectables.** Once you're full up on the culinary market, make your way across town for a different kind of market. The **Portland Saturday Market** runs along the waterfront and provides more than 350 Pacific Northwest craft vendors space to sell their wares. Makers, artists, and musicians of all types come together into a superstore of state-shaped cutting boards, batik baby onesies, dog treats, miniature fairy garden doors, and original works of fine art.

If none of the market's many food vendors filled you up, make your way to any of Portland's famous food cart pods, like the 3rd Avenue one that isn't far away and has a wide selection. But if you need to sit down, head out to **Kargi Gogo,** a former food truck that now serves their Georgian food—dumplings and cheese bread—from an adorable café on Alberta Street.

Then you'll be well placed to begin your afternoon of shopping: the Alberta Arts District, running along NE Alberta Street, includes adorable boutiques of all types, from **The Pencil Test**—a bra shop for women with D-cups and larger—to kid toys at **Grasshopper.** In between, browse galleries, vintage clothing stores, and yarn shops.

By the time you get to dinner at **Erizo,** you will want to sit for a nice long time with many glasses of wine—which is just what you'll get from this 20-course tasting menu of ultrasustainable seafood, some of it fished and foraged by the chef himself, others saved from becoming food waste and instead turned into fine-dining food.

More than 10,000 varieties provide plenty of color at Portland's International Rose Test Garden.

Day 3

Start your day with a taste of Portland's strong Mexican cuisine at **Mi Mero Mole,** where house-made tortillas come from freshly nixtamalized corn and the café de olla smells like waking up in Mexico City. Take a slow stroll up Burnside to a Portland classic: **Powell's City of Books.** Wander the color-coded rooms through multiple floors of new and used books, talk to the well-read, effusively helpful staff members to get recommendations, and just try not to leave with more than you can carry home.

Though newer than Powell's, **Tasty n' Alder** might just be as beloved. The eclectic restaurant from John Gorham serves a radicchio salad, Korean-inspired chicken, and pillow-light potato bravas that keep people in line for an hour, along with everything from lemon ricotta pancakes to Gaucho-style rib-eye steaks.

Continuing the tour of the city's best and brightest, take your pick of any of the famous gardens. The **International Rose Test Garden** features 10,000 varieties of the plant that gave the Rose City its nickname—and a darn good view of its most famous peak, Mt. Hood, too. Not far away, the **Portland Japanese Garden** shares the stunning mountain panorama as visitors crisscross along the walkways through the manicured plants, streams, and rocks. The **Lan Su Chinese Garden** keeps visitors closer to town and offers a little more covered walking areas along its paths and bridges centered on a man-made lake.

Finish off the trip with one final reminder of how Portland lets chefs take a good idea and turn it into a phenomenal restaurant at **Gado Gado,** where Indonesian culinary traditions meet playful modern cooking and trendy patterned wallpaper decorated with birds and shrimp. Dishes like a foie gras version of kaya toast and roti canai served with corn and cheese dip instead of curry.

Recommendations

Sights

Alberta Arts District. ⊠ *N.E. 15th St. and N.E. Alberta St., Portland, OR* ⊕ *www. albertamainst.org* ⊆ *Free.*

International Rose Test Garden. ⊠ *400 S.W. Kingston Ave., Portland, OR* ☎ *503/823–7529* ⊕ *www.portlandoregon.gov/parks* ⊆ *Free.*

Lan Su Chinese Garden. ⊠ *239 N.W. Everett St., Portland, OR* ☎ *503/228–8131* ⊕ *www.lansugarden.org* ⊆ *Free.*

Portland Japanese Garden ⊠ *611 S.W. Kingston Ave., Portland, OR* ☎ *503/223–1321* ⊕ *www.japanesegarden.org* ⊆ *Free.*

🍴 Restaurants

Eem. $ *Average main: $10* ⊠ *3808 N. Williams Ave., Portland, OR* ☎ *971/295–1645* ⊕ *www.eemto-you.com.*

Erizo. $ *Average main: $50* ⊠ *215 S.E. 9th Ave., Portland, OR* ☎ *503/206–8619* ⊕ *www.erizopdx.com* ⊗ *Closed Sun., Mon., and Wed.*

Gado Gado. $ *Average main: $10* ⊠ *1801 N.E. Cesar E Chavez Blvd., Portland, OR* ☎ *503/206–8778* ⊕ *www.gadogadopdx. com.*

Kachka. $ *Average main: $8* ⊠ *960 S.E. 11th Ave., Portland, OR* ☎ *503/235–0059* ⊕ *www.kachkapdx.com.*

Kargi Gogo. $ *Average main: $8* ⊠ *3039 N.E. Alberta St., Portland, OR* ☎ *503/764–9552* ⊕ *www. kargigogo.com* ⊗ *Closed Mon.*

Mi Mero Mole. $ *Average main: $10* ⊠ *32 N.W. 5th Ave., Portland, OR* ☎ *971/266–8575* ⊕ *www.mmmtacospdx.com* ⊗ *Closed Sun. and Mon.*

Tasty n' Alder. $ *Average main: $28* ⊠ *580 S.W. 12th Ave,. Portland, OR* ☎ *503/621–9251* ⊕ *www.tastynalder. com* ⊗ *Closed Mon. and Tues.*

☕ Coffee and Quick Bites

Mio's Delectables. $ *Average main: $5* ⊠ *611 S.W. Kingston Ave., Portland, OR* ☎ *503/223–1321* ⊕ *www.www.miosdelectables.com.*

Obon Shokudo. $ *Average main: $6* ⊠ *722 S.E. 10th Ave., Portland, OR* ☎ *503/660–3176* ⊕ *www.obonpdx.com* ⊗ *Closed Mon.*

Pine State. $ *Average main: $35* ⊠ *1717 N.W. 23rd Ave., Portland, OR* ☎ *971/407–3621* ⊕ *www.pinestatebiscuits.com.*

🛏 Hotels

Jupiter Next. $ *Rooms from: $129* ⊠ *900 E. Burnside St., Portland, OR* ☎ *503/230–9200* ⊕ *www.jupiterhotel.com/jupiter-next-rooms* ⦿ *No meals.*

The Nines. $ *Rooms from: $279* ⊠ *525 S.W. Morrison St., Portland, OR* ☎ *503/222–9996* ⊕ *www.thenines.com* ⦿ *No meals.*

🍸 Nightlife

Alberta Rose Theatre. ⊠ *3000 N.E. Alberta St., Portland, OR* ☎ *503/719–6055* ⊕ *www.albertarosetheatre.com.*

Base Camp. ⊠ *930 S.E. Oak St., Portland, OR* ☎ *503/477–7479* ⊕ *www.www.basecampbrewingco.com.*

Breakside. ⊠ *820 Northeast Dekum St., Portland, OR* ☎ *503/719–6475* ⊕ *www. breakside.com.*

Doug Fir Lounge. ⊠ *830 E. Burnside St,, Portland, OR* ☎ *503/231–9663* ⊕ *www. dougfirlounge.com.*

Gigantic. ⊠ *5224 S.E. 26th Ave,, Portland, OR* ☎ *503/208–3416* ⊕ *www.giganticbrewing.com.*

Hair of the Dog. ⊠ 61 S.E. Yamhill St., Portland, OR ☎ 503/232–6585 ⊕ www. hairofthedog.com.

Hopworks. ⊠ 2944 S.E. Powell Blvd., Portland, OR ☎ 571/982–0358 ⊕ www. hopworksbeer.com.

Laurelwood. ⊠ 5115 N.E. Sandy Blvd., Portland, OR ☎ 508/282–0622 ⊕ www. laurelwoodbrewpub.com.

Revolution Hall. ⊠ 1300 S.E. Stark St., Portland, OR ☎ 971/808–5094 ⊕ www. revolutionhall.com.

Wonder Ballroom. ⊠ 128 N.E. Russell St., Portland, OR ☎ 503/284–8686 ⊕ www. wonderballroom.com.

 Shopping

Grasshopper. ⊠ 1816 N.E. Alberta St., Portland, OR ☎ 503/335–3131.

The Pencil Test. ⊠ 2407 N.E. Alberta St., Portland, OR ☎ 971/266–8611 ⊕ www. thepenciltest.com.

Portland Farmers Market. ⊠ 240 N. Broadway, Portland, OR ☎ 503/241–0032 ⊕ www.portlandfarmersmarket.org.

Portland Saturday Market. ⊠ 2 S.W. Naito Pkwy., Portland, OR ☎ 503/222–6072 ⊕ www.portlandsaturdaymarket.com.

Powell's City of Books. ⊠ 1005 W. Burnside St., Portland, OR ☎ 800/878–7323 ⊕ www.powells.com/locations/ powells-city-of-books.

Steven Smith Teamaker. ⊠ 110 S.E. Wash-ington St., Portland, OR ☎ 503/719–8752 ⊕ www.smithtea.com.

San Diego, CA

120 miles (approx. 2½ hours) from Los Angeles.

San Diego is the perfect getaway from Los Angeles—it's just far away enough to feel like a real vacation, while it's not too

long of a drive for a weekend (especially for an Angelino who is probably already in the cart way too much). There's a little bit for everyone here: gorgeous beaches, waterfront brunches spots and kitschy tiki bars, and a fun and lively downtown area that you may only know from the dinosaur rampage in *The Lost World: Jurassic Park.*

Planning

GETTING THERE AND BACK
From Los Angeles, San Diego is a straight shot down the I–5 S, getting you there in about 2½ hours. You can also take CA 73 S and I–5 S in roughly the same amount of time.

WHEN TO GO
June through September is obviously the best time to visit San Diego, but note that June will be gloomy (though you might be able to find a deal because of this). The best month is September, when the rates will be more reasonable and the weather will still be warm. Rates are lowest, however, from September through November.

WHERE TO STAY
Maybe the best bang for your buck is the surf-theme **Pacific Beach Surf Beachside Inn.** For something a little more upscale, there's nearby **Pacific Terrace Hotel,** with rooms and a pool overlooking the beach and boardwalk. If you'd rather stay in La Jolla, **La Jolla Shore Hotel** also sits right on the beach.

Day 1

Assuming you leave by 10 am at the latest, you'll roll into San Diego around 1 pm. Check into your accommodations, preferably in the neighborhood of Pacific Beach. Grab lunch at **Rocky's Crown Pub** (arguably the best burgers in San Diego). If you'd rather have a quick bite, the casual **Da Kine's Plate Lunches** serves

The year-round warm weather and beautiful coastline are among the top draws in San Diego.

Hawaiian food near the beach. It recently reopened after an 11-year hiatus, and the food is truly incredible). After lunch, take a walk to nearby Garnet Avenue, where you'll find a melange of antique stores, clothing boutiques, and surf shops, along with great vintage duds at **Buffalo Exchange.** There's also a **Mr. Frostie Ice Cream** where you can pop in for a tasty little cone. If shopping isn't your style, catch a wave at **Tourmaline Surfing Park Beach,** also in Pacific Beach.

After an afternoon of exploring downtown Pacific Beach, head over to **Pacific Beach Shore Club** for fish tacos and creative cocktails in a rooftop bungalow. Stick around after dinner for the beach-party atmosphere, or enjoy a change of scenery at **Amplified Ale Works** or **Modern Times Beer** (two nearby breweries) or head over to trendy Mexican restaurant **El Prez** for margaritas paired with gorgeous views of the boardwalk and Pacific Beach.

Day 2

Begin your day the only way anyone should in San Diego—by standing in line for burritos at **Kono's Surf Club Cafe** on Pacific Beach, right by Crystal Pier. This is—hands down—the city's best place for an all-day breakfast (burritos or otherwise). A second eatery, **Konito's Cafe,** recently opened up about a mile east and caters to those who are there for the good food and not to stare at the beach.

To walk off your breakfast, take a short drive to La Jolla for a pleasant and not-too-difficult beach trek on the La Jolla Coast Walk Trail. From end to end it crosses more than 10 different beaches. Afterwards you can make your way to **Mitch's Seafood** for locally caught fish and craft beer from many local San Diego breweries. It's right on the marina, so the waterfront views are the loveliest possible.

After lunch, head to Balboa Park, where you can visit the **San Diego Natural History**

Museum or stroll through the beautiful gardens surrounding it. One displays cacti, another desert plants, another plants native to California—you've got plenty of options, and they're all gorgeous. If you're an animal lover, the world-famous **San Diego Zoo** is also located in Balboa Park.

Next up, head to **Bali Hai Restaurant,** a sprawling Polynesian-style destination known for its mai tais (and other tropical drinks) and breathtaking bay views. There's a killer happy hour menu (coconut shrimp and other delicious appetizers) and an impressive dinner menu. The place is so beautiful you'll want to stick around for a few hours. After dinner, spend the early part of your evening wandering nearby **Seaport Village,** a waterfront shopping complex next to the San Diego Bay. It is touristy, sure, but it's also a pleasant place to pass the time.

In the evening, make your way to the Gaslamp District for the unbeatable nightlife. **Coin-Op Game Room** is an 1980s theme arcade where you can drink beers and show off your skills, and **Trailer Park After Dark,** is a kitschy bar decorated like an actual trailer park.

Day 3

Check out of your accommodations—we're headed to nearby Del Mar, the fanciest neighborhood in San Diego County. It's our last day, so we're heading to **Torrey Pines Reserve** in Del Mar for an early morning hike and gorgeous beach views from the various lookout points. Immediately afterward, proceed directly to **Jake's Del Mar,** the spot for brunch in Del Mar. This upscale eatery boasts incredible ocean vistas from the patio or the dining room (floor to ceiling windows, of course). Brunch starts at 10 am and ends at 2 pm, so get there early to snag a seat.

After brunch, take some time to lounge around on Del Mar City Beach. Nearby **Del Mar Village** has upscale clothing boutiques (for men and women), kitschy beach stores, and souvenir shops. Del Mar Village also hosts your happy-hour destination for when you're shopped out: **Viewpoint Brewing Co.** It has a real gastropub atmosphere with communal seating. Have a pint or two before heading to **Pacifica Del Mar,** an upscale eatery serving seafood, steaks, pasta, and more than 200 types of vodka. After dinner, linger on the beach for a bit before heading back to Los Angeles.

Recommendations

Sights

San Diego Natural History Museum. ✉ *1788 El Prado, San Diego, CA* ☎ *877/946–7797* 🌐 *www.sdnhm.org* 🎟 *$11.*

San Diego Zoo. ✉ *2920 Zoo Dr., San Diego, CA* ☎ *619/231–1515* 🌐 *www.sandiegozoo.org* 🎟 *$58.*

Torrey Pines Reserve. ✉ *12600 N. Torrey Pines Rd., La Jolla, CA* ☎ *858/755–2063* 🌐 *www.torreypine.org* 🎟 *Free.*

Tourmaline Surfing Park Beach. ✉ *La Jolla Blvd., and Tourmaline St., La Jolla, CA* ☎ *858/405–4004* 🌐 *www.lajolla.com/profiles/tourmaline-surf-park-beach* 🎟 *Free.*

Restaurants

Bali Hai Restaurant. [$] *Average main: $10* ✉ *2230 Shelter Island Dr., San Diego, CA* ☎ *619/222–1181* 🌐 *www.balihairestaurant.com.*

Da Kine's Plate Lunches. [$] *Average main: $10* ✉ *5401 Linda Vista Rd., San Diego, CA* ☎ *858/302–2096* 🕒 *Closed Mon.*

El Prez. [$] *Average main: $10* ✉ *4190 Mission Blvd., San Diego, CA* ☎ *858/274–8785* 🌐 *www.elprezpb.com.*

Jake's Del Mar. $ *Average main: $15* ⊠ *1660 Coast Blvd., Del Mar, CA* ☎ *858/755–2002* ⊕ *www.jakesdelmar. com.*

Konito's. $ *Average main: $19* ⊠ *1730 Garnet Ave., San Diego, CA* ☎ *858/230–7355* ⊕ *www.konoscafe.com.*

Kono's Surf Club Cafe. $ *Average main: $10* ⊠ *704 Garnet Ave., San Diego, CA* ☎ *858/483–1669* ⊕ *www.konoscafe.com.*

Mitch's Seafood. $ *Average main: $15* ⊠ *1403 Scott St., San Diego, CA* ☎ *619/222–787* ⊕ *www.mitchsseafood. com.*

Pacifica Del Mar. $ *Average main: $55* ⊠ *1555 Camino Del Mar, Del Mar, CA* ☎ *858/792–0476* ⊕ *www.pacificadelmar. com.*

Pacific Beach Shore Club. $ *Average main: $15* ⊠ *4343 Ocean Blvd., San Diego, CA* ☎ *858/272–7873* ⊕ *www. pbshoreclub.com.*

Rocky's Crown Pub. $ *Average main: $10* ⊠ *3786 Ingraham St., San Diego, CA* ☎ *858/273–9140* ⊕ *www.rockyburgers. com.*

☕ Coffee and Quick Bites

Mr. Frostie Ice Cream. $ *Average main: $8* ⊠ *1470 Garnet Ave., Pacific Beach, CA* ☎ *858/274–9977* ⊕ *www.mrfrostiespb. com.*

🛏 Hotels

La Jolla Shore Hotel. $ *Rooms from: $219* ⊠ *8110 Camino Del Oro, La Jolla, CA* ☎ *855/923–8058* ⊕ *www.ljshoreshotel. com* ❑ *No meals.*

Pacific Beach Surf Beachside Inn. $ *Rooms from: $99* ⊠ *4760 Mission Blvd., San Diego, CA* ☎ *858/483–6780* ⊕ *www. pbsurfinn.com* ❑ *Free breakfast.*

Pacific Terrace Hotel. $ *Rooms from: $279* ⊠ *610 Diamond St., San Diego, CA* ☎ *858/581–3500* ⊕ *www.pacificterrace. com* ❑ *No meals.*

Nightlife

Amplified Ale Works. ⊠ *4150 Mission Blvd., San Diego, CA* ☎ *858/270–5222* ⊕ *www.amplifiedales.com.*

Coin-Op Game Room. ⊠ *3926 30th St., San Diego, CA* ☎ *619/255–8523* ⊕ *www. coinopsd.com.*

Modern Times Beer. ⊠ *3725 Greenwood St., San Diego, CA* ☎ *619/546–9694* ⊕ *www.moderntimesbeer.com.*

Trailer Park After Dark. ⊠ *835 5th Ave., San Diego, CA* ☎ *619/236–1550* ⊕ *www. trailerparkafterdark-sandiego.com.*

Viewpoint Brewing Co. ⊠ *2201 San Die-guito Dr., Del Mar, CA* ☎ *858/356–9346* ⊕ *www.viewpointbrewing.com.*

Shopping

Buffalo Exchange. ⊠ *1079 Garnet Ave., San Diego, CA* ☎ *858/273–6227* ⊕ *www. buffaloexchange.com.*

Del Mar Village. ⊠ *1104 Camino Del Mar, Del Mar, CA* ☎ *858/735–3650* ⊕ *www. visitdelmarvillage.com.*

Seaport Village. ⊠ *849 W. Harbor Dr., San Diego, CA* ☎ *619/530–0704* ⊕ *www. seaportvillage.com.*

San Luis Obispo, CA

189 miles (approx. 3 hours) from Los Angeles, 231 miles (approx. 3½ hours) from San Francisco.

Looking for all the things you love about California but at a more (well, even more) laid-back pace? Look no further than San Luis Obispo. Located roughly halfway between San Francisco and Los Angeles, this coastal college town is home to (or in easy striking distance of) everything you could want from the Golden State.

No expense was spared during the construction of Hearst Castle, one of Central California's most eye-catching attractions.

You want beaches? Not only does the region have plenty of beaches, but it boasts the only one where you can career across the dunes on your ATV. You want the California wine country experience? Winemakers in nearby Paso Robles craft world-class vintages, but with a signature devil-may-care spirit. You want Golden Age of Hollywood glamour? Look no further than the unrestrained decadence of Hearst Castle.

Planning

GETTING THERE AND BACK
From Los Angeles, it's about a three-hour drive (without traffic) via the 101 N or a (roughly) five- to six-hour Amtrak ride from Union Station in downtown Los Angeles. From San Francisco, the drive is about three and a half hours (without traffic) via the 101 S or a (roughly) five- to six-hour Amtrak ride from the Emeryville station.

INSPIRATION
Lyrics fixated on death, sex, violence, surrealist films, and earthquakes co-mingle with grungy, poppy, surfy melodies on the Pixie's 1989 album *Doolittle*. This album, along with the band's previous album *Surfer Rosa*, were hugely influential on the grunge and alt-rock musicians of the 1990s and beyond. It's the perfect thing to put yourself in the college radio state of mind.

PIT STOPS
The Gaviota northbound rest stop is well maintained (aka the bathrooms are clean) as well as picturesque, making it a great spot to stretch your legs and breathe in the salt air.

WHEN TO GO
San Luis Obispo's climate is mild year-round and hardly ever too warm or too cold, making it an excellent place for a quick, low-key getaway no matter the season.

WHERE TO STAY

Get the full **Madonna Inn** experience when you check in for a stay in one of its variously opulent and theme rooms. If you're looking for a more subdued stay, you can relax at **Sycamore Mineral Springs Resort & Spa,** where each room comes equipped with a hot tub filled with piped in mineral water. If you'd like to stay situated in the heart of San Luis Obispo proper, **The Kinney** makes for the perfect base of operations for exploring Central Coast California.

Day 1

Once you've reached your destination, there's no sense in beating around the bush—it's beach time. **Pismo Beach** offers a wide, sandy shore great for stretching out for sunbathing and gorgeous waves perfect for a surf session. The beach also features a 1,200-foot pier built in 1928 that stretches out over the water, offering stunning views of this classic California beach town.

With your freshly worked-up appetite in tow, stop by **Firestone Grill** for lunch. This barbecue spot is beloved for its tri-tip sandwich—like, really beloved. As in, be prepared to wait in line. But rest assured, once you're hunkered down with your food and a glass of cold beer you'll understand why. **Big Sky Cafe** is a great alternate.

Though wine grapes were introduced to the region by the Spanish in the late 18th century, Paso Robles' wine industry has boomed over the last several decades with more than 200 wineries taking advantage of the unique terroir created by the area's various microclimates. There are any number of worthy tasting rooms (Paso Robles' downtown area makes it easy to visit several tasting rooms all in one spot), but for a delicious Cabernet paired with a gorgeous view, a visit to **DAOU Vineyards** is a must. Another local favorite is **Calcareous Vineyard.**

Close out your day comfortably ensconced in the welcoming, old school atmosphere of **Café Roma.** This fixture of San Luis Obispo's Historic Railroad District serves classic Italian favorites made from ingredients that have been sourced from local farmers, ranchers, and fishermen.

Day 2

The **Apple Farm Restaurant** has become a favorite spot for comfort food, breakfast staples, and its apple dumpling. Breakfast here is a blissfully straightforward affair (think pancakes, omelets, and Benedicts) where ingredients are sourced from Central Coast farmers markets. Loals also love **SLO Provisions.**

Up the coast in San Simeon, atop La Cuesta Encantada ("The Enchanted Hill") sits an estate so measureless in its decadence the fictional version that appears in Citizen Kane was dubbed Xanadu. Newspaper magnate William Randolph Hearst commissioned architect Julia Morgan to execute a vision that would become **Hearst Castle.** Construction started in 1919 and would take more than 20 years to complete. The result is a 127-acre property outfitted with countless rooms, fireplaces, gardens, priceless collections of art, pools, and a range of architectural styles. The property was donated to the state of California in 1958 and has since become a quintessential stop on any visit to Central California.

Hop on the Pacific Coast Highway and start heading back south for lunch at **Tognazzini's Dockside Restaurant** in the impossibly charming beach town of Morro Bay. Dine indoors at the original restaurant or opt for the more casual outdoor location—either way, you'll find a menu chock full of local seafood that's as delicious as it is fresh. Another must-visit is the **Great American Fish Company.**

Despite the state's hundreds of miles of coast, there are very few where it's legal to drive on the beach. This makes **Oceano Beach** a must for anyone who's ever wanted to hop on a dune buggy and cruise along the shore literally just steps from the water. Not much of a thrill seeker? Oceano is also one of the few California beaches where you don't have to clamor for one of a few precious cement fire pits if you want to have a bonfire. The only thing you need here is some firewood and a can-do attitude.

For dinner, stop by **Novo Restaurant & Lounge.** The menu here is inspired by elements of cuisine from all over the world and realized using local ingredients. If you can, snag a table on their outdoor patio which overlooks the verdantly shaded San Luis Creek. If you want to try Peruvian fare, head to **Mitsura.**

Truly no stop in San Luis Obispo is complete without a pilgrimage to the wondrously kitschy **Madonna Inn.** The hotel is famous for its top-to-bottom every-shade-of-pink color scheme and baroque maximalist fever dream décor. It's truly a seeing is believing experience, so don your finest cat-print-of-your-choice and order up the hotel bar's signature drink—the Pink Cloud—and toast to a day well-spent.

Day 3

Get your morning caffeine fix at **Kreuzberg California,** which takes inspiration from the café scene of Berlin (as in, it also makes a great place to revisit during lunch and cocktail hours). Pair your espresso with a Classic Two Egg Brekky or a San Luis Obispbowl (aka an acai bowl) for a well-rounded start to your day. And there's lovely garden seating at **Linnaea's Cafe.**

Cal Poly's Design Village (also known as the Architecture Graveyard) looks a bit like the part of The Shire where

you'd go to hang out with the hobbits that got really into the counterculture. Nestled against a backdrop of gently rolling hills are experimental structures and sculptures designed by Polytechnic State University's design, architecture, and engineering students as part of the Design Challenge. During the annual event, competitors assemble structures designed around a theme (such as "Balance" or "Synthesis") that must be built in 12 hours and shelter the team for an entire weekend. Some of the structures still remain, a unique testament to their builders' innovation and creativity. Getting there isn't quite strenuous enough to be a full blown hike, but it's about a two-mile round-trip walk, so wear a comfy pair of walking shoes.

Pismo Beach is famous for its clams, so you'd be remiss if you left town without sampling some steamed clams or clam chowder from **Splash Café.** You'll likely encounter a line outside this no-frills stand but a seafood lunch this satisfying is worth the wait.

Before you start the trek back home, stop by Piedras Blancas for a chance at glimpsing a beach full of elephant seals as they sun their generously proportioned tummies and occasionally do battle in the surf (bulls will be bulls!). The seals return to this six mile stretch of shore consistently throughout the year but their peak season is between December and March.

Recommendations

Sights

Calcareous Vineyard. ✉ 3430 Peachy Canyon Rd., Paso Robles, CA ☎ 805/239–0289 ⊕ www.calcareous.com 🖾 Tastings $20.

Cal Poly Design Village. ✉ San Luis Obispo, CA ☎ 805/756–1111 ⊕ www.architecture.calpoly.edu 🖾 Free.

DAOU Vineyards. ✉ *2777 Hidden Mountain Rd., Paso Robles, CA* ☎ *805/226–5460* 🌐 *www.daouvineyards.com* 🎫 *Tastings $20.*

Hearst Castle. ✉ *750 Hearst Castle Rd., San Simeon, CA* ☎ *800/444–4445* 🌐 *www.hearstcastle.org* 🎫 *$25.*

Oceano Beach. ✉ *West end of Pier Ave., Oceano, CA* ☎ *805/473–7220* 🌐 *www.parks.ca.gov* 🎫 *$5 per vehicle.*

Pismo Beach. ✉ *760 Mattie Rd., Pismo Beach, CA* ☎ *805/773–4657* 🌐 *www.pismobeach.org* 🎫 *Free.*

Restaurants

The Apple Farm. [$] *Average main: $17* ✉ *2015 Monterey St., San Luis Obispo, CA* ☎ *800/255–2040* 🌐 *www.applefarm.com.*

Café Roma. [$] *Average main: $17* ✉ *1020 Railroad Ave., San Luis Obispo, CA* ☎ *805/541–6800* 🌐 *www.caferomaslo.com* 🕒 *Closed Sun.*

Firestone Grill. [$] *Average main: $8* ✉ *1001 Higuera St., San Luis Obispo, CA* ☎ *805/783–1001* 🌐 *www.firestonegrill.com.*

Great American Fish Company. [$] *Average main: $10* ✉ *1185 Embarcadero, Morro Bay, CA* ☎ *805/772–4407* 🌐 *www.bestfishrestaurantmorrobay.com.*

Kreuzberg California. [$] *Average main: $5* ✉ *685 Higuera St., San Luis Obispo, CA* ☎ *805/439–2060* 🌐 *www.kreuzbergcalifornia.com.*

Linnaea's Café. [$] *Average main: $8* ✉ *1110 Garden St., San Luis Obispo, CA* ☎ *805/541–5888* 🌐 *www.linnaeas.com.*

Mistura. [$] *Average main: $16* ✉ *570 Higuera St., San Luis Obispo, CA* ☎ *805/439–3292* 🌐 *www.misturarestaurants.com.*

Novo Restaurant & Lounge. [$] *Average main: $16* ✉ *726 Higuera St., San Luis Obispo, CA* ☎ *805/543–3986* 🌐 *www.novorestaurant.com.*

SLO Provisions. [$] *Average main: $11* ✉ *1255 Monterey St., San Luis Obispo, CA* ☎ *805/439–4298* 🌐 *www.sloprovisions.com* 🕒 *Closed Sun.*

Splash Café. [$] *Average main: $10* ✉ *1491 Monterey St., San Luis Obispo, CA* ☎ *805/544–7567* 🌐 *www.splashcafe.com.*

Tognazzini's Dockside Restaurant. [$] *Average main: $32* ✉ *1245 Embarcadero, Morro Bay, CA* ☎ *805/772–8100* 🌐 *www.morrobaydockside.com.*

Hotels

The Kinney. [$] *Rooms from: $115* ✉ *1800 Monterey St., San Luis Obispo, CA* ☎ *805/544–8600* 🌐 *www.thekinneyslo.com* 🍴 *No meals.*

Madonna Inn. [$] *Rooms from: $209* ✉ *100 Madonna Rd., San Luis Obispo, CA* ☎ *805/543–3000* 🌐 *www.madonnainn.com* 🍴 *No meals.*

Sycamore Mineral Springs Resort & Spa. [$] *Rooms from: $195* ✉ *1215 Avila Beach Dr., San Luis Obispo, CA* ☎ *805/595–7302* 🌐 *www.sycamoresprings.com* 🍴 *No meals.*

Santa Barbara, CA

90 miles (approx. 1¾ hours) from Los Angeles.

Thanks to its Mediterranean climate and a refined atmosphere that's long catered to the sensibilities of well-heeled locals and the visiting Hollywood elite, the small coastal city of Santa Barbara has been nicknamed "the American Riviera." But don't let its patrician reputation lead you to think that Santa Barbara is solely the realm of the hoity and the toity. At the end of the day, when you're in Santa Barbara you're squarely in Coastal

Founded in 1786, massive Mission Santa Barbara is known as the "Queen of the Missions."

California territory. That means there's still plenty of space for a more down-to-earth weekend of hitting the beach, riding the waves, and exploring a food and drink scene that's as exciting (not to mention as delicious) as anything you'll find back in LA.

Planning

GETTING THERE AND BACK

The most direct route from Los Angeles will be via I-405 to U.S. 101 (which will take you about 1¾ to 2 hours), or you can opt for the scenic route and start off on the Pacific Coast Highway, enjoying the Malibu coastline, and then hop on the 101 around Oxnard. (This will add an hour or so to your travel time, but it's unlikely you'll regret taking in such wonderful views.) Santa Barbara is also an easy trip on Amtrak from Union Station in LA.

WHEN TO GO

Santa Barbara's famously mild weather means there's truly no bad time for a visit. If you want to see the city at its most festive, visit during Old Spanish Days (or simply "Fiesta"), an event that, over the course of five days each summer, celebrates the area's Spanish heritage.

WHERE TO STAY

The **San Ysidro Ranch** has been a fixture of the Santa Barbara area as early as 1839. This luxury resort is famous for having hosted Jacqueline and John F. Kennedy on their honeymoon. If you like your luxury stay to come with an oceanfront view, check in to the **Four Seasons Resort The Biltmore** where you'll have easy access to the resort's pool, gardens, and Butterfly Beach. If you're in the market for something a little more low-key, though no less central, check out **The Wayfarer,** where you'll only be mere steps away from the Funk Zone's myriad of bars and restaurants.

Day 1

Whether you took the more direct route via the 101 or opted for the longer but more scenic route via the Pacific Coast

Highway, you'll likely land in Santa Barbara in the mood for a little lunch. Stop by **Santa Barbara Public Market,** which plays host to a variety of vendors serving a variety of cuisine and wine that's been locally sourced. The food hall is especially well-suited to groups that have trouble reaching a consensus. Another great option is **Lilly's Taqueria.**

After you've reenergized, find your way to what is perhaps the city's most famous landmark, **Mission Santa Barbara.** Founded in 1786 by Spanish missionaries, the mission is an impressively scaled structure with a Neoclassical facade, a Moorish fountain, and a collection of colonial artwork. Consequently, the Mission Santa Barbara has come to be regarded as "The Queen of the Missions."

Kick off the evening in the Funk Zone, a formerly run-down industrial neighborhood transformed into a hip hangout, with some predinner cocktails at **Pearl Social.** This intimate spot serves up impossibly pretty cocktails and live music nightly. Larger parties enjoy sharing one of their punch bowls.

Barbareño defines its cuisine as "Central Coast Californian"—something you might not be able to define off the top of your head. But after dining in this restaurant's relaxed yet sophisticated atmosphere on tri-tip steak served with chimichurri, grilled avocado bowls, and pinquito beans you'll understand exactly what it means. For desert, treat yourself to Barbareño's delicious homemade ice cream.

Day 2

Start your morning with an excellent cup of coffee from **Handlebar Coffee Roasters.** The café and roasting company was opened in 2011 by two former professional cyclists, and since then have focused on crafting excellent coffee. Along with your caffeine boost you can chow down on a pastry or some next-level avocado or smoked-salmon toast.

After breakfast, it's time to turn your attentions toward Santa Ynez Mountains—they're not just a beautiful backdrop for the city—and hike your way to Inspiration Point. It's a moderately challenging 3½-mile trek, but once you reach the top you'll understand how the spot got its name. You'll be rewarded with a stunning view of the city, the ocean, and the Channel Islands.

For a hearty posthike lunch, stop by **Cold Spring Tavern.** More than a BBQ spot, Cold Spring Tavern is a quintessential piece of Santa Barbara history, having served as a favorite stop for stagecoach passengers. Weekends here mean the restaurant will be serving its famous tri-tip sandwiches—a delicious tradition you'll be very glad to have taken part in.

There's no shortage of beaches in the Santa Barbara area, which also means there's no shortage of places for basking in a Californian sunset. But for something extra special, find your way to **Butterfly Beach** in Montecito, which, unlike most of the area's beaches, faces the west instead of south. It's a little off the beaten path, so you'll find pristine sand and a more intimate atmosphere. You might even see some dolphins to round out the day.

For dinner, find your way to the patio at **Oliver's** for a vegan experience that will win over even the staunchest of carnivores. The menu is populated by such delicious and satisfying dishes as kung pao cauliflower and jackfruit tacos served in a romantic, upscale setting.

For after-dinner drinks in a space designed with Santa Barbara's "American Riviera" rep in mind, head to **The Good Lion.** The cocktail menu rotates on a weekly basis, so that the drinks are consistent with whatever fruits and herbs are currently in season. Rest assured though, anything you order is sure to be completely and utterly delicious.

Day 3

For a hearty breakfast, head to **Jeannine's Restaurant and Bakery.** This Santa Barbara institution serves what is perhaps the platonic ideal of breakfast food: straightforward, made with natural ingredients, and served alongside a big cup of coffee—or a bottle of bubbly. Whichever you're in the mood for.

It's time to head north to Los Olivos, a 40-or-so minute drive that will take you past Cachuma Lake into the Santa Ynez Valley. And one of the best ways to take in all this natural beauty is on a bicycle. It's easy enough to sign up for a guided tour with **Santa Barbara Wine Country Cycling Tours,** or simply rent a bike and explore the picturesque countryside on your own.

Stop in for lunch at **Los Olivos Wine Merchant Cafe,** where you'll find delicious salads, sandwiches, pizzas, and pastas. But no matter what you order, you'll be able to pair your meal with a plethora of wines. The "Wine Merchant" part of this spot features more than 500 wines and specializes in wine from California's Central Coast, naturally.

You may recognize the Santa Ynez wine country as the setting for the movie *Sideways.* You can opt for going very slightly afield to wineries like **Beckmen Vineyards, Foxen Vineyard and Winery,** or any number of vineyards that populate the Santa Ynez Valley from Solvang to Santa Maria. Or you can stay put right in Los Olivos, where a staggering number of tasting rooms—such as **Blair Fox Cellars, Refugio Ranch Vineyards, The Hideaway LO** to truly name a few—populate the two-or-so blocks that make up the heart of the town. Round out your afternoon at **Coquelicot Estate Vineyard's** tasting room and inviting backyard space (complete

with bocce ball) perusing an art at **Gallery Los Olivos.**

Recommendations

◉ Sights

Beckmen Vineyards. ✉ *2670 Ontiveros Rd., Los Olivos, CA* ☎ *805/688–8664* ⊕ *www.beckmenvineyards.com* ✉ *Tastings $20.*

Blair Fox Cellars. ✉ *2477 Alamo Pintado Ave., Los Olivos, CA* ☎ *805/691–1678* ⊕ *www.blairfoxcellars.com* ✉ *Tastings $12* ◷ *Closed Tues. and Wed.*

Butterfly Beach. ✉ *1260 Channel Dr., Montecito, CA* ☎ *805/681–4200* ✉ *Free.*

Coquelicot Estate Vineyard. ✉ *2884 Grand Ave., Los Olivos, CA* ☎ *805/688–1500* ⊕ *www.coquelicotwines.com* ✉ *Tastings from $15.*

Foxen Vineyard and Winery. ✉ *7600 Foxen Canyon Rd., Santa Maria, CA* ☎ *805/937–4251* ⊕ *www.foxenvineyard.com* ✉ *Tastings $20.*

The Hideaway LO. ✉ *2990 Grand Ave., Los Olivos, CA* ☎ *805/697–7892* ⊕ *www.thehideawaylo.com* ✉ *Tastings $15.*

Mission Santa Barbara. ✉ *2201 Laguna St., Santa Barbara, CA* ☎ *805/682–4713* ⊕ *www.santabarbaramission.org* ✉ *$12.*

Refugio Ranch Vineyards. ✉ *2990 Grand Ave., Los Olivos, CA* ☎ *805/697–5289* ⊕ *www.refugioranch.com* ✉ *Tastings $20.*

🍴 Restaurants

Barbareño. Ⓢ *Average main: $21* ✉ *205 W. Canon Perdido St., Santa Barbara, CA* ☎ *805/963–959* ⊕ *www.barbareno.com.*

Cold Springs Tavern. Ⓢ *Average main: $25* ✉ *5995 Stagecoach Rd., Santa Barbara, CA* ☎ *805/967–0066* ⊕ *www.coldspringtavern.com.*

The Good Lion. $ *Average main: $25* ✉ *1212 State St., Santa Barbara, CA* ☎ *805/845–8754* ⊕ *www.goodlioncocktails.com.*

Lilly's Taqueria. $ *Average main: $4* ✉ *310 Chapala St., Santa Barbara, CA* ☎ *805/966–9180* ⊕ *www.lillystacos.com.*

Los Olivos Wine Merchant Cafe. $ *Average main: $15* ✉ *2879 Grand Ave., Los Olivos, CA* ☎ *805/688–7265* ⊕ *www.winemerchantcafe.com.*

Oliver's. $ *Average main: $15* ✉ *1198 Coast Village Rd., Santa Barbara, CA* ☎ *805/969–0834* ⊕ *www.oliversofmontecito.com* ☾ *Closed Mon.*

☕ Coffee and Quick Bites

Handlebar Coffee Roasters. $ *Average main: $20* ✉ *128 E. Canon Perdido St., Santa Barbara, CA* ☎ *719/201–3931* ⊕ *www.handlebarcoffee.com.*

Jeannine's Restaurant and Bakery. $ *Average main: $50* ✉ *15 E. Figueroa St., Santa Barbara, CA* ☎ *805/966–1717* ⊕ *www.jeannines.com.*

🛏 Hotels

Four Seasons Resort The Biltmore. $ *Rooms from: $645* ✉ *1260 Channel Dr., Santa Barbara, CA* ☎ *805/969–2261* ⊕ *www.fourseasons.com* ❍ *No meals.*

San Ysidro Ranch. $ *Rooms from: $841* ✉ *900 San Ysidro La., Santa Barbara, CA* ☎ *805/565–1700* ⊕ *www.sanysidroranch.com* ❍ *Free breakfast.*

The Wayfarer. $ *Rooms from: $139* ✉ *12 E. Montecito St., Santa Barbara, CA* ☎ *805/845–1000* ⊕ *www.wayfarersb.com* ❍ *No meals.*

🍸 Nightlife

Pearl Social. ✉ *131 Anacapa St., Santa Barbara, CA* ☎ *805/284–0380* ⊕ *www.pearlsocialsb.com.*

🛍 Shopping

Gallery Los Olivos. ✉ *2920 Grand Ave., Los Olivos, CA* ☎ *805/688–7517* ⊕ *www.gallerylosolivos.com.*

Santa Barbara Public Market. ✉ *38 W. Victoria St., Santa Barbara, CA* ☎ *805/770–7702* ⊕ *www.sbpublicmarket.com.*

🏃 Activities

Santa Barbara Wine Country Cycling Tours. ✉ *1693 Mission Dr., Solvang, CA* ☎ *888/557–8687* ⊕ *www.winecountrycycling.com* ⊠ *$100 per person.*

Sequoia and Kings Canyon National Parks, CA

Sequoia National Park is 223 miles (approx. 4 hours) from Los Angeles and 260 miles (approx. 4½ hours) from San Francisco.

The word "exceptional" best describes virtually every corner of Sequoia and Kings Canyon National Parks. The two adjacent national parks encompass 865,964 wild and scenic acres (95% is protected) between the foothills of California's Central Valley and its eastern borders along the craggy ridgeline of the Sierra's highest peaks, including Mount Whitney, the tallest mountain in the lower 48. This magnificent wonderland offers some of the nation's greatest escapes. Wander among giant sequoias and gaze in awe at some of the largest and oldest living things on the planet. This rare species of trees grows only at certain elevations and in particular environments on the western slopes of the Central Sierra. Drive along byways that deliver stunning vistas at nearly every turn, including a road that drops 30 miles from Grants Village down to the Kings River

Spread out along Generals Highway, Giant Forest contains some of the tallest trees in Sequoia National Park.

Canyon, several thousand feet deeper than the Grand Canyon. Elevations at visitor centers range from 1,700 feet at the southern Ash Mountain entrance to 6,720 feet at Lodgepole in the Giant Forest area, and down again to 4,635 feet at Cedar Grove, near the Kings River. The extraordinary variations in ecosystems and more than 800 miles of maintained hiking trails provide a wealth of opportunities for repeat adventures.

Planning

GETTING THERE AND BACK

Driving is the best option for visiting the parks. From Los Angeles follow I–5 N to Highway 99 and continue north to Visalia and Highway 198 E to tiny Three Rivers, 7 miles from Sequoia National Park's southern entrance. From San Francisco, travel south on I–5 or Highway 99 to Visalia and east on Highway 198 to Three Rivers. If you reverse the itinerary, take Route 180 from Fresno to the Kings Canyon entrance near Grant Grove Village,

56 miles east of Fresno. The 46-mile Generals Highway traverses the two parks from north to south.

Note: if your vehicle is longer than 22 feet, it's not allowed on the narrow, steep, and curvy 16-mile section of General's Highway from the visitor center up to the Giant Forest. You should enter and leave the parks via Highway 180 instead. Free shuttles run between sights in the Lodgepole/Giant Forest area in summer and some holiday periods.

WHEN TO GO

Sequoia is a year-round destination, but spring and fall—when temperatures are mild and fewer visitors clog the narrow roadways and parking lots—are the best times to visit, hike, fish, and bike. Winter draws outdoor enthusiasts for cross-country skiing and snowshoeing along pristine forest trails and around the powdery groves. Some roads and services close from mid-October through April.

WHERE TO STAY

If you want to stay in the parks where you have easy access to trails and activities, your options are limited and you should reserve well in advance. The 102-room, full-service **Wuksachi Lodge,** 2 miles north of the Lodgepole Visitor Center, is your best bet in Sequoia National Park. Kings Canyon holds the 36-room **John Muir Lodge** and **Grant Grove Cabins** in Grant Grove Village near the Big Stump entrance, and the remote 21-room **Cedar Grove Lodge** (closed winter) 30 miles to the east. Rooms range from rustic bunk rooms to upscale cabin suites at **Montecito-Sequoia Lodge,** on private lakefront property between the two parks.

If the park lodges are full (especially in summer and holiday weekends), you'll find a range of options, from tiny inns, riverside cabins, and chain motels in Three Rivers, about 6 miles from the Ash Mountain entrance. Some of our faves include **Rio Sierra Riverhouse,** with four rooms, a cabin, and sandy beach, and **Buckeye Tree Lodge,** a riverside collection of 12 rooms and 10 cabins.

Day 1

Depart as early as possible so you can grab lunch in Visalia or Three Rivers before heading up the mountain to explore sequoia groves before sunset. In Visalia, splurge at the sophisticated **Vintage Press** or **Café 225,** or go more budget and casual at **Quesadilla Gorilla, Pita Kabob** gastropub, or **Planing Mill Pizza** in the craft beer district. Top picks in Three Rivers include the boho-chic **Buckaroo Diner,** where you can feast on seasonal, organic dishes and river views, and **Sierra Subs,** with tasty sandwiches perfect for an on-the-go lunch. Quench your thirst and shift into "relax mode" at the **Three Rivers Brewery, The River View,** or the **Gateway Restaurant,** where you can sit at the river's edge and watch whitewater tumble downslope toward the valley.

After you've fueled up or procured picnic provisions, it's time to head into the woods along Generals Highway. If you haven't already purchased a pass, pay $35 at the Sequoia National Park entrance kiosk for a pass that covers both parks for seven days. Stop at the **Foothills Visitor Center,** just a mile north, to get the latest information and touring tips.

The next portion of your trip—15 miles and 3,500 feet up one of the steepest, curviest roads you'll ever travel—requires great concentration and nerves of steel. Resist the urge to ooh and ahh at the stunning Sierra views while at the wheel—save the shock and awe moments for when you're safely parked at one of the multiple vista points along the way.

About 45 minutes after you begin your ascent, the road wends through the **Giant Forest,** where magnificent sequoia trees surround you at every turn. Learn all about sequoias—their remarkable evolution, habitat, and need for occasional fires to ensure rebirth of the species—in the **Giant Forest Museum.** Stroll along the wheelchair-accessible Big Trees Trail that circles Round Meadow.

Jump back in the car and continue a few miles up the road to come face-to-face with **General Sherman,** the world's largest tree (measured in volume), and also one of the world's tallest and oldest sequoias. Crane your neck and take a super-long pano shot (flip your phone camera to horizontal and start from the base of the tree). Walk along the paved, 2-mile loop Congress Trail—one of the park's finest—to view The President (the world's second largest tree) and two superb sequoia clusters, Senate and House. Now it's time for a break and sustenance. Drive 2 miles north to check out the **Lodgepole Visitor Center** complex, with exhibits, an informative film, deli, market, and snack shop. Check into Wuksachi Lodge, 2 miles north of Lodgepole, and relax with a drink before dinner at **The Peaks** (reserve in advance).

Day 2

Savor a hearty mountain breakfast at either Wuksachi or Lodgepole, then drive or (in summer) hop aboard the free shuttle to massive **Moro Rock** and 360-degree views, followed by a peek at iconic **Tunnel Log,** a 275-foot fallen tree with a man-made hole large enough for vehicle passage. Next, walk the mile-long trail around lush Crescent Meadow, which John Muir called "the gem of the Sierra." Tuck back in your car and continue north on General's Highway to the panoramic Kings Canyon Overlook before stretching your legs at the **Kings Canyon Visitor Center** in Grant Grove Village. Lunch on farm-fresh fare at the **Grant Grove Restaurant** or pick up items at the village market for a picnic along the way.

Point your car east along Highway 180 to follow the spectacular, 30-mile **Kings Canyon Scenic Byway.** The drive without stops takes about an hour each way. Pull over at Junction View, where you can gawk at the jagged peaks that loom over Kings Canyon. Continue to **Grizzly Falls,** then to Cedar Grove Village, on the canyon floor. Grab a snack at the snack bar, or at a table by the South Fork of the Kings River.

Stroll or hike around Zumwalt Meadow, a few miles up the road, to view Grand Sentinel and North Dome before turning around at Road's End, a backpacker wilderness trailhead. Stop at Roaring River Falls on your way back to Grant Grove Village and check into your cozy digs at Grant Grove Cabins or John Muir Lodge. Relax over drinks and dinner by the fireplace at the lodge restaurant or at Grant Grove Restaurant.

Day 3

Rise early to fuel up for the day at one of the village restaurants. Drive a mile east to Grant Grove to greet another gentle giant, the **General Grant Tree,** and amble along the paved trails in the groves. By midmorning head to Panoramic Point for jaw-dropping views of Hume Lake and the High Sierra.

Stay in the park as long as you can before heading down the mountain via Highway 180. If you're heading back to the San Francisco Bay Area, stop at **The School House,** a rustic-upscale locavore restaurant and tavern in an historic building in Sanger, on Highway 180 about 16 miles east of Fresno. Returning to Los Angeles? Take a break at one of the aforementioned eateries in Three Rivers or Visalia.

If you have extra time to spend in the region, add a journey from Three Rivers up twisty Mineral King Road up to a splendid valley (7,500 feet elevation) with myriad trails far from the madding crowd (open summer and early fall). Also try to visit **Giant Sequoia National Monument** and trek to Alder Creek forest, a 530-acre formerly private sequoia grove in the Mineral King area acquired by the Save the Redwoods League in late 2019 and home to one of the world's five largest trees.

Recommendations

Sights

General Grant Tree. ⊠ Grant Tree Rd., Kings Canyon National Park, CA ☎ 559/565–3341 ⊕ www.nps.gov/seki/learn/nature/grant.htm ⊠ $35 per vehicle.

General Sherman Tree. ⊠ Giant Forest, Wolverton Rd., Sequoia National Park, CA ☎ 559/565–3341 ⊕ www.nps.gov/seki/learn/nature/sherman.htm ⊠ $35 per vehicle.

Giant Forest. ⊠ *Generals Hwy., Sequoia National Park, CA* ☎ *559/565–3341* ⊕ *www.nps.gov/seki/planyourvisit/gfday-hikesum.htm* ⬤ *$35 per vehicle.*

Giant Forest Museum. ⊠ *47050 Generals Hwy., Sequoia National Park, CA* ☎ *559/565–3341* ⊕ *www.nps.gov/seki/learn/historyculture/gfgfm.htm* ⬤ *$35 per vehicle.*

Giant Sequoia National Monument. ⊠ *Rte. 180, Porterville, CA* ☎ *559/920–1588* ⊕ *www.fs.usda.gov/visit/destination/giant-sequoia-national-monument-0* ⬤ *$35 per vehicle.*

Grizzly Falls. ⊠ *Rte. 180, Kings Canyon National Park, CA* ☎ *559/565–3341* ⊕ *www.fs.usda.gov/recarea/sequoia/recarea/?recid=79509* ⬤ *$35 per vehicle.*

Kings Canyon Scenic Byway. ⊠ *Rte. 180, Kings Canyon National Park, CA* ☎ *559/565–3341* ⊕ *www.nps.gov/seki/planyourvisit/byways.htm.*

Moro Rock. ⊠ *Crescent Meadow Rd., Sequoia National Park, CA* ☎ *559/565–3341* ⊕ *www.nps.gov/seki/planyourvisit/moro.htm* ⬤ *$35 per vehicle.*

🍴 Restaurants

Buckaroo Diner. Ⓢ *Average main: $13* ⊠ *41695 Sierra Dr., Three Rivers, CA* ☎ *559/465–5088* ⊕ *www.theolbuckaroo.com* ⊙ *Closed Tues.*

Café 225. Ⓢ *Average main: $18* ⊠ *225 W. Main St., Visalia, CA* ☎ *559/733–2967* ⊕ *www.cafe225.com.*

The Gateway Restaurant. Ⓢ *Average main: $18* ⊠ *45978 Sierra Dr., Three Rivers, CA* ☎ *559/561–4133* ⊕ *www.gateway-sequoia.com.*

The Peaks. Ⓢ *Average main: $22* ⊠ *64740 Wuksachi Way, Sequoia National Park, CA* ☎ *559/625–7700* ⊕ *www.nps.gov/seki/planyourvisit/wheretoeat.htm.*

Pita Kabob. Ⓢ *Average main: $10* ⊠ *5101 W. Walnut Ave., Visalia, CA* ☎ *559/627–2337* ⊕ *www.pitakabob.com* ⊙ *Closed Sun.*

Planing Mill Pizza. Ⓢ *Average main: $9* ⊠ *778 E. Center Ave., Visalia, CA* ☎ *559/713–0818* ⊕ *www.planingmillpizza.com* ⊙ *Closed Mon.*

Quesadilla Gorilla. Ⓢ *Average main: $9* ⊠ *302 W. Main St., Visalia, CA* ☎ *559/646–6475* ⊕ *Quesadillagorilla.com.*

The River View. Ⓢ *Average main: $11* ⊠ *42323 Sierra Dr., Three Rivers, CA* ☎ *559/561–2211.*

Sierra Subs. Ⓢ *Average main: $9* ⊠ *41651 Sierra Dr., Three Rivers, CA* ☎ *559/561–4810* ⊕ *www.sierrasubsandsalads.com* ⊙ *Closed Sun. and Mon.*

Three Rivers Brewery. Ⓢ *Average main: $10* ⊠ *41763 Sierra Dr, Three Rivers, CA* ☎ *559/909–5483.*

Vintage Press. Ⓢ *Average main: $28* ⊠ *216 N. Willis St., Visalia, CA* ☎ *559/733–3033* ⊕ *www.thevintagepress.com* ⊙ *Closed Mon.*

🛏 Hotels

Buckeye Tree Lodge. Ⓢ *Rooms from: $149* ⊠ *46000 Sierra Dr., Three Rivers, CA* ☎ *559/561–5900* ⊕ *www.buckeyetreelodge.com* ⦿ *Free breakfast.*

Cedar Grove Lodge. Ⓢ *Rooms from: $151* ⊠ *86724 CA 180, Kings Canyon National Park, CA* ☎ *866/807–3598* ⊕ *www.nationalparkreservations.com/lodge/sequoiakingscanyon-cedar-grove-lodge* ⦿ *No meals.*

Grant Grove Cabins. Ⓢ *Rooms from: $51* ⊠ *86728 CA 180, Kings Canyon National Park, CA* ☎ *866/807–3598* ⊕ *www.nationalparkreservations.com/lodge/sequoiakingscanyon-grant-grove-cabins* ⦿ *No meals.*

John Muir Lodge. $ *Rooms from: $116* ✉ *Panoramic Point,, Kings Canyon National Park, CA* ☎ *866/807–3598* ⊕ *www. nationalparkreservations.com/lodge/ sequoiakingscanyon-john-muir-lodge* ❘⊙❘ *No meals.*

Montecito-Sequoia Lodge. $ *Rooms from: $119* ✉ *63410 Generals Hwy., Sequoia National Park, CA* ☎ *559/565–3388* ⊕ *www.mslodge.com* ❘⊙❘ *No meals.*

Rio Sierra Riverhouse. $ *Rooms from: $225* ✉ *41997 Sierra Dr., Three Rivers, CA* ☎ *833/239–7450* ⊕ *www.rio-sierra. com* ❘⊙❘ *Free breakfast.*

Wuksachi Lodge. $ *Rooms from: $123* ✉ *64740 Wuksachi Way, Sequoia National Park, CA* ☎ *866/807–3598* ⊕ *www. nationalparkreservations.com* ❘⊙❘ *No meals.*

Sonoma County, CA

44 miles (approx. 1 hour) from San Francisco.

More stylish than Mendocino and more laid back than Napa, Sonoma County is a place you'll never want to leave. Experience the best of Northern California's iconic vineyards and idyllic beaches in this gorgeous weekend destination just a short drive from San Francisco. A weekend in Sonoma is all about eating and drinking well and reveling in the sunkissed landscapes of golden beaches and vine-covered hills. Let the bacchanal begin.

Planning

GETTING THERE AND BACK
From San Francisco, head north on the 101, which will take you through Petaluma on to Santa Rosa and Healdsburg, one of the cutest towns in California and a great place to use as your home base for the weekend.

PIT STOPS
Santa Rosa is home to the **Russian River Brewing Company,** whose Pliny the Elder beer has attained cult status. Stop by for a taste (or a to-go growler) of what's been called "the best beer in America."

WHEN TO GO
California is perfect year-round, but the weather is especially lovely in the fall, from September to November. Unfortunately, this is also prime fire season, so plan accordingly.

WHERE TO STAY
Hotel Healdsburg is centrally located just a block from the town square. Rooms have a hip minimalist design, and the pool is a perfect afternoon oasis. For something truly unique, **Autocamp Russian River** in Guerneville is a hip glamping resort with airstream trailers, tents, and cabins.

Day 1

Driving north on the 101 from San Francisco, make your way up to Geyserville, a tiny town in the northeast corner of the county, where you can stop for lunch at **Diavolo** for indulgent Neapolitan-style pizza with farm fresh ingredients.

The town of Geyserville is cute and quirky with some Wild West vibes, so take a stroll down the street to the **Geyserville Gun Club** (a bar) for a drink to explore a bit.

After lunch, drive south to Healdsburg to check in to your hotel. Healdsburg is a beautiful small town centered around a palm tree-lined town square. Window shop at the art galleries and upscale boutiques and pop into any of the tasting rooms scattered around town. Have fun walking around town and exploring without a set destination in mind—there's plenty to discover here. Just make sure to stay relatively sober and save room for a special dinner.

The gently rolling countryside gives way to vast vineyards in the Sonoma Valley.

Be sure to make reservations well in advance at the three-Michelin-starred **SingleThread Farms** in Healdsburg, considered one of the best restaurants in the world. You'll be treated to a multicourse sensory experience. Dishes here elevate simple and fresh ingredients with innovative textures and flavors, making every course into a delight and a surprise. It costs a fortune, but it's a once-in-a-lifetime dining experience you won't soon forget.

Day 2

You're going to need a designated driver today to explore the Alexander Valley and the Dry Creek Valley. If you're not traveling with somebody who wants to stay sober, not a problem—it's very easy (although a bit pricey) to hire a driver for the day with **Wine Tour Drivers.** Alternately, you can also rent bikes and modify your route to stop at just one or two wineries closer to town.

Start your morning off with a fancy coffee at **Flying Goat** in Healdsburg—you're going to need all the energy you can get today. Next, stock up on picnic supplies at **Oakville Grocery**—sandwiches, beverages, cheese, cookies, and anything else you might need for a lazy wine-fueled lunch.

The Dry Creek Valley and Alexander Valley are much more laid back than the Napa Valley, but it's still a good idea to call ahead to make a reservation for a tasting, especially if you're traveling with three or more people.

The best way to tackle this wine tasting extravaganza is to start early and pace yourself. Factor in about 45 minutes for each stop, longer if you plan to picnic. Some of the can't-miss wineries in the area include **Bella Winery, Hop Kiln Estate,** and **Truett Hurst,** which is a great place to have lunch. **Seghesio Family Vineyards,** back in Healdsburg, is a great place to end your day of wine tasting.

Tonight, opt for something casual and low key—tacos and burritos at **El Farolito** are always a good idea, or if you want something a bit more upscale, **Barndiva** has a great outdoor patio with farm-to-table California classics. If you're in the mood to drink something besides wine, **Duke's** on the main square has craft cocktails and great people watching.

Day 3

Today's drive home will be long and lazy, taking you to coastal Sonoma county to bask in the sun. **Cousteaux Bakery** in Healdsburg will get you ready for the day with coffee and pastries before you hop in the car and make your way to the town of Petaluma. Park the car and explore by foot, stopping by **Vintage Bank Antiques** and the **Petaluma Historical Library and Museum.** There are also a couple of vintage stores and boutiques, and the **Petaluma Seed Bank** is worth browsing for a unique souvenir to take home and plant in your own garden.

When you've worked up an appetite, visit **Della Fattoria** for lunch—you can't go wrong with ordering any of the sandwiches served on freshly baked bread.

After lunch, it's time to get back in the car for a drive to the coast. It's a short but picturesque drive from Petaluma to Tomales Bay. Stop for a plate of fresh oysters at **Nick's Cove** before detouring to **Point Reyes National Seashore** and visiting the lighthouse and visitors center, built in 1870. You can go for a hike or enjoy the beach before continuing on to Stinson Beach and the "hidden" town of Bolinas on Highway 1 in time to catch the sunset before heading back to San Francisco.

Recommendations

Sights

Bella Winery. ⊠ 9711 W. Dry Creek Rd., Healdsburg, CA ☎ 707/473–9171 ⊕ www.landmarkwine.com ⟐ Tastings $15.

Hop Kiln Estate. ⊠ 6050 Westside Rd., Healdsburg, CA ☎ 707/433–6491 ⊕ www.landmarkwine.com ⟐ Tastings $30.

Petaluma Historical Library and Museum. ⊠ 20 4th St., Petaluma, CA ☎ 707/778–4398 ⊕ www.petalumamuseum.com ⟐ Free.

Point Reyes National Seashore. ⊠ 1 Bear Valley Rd., Point Reyes Station, CA ☎ 415/464–5100 ⊕ www.nps.gov ⟐ Free.

Seghesio Family Vineyards. ⊠ 700 Grove St., Healdsburg, CA ☎ 707/433–3579 ⊕ www.seghesio.com ⟐ Tastings $20.

Truett Hurst. ⊠ 5610 Dry Creek Rd., Healdsburg, CA ☎ 707/433–9545 ⊕ www.truetthurstwinery.com ⟐ Tastings $20.

Restaurants

Barndiva. $ Average main: $18 ⊠ 231 and 237 Center St., Healdsburg, CA ☎ 707/431–0100 ⊕ www.barndiva.com ⊘ Closed Mon. and Tues.

Della Fattoria. $ Average main: $14 ⊠ 143 Petaluma Blvd. North Petaluma, CA ☎ 707/763–0161 ⊕ www.dellafattoria.com.

Diavolo. $ Average main: $20 ⊠ 21021 Geyserville Ave., Geyserville, CA ☎ 707/814–0111 ⊕ www.diavolapizzeria.com.

El Farolito. $ Average main: $15 ⊠ 128 Plaza St., Healdsburg, CA ☎ 707/433–2807 ⊕ www.elfarolito2000.com ⊘ Closed Sun.

Nick's Cove. $ *Average main: $18* ✉ *23240 Hwy. 1, Marshall, CA* ☎ *415/663–1033* ⊕ *www.nickscove.com.*

SingleThread Farms. $ *Average main: $35* ✉ *131 North St., Healdsburg, CA* ☎ *707/723–4646* ⊕ *www.singlethreadfarms.com.*

Coffee and Quick Bites

Cousteaux Bakery. $ *Average main: $15* ✉ *417 Healdsburg Ave., Healdsburg, CA* ☎ *707/433–1913* ⊕ *www.costeaux.com.*

Flying Goat. $ *Average main: $18* ✉ *324 Center St., Healdsburg, CA* ☎ *707/433–9081* ⊕ *www.flyinggoatcoffee.com.*

🛏 Hotels

Autocamp Russian River. $ *Rooms from: $269* ✉ *14120 Old Cazadero Rd., Guerneville, CA* ☎ *888/405–7553* ⊕ *www.autocamp.com* ⊙ *Free breakfast.*

Hotel Healdsburg. $ *Rooms from: $509* ✉ *25 Matheson St. Healdsburg, CA* ☎ *707/431–2800* ⊕ *www.hotelhealdsburg.com* ⊙ *Free breakfast.*

🍸 Nightlife

Duke's. ✉ *111 Plaza St., Healdsburg, CA* ☎ *707/431–1060* ⊕ *www.drinkatdukes.com.*

Geyserville Gun Club. ✉ *21025 Geyserville Ave., Geyserville, CA* ☎ *707/814–0036* ⊕ *www.geyservillegunclub.com.*

Russian River Brewing Company. ✉ *725 4th St., Santa Rosa, CA* ☎ *707/545–2337* ⊕ *www.russianriverbrewing.com.*

🛍 Shopping

Oakville Grocery. ✉ *124 Matheson St., Healdsburg, CA* ☎ *707/433–3200* ⊕ *www.oakvillegrocery.com.*

Petaluma Seed Bank. ✉ *110 Petaluma Blvd. N, Petaluma, CA* ☎ *707/773–1336* ⊕ *www.rareseeds.com.*

Vintage Bank Antiques. ✉ *101 Petaluma Blvd. N, Petaluma, CA* ☎ *707/769–3097* ⊕ *www.vintagebankantiques.net.*

🏃 Activities

Wine Tour Drivers. ☎ *707/584–6994* ⊕ *www.winetourdrivers.com* ⊠ *$45 per hr.*

Walla Walla, WA

261 miles (approx. 4¼ hours) from Seattle.

Washington's quintessential wine destination brings Seattleites across the mountains in search of copious amounts of sunshine, a small-town feel, and big Syrahs. The wine scene's wide array of grape varieties makes it an appealing destination for wine nerds and their rookie taster friends, as does the casual feel at even the internationally acclaimed wineries. Slow days of meandering the rolling hills of grapevines and wheat fields end with legendary sunsets and meals from the outsize culinary scene, which draws on the area's agricultural roots to feature local produce like the town's eponymous onions.

Planning

GETTING THERE AND BACK
There's no fast way to get to Walla Walla, but at least the 4½-hour drive is about as scenic as they come. After rolling down the east side of Snoqualmie Pass, you split from the interstate to cross the Columbia River Gorge at the town of Vantage, then follow the river south before heading east through wine country.

Besides its dozens of vineyards, Walla Walla is also known for its spectacular scenery.

WHEN TO GO

The sun almost always shines in Walla Walla, but the temperature rises and falls—a lot. The cold winters and warm summers make spring and fall the best times to go—but check ahead if you'll be there for either season's release weekend. If you like parties, head over then to see each vineyard unveil its new wines. If you prefer a more laid-back feel, come another weekend.

WHERE TO STAY

The **Inn at Abeja** fulfills pastoral, luxurious wine country dreams, renting suites, cottages, and a whole farmhouse on the winery's 38 acres of land, and your room includes a welcome glass of wine, a tasty breakfast, and a wine tasting. Alternatively, **The Finch** sits right in the center of town, adorned with works by local artists and offering affordable spaces for people looking to spend more time out of the room than in it.

Day 1

Leaving Seattle midmorning will get you to Ellensburg just in time to grab a "Sweet and Salty" ham and Swiss sandwich at **Daily Bread and Mercantile** and arrive just in time for the appointment you made (you did make it, right?) at **Abeja Winery** to taste their estate wines, complete with a walking tour of the historic farmstead and a charcuterie spread to tide you over until dinner. On Fridays, you'll also need an appointment to taste at **àMaurice Cellars,** where Anna Schafer creates ambitious, complex wines that show off her fifth-generation Washingtonian connection to the land.

In winter, you'll probably want to just cozy down deep in your hotel room with some takeout from **Granny's Tamales,** but in summer, keep the evening going at **Three Rivers Winery's** Friday evening live music series. You can dance the evening away under the waning sun and pick up some dinner and drinks on-site from a local restaurant.

Day 2

If you're staying at Abeja, your breakfast is included. If not, **Maple Counter's** Swedish pancakes with lingonberries will get you ready for the day. Take advantage of Walla Walla's typically dry skies with a round at the **Wine Valley Golf Club,** which uses the area's natural undulations and stunning landscape to create a top-notch course for players of every level. If the weather or the sport don't appeal, take a scenic drive south across the border to Oregon to tour the **Historical Pendleton Woolen Mill** and pick up one of those famous blankets, and visit the **Tamástslikt Cultural Institute** to learn about the area's Indigenous people.

Back in town for lunch, head to the gas station. The best food around comes from **Andrae's Kitchen,** a counter inside the Cenex that features an eclectic menu of tacos, Halal-style chicken, and poutine, among other things, cooked by a formally trained chef. Once a quiet secret, the lines can get long on weekends, but the beignets are well worth the wait.

After lunch, hit Walla Walla's biggest attraction: the wineries. With such a variety of incredible wines of different styles, you want to look for places that specialize in whatever you like, as well as visit classics like **L'Ecole No. 41,** named for the historic school building in which it makes its famous wines, and newer spots that keep the dynamic region moving forward, too, like **Elephant 7**—the state's only Filipino-owned winery. End at **Castillo de Feliciana** with a glass of their seasonal sangria and a stunning view to check out as you sip.

Make sure you save room for handmade pasta at **Passatempo Taverna,** though. Hearty, rustic Italian dishes like orecchiette with oxtail ragu or carrots with toasted fennel will soak up that sangria. Try to snag a seat at the long bar, because

renowned barman Jim German etched the drinks list deep with his cocktail knowledge and impeccable taste.

Day 3

Hit **Bacon and Eggs** for breakfast standards made with far more thought than was given to the restaurant's name— everything from shrimp or grits to chilaquiles to brioche French toast and crab cakes Benedict is made from scratch using local ingredients. Don't let a heavy breakfast weigh you down, though: get the best view in town by chartering a ride with **Blue Mountain Balloons,** who will float you over the valley. Peer down at the wheat fields and vineyards, the town, and, of course, Columbia River.

Back in town, grab lunch from **Saffron,** when the Mediterranean restaurant's crowds are a little lighter, but leave yourself plenty of time to shop the extensive olive oil and vinegar selection at **D'Olivo,** as well as their olive oil skin care before you have to head home—stopping on the way for a classic road trip-style dinner at Prosser's **Davy's Burger Ranch,** where the old-school burger meets seasonal local specials like deep-fried asparagus and blackberry-lavender lemonade.

Recommendations

Sights

Abeja Winery. ⊠ *2014 Mill Creek Rd., Walla Walla, WA* ☏ *509/526–7400* ⊕ *www. abeja.net* ☕ *Tastings $30.*

àMaurice Cellars. ⊠ *178 Vineyard La., Walla Walla, WA* ☏ *509/522–5444* ⊕ *www. amaurice.com* ☕ *Tastings $10* ☉ *Closed Mon.–Thurs.*

Castillo de Feliciana. ⊠ *85728 Telephone Pole Rd., Milton-Freewater, OR* ☏ *541/558–3656*

⊕ castillodefeliciana.com 🍷 Tastings $10 ⊙ Closed Mon.–Thurs.

Elephant 7 Winery. ✉ 134 W. Poplar St., Walla Walla, WA ☎ 206/679–8705 ⊕ www.elephantsevenwine.com 🍷 Tastings $10 ⊙ Closed Mon.–Thurs.

L'Ecole No. 41. ✉ 41 Lowden School Rd., Lowden, WA ☎ 509/525–0940 ⊕ www. lecole.com 🍷 Tastings $15.

Pendleton Woollen Mill. ✉ 1307 S.E. Court Pl., Pendleton, OR ☎ 800/760–4844 ⊕ www.pendleton-usa.com/mill-tours. html 🍷 Free ⊙ Closed Sun.

Tamástslikt Cultural Institute. ✉ 47106 Wildhorse Blvd., Pendleton, OR ☎ 541/429–7700 ⊕ www.tamastslikt.org 🍷 $10 ⊙ Closed Sun.

Three Rivers Winery. ✉ 5641 U.S. 12, Walla Walla, WA ☎ 509/526–9463 ⊕ www. threeriverswinery.com 🍷 Tastings $10.

 Restaurants

Andrae's Kitchen. $ Average main: $12 ✉ Walla Walla Convenience Store. 706 W. Rose St., Walla Walla, WA ☎ 509/572–0728 ⊕ www.andraeskitchen.com.

Bacon and Eggs. $ Average main: $12 ✉ 57 E. Main St., Walla Walla, WA ☎ 509/876–4553 ⊕ www.baconandeggs-wallawalla.com ⊙ Closed Tues.–Thurs. No dinner.

Davy's Burger Ranch. $ Average main: $7 ✉ 1305 Meade Ave., Prosser, WA ☎ 509/786–2720.

Granny's Tamales. $ Average main: $6 ✉ 203 Wildwood St., Walla Walla, WA ☎ 509/876–2335 ⊙ Closed Sun.

Maple Counter Café. $ Average main: $13 ✉ 209 E. Alder St., Walla Walla, WA ☎ 509/876–2527 ⊕ www.maplecounter-cafe.com ⊙ No dinner.

Passatempo Taverna. $ Average main: $10 ✉ 215 W. Main St., Walla Walla, WA ☎ 509/876–8822 ⊕ www.passatempow-allawalla.com ⊙ Closed Wed.

Saffron Mediterranean Kitchen. $ Average main: $35 ✉ 330 W. Main St., Walla Walla, WA ☎ 509/525–2112 ⊕ www. saffronmediterraneankitchen.com ⊙ Closed Mon.

 Coffee and Quick Bites

Daily Bread and Mercantile. $ Average main: $5 ✉ 306 S. Main St., Ellensburg, WA ☎ 509/925–2253 ⊕ www.daily-breadeburg.com.

 Hotels

The Finch. $ Rooms from: $98 ✉ 325 E. Main St., Walla Walla, WA ☎ 509/956–4994 ⊕ www.finchwallawalla.com ⊙ No meals.

The Inn at Abeja. $ Rooms from: $369 ✉ 2014 Mill Creek Rd., Walla Walla, WA ☎ 509/522–1234 ⊕ www.abeja.net ⊙ Free breakfast.

 Shopping

D'Olivo Tasting Bar. ✉ 10 E. Main St., Walla Walla, WA ☎ 509/529–7537 ⊕ www. dolivotastingbar.com.

Activities

Blue Mountain Balloons. ☎ 509/529–2112 ⊕ www.bluemountainballoons.com 🍷 $245.

Wine Valley Golf Club. ✉ 176 Wine Valley Rd., Walla Walla, WA ☎ 509/525–4653 ⊕ www.winevalleygolfclub.com 🍷 Greens fee $135.

Orcas Island is home to Mount Constitution, the highest spot in the San Juan Islands.

Whidbey and the San Juan Islands, WA

35 miles (approx. 1 hour) from Seattle.

"Getting there is half the fun" served as an advertising slogan for transatlantic ships in the 1950s, but it could just as easily have been invented for the Washington State Ferries, which whisk people from their urban and suburban homes and transport through the cold-water straits of Puget Sound, through a maze islands blanketed in old growth forests. Bountiful shellfish, windswept cliffs, and winding pastoral roads make Whidbey Island and San Juan Islands like Orcas and Lopez appealing escapes for anyone who wants to slow down and feel the breeze blow their worries away as they sip a glass of something cool.

Planning

GETTING THERE AND BACK

Careful planning and booking ahead is essential to a low-stress trip to the San Juans. Check the somewhat complicated Washington State Ferries process for reserving to get your spot two months, two weeks, or two days head. Whidbey is a quick drive if everything is booked up.

WHEN TO GO

Summer is high season, when everything is open, in service, and likely packed. Outside of that, hours will be adjusted and businesses may be on break—and you're less likely to spot any whales on your journey.

WHERE TO STAY

Lopez offers few formal lodgings, so it's just a matter of finding the perfect rental home. Orcas spans the full array of options, from a luxury room at the **Rosario Resort and Spa** to the yurts and basic cabins at **Doe Bay Resort and Retreat.** On Whidbey, the **Captain Whidbey Inn** offers an enticing boutique feel with Filson-outfitted cabins, while the high-end **Inn at Langley** awaits your splurge for the balcony view rooms looking over the water.

Day 1

If you're heading to Whidbey, a midmorning boat will leave you plenty of time to get across the water in time for a lunch of mussels from nearby Penn Cove on the deck. If you're headed to Lopez, try to time yourself to pick up an early lunch at the **Shrimp Shack** to eat on the ferry. Once you get to the other side and drop your bags, make your way to Iceberg Point to spend the afternoon hiking out to one of the best views in the islands. For dinner, taste the essence of the island at **Ursa Minor,** where chef Nick Coffey slices, ferments, churns, and cooks the local flora, fauna, and seaweed into dishes that showcase the best of the region. On Whidbey, find a similar flavor in a much more high-end form at the three-hour, many-course meal served by the Inn at Langley.

Day 2

On Lopez, start your day with a healthful drink from the **Vortex Café & Juice Bar,** then hop on a bike from **Lopez Bike Works** to make your way around the island, a flat ride that can be done in loops of various lengths. Get back into town in time to grab lunch overlooking the water at **Haven.**

Nothing can compete with the fun of playing in the old naval forts that once guarded the waterfront. Duck into bunkers and climb the old cannons at **Fort Casey Historical State Park** before stopping for a light lunch at **Toby's Tavern.** While away the afternoon at the nearby **Penn Cove Brewing Company** until the **Oystercatcher** opens for dinner. The tiny spot specializes in using the local bivalves in

creative ways, like pork belly and scallops with curried crème fraîche and kimchi.

The reason for the early dinner comes in the form of your date night at the drive-in. Oak Harbor's **Blue Fox Drive-In** keeps the old tradition alive, with low-cost second-run movies played on a big screen for you to watch from the comfort of your car.

If you've made your way to Orcas, take the opportunity to make your way to the top of Mount Constitution, the highest point in the San Juan Islands, and look out from the top of the tower. If the weather cooperates, rent a kayak at the bottom in **Moran State Park,** and take a paddle around the lake. For dinner, choose between two options at the same restaurant: the casually spectacular many-course tasting menu at **Aelder** or the less spendy (but no less burgeoning with fresh local oysters, green garlic and more) pizza shop **Hogstone.** Either way, end the night with a cocktail at the nautically themed **Barnacle.**

Day 3

Grab brunch on Orcas at **Roses Bakery Café,** digging into their baked eggs with Gruyere or polenta and eggs with red chile sauce before you hop on an **Eclipse Charters** boat for a whale-watching tour (which guarantees whale sightings in summer). When you get back, have a late-afternoon snack to tide you over at **Buck Bay Shellfish Farm,** where you can buy oysters, crabs, or other treats and picnic out front—they'll give you a shucking lesson, if you need it. Finish the trip with a dip in the clothing-optional soaking tubs at Doe Bay Resort and retreat and dinner at the attached café before you grab a ferry back.

If you stayed on Whidbey, sit down to so much more than the name implies at **Whidbey Donuts,** where the standard diner does sneak in a few treats like the doughnut French toast. Play the day away at **Fort Ebey State Park,** hiking, surfing, or foraging for seaweed, before ending your trip on the patio at the **Captain Whidbey,** looking out over the water and slurping up oysters that were recently in it.

Recommendations

Sights

Fort Casey Historical State Park. ⊠ 1280 Engle Rd., Coupeville, WA ☎ 360/902–8844 ⊕ www.parks.state.wa.us/505/Fort-Casey 🎫 Free.

Fort Ebey State Park. ⊠ 400 Hill Valley Dr., Coupeville, WA ☎ 360/678–4636 ⊕ www.parks.state.wa.us/507/Fort-Ebey 🎫 Free.

Moran State Park. ⊠ 3572 Olga Rd., Olga, WA ☎ 360/376–2326 ⊕ www.parks.state.wa.us/547/Moran 🎫 Free.

🍴 Restaurants

Aelder. Ⓢ Average main: $25 ⊠ 460 Main St., Eastsound, WA ☎ 360/376–4647 ⊕ www.www.hogstone.com/aelder ⊙ Closed Tues.–Thurs. No lunch.

Captain Whidbey. Ⓢ Average main: $35 ⊠ 2072 W. Capt. Whidbey Inn Rd., Coupeville, WA ☎ 360/678–4097 ⊕ www.www.captainwhidbey.com.

Haven Bar & Kitchen Ⓢ Average main: $20 ⊠ 9 Old Post Rd., Lopez Island, WA ☎ 360/468–3272 ⊕ www.lopezhaven.com ⊙ Closed Sun.–Tues.

Hogstone. Ⓢ Average main: $20 ⊠ 460 Main St., Eastsound, WA ☎ 360/376–4647 ⊕ www.hogstone.com ⊙ Closed Tues.–Thurs. No lunch.

The Oystercatcher. Ⓢ Average main: $40 ⊠ 901 Grace St. NW, Coupeville, WA ☎ 360/678–0683 ⊕ www.oystercatcher-whidbey.com ⊙ Closed Tues. and Wed.

Penn Cove Brewing Company. Ⓢ Average main: $8 ⊠ 103 S. Main St., Coupeville, WA ☎ 360/682–5747 ⊕ www.penncovebrewing.com/coupeville ⊙ Closed Mon.–Wed.

Roses Bakery Café. Ⓢ Average main: $22 ⊠ 382 Prune Alley, Eastsound, WA ☎ 360/376–4292 ⊕ www.rosesbakerycafe.com ⊙ Closed Sun. and Mon.

Shrimp Shack. Ⓢ Average main: $12 ⊠ 6168 WA 20, Anacortes, WA ☎ 360/293–2531 ⊕ www.shrimpshack.us.

Toby's Tavern. Ⓢ Average main: $5 ⊠ 8 N.W. Front St., Coupeville, WA ☎ 360/678–4222 ⊕ www.tobysuds.com.

Ursa Minor. Ⓢ Average main: $40 ⊠ 210 Lopez Rd., Lopez Island, WA ☎ 360/622–2730 ⊕ www.ursaminorlopez.com ⊙ Closed Tues.–Thurs.

Whidbey Donuts. Ⓢ Average main: $10 ⊠ 5603 Bayview Rd, Langley, WA ☎ 360/321–4653 ⊕ www.whidbeydoughnuts.com.

☕ Coffee and Quick Bites

Vortex Café & Juice Bar. Ⓢ Average main: $10 ⊠ 135 Lopez Rd., Lopez Island, WA ☎ 360/468–4740 ⊕ www.vortexonlopez.com.

🏨 Hotels

Captain Whidbey Inn. Ⓢ Rooms from: $270 ⊠ 2072 W. Capt. Whidbey Inn Rd., Coupeville, WA ☎ 360/678–4097 ⊕ www.captainwhidbey.com ⏹ No meals.

Doe Bay Resort and Retreat. Ⓢ Rooms from: $100 ⊠ 107 Doe Bay Rd., Olga, WA ☎ 360/376–2291 ⊕ www.doebay.com ⏹ No meals.

Inn at Langley. Ⓢ Rooms from: $325 ⊠ 400 1st St., Langley, WA ☎ 360/221–3033 ⊕ www.innatlangley.com ⏹ Free breakfast.

Rosario Resort and Spa. $ *Rooms from: $199* ✉ *1400 Rosario Rd., Eastsound, WA* ☎ *360/376–2222* ⊕ *www.rosarioresort. com* ⦿ *No meals.*

☥ Nightlife

The Barnacle. ✉ *249 Prune Alley, Eastsound, WA* ☎ *360/622–2675* ⊕ *www. thebarnaclebar.com.*

Penn Cove Brewing Company. ✉ *780 S.E. Bayshore Dr., Oak Harbor, WA* ☎ *360/682–2247* ⊕ *www.penncovebrewing.com.*

Shopping

Buck Bay Shellfish Farm. ✉ *117 E. J. Young Rd., Olga, WA* ☎ *360/376–5280* ⊕ *www. buckbayshellfishfarm.com.*

Activities

Eclipse Charters. ✉ *8368 Orcas Rd., Orcas, WA* ☎ *360/376–6566* ⊕ *www. orcasislandwhales.com* ⛟ *$79 per person.*

Lopez Bike Works. ✉ *2847 Fisherman Bay Rd., Lopez Island, WA* ☎ *360/468–2847* ⊕ *www.lopezkayaks.com* ⛟ *Rentals from $35.*

Yosemite National Park, CA

172 miles (approx. 3½ hours) from San Francisco, 280 miles (approx. 4½ hours) from Los Angeles.

Anchored by Half Dome's famous colossal face, Yosemite's granite beauty doesn't need an introduction. Established as a national park in 1890, largely due to the efforts of Scottish naturalist John Muir, it was home to the Miwok for thousands of years. Their word ahwahnee means "valley that looks like a gaping mouth," a spot-on description of this spectacular glacier-gouged gash across the High Sierra.

The heart of it all is Yosemite Valley, surrounded by its towering granite monuments, including 8,842-foot Half Dome and 7,569-foot El Capitan, the world's tallest exposed granite monolith. To the south awaits Mariposa Grove, with its sky-high sequoias, and to the north, Tioga Pass Road climbs into the Sierra High Country, accessing Tuolumne Meadows and Tenaya Lake.

You'll find some of the world's best hiking here, for beginners and hardcore; fabulous summer fishing; world-class rock climbing; primo camping; and a jaw-dropping dose of Mother Nature.

Planning

GETTING THERE AND BACK
Yosemite National Park is a four-hour drive from San Francisco, via I–580 and CA 120; if you exit the park's eastern entrance, the trip back home will take 5½ hours, via U.S. 50 and I–80. You'll be going against traffic on your way there, though leave early or after 9 am to avoid the rush. You can also take Amtrak, with the last stretch aboard the YARTS bus line, with a travel time of six hours.

Yosemite is also a good getaway from Los Angeles, with a drive time of 4½ hours (280 miles) via CA 99.

WHEN TO GO
Summer is Yosemite's most popular time of year; it's also the best time to ensure that you can access all parts of the park via car. Tioga Road can be closed until late May or early June. That said, the best months, with the best weather and fewer crowds, are May and September. Avoid summer holiday weekends.

WHERE TO STAY
Yosemite is an outdoorsy destination, with plenty of campgrounds and tent cabins for the truly rustic, stars-overhead

The peaks known as Three Brothers rise above the Merced River in Yosemite National Park.

experience. For something a little more upscale, you can have your own private hideaway in a two-bedroom cabin, complete with kitchen and inviting porch, at the Explorer Cabins at the **Tenaya Lodge at Yosemite.** And **AutoCamp Yosemite,** in nearby Mariposa, offers Airstreams, modern cabins, and luxury tents, all with private patios and firepits; a midcentury clubhouse has a heated pool and sundeck, and daily shuttles take you in and out of the national park.

Day 1

From San Francisco, the three-hour drive to **Yosemite National Park** is a destination unto itself, as the landscape rises from rolling golden foothills to ever higher, ever more majestic mountains the deeper you delve into the High Sierra. Once you hit Yosemite Valley, stop by the visitor center and Ansel Adams Gallery (the photographer lived much of his life here), and breathe in the breathtaking beauty of the Yosemite icons surrounding you: Half

Dome, El Capitan, Yosemite Falls, and Bridalveil Fall. Given the fact that most visitors target this 7-mile-long valley, a mere 1% of the entire park, it's time to find your own solitude. And there's no better place for that than along one of the park's lesser known trails.

If you're up for a 7-mile hike, one of the best is Inspiration Point, departing from the Bridalveil Veil parking lot and snaking up the valley's south side to Inspiration Point. This old stagecoach route is not exceedingly famous, though you're following in the footsteps of the first Westerners who visited the valley. At the end awaits the classic postcard view of Yosemite's monoliths—El Capitan, Half Dome, Sentinel Dome, Cathedral Spires—rising from the valley floor, the same stunning scene made famous in Ansel Adams's 1934 photograph.

Those short on time can obtain the same view by following the sinuous turns of the Wawona Road south to the famed Tunnel View, just before Wawona Tunnel, typically full of camera-snapping crowds.

Here, hop on the 2½-mile trail, climbing 500 feet to Inspiration Point—you'll have it all to yourself, guaranteed.

If you continue south on Wawona Road, you'll come to the park's famous **Mariposa Grove,** with its sky-high giant sequoias—and crowds. A lesser known sequoia grove awaits in **Tuolumne Grove,** an 18-mile drive northwest of valley, just off Tioga Road. Here, the 2½-mile round-trip trail brings you into the hushed, cathedral-like ambience of these ancient trees. There's even one you can walk through.

For dinner, head into the cute little town of Mariposa, just outside the park, to the **1850 Restaurant and Brewery.** Creative takes on American favorites include fried chicken with wasabi, salmon cake salad with strawberry vinaigrette, and the 1850 burger doused in 1,000 Island dressing.

Day 2

El Capitan is, hands down, one of the world's bucket list climbs, made even more famous by movies such as *The Dawn Wall* and *Free Solo.* What's lesser known is that you can hike El Capitan—a 15½-mile trek that brings you to El Cap's apex, taking in majestic views of Taft Point, Dewey Point, Half Dome, Clouds, Rest, and North Dome. This is one of those experiences you'll remember for a lifetime—and, chances are, it will take all day. So that's one option for you today (and a great alternative to the superpopular, hard-to-get-permits-for Half Dome hike).

If you're not quite so hardcore, kick off the day with breakfast at the legendary **Ahwahnee Hotel Dining Room,** with 34-foot ceilings, chandeliers, and massive windows looking out on Yosemite Valley. Here, masterfully crafted dishes, such as the eggs Benedict with tomato, spinach, and Canadian bacon; steak and eggs; and the smoked salmon platter will fortify you for an active day.

After, drive up to Washburn Point, the less famous version of Glacier Point. Here you'll get your first glimpse of Half Dome from Glacier Point Road. The vista itself takes in a unique perspective of Half Dome and Vernal and Nevada Falls. Glacier Point is just up the road. Though potentially crowded, it's the perfect spot to unpack a picnic. Amble a short way down Four Mile Trail, which descends from here through tree-shaded, rocky terrain, offering million-dollar views overlooking the valley floor. If you decide to go the entire way, be forewarned: it's strenuous, but so worth it.

If you still have time, you can rent a bike and take a spin around the valley's scenic trails or raft the Merced (rafts available at Curry Village). You can never get enough of those views.

For predinner cocktails, head to the patio at the **Mountain Room Lounge,** part of Yosemite Valley Lodge, where a Hiker's Jubilee cocktail (whiskey, grenadine Disaronno, and Pepsi) is the perfect accompaniment to the surrounding views. You can extend the evening with dinner from the bar menu (California shrimp salad, beef chili, house-smoked pork sandwich), or head next door to the fancier **Mountain Room Restaurant,** offering steaks, seafood, and fresh California salads.

Day 3

Today, grab a quick but hearty breakfast at **Basecamp Eatery,** then make your way to **Tuolumne Meadows,** a 1½-hour drive up Tioga Road (open late May or early June and closed with November snowfalls). Here, you have your choice of backcountry hikes, each one more gorgeous than the next. Seek out Olmsted Point, where a short trail showcases epic views of the wide-open high country. You'll see Tenaya Lake, perhaps the most gorgeous of all Yosemite lakes and popular for kayaking, boating, swimming, and sunbathing.

Ten miles farther along Tioga Road you come to Tuolumne Meadows Visitor Center. This is a good stop for more hiking (the Soda Springs Trail is an easy 1½-mile round trip). Or, farther east on Tioga Road near the park's eastern entrance, the 3-mile Gaylor Lakes Trail hikes up (and up and up) to two stunning alpine lakes.

From here, you can make your way back to San Francisco. One last stop to consider is **Mono Lake** as you exit the park. This surprisingly salty lake features spectacular tufa towers, resembling a city skyline against the surrounding peaks. Check them out at Mono Lake Tufa State Natural Reserve. It's also a popular bird-watching spot.

Recommendations

Sights

Mariposa Grove. ⊠ *Mariposa Grove Rd., Yosemite National Park, CA* ☎ *209/372-0200* ⊕ *www.nps.gov/yose/planyourvisit/mg.htm* 🗺 *$35 per vehicle.*

Mono Lake Tufa State Natural Reserve. ⊠ *Hwy. 395, Lee Vining, CA* ☎ *760/647-6331* ⊕ *www.monolake.org* 🗺 *Free.*

Tuolumne Grove. ⊠ *Rte. 120, Yosemite National Park, CA* ☎ *209/372-0200* ⊕ *www.nps.gov/yose/planyourvisit/sequoias.htm* 🗺 *$35 per vehicle.*

Tuolumne Meadows. ⊠ *Rte. 120, Yosemite National Park, CA* ☎ *209/372-0200* ⊕ *www.nps.gov/yose/learn/nature/tuolumne.htm* 🗺 *$35 per vehicle.*

Yosemite National Park. ⊠ *Yosemite Valley Visitor Center, 9035 Village Dr., Yosemite Valley, CA* ☎ *209/372-0200* ⊕ *www.nps.gov/yose/planyourvisit/yv.htm* 🗺 *$35 per vehicle.*

Restaurants

Ahwahnee Hotel Dining Room. 🔢 *Average main: $35* ⊠ *9013 Village Dr., Yosemite National Park, CA* ☎ *888/413-8869* ⊕ *www.travelyosemite.com.*

Basecamp Eatery. 🔢 *Average main: $12* ⊠ *9006 Yosemite Lodge Dr., Yosemite National Park, CA* ☎ *888/413-8869* ⊕ *www.travelyosemite.com.*

1850 Restaurant and Brewery. 🔢 *Average main: $22* ⊠ *5114 Yosemite All-Year Hwy., Mariposa, CA* ☎ *209/966-222* ⊕ *www.1850restaurant.com.*

Mountain Room Restaurant. 🔢 *Average main: $29* ⊠ *Yosemite Valley Lodge, 9006 Yosemite Lodge Dr., Yosemite Valley, CA* ☎ *209/372-1403* ⊕ *www.travelyosemite.com.*

🛏 Hotels

AutoCamp Yosemite. 🔢 *Rooms from: $409* ⊠ *6323 CA 140, Midpines, CA* ☎ *888/405-7553* ⊕ *www.autocamp.com* 🍽 *Free breakfast.*

Tenaya Lodge at Yosemite. 🔢 *Rooms from: $289* ⊠ *1122 Hwy. 41, Fish Camp, CA* ☎ *888/514-2167* ⊕ *www.tenayalodge.com* 🍽 *No meals.*

🍸 Nightlife

Mountain Room Lounge. ⊠ *Yosemite Valley Lodge, 9006 Yosemite Lodge Dr., Yosemite Valley, CA* ☎ *209/372-1403* ⊕ *www.travelyosemite.com.*

Chapter 2

SOUTHWEST AND NORTHERN PLAINS

WELCOME TO
SOUTHWEST AND NORTHERN PLAINS

TOP REASONS
TO GO

★ **Bucket List Sights:**
Zion, Grand Teton, and
Great Basin are waiting
to be explored.

★ **Views for Days:**
The South Rim is the
best spot for taking in
the Grand Canyon.

★ **Rocky Mountain High:**
You can almost literally
"touch the sky" from
atop Pike's Peak.

★ **Desert Expeditions:**
Marvel at giant cacti in
Saguaro and massive
dunes at White Sands.

★ **Head to the Hills:**
Stunning sunsets
draw travelers to
Texas Hill Country.

Many of the country's most spectacular drives are found in the Southwest and Northern Plains. The stunning mountain terrain of Colorado and Utah eventually give way to the expansive deserts in Arizona and New Mexico. The topography flattens out in Oklahoma and Texas, eventually dropping you off at the broad beaches along the Gulf of Mexico.

Texas is the second largest state, so it takes two hub cities to hit most destinations. **Houston** is fairly close to the coast, so it's a perfect place to depart for beach destinations like South Padre Island. **Dallas** is farther north, which makes it an ideal starting point for to places like Waco and Oklahoma City. And if Austin or San Antonio are your dream trip, either city makes an excellent base. It's no surprise that **Denver** is a gateway to the Colorado Rockies, but it's also within driving distance of far-flung destinations like the Badlands of South Dakota. **Salt Lake City** is a short distance from some of the country's natural wonders, including national parks like Zion, Grand Teton, and Great Basin. **Albuquerque** is near White Sands National Park, while **Phoenix** is perfectly positioned for Tucson, Sedona, and the one place on everyone's bucket list, the Grand Canyon.

Austin, TX

162 miles (approx. 3 hours) from Houston.

Gear up for a weekend in the Live Music Capital of the World, just a three-hour drive west of Houston. With music venues galore, extensive outdoor activities, and ample food and drink, there's plenty for everyone to do in Texas' capital city. Bring your cowboy boots but don't expect the conventional—this funky town thrives on its reputation of being weird.

Planning

GETTING THERE AND BACK

From Houston, Austin is a quick drive west on I–10 to TX 71W. Make sure your air-conditioning is working from February to November. Consider listening to Willie Nelson along the way for peak iconoclast vibes.

PIT STOPS

If you need to stop for gas, snacks, or a bathroom, don't mess it up by going anywhere that's not a **Buc'ees.** First, they boast the cleanest bathrooms in America; second, this place is a rest stop on acid. Why are there stuffed beavers everywhere? Who is buying these faux antiques? What's with all the Czech pastries? How many flavors of Icee really exist? You'll have plenty of time to ask

One of the Austin area's most beautiful destinations is the lush Barton Creek Greenbelt.

the hard questions in the world's longest car wash.

WHEN TO GO

Spring and fall are prime for good weather. Beware Austin heat in peak summer—it's not for the thick-blooded.

WHERE TO STAY

Built in 1886 and impeccably restored, the **Driskill** represents a time when people mingled in grandiose settings. The lobby is highlighted by vaulted ceilings, decorative columns, and chandeliers. The uber-hip **Hotel San José** is a boutique hotel in the midst of the South Congress Avenue action. The **Austin Motel** is the preferred budget option.

Day 1

When you roll into town, you're probably going to be hungry. Everywhere you look is an adorable food truck or charming mom-and-pop restaurant. Austin has no shortage of lunch temptations. Start at the **Pangea Lounge** on East 6th Street, a

cluster of food trucks offering everything from Philly cheesesteaks to Indian, Greek, Halal, and Thai favorites. Grab a hammock in the shade or peruse artisan wares on the weekend. This will give you a good vantage point for the weekend ahead—all around you are bars, restaurants, and music venues, restaurants filled with cool-looking people doing cool-looking stuff.

If you're going to Austin, you're probably planning to "keep it weird" anyway, so consider staying in one of the funky lodgings. Historical opposites are the legendary **Austin Motel** ("so close, yet so far out") and the regal **Driskill Hotel**. The boutique **San Jose Hotel** is sleek as heck. Get your bearings of the city from the best view of Austin atop **Mount Bonell.** The super short, very easy hike (but bring plenty of water because it's Texas) puts you in a prime viewing location of downtown all the way to the 360 Bridge. Isn't Lake Austin lovely?

All that sunshine and walking is sure to have built up your appetite again. Now is the time to remind yourself that this is a huge part of what you came to Austin for: the opportunity to stuff yourself silly. **Polvo's** will help you out with that. The Mexican and Tex-Mex plates aren't messing around—you can easily share the fajitas, burritos, enchiladas, and more, but why would you want to? You'll want your leftovers later tonight. Don't forget a spin around the salsa bar, and everything tastes better with a pitcher of margaritas.

The historic Rainey Street district was once a sleepy neighborhood of bungalow homes but has since transformed into a hopping nightlife scene of bars and restaurants. Catch live music, rowdy beer gardens, and games of cornhole, but don't miss **Lustre Pearl,** an Austin drinking landmark where "it takes all kinds" truly comes to life.

Day 2

There are two trucks serving **Veracruz All Natural Mexican Food** in Austin, but head to the one farther south to be closer to where you're hanging out today. Grab a juice or smoothie and partake in a famous Austin tradition: a breakfast taco from the taco truck. Don't miss the miga tacos with scrambled eggs, peppers, and cheese. This is Austin breakfast.

Grab an iced coffee at **Jo's** (and take a selfie next to the "I Love You So Much" mural) because you are in for a busy day of window shopping, people-watching, and hanging out along South Congress Avenue. Here you'll find an eclectic array of boutiques, restaurants, and music venues. Don't miss **Uncommon Objects,** where you can buy your next completely unique antique; **Lucy in Disguise With Diamonds** for when you want to go incognito; **Monkey See Monkey Do** for the gifts and souvenirs; and **South Congress Books** for something to read. You can try not to eat and drink along the way, but why would you do that?

There are so many interesting people to watch in Austin, and they all seem to convene at **Bouldin Creek Cafe** for lunch. That's a good thing, since the food here is tasty. Vegetarian and vegan options don't come easy in Texas, but Bouldin Creek provides a healthy twist on all your favorites. Don't skip on an iced coffee pick-me-up.

When you get to **Barton Springs,** you'll feel like you've finally arrived. This is peak Austin: a lawn full of gorgeous humans languidly splayed out around a natural spring water pool. With plenty of shade and space, you'll want to post up for at least the afternoon, napping and enjoying the laid-back atmosphere. The chilly water is only bearable for a quick dip to shake off that Texas heat.

Another can't-miss landmark is **The Salt Lick,** in nearby Driftwood. The open-pit barbecue joint serves brisket, sausages, and pork ribs alongside a bevy of traditional sides like beans, coleslaw, and potato salad. Don't miss out on pie for dessert, and BYOB.

Tonk up your honk at **The White Horse,** which has live music seven nights a week. There ain't nothing like two-stepping around this classic bar with a Lonestar in your hand. Whether you're an old-school cowboy or swanky hipster queen, there's a place for you to extra out at The White Horse. Hit that patio for gulps of fresh air between sets, and grab a taco to load up for the next dance. Just try not to have a blast—it's an impossible task.

Day 3

Church has never been this fun, or delicious. Sunday morning at **Stubb's BBQ** isn't your regular service. From the Bloody Mary bar to the brisket carving station, Gospel Brunch is one holy experience. The choir serenades you all through your meal, though you might find yourself on your feet clapping and stomping before you've finished breakfast.

When it's not in a drought, Austin is famous for its lush scenery. Take in the views at **Barton Creek Greenbelt,** where you can hike, bike, climb, and swim through the verdant park. The best entrance for a short trip is the Main Access Point along Capital of Texas Highway. You'll love the limestone bluffs, live oak trees, and fields of wildflowers. Wear a bathing suit so you can cool off along the way.

Austin loves its fusion food—it's the perfect representation of a city that welcomes everyone. **The Whip-In** is exactly that sort of place, a mashup of gastropub, convenience store, bar, and music venue that serves contemporary Indian-Tex-Mex cuisine. Pull up a seat on the patio with a cold craft beer, and stock up on delicious gourmet snacks for your ride home.

There's a lot of discourse around what's authentically Austin, but the undisputed truth is that Chicken Shit Bingo is what legends are made of. Every Sunday afternoon at **The Little Longhorn Saloon,** crowds gather around the bingo board to eat chili dogs, drink incredibly cheap beer, and holler at chickens who walk about the bingo board and peck at the numbers. You could win big, but even if you don't, this is a hilariously good time you'll never forget.

Recommendations

Sights

Barton Creek Greenbelt. ✉ *3755 S. Capital of Texas Hwy. B, Austin, TX* ☎ *512/974–6700* 🌐 *www.austinparks.org/barton-creek-greenbelt* 🎟 *Free.*

Barton Springs. ✉ *2131 William Barton Dr., Austin, TX* ☎ *512/974–6300* 🌐 *www.austintexas.gov/page/pools-splash-pads* 🎟 *Free.*

Mount Bonell. ✉ *3800 Mount Bonnell Rd., Austin, TX* ☎ *512/974–6700* 🌐 *www.austintexas.org/listings/covert-park-at-mt-bonnell/2925* 🎟 *Free.*

Restaurants

Bouldin Creek Cafe. [$] *Average main: $5* ✉ *1900 S. 1st St., Austin, TX* ☎ *512/416–1601* 🌐 *www.bouldincreekcafe.com.*

Jo's. [$] *Average main: $11* ✉ *242 W. 2nd St., Austin, TX* ☎ *512/469–9003* 🌐 *www.joscoffeeshop.com.*

Pangea Lounge. [$] *Average main: $11* ✉ *1211 E. 6th St, Austin, TX* ☎ *512/4507–9459* 🌐 *www.facebook.com/pangeaLoungeatx.*

Polvo's. [$] *Average main: $12* ✉ *14735 Bratton La., Austin TX* ☎ *512/ 251–5596* 🌐 *www.polvosaustin.com* 🕓 *Closed Sun.*

The Salt Lick. [$] *Average main: $25* ✉ *18300 Farm to Market Rd., Driftwood, TX* ☎ *512/530-2900* 🌐 *www.saltlickbbq.com.*

Stubb's BBQ. [$] *Average main: $6* ✉ *801 Red River St., Austin, TX* ☎ *512/480–8341* 🌐 *www.stubbsaustin.com.*

Veracruz All Natural Mexican Food. [$] *Average main: $4* ✉ *4208 Menchaca Rd., Austin, TX* ☎ *512/981–1760* 🌐 *www.veracruzallnatural.com* 🕓 *No Dinner Mon.–Thurs.*

The Whip-In. [$] *Average main: $10* ✉ *1950 S. IH 35 Frontage Rd., Austin, TX* ☎ *512/442–5337* 🌐 *www.whipin.com.*

Hotels

Austin Motel. [$] *Rooms from: $196* ✉ *1220 S. Congress Ave., Austin, TX* ☎ *512/441–1157* 🌐 *www.austinmotel.com* 🍴 *No meals.*

Driskill Hotel. [$] *Rooms from: $339* ✉ *604 Brazos St., Austin, TX* ☎ *512/439–1234* 🌐 *www.hyatt.com/en-US/hotel/texas/the-driskill/aushd* 🍴 *No meals.*

San Jose Hotel. $ *Rooms from: $286* ⊠ *1316 S. Congress Ave., Austin, TX* ☎ *512/444–7322* ⊕ *www.sanjosehotel. com* ⍟ *No meals.*

 Nightlife

The Little Longhorn Saloon. ⊠ *5434 Burnet Rd., Austin, TX* ☎ *512/524–1291* ⊕ *www. thelittlelonghornsaloon.com.*

Lustre Pearl. ⊠ *114 Linden St., Austin, TX* ☎ *512/524–1143* ⊕ *www.east.lustre- pearlaustin.com.*

The White Horse. ⊠ *500 Comal St., Austin, TX* ☎ *512/553–6756* ⊕ *www.thewhite- horseaustin.com.*

 Shopping

Buc'ees. ⊠ *1700 TX-71, Bastrop, TX* ☎ *979/238–6390* ⊕ *www.buc-ees.com.*

Lucy in Disguise With Diamonds. ⊠ *1506 S. Congress Ave., Austin, TX* ☎ *512/444– 2002* ⊕ *www.lucyindisguise.com.*

Monkey See Monkey Do. ⊠ *1712 S. Congress Ave., Austin, TX* ☎ *512/443– 4999* ⊕ *www.facebook.com/ MonkeySeeMonkeyDoAustin.*

South Congress Books. ⊠ *1608 S. Con- gress Ave., Austin, TX* ☎ *512/916–8882* ⊕ *southcongressbooks.com.*

Uncommon Objects. ⊠ *1602 Fortview Rd., Austin, TX* ☎ *512/442–4000* ⊕ *www. uncommonobjects.com.*

Bisbee and Tombstone, AZ

Bisbee is 207 miles (approx. 3¼ hours) from Phoenix.

Squared off like a pair of old-time gun- slingers in southern Arizona, Bisbee and Tombstone stake a claim on Gold Rush history. Mines in Bisbee once gushed silver and gold, drawing fortune hunters who turned a dot on the map into a boom town. Nearby Tombstone made a name with gambling, dance halls, and deadly duels.

Today, decades after the mines went dry, the two communities couldn't be more different. Bisbee offers a mix of art, history, and mining lore in a town that thrives on offbeat culture. Tombstone is like a Wild West theme park, but the attractions—from the OK Corral to Boot Hill Graveyard—are real (mostly). For travelers, they're a taste of a bygone time in Arizona's past, and you'll still find venerable saloons, frontier trading posts, and ghosts around every corner.

Planning

GETTING THERE AND BACK
Follow I–10 E to exit 303, then take AZ 80 E to Bisbee.

INSPIRATION
Listen to the soundtrack *Once Upon a Time in the West,* by Italian composer Ennio Morricone, created for the Sergio Leone movie of that same name. From jangly saloon music to gunfight-ready tracks, it's just the thing for getting in the dusty, Old West spirit.

PIT STOPS
Along the way, duck off the Interstate into **Saguaro National Park,** where the 8-mile Cactus Forest Drive loops through dramatic desert punctuated by oversized cacti.

WHEN TO GO
While Bisbee is a year-round destination, summer highs can climb well into the 90s. In the spring and fall, things get more comfortable, with mild weather all day. By midwinter, there's still plenty of sun, but temperatures can drop to freezing at night. If you're coming to see Sandhill Cranes migrating near Bisbee, the season is from mid-September to mid-February.

Looking like a movie set, the tiny town of Tombstone has an entertaining Old West vibe.

WHERE TO STAY

Shack up in a shiny Airstream at Bisbee's **Shady Dell Vintage Trailer Court** for a bracing dose of old-school quirk that's also budget-friendly. There are more than Airstreams, actually—options range from a 1947 Tiki bus to the 1959 Boles Aero— and each spot comes with an outdoor charcoal grill. For a few more creature comforts, opt for the **Letson Loft Hotel,** an 1883 Main Street building with eight restored guest rooms.

Day 1

Perk up after a long drive with cold-brew coffee and a burrito at **Bathtub Coffee,** whose playfully odd vibe is the perfect introduction to Bisbee. (Their "Karmic Forwarding" program invites visitors to fill out postcards that are mailed to random addresses in town.)

Next, go underground the desert landscape on a tour of the **Copper Queen Mine**; you'll get a miner's lamp, hard hat, and slicker, and fill up on a mix of mining history and tall tales. Gold, copper, silver, lead, and zinc once poured from the earth here, but the Bisbee mines closed for good in 1975.

When you're back in the sunshine, head back to historic Bisbee to check out some of the town's art galleries. Find eccentric contemporary work in the **Sam Poe Gallery**; a stone's throw away is the **Belleza Gallery,** with a focus on fine art that ranges from oil paintings to mixed media. It's just a few more steps to **55 Main Gallery,** another contemporary collection with some vintage thrown in for good measure.

For dinner, head to **Café Roka,** the long-time star of the local dining scene. Prix-fixe menus feature continent-hopping flavors, with an impressive wine list to go alongside. Since there's live jazz on most Friday nights, it's worth booking well in advance to score a table at this destination eatery in a historic art deco building.

After your meal, dive into Bisbee's dark side with an evening at the **Bisbee Séance**

Room, where intimate magic shows mash up card-trick sleight of hand with the creepiest tidbits of local history. Magic Kenny Bang Bang is the one-man-show's charismatic ringmaster.

Day 2

Sidle up to the squiggle-shape counter at **Bisbee Breakfast Club** for classics from the griddle: think big flapjacks, generous omelets, and huevos rancheros. Check out the abandoned gas station next door for a few essential Instagram shots, then head half a mile west to the Lavender Pit, a disused copper pit mine that resembles a mold in a mountain. There's not much to do here aside from peering inside, but it's a truly impressive sight.

Now it's time to saddle up and head to Tombstone. (Really you should drive, but do it while imagining something a little more Wild West.) This is where Wyatt Earp and Doc Holliday had their shootout at the **OK Corral**—probably—and where gunslinging legends were laid to rest in the **Boot Hill Graveyard.** Equal parts authentic history, tourist trap, and cowboy cosplay, Tombstone can be great fun if you're willing to go all-in.

Start at the OK Corral, where dramatized gunfights are staged a few times a day. Your tickets also get you access to the Historama next door, including a multimedia presentation that benefits from gravelly voiced, high-drama narration by Vincent Price.

Next, pay your respects to fallen gunslingers at Boot Hill Graveyard—Boot Hill used to be a common name for cemeteries for those who "died with their boots on." It's an odd place, and most people wander around just looking for funny epitaphs, but it's worth checking out the memorial to Jewish pioneers and "their Indian friends," plus the section cordoned off for Chinese residents. They're a

reminder that Arizona history didn't resemble an all-white cowboy movie.

Take a break for lunch at the **Crystal Palace Saloon,** a bar with a long, rowdy history. The menu of burgers, sandwiches, and pub food is fine, but the real pleasure is in the atmospheric room, the mirrored mahogany bar, and the authentic tin ceilings. (The staffers wear costumes that are both corny and fun.)

Find a little more history and a little less showmanship at the **Tombstone Courthouse State Historic Park,** a two-story Victorian-era building that's now a museum. The exhibits include stories about Wyatt Earp, silver mining, and ranching. The final stop on your Wild West tour of Tombstone has to be the **Bird Cage Theatre,** once known for bawdy entertainment and epic poker duels. Rumors of ghosts abound—tours of the historic spot feature all the grisly details.

Now that you've ticked off the Tombstone essentials, head back to Bisbee for a patio dinner at **Poco,** choosing from a menu of Mexican-inspired vegan fare including burritos, bowls, and chimichangas. Nachos come draped in a thick layer of "cheezy" sauce. Some weekend nights feature live music, but if things are quiet go check out the scene at the nearby **Old Bisbee Brewing Company.** Beers here range from a crisp Pilsner to a creamy stout that could double as dessert.

Day 3

Stroll to **Bisbee Coffee Company** to wake up with a cup of locally roasted coffee and a pastry; this is the perfect place to linger over a slow breakfast, as the outside seating offers prime people-watching.

Before heading home, make a side trip to the vineyards of the Sonoita and Elgin area, an hour northwest of Bisbee. The first stop is the off-grid **Rune Wines,** which consists of an Airstream trailer and a Quonset hut; in cold weather, tastings are in the hut, while on nice days the whole operation migrates outdoors. The Petite Syrah wins raves, and there's even an unusual wild fermented Syrah.

A short drive away in Sonoita is **Arizona Hops and Vines,** a hilltop spot with a decidedly youthful vibe. Food pairings at wine tastings might include Cheetos, Coco Puffs, and flavored potato chips, and wines get irreverent names—La Petite Mort, The Peacemaker—that will wash away any pinkies-out snobbery you associate with wine tasting.

For lunch, make a final stop at the **Copper Brothel Brewery,** which has a full lineup of house made beers and a hearty pub food menu. The Colorado-style pork green chile is a favorite, but there are also salads, sandwiches, tacos, and Southwestern pub fare.

Recommendations

Sights

Arizona Hops and Vines. ✉ *3450 AZ 82, Sonoita, AZ* ☎ *301/237–6556* 🌐 *www.azhopsandvines.com* 🎟 *$15.*

Bird Cage Theatre. ✉ *535 E. Allen St., Tombstone, AZ* ☎ *800/457–3423* 🌐 *www.tombstonebirdcage.com* 🎟 *$14.*

Boot Hill Graveyard. ✉ *408 AZ 80, Tombstone, AZ* ☎ *520/457–2540* 🌐 *tombstone-boothillgiftshop.com* 🎟 *$3.*

Copper Queen Mine. ✉ *478 N. Dart Rd., Bisbee, AZ* ☎ *520/432–2071* 🌐 *www.queenminetour.com* 🎟 *$14.*

OK Corral. ✉ *326 Allen St., Tombstone, AZ* ☎ *520/457–3456* 🌐 *www.ok-corral.com* 🎟 *$6.*

Rune Wines. ✉ *3969 AZ 82, Sonoita, AZ* ☎ *520/338–8823* 🌐 *www.runewines.com* 🕒 *Closed Tues.*

Saguaro National Park. ✉ *Rincon Mountain Visitor Center, 3693 S. Old Spanish Trail, Tucson, AZ* ☎ *520/733–5153* 🌐 *www.nps.gov/sagu* 🎟 *$25 per vehicle.*

Restaurants

Bisbee Breakfast Club. [$] *Average main: $12* ✉ *75 Erie St., Bisbee, AZ* ☎ *520/432–5885* 🌐 *www.bisbeebreakfastclub.com* 🕒 *No dinner.*

Café Roka. [$] *Average main: $14* ✉ *3112 AZ 83, Sonoita, AZ* ☎ *520/405–6721* 🌐 *www.copperbrothelbrewery.com.*

Copper Brothel Brewery. [$] *Average main: $14* ✉ *3112 AZ 83, Sonoita, AZ* ☎ *520/405–6721* 🌐 *www.copperbrothel-brewery.com.*

Crystal Palace Saloon. [$] *Average main: $10* ✉ *15 Main St., Bisbee, AZ* ☎ *520/314–5929* 🌐 *www.facebook.com/pocobzb.*

Poco. [$] *Average main: $10* ✉ *15 Main St., Bisbee, AZ* ☎ *520/314–5929* 🌐 *www.facebook.com/pocobzb.*

Coffee and Quick Bites

Bathtub Coffee. [$] *Average main: $5* ✉ *31 Subway St., Bisbee, AZ* ☎ *520/276–4955* 🌐 *cup-of-swords-llc.square.site* 🕒 *No dinner.*

Bisbee Coffee Company. [$] *Average main: $5* ✉ *2 Copper Queen Plaza, Bisbee, AZ* ☎ *520/266–2438* 🌐 *bisbeecoffee.com* 🕒 *No dinner.*

Hotels

Letson Loft Hotel. [$] *Rooms from: $150* ✉ *26 Main St., Bisbee, AZ* ☎ *520/432–3210* 🌐 *www.letsonlofthotel.com* 🍴 *Free breakfast.*

Shady Dell Vintage Trailer Court. [$] *Rooms from: $70* ✉ *1 Old Douglas Rd., Bisbee, AZ* ☎ *520/432–3567* 🌐 *heshadydell.com* 🍴 *No meals.*

Nightlife

Bisbee Séance Room. ✉ *26 Brewery Ave., Bisbee, AZ* ☎ *520/203–3350* ⊕ *thebisbeeseanceroom.com.*

Old Bisbee Brewing Company. ✉ *200 Review Alley, Bisbee, AZ* ☎ *520/432–2739* ⊕ *www.oldbisbeebrewingcompany.com.*

Shopping

Belleza Gallery. ✉ *27 Main St., Bisbee, AZ* ☎ *520/432–5877* ⊕ *bellezagallery.org.*

55 Main Gallery. ✉ *55 Main St., Bisbee, AZ* ☎ *520/432–4694* ⊕ *www.facebook.com/55maingallery.*

Sam Poe Galery. ✉ *33 Subway St., Bisbee, AZ* ☎ *520/432–5338* ⊕ *www.sampoegallery.com.*

Breckenridge, CO

81 miles (approx. 1½ hours) from Denver.

Breckenridge gets more snow than any other town in Colorado, making it a mecca for powder hounds and winter sports enthusiasts. But whether you're bombing the back bowls or staking out the best spot for après, there's more than one way to earn your turns on a Breckenridge weekender.

Breckenridge's appeal extends far beyond the slopes. A former gold rush town turned resort destination, it's an easy getaway for both adventure enthusiasts and those looking for a relaxing, rejuvenating mountain retreat. With an eclectic downtown, the largest historic district in Colorado, and more than 300 days of sunshine a year, it appeals to a wide variety of Front Range visitors and locals alike.

Planning

GETTING THERE AND BACK

What should be a straightforward 1½-hour drive down I–70 is often confounded by ski traffic, weather conditions, and accidents pretty predictably November through April, causing hours of delays. If you are going to drive, avoid leaving Friday after work (4 to 8 pm) or Saturday morning after 6 am, and don't attempt to return Sunday between 11 and 6.

If you'd rather skip the headache, there are private and shared shuttles from Denver International Airport to the mountains. Or if you have time to spare, you can take the Bustang West bus from Denver to Frisco and then hop on a transfer. Since Breckenridge has a free shuttle around town, you really don't need a car once you get there.

WHEN TO GO

Winter is prime time for powder hounds, but don't discount summer or fall for warm-weather fun like hiking and biking. Ski season generally runs from November through May and sometimes into June, weather permitting. It gets especially busy during the holiday season.

WHERE TO STAY

As a major resort destination, Breckenridge has a plethora of accommodations, many of which are right on the mountain. **One Ski Hill Place** is one of the most accessible, pampered properties. For a more affordable getaway, **The Bivvi** is a chic hostel designed to serve as a crash pad for adventurers.

Day 1

After braving I–70's notoriously soul-sucking traffic, you're instantly rewarded with Breck's picture-perfect views. Shake off the last bits of stress with a margarita and Mexican food from **Mi Casa**. A local favorite for more than 30 years, it's

A favorite winter destination, Breckenridge caters to skiers and snowboarders of all skill levels.

known for its award-winning mango duck quesadillas and sizzling fajitas.

You're likely to be antsy to stretch your legs, so before you get settled into your hotel, take some time to explore. You can wander the eight-block downtown on your own, or get acquainted on a (Fat) Bike and Brew Tour, which is run year-round by **Ridden.** You'll visit the world's highest distillery and one of Breckenridge's most popular local breweries, **Broken Compass,** to toss a few back and fully ease into vacation mode.

After you're sufficiently loosened up, throw on your warmest layers, because it's time to experience a true winter wonderland. The magical evening begins with a sleigh ride to a chuckwagon dinner under the stars. Themed shows can be cheesy, but **Two Below Zero** does a great job appealing to guests of all ages while paying homage to Colorado's cowboy culture. A riveting Wild West performance with on-site country crooners sets the tone for the evening as you fill your belly next to a roaring fire that slowly lulls you

to sleep. In summer, their backcountry cookouts and wagon rides are equally entertaining, so no matter when you visit, you're in for a unique treat.

Day 2

If you're anxious to make the most of the day, snag a French Toast sandwich or signature green chili burrito at **BreckFast.** One of Breck's most popular fast-casual eateries, they'll get you fueled up and out on the slopes in time for first tracks.

If you've never skied or snowboarded before, definitely take a lesson so you don't leave with a bruised ego or backside. With five peaks, four terrain parks, more than 150 trails, nearly 3,000 skiable acres, and the tallest chairlift in North America, you could spend days exploring the insane topography and still not even make a dent. To begin to get your bearings, the gondola operates just about year-round and is completely free, whether you have a lift ticket or not. A breathtaking ride over Colorado's looming peaks, gawk in awe of the outdoor playground that unfolds below you.

If the idea of flying downhill is intimidating, Breckenridge is also home to two Nordic centers, which boast more than 30 miles of cross-country skiing and snowshoeing trails, meaning you can still enjoy some alpine fun and take in the landscape on flat land. Spend the morning playing in the snow however you see fit.

When you're ready for a lunch break, **Pioneer Crossing** is Breck's newest on-mountain dining option. A cozy cabin to warm up, their menu boasts everything from crepes and burgers to local Colorado lamb. If by now your calves are screaming or you'd rather head back to town, **The Canteen Tap House & Tavern** has burgers that are always crowd-pleasers.

You can either spend the afternoon perfecting your turns, trying another sport like snowmobiling, or warming up with a scenic Snowcat ride.

In the warmer months, the ski runs are converted into mountain biking trails with other on-mountain activities like alpine slides and ziplines to keep the adrenaline going. There are hiking trails for all abilities and agilities, from gentle inclines to awe-inspiring fourteeners (peaks with an elevation above 14,000 feet). Just steps from Main Street, Blue River and Maggie Pond provide watery adventures like fly fishing, paddle boarding, and kayaking, or local tour operators can take you whitewater rafting for the day.

No matter the season, après is always the best time of day. On the mountain, **Robbie's Tavern** and **TBar** are great places to tip one back and relax slopeside. In town, **Rocky Mountain Underground** (RMU to locals), boasts an insanely popular backyard beer garden with rotating beer (and cocktails) on tap.

You can fill up on nibbles and happy hour bites, or treat yourself to dinner at **Hearthstone Restaurant**. A local favorite for decades, it serves hearty hand-cut steaks, wild game, and fresh seafood in a beautifully appointed Victorian home where sensuous blackberry elk and Alaskan black cod magically replenish your tired bones. Tuck in early, because you have another long day ahead.

Day 3

Start the morning with a leisurely breakfast at **The Crown,** which has a cozy coffee shop vibe. Come for the house-made cold brew, but stay for the extra spicy Bloody and bagel sandwiches.

Of course, you can ski or snowboard again (practice makes perfect), but if you're sore or seeking a more memorable adventure, why not give dogsledding a try? You'll take turns mushing and riding in the sleigh while being pulled by a team of beautiful huskies ready to run. And yes, you can play with the puppies after.

Warm-up with a bowl from **Soupz On,** where you can sample the flavors before committing. Best known for the elk stroganoff, they also have creative palate pleasers like chicken chowder, jalapeno asiago, and English cottage pie.

Before you head home, indulge in one last cold-weathered adventure. You can try ice skating at **Stephen C. West Ice Arena,** sledding at **Carter Park,** or tubing at **Frisco Adventure Park.**

Recommendations

Sights

Carter Park. ⊠ *300 S. High St., Breckenridge, CO* ☏ *970/453–1734* ⊕ *www. breckenridgerecreation.com* ▨ *Free.*

Frisco Adventure Park. ⊠ *616 Recreation Way, Frisco, CO* ☏ *970/668–2558* ⊕ *www.townoffrisco.com* ▨ *$25.*

Stephen C. West Ice Arena. ✉ *189 Boreas Pass Rd., Breckenridge, CO* ☎ *970/547–9974* ⊕ *www.breckenridgerecreation. com* 🎫 *$8.*

Restaurants

BreckFast. 💲 *Average main: $8* ✉ *500 S. Main St., Breckenridge, CO* ☎ *970/771–3456* ⊕ *www.breckfastcolorado.com.*

The Canteen Tap House & Tavern. 💲 *Average main: $10* ✉ *208 N. Main St., Breckenridge, CO* ☎ *970/453–0063* ⊕ *www. thecanteenbreck.com.*

The Crown. 💲 *Average main: $8* ✉ *215 S. Main St., Breckenridge, CO* ☎ *970/453–6022* ⊕ *www.facebook.com/ thecrownbreckenridge.*

Hearthstone Restaurant. 💲 *Average main: $41* ✉ *130 S. Ridge St., 1613 Breckenridge, CO* ☎ *970/453–1148* ⊕ *www. hearthstonebreck.com.*

Mi Casa. 💲 *Average main: $13* ✉ *600 S. Park Ave., Breckenridge, CO* ☎ *970/453–2071* ⊕ *www.micasabreck.com.*

Pioneer Crossing. 💲 *Average main: $15* ✉ *Columbine Rd., Breckenridge, CO* ☎ *970/453–3272* ⊕ *www.breckenridge. com.*

Soupz On. 💲 *Average main: $7* ✉ *City Market Center, 400 N. Park Ave., Breckenridge, CO* ☎ *970/547–4797* ⊕ *www. soupzon.net.*

🛏 Hotels

The Bivvi. 💲 *Rooms from: $70* ✉ *9511 C0 9, Breckenridge, CO* ☎ *970/423–6553* ⊕ *www.thebivvi.com* ⦿ *Free breakfast.*

One Ski Hill. 💲 *Rooms from: $494* ✉ *1521 Ski Hill Rd., Breckenridge, CO* ☎ *800/290–3604* ⊕ *www.oneskihill. rockresorts.com* ⦿ *No meals.*

▶ Nightlife

Broken Compass. ✉ *68 Continental Ct., Breckenridge, CO* ☎ *970/398–2772* ⊕ *www.brokencompassbrewing.com.*

Robbie's Tavern. ✉ *1627 Ski Hill Rd., Breckenridge, CO* ☎ *970/547–8785* ⊕ *www. robbiestavern.com.*

TBar. ✉ *1521 Ski Hill Rd., Breckenridge, CO* ☎ *970/547–8837* ⊕ *www.breckenridge.com.*

🏃 Activities

Ridden. ✉ *Breckenridge, CO* ☎ *970/453–2055* ⊕ *www.breckenridgebiketours.com* 🎫 *$70.*

Two Below Zero. ✉ *616 Recreation Way, Breckenridge, CO* ☎ *970/453–1520* ⊕ *www.dinnersleighrides.com* 🎫 *$84.*

Carlsbad Caverns National Park, NM

302 miles (approx. 4¾ hours) from Albuquerque.

A weekend getaway to Carlsbad Caverns National Park is tailor-made for outdoor adventurers and aficionados of the otherworldly. The subterranean landscape at New Mexico is one of the deepest and most ornate in the world and its caves, the well-lit Big Room and the park's lesser known undeveloped chambers, are well worth the almost five hour drive from Albuquerque. On the way, get a gander at Roswell, a mecca for the UFO-curious since 1947.

Planning

GETTING THERE AND BACK

Carlsbad Caverns National Park is 302 miles from Albuquerque, just north of the Texas border in the Guadalupe Mountains. The drive heads east out of

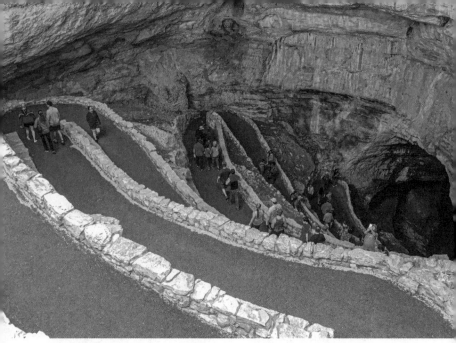

Winding trails take you into the underground caves at Carlsbad Caverns National Park.

the New Mexico capital, tracing historic Route 66 on I–40 for 62 miles. At Clines Corners, turn onto Highway 285 and drive south through the state's rural hinterlands.

PIT STOPS
A 58-mile detour from Vaughn on Highway 285 lands you in the final resting place of notorious outlaw Billy the Kid. Visit the **Billy the Kid Museum,** packed with ephemera from the 19th century, then pay your respects to the man himself in the Old Fort Sumner Cemetery.

WHEN TO GO
Carlsbad Caverns National Park is an all-season getaway. Even when temperatures are soaring outside, inside the caves it's a cool 56 degrees. Summertime draws the most crowds, but it's also the season (late April through October) when the park's famed bats make their nightly exodus from the cave.

WHERE TO STAY
The most enchanting place to stay at Carlsbad Caverns is also the most rustic. The national park has no lodgings, but allows backcountry camping. For running water and other amenities, overnight in the town of Carlsbad 20 miles north of the park. The charming **Fiddler's Inn** bed-and-breakfast has lots of creature comforts.

Day 1

It's a long drive from Albuquerque to **Carlsbad Caverns National Park**—just under five hours—so hit the road as soon as you are able. The route, which largely passes through New Mexico's vast ranchlands, is somewhat monotonous, but pleasant enough with panoramas that stretch all the way to the Guadalupe Mountains in the south.

For dinner, make a pit stop in Roswell, site of the country's most mythic UFO sighting. **The Cowboy Cafe,** a throwback diner with a meat-heavy menu full of burgers, steak, and fried chicken is a local favorite. Find a wider menu (including some vegetarian options) at the Southwest-Mex-style **Peppers Grill & Bar.**

After dinner, you're only about 80 minutes from your destination. Since the visitor center, which issues camping permits, will likely be closed by the time you arrive, plan to spend Friday night in the town of Carlsbad, 20 miles north of the park. If you intend to camp on Saturday night, hit the grocery store before you hit the sack.

Day 2

Before heading into the park this morning, make a quick stop for breakfast at the **Blue House Bakery & Cafe,** a cute coffee shop with pastries, bagels, and more that opens bright and early at 6 am.

Carlsbad Caverns' most stunning attraction is its Big Room, but if you've got a pair of sturdy shoes and a sense of adventure, your first order of business today should be taking a guided tour of one of the less accessible caves. Slaughter Canyon is among the more challenging, requiring visitors to hike half a mile up to the cave, then traverse narrow, slippery unpaved trails in complete darkness (they provide you with headlamps and helmets). The Hall of the White Giant, which requires ladder climbing and crawling through tight passageways, is perhaps the most challenging of the bunch, while Left Hand Tunnel is significantly easier, with a relatively flat, dry dirt trail. The tours leave between 8:30 to 9:30 am, but some don't run daily.

After your tour is over, stop in at the Carlsbad Caverns visitor center to fuel up (and to grab a camping permit if you plan on staying in the park overnight). The **Carlsbad Caverns Trading Company** has basic grab-and-go sandwiches, salads, and snacks, as well as a hot food counter.

After lunch, grab a ticket for the Big Room and get in line for the elevator, which plunges 750 feet straight down. From there, step onto the paved trail in a self-guided tour that winds 1.25 miles among the spotlit speleothems of the underground chamber. If you've still got some energy to spare when you've completed the circuit, hike up the steep 1.25 mile Natural Entrance Trail into the light. If you're running on fumes, the elevators ascend to the visitor's center until 5 pm.

As the sun begins to set, hundreds of thousands of Carlsbad Caverns' Brazilian free-tailed bats emerge in a frenzied flight for food. Get the best view from the outdoor amphitheater, a five-minute walk from the visitor center. Though the bats begin their evening ritual mid- to late April, the ranger-led bat flight programs only run from late May through October.

If you are camping in the park overnight, head to your site when the show is over for dinner and stargazing. Otherwise, drive back to Carlsbad for a hot meal. The historic log-cabin **Red Chimney Pit Bar-B-Q** has brisket, ribs, burgers, and all the fixins. Steak, pasta, and seafood are on the menu at the cozy, casual fine-dining restaurant **Yellow Brix.**

Day 3

Before hitting the long road back to Albuquerque, stop in at the **Pecos River Cafe** for a hearty breakfast heaped with pancakes, huevos rancheros, and other classic and Southwestern-inspired options. When you've had your fill, make a beeline for Roswell and the bizarre little **International UFO Museum and Research Center.** If you aren't already a believer, they'll do your best to make you one.

Ninety minutes down the road, pull into **Pedro's Burritos** for lunch where authentic burritos start at just $3. Go ahead and grab an iced coffee while you're at it: there's just over 100 miles to go before

110

you reach Albuquerque and the end of an epic weekend getaway.

Recommendations
 Sights

Billy the Kid Museum. ✉ *1435 Sumner Ave., Fort Sumner, NM* ☎ *575/355–2380* ⊕ *www.billythekidmuseumfortsumner. com* 🗐 *$5 per person* ⊙ *Closed Sun. in winter.*

Carlsbad Caverns National Park. ✉ *727 Carlsbad Cavern Hwy., Carlsbad, NM* ☎ *575/785–2232* ⊕ *www.nps.gov* 🗐 *$15 per person.*

International UFO Museum and Research Center. ✉ *114 N. Main St., Roswell, NM* ☎ *575/625–9495* ⊕ *www.roswellufomuseum.com* 🗐 *$5 per person.*

 Restaurants

Blue House Bakery & Cafe. Ⓢ *Average main: $5* ✉ *609 N. Canyon St., Carlsbad, NM* ☎ *575/628–0555* ⊕ *www.facebook. com/bluehousebakeryandcafe* ⊙ *Closed Sun. No dinner.*

Carlsbad Caverns Trading Company. Ⓢ *Average main: $9* ✉ *727 Carlsbad Caverns Hwy., Carlsbad, NM* ☎ *575/785–2281* ⊕ *carlsbadcavernstradingco.com* ⊙ *No dinner.*

The Cowboy Cafe. Ⓢ *Average main: $11* ✉ *1120 E. 2nd St., Roswell, NM* ☎ *575/622–6363* ⊕ *www.thecowboy. cafe.*

Pecos River Cafe. Ⓢ *Average main: $6* ✉ *409 S. Canal St., Carlsbad, NM* ☎ *575/887–8882* ⊕ *www.facebook.com/ pecosrivercafe* ⊙ *Closed weekends.*

Pedro's Burritos. Ⓢ *Average main: $5* ✉ *1005 U.S. Hwy 285, Vaughn, NM* ☎ *No phone* ⊕ *www.facebook.com/pedrosburritos54* ⊙ *Closed Mon.*

Peppers Grill and Bar. Ⓢ *Average main: $10* ✉ *2249 S. Canal St., Carlsbad, NM* ☎ *575/628–1275* ⊕ *www.peppers-grill. com* ⊙ *Closed Sun.*

Red Chimney Pit Bar-B-Q. Ⓢ *Average main: $8* ✉ *817 N. Canal St., Carlsbad, NM* ☎ *575/885–8744* ⊕ *www.redchimneybbq. com* ⊙ *Closed Sun. and Mon.*

Yellow Brix. Ⓢ *Average main: $16* ✉ *201 N. Canal St., Carlsbad, NM* ☎ *575/941–2749* ⊕ *www.yellowbrixrestaurant.com.*

 Hotels

Fiddler's Inn. Ⓢ *Rooms from: $163* ✉ *705 N. Canyon St., Carlsbad, NM* ☎ *575/725–8665* ⊕ *www.fiddlersinnbb.com.*

Colorado Springs, CO

75 miles (approx. 1 hour) from Denver.

At the base of Pikes Peak mountain, the city of Colorado Springs contains multitudes that often contradict each other. An Air Force Academy and a liberal arts college; a Focus on the Family headquarters and an Olympic Training Center; a historical luxury resort and a geological wonder—are just some of the icons that make up its identity.

The red sandstone playground of Garden of the Gods—a sculpture garden of eroded formations dating back hundreds of millions of years—is probably the most appealing and unique feature to Colorado Springs. Glacier-built Plke's Peak is the tallest (14,115-foot) summit in this city's majestic mountain backdrop, and can be ascended by foot or car. When you aren't communing with nature, the stately Broadmoor Resort, and the old timey, quirky charms of Manitou Springs and Old Colorado City, will pamper and entertain.

The history and traditions of Ancestral Puebloans are on display at the Manitou Cliff Dwellings.

Planning

GETTING THERE AND BACK

It's about an hour (70-mile) drive south on I–25 from Denver to Colorado Springs. The idea of extending Denver's train system all the way to C-Springs (and the rest of the Front Range) has been up in the air for years; for now, there is a reliable bus route that takes about two hours. Several airlines make the 45-minute flight from Denver International Airport (DIA) to Colorado Springs' airport, but unless you are already en route this option rarely makes the most sense.

WHEN TO GO

This region of Colorado definitely earns its name as the real "Sunshine State," boasting an average of some 300 days of sunshine a year. Through early winter, you'll need little more than a light jacket or sweater, though it's significantly colder (mid-20s) at night, and there's regular snow.

WHERE TO STAY

Both **The Broadmoor** and **Garden of the Gods Club and Resort** can be prohibitively expensive for a whole weekend stay, but are worth a special night or two. The views, the grounds, and the access to amenities (like the Garden of the Gods infinity pool, with stunning views of the park and mountain range) feel exclusive and luxurious in the way a good retreat should. **Cheyenne Mountain Resort** is another option in this range, and sometimes offers better deals. The **Antlers Hilton Colorado Springs** is more moderately priced, still with some doses of Southwest charm, and gives you the added benefit of being directly downtown.

Day 1

It's such a short drive from Denver to Colorado Springs, so you have plenty of time to explore today. Start in Manitou Springs, a funky mountain town a 15-minute drive west of C-Springs, that boasts medicinal waters—and an odd number of Wiccans.

Have lunch at **Adam's Mountain Cafe,** where vegetarian and organic choices meet comfort food, before indulging both in the natural and the funky human side of Manitou Springs. Downtown is full of hippie shops (and whispers of Pagan witchcraft), Native American artifacts, arcades, art galleries, and quite a lot of flair.

After walking through downtown, spend a few hours checking out Manitou Springs' natural beauty in **Manitou Cliff Dwellings** and **Cave of the Winds.**

After freshening up at your hotel, head to Old Colorado City, an offshoot of Colorado Springs, featuring a main street of 19th-century buildings and fun gift shops. Dine on local game and Colorado beer at **Front Range Barbecue,** where you can usually catch some live music as well. Before bed, go for a fun drink at **IvyWild School,** an elementary school–turned–hipster cocktail bar (and brewery, boutique shop, and more) downtown.

Day 2

Grab your sunblock and water bottle for a full, active day in the Colorado sunshine. For breakfast, opt for a breakfast burrito from a taco shop like **Monica's** or **Daniel's** and enjoy it outside before ascending **Pike's Peak.** This is a very accessible big mountain: the summit can be reached by car, and there are plans in the works for the historic **Pikes Peak Cog Railway** to be up and running again. There are several hiking trails up and around Pike's Peak, Barr Trail being the longest (about 12 miles) and most challenging. Alternatively, follow the steps former rail tie-steps up the Manitou Incline, an incredibly strenuous 1-mile ascent and favorite cardio activity for active locals and visitors.

Despite the awe-inducing appearance of its giant geological formations, hikes around **Garden of the Gods** are moderate and very accessible. Plan to spend the afternoon walking around here, even if you clocked in many miles and elevation this morning. For respite, you can always stop at **Garden of the Gods Trading Post,** which has a gift shop, art gallery, and substantial restaurant, or go for a sandwich at **Mountain Shadows Restaurant** if you want more local flair. If you need some extra pampering, sign up for spa treatments at the **Garden of the Gods Club and Resort.**

Time to switch gears. Head back to your hotel to change into something festive before cabbing it to the Broadmoor for a fancy drink on the terrace. This impressive resort is made up of a series of formidable pink stucco buildings surrounding a lagoon and immaculate grounds. While it has seen some updates over the last century, it still has the feel of a sophisticated European retreat.

For extra fun, check out the **Golden Bee,** the Broadmoor's authentic 19th-century English pub (the walls were literally imported from England) and definitely the most raucous, cheerful place on campus. Nightly piano singalongs start at 7:30, and you can order beers and ales by the yard.

Later, enjoy a late dinner back downtown at **The Rabbit Hole,** an underground cellar with a chic cocktail menu and interesting share plates, charcuterie boards full of items like duck wings and buffalo ribs.

Day 3

As a college town, Colorado Springs has some quality greasy spoons, so plan to grab a big satisfying breakfast as your last meal before leaving town. Breakfast burritos and potato-heavy plates, both smothered in green chile, are served in a goofy setting (plastered in purple and yellow) at **King's Chef Diner.** There's also an all-day Southwestern breakfast at **Bon Ton's Cafe.**

You have a few options for a great after-breakfast hike. There's **North Cheyenne Cañon Park,** with a couple moderate (3-mile) and great views of the city, or **Broadmoor Seven Falls,** with its scenic cascades and recreation area.

For a last activity before heading back to Denver, consider checking out several breweries in town; **Phantom Canyon Brewing, Bristol Brewing Co.,** and **Cerberus Brewing Co.** are among the favorites. As an alternative, check out the slightly goofy **Ghost Town Museum,** where interactive activities include gold panning, old arcade games, and a player piano.

Recommendations

Sights

Broadmoor Seven Falls. ✉ *1045 Lower Gold Camp Rd., Colorado Springs, CO* ☎ *855/923–7272* 🌐 *www.broadmoor.com* 🎟 *$12* 🕒 *Closed Mon.–Thurs.*

Cave of the Winds. ✉ *100 Cave of the Winds Rd., Manitou Springs, CO* ☎ *719/685–5444* 🌐 *www.caveofthewinds.com* 🎟 *$14.*

Garden of the Gods. ✉ *1805 N. 30th St., Colorado Springs, CO* ☎ *719/634–6666* 🌐 *www.gardenofgods.com* 🎟 *Free.*

Ghost Town Museum. ✉ *400 S. 21st St., Colorado Springs, CO* ☎ *719/634–0696* 🌐 *www.ghosttownmuseum.com* 🎟 *$7.*

Manitou Cliff Dwellings. ✉ *10 Cliff Dwellings Rd., Manitou Springs, CO* ☎ *719/685–5242* 🌐 *www.cliffdwellingsmuseum.com* 🎟 *$12.*

North Cheyenne Cañon Park. ✉ *2120 S. Cheyenne Canyon Rd., Colorado Springs, CO* ☎ *719/385–6086* 🌐 *www.coloradosprings.gov* 🎟 *Free.*

Pike's Peak. ✉ *High point of El Paso County, 30 miles northwest of Colorado Springs, CO* ☎ *719/684–9383* 🌐 *www.pikespeak.us.com* 🎟 *$12.*

Pikes Peak Cog Railway. ✉ *515 Ruxton Ave., Manitou Springs, CO* ☎ *719/685–5401* 🌐 *www.colorado.com* 🎟 *$15.*

Restaurants

Adam's Mountain Cafe. [$] *Average main: $20* ✉ *26 Manitou Ave., Manitou Springs, CO* ☎ *719/685–1430* 🌐 *www.adamsmountaincafe.com* 🕒 *Closed Sun. and Mon.*

Bon Ton Cafe. [$] *Average main: $14* ✉ *2601 W. Colorado Ave., Colorado Springs, CO* ☎ *719/634–1007* 🌐 *www.bontonscafe.com.*

Daniel's. [$] *Average main: $3* ✉ *6815 Space Village Ave., Colorado Springs, CO* ☎ *719/574–2992* 🌐 *www.danielsfund.org* 🕒 *Closed Sun.*

Garden of the Gods Trading Post. [$] *Average main: $8* ✉ *324 Beckers La., Manitou Springs, CO* ☎ *719/685–9045* 🌐 *www.gardenofthegodstradingpost.com.*

King's Chef Diner. [$] *Average main: $10* ✉ *131 E. Bijou St., Colorado Springs, CO* ☎ *719/636–5010* 🌐 *www.cosdiner.com.*

Monica's. [$] *Average main: $6* ✉ *30 E. Fillmore St., Colorado Springs, CO* ☎ *719/473–1996.*

Mountain Shadows Restaurant. [$] *Average main: $10* ✉ *2223 Colorado Ave., Colorado Springs, CO* ☎ *719/633–2122* 🌐 *www.mtnshadowsrestaurant.com.*

The Rabbit Hole. [$] *Average main: $23* ✉ *101 N. Tejon St., Colorado Springs, CO* ☎ *719/203–5072* 🌐 *www.rabbitholedinner.com.*

Hotels

Antlers Hilton Colorado Springs. [$] *Rooms from: $139* ✉ *4 S. Cascade Ave., Colorado Springs, CO* ☎ *719/955–5600* 🌐 *www.antlers.com.*

The Broadmoor. [$] *Rooms from: $875* ✉ *1 Lake Ave., Colorado Springs, CO* ☎ *800/755–5011* 🌐 *www.broadmoor.com.*

Cheyenne Mountain Resort. [$] *Rooms from: $146* ✉ *3225 Broadmoor Valley Rd., Colorado Springs, CO* ☎ *719/538–4000* 🌐 *www.cheyennemountain.com.*

Garden of the Gods Club and Resort. [$] *Rooms from: $241* ✉ *3320 Mesa Rd., Colorado Springs, CO* ☎ *719/632–5541* 🌐 *www.gardenofthegodsresort.com.*

🍸 Nightlife

Bristol Brewing Co. ✉ *1604 S. Cascade Ave., Colorado Springs, CO* ☎ *719/633–2555* 🌐 *www.bristolbrewing.com.*

Cerberus Brewing Co. ✉ *702 W. Colorado Ave., Colorado Springs, CO* ☎ *719/636–2337* 🌐 *www.cerberusbrewingco.com.*

Golden Bee. ✉ *1 Lake Ave., Colorado Springs, CO* ☎ *719/577–5733* 🌐 *www.broadmoor.com.*

IvyWild School. ✉ *1604 S. Cascade Ave., Colorado Springs, CO* ☎ *719/368–6100* 🌐 *www.ivywildschool.com.*

Phantom Canyon Brewing. ✉ *2 E. Pikes Peak Ave., Colorado Springs, CO* ☎ *719/635–2800* 🌐 *phantomcanyon.com.*

Durango, CO

337 miles (approx. 6 hours) from Denver.

Durango is the largest city in Southern Colorado and a hub for adventure. With distinct Old-West vibes, this reformed boomtown highlights both the Rocky Mountain State's mining past and intrepid mountainous pursuits.

While the town itself is a draw, its proximity to national parks, towering peaks, desert landscapes, historical monuments, and natural attractions are equally as appealing in a part of the state many have yet to explore fully. You could spend days or weeks adventuring around Southern Colorado, so this quick weekend getaway is really just the tip of the iceberg.

Planning

GETTING THERE AND BACK

The most direct route from Denver to Durango is a six-hour drive down 285 S and 160 W, but if you cut down I–25 and add 30 minutes, you'll pass Colorado Springs and Pueblo and can hit Great Sand Dunes National Park and Pagosa Springs on the way.

PIT STOP

If you have a couple of extra days or some time to kill, you can also head back a different route up the Million Dollar Highway through Ouray and Telluride to hit a third national park, **Black Canyon of the Gunnison.**

WHEN TO GO

With more than 300 days of sunshine a year, Durango is a year-round destination, although the summer and winter seasons have quite a different appeal. The train runs year-round, but summer typically gives you more flexibility with routes and options.

WHERE TO STAY

Durango has a variety of accommodations from rustic cabins and B&Bs to your basic no-frills hotels and motels. **The Rochester Hotel** is one of the nicest, which was once a historic apartment complex converted into a boutique hotel. A more affordable option is the **Strater Hotel,** which bills itself as a living history museum. The Victorian property is home to the world's largest collection of antique walnut furniture. For an equally unique experience, **Colorado Trails** is an all-inclusive dude ranch that features horseback riding, fly-fishing, and cookouts over the fire.

Durango's stunning scenery is best seen from the Durango & Silverton Narrow Gauge Railroad.

Day 1

From Denver, it's a four-hour drive to **Great Sand Dunes National Park,** the tallest dunes in North America. You'll want to pack snacks because there aren't many food stops past Pueblo. Swing through Alamosa to rent a sandboard or sled before you arrive.

It's such a strange sight to see towering dunes rise out of nowhere in front of the mountainous backdrop. Take a moment to pause and let the beauty soak in. Once you've gotten your bearings, splash around in Medano Creek, which you have to cross to get to the dunes, and spend some time playing in the world's largest sandbox.

From there, it's another two hours to Pagosa Springs to rest and fuel up. By now, you're probably starving, which is fine because there are plenty of restaurants in town. **Alley House Grille** is a local favorite for its upscale, Asian-inspired

cuisine. Snag a seat on the deck and feast on crispy pork belly and fillets.

One of Colorado's best natural mineral springs, the area is certified by Guinness World Records as the World's Deepest Geothermal Hot Spring Aquifer. There are three hot springs resorts, but **The Springs Resort & Spa** is the largest and most popular with 23 pools of varying sizes, shapes, and temperatures. There's even an adults-only section if you're looking to rekindle the romance that's especially beautiful in the inky moonlight.

Day 2

Cozy up for breakfast at **Oscar's Café.** With blue plate specials, pancakes, and omelets, it's a tasty, no-frills morning meal.

One of the indisputable highlights of the area is the **Durango & Silverton Narrow Gauge Railroad.** This classic coal-powered steam engine takes you up the mountain to Colorado's old mining towns. Trips can be as short as two hours and are a great way to see the high country and some of the smaller mountain communities.

When you've returned, head to **El Moro Tavern,** once home to Durango's strangest shootout. The saloon was raided during a poker game in the early 1900s and has plenty of stories in its walls, although today, it's more known for its hot chicken sandwiches and burgers.

Spend the afternoon taking advantage of the landscape with a half-day whitewater rafting trip, horseback riding excursion, or ziplining adventure. In winter, there's skiing, snowmobiling, ice climbing, and dogsledding to get your blood pumping.

For dinner, head back to town to unwind at **Ken & Sue's.** Your classic American bistro, it has seafood creations like pistachio-crusted grouper or carnivorous plates of prime rib. If you're not in a food coma, embark on a bar crawl at one of three local breweries, pick up a sweet treat from **Animas Chocolate & Coffee Company,** catch some live music at **Balcony Bar & Grill,** or hit up the **Diamond Belle Saloon,** where ragtime entertainers will transport you back to the turn of the last century.

Day 3

For your last day in town, fuel up at the **Lone Spur Café,** which touts authentic cowboy cuisine like Spanish skillets and chorizo scrambles. Spend the rest of the morning exploring the Native American cliffside pueblos of **Mesa Verde National Park.** Spanish for "green table," the park has nearly 5,000 known archaeological sites, including 600 cliff dwellings. You can see them by driving the Mesa Top Loop Road, which takes you to a dozen sites and a handful of overlooks in a 6-mile loop. Or, if you'd rather hike, trails of varying difficulties and distances can take you closer to the ruins and petroglyphs. There are also ranger-led tours.

Before you head home, you can choose to continue on to **Four Corners National Monument** to snag that iconic photo standing in four states at once.

Recommendations

Sights

Black Canyon of the Gunnison. ✉ *102 Elk Creek, Gunnison, CO* ☎ *970/641–2337* 🌐 *www.nps.gov* 🎟 *$15.*

Durango & Silverton Narrow Gauge Railroad. ✉ *479 Main Ave., Durango, CO* ☎ *970/247–2733* 🌐 *www.durangotrain.com* 🎟 *$64.*

Four Corners National Monument. ✉ *597 NM 597, Teec Nos Pos, AZ* ☎ *928/871–6647* 🌐 *www.navajonationparks.org/tribal-parks/four-corners-monument* 🎟 *$10 per vehicle.*

Great Sand Dunes National Park. ✉ *Great Sand Dunes Visitor Center, 11999 State Hwy. 150, Mosca, CO* ☎ *719/378–6395* 🌐 *www.nps.gov/grsa* 🎟 *$25 per vehicle.*

Mesa Verde National Park. ✉ *Mesa Verde Visitor and Research Center, 7 Headquarters Loop Rd., Mesa Verde National Park, CO* ☎ *970/529–4465* 🌐 *www.nps.gov* 🎟 *$30 per vehicle.*

Restaurants

Alley House Grille. [$] *Average main: $24* ✉ *214 Pagosa St., Pagosa Springs, CO* ☎ *970/264–0999* 🌐 *www.alleyhousegrille.com* 🕒 *Closed Mon.–Wed.*

El Moro Tavern. [$] *Average main: $10* ✉ *945 Main Ave., Durango, CO* ☎ *970/259–5555* 🌐 *www.elmorotavern.com.*

Ken & Sue's. [$] *Average main: $11* ✉ *636 Main Ave., Durango, CO* ☎ *970/385–1810* 🌐 *www.kenandsues.com* 🕒 *No lunch on weekends.*

Lone Spur Café. $ *Average main: $10* ✉ *619 Main Ave., Durango, CO* ☎ *970/764–4280* ⊕ *www.lonespurcafe. com.*

Oscar's Café. $ *Average main: $10* ✉ *18 Town Plaza, Durango, CO* ☎ *970/247– 0526* ⊕ *breakfastdurango.com* ☾ *No dinner.*

☕ Coffee and Quick Bites

Animas Chocolate & Coffee Company. $ *Average main: $12* ✉ *920 Main Ave., Durango, CO* ☎ *970/317–5761* ⊕ *www. animaschocolatecompany.com.*

🛏 Hotels

Colorado Trails Ranch. $ *Rooms from: $400* ✉ *12161 Colorado Rd. 240, Durango, CO* ☎ *970/247–5055* ⊕ *www. coloradotrails.com* ⍟ *Free breakfast.*

Rochester Hotel. $ *Rooms from: $199* ✉ *726 E. 2nd Ave., Durango, CO* ☎ *970/385–1920* ⊕ *www.rochesterhotel. com* ⍟ *Free breakfast.*

The Springs Resort & Spa. $ *Rooms from: $359* ✉ *323 Hot Springs Blvd., Pagosa Springs, CO* ☎ *800/225–0934* ⊕ *www.pagosahotsprings.com* ⍟ *Free breakfast.*

Strater Hotel. $ *Rooms from: $159* ✉ *699 Main Ave., Durango, CO* ☎ *800/247–4431* ⊕ *www.strater.com* ⍟ *No meals.*

▼ Nightlife

Balcony Bar & Grill. ✉ *600 Main Ave., Durango, CO* ☎ *970/422–8008* ⊕ *www. balconybarandgrill.com.*

Diamond Belle Saloon. ✉ *699 Main Ave. Durango, CO* ☎ *800/247–4431* ⊕ *www. strater.com.*

Estes Park and Rocky Mountain National Park, CO

66 miles (approx. 1½ hours) from Denver.

The basecamp of Rocky Mountain National Park and the inspiration for one of John Denver's most famous songs, Estes Park is one of the most accessible mountain getaways from Denver. It is one of the most visited national parks in the country and offers visitors a plethora of outdoor pursuits, breathtaking landscapes, and interesting wildlife. Perfect for both travelers looking to get off the grid and get back to nature and those looking for an adrenaline rush, Estes Park is a "choose your own adventure" kind of vacation that puts Colorado's rugged beauty on full display.

Planning

GETTING THERE AND BACK

The quickest way to get to Estes Park from Denver is a straight shot past Boulder on U.S. 36 W. But if you have extra time, the Peak to Peak Scenic Byway is a worthy detour, especially in fall. The longer route takes roughly three hours and promises views of old mining towns, creeks, and alpine lakes.

PIT STOPS

Stop for afternoon tea at the **Boulder Dushanbe Teahouse.** The ornate building was handcrafted by more than 40 artisans in Tajikistan, shipped overseas, and rebuilt tile by tile.

WHEN TO GO

Rocky Mountain National Park is a year-round destination, albeit the attractions vary wildly by season. Summer and fall are the most popular times to visit and are very crowded, which means you'll likely need to utilize the park-and-ride shuttle, as parking lots fill up fast. Trail

Colorado's rugged beauty on full display at Rocky Mountain National Park.

Ridge Road is open May to October, with elk mating season a major draw in September and October when the animals are especially active. The snowy calm of winter has its own appeal if you don't mind a little cold-weather fun.

WHERE TO STAY

Hard to miss, the stately **Stanley Hotel** sits atop a hill overlooking the city. This early 1900s beauty with an opulent interior inspired Stephen King to write *The Shining*. Most visitors opt for the property's cozy cabins or cottages, which have amenities like hot tubs.

Day 1

A quick 90-minute drive from Denver and you'll be feeling worlds away from the hustle and bustle of the city. If you leave early enough, you can arrive by midmorning to take full advantage of the day. Whether you make it a lazy, late brunch or grab a quick lunch to-go, the **Egg of Estes** is one of the town's most beloved breakfast joints. Splurge on

apple-cinnamon pancakes, strawberry-banana waffles, or fill up with a hearty Benedict or scramble. If you'd rather keep rolling, keep it light with a fresh-pressed juice for the road.

Since you've been in the car and probably want to stretch your legs, start with an easy-two miler to warm up and adjust to the altitude. The appropriately named Dream Lake is one of the most popular hikes in **Rocky Mountain National Park** for insane snow-capped peaks that reflect brilliantly off the water. Take in the beauty and breathe in the crisp mountain air. From here, you can either head to your hotel to freshen up, or if you have the time and energy, keep exploring. Many trails connect to make it a longer loop.

Settle in for dinner at the Stanley Hotel's restaurant, **Cascades,** a classic American steak house. Fill up on locally caught trout and wild game before sauntering over to the **Whiskey Bar** for the state's largest selection of whiskeys and single malt scotches. Once you're feeling all warm and fuzzy and get to chatting with the bartender, the hotel's mysteries start revealing themselves. Curious to see for yourself? The hotel's after-dark ghost tours are sure to make your skin crawl as whispers of strange occurrences suddenly seem commonplace. Whether you leave believing in spirits or simply spirited is up to you.

Day 2

Shake off the reverberations of last night because you have a big day ahead. Fuel up with a hearty morning meal at **Notch-top Bakery & Café.** Mexican favorites like the massive Colorado burrito or breakfast tacos bring the heat, while the banana split waffle and banana bread French toast provide a much-needed sugar high.

When you're finally ready to roll out of there, it's time to explore Rocky Mountain National Park's 265,769 acres from top to bottom. You can tour the park on two legs, four wheels, or four hooves on a trolley, ATV, or horseback riding tour, depending on your interests and fitness level.

But first, get your bearings with a harrowing drive up **Trail Ridge Road.** One of Colorado's most impressive National Scenic Byways, it's the highest continuous road in the United States and holds the distinction of being one of just a handful of roads included on the National Register of Historic Places. Full of hairpin turns, insane elevation gains, and a surprising lack of guard rails, you'll cross the Continental Divide as you take in glacier-carved valleys, jagged peaks, and shimmering alpine lakes. The drive takes two to three hours to complete, depending on how hard you're riding the brakes.

If you prefer to leave the driving to someone else, **Estes Park Trolleys** offers two- to five-hour tours to the park's major attractions, which are perfect for those looking to sit back, relax, and enjoy the ride, worry-free.

If you really want to explore, you have to get off the beaten path. For restless spirits looking to get off the grid, there are ATV, jeep, and horseback riding tours and rentals to tackle the backcountry. Depending on how comfortable you are getting wonderfully lost will determine if you need a guide or feel confident going at it on your own.

Once you've worked up an appetite, head back into town to grab a sandwich or wrap from **Scratch** and keep on rolling. For the land lopers, there's rock climbing, hiking, and biking still to try. Or, for those looking to beat the heat, half-day white-water rafting, kayaking, paddleboarding, or fly-fishing excursions may be just what the doctor ordered. In winter, a whole other set of adventures await. There's skiing, ice climbing, snowmobiling, and snowshoe tours in the area.

When you've had your fill of adventure, unwind with beer and bites at **The Rock Inn.** Built in the 1930s as a dance hall (they still regularly host live music at happy hour), it promises epic brews and views under the setting sun.

Day 3

For your last day, ease your sore muscles and tired body with a slower-paced morning, soaking in all Colorado has to offer. Meander the **Riverwalk,** which runs along the main drag of Elkhorn Avenue. Babbling brooks interspersed with boutiques, galleries, and public art of all types offer the quintessential mountain town vibe. Get a java jolt with an espresso from **Kind Coffee,** or indulge your sweet tooth at **Cinnamon's Bakery,** if you can snag one of their coveted buns before they run out for the day. Treat yourself to a massage, shop for souvenirs, or tip one back at one of the local breweries.

For one last parting view, the **Estes Park Aerial Tram** gives you a taste of the ski gondola in summer. One of just a handful of European-style cable cars operating in the United States, the five-minute ride takes you above treeline for a stunning bird's-eye view from above. Snap some photos and soak in every last bit of that mountain magic before heading home.

Recommendations

Sights

Estes Park Aerial Tram. ✉ *420 E. Riverside Dr., Estes Park, CO* ☎ *970/475–4095* 🌐 *www.estestram.com* 🎟 *$14.*

Riverwalk. ✉ *George Hix Riverside Plaza, 111 E. Riverside Dr., Estes Park, CO* ☎ *970/586–0500* 🌐 *www.visitestespark.com* 🎟 *Free.*

Rocky Mountain National Park. ✉ *Beaver Meadows Visitor Center, 1000 U.S. 36, Estes Park, CO* ☎ *970/586–1206* 🌐 *www.nps.gov* 🎟 *$15.*

Trail Ridge Road. ✉ *U.S. 34, Estes Park, CO* 🌐 *www.nps.gov/romo/planyourvisit/trail_ridge_road.htm.*

Restaurants

Boulder Dushanbe Teahouse. [$] *Average main: $25* ✉ *1770 13th St., Boulder, CO* ☎ *303/442–4993* 🌐 *www.bouldertea-house.com.*

Cascades. [$] *Average main: $19* ✉ *333 Wonderview Ave. Estes Park, CO* ☎ *970/577–4000* 🌐 *www.stanleyhotel.com.*

Egg of Estes. [$] *Average main: $10* ✉ *393 E. Elkhorn Ave., Estes Park, CO* ☎ *970/316–0133* 🌐 *www.eggofestes.com.*

Notchtop Bakery & Café. [$] *Average main: $29* ✉ *1675 CO 66, Estes Park, CO* ☎ *970/586–4116* 🌐 *www.rockinnestes.com.*

Scratch. [$] *Average main: $12* ✉ *911 Moraine Ave., Estes Park, CO* ☎ *970/586–8383* 🕒 *Closed Wed.*

Coffee and Quick Bites

Cinnamon's Bakery. [$] *Average main: $4* ✉ *920 W. Elkhorn Ave., Estes Park, CO* ☎ *970/480–1501* 🌐 *www.cinnamons-estespark.com* 🕒 *Closed Mon.–Wed.*

Kind Coffee. [$] *Average main: $4* ✉ *470 E. Elkhorn Ave., Estes Park, CO* ☎ *970/586–5206* 🌐 *www.kindcoffee.com.*

Hotels

Stanley Hotel. [$] *Rooms from: $189* ✉ *333 Wonderview Ave., Estes Park, CO* ☎ *970/577–4000* 🌐 *www.stanleyhotel.com* 🍴 *No meals.*

Nightlife

Whiskey Bar. ✉ *333 Wonderview Ave., Estes Park, CO* ☎ *970/577–4000* 🌐 *www.stanleyhotel.com.*

Activities

Estes Park Trolleys. ✉ *1360 Big Thompson Ave., Estes Park, CO* ☎ *970/481–8531* 🌐 *www.estesparktrolleys.com* 🎟 *From $50.*

Flagstaff and Grand Canyon, AZ

149 miles (approx. 2½ hours) from Phoenix.

Surrounded by breezy, beautiful Arizona pines, the laid-back town of Flagstaff is a haven for outdoors lovers. With national forests and other preserved lands on every side, it's all about getting outside here: warm weather means hiking, biking, and rock climbing, while winter brings skiing and snowboarding.

Grand Canyon National Park is just an hour and a half north, so it's easy to add a jaunt to the spectacular South Rim. And while Flagstaff isn't known for raucous nightlife, there's plenty going on after dark; designated an "International Dark Sky City," Flagstaff has incredible stargazing that rewards travelers who stay up late.

Planning

GETTING THERE AND BACK
From Phoenix, it's a quick trip north on I–17 to get to Flagstaff.

PIT STOPS
The cliff-dwellings at **Montezuma Castle National Monument** make the perfect stopover, with a 0.3-mile paved trail to a viewing area where you can check out the ruins.

WHEN TO GO
Mountain air keeps Flagstaff cool through the summer, when highs are in the high 70s and low 80s. It's a great time to visit, but summer also brings crowds at the Grand Canyon. Fall and spring have a magical blend of warm weather and uncrowded trails. By November, things get chilly; ski season generally lasts from mid-November through late April.

WHERE TO STAY
Many Flagstaff accommodations cater to tourists moving quickly to other destinations, but there's character to be found here, too. Channel vintage road-trip vibes at **Motel du Beau,** a quirky budget pick located on historic Route 66 in downtown Flagstaff. (It was built in 1929 to host the new "auto tourists" hitting the road in their own cars.) If it's in your budget, the upscale **Inn at 410** is the town's coziest bed and breakfast, with comfortable themed rooms and a location that's easy walking distance from downtown. Winter brings crowds to the **Arizona Snowbowl** resort.

Day 1

Settle into the college-town energy at teeny **Diablo Burger,** whose thick, juicy patties are made with local, organic, grass-fed beef. Patties are on English muffins, which keeps the focus on the meat and toppings. (Don't miss the hatch chile mayo.)

Next, tie on your hiking boots for a trip into **Coconino National Forest,** where you can go underground to walk the Lava River Cave. Bring a flashlight, then venture into the long lava tube, which tapers from a cavernous, 40-foot ceiling to a tight squeeze that requires hikers to duck low.

If an underground hike isn't your thing, opt for the popular Kachina Trail. Threading along the southern flanks of the San Francisco Peaks, this 5-mile path weaves through aspen groves that turn golden in autumn, plus a fascinating lava flow, lush fern meadows, and a series of pretty canyons.

For dinner, check out the Neapolitan-style pies at **Pizzicletta,** known for crusts that blister a mottled black in wood-fired ovens. While pizza is the main event here, the house-made gelato and burrata appetizers win serious raves from locals.

Instead of going out on the town, head to the historic **Lowell Observatory** to check in with the night sky. Six high-tech telescopes on their public observatory deck offer views of faraway celestial objects. Nightly stargazing sessions offer guided tours of the twinkling constellations; inside the visitor center, evening programs fill you in on the secrets of the stars and galaxies.

Day 2

Founded in 1926 as a boarding house for Basque shepherds, the **Tourist Home All Day Café** is now a Flagstaff breakfast

The Colorado River slices through Grand Canyon National Park.

institution. The overstuffed breakfast burrito alone is worth a trip to Flagstaff, but there are also fresh-made donuts, egg dishes, and a full lineup of pastries.

Start there: it's fuel for a day in **Grand Canyon National Park,** whose South Rim queues up oversized views of red-rock layers and the Colorado River below. It's also a site that draws visitors from around the world; that means it's worth hatching a strategic plan to avoid spending the day in traffic.

Start by renting a pair of wheels from **Bright Angel Bikes,** a shop located right by the Grand Canyon Visitor Center. That gives you access to the wiggling curves of 7-mile long Hermit Road to the west. It's closed to private-vehicle traffic from March through November, and features a series of nine overlooks.

By the time you make it back to the bike shop, it will be time for lunch at the **El Tovar Hotel,** a historic landmark that opened in 1905 on the edge of the canyon itself. While the food isn't

memorable, it's well worth making advance reservations to enjoy a meal in a lodgelike dining room with unmatched views.

Next, hop the Kaibab/Rim Route shuttle bus east to the South Kaibab Trailhead. It's the starting point for a leg-burning hike that drops all 4,780 feet to the Colorado River, but that's too far to go with just an afternoon to hike. Enjoy some of the finest parts of the trail, without the epic trek, on a 1.8-mile, round-trip walk down to the perfectly named Ooh-Aah Point. (Bring plenty of water, as there's none available along the trail.)

It's worth sticking around for sunset— that's when the colors really get bright— and there's plenty more on the South Rim to occupy the late afternoon. One of the literal high points of the area is the 70-foot Desert Watchtower, where vistas stretch to the distant Vermilion Cliffs and Painted Desert. Another worthwhile destination is **Kolb Studio,** a photography workshop-turned-museum that features early footage of Colorado River exploration.

When the sky starts to get dusky, stake your claim on a sunset spot; both Hopi Point and Yavapai Point are justifiably popular. After the show, start the drive back to Flagstaff, for dinner along the Flagstaff Brewery Trail.

Start with a Hazy Angel IPA at **Lumberyard Brewing Company,** the perfect pairing with a plate of chicken wings or the breaded cauliflower "wings." Just across the street is **Flagstaff Brewing Company,** offering small-batch beers that range from a crisp, single-hop Kolsch to the creamy Sasquatch Stout. (Food and ping-pong tables are great, too.) If you can manage one more brewery, make it the nearby **Dark Sky Brewing**; they've made hundreds of beers, and are known for experimental flavors.

Day 3

Wake up with a cappuccino from **Macy's Coffee,** a beloved hangout whose sign is a local touchstone. (Note the naked guy bathing in a steaming cup of joe.) From there, it's a quick stroll to **The Artist's Gallery,** a cooperative arts and crafts space featuring work by a long list of local artists. This is an excellent place to pick up souvenirs, including jewelry, pottery, and prints.

Next, head to **Riordan Mansion State Historic Park,** an Arts-and-Crafts–style mansion designed by the same architect who created the Grand Canyon's El Tovar. Hour-long guided tours take in the beautifully detailed home's original Craftsman furnishings; the free-to-access visitor center has historic photographs and a collection of period tools.

Make your final sightseeing stop at the extraordinary **Museum of Northern Arizona,** whose permanent collections explore the Indigenous art, history, and cultures

of the entire Colorado Plateau. (There's a great museum gift shop, too.) After you see the exhibits inside the museum, check out the gardens: the medicinal plant garden features a wide range of the healing plants traditionally used in the region.

Before you hit the road, duck into the deceptively named **MartAnne's Breakfast Palace,** where breakfast—and lunch—are served all day. Southwestern favorites including burritos, enchiladas, and chilaques arrive in hefty portions. If you can, save room for the house-made desserts, or just take an order of mini Mexican donuts to go.

Recommendations

Sights

Coconino National Forest. ⊠ *1824 S. Thompson St., Flagstaff, AZ* ☎ *928/527–3600* ⊕ *www.fs.usda.gov* 🖃 *$5 for Red Rock.*

Grand Canyon National Park. ⊠ *Grand Canyon National Park Visitor Center, S. Entrance Rd., Grand Canyon Village, AZ* ☎ *928/638–7888* ⊕ *www.nps.gov* 🖃 *$35 per vehicle.*

Kolb Studio. ⊠ *Village Loop Dr., Grand Canyon Village, AZ* ☎ *928/638–2771* ⊕ *www.grandcanyon.org* 🖃 *Free.*

Lowell Observatory. ⊠ *1400 W. Mars Hill Rd., Flagstaff, AZ* ☎ *928/774–3358* ⊕ *www.lowell.edu* 🖃 *$22.*

Museum of Northern Arizona. ⊠ *3101 N. Ft. Valley Rd., Flagstaff, AZ* ☎ *928/774–5213* ⊕ *www.musnaz.org* 🖃 *$12.*

Riordan Mansion State Historic Park. ⊠ *409 W. Riordan Rd., Flagstaff, AZ* ☎ *928/779–4395* ⊕ *www.arizonahistoricalsociety.org* 🖃 *$10.*

Restaurants

Diablo Burger. $ *Average main: $13* ✉ *120 N. Leroux St., Flagstaff, AZ* ☎ *928/774-3274* ⊕ *www.diabloburger. com.*

El Tovar Hotel. $ *Average main: $30* ✉ *1 El Tovar Rd., Grand Canyon, AZ* ☎ *928/638-2631* ⊕ *www.grandcanyon-lodges.com.*

Macy's Coffee. $ *Average main: $8* ✉ *14 S. Beaver St., Flagstaff AZ* ☎ *928/774-2243* ⊕ *www.macyscoffee.net.*

MartAnne's Breakfast Palace. $ *Average main: $13* ✉ *112 E. Rte. 66, Flagstaff, AZ* ☎ *928/773-4701* ⊕ *www.martannes. com.*

Pizzicletta. $ *Average main: $15* ✉ *203 W. Phoenix Ave., Flagstaff, AZ* ☎ *928/774-3242* ⊕ *www.pizzicletta.com.*

Tourist Home All Day Café. $ *Average main: $12* ✉ *52 S. San Francisco St., Flagstaff AZ* ☎ *928/779-2811* ⊕ *www. touristhomecafe.com.*

Hotels

Arizona Snowbowl. $ *Rooms from: $85* ✉ *9300 N. Snowbowl Rd., Flagstaff, AZ* ☎ *928/779-1951* ⊕ *www.snowbowl.ski* ⦿ *No meals.*

Inn at 410. $ *Rooms from: $162* ✉ *410 Leroux St., Flagstaff, AZ* ☎ *928/774-0088* ⊕ *www.inn410.com* ⦿ *Free breakfast.*

Motel du Beau. $ *Rooms from: $58* ✉ *19 W. Phoenix Ave., Flagstaff, AZ* ☎ *928/774-6731* ⊕ *www.modubeau.com* ⦿ *Free breakfast.*

Nightlife

Dark Sky Brewing. ✉ *117 N. Beaver St., Flagstaff, AZ* ☎ *928/440-5151* ⊕ *www. darkskybrewing.com.*

Flagstaff Brewing Company. ✉ *16 E. Rte. 66, Flagstaff, AZ* ☎ *928/773-1442* ⊕ *www.flagbrew.com.*

Lumberyard Brewing Company. ✉ *5 S. San Francisco St., Flagstaff, AZ* ☎ *928/779-2739* ⊕ *www.lumberyardbrewingcompany.com.*

Shopping

The Artist's Gallery. ✉ *17 N. San Francisco St., Flagstaff, AZ* ☎ *928/773-0958* ⊕ *www.theflagstaffartistsgallery.com.*

Activities

Bright Angel Bikes. ✉ *10 S. Entrance Rd., Grand Canyon, AZ* ☎ *928/679-0992* ⊕ *www.bikegrandcanyon.com* ⬚ *Bike Rental starts from $10.*

Grand Junction, CO

243 miles (approx. 4 hours) from Denver.

Nestled among Colorado's western slope, the Grand Junction area is close to the state border and about equidistant from Denver and Salt Lake City. Many people breeze by on their way to Moab National Park, but that's a mistake. Flanked by both the Colorado Plateau and the Rocky Mountains, the area is an outdoor lover's dream, but the bigger draw is Colorado's largely unknown agricultural region.

A true hidden gem, Palisade, Colorado's wine country, makes for a cozy couple's retreat or raucous girlfriend getaway. Downtown Grand Junction teems with galleries, outdoor art, and performance venues, ensuring there's plenty for adventure enthusiasts, culture vultures, and foodies alike. Here's how to see the best of the west on this surprising weekend trip from the Mile High.

Unique rock formations dot the landscape at Colorado National Monument.

Planning

GETTING THERE AND BACK

Virtually four hours straight west, Grand Junction is the last major stop in Colorado before you cross the Utah border. You'll take I–70 through high country, so pause in Breckenridge or Vail if you need to stretch your legs or can't pass up the scenic overlooks.

WHEN TO GO

Autumn is the best time to visit, because the colors on the Western Slope are stunning. There are festivals virtually every weekend in spring and fall, but summer is also a busy time for picking fruit at the orchards, browsing the farmer's markets, and floating the river. While snow could complicate winter explorations, winter is milder than elsewhere in Colorado, making it a good choice if you're looking for somewhere to escape the cold.

WHERE TO STAY

The good news is none of the lodgings are particularly expensive in Grand Junction. **Spoke and Vine** is one of the nicer accommodation options, albeit they very clearly state, don't expect the Ritz. For a more memorable retreat, you can stay right in the vineyards at the **Colorado Wine Country Inn.** The boutique property is Colorado's first wine-themed hotel and features afternoon tastings set on 21-acres of sprawling vines. The **Chateau at Two Rivers Winery** is another that lets you sleep among the grapes with elegantly appointed French touches.

Day 1

If you leave early enough, you'll arrive in time for lunch and have the afternoon to explore. Grab a table on the patio at **Spoons Bistro & Bakery,** which is the place to fill your stomach and appease your soul. A humanitarian food venture, all proceeds benefit HopeWest, a local non-profit dedicated to those facing serious illnesses. Their rosemary chicken isn't half bad, either.

It's been a long morning in the car, but you can't not see **Colorado National Monument.** With twisty red outcrops and deep sandstone towers, it's often described as the little Grand Canyon. Teeming with wildlife, natural history, and unique geological formations, the 23-mile Rim Rock Drive will take you to awe-inspiring views, but if you'd rather get some exercise, the 2-mile Serpent's Trail or half-mile Otto's Trail are popular places to take in the landscape while stretching your legs.

For the best sunset spot, head up to **Grand Mesa National Forest,** where the aspens are a brilliant yellow in fall. The largest flattop mountain in the world, the area is home to endless forests and more than 300 high alpine lakes. In winter, there's cross-country skiing, ice fishing, and snowmobiling on the Grand Mesa or downhill skiing at nearby **Powderhorn Mountain** to soak in the setting.

Spend some time hiking around or head back to the hotel to freshen up. When you're ready to fill your belly, **Bin 707 Foodbar** features seasonal Colorado cuisine with the area's farm-fresh roots on full display. There's everything from burgers and tacos to game meats. Tuck in early and rest up, because you have a long day of sipping and swirling ahead.

Day 2

Grab a coffee and fill up on scratch-made pastries at **Slice O' Life Bakery** because you'll need something in your belly for a long day of wine tasting. The **Palisade Fruit & Wine Byway** boasts 25 stops for vineyard tours and winemaking demonstrations. The most popular way to explore is by renting a bike and following one of the 5- to 25-mile routes. If you'd prefer to cover more ground, don't like cycling, or are worried about getting tipsy on two wheels, you can also charter a limo, pedicab, open-air safari vehicle, or even a horse and buggy to get around.

Each winery has its own vibe and varietals, with many of the tasting rooms free or less than $10. A few not-to-miss stops include **Varaison Vineyards & Winery** for their rose garden and hard ciders, **Talon Winery,** which is really three-stops in one with St. Kathryn Cellars and Meadery of the Rockies' sweet honey wines and fruit pours, and **Restoration Vineyards,** which breaks up the day of drinking with complimentary cheese pairings.

If a liquid lunch isn't cutting it, swing by **Palisade Café 11.0** for a quick bite. Farm-to-table fresh, they have rotating sandwich specials, burgers, or salads with a slight Spanish influence.

Another good midday recovery stop is **Suncrest Orchard Alpacas and Fiber Works,** where you can make some fuzzy new friends. Alpacas are hilarious creatures you can feed or take for a walk before touring the mill and shopping for handmade yard and woven souvenirs.

Locals know Palisade Brewing Company is the place to unwind after a day of drinking. Smoked meat platters (hello, jalapeño cheddar brisket) and fried foods are just what the doctor ordered. They regularly have live music, which means the place turns into a patio party. If by some chance you're still thirsty, they're right down the block from **Peach Street Distillers,** which you can also tour.

Day 3

When you finally pull yourself out of bed, it's off to **Dream Cafe** for hangover brunch. There are Bloody Marys and Mimosas for a little hair of the dog, or stick to carbo-loading. Appease your appetite with the baked avocado Benedict, pineapple upside-down pancakes, or breakfast pot pies.

For one last adventure, marvel at mustangs. **The Little Book Cliffs Wild Horse Area** is one of just three in the western United States where wild horses roam. With 30,000 acres of open space, you can go on a trail ride, hike, mountain bike, or hop on a 4x4 before hitting the road. At any given time, there are 80 to 120 mustangs galloping and grazing, which makes for a pretty magical morning in the mountains.

On the way out of town, be sure to snag some peaches (Palisade's other claim to fame) to bring home with you or for a car snack from one of the roadside fruit stands or farms.

Recommendations

Sights

Colorado National Monument. ✉ *Rimrock Dr., Fruita, CO* ☎ *970/858–3617* 🌐 *www.nps.gov/colm* 🎟 *$15 per vehicle.*

Grand Mesa National Forest. ✉ *2250 Hwy. 50, Delta, CO* ☎ *970/874–6600* 🌐 *www.fs.usda.gov* 🎟 *Free.*

Little Book Cliffs Wild Horse Area. ✉ *952 I–70, 8 miles northeast of Grand Junction, Palisade, CO* ☎ *970/244–3000* 🌐 *www.blm.gov* 🎟 *Free.*

Restoration Vineyards. ✉ *3594 E 1/2 Rd., Palisade, CO* ☎ *970/985–0832* 🌐 *www.restorationvineyards.com* 🎟 *Tastings $5.*

Talon Winery. ✉ *785 Elberta Ave., Palisade, CO* ☎ *970/464–9288* 🌐 *www.talonwinebrands.com* 🎟 *Tastings $3.*

Varaison Vineyards & Winery. ✉ *405 W. 1st St., Palisade, CO* ☎ *970/464–4928* 🌐 *www.varaisonvineyards.com* 🎟 *Tastings free.*

Restaurants

Bin 707 Foodbar. [$] *Average main: $23* ✉ *225 N. 5th St., Grand Junction, CO* ☎ *970/243–4543* 🌐 *www.bin707.com.*

Dream Cafe. [$] *Average main: $11* ✉ *314 Main St., Grand Junction, CO* ☎ *970/424–5353* 🌐 *www.dreamcafegj.com*

Palisade Brewing Company. [$] *Average main: $14* ✉ *200 Peach Ave., Palisade, CO* ☎ *970/464–1462* 🌐 *www.palisadebrewingcompany.com.*

Palisade Cafe 11.0. [$] *Average main: $11* ✉ *113 E. 3rd St., Palisade, CO* ☎ *970/464–2888* 🌐 *www.palisadecafe11.com* 🕓 *Closed Mon. and Tues. No Lunch Wed., Thurs., and Sun.*

Spoons Bistro & Bakery. [$] *Average main: $9* ✉ *3090 N. 12th St., Grand Junction, CO* ☎ *970/255–7237* 🌐 *www.spoonsbistroandbakery.com.*

Coffee and Quick Bites

Slice O' Life Bakery. [$] *Average main: $20* ✉ *105 W. 3rd St., Palisade, CO* ☎ *970/464–0577* 🕓 *Closed Sun. and Mon.*

Hotels

The Chateau at Two Rivers Winery. [$] *Rooms from: $92* ✉ *2087 Broadway, Grand Junction, CO* ☎ *970/255–1471* 🌐 *www.tworiverswinery.com* 🍴 *Free breakfast.*

Colorado Wine Country Inn. [$] *Rooms from: $99* ✉ *777 Grande River Dr., Palisade, CO* ☎ *970/464–5777* 🌐 *www.coloradowinecountryinn.com* 🍴 *Free breakfast.*

Spoke and Vine. [$] *Rooms from: $99* ✉ *424 W. 8th St. Palisade, CO* ☎ *970/464–2211* 🌐 *www.spokeandvinemotel.com* 🍴 *Free breakfast.*

Nightlife

Peach Street Distillers. ✉ *144 S. Kluge Ave., Palisade, CO* ☎ *970/464–1128* 🌐 *www.peachstreetdistillers.com.*

🛍 Shopping

Suncrest Orchard Alpacas and Fiber Works. ✉ *3608 E. 1/4 Rd., Palisade, CO* ☎ *970/464–4862* ⊕ *www.suncrestorchardalpacas.net.*

🏃 Activities

Emerald Coast Paddleboard. ✉ *48338 Powderhorn Rd., Mesa, CO* ☎ *970/268–5700* ⊕ *www.powderhorn.com* ✉ *$399.*

Great Basin National Park, NV

234 miles (approx. 3¾ hours) from Salt Lake City.

Mountains, lakes, deserts, grasslands, abandoned mines, and even a glacier—Great Basin National Park in Nevada has a little bit of everything within its 77,000 acres. Everything except people, that is. With just 131,802 visitors in 2019, it's one of the least visited national parks in the country, providing for a truly special experience. Though it's a bit remote, Great Basin is worth the trek, particularly for outdoorsy folk. But you don't need to be a survivalist to enjoy the park's top sights, from the Lehman Caves to Wheeler Peak, as well as the incredible astronomy programming (Great Basin is an International Dark Sky Park, which is hardly surprising given that the nearest major city is Salt Lake City, more than 200 miles away).

Planning

GETTING THERE AND BACK

From Salt Lake City, drive south along I–15 to UT 68 or UT 132 to U.S. 6, then head west on U.S. 6 and U.S. 50, the latter being a cross-country road known as the Loneliest Road in America, as it cuts through some pretty desolate stretches of land.

PIT STOPS

Just after Route 50's marker 81 is the Hinckley Shoe Tree, a barren tree covered in shoes. It's the only noticeable landmark for miles along the highway, so it's pretty hard to miss. At the very least, it makes for a good photo op and gives you the chance to stretch your legs!

WHEN TO GO

Though Great Basin is open year-round, summer is peak season, while fall comes in second place. Winter and spring are quieter—a good portion of the park is inaccessible by road due to snow—but beautifully serene. The weather varies greatly throughout the park, as there are numerous microclimates over an 8,000-foot elevation range between the highest peak and the lowest valley. Expect vastly different temperatures, unexpected thunderstorms, and snow any time of year. The biggest event at Great Basin is the Great Basin Astronomy Festival in September, which is also a great month for fall foliage.

WHERE TO STAY

If you want to stay in the Great Basin itself, you'd better bring your tent—the only options are a number of small, rustic campsites. The nearest RV park is in Baker, just 5 miles outside of the park, which is also where the closest permanent lodgings are. Our recommendations are the 10-room **Stargazer Inn** or the **Hidden Canyon Retreat,** a 375-acre ranch that's rather upscale as far as Baker accommodations go.

Day 1

Hit the road early and travel 3½ hours southwest of Salt Lake City to Baker, Nevada, the gateway town to **Great Basin National Park.** Try to arrive by 9 am so you can take advantage of the whole day. Start by getting your bearings at the Great Basin Visitor's Center, where you can chat with rangers about your plans, watch an orientation film, and view

Great Basin National Park's Alpine Lakes Loop Trail winds past pristine lakes.

exhibits about the park. Grab a caffeine pick-me-up and a quick bite at the Magic Bean Coffee Cart before heading into the park itself, just five miles down the road. If you plan on camping in the park throughout the weekend, remember that Baker is the last place you'll be able to stock up on supplies.

Your first order of business in Great Basin should be the impressive **Lehman Caves,** open year-round. There's a second visitor's center here where you can buy tickets for the guided tour (necessary for entrance to the caves). Afterward, enjoy a late lunch at the Great Basin Cafe in the visitor's center, the only restaurant in the entire park, and a seasonal one at that. If you're visiting in the late spring, the summer, or the fall, take the 12-mile Wheeler Peak Scenic Drive through the mountains toward the summit of Wheeler Peak, Nevada's second tallest mountain at 13,064 feet tall. The view is incredible no matter the season, but fall foliage really makes the landscape look spectacular.

Grab an early dinner at **Great Basin Cafe,** the place for soups and sandwiches at the Lehman Caves Visitor Center. Stay in the park to catch ranger-led astrology programs. Between the park's lack of light pollution and the dry desert air, the stars are crystal clear.

Day 2

Summertime visitors should rise with the sun, drop by the Magic Bean Coffee Cart for breakfast, then head to the Wheeler Peak Summit Trail, located at the end of the Wheeler Peak Scenic Drive. Park rangers suggest doing the hike first thing in the morning, because afternoon thunderstorms are known to pop up and make the hike a little treacherous. The trail is nearly 9 miles out and back, and it's not for beginners between the high elevation, the 2,900-foot elevation gain from the trailhead to the summit, potentially high winds, and the steep, rocky route that requires some scrambling.

Pack your lunch for during or after the hike.

In the afternoon, don't miss the much easier 2.8-mile Bristlecone Trail that takes you through a grove of bristlecone pines, which can live more than 4,000 years. You can also tack on the Glacier Trail to this hike, which adds another 1.8 miles and brings you close to Nevada's only glacier, a scant remnant of its former glory.

If you're staying in Baker, drive back into town for dinner at **Kerouac's,** the on-property eatery of the Stargazer Inn, which is open seasonally. For evening entertainment, there's a teeny "casino" at the **Border Inn.**

Day 3

For the most ambitious hikers in the summer, today's plan should be to drive to the remote south side of the park, where backcountry explorers have free rein—quite literally, as you're allowed to ride horses here. We recommend the marked Lexington Arch Trail, which ends at a naturally formed 75-foot-tall limestone arch. It's 5.4 miles out and back and is appropriate for intermediate hikers. But remember, this is in the backcountry, so some experience is definitely necessary. As an alternative, a slightly less intense journey would be the Alpine Lakes Loop Trail, a 2.7-mile loop that passes Stella Lake and Teresa Lake.

By late afternoon, you should start your drive back to Salt Lake City to get a good night's sleep after all the physical activity.

Recommendations

◉ Sights

Great Basin National Park. ✉ Great Basin Visitor Center, 100 Great Basin, Baker, NV ☎ 775/234–7510 ⊕ www.nps.gov/grba/ 🖼 Free.

Lehman Caves. ✉ Lehman Caves Visitor Center, 5500 NV 488, Baker, NV ☎ 775/234–7331 ⊕ www.nps.gov/grba/planyourvisit/lehman-caves-tours.htm 🖼 Free ⊙ By tour only.

🍴 Restaurants

Great Basin Cafe. 💲 Average main: $6 ✉ Lehman Caves Visitor Center, 5500 NV 488, Baker, NV ☎ 775/234–7200 ⊕ www.greatbasincafe.com.

Kerouac's. 💲 Average main: $14 ✉ 115 S. Baker Ave., Baker, NV ☎ 775/234–7323 ⊕ www.stargazernevada.com ⊙ Closed Tues. and Wed.

🛏 Hotels

Hidden Canyon Retreat. 💲 Rooms from: $164 ✉ 2000 Hidden Canyon Pkwy., Baker, NV ☎ 775/234–7172 ⊕ www.hiddencanyonretreat.com ⦿ Free breakfast.

Stargazer Inn. 💲 Rooms from: $78 ✉ 115 S. Baker Ave., Baker, NV ☎ 775/234–7323 ⊕ www.stargazernevada.com ⦿ Free breakfast.

🍸 Nightlife

Border Inn. ✉ Hwy. 6, Baker, NV ☎ 775/234–7300 ⊕ www.borderinncasino.com.

Jackson, Grand Teton, and Yellowstone, WY

Jackson is 277 miles (approx. 4½ hours) from Salt Lake City.

Let's start with a little geography. Jackson is a city, and it's located at the south end of Jackson Hole Valley in northwest Wyoming. The valley marks the southern end of spectacular Grand Teton National Park, which begins at the southern end of Yellowstone National Park—America's

Yellowstone National Park's geysers show off brilliant shades of blue and green.

first national park, covering 3,500 square miles in Wyoming, Montana, and Idaho.

For today's travelers, Jackson is a dreamy destination to nestle yourself in nature. By day, discover all manner of recreational activities. By night, stroll around the rustic-chic town square, dance to live music, and dine and drink alfresco. Just like all the celebrities, you're sure to fall hard for this debonair cowboy enclave.

Planning

GETTING THERE AND BACK
This is one gorgeous drive. From Salt Lake City, travel north on I-15 into Idaho, connecting to U.S. 30 E where you'll enjoy part of the Bear Lake Scenic Byway. At Soda Springs, get onto ID 34 and U.S. 89 (which becomes U.S. 191) and cruise right into Jackson.

INSPIRATION
In the Cowboy State, your tunes should skew towards country music. There's nothing wrong with listening to Johnny Cash and June Carter Cash's "Jackson," but it's actually about a Tennessee town. So roll with John Denver's "Song of Wyoming," George Strait's "I Can Still Make Cheyenne," Gene Autry's "Hills of Wyoming," or Chris LeDoux's "Paint Me Back Home in Wyoming."

PIT STOPS
Bear Lake Scenic Byway is an irresistible opportunity to soak in the hot mineral pools in the town of Lava Hot Springs, home to a popular water park. In Soda Springs, don't miss **Geyser Park,** said to be the only "captive geyser" in the world, meaning it's capped and controlled by a timer that allows its 100-foot-high eruption every hour. At nearby **Hooper Springs Park,** get yourself a free bottle of natural soda water.

WHEN TO GO
Jackson is a year-round destination, always inviting active travelers to bike, hike, ride horses, raft, and ski its many slopes. The city's at an elevation of 6,200 feet, though, so pack clothes for temperatures that fluctuate from balmy days

to frigid nights. In winter, expect heavy snowfall and subzero temperatures. Annual rodeos, concerts, festivals, and other events take place all year, led by the Teton County Fair every July.

WHERE TO STAY

Jackson and the surrounding area offer lots of lodging choices all year round, both big brands and indie hotels. **Spring Creek Ranch,** just north of town, offers an outdoor pool and a relaxing spa. In downtown, there's the **Antler Inn,** one of the boutique properties of the family-owned Town Square Inns.

Day 1

On your way toward downtown Jackson, Highway 191 becomes West Broadway, lined by hotels and restaurants on both sides. Stop along the way for your welcome lunch at **Sidewinders American Grill** for filling gastropub fare, draft wine and beer, plus unexpected dishes like burrata with house-made chimichurri, and fresh kale and farro salad.

Proceed toward the historic town square, officially named George Washington Memorial Park, and marked by its four arches made of elk antlers (which are either cool or creepy, your call). You'll notice right off how compact Jackson is, so park your car and let yourself wander.

If you're planning sporty adventure time, you may want to gear up or check in at **Grand Teton Fly Fishing, Teton Whitewater,** or **Jackson Hole Grand Expeditions,** the latter offering year-round wildlife safaris and photography excursions. You could also rent a bike from a spot like **Hoback Sports** or **Teton Mountain Bike Tours,** and dive right into some gorgeous trail cycling. Or check out the busy local club Jackson Hole Babe Force, offering women-only mountain adventures.

If you're more artsy than sporty, you'll enjoy the abundant art galleries around

downtown. The **Jackson Hole Center for the Arts** is a hot spot for live music and other events. Just north of town, the **National Museum of Wildlife Art** beguiles visitors with its unique hillside architecture and exhibits of wild-animal art from around the world.

Plan ahead with a reservation at local favorite **Snake River Grill,** serving mountain cuisine in a white-tablecloth bedecked log cabin. The founders translate local ingredients into sophisticated dishes that resonate with foodie types. You can enjoy its smoked trout chowder, venison carpaccio, buffalo short ribs, and other delights alongside an international beer and wine menu. Follow it with a delicious craft cocktail a block away at **The Rose,** an atmospheric lounge with diamond-tufted banquettes and locally distilled spirits.

Day 2

Today will be devoted to the main course of this trip, **Yellowstone National Park,** whose entrance is about an hour away from Jackson.

Just off the square is a log cabin serving Jackson's Southern-tinted, "inspired home cooking." Look for **Café Genevieve's** mint-green sign and shady dining terrace, and get your fill of brunch, be it biscuits with Cajun gravy, chicken and waffles, or classic grilled cheese and tomato soup.

Before you leave for Yellowstone, stop by family-owned **Persephone Bakery** just east of town square to procure sandwiches and other freshly made picnic items to lunch on in the park. There are a few stores and cafés inside Yellowstone, but wise travelers know that Persephone's treats will be a hundred times tastier. A big plus: they're pleasantly portable.

It's about 60 miles north on U.S. 191 from Jackson to Yellowstone's South Entrance, and another 20 miles to West

Thumb on the western shore of Yellowstone Lake. From there, you could easily spend the full day or several days exploring this magnificent, preserved wonder. Keep an eye out for wildlife. There are more than 60 species of mammals here, like bears, wolves, bison, elk, and lynxes.

You'll have to choose what's most important, but the big draws include Old Faithful, the most famous of Yellowstone's regularly erupting geysers; the Grand Canyon of the Yellowstone River; Grand Prismatic Spring in the Midway Geyser Basin; and the 132-foot-tall Tower Fall waterfall.

Leave time for a night out in Jackson, because the historic **Million Dollar Cowboy** is calling. Open since 1937, the Cowboy is easy to find—just look for the giant neon bucking bronco on the west side of the square. Head to the underground dining room for elk chops, steelhead trout, dry-aged rib eye, or another hearty dish. Then join the fun for two-stepping and line dancing in the big barroom, which hosts live bands every weekend and most weeknights.

Day 3

There are plenty of posh brunch spots in Jackson, but seven miles west in the town of Wilson is family-run **Nora's Fish Creek Inn,** where you can wake up to country-style mornings with biscuits and hotcakes, Mexican breakfasts, French toast, and more.

To round out your third day here, saddle up for a one- or two-hour ride on horseback atop East Gros Ventre Butte with Spring Creek Ranch's **Castagno Outfitters.** You'll take in grand views of the Teton Range, downtown Jackson, and surrounding peaks and valleys. If you'd prefer quality time in town, wander through Gaslight Alley just off the square on North Cache Street. It's a collection of locally owned and operated shops selling uncommon goods. Some favorites are **Made** (for handmade, repurposed, and found goods) and **Valley Bookstore** (a favorite independent for nearly 50 years).

Grab a beverage at **Cowboy Coffee,** roasted in town, along with fresh-baked cinnamon rolls and croissants. Saunter over to **Mountain Dandy** on West Pearl Street to browse provisions for home and gentlemen. Quality cowboy boots, belts, hats, and other rugged wear are ready for you at **Beaver Creek Hats & Leather** on East Broadway.

Alternatively, if you want to do some more national park exploring, **Grand Teton National Park** sits on Jackson's doorstep. The Craig Thomas Discovery & Visitor Center is only 18 miles from downtown Jackson, about 25 minutes by car. You have a couple of choices if you have only a half-day. If you arrive early, take a two-hour, guided Snake River scenic float trip (make required reservations with one of the half-dozen outfitters that offer the trip). When you're back on dry ground, drive north on Teton Park Road, stopping at scenic turnouts—don't miss Teton Glacier—until you reach South Jenny Lake Junction where you can take in the views or take another 20-minute boat trip to the lake's west shore, where you can take a breathtaking but short hike to Hidden Falls or Inspiration Point. You'll be done and ready to head back to Jackson by early afternoon for a late lunch.

Don't miss a last souvenir to go from **Yippy I-O Candy Co.,** selling homemade fudge, caramel popcorn, saltwater taffy, and huckleberry jams. At the long-running **Mursell's Sweet Shop,** pick up old-school candy bars. Both let you savor Jackson's sweetness all the way home.

Recommendations

👁 Sights

Geyser Park. ✉ 39 W. 1st St., Soda Springs, ID ☎ 208/547–2600 ⊕ www.sodaspringsid.com/recreation/geyser_park 💲 Free.

Grand Teton National Park. ✉ Moose, WY ☎ 307/739–3399 ⊕ www.nps.gov/grte 💲 $35.

Hooper Springs Park. ✉ 1805 Government Dam Rd., Soda Springs, ID ☎ 208/547–2600 ⊕ www.sodaspringsid.com/recreation/hooper_springs_park 💲 Free.

National Museum of Wildlife Art. ✉ 2820 Rungius Rd., Jackson, WY ☎ 307/733–5771 ⊕ www.wildlifeart.org 💲 $15 ⊙ Closed Sun. and Mon.

Yellowstone National Park. ✉ Yellowstone National Park, WY ☎ 307/344–7381 ⊕ www.nps.gov/yell 💲 $15.

🍴 Restaurants

Café Genevieve. 💲 Average main: $28 ✉ 135 E. Broadway Ave., Jackson, WY ☎ 307/732–1910 ⊕ genevievejh.com ⊙ Closed Mon. and Tues.

Million Dollar Cowboy. 💲 Average main: $30 ✉ 25 N. Cache St., Jackson, WY ☎ 307/733–2307 ⊕ www.milliondollarcowboybar.com.

Nora's Fish Creek Inn. 💲 Average main: $12 ✉ 5600 WY 22, Wilson, WY ☎ 307/733–8288.

Sidewinders American Grill. 💲 Average main: $22 ✉ 945 W. Broadway, Jackson, WY ☎ 307/734–5766 ⊕ www.sidewinderstavern.com.

Snake River Grill. 💲 Average main: $28 ✉ 84 E. Broadway Ave., Jackson, WY ☎ 307/733–0557 ⊕ www.snakerivergrill.com ⊙ No lunch.

☕ Coffee and Quick Bites

Cowboy Coffee. 💲 Average main: $5 ✉ 125 N. Cache St., Jackson, WY ☎ 307/733–7392 ⊕ cowboycoffee.com.

Persephone Bakery. 💲 Average main: $5 ✉ 145 E. Broadway Ave., Jackson, WY ☎ 307/200–6708 ⊕ persephonebakery.com.

🛏 Hotels

Antler Inn. 💲 Rooms from: $142 ✉ 330 W. Pearl Ave., Jackson, WY ☎ 307/733–7550 ⊕ www.townsquareinns.com/properties/antler-inn 🍽 No meals.

Spring Creek Ranch. 💲 Rooms from: $298 ✉ 1600 N.E. Butte Rd., Jackson, WY ☎ 301/733–8833 ⊕ www.springcreekranch.com 🍽 Free breakfast.

🍸 Nightlife

The Rose. ✉ 50 W. Broadway, Jackson, WY ☎ 307/733–1500 ⊕ www.facebook.com/therosejh.

🎭 Performing Arts

Jackson Hole Center for the Arts. ✉ 265 S. Cache St., Jackson, WY ☎ 307/734–8956 ⊕ jhcenterforthearts.org.

👜 Shopping

Beaver Creek Hats & Leather. ✉ 36 E. Broadway Ave., Jackson, WY ☎ 307/733–1999 ⊕ www.beavercreekhats.com.

Made. ✉ Gaslight Alley, 125 N. Cache St., Jackson, WY ☎ 307/690–7957 ⊕ www.madejacksonhole.com.

Mountain Dandy. ✉ 265 W. Pearl Ave., Jackson, WY ☎ 307/690–2896 ⊕ mountaindandy.com.

Mursell's Sweet Shop. ✉ 125 N. Cache St., Jackson, WY ☎ 307/264–1508 ⊕ mursells.com.

Valley Bookstore. ⌧ *125 N. Cache St., Jackson, WY* ☎ *307/733–4533* ⊕ *www. valleybookstore.com.*

Yippy I-O Candy Co. ⌧ *84 E. Broadway Ave., Jackson, WY* ☎ *307/739–3020* ⊕ *www.yippyi-ocandy.com.*

 ## Activities

Castagno Outfitters. ⌧ *25515 Buffalo Run, Moran, WY* ☎ *877/559–3585* ⊕ *www. castagnooutfitters.com* ⌨ *Trail rides from $49.*

Grand Teton Fly Fishing. ⌧ *225 W. Broadway, Jackson, WY* ☎ *307/690–0910* ⊕ *www.grandtetonflyfishing.com* ⌨ *Trips from $150.*

Hoback Sports. ⌧ *520 W. Broadway, Jackson, WY* ☎ *307/733–5335* ⊕ *hoback-sports.com* ⌨ *Bike rentals from $30.*

Jackson Hole Grand Expeditions. ☎ *307/543–6025* ⊕ *www.jacksonhole-grandexpeditions.com* ⌨ *Tours from $125.*

Teton Mountain Bike Tours. ⌧ *545 N. Cache St., Jackson, WY* ☎ *307/733–0712* ⊕ *www.tetonmtbike.com* ⌨ *Bike rentals from $30.*

Teton Whitewater. ⌧ *260 N. Cache St., Jackson, WY* ☎ *307/733–2285* ⊕ *www. tetonwhitewater.com* ⌨ *Rafting from $70.*

Moab, Arches, and Canyonlands, UT

355 miles (approx. 5½ hours) from Denver; 234 miles (approx. 4 hours) from Salt Lake City.

With two national parks just 30 minutes from each other, Moab is Utah's basecamp for adventure. An outdoor lover's dream, you could spend your days hiking, biking, and sleeping under the stars as you take in the magnificent red rock formations. One of the Southwest's greatest landscapes, many of the desert playground's most sought-after views are accessible to the casual traveler, but for intrepid adventurers looking to challenge themselves and get off the grid, there's plenty of backcountry to get lost in.

Planning

GETTING THERE AND BACK

An easy 5½-hour drive due west, the route from Denver takes you past scenic mountain towns like Breckenridge, Vail, and Glenwood Springs on I-70. You'll continue through Grand Junction until you reach the Utah border where you've basically made it.

PIT STOPS

Stop in Palisade, Colorado's secret wine region, to pick up provisions en route.

WHEN TO GO

Spring and fall are peak seasons in Moab, as the weather is more attuned to outdoor activities. Summertime can see temperatures soaring above 100 degrees, which makes desert explorations difficult. Winter can be an intriguing time to visit as the crowds have subsided, albeit many of the trails do get icy.

WHERE TO STAY

Most of the area hotels are basic, no frills crash pads, so many people choose to save their money and camp. If that's not your thing, the **Sorrel River Ranch** is the ultimate splurge. As the only luxury resort in Moab, expect the custom-built ranch cabins, signature spa services, and privately guided excursions.

For a more accessible place to rest your head, the **Castle Valley Inn Bed and Breakfast** is a delightful little hideaway with homemade pastries, beautiful grounds, and a garden hot tub to soak in the views.

Hiking to Double Arch is among the most popular diversions at Arches National Park.

Day 1

If you leave early enough, you should arrive by mid-afternoon and can stop at **Moab Brewery** to fuel up. The town's largest restaurant and only microbrewery and distillery, it's basic pub fare like burger and wings, but is a good spot to try some of the local spirits. Their signature pour, Dead Horse Ale, takes its name from the popular viewpoint and should get you amped up and ready to explore.

If you're not too tired of being in the car, the Canyonlands Loop at sunset is simply stunning. **Canyonlands National Park** is much bigger than Arches (almost 5 times the size), and yet sees about half the number of tourists. It's more spread out, which makes touring a challenge, but does have an easy 34-mile drive loop to some of the highlights such as Island in the Sky. Snap some photos, do a short hike or two, and stretch your legs before heading to your hotel to freshen up.

When you're ready, head back out to the main drag for dinner. **Antica Forma** is the town's beloved Italian joint and just the carb-fest you need to prep for tomorrow's activities. Known for their woodfired pizzas made fresh from an oven flown in all the way from Naples, they have traditional red pies and more unique toppings like pistachio. Hit the hay early, because you'll need to rest up for tomorrow's festivities.

Day 2

Grab a coffee and breakfast burrito from **Love Muffin Café**, plus a panini or some snacks for the road. Since you'll be out most of the day, you'll want to pack sustenance and enough water for a day in the desert.

Home to more than 2,000 natural sandstone arches, **Arches National Park** is the gem of the national park system. Your first stop is one you'll recognize from the Utah license plate. Delicate Arch is the park's most iconic hike and a must-see, which you can view from afar at the Upper Viewpoint or up close on the 3-mile trail.

For a more challenging trek, Devils Garden Loop will take you to a handful of the park's most prominent arches in 2 to 8 miles. They each have varying degrees of difficulty and altitude gain, so plan accordingly and know your endurance level. It can take most of the day if you're keen on covering a lot of ground.

If you plan well enough in advance, Fiery Furnace is another coveted adventure in Arches National Park. Reservations and permits are required to hike this naturally formed rock labyrinth. You'll either have to go with a guide or watch a video at the ranger station to learn how to maneuver your way out of the twists and turns of this intriguing canyon maze that has no trails or markers.

You can spend the full day at Arches, but if you'd rather beat the heat, river trips are also extremely popular. Full day or half-day whitewater excursions down the Colorado and Westwater Canyon range in difficulty from Class II to V. Whether you're looking for a lazy day on the water or roaring rapids, whitewater rafting in Moab is another summer must.

After a long day of exploring, head to **Moab Garage** for a sweet treat. Their liquid nitrogen ice cream, ice cream sandwiches, and donuts are the perfect midafternoon pick-me-up. Looking as much like a science experiment as a snack, the cold feels great after a long day in the blazing sun.

Once you've showered and cleaned up, stake out a seat at **Blu Pig** patio, which boasts barbecue and blues. With live music seven nights a week, it's undoubtedly the town gathering place. Cooked slow and low, tender ribs and tri-tip taste even better to a soundtrack of reckless abandon before you tuck in for the evening.

Day 3

You have time for one more half-day excursion, so make it count. Mountain biking, rock climbing, and ATV tours are all wildly popular ways to explore the insane scenery, which makes it a bit of a "choose your own" adventure.

Give canyoneering a try, as it's one of those sports uniquely attuned to the landscape that you can't do just anywhere. Essentially the opposite of rock climbing—by the laws of physics, what goes up must come down. Rappelling, scrambling, and wading through the slot canyons over waterfalls, it's an amazing, surprisingly less technical adventure suitable for just about any fitness level.

Once you've dried off and packed up, mingle over one last meal before you head back. Open since the 1960s, **Moab Diner** is the quintessential roadside café that can satisfy any carb craving. From big juicy burgers to runny eggs, splurge on a malt, brown butter sundae, or banana split before hitting the road in time to make it back for dinner.

Recommendations

👁 Sights

Arches National Park. ✉ *Arches National Park Visitor Center, Arches Entrance Rd., Moab, UT* ☎ *435/719–2299* 🌐 *www.nps.gov/arch* 🎟 *$30 per vehicle.*

Canyonlands National Park. ✉ *Island in the Sky Visitor Center, Grand View Point Rd, Moab, UT* ☎ *435/719–2313* 🌐 *www.nps.gov/cany* 🎟 *$30 per vehicle.*

🍴 Restaurants

Antica Forma. [$] *Average main: $20* ✉ *267 N. Main St., Moab, UT* ☎ *435/355–0167* 🌐 *www.anticaforma.com.*

Blu Pig. [$] *Average main: $20* ✉ *811 S. Main St., Moab, UT* ☎ *435/259–3333* 🌐 *www.blupigbbq.com.*

Love Muffin Café. [$] *Average main: $11* ✉ *139 N. Main St., Moab, UT* ☎ *435/259–6833* 🌐 *www.lovemuffincafe.com* 🍴 *No dinner.*

Moab Brewery. [$] *Average main: $10* ✉ *686 S. Main St., Moab, UT* ☎ *435/259–6333* 🌐 *www.themoabbrewery.com.*

Moab Diner. [$] *Average main: $13* ✉ *189 S. Main St., Moab, UT* ☎ *435/259–4006* 🌐 *www.moabdiner.com.*

Coffee and Quick Bites

Moab Garage. [$] *Average main: $10* ✉ *78 N. Main St., Moab, UT* ☎ *435/554–8467* 🌐 *www.facebook.com/MoabGarageCo* 🍴 *Closed Tues.–Thurs. No dinner.*

Hotels

Castle Valley Inn Bed and Breakfast. [$] *Rooms from: $155* ✉ *424 Amber La., Moab, UT* ☎ *435/259–6012* 🌐 *www.castlevalleyinn.com* 🍴 *Free breakfast.*

Sorrel River Ranch. [$] *Rooms from: $649* ✉ *Mile 17, UT 128, Moab, UT* ☎ *435/259–4642* 🌐 *www.sorrelriver.com* 🍴 *No meals.*

Oklahoma City, OK

206 miles (approx. 3 hours) from Dallas.

They call Oklahoma City "the modern frontier," inviting travelers to summon the pioneer spirit of the Great Plains as they savor 21st-century culture. It's remarkable how the contemporary part of OKC keeps its cowboy roots kicking. A weekend getaway allows you time enough to really explore the state capital, sampling Americana like chicken-fried steak and Route 66, plus surprises like incredible Vietnamese restaurants and a world-class arts collective.

Planning

GETTING THERE AND BACK

At 6½ hours, it's a long drive from Houston up to Oklahoma City, so the 3½-hour drive from Dallas seems zippy by comparison. I–35 is a long, mostly straight line across the state border. If you're game for a smaller highway, consider U.S. 77, which opened in 1926 and spans 1,305 miles from the Mexican border up all the way to Sioux City, Iowa.

INSPIRATION

The list of famous Oklahoman musicians is incredible: Garth Brooks and Roy Clark (Tulsa), Reba McEntire (McAlester), Toby Keith (Clinton), Carrie Underwood (Muskogee), Vince Gill (Norman), Blake Shelton (Ada), Conway Twitty (born in Mississippi but lived for many years in Oklahoma City), and many more. But don't miss Gene Autry's biggest, catchiest hit, "Back in the Saddle Again." Although born in Texas, Autry established his Flying A Ranch in Berwyn at the height of his fame in the early 1940s, and the town even changed its name to "Gene Autry, OK."

PIT STOPS

Just off I–35, the **Gene Autry Oklahoma Museum** (in the town of Gene Autry, near Ardmore) is a fitting stop along the way. For a bit of quirk, just across the interstate is the town of Springer's famous Magnetic Hill, where you can put your car in neutral, then feel it mysteriously accelerate up a hill. (It's actually an optical illusion, but fun nonetheless!)

WHEN TO GO

The Great Plains climate comes with a few weather extremes, like snowy winters and very hot summers (90 to 100 degrees much of the season). March through June and October tend to be the months that bring tornadoes, so keep an eye on weather forecasts when planning your getaway.

Giant bronze sculptures at Oklahoma City's Centennial Land Run Monument.

WHERE TO STAY

It's easy to book a room at one of the hotel chains dotting the OKC map, including big names like Marriott, Sheraton, Hilton, Hyatt, and their boutique brands. For an independent hotel, **The Colcord** is in a nice spot by the botanical gardens, with modern accommodations in a historic high rise. The **Ambassador Hotel Oklahoma City** has art deco details and a rooftop pool, while **21c Museum Hotel Oklahoma City** is part of the Museum Hotels collection, featuring art galleries and the eatery **Mary Eddy's.**

Day 1

The first meal in a new city can set the tone for your whole trip. Luckily, local chef Kathryn Mathis has two great options for you: **Back Door Barbecue** or **Big Truck Tacos.** Both are casual, affordable, delicious, and filling, plus they're only three blocks apart in Paseo, in case you need to sample both saucy ribs and creative tacos.

You'll soon notice that Oklahoma City is laid out like a grid with numerical streets, making navigation easy. So from Paseo on the north side of town, head south to Midtown, where you can pay respects at the powerful **Oklahoma City National Memorial & Museum,** which commemorates the 1995 Murrah Building bombing.

A few blocks away, shift to a bit of beautiful nature at the **Myriad Botanical Gardens,** a 17-acre wonderland of foliage featuring a tropical conservatory and carousel. Nearby, the **Oklahoma City Museum of Art** inspires visitors with a variety of visual art, including robust photography and contemporary galleries, and one of the world's largest public collections of Dale Chihuly glass.

By now you can head over to historic Automobile Alley, along North Broadway, for shopping, dining, and nightlife. Stop by **Sidecar Barley & Wine Bar** for fine libations and snacks in the elegant lounge or outdoor patio. For dinner, try inventive Mexican dishes and margaritas at **Barrios,** or sample seasonal American dishes at

Packards. If you planned ahead and made a reservation, you'll love the inventive 10-course tasting menu at compact **Nonesuch.**

Day 2

Launch your day with a tasty breakfast at **Hatch** for excellent "early mood food" that will rouse your taste buds with daring omelets, waffles, benedicts, sandwiches, and "coffee cocktails."

Then it's an easy jaunt to one of the city's wildest stops, **Factory Obscura Mix-Tape.** Housed in a converted industrial space that was originally outfitted by indie band the Flaming Lips, Factory Obscura is a local arts collective that stages immersive multisensory installations—an artsy, psychedelic outpost unlike anything else you'll experience.

Shift to Western mode next, with a trip to the **National Cowboy & Western Heritage Museum.** The museum started in 1955 as the Cowboy Hall of Fame, before evolving into one of Oklahoma City's top attractions, with nearly 30,000 Western and American Indian artifacts and artworks, not to mention the world's biggest collection of rodeo trophies, photographs, saddlery, and more authentic frontier relics.

A short jaunt from the museum is the famous **Oklahoma City Zoo,** with animal shows and Outdoor Safari Walk tickets available by reservation.

Next, head to the old industrial district known as Bricktown, where you can grab a latte and snack from locally owned **Landing Coffee Co.** roastery and café. Then stroll through River Walk Park to see the **Centennial Land Run Monument** at the end of the Bricktown Canal. The monument is a striking assemblage of giant bronze statues depicting 45 early settlers frozen in motion as they race to claim new homesteads.

Keep walking south to join an hour-long tour on the **Bricktown Water Taxi** on the Oklahoma River. If you're feeling splashy, head to **Riversport Adventures** on the north shore for on-site ziplining, slides, climbing walls, whitewater rafting, and more.

By now you should be feeling the real-deal country vibes of OKC, so it's time to browse the big hats at **Shorty's Hattery,** or browse boots and more Western wear at **Langston's.** Both are in the Stockyards City Main Street historic district on the south shore of the river, where you'll find **Oklahoma Native Art & Jewelry** boutique, the free and funky **Rattlesnake Museum,** and the **Rodeo Opry** live music venue.

The Stockyards is also home of one of Oklahoma's preeminent steakhouses. **Cattlemen's Steakhouse** has been serving prime USDA beef since 1945, and is now considered a local institution serving all cuts of steak, "lamb fries," fried catfish, and a mighty fine chicken-fried steak with gravy.

Day 3

You can channel the early days of road-tripping with quality time along Route 66, which traverses the northwest corner of Oklahoma City. Start with diner-style breakfast at family-owned **Stray Dog Café,** or hit up **Ann's Chicken Fry House** for its famous chicken-fried steak and eclectic Route 66 décor—both of them on America's Mother Road (locally known as NW 39th Street).

Nearby, take a walk around Lake Overholser, where you can walk a nature trail, rent a paddleboat, and climb up the Cyrus Avery Observation Tower inside Route 66 Park. Top it off with a come from **Braum's Ice Cream and Dairy Store,** a regional chain that first opened in Oklahoma City in 1968.

Since this is the Oklahoma capital, you'd be right to check out Historic Capitol Hill for its century-old low-rise architecture, and its grand **State Capitol** on North Lincoln Boulevard. Its grounds span 100 acres and you can't miss its towering Greco-Roman dome, open for self-guided or volunteer-led tours (call ahead for times and reservations).

The stately 1928 Governor's Mansion is uptown on N.E. 23rd Street, near the Oklahoma History Center. While you're in the area, don't miss a photo opp by the city's iconic 1958 **Gold Dome Building,** a geodesic dome that's now a local landmark just off Route 66.

One of the bigger surprises in OKC is the strong local Vietnamese community and food culture. So cap off your visit with a fresh pho soup, banh-mi sandwich, and bubble tea in the Oklahoma City Asian District, sometimes called "Little Saigon." You'll find a busy cluster of Vietnamese-specific and pan-Asian restaurants there. **Pho Lien Hoa** is a local favorite, but there are plenty of other good ones, like **Pho Cuong,** and **Lee's Sandwiches.** So fill up for your drive home, or invest in a tasty lunch to go.

Recommendations

Sights

Centennial Land Run Monument. ☒ 200 Centennial Ave., Oklahoma City, OK ☎ 405/297–8912 💲 Free.

Factory Obscura Mix-Tap. ☒ 25 N.W. 9th St., Oklahoma City, OK ☎ No phone ⊕ www.factoryobscura.com/mixtape 💲 $25 ۞ Closed Mon. and Tues.

Gene Autry Oklahoma Museum. ☒ 47 Prairie St., Gene Autry, OK ☎ 580/294–3276 ⊕ www.geneautryokmuseum.org 💲 Free ۞ Closed Mon.–Wed.

The Gold Dome. ☒ 1112 N.W. 23rd St., Oklahoma City, OK.

Myriad Botanical Gardens. ☒ 301 W. Reno Ave., Oklahoma City, OK

☎ 405/445–7080 ⊕ oklahomacitybotanicalgardens.com 💲 $2.

National Cowboy & Western Heritage Museum. ☒ 1700 N.E. 63rd St., Oklahoma City, OK ☎ 405/478–2250 ⊕ www.nationalcowboymuseum.org 💲 $13.

OKC Rattlesnake Museum. ☒ Corner of 15th and S. Agnew Sts., Oklahoma City, OK ☎ 405/850–5905 💲 Free.

Oklahoma City Museum of Art. ☒ 415 Couch Dr., Oklahoma City, OK ☎ 405/236–3100 ⊕ www.okcmoa.com 💲 $12 ۞ Closed Mon. and Tues.

Oklahoma City National Memorial & Museum. ☒ 620 N. Harvey Ave., Oklahoma City, OK ☎ 405/235–3313 ⊕ www.memorialmuseum.com 💲 $15.

Oklahoma City Zoo. ☒ 2000 Remington Pl., Oklahoma City, OK ☎ 405/850–5905 ⊕ www.okczoo.org 💲 $12.

Oklahoma State Capitol. ☒ 2300 N. Lincoln Blvd., Oklahoma City, OK ☎ 405/521–3356 ⊕ www.ok.gov 💲 Free ۞ Closed weekends.

🍴 Restaurants

Ann's Chicken Fry House. 💲 Average main: $11 ☒ 4106 N.W. 39th St., Oklahoma City, OK ☎ 405/943–8915 ⊕ www.theroadwanderer.net ۞ Closed Sun. and Mon.

Back Door BBQ. 💲 Average main: $15 ☒ 315 N.W. 23rd St., Oklahoma City, OK ☎ 405/525–7427 ⊕ backdoorbarbecue.com.

Barrios. 💲 Average main: $12 ☒ 1000 N. Hudson Ave., Oklahoma City, OK ☎ 405/702–6922 ⊕ www.barriosmexicanokc.com ۞ Closed Mon.

Big Truck Tacos. 💲 Average main: $10 ☒ 530 N.W. 23rd St., Oklahoma City, OK ☎ 405/525–8226 ⊕ www.bigtrucktacos.com.

Cattlemen's Steakhouse. $ *Average main: $18* ⊠ *1309 S. Agnew, Oklahoma City, OK* ☎ *405/236–0416* ⊕ *www.cattlemensrestaurant.com.*

Hatch. $ *Average main: $11* ⊠ *Buick Bldg., 1101 N. Broadway Ave., Oklahoma City, OK* ☎ *405/609–8936* ⊕ *www.hatchearlymoodfood.com* ◷ *No dinner.*

Lee's Sandwiches. $ *Average main: $10* ⊠ *3300 N. Classen Blvd., Oklahoma City, OK* ☎ *405/601–2161* ⊕ *www.leesandwiches.com.*

Mary Eddy's. $ *Average main: $24* ⊠ *21C Museum Hotel, 900 W. Main St., Oklahoma City, OK* ☎ *405/982–6960* ⊕ *www.maryeddysokc.com.*

Nonesuch. $ *Average main: $60* ⊠ *803 N. Hudson Ave., Oklahoma City, OK* ☎ *405/601–9131* ⊕ *www.nonesuchokc.com* ◷ *Closed Sun.–Tues. No lunch.*

Packard's. $ *Average main: $15* ⊠ *201 N.W. 10th St., Oklahoma City, OK* ☎ *405/605–3771* ⊕ *www.packardsokc.com*

Pho Cuong Restaurant. $ *Average main: $10* ⊠ *3016 N. Classen Blvd., Oklahoma City, OK* ☎ *405/601–9131.*

Stray Dog Café. $ *Average main: $10* ⊠ *6722 N.W. 39th Expy., Bethany, OK 73008* ☎ *405/470–3747.*

Coffee and Quick Bites

Braum's Ice Cream and Dairy Store $ *Average main: $5* ⊠ *1129 W. Memorial Rd., Oklahoma City, OK* ☎ *405/752–0700* ⊕ *www.braums.com.*

Landing Coffee Co. $ *Average main: $4* ⊠ *229 E. Sheridan Ave., Oklahoma City, OK* ☎ *405/361–6368* ⊕ *www.landingcoffeeco.com.*

Hotels

Ambassador Hotel Oklahoma City. $ *Rooms from: $220* ⊠ *1200 N. Walker Ave., Oklahoma City, OK* ☎ *405/600–6200* ⊕ *www.marriott.com* ⦿ *No meals.*

The Colcord. $ *Rooms from: $213* ⊠ *15 N. Robinson Ave., Oklahoma City, OK* ☎ *405/601–4300* ⊕ *www.colcordhotel.com* ⦿ *No meals.*

21c Museum Hotel Oklahoma City. $ *Rooms from: $159* ⊠ *900 W. Main St., Oklahoma City, Oklahoma* ☎ *405/982–6900* ⊕ *www.21cmuseumhotels.com* ⦿ *No meals.*

☍ Nightlife

Sidecar Barley & Wine Bar. ⊠ *13230 Pawnee Dr., Oklahoma City, OK* ☎ *405/286–9307* ⊕ *www.sidecarbarleyandwine.com.*

☖ Shopping

Langston's Western Wear. ⊠ *2224 Exchange Ave., Oklahoma City, OK* ☎ *405/235–9536* ⊕ *www.langstons.com.*

Oklahoma Native Art & Jewelry. ⊠ *2204 Exchange Ave., Oklahoma City, OK* ☎ *405/604–9800* ⊕ *www.oknativeart.com.*

Shorty's Hattery. ⊠ *1007 S. Agnew Ave., Oklahoma City, OK* ☎ *405/232–4287* ⊕ *www.shortyshattery.com* ◷ *Closed Sun.*

☍ Activities

Bricktown Water Taxi. ⊠ *111 S. Mickey Mantle Dr., Oklahoma City, OK* ☎ *405/234–8294* ⊕ *www.bricktownwatertaxi.com* ⛵ *$12.*

Riversport Adventures. ⊠ *800 Riversport Dr., Oklahoma City, OK* ☎ *405/552–4040* ⊕ *www.riversportokc.org* ⛵ *From $20.*

Park City and the Wasatch Range, UT

32 miles (approx. 45 minutes) from Salt Lake City.

The preeminent ski town in Utah, Park City is a ski bum's paradise—well, a wealthy ski bum, anyway, given that the town is one of the most expensive places to live in the state. But luckily those dollar signs don't have to apply to visitors coming from nearby Salt Lake City, and there are activities and accommodations for all price points. Park City is famous for two reasons: skiing, and the annual Sundance Film Festival in January. But there's also hiking or rafting and shopping and dining in downtown Park City.

Planning

GETTING THERE AND BACK

From Salt Lake City, Park City is only a 40-minute drive through the mountains on I–80, making it a super-easy weekend getaway.

PIT STOPS

If you want to take a slightly more leisurely route, head through Emigration Canyon and stop at **Ruth's Diner,** the second oldest restaurant in Utah, which opened in 1930.

WHEN TO GO

Park City is a year-round destination, offering both indoor and outdoor activities during each season. Peak seasons are summer and winter, especially for spending time outdoors, while the best deals can be found in the spring and the fall. Park City's premier event is the Sundance Film Festival, held in January—yes, you might be able to rub elbows with celebrities, but be prepared for huge crowds everywhere.

WHERE TO STAY

Park City is undoubtedly an upscale town, known for its ultraluxe ski resorts like **Stein Eriksen Lodge Deer Valley,** a stalwart that has drawn return guests for decades, and **The Lodge at Blue Sky,** set on a 3,500-acre ranch just outside of town. For a boutique experience, stay at the **Washington School House,** built in 1889 and converted into a charming 12-room hotel.

Day 1

Don't worry about getting an early start—Park City is well under an hour away from Salt Lake City, so you can sleep in. We recommend heading just outside of town to the **High West Distillery** in Wanship to kick off your weekend. Take the first free tour of the day (definitely opt for the whiskey flight, which costs extra), then stick around for lunch and a whiskey cocktail in the kitchen.

Afterward, drive to downtown Park City, 25 minutes away, and spend the afternoon strolling Main Street. There are more than 100 boutiques and galleries in town, so you'll have plenty to peruse. Don't miss the charming **Atticus Coffee, Books & Teahouse** if you need a little caffeine pick-me-up. After your shopping spree, drop by **Old Town Cellars** for a pred-inner wine tasting accompanied by bites.

Make a dinner reservation at **Fletcher's,** an American eatery known for its shared plates and delicious butter cake, before checking out the evening's live event at the **Egyptian Theatre,** which puts on plays, concerts, and other performances throughout the year. For your nightcap, we recommend a stiff cocktail at the elegant **St. Regis Bar.**

Chair lifts hoist skiers to the top of the slopes around Park City.

Day 2

Today's the day for outdoor adventures, no matter what season you visit. Start your day at **Deer Valley Grocery Cafe** with a coffee and a hearty breakfast. Then, if you're visiting in winter, head uphill at Deer Valley Resort or Park City Mountain for your first of many ski runs. There are lessons for beginners, of course, but you can also partake in other wintry activities like snow tubing or snowmobiling if you're hesitant to ski or snowboard. And if you're in town when there's no snow on the ground, you can still spend the morning on the mountain—trek one of the many scenic hiking paths, go mountain biking, or simply take a scenic ride on the lifts.

For a casual lunch, grab soup, a salad, a sandwich, or pizza at the laid-back **Silver Star Cafe,** or if you were a big fan of High West, you can try their in-town location **High West Saloon,** the world's only ski-in distillery. Then go back into the great outdoors for a second round of outdoor activities. Avid skiers might wish to return to the slopes, but for those who desire a little variety, you can visit **Utah Olympic Park** for ziplining and bobsledding on the site of the 2002 Winter Olympics—both activities are available year-round. Other nonwinter options for afternoon excursions include fly fishing, rafting, and horseback riding, which are available through tour operators like **Destination Sports, North Forty Escapes,** and **Park City on the Fly,** among others.

Make a dinner reservation at Riverhorse on Main, an upscale yet relaxed American restaurant that's one of the most popular spots in town. On weekends, they often have live music. For after-dinner drinks, kick back and relax at **No Name Saloon & Grill** just down the street for a more raucous time.

Day 3

After your action-packed day yesterday, treat yourself to a relaxing morning. Grab a light breakfast and a coffee at

Aussie-inspired café **Five5Seeds** before heading to one of the many spas in town. Most of the major hotels have their own spas that are open to nonguests—we recommend the **Spa at Hotel Park City** and its Pure Indulgence treatment that combines a scrub, a soak, and a massage. But you can also try an independent day spa, like **Aura Spa & Boutique** or the **SYNC Float Center,** where you can unplug in a sensory deprivation tank.

Once you're blissed out, drive 30 minutes east for biscuits at **Woodland Biscuit Company**—trust us, it's worth it. There are delectable all-day breakfast sandwiches if you want something a little more robust than your prespa meal, or you can opt for a burger.

Wrap up your weekend getaway with a long scenic drive and an afternoon snowshoe trek or a hike, depending on the season. In the winter, head to Robert Redford's iconic **Sundance Mountain Resort,** where you can explore more than 6 miles of snowshoeing trails with views of Mt. Timpanogos. In the summer, continue past Sundance on Alpine Loop Scenic Byway, which is open from late May through late October, for one of the most beautiful drives in the Uinta-Wasatch-Cache National Forest, especially during fall foliage season. Make stops at **Timpanogos Cave National Monument** and **Cascade Springs** before driving back through Provo on your way to Salt Lake City.

Recommendations

Sights

Cascade Springs. ✉ *Cascade Scenic Dr., Provo, UT* ☎ *801/785–3563* 🌐 *www.gohebervalley.com* 🎟 *Free.*

Sundance Mountain Resort. ✉ *8841 Alpine Loop Scenic Byway, Sundance, UT* ☎ *801/225–4107* 🌐 *www.sundanceresort.com* 🎟 *Free.*

Timpanogos Cave National Monument. ✉ *2038 Alpine Loop Rd., American Fork, UT* ☎ *801/756–5239* 🌐 *www.nps.gov/tica* 🎟 *Free.*

Utah Olympic Park. ✉ *3419 Olympic Pkwy., Park City, UT* ☎ *435/658–4200* 🌐 *www.utaholympiclegacy.org* 🎟 *Tours $12.*

Restaurants

Deer Valley Grocery Cafe. [$] *Average main: $13* ✉ *1375 Deer Valley Dr., Park City, UT* ☎ *435/615–2400* 🌐 *www.deervalley.com.*

Five5 Seeds. [$] *Average main: $13* ✉ *1600 Snow Creek Dr., Park City, UT* ☎ *435/901–8242* 🌐 *www.five5eeds.com.*

Fletcher's. [$] *Average main: $15* ✉ *562 Main St., Park City, UT* ☎ *435/649–1111* 🌐 *www.fletcherspc.com* 🕐 *Closed Tues. and Wed.*

Riverhorse on Main. [$] *Average main: $19* ✉ *540 Main St., Park City, UT* ☎ *435/649–3536* 🌐 *www.riverhorseparkcity.com.*

Ruth's Diner. [$] *Average main: $7* ✉ *4160 Emigration Canyon Rd., Salt Lake City, UT* ☎ *801/582–5807* 🌐 *www.ruthsdiner.com.*

Silver Star Cafe. [$] *Average main: $12* ✉ *1825 Three Kings Dr., Park City, UT* ☎ *435/655–3456* 🌐 *www.thesilverstarcafe.com.*

Woodland Biscuit Company. [$] *Average main: $5* ✉ *2734 E. State Hwy. 35, Hideout, UT* ☎ *435/783–4202* 🌐 *www.woodlandbiscuitcompany.com.*

Coffee and Quick Bites

Atticus Coffee, Books & Teahouse. [$] *Average main: $7* ✉ *738 Main St., Park City, UT* ☎ *435/214–7241* 🌐 *www.atticustea.com.*

Hotels

The Lodge at Blue Sky. [$] *Rooms from: $999* ✉ *27649 Old Lincoln Hwy., Wanship, UT* ☎ *435/571–0349* 🌐 *www.aubergeresorts.com* 🍴 *No meals.*

Stein Eriksen Lodge Deer Valley. [$] *Rooms from: $360* ✉ *7700 Stein Way, Park City, UT* ☎ *844/207–8273* 🌐 *www.steinlodge.com* 🍴 *No meals.*

Washington School House. [$] *Rooms from: $509* ✉ *543 Park Ave., Park City, UT* ☎ *435/649–3800* 🌐 *www.washington-schoolhouse.com* 🍴 *No meals.*

Nightlife

High West Distillery. ✉ *27649 Old Lincoln Hwy., Wanship, UT* ☎ *435/649–8300* 🌐 *www.highwest.com.*

High West Saloon. ✉ *703 Park Ave., Park City, UT* ☎ *435/649–8300* 🌐 *www.highwest.com.*

No Name Saloon & Grill. ✉ *447 Main St., Park City, UT* ☎ *435/649–6667* 🌐 *www.nonamesaloon.net.*

Old Town Cellars. ✉ *408 Main St., Park City, UT* ☎ *435/649–3759* 🌐 *www.otcwines.com.*

St. Regis Bar. ✉ *St. Regis Deer Valley, 2300 Deer Valley Dr. E, Park City, UT* ☎ *435/940–5700* 🌐 *www.marriott.com.*

Performing Arts

Egyptian Theatre. ✉ *328 Main St., Park City, UT* ☎ *855/745–7469* 🌐 *www.egyptiantheatrecompany.org.*

Shopping

Aura Spa & Boutique. ✉ *405 Main St., Park City, UT* ☎ *435/658–2872* 🌐 *www.auraspaforthespirit.com.*

Spa at Hotel Park City. ✉ *2001 Park Ave., Park City, UT* ☎ *435/940–5080* 🌐 *www.hotelparkcity.com.*

SYNC Float Center. ✉ *1200 W. Lori La., Kamas, UT* ☎ *435/333–7962* 🌐 *www.syncfloat.com.*

Activities

Destination Sports. ✉ *1025 Empire Ave., Park City, UT* ☎ *435/649–8092* 🌐 *www.destinationsports.com* 🎟 *Rafting from $55.*

North Forty Escapes. ✉ *1 Stillman Ranch Rd., Oakley, UT* ☎ *435/640–3239* 🌐 *www.northfortyescapes.com* 🎟 *Skeet shooting ifrom $109.*

Park City on the Fly. ✉ *1109 Park Ave., Park City, UT* ☎ *435/649–6707* 🌐 *www.parkcityonthefly.com* 🎟 *Fishing from $295.*

Rapid City, the Black Hills, and the Badlands, SD

389 miles (approx. 6 hours) from Denver.

Rapid City, South Dakota, is best known for its proximity to Mt. Rushmore, but that's hardly the only reason it's been voted the most patriotic city in the United States. Nestled between Black Hills National Forest and Badlands National Park with a handful of monuments and additional national parks within an hour's drive, the city's charming downtown is home to the most presidential sculpture installation and the family-friendly atmosphere of area attractions set the scene for one of the most all-American weekends you'll find outside of the capital.

Planning

GETTING THERE AND BACK

The route from Denver to Rapid City is a solid six-hour drive, so you'll likely want to take the quickest possible path to maximize your time there, and that's via

One of South Dakota's most stunning drives takes you through Badlands National Park.

I–25 N from Denver. Halfway through Wyoming, make your first turn onto U.S. 18 E before veering off into South Dakota and making a second turn on SD 79 N.

INSPIRATION

Get into the Black Hills spirit by listening to the audiobook of *Deadwood* by National Book Award winner Pete Dexter on the way.

PIT STOPS

If you're making great time, consider a pit stop at the free Wyoming Pioneer Museum just 20 minutes off-route by staying on I–25 N for an additional 15 miles instead of turning onto U.S. 18 E.

WHEN TO GO

Unsurprisingly, summer is peak tourism season in Rapid City, where parks and wildlife are the star attractions, but the spring and fall shoulder seasons are equally beautiful and see a slight reduction in prices. Don't pass up winter visits, though, when already-low rates are even further reduced, and there's still plenty to see and do.

WHERE TO STAY

The Foothills Inn provides cozy rooms with a standard business-travel atmosphere that offers all the necessities without much fuss in downtown Rapid City. **Hotel Alex Johnson** offers a well-appointed, modern stay in a historic 1920s property just one block from Main Street. It comes complete with a salon, spa, pub, shops, and a rooftop bar. The Germanic Tudor–style architecture and Native American interior design inspire quick immersion into the region's two largest ethnic influences.

Day 1

Arrive in Rapid City in the early afternoon and check into a downtown hotel for a convenient home base. Drop your bags, freshen up, and walk a few minutes to **Kōl** for a late lunch from the restaurant's massive coal-fired oven. Try one of more than a dozen specialty pizzas like the Sausage Pistachio or Figgy, Piggy, Parm for a quick pick-me-up before exploring the downtown area.

Step outside and meander the surrounding blocks, where life-size bronzes of all former presidents, through Obama, are randomly scattered to honor the legacy of each American leader in the City of Presidents installation. Pop in and out of shops at will as you acquaint yourself with the downtown area, but be sure not to miss **Prairie Edge** for a sprawling showcase of Northern Plains Indian arts and heritage in a block-wide facility that serves as both a gallery and shopping venue offering authentic jewelry, books, music, art, and more. If you're craving more creativity, head to the free galleries at the **Dahl Arts Center** to explore contemporary works or, if you're more in the mood to dig into the past, check out the **Museum of Geology** for some free exploration of South Dakota mineralogy and paleontology, dinosaur fossils included.

Chow down on Rapid City flavors with dinner at **Murphy's Pub and Grill** where local ingredients produce hearty regional favorites like buffalo stew and buffalo meatloaf. Be sure to start with the restaurant's famous Dakota Pulled Pork Chips, hand-cut and topped with slow-roasted, red-wine pork and cheese. Feel free to pair a couple pints with your meal—you can walk back to your hotel.

Day 2

Start your day early at local favorite breakfast spot **Black Hills Bagels,** where more than 20 varieties of bagels range from cinnamon raisin to white chocolate chip and can be enhanced with an array of toppings on the build-your-own sandwich menu (or just choose from the five signature sandwiches if endless options aren't your thing). Take your breakfast sandwich to-go (consider grabbing something extra for the long morning ahead) and drive 30 minutes to **Mount Rushmore National Memorial.** The best photo ops here are in

the morning hours before the sun begins to add plenty of shadows to the massive presidential faces around noon, and crowds tend to be lighter the earlier you arrive. Aim to arrive by 8 and spend an hour walking the trails and snapping pics before hitting the road again by 9.

From here, it's just under an hour to **Custer State Park's** Wildlife Loop, where you'll enjoy spectacular natural scenery. Bighorn sheep, elk, prairie dogs, and more can be found along the 18-mile loop, but never leave your vehicle when you spot impressive creatures. The drive should take about an hour and a half, barring buffalo traffic jams (yes, that's real). The animals are most active in the morning and in late evening, so feel free to begin your day even earlier if you'd rather to arrive before 10.

Drive 30 minutes to **Crazy Horse Memorial** to spend an hour in the museum and checking out the impressive sculpture itself. You don't need to spend the extra cash or time on the optional bus ride to get a closer view; you'll get the picture with a standard visit and will be getting hungry for lunch, so hop back in the car and head 10 minutes north to the **Alpine Inn.** This is one of the region's best restaurants, and the lunch menu presents German favorites traditional to the area's early immigration. Start with the Black Forest Meat and Cheese Board before moving on to schnitzel, spaetzle, or The German Plate (bratwurst, potato salad, sauerkraut, red cabbage, and German bread).

The **South Dakota Air and Space Museum** is a 45-minute drive from here, giving you just enough time for about 1½ hours of exploring the free indoor exhibits and outdoor collection of aircraft before it closes at 4:30 in the off-peak season, or 6 if you visit in summer. Downtown Rapid City is just 20 minutes from here, and you'll want to head back to your hotel to shower and change before dinner.

Recharge from your busy day in style with an elegant steak dinner at **Delmonico Grill.** The steak for two is the signature splurge here, but there are plenty of other more sensibly sized rib-eye options available, along with a smattering of additional entrées, upscale burgers, and even vegetarian options. If you're somehow not starving, consider the honey bourbon steak tips with peppers and cornbread for a (somewhat) lighter taste of the house's specialty.

Day 3

Depending on your early morning energy level, walk or drive to the **Millstone Family Restaurant** for a satisfying country breakfast before starting your final day in Rapid City. Breakfast is so beloved here that it's served all day and includes an extensive array of omelets, waffles, pancakes, and more, but the skillets menu is most worth your attention. Simple tastes will appreciate the straightforward Corned Beef Hash Skillet while more decadent desires will lean toward the Rushmore Skillet, featuring ham and bacon over hash browns, eggs, and toast slathered in a creamy hollandaise sauce.

Plan to hit the road by 9 for the one-hour drive to **Badlands National Park,** where stunning geological formations are home to an array of ancient fossils and plenty of impressive creatures still roam the nearly quarter million acres of protected land. Spend a half hour at the visitor center checking out exhibits and the worthwhile film, then feel free to hit some of the moderate trails just beyond the center or head straight for the park's famous 30-mile Badlands Loop. This scenic drive includes 16 fabulous lookout spots, otherworldly rock formations, and plenty of opportunity for wildlife spotting, including the endangered and adorable black-footed ferret. Plan to spend about four hours in the park before heading back to downtown Rapid City, packing up, and hopping back on the road to head home by 4.

Recommendations

Sights

Badlands National Park. ✉ *Ben Reifel Visitor Center, 25216 Ben Reifel Rd., Interior, SD* ☎ *605/433–5361* ⊕ *www.nps.gov/badl/planyourvisit/index.htm* 🎟 *$15.*

Crazy Horse Memorial. ✉ *12151 Ave. of the Chiefs, Crazy Horse, SD* ☎ *605/673–4681* ⊕ *www.crazyhorsememorial.org* 🎟 *$12.*

Custer State Park. ✉ *13400 U.S. 16A, Custer, SD* ☎ *605/2237660* ⊕ *gfp.sd.gov/parks/detail/custer-state-park* 🎟 *$20 per vehicle.*

Dahl Arts Center. ✉ *713 7th St., Rapid City, SD* ☎ *605/394–4101* ⊕ *www.thedahl.org* 🎟 *Free* ⊗ *Closed Sun.*

Mount Rushmore National Memorial. ✉ *13000 SD 244, Keystone, SD* ☎ *605/574–2523* ⊕ *www.nps.gov/moru/planyourvisit/index.htm* 🎟 *Free.*

Museum of Geology. ✉ *501 E. St. Joseph St., Rapid City, SD* ☎ *605/394–2467* ⊕ *www.museum.sdsmt.edu* 🎟 *Free.*

South Dakota Air and Space Museum. ✉ *2890 Davis Dr., Ellsworth Air Force Base, SD* ☎ *605/385–5189* ⊕ *www.sdairandspacemuseum.com* 🎟 *Free* ⊗ *Closed Sun.*

Wyoming Pioneer Museum. ✉ *400 W. Center St., Douglas, WY* ☎ *307/358–9288* ⊕ *wyoparks.wyo.gov/index.php/places-to-go/wyoming-pioneer-museum* 🎟 *$6* ⊗ *Closed Sun. and Mon.*

Restaurants

Alpine Inn. $ *Average main: $13* ✉ *133 Main St., Hill City, SD* ☎ *605/574–2749* ⊕ *www.alpineinnhillcity.com.*

Black Hills Bagels. $ *Average main: $9* ✉ *913 Mt. Rushmore Rd., Rapid City, SD* ☎ *605/399–1277* ⊕ *www.blackhillsbagels.com.*

Delmonico Grill. $ *Average main: $9* ✉ *609 Main St., Rapid City, SD* ☎ *605/791–1664* ⊕ *www.delmonicogrill.com* ⊘ *Closed Sun.*

Kōl. $ *Average main: $15* ✉ *504 Mt. Rushmore Rd., Rapid City, SD* ☎ *605/791–1600* ⊕ *www.kolfired.com* ⊘ *Closed Mon.*

Millstone Family Restaurant. $ *Average main: $10* ✉ *1520 N. Lacrosse St., Rapid City, SD* ☎ *605/348–9022* ⊕ *www.bhmillstone.com.*

Murphy's Pub and Grill. $ *Average main: $10* ✉ *510 9th St., Rapid City, SD* ☎ *605/791–2244* ⊕ *www.murphyspubandgrill.com.*

Hotels

The Foothills Inn. $ *Rooms from: $250* ✉ *1625 N. Lacrosse St., Rapid City, SD* ☎ *605/348–5640* ⊕ *www.thefoothillsinn.com* ❮❮❯ *Free breakfast.*

Hotel Alex Johnson. $ *Rooms from: $173* ✉ *523 6th St., Rapid City, SD* ☎ *605/342–1210* ⊕ *www.alexjohnson.com* ❮❮❯ *No meals.*

Shopping

Prairie Edge. ✉ *606 Main St., Rapid City, SD* ☎ *605/342–3086* ⊕ *www.prairieedge.com* ⊘ *Closed Sun. and Mon.*

St. George and Zion National Park, UT

301 miles (approx. 4¼ hours) from Salt Lake City.

Spectacular parks ring the town of St. George, a desert outpost offering easy access to some of the finest rock-and-sand landscapes in southwest Utah. Zion National Park is under an hour away, with world-class scenery that's an unmissable highlight. Even closer to town are the hiking, biking, and horseback riding trails of Snow Canyon State Park, Sand Hollow State Park, and Gooseberry Mesa.

While many travelers use St. George as a starting point for wilderness trips, a weekend in town pays off with appealing dining, comfortable accommodations, and the chance to catch outdoor performances at the Tuacahn Theatre. Suntanned retirees rub shoulders with adventurous desert rats in St. George's cute, historic downtown, for an inviting scene that can be as rugged—or as relaxed—as you want.

Planning

GETTING THERE AND BACK

From Salt Lake City, it's a straight shot on I–15 S to downtown St. George.

INSPIRATION

Along the way, listen to an audiobook of *Desert Solitaire,* Edward Abbey's classic tale of life and adventure in the Utah desert.

WHEN TO GO

Temperatures soar into the 90s and above from June through September, which can be blissful if you're swimming in Sand Hollow Reservoir or keeping to the shade at midday. For all-day hikes, the milder months in early spring and late fall are the ideal time to visit. While winter temperatures can be cool—the average high in December is 52 degrees—plenty of sun means it's still a popular time to travel.

WHERE TO STAY

Campgrounds dot the terrain surrounding St. George, but one of the finest is the 31-site campground at Snow Canyon State Park, which has red-and-white striped sandstone cliffs for a backdrop. If

Southwestern Utah's most revered hiking destination is Zion National Park.

you'd rather sleep indoors, options range from cheaper chain hotels to golf resorts.

Spectacular views from guestrooms and the pool make the **Inn on the Cliff** a standout, and it's also a bargain at mid-range prices. Set off in the quiet of the desert is the more luxurious **Red Mountain Resort,** a spa with great access to hiking, biking, and golf.

Day 1

Shake off the road dust over cold brew coffee and lunch at **Xetava Gardens Café,** whose desert-toned architecture plays perfect harmony with the surrounding landscape. The café itself is a work of art, from the hand-carved double doors to a rosy pile of giant boulders in the center of the dining room. It's also part of the super-browsable **Kayenta Art Village,** a cluster of art galleries plus a red-rock, open-air labyrinth.

Instead of checking in to your hotel, head to nearby **Snow Canyon State Park,** a natural maze of lava cones, cactus, and sand dunes. Activities here include biking, climbing, and hiking—one favorite walk is the 1.2-mile Petrified Dunes Trail, which traverses a series of mounds that were once soft, shifting sand.

For dinner, head to **Wood Ash Rye** in downtown St. George, whose chefs prepare regionally sourced contemporary dishes and chic cocktails in an open kitchen. (The mozzarella salad is a standby that wins raves from regulars.) Should your trip coincide with an outdoor performance at the **Tuacahn Amphitheatre,** it's worth snagging tickets for a night under the stars. Lineups go from concerts to musical theater, but the location is just as good as whatever's on stage; 1,500-foot cliffs make a truly impressive backdrop.

Day 2

Start the morning cowboy-style at the down-home **Wagon Wheel Diner,** where locals come for thick sausage gravy poured onto oversize, house-baked buttermilk biscuits. It's ideal fuel for a day in and around **Zion National Park,** an extraordinary playground of soaring cliffs, deeply creased canyons, and hiking trails that are among southwestern Utah's great treasures.

The most popular hikes here can get crowded on weekend days, but fortunately the beauty goes way beyond the best-known areas. One gorgeous option is the 3-mile Watchman Trail, which leaves from a trailhead near the Zion Canyon Visitor Center and gives great views of the Springdale area. In spring, see blooming prickly pear cactus while switch-backing up the gradual slope; look up and you'll catch morning light on the sheer angle of Watchman spire.

By the time you're back to the trailhead, you'll be perfectly placed for a light lunch at **Café Soleil**—dine on the patio or grab a take-out sandwich for the drive into the park itself, following the Virgin River to **Zion National Park Lodge.** When the road ends, continue on foot along the Riverside Walk, a mostly flat trail with hanging gardens dangling high above the valley floor.

Throughout your time in Zion, watch for the tiny figures of rock climbers scaling impossible-looking cliffs. Even if you're not an expert alpinist, you can get a taste of that thrill by spending the afternoon with **Zion Adventures** at Eye of the Needle, located just outside Zion National Park. Metal rungs are fixed solidly into the stone, so you can venture into vertical playgrounds while secured into a climbing harness, and descend a 400-foot waterfall via a series of dramatic rappels.

Finish your afternoon hiking by dusk. That's when you should stop and watch the sunset, a dramatic show that brings out every hue of the multicolor sandstone cliffs. A great spot to catch sunset light is Canyon Junction Bridge, where you'll have views of Watchman Mountain and the Virgin River.

When the light fades, head back out of the park for dinner at **Zion Brewery,** whose gardenlike beer patio opens to the sky and surrounding cliffs. Along with a rotating cast of house-brewed beers, find burgers and pub favorites on the menu, plus a hearty buffalo meatloaf that's a standout favorite.

Day 3

Pick up pan dulce and coffee from **Neto's** as you head out for a final morning in the desert. Today, choose between single-track mountain biking at **Gooseberry Mesa** and a trip to **Sand Hollow State Park.**

If you're riding, enjoy your baked goods on the 22-minute drive east to Hurricane, the starting point for most trails on Gooseberry Mesa. You can rent a mountain bike at **Over the Edge,** which is also a great place to get tips on where to ride. (Advanced riders should consider the 24-mile Hurricane Rim Loop, a gorgeous trail that's earned kudos from the International Mountain Bike Association.)

If you'd rather tackle the terrain with the motorized boost of an ATV, visit Sand Hollow State Park for an adventure with **Zion Country Off-Road Tours.** Here, you'll find sand dunes to play in and open views across the surrounding sagebrush country. When you've had enough of dry land, cool off in Sand Hollow Reservoir, where a broad beach slopes to warm, super-swimmable water. There's also a scuba-diving park in the reservoir, where divers can spot a submerged airplane and other features.

Make your final meal in St. George a stop at the Peruvian rotisserie **Viva Chicken,** where tender, slow-cooked chicken comes with the creamy sauces that are hugely popular in Peru. (Salads and fresh juices are big here, too.)

Recommendations

👁 Sights

Gooseberry Mesa. ✉ *300 N. State St., Salt Lake City, UT* ☎ *800/200–1160* ⊕ *www. visitutah.com* 🏷 *Free.*

Sand Hollow State Park. ✉ *3351 Sand Hollow Rd., Hurricane, UT* ☎ *435/680–0715* ⊕ *stateparks.utah.gov/parks/sand-hollow* 🏷 *$15 per vehicle.*

Snow Canyon State Park. ✉ *1002 Snow Canyon Dr., Ivins, UT* ☎ *435/628–2255* ⊕ *stateparks.utah.gov/parks/snow-canyon* 🏷 *$10 per vehicle.*

Zion National Park. ✉ *Zion Canyon Visitor Center, Mount Carmel Hwy., Springdale, UT* ☎ *435/772–3256* ⊕ *www.nps.gov/zion/index.htm* 🏷 *$20.*

🍴 Restaurants

Café Soleil. 💲 *Average main: $8* ✉ *205 Zion Park Blvd., Springdale, UT* ☎ *435/772–0505* ⊕ *www.cafesoleilzionpark.com* 🕙 *No dinner.*

Viva Chicken. 💲 *Average main: $14* ✉ *1183 E. 100 S, St. George, UT* ☎ *435/628–8855* ⊕ *www.vivachicken.com.*

Wagon Wheel Diner. 💲 *Average main: $7* ✉ *2654 E. Red Cliffs Dr., St. George, UT* ☎ *435/652–4352* 🕙 *No dinner.*

Wood Ash Rye. 💲 *Average main: $26* ✉ *Advenire Hotel, 25 W. St. George Blvd., St. George, UT* ☎ *435/522–5020* ⊕ *www.theadvenirehotel.com.*

Xetava Gardens Café. 💲 *Average main: $16* ✉ *815 Coyote Gulch Ct., Ivins, UT* ☎ *435/656–0165* ⊕ *www.xetava.com.*

Zion Brewery. 💲 *Average main: $20* ✉ *142 N. Main St., St. George, UT* ☎ *435/673–7644* ⊕ *www.zionbrewery.com.*

☕ Coffee and Quick Bites

Neto's. 💲 *Average main: $6* ✉ *1091 N. Bluff St, St. George, UT* ☎ *435/216–1590.*

🛏 Hotels

Inn on the Cliff. 💲 *Rooms from: $179* ✉ *511 S. Airport Rd., St. George, UT* ☎ *435/216–5864* ⊕ *www.innonthecliff.com* 🍴 *Free breakfast.*

Red Mountain Resort. 💲 *Rooms from: $225* ✉ *1275 Red Mountain Circle, Ivins, UT* ☎ *435/673–4905* ⊕ *www.redmountainresort.com* 🍴 *No meals.*

Zion National Park Lodge. 💲 *Rooms from: $209* ✉ *1 Zion Lodge, Springdale, UT* ☎ *435/772–7700* ⊕ *www.zionlodge.com* 🍴 *No meals.*

🎭 Performing Arts

Tuacahn Center for the Arts. ✉ *1100 Tuacahn Dr., Ivins, UT* ☎ *435/652–3200* ⊕ *www.tuacahn.org.*

👜 Shopping

Kayenta Art Village. ✉ *851 Coyote Gulch Ct., Ivins, UT* ☎ *435/688–8535* ⊕ *www.coyotegulchartvillage.com.*

🏃 Activities

Over the Edge. ✉ *76 E. 100 S, Hurricane, UT* ☎ *435/635–5455* ⊕ *otesports.com* 🏷 *Rentals from $90.*

Zion Adventures. ✉ *36 Lion Blvd., Springdale, UT* ☎ *435/772–1001* ⊕ *www.zionadventures.com* 🏷 *Canyoneering from $159.*

Zion Country Off-Road Tours. ✉ *1437 S. 160 W, Hurricane, UT* ☎ *435/767–7956* ⊕ *www.zionatvjeeptours.com* 🏷 *Jeep tours from $250.*

Southwest and Northern Plains ST. GEORGE AND ZION NATIONAL PARK, UT

San Antonio, TX

197 miles (approx. 3 hours) from Houston, 273 miles (approx 4½ hours) from Dallas.

San Antonio has always been a fun destination, with its theme parties, its famous Riverwalk, and, of course, The Alamo. The last decade has seen increasing growth in tourism as the city increasingly focuses on culture, dining, and the arts, reinvigorating to some of the city's older districts. It would be easy to just eat your way through San Antonio and be happy, but you'll definitely want to check out some of the great museums, historical buildings, and even some of the fun tourist traps.

Planning

GETTING THERE AND BACK

San Antonio is a straight shot down I–30 W from Houston, clocking in at right around three hours for the journey.

INSPIRATION

There is no shortage of delightful songs about San Antonio, so make your own playlist before you go, and you'll be toe-tapping along to Bob Wills, Tanya Tucker, Alejandro Escovedo, Tish Hinojosa, Flaco Jimenezz, and more during your trip.

PIT STOPS

Make a pit stop at **Buc-ee's** in Luling, because you're pretty much required by Texas law to stop there for snacks and souvenirs.

WHEN TO GO

San Antonio is a great place to visit year-round, but the one holiday that it's really becoming known for is *Dia de los Muertos* (Day of the Dead). This weeklong celebration takes over the week after Halloween. Since this itinerary doesn't involve a lot of water activities, visiting during late fall and winter and spring will be more pleasant than the blistering heat of a Texas summer.

WHERE TO STAY

San Antonio boasts some of the nicest, most creative hotels around, thanks to its growing popularity as a weekend destination. That makes it a little harder to choose a hotel, but if you don't mind hotel-hopping, that's always an option. Consider staying your second night at **The Hotel Emma,** housed in the luxuriously restored former Pearl Brewery, and one of the anchors of the popular Pearl District. For options near the city center, **Hotel Valencia Riverwalk** and **Mokara Hotel & Spa** give ample opportunities to treat yourself in style.

Day 1

Once you reach San Antonio, start making your way north toward the city center on Probandt Street. From there you can grab a bite at **Burgerteca** for lunch, a place where the humble burger is elevated in surprising ways by traditional Mexican flavors. Try the mole fries, a chilaquiles burger, and wash it all down with an agua fresca. After lunch, grab coffee at **Halcyon Southtown** and pop into some of the art museums of the Southtown District. Find wonderful options for contemporary art at **Ruby City,** a highly acclaimed contemporary art museum that opened in 2019, as well as **Blue Star Contemporary** that includes a special gallery space for local student artists.

After a leisurely early afternoon, check into your accommodations, get settled, then head over to **Historic Market Square,** the largest Mexican market in San Antonio. The outdoor plaza stretches over three blocks where you'll find plenty of specialty and produce vendors. Even if you don't want to shop, you'll have fun just window shopping and taking in the area culture. There are plenty of places to eat in the area, but **La Margarita** will really do you right. Enjoy a two- or

In San Antonio, the Alamo is the most popular historic site in Texas.

three-margarita dinner over Gulf oysters and shrimp, enchiladas, and fajitas. After that dinner, you may be tempted to head to your room, but try to muster up a second wind and stroll over to **Mariachi Bar** for cold beers, stiff drinks (and tequila flights), and live music from Mariachi Oro y Plata every night of the week.

Day 2

Saturday may be a busy day to spend on San Antonio's famed Riverwalk, but being part of the bustling crowds is part of the fun. Though you'll be pretty busy today, if you want to, start off at one of the state's most historical sites, **The Alamo.** Get to know "a story bigger than Texas" through a guided tour, an audio tour, or by just walking around the grounds. After your time at the Alamo, it's probably close to lunch time, and the Riverwalk is calling.

Lunch time includes plenty of options; consider trying barbecue at **The County Line** or a gourmet sandwich or salad at **Boudro's Texas Bistro.** For Mexican food,

try **Casa Rio.** They've been around since 1946, so they know a thing or two about the cuisine. After lunch, head out to explore more of the Riverwalk. When you're ready, take a break to have fun at a real tourist trap (in a good way), **Dick's Last Resort.** The servers are funny, sarcastic, and they make for a great time while you enjoy drinks and an appetizer. If you're not up for drinks, experience a leisurely view of the Riverwalk on a boat tour from **Go Rio.** They offer 35-minute narrated cruises that help to connect visitors with the city's history, culture, and architecture.

You'll be spending this evening at the famed Pearl District, which has sprung up from the old Pearl Brewery. Make the difficult decision about where to eat before you head out (some places may need a reservation). For a more casual, healthy vibe try the menu at **Green** for the city's only 100% kosher vegetarian restaurant. A unique dining option is available at **Savor,** where advanced Culinary Institute of America students offer up three- or four-course meals that are delicious and educational. **Southerleigh** is another wonderful choice, thanks to its tasty Texas-based cuisine with a coastal flare and its on-site brewery that's bringing beer-making back to Pearl.

Day 3

Wake up and start your day fresh by visiting the **Pearl Farmers Market** early in the morning to pick up locally made products, food items, and produce. You may be tempted to eat there, and to linger a bit, and that's fine. If you'd rather grab breakfast nearby, however, **Bakery Lorraine** is a great bet for a beautiful, tasty meal, plus treat to take home. After breakfast, spend the morning and early afternoon visiting the wide array of museums in the San Antonio Museum District that surrounds Mahncke Park. Choose your own adventure by spending your time at just one museum, or try to squeeze in as many as you can before heading home. The **San Antonio Museum of Art** is in the Pearl District, so if you're museum-hopping and love art, make this largest collection of Latin American art in the country your first stop.

The **San Antonio Botanical Garden** recently celebrated its 40th anniversary with a $20 million expansion and renovation. Not only does it have the incredible flowers, trees, and plants you'd expect to see in a botanical garden, but you can also learn how to cook, grow your own food, and even make tasty cocktails in the outdoor garden kitchen. The **Japanese Tea Garden** is also a nice place for plant lovers looking for a bit of quiet reflection among the pathways, koi ponds, waterfall, and beautiful plant life. The **Witte Museum** is a good choice to experience a little bit of everything—Texas culture, nature, and science are all represented through a variety of exhibits. If you have kids with you, the **DoSeum** is a must-visit with

plenty of hands-on experiences to make learning memorable and fun.

After the museums, head further south to grab a late lunch before getting on the road. There are two great options in Southtown, both viable contenders for best Mexican food in San Antonio; you'll have to make the tough choice between **Rosario's** and **Queso Pan y Vino** on your own, but you can't go wrong, either way, as you say farewell to San Antonio, its food, its culture, and its people.

Recommendations

Sights

The Alamo. ⊠ 300 Alamo Plaza, San Antonio, TX ☎ 210/225–1391 ⊕ www.thealamo.org 🖾 Free.

Blue Star Contemporary. ⊠ Blue Star Arts Complex, 116 Blue Star, San Antonio, TX ☎ 210/227–6960 ⊕ www.bluestarcontemporary.org 🖾 Free ⊘ Closed Mon. and Tues.

DoSeum. ⊠ 2800 Broadway St., San Antonio, TX ☎ 210/212–4453 ⊕ www.thedoseum.org 🖾 $14.

Historic Market Square. ⊠ 514 W. Commerce St., San Antonio, TX ☎ 210/207–8600 ⊕ www.marketsquaresa.com 🖾 Free.

Japanese Tea Garden. ⊠ 3853 N. St. Mary's St., San Antonio, TX ☎ 210/559–3148 ⊕ www.saparksfoundation.org 🖾 Free.

Ruby City. ⊠ 150 Camp St., San Antonio, TX ☎ 210/227–8400 ⊕ www.rubycity.org 🖾 Free ⊘ Closed Mon.–Wed.

San Antonio Botanical Garden. ⊠ 555 Funston Pl., San Antonio, TX ☎ 210/536–1400 ⊕ www.sabot.org 🖾 $12.

San Antonio Museum of Art. ⊠ 200 W. Jones Ave., San Antonio, TX ☎ 210/978–8100 ⊕ www.samuseum.org 🖾 $20 ⊘ Closed Mon.

Witte Museum. ✉ *3801 Broadway St., San Antonio, TX* ☎ *210/357–1900* 🌐 *www.wittemuseum.org* 🎟 *$14.*

🍴 Restaurants

Bakery Lorraine. [$] *Average main: $8* ✉ *306 Pearl Parkway #110, San Antonio, TX* ☎ *210/862–5582* 🌐 *www.bakerylorraine.com*

Boudro's Texas Bistro. [$] *Average main: $25* ✉ *421 E. Commerce St., San Antonio, TX* ☎ *210/224–8484* 🌐 *www.boudros.com.*

Burgerteca. [$] *Average main: $12* ✉ *403 Blue Star, San Antonio, TX* ☎ *210/635–0016* 🌐 *www.chefjohnnyhernandez.com.*

The County Line. [$] *Average main: $16* ✉ *111 W. Crockett St. #104, San Antonio, TX* ☎ *210/229–1941* 🌐 *www.countyline.com.*

Green. [$] *Average main: $10* ✉ *Pearl Brewery, 200 E. Grayson St., San Antonio, TX* ☎ *210/320–5865* 🌐 *www.eatatgreen.com* 🕒 *Closed Sat.*

La Margarita. [$] *Average main: $11* ✉ *120 Produce Row, San Antonio, TX* ☎ *210/227–7140* 🌐 *www.lamargarita.com.*

Queso Pan y Vino. [$] *Average main: $10* ✉ *727 S. Alamo St., San Antonio, TX* ☎ *210/263–9729* 🌐 *www.facebook.com/qpvsa* 🕒 *Closed Sun. and Mon.*

Rosario's. [$] *Average main: $13* ✉ *9715 San Pedro Ave., San Antonio, TX* ☎ *210/481–4100* 🌐 *www.rosariossa.com* 🕒 *Closed Sun.*

Savor. [$] *Average main: $16* ✉ *116 Isleta St., San Antonio, TX* ☎ *210/554–6484* 🌐 *www.ciarestaurantgroup.com.*

Southerleigh. [$] *Average main: $16* ✉ *136 E. Grayson St., San Antonio, TX* ☎ *210/455–5701* 🌐 *www.southerleigh.com.*

☕ Coffee and Quick Bites

Halcyon Southtown. [$] *Average main: $12* ✉ *1414 S. Alamo St., San Antonio, TX* ☎ *210/277–7045* 🌐 *www.halcyoncoffeebar.com.*

🛏 Hotels

Hotel Emma. [$] *Rooms from: $345* ✉ *136 E. Grayson St., San Antonio, TX* ☎ *210/448–8300* 🌐 *www.thehotelemma.com* 🍽 *No meals.*

Hotel Valencia Riverwalk. [$] *Rooms from: $187* ✉ *150 E. Houston St., San Antonio, TX* ☎ *210/227–9700* 🌐 *www.hotelvalencia-riverwalk.com* 🍽 *No meals.*

Mokara Hotel & Spa. [$] *Rooms from: $259* ✉ *212 W. Crockett St., San Antonio, TX* ☎ *210/396–5800* 🌐 *www.omnihotels.com* 🍽 *No meals.*

🍸 Nightlife

Dick's Last Resort. ✉ *223 Losoya St., San Antonio, TX* ☎ *210/224–0026* 🌐 *www.dickslastresort.com.*

Mariachi Bar. ✉ *218 Produce Row, San Antonio, TX* ☎ *210/225–1262* 🌐 *www.mariachibar.com.*

🛍 Shopping

Buc-ee's. ✉ *2760 I-35, New Braunfels, TX* ☎ *979/238–6390* 🌐 *www.buc-ees.com.*

Pearl Farmers Market. ✉ *312 Pearl Pkwy., San Antonio, TX* ☎ *210/212–7260* 🌐 *www.atpearl.com.*

🏃 Activities

Go Rio. ✉ *809 River Walk St., San Antonio, TX* ☎ *210/227–4746* 🌐 *www.goriocruises.com* 🎟 *Cruises $14.*

Santa Fe and Taos, NM

64 miles (approx. 1 hour) from Albuquerque, 356 miles (approx. 6 hours) from Denver.

A hub of art and culture, Santa Fe is the oldest continuously inhabited city in the United States, with most of the downtown designated as a historic district. The distinct adobo architecture, bustling street markets, and unique blend of Spanish and Native American make it a fascinating place to explore. It's also a great base for trips into the Sangre de Cristo Mountains.

While typically thought of as a ski destination, Taos is much more than just a sleepy resort town. Home to one of America's leading art colonies and tons of native tradition, it's well worth a few hours to experience the unique culture. Here's how to experience the best of the Southwest with a weekend in Santa Fe and Taos.

Planning

GETTING THERE AND BACK

It's a quick hour-long drive from Albuquerque to Santa Fe northeast on I–25. From Denver to Santa Fe, it's a six-hour drive south on I–25. If you add a stop in Taos, the detour takes about 30 minutes on U.S. 160 W.

PIT STOPS

No matter which route you take, you can stop in Colorado Springs to feed the giraffes at **Cheyenne Mountain Zoo** or in Pueblo to stretch your legs along the **Historic Arkansas Riverwalk.**

WHEN TO GO

Santa Fe is a year-round destination, albeit summer in the desert can get very hot. Fall is the most popular time to visit as the weather is milder, and the Albuquerque Balloon Fiesta is a big draw.

WHERE TO STAY

The **Inn of the Five Graces** is a luxurious adobo villa with a soothing east-meets-west vibe. Trinkets from the Silk Road contrast with Spanish touches, creating a unique Southwest sanctuary. For a more affordable escape, **Hotel Santa Fe Hacienda & Spa** is a rustic-chic retreat with plenty of Native American touches. Santa Fe also has glamping casitas, yurts, and tipis for the photo inclined.

Day 1

It's a 4½-hour drive from Denver to Taos, so if you leave early you can make it by lunchtime. Get your first taste of New Mexico's regional fare at **La Cueva Café.** Lunch and brunch favorites like hatch chile rellenos and chicken mole enchiladas are characterized by an abundance of flavors and colors. Now that you've satisfied the hunger pangs, it's time to tour **Taos Pueblo,** the shining jewel of the state. Both a UNESCO World Heritage Site and a National Historic Landmark, it's one of the oldest continuously inhabited areas of the United States. Take a guided tour of the millennia-old adobe buildings, sample some tasty fry bread, and shop for handmade art and jewelry.

While in Taos, you'll also want to pay a visit to the **Ghost Ranch** to see the multicolor canyons and cliffs that inspired painter Georgia O'Keeffe. You can hike the paths, saddle up for a trail ride, and, if you have time, take a meditation class to find your om. Once you've worked up an appetite, fuel up with authentic Southwest fare like stuffed sopapillas at **Michael's Kitchen.** The casual family eatery produces 50 gallons of red and green chile sauce a day, which is just one of the reasons they've been a local landmark since the 1970s.

Jump back in the car, and in another hour and a half you'll have made it to Santa Fe for the night.

The adobe buildings at Taos Pueblo have been continuously inhabited for more than 1,000 years.

Day 2

The pulse of Santa Fe is notably slower, so enjoy a leisurely start the day at **Cafe Pasqual's.** The go-to brunch spot has hand-painted tiles and colorful murals that make it resemble an art gallery. The smoked trout hash and huevos motulenos (eggs sautéed with banana, salsa, and feta) are crowd-pleasers for their surprising flavor profiles. When you're ready, make your way around **Santa Fe Plaza,** the town's main square and its heart and soul. As the country's third-largest art market, the entire plaza is essentially one massive indoor/outdoor gallery with more than 300 vendors.

Depending on your level of shopping enthusiasm, you could spend all day scouring for treasures. If you'd prefer not to explore alone, guided tram rides and walking tours give you an introduction to the area's Native American art and culture. Keep your eyes peeled, as there's always a festival or parade taking place. Settle in for lunch at **The Shed,** a James

Beard award winner for its classic, timeless traditions. You can stick to lighter bites like posole and salads, or fill up on a cravable carne plate to ensure you have enough energy for the rest of the day.

The art enthusiasts should spend the afternoon meandering **Canyon Road,** which has more than 100 galleries and studios in a half-mile. For the history lovers, Museum Hill has four iconic cultural institutions: the **Museum of Indian Arts and Culture,** the **Wheelwright Museum of the American Indian,** the **Museum of Spanish Colonial Art,** and the renowned **International Folk Art Museum.** If you'd rather take advantage of the landscape, **Santa Fe National Forest** has more than 1,000 miles of hiking, biking, and horseback riding trails.

When it's time to unwind, grab a bite and a brew at The Railyard, an entertainment district that's one of the city's newest hotspots. Grab some pub grub from **Second Street Brewery,** then catch some live music or check out an indie flick at the **Violet Crown,** a cinema that also has 30 beers on tap and a full café menu.

Day 3

A Santa Fe staple, **The Pantry** has been dishing up cozy Southwest comfort food for decades. Fill up on one last good meal of beef brisket or green chile before heading out. Spend the morning deciphering the mystery that is **Meow Wolf,** Santa Fe's most befuddling attraction. Part immersive art installation, part murder mystery, the "House of Eternal Return," is a multimedia sensory experience. But be warned: you'll leave with more questions than answers.

If you have time before you leave, swing by the **Puye Cliff Dwellings.** A National Historic Landmark, the abandoned pueblo ruins offer one last parting look at Native American life before hitting the road.

Recommendations

👁 Sights

Ghost Ranch. ✉ *280 Private Dr. 1708, Abiquiu, NM* ☎ *505/685–1000* 🌐 *www.ghostranch.org* 🎫 *$100.*

International Folk Art Museum. ✉ *Museum Hill, 706 Camino Lejo, Santa Fe, NM* ☎ *505/476–1200* 🌐 *www.internationalfolkart.org* 🎫 *$12.*

Meow Wolf. ✉ *1352 Rufina Circle, Santa Fe, NM* ☎ *505/395–6369* 🌐 *www.meowwolf.com* 🎫 *$25.*

Museum of Indian Arts and Culture. ✉ *710 Camino Lejo, Santa Fe, NM* ☎ *505/476–1269* 🌐 *www.miaclab.org* 🎫 *$12* 🕒 *Closed Mon.*

Museum of Spanish Colonial Art. ✉ *750 Camino Lejo, Santa Fe, NM* ☎ *505/982–2226* 🌐 *www.spanishcolonial.org* 🎫 *$10.*

Puye Cliff Dwellings. ✉ *Puye Visitor Center, Santa Clara Canyon Rd., Española, NM* ☎ *505/917–6650* 🌐 *www.puyecliffdwellings.com* 🎫 *$20.*

Santa Fe National Forest. ✉ *11 Forest La., Santa Fe, NM* ☎ *505/438–5300* 🌐 *www.fs.usda.gov/santafe* 🎫 *Free.*

Santa Fe Plaza. ✉ *63 Lincoln Ave., Santa Fe, NM* ☎ *505/955–6200* 🌐 *www.santafe.org* 🎫 *Free.*

Taos Pueblo. ✉ *120 Veterans Hwy., Taos, New Mexico* ☎ *575/758–1028* 🌐 *www.taospueblo.com* 🎫 *$16.*

Wheelwright Museum of the American Indian. ✉ *704 Camino Lejo, Santa Fe NM* ☎ *505/982–4636* 🌐 *www.wheelwright.org* 🎫 *$8.*

🍴 Restaurants

Cafe Pasqual's. [$] *Average main: $18* ✉ *121 Don Gaspar, Santa Fe, NM* ☎ *505/983–9340* 🌐 *www.pasquals.com.*

La Cueva Café. [$] *Average main: $12* ✉ *135 Paseo Del Pueblo Sur, Taos, NM* ☎ *575/758–7001* 🌐 *www.lacuevacafe.com* 🕒 *Closed Sun.*

Michael's Kitchen. [$] *Average main: $20* ✉ *304-C N. Pueblo Rd., Taos, NM* ☎ *575/758–4178* 🌐 *www.michaelskitchen.com* 🕒 *No dinner.*

The Pantry. [$] *Average main: $12* ✉ *1820 Cerrillos Rd., Santa Fe, NM* ☎ *505/986–0022* 🌐 *www.pantrysantafe.com.*

Second Street Brewery. [$] *Average main: $15* ✉ *2920 Rufina St., Santa Fe, NM* ☎ *505/954–1068* 🌐 *www.secondstreetbrewery.com.*

The Shed. [$] *Average main: $13* ✉ *113½ E. Palace Ave., Santa Fe, NM* ☎ *505/982–9030* 🌐 *www.sfshed.com* 🕒 *Closed Sun.*

🛏 Hotels

Hotel Santa Fe Hacienda & Spa. [$] *Rooms from: $220* ✉ *1501 Paseo de Peralta, Santa Fe, NM* ☎ *855/825–9876* 🌐 *www.*

hotelsantafe.com/sleep/hacienda-santa-fe
🍽 *No meals.*

Inn of the Five Graces. 💲 *Rooms from: $425* ✉ *150 E. De Vargas St., Santa Fe, NM* ☎ *505/992–0957* ⊕ *www.fivegraces. com* 🍽 *Free breakfast.*

ⓨ Nightlife

Violet Crown. ✉ *1606 Alcaldesa St., Santa Fe, NM* ☎ *505/216–5678.*

Sedona, AZ

116 miles (approx. 3 hours) from Phoenix, 351 miles (approx. 5½ hours) from Albuquerque.

Sedona's otherworldly landscapes attract spirituality seekers from around the world. Some believe the area is an energy vortex, and you could spend a weekend here just stocking up on crystals, joining healing ceremonies, and peering into the future. But the area is also an extraordinary playground for nature lovers, with desert canyons and stunning red mesas spreading out in every direction. While you'll find rugged adventure throughout the Southwest, Sedona also has a luxurious side that most other trail towns can't match, including tranquil spas that make for the perfect escape from daily life.

An hour and a half away, the town of Prescott is waiting to bring you back down earth. It's all about breezy pine forests and frontier history, plus a beautiful downtown that invites leisurely strolling.

Planning

GETTING THERE AND BACK
Take I–17 N from Phoenix for most of the journey, switching to Highway 179 N for the last half hour. From Albuquerque, take I–40 E.

PIT STOPS
Pause along the way in the ghost town of Bumble Bee, which was once a stagecoach stop on the historic Prescott–Phoenix route. If you're coming from Albuquerque, stretch your legs at the psychedelic wonderland of **Petrified Forest National Park,** where trees have been fossilized by rainbow-hued minerals.

WHEN TO GO
Spring wildflowers and mild weather from March to May make this a popular time to visit. Temperatures spike in the summer months, but then things cool back down in September, October, and November, bringing plenty of sun and great hiking conditions. Winter highs are only in the 50s and 60s, but uncrowded trails and lower rates mean it's still worth the trip.

WHERE TO STAY
Accommodations in Sedona tend to be pricey, with most budget-friendly options limited to motels along the main strip. An appealing alternative is a cabin at **The Canyon Wren,** a rustic, quiet property near Oak Creek Canyon. Located on Airport Mesa, **Sky Ranch Lodge** has gorgeous views of the desert from private patios that are worth paying extra for.

Day 1

It would be a shame to spend your first hours in Sedona cooped up indoors; fortunately, the teensy **Sedona Memories** bakery and café has all your picnic needs covered. Call in an order for a hefty sandwich on house-baked bread—you might want to throw in a cookie—and you'll be on the road in no time.

The perfect lunch spot is just up the road at **Midgley Bridge Picnic Area,** where you'll have views of Mitten Ridge and the tip of Oak Creek Canyon. If it's a hot day, this doubles as a place to cool off. A trail from the parking lot winds down below the bridge to Oak Creek, a 15-minute

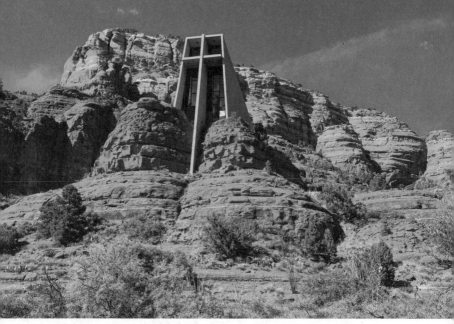

Near Sedona, the Chapel of the Holy Cross is built on the side of a 1,000-foot rock wall.

hike that pays off with a gorgeous place to swim.

Flanked in red rocks and green trees, Oak Creek Canyon is among the most popular hiking spots in Sedona. West Fork Trail, 9 miles north of Midgley Bridge, is a justifiably beloved walk that hops back and forth across the west fork of Oak Creek until the canyon walls close in just past the 7 mile point.

After your hike, head back into town via the **Sedona Arts Center,** a gallery featuring the work of local artists. It's also a hub of First Friday events each month, with a free shuttle taking you to galleries around town.

From there, it's just a short drive to dinner at **The Hudson,** where an outdoor patio has some of the area's finest sunset views. Craft cocktails pair nicely with a vaguely Southwestern menu featuring specialties like prickly pear baby back ribs.

Day 2

Set an alarm for the predawn hours: it's worth it to catch sunrise at the remarkable **Chapel of the Holy Cross,** a modernist landmark built in 1956 on the side of a 1,000-foot rock wall. (If you'd rather come when the church itself is open, visit a little later in the day.)

Once the early colors fade, head back into town for breakfast at the appealingly kitschy **Coffee Pot Restaurant,** known for great huevos rancheros, hefty omelets, and lofty, house-made biscuits. Just north of here is Coffee Pot Rock, a red-rock formation that's a dead ringer for an old-fashioned percolator.

Rent a pair of wheels from **Over the Edge Bikes** or **Absolute Bikes.** Both places have experts who can advise you on the best trails to start exploring. One beginner-friendly option is the 2-mile Big Park Loop Mountain Bike Trail, which will get you out among the rock formations without the tougher sections found on other Sedona-area rides.

For something a little more challenging, check out the 13-mile West Sedona Tour, a series of linked trails that include a few rocky patches requiring some dexterous moves. A good alternative to exploring on your own are the excellent mountain bike tours from **360 Adventures** or **Hermosa Tours.**

When you're ready for a light lunch, head to **Local Juicery,** which has colorful salads, raw bowls, and an eclectic array of smoothies. It's a virtuous way to kick off an afternoon at one of Sedona's many spas: One favorite is **Mii amo,** where outdoor pools have views across the rock walls of Boynton Canyon. Services here run from classic massages to quirkier experiences that draw on Sedona's spiritual side: interactive aura photography, crystal grotto blessings, or past-life regressions.

If you can tear yourself away from the spa, make a sunset trip to Airport Mesa, one of the main vortex sites around Sedona. Evening light is a major draw here, and it's fun to join the crowd that shows up for the event—decide for yourself whether you're feeling that energy.

The throng lends a holiday feel to the nearby **Mesa Grill,** where you can catch the last, lingering rays of light as you dine by a fire pit on the outdoor patio. Excellent margaritas and local craft beers whet your appetite for a menu of pub food spiked with plenty of vegetables. Stick around after dark for a stargazing outing with **Evening Sky Tours,** which gets you access to a high-powered telescope.

Day 3

Check out early, then hit the road to spend your final morning in Prescott, picking up beverages at **Creekside Coffee** on your way out of town. By the time you get to Prescott, you'll be ready for a

cowboy-style breakfast at the **Lone Spur Café,** whose booths are illuminated by giant antler chandeliers that lend the diner an Old-West flair.

On weekend mornings, local volunteers lead free walking tours of the town's fascinating historic district, spilling details of the saloons, statues, and memorials you'll find there. Visit the town's excellent **Sharlot Hall Museum,** named for a self-educated frontier woman who worked to preserve Arizona history at the turn of the 20th century. The 4-acre museum includes the 1864 Governor's Mansion, a classic stagecoach, and exhibits on Native American burden baskets.

Before heading home, make a final lunch stop at **The Palace,** a saloon that first opened in 1877. It's a local legend: during the Whiskey Row Fire in 1900, the saloon went up in flames, but patrons carried the beautifully carved bar away to safety. Find a spot at that very same bar for a bowl of corn chowder or a buffalo burger.

Recommendations

Sights

Chapel of the Holy Cross. ⊠ 780 Chapel Rd., Sedona, AZ ☎ 928/282–4069 ⊕ www.chapeloftheholycross.com.

Midgley Bridge Picnic Area. ⊠ Rte. 89A, 1½ miles north of Sedona, AZ ☎ 928/203–2900 ☒ Red Rock day pass $5.

Petrified Forest National Park. ⊠ 1 Park Rd., Petrified Forest National Park ☎ 928/524–6228 ⊕ www.nps.gov/pefo ☒ $5.

Sedona Arts Center. ⊠ 15 Art Barn Rd., Sedona, AZ ☎ 928/282–3809 ⊕ www.sedonaartscenter.com ☒ Free ⊗ Closed Mon.–Thurs.

Sharlot Hall Museum. ⊠ 415 W. Gurley St., Prescott, AZ ☎ 928/445–3122 ⊕ www.sharlothallmuseum.org ☒ $12 ⊗ Closed Mon.

🍴 Restaurants

Coffee Pot Restaurant. [$] *Average main: $8* ✉ *2050 W. Rte. 89A, Sedona, AZ* ☎ *928/282–6626* ⏲ *No dinner.*

The Hudson. [$] *Average main: $30* ✉ *Hillside Shopping Center, 671 Rte. 179, Sedona, AZ* ☎ *928/862–4099* 🌐 *www.thehudsonsedona.com.*

Local Juicery. [$] *Average main: $10* ✉ *3150 W. Rte. 89A, Sedona, AZ* ☎ *928/282–8932* 🌐 *www.localjuicery.com.*

Lone Spur Café. [$] *Average main: $10* ✉ *106 W. Gurley St., Prescott, AZ* ☎ *928/445–8202* 🌐 *www.lonespurcafe.com* ⏲ *No dinner.*

Mesa Grill. [$] *Average main: $23* ✉ *1185 Airport Rd., Sedona, AZ* ☎ *928/282–2400* 🌐 *www.mesagrillsedona.com.*

The Palace. [$] *Average main: $28* ✉ *120 S. Montezuma St., Prescott, AZ* ☎ *928/541–1996* 🌐 *www.whiskeyrowpalace.com.*

Sedona Memories. [$] *Average main: $9* ✉ *321 Jordan Rd., Sedona, AZ* ☎ *928/282–0032* ⏲ *No dinner.*

☕ Coffee and Quick Bites

Creekside Coffee. [$] *Average main: $6* ✉ *251 SR 179, Suite C2, Sedona, AZ* ☎ *928/955–9888* 🌐 *www.creekside.coffee* ⏲ *No dinner.*

🛏 Hotels

The Canyon Wren. [$] *Rooms from: $185* ✉ *6425 N. AZ 89A, Sedona, AZ* ☎ *928/282–6900* 🌐 *www.canyonwrencabins.com* 🍽 *Free breakfast.*

Sky Ranch Lodge. [$] *Rooms from: $200* ✉ *1105 Airport Rd., Sedona, AZ* ☎ *928/282–6400* 🌐 *www.skyranchlodge.com* 🍽 *No meals.*

🏃 Activities

Absolute Bikes. ✉ *6101 Rte. 179, Suite B, Oak Creek, Sedona, AZ* ☎ *928/284–1242* 🌐 *www.absolutebikes.net* 🎫 *From $40.*

Evening Sky Tours. ✉ *Sedona, AZ* ☎ *928/203–0006* 🌐 *www.eveningskytours.com* 🎫 *From $117.*

Hermosa Tours. ✉ *Over the Edge Bike Shop, 1695 Rte. 89A, Sedona, AZ* ☎ *877/765–5682* 🌐 *www.hermosatours.net* 🎫 *From $180.*

Mii amo. ✉ *525 Boynton Canyon Rd., Sedona, AZ* ☎ *928/203–8500* 🌐 *www.miiamo.com* 🎫 *From $165.*

Over the Edge Bikes. ✉ *1695 Rte. 89A, Sedona, AZ* ☎ *928/282–1106* 🌐 *www.otesports.com* 🎫 *From $95.*

360 Adventures. ✉ *Sedona, AZ* ☎ *480/722–0360* 🌐 *www.360-adventures.com* 🎫 *From $205.*

South Padre Island, TX

377 miles (approx. 6 hours) from Houston.

Though its reputation as a Spring Break destination tends to be the first thing that Texans think about when they hear South Padre Island, there's a whole lot more to this fun and friendly coastal town. South Padre likes to boast about its warm weather and nearly 300 days of sunshine a year, making outdoor activities the perfect bet at this coastal destination. The cleanliness of the Gulf water in this area is also a big draw, and frequent dolphin sightings are just one of the many ways you can get to know the wildlife of the area better.

Planning

GETTING THERE AND BACK

You'll keep your drive at just under six hours if you don't linger too long at stops and take the U.S. 59 S and U.S. 77 S route.

WHEN TO GO

If you don't want to party like a spring breaker, you'll want to avoid the island during March, when it becomes a hedonistic paradise for college crowds. Highs in the southerly island rarely dip below the low 70s, making it a good place to visit year-round.

WHERE TO STAY

For a relaxing experience, **Pearl South Padre Beachfront Resort** is a great choice, complete with spa, restaurants (including a swim-up bar), and a kids camp. The **Isla Grand Beach Resort** is another good option, with tennis courts, golfing, two huge pools, and dining with live music. **La Copa Inn** is a more affordable version of these resorts that includes a pool and a boardwalk to the beach.

Day 1

Heading in from Houston, you should arrive at South Padre Island around lunchtime. Before grabbing a bite, stop at the **Port Isabel Lighthouse** to experience panoramic views of the area you're about to visit. On a clear day, you can see up to 16 miles in any direction. Once you're back in the car, cross over the Queen Isabella Causeway and head straight to **Dirty Al's** to see if their claims to fame really stack up: "best seafood on South Padre Island" and "world's best fried shrimp" are pretty tall orders, but Dirty Al's doesn't disappoint; neither does the cold beer and beautiful harbor views.

Some of South Padre's most famous residents are its sea turtles and starting off your trip with a quick visit to **Sea Turtle Inc.** to learn about their local rescue and rehabilitation efforts is a great way to get to know them. Arrive around 2 to explore the facility on a self-guided tour, then head to the rehabilitation center to watch some enrichment feeding at 3 pm. You should be finishing up just in time to check into your accommodations and freshen up for happy hour and dinner.

First stop when heading back out: **Padre Island Brewing Company** for a locally brewed craft beer and a great happy hour. This is your place to indulge in Gulf oysters (when in season) and inexpensive craft beer while lounging on the large patio. After a couple of beers, move on to **Sea Ranch Restaurant** to linger over a late dinner of fish, seafood, steaks, and cocktails. After a busy day, hit the hay and get ready for an even busier day to follow.

Day 2

Start an active day off with a big, Texas-size breakfast at **Pier 19** and treat yourself to their famous giant cinnamon rolls, omelets, or huevos rancheros along with well-priced mimosas and bloody marys. Be sure to keep your eyes on the water, as dolphins enjoy playing in this area. After that heavy breakfast, but before you hit the beach to enjoy your day, make a pit stop at the small counter restaurant, **Ceviche Ceviche,** to build your own ceviche bowl, then stick it in a cooler to enjoy for a beach lunch later.

Now is the time to choose your beach spot, and **Isla Blanca Park** at the southern part of the island is always a great bet, with concessions, facilities, and a fishing area, it's great for families. However, if you want to end your day with a Turbo Pina Colada in hand as you watch the sunset, set up your spot in front of **Wanna Wanna Beach Bar** a bit farther north. If you're still feeling beachy, grab dinner there at Wanna Wanna, but if you want to treat yourself to one of the best dining experiences on the island, get cleaned up

The gentle waters of the Gulf of Mexico lap the shores of South Padre Island.

and grab a table at **F&B,** where the food looks as good as it tastes.

If you still have some energy after that long day, South Padre is definitely a good place for nightlife. There are plenty of options for live music, mariachi bands, and nightclubs. **Louie's Backyard** is always a great choice, with a vibrant atmosphere and the famous Charlie's Cherry drink.

Day 3

Eggs Benedict, french toast, and some killer iced coffee awaits at **Yummies Bistro**, the perfect place to fuel up before starting your day. After breakfast, pop into **South Padre Island Dolphin Research & Sealife Nature Center** to get up close and personal with a variety of rescue animals including turtles, iguanas, and non-native fish, as well as the dolphins through their bay view education center.

Ready to get back in the ocean? Of course you are, that's why you chose South Padre Island. Instead of spending your last day relaxing, get a little wild and try booking a fun ocean activity for the late morning. There are plenty of things to choose from ranging from a banana boat ride from **Parrot Eyes Watersports** to something a bit more daring like parasailing at **Sonny's Beach Service.** Grab lunch at a local favorite, **Chillito Pikin,** for authentic Mexican and Tex-Mex food. If you have kids, head to the **Beach Park at Isla Blanca** water park for the day (enjoy lunch and cocktails there, as well). If you want to squeeze in one more activity before heading home, a sunset cruise will certainly leave a beautiful, lasting memory of your trip.

Recommendations

Sights

Beach Park at Isla Blanca. ✉ *33261 State Park Rd. 100, South Padre Island, TX* ☎ *956/772–7873* ⊕ *www.beachparktx. com* 🎟 *$44.*

Isla Blanca Park. ✉ *33174 State Park Rd. 100, South Padre Island, TX* ☎ *956/761–5494* 🌐 *www.cameroncounty.us* 🎟 *$12 per car.*

Port Isabel Lighthouse. ✉ *421 E. Queen Isabella Blvd., Port Isabel, TX* ☎ *956/943–7602* 🌐 *www.portisabelmuseums.com* 🎟 *$4.*

Sea Turtle Inc. ✉ *6617 Padre Blvd., South Padre Island, TX* ☎ *956/761–4511* 🌐 *www.seaturtleinc.org* 🎟 *$10* 🕒 *Closed Mon.*

South Padre Island Dolphin Research & Sealife Nature Center. ✉ *TX 100, Port Isabel, TX* ☎ *956/299–1957* 🌐 *www.spinaturecenter.com* 🎟 *$3.*

🍴 Restaurants

Ceviche Ceviche. [$] *Average main: $10.* ✉ *1004 Padre Blvd., South Padre Island, TX* ☎ *956/772–1555* 🌐 *www.facebook.com/cevichecevichesouthpadreisland.*

Chillito Pikin. [$] *Average main: $14* ✉ *3305 Padre Blvd., South Padre Island, TX* ☎ *956/433–5484* 🕒 *Closed Sun.*

Dirty Al's. [$] *Average main: $12* ✉ *33396 State Park Rd. 100, South Padre Island, TX* ☎ *956/761–4901* 🌐 *www.dirtyalspi.com.*

F&B. [$] *Average main: $30* ✉ *3109 Padre Blvd., South Padre Island, TX* ☎ *956/772–8114* 🌐 *www.fandbspi.com* 🕒 *No lunch Mon.–Sat.*

Pier 19. [$] *Average main: $18* ✉ *1 Padre Blvd., South Padre Island, TX* ☎ *956/761–7437* 🌐 *www.pier19.us.*

Sea Ranch Restaurant. [$] *Average main: $28* ✉ *33330 State Park Rd. 100, South Padre Island, TX* ☎ *956/761–1314* 🌐 *www.searanchrestaurant.com* 🕒 *No lunch.*

Yummies Bistro. [$] *Average main: $5* ✉ *700 Padre Blvd., South Padre Island, TX* ☎ *956/761–2526* 🌐 *www.facebook.com/yummies.bistro* 🕒 *No dinner.*

🛏 Hotels

Isla Grand Beach Resort. [$] *Rooms from: $134* ✉ *500 Padre Blvd., South Padre Island, TX* ☎ *956761–6511* 🌐 *www.isla-grand.com* 🍽 *No meals.*

La Copa Inn. [$] *Rooms from: $135* ✉ *350 Padre Blvd., South Padre Island, TX* ☎ *956/761–6000* 🌐 *www.lacoparesort.com* 🍽 *Free breakfast.*

Pearl South Padre Beachfront Resort. [$] *Rooms from: $149* ✉ *310 Padre Blvd., South Padre Island, TX* ☎ *956/761–6551* 🌐 *www.pearlsouthpadre.com* 🍽 *No meals.*

🍸 Nightlife

Louie's Backyard. ✉ *2305 Laguna Blvd., South Padre Island, TX* ☎ *953/761–6406* 🌐 *www.lbyspi.com.*

Padre Island Brewing Company. ✉ *3400 Padre Blvd., South Padre Island, TX* ☎ *956/761–9585* 🌐 *www.pibrewingcompany.com.*

Wanna Wanna Beach Bar ✉ *5100 Gulf Blvd., South Padre Island, TX* ☎ *956/761–7677* 🌐 *www.wannawanna.com.*

🏃 Activities

Parrot Eyes Watersports. ✉ *5801 Padre Blvd., South Padre Island, TX* ☎ *956/761–9457* 🌐 *www.parroteyesspi.com* 🎟 *Parasailing from $80.*

Sonny's Beach Service. ✉ *310 Padre Blvd., South Padre Island, TX* ☎ *956/761–5556* 🌐 *www.sonnysbeachservice.com* 🎟 *Parasailing from $75.*

Sun Valley, ID

294 miles (approx. 4¾ hours) from Salt Lake City.

As America's oldest ski resort, Sun Valley has long been a playground for celebrities, athletes, and ski bums. The resort is known more for sun than snow, but world-class snowmaking equipment ensures a long season here when other ski resorts are dry. With two different ski hills (Dollar and Baldy), 3,400 vertical feet, and more than 2,000 acres of varied terrain, Sun Valley has something for every skier, from beginners to terrain-park experts and from lodge-hopping snow bunnies to side-country powder hounds.

If skiing isn't your thing, don't worry. With two film festivals, a writer's conference, a state-of-the-art outdoor concert pavilion, and countless art galleries, Sun Valley is a cultural mecca. At night, the town of Ketchum, the town at the base of Sun Valley Ski Resort, comes alive with rustic steakhouses, old-school pubs, hip hangouts, and live music.

Planning

GETTING THERE AND BACK

Sun Valley is hard to get to, and most of the people who love the town are eager to keep it that way. The tiny airport is serviced by just a few direct flights (many of them operating seasonally) from Salt Lake City, Los Angeles, San Francisco, Seattle, Denver, and Chicago. It's an easy weekend trip for West Coasters (especially the drive along I–84 from Salt Lake City), but East Coasters may want to take an extra day off to make the long journey worth it.

WHEN TO GO

Sun Valley thrives in the summer when mountains beckon adventure seekers for fishing, camping, hiking, mountain biking, whitewater rafting, swimming, and more. But winter is truly magical, with a soft blanket of snow covering the valley and twinkling lights illuminating the night. Pack your coziest après-ski gear and visit in February or March, after the holiday crowds have gone home but the skiing is still prime.

WHERE TO STAY

Compared to other ski towns, Sun Valley doesn't have a very diverse portfolio of hotels, but there are some fabulous options depending on your budget and travel style. Those traveling with the very young or the very old should stay at the iconic **Sun Valley Lodge**, where you'll find plenty of dining options, comfortable and accessible rooms, and tons of family-friendly activities. More mature couples will enjoy the coziness and comfort of the luxurious **Knob Hill Inn** (with a fabulous restaurant attached), while young families will love the happening kid-friendly lobby and giant hot tub at the **Limelight Hotel. Hotel Ketchum** is the hippest place to stay and is perfect for young couples, groups, or more budget-conscious travelers.

Day 1

After you've checked in to your accommodations, it's time to make the most of the afternoon. Any visitor's first stop in Sun Valley should be the **Sun Valley Lodge,** a sprawling resort that's actually more of a small village, with a few shops, restaurants, and two different hotels. You can take a stroll through the Tyrolean-inspired Sun Valley village, shopping for cashmere sweaters, jewelry, or ski equipment. You can also shop for postcards at the souvenir store and walk over to the post office to send them. The lodge itself is a little slice of history, built in 1936 (but renovated in 2017, which stripped the hotel of some of its old-school charm). Peruse the framed photos of celebrities hung in the lobby, or grab a hot chocolate or a hot toddy and sit outside to watch

More like a small village, sprawling Sun Valley Lodge is a four-season destination.

the figure skaters at the outdoor ice rink. Chances are, you'll see at least one Olympic medalist. If you're feeling brave, you can even rent a pair yourself and go for a spin around the rink.

For dinner make your way back to town for a classic Idaho dish of steak and a baked potato at the **Pioneer Saloon,** a Wild West–inspired restaurant filled with taxidermy and cattle ranch-theme decor (it's not as cheesy as it sounds). Dinner here is a must, but it can be quite the production as the restaurant doesn't take reservations. Arrive early and cozy up at the bar while you wait. After dinner, it's best to get a good night's sleep. There's a lot of exploring to be done.

Day 2

Wake up early and eat a big breakfast, because you're hitting the slopes today. **Wrap City,** right on Main Street, serves perfect breakfast burritos for a quick meal on your way to the mountain, or if you're a latte and a pastry kind of person,

head to **Java** for a "bowl of soul" (a secret recipe mocha with homemade whipped cream) and a scone.

The lifts open at 9 am and depending on the conditions, you'll want to time your start accordingly. On bluebird powder days (where it's snowed the day before but the skies today are blue) or warmer spring days, you'll want to make sure you're there when the lifts open and the snow isn't scraped off or melted. If it's still snowing, a lazy start is fine since there will be plenty of powder through-out the day. On supercold mornings, feel free to stay inside and linger over breakfast while you wait for the day to warm up and the snow to soften.

Sun Valley is a fun mountain full of long and steep groomed runs where you can really carve your way down the mountain. Off the main trails, there's plenty to explore in side-country areas and tree runs. Expert and beginner runs can be found all over the mountain. It's almost impossible to get yourself into a situation where the only way back to the lift is via a double-black diamond expert run, so feel free to get a little lost.

For lunch, make a reservation at **The Roundhouse,** one of the coolest on-mountain dining experiences in the United States. The round building (hence the name) was built in 1939 and offers a white tablecloth sit-down lunch with jaw-dropping views of the surrounding mountains. Drinking red wine and dining on steak frites while wearing ski boots is a surreal experience that's reminiscent of Europe's poshest ski resorts.

After lunch, it's honestly okay to quit for the day. You've done a lot already, and nobody is going to judge you for taking one last run and calling it a day. You can even take the gondola down if you're feeling lazy enough.

When you've changed out of your ski clothes, make your way into town for a little bit of shopping at one of Ketchum's many boutiques. Thrifters will love pawing through the racks of vintage ski wear and cozy flannel at the **Gold Mine,** while those looking to spend a bit more can shop for Prada at **Elle Rose,** fashion-forward streetwear at **Theodore,** and exquisite vintage clothes at **Deja Vu.** There's more than just clothing for sale though, with galleries scattered along Main Street and Sun Valley Road, a cozy bookstore called **Chapter One** that's full of great recommendations, a few wonderfully tacky souvenir shops, and a coffee shop/vintage store combo called **Maude's** with a great jewelry selection.

After you've explored the town, it's time for any local's favorite sunset activity: hot tubbing, preferably with an alcoholic beverage in hand. Most, if not all, of the hotels in the area have a hot tub on-site, but if you want to venture somewhere that's more than just a run-of-the-mill plastic tub, look no further than the Sun Valley Resort, whose gigantic hot pool is open to the public (for a fee). There's even a server that comes around taking drink orders.

Now that you've been refreshed and energized, it's time to hit the town. Last night was an old classic, so tonight is something new. **The Covey,** one of the buzziest restaurants in town, feels like a chic farmhouse with a locally inspired seasonal menu full of small plates, seafood, and pasta. After dinner, you can opt for a craft cocktail at **The Hangout,** a glass of wine at **Enoteca,** a pint of Guinness at **The Cellar,** or a martini at **The Sawtooth Club** before making mischief at **Whiskey Jacques,** a huge bar with a varied lineup of musical acts, rollicking cover bands, and DJs who will get you dancing.

Day 3

You might be too hungover to ski today, and that's totally okay. But either way, there's a burger and fries in your future. If you're skiing, visit the "local's" side of the mountain, Warm Springs, for lunch at **Apple's,** where you can get your burger with a side of tater tots (Idaho loves tater tots; they are a nearly perfect food). If you've decided to sleep in instead of ski, you're headed to **Grumpy's** for lunch for a perfect quarter pounder and fries that's (perhaps) washed down with a little hair of the dog.

If you have time before your flight, it's good to get one last dose of fresh mountain air. If you've rented a car, take a drive north to Galena Lodge, Smiley Creek Lodge, or the town of Stanley, Idaho for a bit of cross country skiing, snowmobiling, or fishing. If you're without wheels, don't worry. The **Sun Valley Nordic Center** is a quick bus ride away and will outfit you with everything you need for a fun and easy afternoon in the snow before it's time to head home.

Recommendations

👁 Sights

Sun Valley Lodge. ✉ *1 Sun Valley Rd., Sun Valley, ID* ☎ *800/786–8258* ⊕ *www. sunvalley.com* 🍴 *Free.*

🍴 Restaurants

Apple's. 💲 *Average main: $9* ✉ *205 Picabo St., Ketchum, ID* ☎ *208/726–7067* ⊕ *www.applesandbigwoodbarandgrill. com* ⊘ *Closed weekends.*

The Covey. 💲 *Average main: $17* ✉ *520 Washington Ave., Ketchum, ID* ☎ *208/726–3663* ⊕ *www.thecovey.com* ⊘ *No lunch Mon. and Tues.*

Grumpy's. 💲 *Average main: $7* ✉ *860 Warm Springs Rd., Ketchum, ID* ☎ *208/720–3171* ⊕ *www.grumpyssunvalley.com.*

Pioneer Saloon. 💲 *Average main: $23* ✉ *320 N. Main St., Ketchum, ID* ☎ *208/726–3139* ⊕ *www.pioneersaloon. com.*

The Roundhouse. 💲 *Average main: $19* ✉ *Bald Mountain, NF 135, Ketchum, ID* ☎ *208/622–2012* ⊕ *www.sunvalley.com* ⊘ *Closed Mon.–Wed.*

Wrap City. 💲 *Average main: $5* ✉ *180 Main St. S, Ketchum, ID* ☎ *208/727–6766* ⊕ *www.wrapcitycafe.com* ⊘ *Closed Sun.*

☕ Coffee and Quick Bites

Java. 💲 *Average main: $4* ✉ *191 4th St. W, Ketchum, ID* ☎ *208/726–2882* ⊕ *www.javabowlofsoul.com.*

🛏 Hotels

Hotel Ketchum. 💲 *Rooms from: $136* ✉ *600 N. Main St., Ketchum, ID* ☎ *208/471–4716* ⊕ *www.hotelketchum. com* 🍴 *Free breakfast.*

Knob Hill Inn. 💲 *Rooms from: $299* ✉ *960 N. Main St., Ketchum, ID* ☎ *208/726–8010* ⊕ *www.knobhillinn.com* 🍴 *Free breakfast.*

Limelight Hotel. 💲 *Rooms from: $339* ✉ *151 Main St. S, Ketchum, ID* ☎ *208/726–0888* ⊕ *www.limelighthotels. com* 🍴 *Free breakfast.*

Sun Valley Lodge. 💲 *Rooms from: $319* ✉ *1 Sun Valley Rd., Sun Valley, ID* ☎ *800/786–8259* ⊕ *www.sunvalley.com* 🍴 *No meals.*

🍸 Nightlife

The Cellar. ✉ *400 Sun Valley Rd., Ketchum, ID* ☎ *208/622–3832* ⊕ *thecellarpub.com.*

Enoteca. ✉ *300 N. Main St., Ketchum, ID* ☎ *208/928–6280* ⊕ *www.ketchum-enoteca.com.*

The Hangout. ✉ *600 N Main St., Ketchum, ID* ☎ *208/471–4716* ⊕ *www. hotelketchum.com.*

The Sawtooth Club. ✉ *231 Main St. S, Ketchum, ID* ☎ *208/726–5233* ⊕ *www. sawtoothclub.com.*

Whiskey Jacques. ✉ *251 N. Main St., Ketchum, ID* ☎ *208/726–5297* ⊕ *www. whiskeyjacques.com.*

🛍 Shopping

Chapter One. ✉ *340 2nd St. W, Ketchum, ID* ☎ *208/726–5425* ⊕ *www.facebook. com/chapteronebookstore.*

Elle Rose. ✉ *641 Sun Valley Rd., Ketchum, ID* ☎ *208/726–2271* ⊕ *www.ellerosesv. com.*

Gold Mine. ✉ *331 N. Walnut Ave., Ketchum, ID* ☎ *208/726–3465* ⊕ *www. comlib.org.*

Maude's. ✉ *391 Walnut Ave., Ketchum, ID* ☎ *208/726–6413* ⊕ *www.maudesinketchum.com.*

Theodore. ✉ *511 Leadville Ave., Ketchum, ID* ☏ *208/726–3544* ⊕ *www.theodorebh. com.*

 Activities

Sun Valley Nordic Center. ✉ *Trail Creek Path, Sun Valley, ID* ☏ *208/622–2250* ⊕ *www.sunvalley.com* ✑ *Passes from $10.*

Texas Hill Country, TX

Driftwood is 184 miles (approx. 3 hours) from Houston, 197 miles (approx 3½ hours) from Dallas.

Ah, the Texas Hill Country. With rolling hills, stunning sunsets, and small-town charm, it's quintessentially Texas, with each small town maintaining a personality and spirit of its own. The region has always been popular, thanks to its natural escapes, but in the past 20 years the growth of wineries and distilleries have made it a destination for drinkers who value flavor and quality over quantity. Visiting the Central Texas Hill Country may include a lot of driving, but that's really half the fun.

Planning

GETTING THERE AND BACK
Take I–10 W to TX 71, plus a couple of country roads, and start your Hill Country weekend in Driftwood. Just follow the smell of the Salt Lick BBQ in the air. The drive will take you a little less than three hours, but if you set out early enough, you can make a stop in Austin to stroll along South Congress Avenue and enjoy their various boutiques and vintage stores.

INSPIRATION
This road trip is just begging for an extended Willie Nelson mix; from his "Luckenbach, Texas" to his "Hill Country Theme," Willie embodies his area of residence in many ways.

PIT STOPS
Feel like a kid again by visiting Austin's **Big Top Candy Shop** for treats and **Monkey See, Monkey Do** to find toys for kids of all ages.

WHEN TO GO
A weekend in the Hill Country makes for a nice, relaxing break almost any time of the year, but if you have the option to go in the spring, that's ideal. Seeing the sides of the road painted from the palette of Texas wildflowers is a sight that you just can't find a lot of places, at least not like this.

WHERE TO STAY
There are plenty of options for lodging in the Texas Hill Country. You can go resort style and stay at **Horseshoe Bay Resort,** where you'll never run out of things to do or eat. For more B&B-style accommodations, **Full Moon Inn** is an award-winning, charming option that straddles Fredericksburg and Luckenbach. For a really fun adventure, try **Flite Acres Ranch** where you can stay in their cabins or bunkhouse and take a welding class while you're there.

Day 1

From Houston, head toward Fredericksburg as your destination for your first day. After you've passed through Austin, into the Hill Country, stop for a unique experience at **Desert Door Distillery** in Driftwood. There, you'll learn about and get to taste sotol (similar to tequila and mezcal), at the craft distillery's cozy tasting room. From there, either double back a bit to eat lunch at the famed **Salt Lick BBQ** (just bring a shirt to change into if you don't want to smell like brisket all day) or head toward Johnson City to grab lunch at **Fat Boy Burgers,** which has an incredibly affordable menu that has something for everyone. Afterward, spend some

The pink granite dome of Enchanted Rock State Natural Area is a perfect place for taking in all of Hill Country.

time at the **Science Mill,** which offers immensely fun, interactive exhibits that teaches science and technology to all ages. After the afternoon of fun, keep heading toward Fredericksburg, stopping in Hye along the way. There, you can try one or both of the area beverage makers' wares. At **Garrison Brothers Distillery,** whiskey lovers can delight in a truly Texan whiskey, the first bourbon to be legally made in Texas, with a tour and tasting (and maybe even a hayride). Enjoy great legs and great views at **Westcave Cellars'** new location near Hye; stop for a tasting and enjoy a glass with beautiful vineyard views.

From there, you may want to stop and check into your accommodations. This could be the tricky part, if you're staying somewhere a bit further away from this southern route, so you may need to cut an item or two from your list of fun. If you're staying near Fredericksburg, however, just head that direction and check into your lodging. After you've freshened up, **August E's** in Fredericksburg is your next destination. You'll need to make it there before sunset, because you do not want to miss the incredible views that come along with your dinner with dishes that range from fresh sashimi to quail legs. After dinner, if you have a little bit of energy left, boot scoot on over to the **Luckenbach Dance Hall** for some extra fun. They're only open until 10, so you don't have to make it a really late night.

Day 2

There are two strong options for spending your only full day in the Hill Country: wine or walking (or, more accurately, hiking). Start off in Marble Falls at **Tea Thyme Cafe** for a hearty breakfast and energizing smoothie. As you probably discovered in Day 1, the Hill Country has some of the most stunning landscapes in Texas, the crest of every hill revealing something new and extraordinary as you meander around the area. Today, enjoy those landscapes outside of the car by exploring some of the area's outdoor spaces. **Balcones Canyonlands National Wildlife Refuge** in Marble Falls offers up 27,500 acres of protected space that allows you to get back to nature through hiking, wildlife photography, birding, and other activities. For a little more low-key time outside, **Sweet Berry Farm** is a lot of fun for kids, especially during berry-picking season in the spring and harvest season in the fall.

After your hiking time, head into Marble Falls to grab lunch at **Franks Holy Smoke** barbecue joint, where the food is so tender there's "no teeth required," or **Bill's Burgers** for burgers, wings, and things (including spicy fried pickles). After lunch, head to one of the Hill Country's best swimming holes at **Krause Springs.** This swimming area is tranquil and easy for everyone to enjoy; be sure to spend a little bit of time in the butterfly garden area to appreciate their gorgeous landscaping and lay back for a few in their mammoth-size hammocks.

If your itinerary should focus on wine instead of the outdoors, you can choose your own adventure along the Texas Wine Trail. There's no shortage of options in the Hill Country area, but if you want to mix in some of the other activities (swimming at Krause Springs, for instance), stay close to the Marble Falls wineries including **Fiesta Winery** and **Flat Creek Estate Winery and Vineyard.**

From Krause, you'll want to head to your last major destination for the day, spending the evening soaking up the devastatingly beautiful Texas sunsets atop **Enchanted Rock State Natural Area.** Your drive there must include the beloved Willow City Loop, which offers incredible landscape views that show off some of Texas's true beauty along 13 miles of two-lane country road. If it's springtime, the bluebonnets, Indian paintbrushes, and Mexican poppies will help guide your way. After you've enjoyed the sunset and Hill Country views atop the pink granite dome, it's time to head back to your

accommodations. Keep your eye out for take-out food that you can pick up along the way; you'll want a shower and rest after your busy day.

Day 3

After you've checked out of your accommodations, stop for lunch at **Apis Restaurant and Apiary.** Here you'll enjoy honey-touched drinks, dishes, and desserts at the restaurant that sits on six acres along the Pedernales River. If you're farther south, try lunch at the popular spot **The Leaning Pear** for hearty, creative sandwiches or wood-fired pizzas.

As you start to head back home, make your last stop one that is perfect to leave on: **Blue Hole Regional Park** in Wimberley is one of the most beautiful land and waterscapes in the state. The 126-acre park includes 4.5 miles of hiking trails, picnic tables, playscape, sand volleyball court, and more. The crown jewel, the Blue Hole Swimming Area, is open seasonally, from May through September. The swimming area requires a reservation to help limit traffic and preserve the area, so be sure to plan in advance, as this is a very popular spot.

Recommendations

Sights

Balcones Canyonlands National Wildlife Refuge. ✉ 24518 FM 1431, Marble Falls, TX ☎ 512/339–9432 ⊕ www.fws.gov ✉ Free.

Desert Door Distillery. ✉ 211 Darden Hill Rd, Driftwood, TX ☎ 512/829–6129 ⊕ www.desertdoor.com ✉ Free ⊙ Closed Mon.–Wed.

Enchanted Rock State Natural Area. ✉ 16710 Ranch Rd. 96, Fredericksburg, TX ☎ 830/389–8900 ⊕ www.tpwd.texas.gov ✉ $8.

Fiesta Winery. ✉ *18727 FM 580, Lometa, TX* ☎ *325/628–3433* 🌐 *www.fiestawinery.com* 🎟 *Tastings $15.*

Flat Creek Estate Winery and Vineyard. ✉ *24912 Singleton Bend E, Marble Falls, TX* ☎ *512/267–6310* 🌐 *www.flatcreekestate.com* 🎟 *Tastings $40* 🕓 *Closed Tues. and Wed.*

Garrison Brothers Distillery. ✉ *1827 Hye-Albert Rd., Hye, TX* ☎ *830/392–0246* 🌐 *www.garrisonbros.com* 🎟 *$10.*

Krause Springs. ✉ *424 Co Rd. 404, Spicewood, TX* ☎ *830/693–4181* 🌐 *www.krausesprings.net* 🎟 *$8.*

Science Mill. ✉ *101 S. Lady Bird La., Johnson City, TX* ☎ *844/263–6405* 🌐 *www.sciencemill.org* 🎟 *$11.*

Westcave Cellars. ✉ *683 Ranch Rd. 1320, Johnson City, TX* ☎ *512/431–1403* 🌐 *www.westcavecellars.com* 🎟 *$15.*

Restaurants

Apis Restaurant and Apiary. [$] *Average main: $8* ✉ *23526 TX 71, Spicewood, TX* ☎ *512/436–8918* 🌐 *www.apisrestaurant.com.*

August E's. [$] *Average main: $15* ✉ *203 E. San Antonio St, Fredericksburg, TX* ☎ *830/997–1585* 🌐 *www.august-es.com* 🕓 *Closed Sun. and Mon.*

Bill's Burgers. [$] *Average main: $6* ✉ *307 Main St., Marble Falls, TX* ☎ *830/201–4481* 🕓 *Closed Mon.*

Fat Boy Burgers. [$] *Average main: $6* ✉ *104 U.S. 281, Johnson City, TX* ☎ *830/868–0264* 🌐 *www.fatboyburgerstx.com* 🕓 *Closed Mon.*

Franks Holy Smoke. [$] *Average main: $10* ✉ *705 W. Main St, Ovilla, TX* ☎ *972/515–8898* 🕓 *Closed Sun.*

The Leaning Pear. [$] *Average main: $7* ✉ *111 River Rd., Wimberley, TX* ☎ *512/847–7327* 🌐 *www.leaningpear.com* 🕓 *Closed Mon.*

Salt Lick BBQ. [$] *Average main: $15* ✉ *18300 Farm to Market Rd. 1826, Driftwood, TX* ☎ *512/858–4959* 🌐 *www.saltlickbbq.com.*

Tea Thyme Cafe. [$] *Average main: $7* ✉ *2108 U.S. 281 C, Marble Falls, TX* ☎ *830/637–7787* 🌐 *www.teathymecafe.com* 🕓 *Closed Sun.*

Hotels

Flite Acres Ranch. [$] *Rooms from: $337* ✉ *2595 Flite Acres Rd., Wimberley, TX* ☎ *512/632–0979* 🌐 *www.fliteacresranch.com* 🍴 *No meals.*

Full Moon Inn. [$] *Rooms from: $175* ✉ *3234 Luckenbach Rd., Fredericksburg, TX* ☎ *830/997–2205* 🌐 *www.fullmooninn.com* 🍴 *Free breakfast.*

Horseshoe Bay Resort. [$] *Rooms from: $209* ✉ *200 Hi Circle N, Horseshoe Bay, TX* ☎ *877/611–0112* 🌐 *www.hsbresort.com* 🍴 *No meals.*

Nightlife

Luckenbach Dance Hall. ✉ *412 Luckenbach Town Loop, Fredericksburg, TX* ☎ *830/997–3224* 🌐 *www.luckenbachtexas.com.*

Shopping

Big Top Candy Shop. ✉ *1706 S. Congress Ave., Austin, TX* ☎ *512/462–2220* 🌐 *www.bigtopcandyshop.com.*

Monkey See, Monkey Do. ✉ *1712 S. Congress Ave., Austin, TX* ☎ *512/443–4999* 🌐 *www.facebook.com/monkeyseemonkeydoaustin.*

Sweet Berry Farm. ✉ *1801 FM1980, Marble Falls, TX* ☎ *830/798–1462* 🌐 *www.sweetberryfarm.com.*

Tucson and Saguaro National Park, AZ

113 miles (approx. 1¾ hours) from Phoenix.

Multicultural roots meet college-town energy in Tucson, a creative hotspot framed by a brace of desert peaks. Galleries and studios attest to the thriving arts scene here, and Tucson is the first city in the United States to be designated a UNESCO City of Gastronomy, a tribute to local flavors that range from bacon-wrapped hot dogs to vegan jackfruit tacos.

With a 131-mile network of car-free trails and paths within Tucson itself, it's no surprise that cycling is big. Beyond the city limits, the surrounding desert is a playground for outdoorsy locals and visitors alike, whether you're hiking the Santa Catalina Mountains or dodging saguaro cacti on a mountain bike.

Planning

GETTING THERE AND BACK
From Phoenix, follow I–10 E all the way to Tucson.

PIT STOPS
Make a pit stop at the open-air **Rooster Cogburn Ostrich Ranch,** where you can feed not only ostriches, but also stingrays, boer goats, miniature donkeys, and other adorable creatures.

WHEN TO GO
Mild weather in the spring and fall make these prime times to visit. In April and May and September and October, average highs range from the low 80s to the mid-90s. Summers are hot, with highs around 100 in June, July, and August. The area enjoys plenty of sun all winter; nights can be cool, but there's plenty of warmth during the day.

WHERE TO STAY
Options here run the gamut from basics to top-end luxury. The most stylish yet affordable pick is **Hotel McCoy,** a revamped midcentury hotel with a salt-water pool, local artworks, and a fun oatmeal-bar breakfast. If you're splashing out, do it at **Hacienda del Sol,** at the base of the Santa Catalina Mountains—there are great views of the peaks from the pool. Many of the rooms here have hand-crafted furniture and beautiful wooden ceilings; desert-inspired artwork is scattered throughout the property.

Day 1

Celebrate an early start to the weekend with a giant cup of horchata and Sonoran-style tacos at **Taqueria Pico de Gallo.** Flour and corn tortillas are made in-house, a tasty base layer for *carne asada*, shrimp, chicken, and fish tacos. (With extra zing from chiltepin peppers, the house hot sauce is a fiery highlight that makes bottled versions look wan.)

From there, head to the wonderful **Arizona-Sonora Desert Museum,** where you'll find 98 acres of botanical gardens and animal enclosures, plus a natural history museum, aquarium, and art gallery. The gardens are a highlight, with 1,200 different kinds of plants that range from a prickly cactus garden to alien-like soaptree yuccas in the desert grassland. Docent-led tours of the museum, free with admission, are a great way to get the most out of your visit.

You may also want to take time to visit **Saguaro National Park.** The western section of the park is near the Arizona-Sonora Desert Museum. You can visit the visitor center, do a short loop hike, and take a scenic drive on the Bajada Loop Drive (a graded dirt road) to Signal Hill, from where you can see the Hohokam petroglyphs. If you have time to visit the eastern section, you can duck off the Interstate to take the 8-mile Cactus

Tucson's Mission San Xavier del Bac is a remarkable sight against the desert sky.

Forest Drive through dramatic desert punctuated by oversized cacti, do a quick hike from the visitor center if you have a bit more time.

Take your time on your way back to town, and if sunset is approaching, pull off to enjoy the view from Gates Pass Scenic Overlook in **Tucson Mountain Park.** A few hiking paths depart from here, but it's well worth the side-trip just to see evening light amid the saguaro cactus.

For dinner, raise a glass of small-batch mezcal to the central Mexican cuisine of **Penca Restaurante,** whose menu offers updated takes on traditional dishes such as *esquites* (corn salad), *pozole* (a meaty stew with a hominy base), and *encacahuatadas* (enchiladas made with peanuts). Want to keep the evening going? Stroll a few blocks to the quirky **R Bar,** whose decor includes a surreal steel mural of Tucson backlit with a loungy orange glow.

Day 2

If the fancy brunch scene leaves you cold, go for oversized banana pancakes at **Bobo's Restaurant,** arriving early to beat lines of locals with the same idea. Service is usually lightning fast here— that means you'll get out the door in time for a morning trip to the Santa Catalina Mountains that arc across the north side of Tucson.

A good place to start exploring is Sabino Canyon in **Coronado National Forest.** The 8-mile Sabino Canyon Trail is flanked by saguaro and ocotillo cactus on the way to pretty Sabino Creek, where cottonwood, ash, and sycamore trees cluster around the precious water source. To reach the trailhead, you'll need a ticket for the open-sided electric tram that shuttles hikers through the fragile landscape.

By the time you're back at the trailhead, you'll be ready to cool off during a meal on the shady, garden patio at **La Cocina**— if you're lucky, you'll catch one of their lunchtime live music events as you dine on Tex-Mex with some global favorites thrown in for good measure. (Think chile relleno meets salade Niçoise.)

From there, it's just a quick stroll to the **Tucson Museum of Art,** a blissfully air-conditioned spot with fine collections of pre-Colombian art from Latin America, plus folk art, and Southwestern art. The collection rambles across a whole city block, filling both a modern wing and several converted 19th-century buildings.

Once you take that in, take a walk—or grab a cab—to 4th Avenue, a street with some of the city's most browsable boutiques, shops, and galleries. Find unique souvenirs from local artists and designers at **Pop Cycle**; quirky local screen prints are available a few doors down from **Tiny Town Surplus**; it's all about comic art, collectibles, and zines at **& Gallery.**

When you're ready for dinner, make your way to the pizza restaurant **Anello,** whose short-but-sweet menu is all about simple toppings on sourdough crusts. Save room for Italian desserts including vivid gelato and an almond olive oil cake.

Day 3

Grab a counter seat at **Welcome Diner** for a leisurely brunch, with options that include chicken and biscuits, breakfast burritos, and plates of eggs, all made with superfresh ingredients, many locally sourced. It's a stylish spot with a midcentury feel, and the appealing vegan options are a favorite even for omnivores.

Next, check out **Mission San Xavier del Bac,** a Catholic church founded in 1692. The building's white and sand-color exterior is a remarkable sight against the desert sky; head inside to see statues and frescoes that have earned this spot the nickname "Sistine Chapel of the Southwest."

And now it's time for a bike ride. Head to the South Mercado Station of the **Tugo Bike Share** program, which is located near a portion of The Loop, Tucson's 131-mile network of car-free paths and trails. From the station, pedal north along the Santa Cruz River, passing a series of parks as you ride.

Before leaving town, make one last food stop at **Tito & Pep,** where chefs use a mesquite-fired grill to tease every bit of flavor from a menu of colorful vegetable dishes, meats, and fish. "It's not Mexican, it's Tucsonian," they say, offering a perfect coda to a weekend in the city.

Recommendations

Sights

Arizona-Sonora Desert Museum. ⊠ *2021 N. Kinney Rd., Tucson, AZ* ☎ *520/883–2702* ⊕ *www.desertmuseum.org* ⊠ *$22.*

Coronado National Forest. ⊠ *300 W. Congress St., Tucson, AZ* ☎ *520/388–8300* ⊕ *www.fs.usda.gov* ⊠ *$8 per person.*

Mission San Xavier del Bac. ⊠ *1950 W. San Xavier Rd., Tucson, Arizona* ☎ *520/294– 2624* ⊕ *www.sanxaviermission.org* ⊠ *Free.*

Rooster Cogburn Ostrich Ranch. ⊠ *17599 E. Peak La., Picacho, AZ* ☎ *520/466–3658* ⊕ *www.roostercogburn.com* ⊠ *$15.*

Sabino Canyon Recreation Area. ⊠ *5700 N. Sabino Canyon Rd., Tucson, AZ* ☎ *520/388–8300* ⊕ *www.fs.usda.gov* ⊠ *$8 per vehicle.*

Saguaro National Park. ⊠ *Rincon Mountain Visitor Center, 3693 S. Old Spanish Trail, Tucson, AZ* ☎ *520/733–5153* ⊕ *www.nps. gov/sagu* ⊠ *$25 per vehicle.*

Tucson Mountain Park. ⊠ *8451 W. McCain Loop, Tucson, AZ* ☎ *520/724–9999* ⊕ *www.pima.gov* ⊠ *Free.*

Tucson Museum of Art. ✉ *140 N. Main Ave., Tucson, AZ* ☎ *520/624–2333* ⊕ *www. tucsonmuseumofart.org* 🎫 *$12.*

 Restaurants

Anello. $ *Average main: $12* ✉ *2225 6th St., Tucson, AZ* ☎ *520/347–2710* ⊕ *www. anello.space* ⊗ *Closed Sun. and Mon.*

Bobo's Restaurant. $ *Average main: $6* ✉ *2938 E. Grant Rd., Tucson, AZ* ☎ *520/326–6163* ⊕ *www.bobostucson. com.*

La Cocina. $ *Average main: $13* ✉ *201 N. Court Ave., Tucson, AZ* ☎ *520/622–0351* ⊕ *www.lacocinatucson.com.*

Penca Restaurante. $ *Average main: $11* ✉ *50 E. Broadway Blvd., Tucson, AZ* ☎ *520/203–7681* ⊕ *www.pencarestaurante.com.*

Taqueria Pico de Gallo. $ *Average main: $6* ✉ *2618 S. 6th Ave., Tucson, AZ* ☎ *520/623–8775* ⊕ *www.picodegallo. com.*

Tito & Pep. $ *Average main: $12* ✉ *4122 E. Speedway Blvd., Tucson, AZ* ☎ *520/207–0116* ⊕ *www.titoandpep.com.*

Welcome Diner. $ *Average main: $12* ✉ *902 E. Broadway Blvd., Tucson, AZ* ☎ *520/622–5100* ⊕ *www.welcomediner. net.*

 Hotels

Hacienda del Sol. $ *Rooms from: $164* ✉ *5501 N. Hacienda del Sol Rd., Tucson, AZ* ☎ *520/299–1501* ⊕ *www.haciendadel-sol.com* ⦿ *No meals.*

Hotel McCoy. $ *Rooms from: $99* ✉ *720 W. Silverlake Rd., Tucson, AZ* ☎ *844/782–9622* ⊕ *www.hotelmccoy.com* ⦿ *Free breakfast.*

 Nightlife

R Bar. ✉ *350 E. Congress St., Tucson, AZ* ☎ *520/305–3599* ⊕ *www.rbartucson. com.*

 Shopping

& Gallery. ✉ *419 N. 4th Ave., Tucson, AZ* ☎ *310/754–5190* ⊕ *www.andgallery.art.*

Pop Cycle. ✉ *422 N. 4th Ave., Tucson, AZ* ☎ *520/622–3297* ⊕ *www.popcycleshop. com.*

Tiny Town Surplus. ✉ *408 N. 4th Ave., Tucson, AZ* ☎ *520/907–9309* ⊕ *www. tinytownsurplus.com.*

⚐ **Activities**

Tugo Bike Share. ✉ *930 E. Broadway, Tucson, AZ* ☎ *877/663–8846* ⊕ *www. tugobikeshare.com* 🎫 *Rides $4.*

Waco, TX

97 miles (approx. 1½ hours) from Dallas and 186 miles (approx 3 hours) from Houston.

Since the debut of the hit show *Fixer Upper,* Waco has been known primarily as the home of Chip and Joanna Gaines' Magnolia empire, and it's become something of a pilgrimage site for fans (expect plenty of bachelorette parties, multigeneration family groups, and young couples). Beyond the highly Instagrammable Magnolia businesses, which range from various eateries to a handful of shops, there's also the Waco Mammoth National Monument, the Texas Sports Hall of Fame, the Dr. Pepper Museum, and the Cameron Park Zoo to appease those without an appetite for home renovations.

Planning

GETTING THERE AND BACK

It's an easy 90-minute drive down I-35 from Dallas to Waco, and a longer three-hour drive from Houston along Highway 6.

PIT STOPS

If you're coming from Dallas, you absolutely must make a pit stop at **Czech Stop,** a roadside gas station and market in West, Texas, with the best kolaches around.

WHEN TO GO

Waco has pleasant weather year-round, with summer highs in the mid-90s and the winter highs in the low-60s, but it's most visited in the spring, summer, and fall. Expect bigger crowds on weekends with football games, as well as during big events hosted by Magnolia, like the Silo District Marathon and the Silobration, both in October.

WHERE TO STAY

Waco is filled with your typical chain hotels at budget-to-splurge prices. *Fixer Upper* fans will want to stay at **Magnolia House,** the Gaines' bed and breakfast, but be warned—it books up months in advance.

Day 1

Whether you're coming from Dallas or Houston, plan on getting an early start to make the most of your Friday in Waco. Since weekends are the busiest time to visit **Magnolia Market at the Silos,** arguably the biggest draw in town, beat the crowds by arriving by 10 or 11 am. Start by having a big brunch at **Magnolia Table,** Joanna Gaines' breakfast and lunch restaurant, which is known to have hours-long waits, especially on Saturday.

At Magnolia Market at the Silos, you can shop for your favorite farmhouse-chic home goods in the eponymous market,

purchase gardening supplies from Magnolia Seed + Supply, or lounge on the grass as you digest. If you get hungry for a snack, check out the food trucks that queue up on the lot. Whatever you do, don't miss Silos Baking Co., which sells Joanna's famous and absolutely delicious cupcakes. While the biggest fans could easily spend an entire afternoon at the Silos, not to mention other Fixer Upper–affiliated businesses like the **Little Shop on Bosque** and **Harp Design Co.** Those who tap out on Magnolia after an hour or two can hop on the free Downtown Trolley and hop off near Franklin and Austin Avenues, where you can browse a plethora of boutique shops. Check out **Spice Village** for a single-stop shopping destination.

When it comes time to start thinking about dinner, mosey on over to **Vitek's,** a Waco barbecue icon. It's known for its Gut Pack, a plate piled high with sausage, beans, cheese, and Fritos, among other tasty ingredients. If you're not in a food coma, check out the programming at the **Waco Hippodrome Theatre,** which functions as a dine-in cinema (maybe just stick to cocktails or beer if you're still full).

Day 2

Get your caffeine fix from **Magnolia Press** first thing, and grab a sweet or savory pastry for a light breakfast—everything Joanna bakes is dreamy, so you can't go wrong with your choice. This morning, we recommend a little lesson in Texas history. Visit Baylor University's **Mayborn Museum,** dedicated to natural and cultural history, or perhaps the **Texas Ranger Hall of Fame and Museum,** if that's more your jam. Prefer to spend time outdoors? Visit the **Cameron Park Zoo,** or hit the Brazos River in a kayak, paddleboard, or canoe rental from **Waco Paddle Company** if the weather's nice. Alternatively, you could stroll the 7 miles of the **Waco Riverwalk.**

Waco's Dr. Pepper Museum delivers plenty of nostalgia.

Once you've worked up your appetite, have lunch at **Clay Pot Waco,** a Vietnamese hot spot, and don't forget a bubble tea.

After lunch, we recommend checking out Baylor's sports scene, depending on the season of your visit. The fall, of course, is prime time for football games—a big Texas tradition. But you can also catch everything from basketball to baseball, equestrian to gymnastics. But if you're in town on a quiet weekend, you can head out on a brewery or distillery crawl and visit crowd favorites like **Brotherwell Brewing** and **Balcones Distillery.** Another option if there are no games in town: get to one of Waco's famous sports bars, like **George's,** popular with the college crowd, to catch a game on TV.

For dinner, you won't want to miss **Franklin Ave Mac House,** Waco's only restaurant dedicated to mac and cheese. There are other options, too, like grilled cheese and salads if you're set on being healthy. After your meal, have a nightcap or two at **Dichotomy Coffee and Spirits,** which

starts as a coffee shop in the morning and transitions into a cocktail bar at night.

Day 3

Have a hearty Mexican breakfast—burritos, huevos, and even pancakes are all on the menu—at **Taqueria El Crucero.** A trip to Waco wouldn't be complete without visiting **Waco Mammoth National Monument.** Catch a guided tour of an archaeological dig site filled with mammoth bones (entrance is by tour only), and learn all about Texas's prehistoric past.

For lunch, keep things light after your big breakfast and dine at **D's Mediterranean Grill**—you can't go wrong with a falafel wrap here. Head downtown afterward to visit the **Dr. Pepper Museum,** which has exhibits dedicated to vintage Dr. Pepper paraphernalia, as well as a laboratory for live demos and an old-school pharmacy that serves the beverage 1950s-style.

Before you head home, stop back in town for one more meal. How about a classic burger? **Cupp's Drive-In** is a no-frills joint serving up greasy delights since 1947, and it'll fuel you up for your drive home.

Recommendations

Sights

Cameron Park Zoo. ✉ *1701 N. 4th St., Waco, TX* ☎ *254/750–8400* 🌐 *www.cameronparkzoo.com* 🎫 *$12.*

Dr. Pepper Museum. ✉ *300 S. 5th St., Waco, TX* ☎ *254/757–1025* 🌐 *www.drpeppermuseum.com* 🎫 *$10.*

Mayborn Museum. ✉ *Baylor University, 1300 S. University Parks Dr., Waco, TX* ☎ *254/710–1110* 🌐 *www.baylor.edu* 🎫 *$10.*

Texas Ranger Hall of Fame and Museum. ✉ *100 Texas Ranger Tr., Waco, TX* ☎ *254/750–8631* 🌐 *www.texasranger.org* 🎫 *$8.*

Waco Mammoth National Monument. ✉ *6220 Steinbeck Bend Dr., Waco, TX* ☎ *254/750–7946* 🌐 *www.nps.gov* 🎫 *$5.*

Waco Riverwalk. ✉ *106 Texas Ranger Tr., Waco, TX* ☎ *254/750–8696* 🌐 *www.wacoheartoftexas.com* 🎫 *Free.*

Restaurants

Clay Pot Waco. [$] *Average main: $8* ✉ *416 Franklin Ave., Waco, TX* ☎ *254/756–2721* 🌐 *www.claypotwaco.com* 🕒 *Closed Mon.*

Cupp's Drive-In. [$] *Average main: $6* ✉ *1424 Speight Ave., Waco, TX* ☎ *254/753–9364* 🌐 *www.cuppsdriveinn.com* 🕒 *Closed Sun.*

D's Mediterranean Grill. [$] *Average main: $13* ✉ *1503 Colcord Ave., Waco, TX* ☎ *254/754–6709* 🕒 *Closed Sun.*

Franklin Ave Mac House. [$] *Average main: $6* ✉ *3428 Franklin Ave., Waco, TX* ☎ *254/224–8081* 🌐 *www.machousewaco.com* 🕒 *Closed Sun.*

Magnolia Table. [$] *Average main: $20* ✉ *2132 S. Valley Mills Dr., Waco, TX* ☎ *254/235–6111* 🌐 *www.magnolia.com* 🕒 *Closed Sun.*

Taqueria El Crucero. [$] *Average main: $6* ✉ *2505 N. Robinson Dr., Waco, TX* ☎ *254/662–3359* 🌐 *www.taqueriaelcrucero.com* 🕒 *Closed Mon.*

Vitek's. [$] *Average main: $10* ✉ *1600 Speight Ave., Waco, TX* ☎ *254/752–7591* 🌐 *www.viteksmarket.com.*

Coffee and Quick Bites

Magnolia Press. [$] *Average main: $5* ✉ *418 S. 8th St., Waco, TX* ☎ *254/265–6858* 🌐 *www.magnolia.com* 🕒 *Closed Sun.*

Hotels

Magnolia House. [$] *Rooms from: $347* ✉ *323 S. Madison Ave., McGregor, TX* ☎ *254/235–6111* 🌐 *www.magnolia.com* 🍴 *Free breakfast.*

Nightlife

Balcones Distillery. ✉ *225 S. 11th St., Waco, TX* ☎ *254/755–6003* 🌐 *www.balconesdistilling.com.*

Brotherwell Brewing. ✉ *400 E. Bridge St., Waco, TX* ☎ *254/301–7152* 🌐 *www.brotherwell.com.*

Dichotomy Coffee and Spirits. ✉ *508 Austin Ave., Waco, TX* ☎ *254/717–3226* 🌐 *www.dichotomycs.com.*

George's. ✉ *1925 Speight Ave., Waco, TX* ☎ *254/753–1421* 🌐 *www.georgesrestaurant.com.*

Waco Hippodrome Theatre. ✉ *724 Austin Ave., Waco, TX* ☎ *254/296–9000* 🌐 *www.wacohippodrometheatre.com.*

📁 Shopping

Czech Stop. ✉ *104 S. George Kacir Dr., West, TX* ☎ *254/826–4161* ⊕ *www. czechstop.net.*

Harp Design Co. ✉ *808 N. 15th St., Waco, TX* ☎ *254/230–2054* ⊕ *www.harpdesign-co.com.*

Little Shop on Bosque. ✉ *3801 Bosque Blvd., Waco, TX* ☎ *254/235–0603* ⊕ *www.magnolia.com.*

Magnolia Market at the Silos. ✉ *601 Webster Ave., Waco, TX* ☎ *254/235–0603* ⊕ *www.magnolia.com.*

Spice Village. ✉ *213 Mary Ave., Waco, TX* ☎ *254/757–0921* ⊕ *www.spicewaco. com.*

🏃 Activities

Waco Paddle Company. ✉ *200 S. University Parks Dr., Waco, TX* ☎ *254/424–3253* ⊕ *www.wacopaddlecompany.com* 🎫 *Paddleboaring from $40.*

White Sands National Park, NM

White Sands National Park is 224 miles (approx 3½ hours) from Albuquerque.

Surreal dunes stretch across the Tularosa Basin at White Sands National Park, a dazzling reflection of the big sky above southern New Mexico. It's the largest gypsum dune field on earth. A wonderland for photographers, it's also a playground for outdoors lovers who come for dune-sledding, hiking, and camping. East of the park by 35 miles, the historic railroad town of Cloudcroft offers a scenic base for visiting the desert.

Planning

GETTING THERE AND BACK
Follow I–25 S from Albuquerque to 380 E, turning onto 54 W in Carrizozo.

PIT STOPS
Take a breather in the small town of Carrizozo, where **Tularosa Basin Gallery of Photography** displays work by New Mexico photographers. As you drive through town, watch for Carrizozo's colorful painted burros.

WHEN TO GO
White Sands National Park is a year-round destination. From June through August, temperatures can climb into the 90s and 100s, though hot days are generally followed by cooler, comfortable nights. In July, August, and September, afternoon thunderstorms are common. Days are warm throughout the winter, but from December to February nights are often below freezing.

WHERE TO STAY
Alamogordo is closer, but Cloudcroft's atmosphere is worth the extra drive. The cheery **Cloudcroft Hostel** is a welcoming place to meet other travelers, and offers loaner sleds you can bring to the dunes. With slightly faded, rustic grandeur, **The Lodge Resort and Spa** is Cloudcroft's most elegant option, featuring antiques-filled rooms and excellent service. If you're equipped to carry all your own gear and water, the national park itself has 10 primitive camping sites.

Day 1

Since services are limited within the borders of **White Sands National Park,** come prepared with a picnic that you can enjoy once you get there. Try the **Brown Bag Deli** in nearby Alamogordo, where you'll find generous sandwiches with coleslaw and dill pickles on the side.

Looking like a winter wonderland, desert dunes spread out in every direction at White Sands National Park.

When you arrive at the park, check in at the entrance and continue onto the gorgeous Dunes Drive, a smooth, white road that weaves through the gypsum dunes. Six miles in, find a trio of picnic areas with sun shelters, a lunch spot with spectacular views to the rolling horizon.

Next, bring plenty of water and sun protection for the 5-mile Alkali Flat Trail, crossing an ancient lakebed now piled high with dunes. Despite the name, it's not flat at all: Along the way, spot ridges, pinnacles, and some of the biggest dunes in the park.

Plan to make it back to the visitor center at least one hour before dusk, because that's when the ranger-guided Sunset Stroll departs. You'll see dunes similar to those on the Alkali Flat Trail, but with a local expert to fill you in on the plants, animals, and geology you encounter.

For dinner, head east to the historic mountain town of Cloudcroft for wood-fired pizza and craft beer at the **Cloudcroft Brewing Company.** The chorizo- and green chile-topped pizza is a local favorite, preferably served alongside a pint of Trainwreck IPA.

Day 2

With the best coffee in town, **Black Bear Coffee Shop** is the place to start the morning. Drinks are made with New Mexico–roasted beans, and there's a light menu of breakfast pastries, including gluten-free and vegetarian options. Before leaving town, stock up on everything you'll need for a day in White Sands National Park, including plenty of water and a picnic lunch.

Start the drive to the national park, pausing just west of town to take in the view from the Mexican Canyon Trestle Overlook, where you'll see the impressive wooden structure that once carried trains across the chasm.

When you reach the park, stop by the gift shop to pick up a plastic snow saucer, an essential piece of equipment for a morning of dune sledding. Park staffers are great with tips on the best sites to go sledding, but a good place to start is in the landscape surrounding the half-mile Interdune Boardwalk. Next, tick off the mile-long Dune Life Nature Trail, with a series of signs covering the foxes, birds, reptiles, and other wildlife that live in the sand here.

After a picnic lunch, leave the park behind for a trip to Alamogordo's **New Mexico Museum of Space History,** whose exhibits highlight this region's history of rocket launches and test flights. On the way in, pay your respects to the gravesite of Ham the chimpanzee, who became the first hominid in space in 1961 and is now buried under a plaque dedicated to the "world's first astrochimp." The museum's highlights include the International Space Hall of Fame and a simulated Martian landscape.

By now, it's time for a scoop of pistachio ice cream, best eaten in the shadow of the world's biggest pistachio. **McGinn's Pistachioland** is both a working pistachio farm and an old-fashioned roadside attraction, complete with an ice cream parlor, koi pond, wine tastings, and a mechanical talking cowboy named Pappy. Take a farm tour and graze the pistachio tasting bar before moving on.

Tonight, snag the fanciest table in Cloudcroft for dinner at **Rebecca's,** a restaurant named after the resident ghost at The Lodge Resort and Spa. The food is nicely done, old-school Continental, with entrées including Chateaubriand, prime rib, and steak.

Day 3

For breakfast, settle into the western-kitsch **Dusty Boots Café** for a hearty egg or skillet breakfast, ordering a slice or two of the house-made banana bread

to go. It's a great snack as you steer through the twists and turns of Sacramento Canyon Road on your way to the **Sunspot Solar Observatory,** where scientists from New Mexico State University keep an eye on the sun.

Inside the visitor center are a small museum and gift shop, and a short, paved trail wraps through portions of the campus that are open to the public. A few minutes farther along is the Apache Point Observatory, which can be viewed from the outside.

On your way back through Cloudcroft, pause for lunch at **Mad Jack's Mountaintop Barbecue,** known for Texas-style brisket you can enjoy at picnic tables outside. (The extra-cooked burnt ends get raves from people who know their meat.)

If you have time for one last hike before you hit the road, make it the 7.3-mile Bridal Veil Falls and Grand View Trail, which takes in a 45-foot waterfall, a restored railroad trestle, and a steep desert landscape that offers a rugged contrast to the dune hikes at White Sands.

Recommendations

Sights

McGinn's Pistachioland. ⊠ *7320 U.S. Hwy. 54, Alamogordo, NM* ☎ *800/368–3081* ⊕ *pistachioland.com* 🖅 *$2.*

New Mexico Museum of Space History. ⊠ *3198 State Rte. 2001, Alamogordo, NM* ☎ *575/437–2840* ⊕ *www.nmspace-museum.org* 🖅 *$8.*

Sunspot Solar Observatory. ⊠ *3004 Telescope Loop, Sunspot, NM* ☎ *575/434–7000* ⊕ *sunspot.solar* 🖅 *Free.*

Tularosa Basin Gallery of Photography. ⊠ *401 12th St., Carrizozo, NM* ☎ *575/937–1489* ⊕ *www.photozozo.org* 🖅 *Free* ⊙ *Closed Tues.*

White Sands National Park. ✉ *White Sands National Park Visitor Center, 19955 U.S. 70, Alamogordo, NM* ☎ *575/479–6124* ⊕ *www.nps.gov/whsa* 🖴 *$25 per car.*

🍴 Restaurants

Brown Bag Deli. Ⓢ *Average main: $8* ✉ *900 Washington Ave., Alamogordo, NM* ☎ *575/437–9751.*

Cloudcroft Brewing Company. Ⓢ *Average main: $13* ✉ *1301 Burro Ave., Cloudcroft, NM* ☎ *575/682–2337* ⊕ *www.cloudcroftbrewing.com.*

Dusty Boots Café. Ⓢ *Average main: $9* ✉ *1315 James Canyon Hwy., Cloudcroft, NM* ☎ *575/682–7577* ۞ *Closed Mon.–Wed.*

Mad Jack's Mountaintop Barbecue. Ⓢ *Average main: $15* ✉ *105 James Canyon Hwy., Cloudcroft, NM* ☎ *575/682–7577* ⊕ *www.facebook.com/madjacksbqshack* ۞ *Closed Mon.–Wed.*

Rebecca's. Ⓢ *Average main: $20* ✉ *The Lodge Resort and Spa, 601 Corona Pl., Cloudcroft, NM* ☎ *575/682–3131* ⊕ *www.thelodgeresort.com.*

Coffee and Quick Bites

Black Bear Coffee Shop. Ⓢ *Average main: $5* ✉ *200 Burro Ave., Cloudcroft, NM* ☎ *575/682–1239* ⊕ *www.mybbcoffee.com* ۞ *Closed Mon. and Tues. No dinner.*

🛏 Hotels

Cloudcroft Hostel. Ⓢ *Rooms from: $39* ✉ *1049 U.S. 82, High Rolls, NM* ☎ *575/682–0555* ⊕ *www.cloudcrofthostel.com* ۩ *No meals.*

The Lodge Resort and Spa. Ⓢ *Rooms from: $125* ✉ *601 Corona Pl., Cloudcroft, NM* ☎ *800/395–6343* ⊕ *www.thelodgeresort.com* ۩ *No meals.*

Chapter 3

MIDWEST AND GREAT PLAINS

WELCOME TO
MIDWEST AND GREAT PLAINS

TOP REASONS TO GO

★ **Amazing Architecture:** Frank Lloyd Wright's Fallingwater is just one of the region's masterpieces.

★ **Cheer for the Home Team:** Baseball fans shouldn't miss Kansas City's Negro Leagues Baseball Museum.

★ **Distinctive Distilleries:** Louisville is one of the most important stops on Kentucky's Bourbon Trail.

★ **Sample New Vintages:** Aficionados turn out for the top-notch reds and whites from Michigan Wine Country.

★ **Uncover Works of Art:** Galleries like the Milwaukee Museum of Art are just as impressive outside.

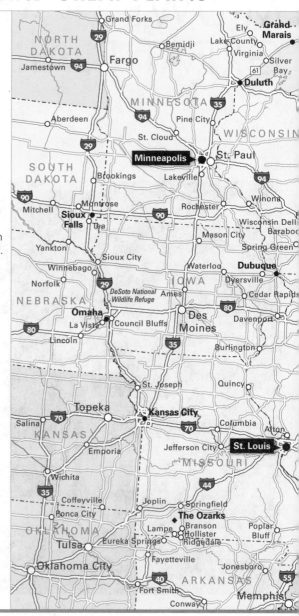

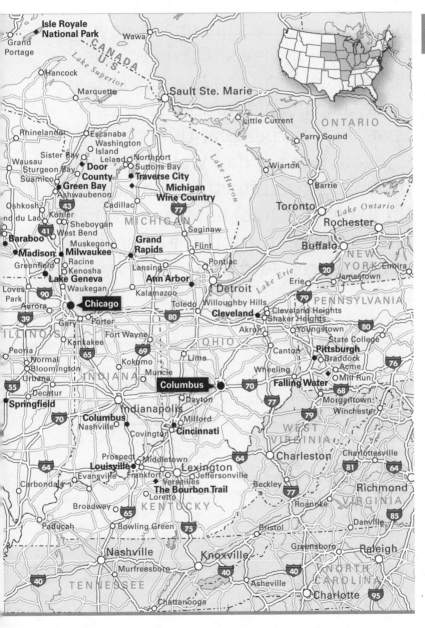

There's never a shortage of surprises in the Midwest and Great Plains region. Looking for a national park where you might be the only ones enjoying the sweeping views? On one of the largest islands in the Great Lakes, lovely Isle Royale National Park gets fewer visitors per year than the Grand Canyon does per day. Want to be wowed by amazing architecture? Columbus (Indiana, not Ohio) has the country's largest concentration of Modernist masterpieces. And there are few wine regions that win as many accolades as those around Michigan's Traverse City.

Chicago makes an excellent starting point for adventures throughout the area. It's within easy driving distance of delightful destinations like Wisconsin's Door County (dubbed the "Malibu of the Midwest" for its surfing culture) and Michigan's Wine Country. It's also perfect for city getaways to places like Milwaukee and Madison. **Minneapolis** is ideal for visiting Minnesota's Grand Marais and secluded Isle Royale National Park. Kentucky's Bourbon Country is a surprisingly short trip from **Columbus.** And the Ozarks—from the family-friendly attractions of Branson to the bubbling waters of Eureka Springs—are just one of the intriguing destinations from **St. Louis.**

Ann Arbor and Grand Rapids, MI

240 miles (approx. 4 hours) from Chicago.

While Michigan's lovely lakefront locales and sweeping wine country get the lion's share of attention from road-trippers, the two very underrated small cities of Ann Arbor (home to the University of Michigan) and Grand Rapids (known for its craft beer scene and dedication to art and culture) deserve your attention. Navigating these two cities in one weekend is very doable.

One of the most popular destinations in Grand Rapids is the 185-acre Frederik Meijer Gardens and Sculpture Park.

Planning

GETTING THERE AND BACK
From Chicago, it's about a four-hour drive along I–94 E to Ann Arbor. To get from there to Grand Rapids, take I–196 W for about two hours. A car is the best way by far to experience both these cities.

PIT STOPS
It would be a shame to drive so close to Lake Michigan and not see it up close. Stop along your way at **Indiana Dunes National Park,** one of the newest additions to the national park system. This waterfront "ecological treasure" is just minutes from the highway.

WHEN TO GO
Summer is the best time to visit, but you'll also find stunning fall foliage in late September and early October and wildflowers and fewer crowds in late spring. Try to avoid Ann Arbor any time the University of Minnesota Wolverines are playing at home.

WHERE TO STAY
CityFlats Hotel is an eco-friendly property in downtown Grand Rapids with a boutique-y feel, tasty street-level eatery, and excellent coffee shop. The **Graduate Ann Arbor,** with its preppy plaid decor and fun vibe, has a cocktail lounge and restaurant. It's a short walk to downtown Ann Arbor as well as sights near the University of Michigan campus.

Day 1

Enjoy your first meal in Ann Arbor at **Zingerman's Deli,** an institution that's been serving hearty sandwiches, salads, and soups since 1982. Walk off your meal at the 94,000-square-foot **University of Michigan Museum of Art,** which has fantastic rotating exhibits, or the **University of Michigan Museum of Natural History,** which has moved into a stunning new location with a state-of-the-art planetarium.

College towns are often known for international cuisine, and Ann Arbor is no exception. Main Street is loaded with options, including **Shalimar** (Indian), and, for happy hour, **Bløm Meadworks** (a mead producer and cidery with a tasting room). Give yourself time to poke into the boutiques along the thoroughfare, including the popular comic book store **Vault of Midnight** and the highly regarded **Literati Bookstore.**

Day 2

Don't depart for Grand Rapids until you've experienced the **Ann Arbor Farmers Market.** It's located in a century-old building and sells much more than fruits and veggies. Maple syrup, coffee beans, smoked fish, and goat's-milk products are also on offer.

Once in Grand Rapids, stretch your legs while absorbing the beauty at **Frederik Meijer Gardens and Sculpture Park,** a 185-acre swath with trails through lovely outdoor gardens. Wear comfortable walking shoes.

Another afternoon activity, particularly if you adore Frank Lloyd Wright's designs, is touring the **Meyer May House,** one of his last designs. Steelcase (a Michigan furniture designer that also produced some of Wright's forward-thinking furnishings) gave this building a top-to-bottom restoration.

If you like craft beer, there's no shortage in Grand Rapids, beginning with **Brewery Vivant,** inside a former funeral chapel in East Hills. Pub fare includes less-common options like drunken noodles and Cuban sandwiches.

Day 3

Grand Rapids has a killer coffee scene, but if you only have time to experience one, make it downtown's **Madcap Coffee Company.** The **Grand Rapids Art Museum,** right across the street, is a gem housing works by renowned artists like Richard Diebenkorn.

Before driving back to Chicago, return to the East Hills neighborhood for eclectic boutique shopping (from kitchen goods at **Art of the Table** to crystals at **Spirit Dreams**). Follow this with a late lunch or early dinner at **The Green Well,** a gastropub that also serves specialties like pierogies and whitefish sandwiches. For a little bit more sass, The **Electric Cheetah** serves 40 craft root beers on tap along with comfort food and "monster cookies" that are perfect for the drive home). Or drop by **Furniture City Creamery** for an ice-cream cone.

Recommendations

Sights

Frederik Meijer Gardens and Sculpture Park. ⊠ *1000 E. Beltline Ave. NE, Grand Rapids, MI* ☎ *616/957–1580* ⊕ *www. meijergardens.org* 🎟 *$15.*

Indiana Dunes National Park. ⊠ *1215 N. Indiana State Rd. 49, Porter, IN* ☎ *219/395–1882* ⊕ *www.nps.gov/indu* 🎟 *$6 per car.*

Meyer May House. ⊠ *450 Madison Ave. SE, Grand Rapids, MI* ☎ *616/246–4821* ⊕ *www.meyermayhouse.steelcase.com* 🎟 *Free* ⊙ *Closed Mon., Wed., Fri., and Sat.*

University of Michigan Museum of Art. ⊠ *525 S. State St., Ann Arbor, MI* ☎ *734/764–0395* ⊕ *www.umma.umich. edu* 🎟 *Free.*

University of Michigan Museum of Natural History. ⊠ *Biological Sciences Bldg., 1105 N. University Ave., Ann Arbor, MI* ☎ *734/764–0478* ⊕ *lsa.umich.edu/ummnh* ⊙ *Free.*

Restaurants

Brewery Vivant. 💲 *Average main: $14* ⊠ *925 Cherry St. SE, Grand Rapids, MI* ☎ *616/719–1604* ⊕ *www.breweryvivant. com* ⊙ *No lunch.*

The Electric Cheetah. [$] *Average main: $15* ✉ *1015 Wealthy St. SE, Grand Rapids, MI* ☎ *616/451–4779* 🌐 *www.electriccheetah.com* 🕑 *Closed Sun.*

The Green Well. [$] *Average main: $20* ✉ *924 Cherry St. SE, Grand Rapids, MI* ☎ *616/808–3566* 🌐 *www.thegreenwell.com.*

Shalimar. [$] *Average main: $10* ✉ *307 S. Main St., Ann Arbor, MI* ☎ *734/663–1500* 🌐 *www.shalimarrestaurant.com.*

Zingerman's Deli. [$] *Average main: $11* ✉ *422 Detroit St., Ann Arbor, MI* ☎ *734/663–3354* 🌐 *www.zingermansdeli.com.*

Coffee and Quick Bites

Furniture City Creamery. [$] *Average main: $8* ✉ *958 Cherry St. SE, Grand Rapids, MI* ☎ *616/920–0752* 🌐 *www.furniturecitycreamery.com* 🕑 *No lunch.*

Madcap Coffee Company. [$] *Average main: $5* ✉ *98 Monroe Center St. NW, Grand Rapids MI* ☎ *888/866–9091* 🌐 *www.madcapcoffee.com* 🕑 *No dinner Sun.*

Hotels

CityFlats Hotel. [$] *Rooms from: $181* ✉ *83 Monroe Center St. NW, Grand Rapids, MI* ☎ *616/608–1720* 🌐 *www.cityflatshotel.com* 🍴 *No meals.*

Graduate Ann Arbor. [$] *Rooms from: $287* ✉ *615 E. Huron St., Ann Arbor, MI* ☎ *734/769–2200* 🌐 *www.graduatehotels.com* 🍴 *No meals.*

Nightlife

Bløm Meadworks. ✉ *100 S. 4th Ave., Ann Arbor, MI* ☎ *734/548–9729* 🌐 *www.drinkblom.com.*

Shopping

Ann Arbor Farmers Market. ✉ *315 Detroit St., Ann Arbor, MI* ☎ *734/794–6255* 🌐 *www.a2farmersmarket.org.*

Art of the Table. ✉ *606 Wealthy St. SE, Grand Rapids, MI* ☎ *616/301–1885* 🌐 *www.artofthetable.com.*

Literati Bookstore. ✉ *124 E. Washington St., Ann Arbor, MI* ☎ *734/585–5567* 🌐 *www.literatibookstore.com.*

Spirit Dreams. ✉ *1430 Lake Dr. SE, Grand Rapids, MI* ☎ *616/456–9889* 🌐 *www.spiritdreamsgr.com.*

Vault of Midnight. ✉ *219 S. Main St., Ann Arbor, MI* ☎ *734/998–1413* 🌐 *www.vaultofmidnight.com.*

Cincinnati, OH

Cincinnati is 295 miles (approx. 4½ hours) from Chicago.

After a speaking engagement there in 1901, Winston Churchill called Cincinnati "the most beautiful of the inland cities of the union," saying that "the city spreads far and wide, its pageant of crimson, purple, and gold laced by silver streams that are great rivers." Meanwhile, novelist Charles Dickens described it as, "cheerful, thriving, and animated." Do these feted Brits flirt with hyperbole? Perhaps, but there's no knocking Cincy's charms. While many dismiss Cincinnati as a sleepy Midwestern town, this southern Ohio hub exudes a unique energy that can't be ignored. The historic Over-the-Rhine (OTR) district has lively Findlay Market, which draws culinary enthusiasts by the carload on the weekends while recent renovations of downtown Cincy's riverfront Great American Ballpark and Fountain Square also speak to Cincy's renaissance. But the bustling municipality has its natural assets, too. There are more than 80 parks throughout the city, adding to its appeal.

Planning

GETTING THERE AND BACK

To get to Cincinnati, drive about three hours south on I–64 from Chicago, then another hour and a half south on I–74.

INSPIRATION

On the drive, check out the podcasts "Around Cincinnati" and "The Cincinnati Edition," great sources for the latest on the city.

WHEN TO GO

Cincinnati's summers are hot and humid, pulling in heat from the Ohio River, and yet there's plenty on the city's calendar during these months. One of the best times to visit Cincinnati is in the fall, when temperatures are ideal, in the 50s and 60s, and the trees show their autumn colors.

WHERE TO STAY

21C Museum Hotel's restoration of the old Metropole Hotel in Cincinnati's historic center helped spur the renaissance of downtown Cincy. Fittingly positioned next to the Contemporary Art Center and across from the Aronoff Center for the Arts, the hotel doubles as an art gallery with rotating exhibitions in the lobby, original art in every guest room, and regular guided tours.

One of the area's hippest hotels, **Hotel Covington,** isn't actually in Cincy itself but a quick jaunt across the Ohio River in nearby Covington, Kentucky. Industrial chic meets time-honored tradition at this trendy hideaway whose past as a department store is on display in everything from its high ceilings to its gigantic window displays. History buffs will want to stay at **Six Acres,** a B&B in the suburb of College Hill about 15 minutes from downtown Cincinnati. It was a stop on the Underground Railroad, housing fugitive slaves as they made their way north to freedom.

Day 1

Leave Chicago early morning and arrive in Cincinnati just in time for lunch at buzzy eatery **Fausto,** inside the downtown **Contemporary Arts Center.** Order the tarragon chicken salad sandwich with pistachios and an iced coffee from the owner's custom-label coffee blend, a collaboration with Cincinnati-based **Deeper Roots Coffee. Nada,** an upscale cantina with outdoor seating, is about five minutes away if you're in the mood for Mexican instead.

After lunch, browse through the Zaha Hadid–designed **Contemporary Arts Center,** which the New York Times called "the best new building since the Cold War." Does the museum's name sound familiar? It made national headlines in 1990 when it was prosecuted for exhibiting sexually charged images by photographer Robert Mapplethorpe. Browse the museum's 11,000 square feet and see new developments in painting, sculpture, photography, architecture, performance art, and new media.

If your caffeine buzz holds out, walk to the nearby 21C Museum Hotel and get lost in the galleries, or visit the neighboring Cincinnati Arts Association's **Weston Art Gallery,** a staging ground for emerging art by local, national, and international artists.

Settle in for a leisurely dinner at **Sotto,** one of the Queen City's most popular restaurants just across the street from CAC. The Italian fare here is raved about by everyone, especially the black kale Caesar salad and short rib cappellacci. In the mood for a nightcap? Hit the patio of the new spot **Night Drop** for a Mezcal and root beer float, or bring your own growlers and fill them up with a selection of craft beers on tap. (And if Italian isn't your thing, you can skip Soto and grab a burger or Cobb salad from Night Drop's bar menu.)

Day 2

Start the day with the lemon ricotta pancakes or one of many omelets at **Maplewood Kitchen & Bar.** For breakfast all day, descend upon the shabby chic **Cheapside Café** for a chorizo and egg sandwich or oatmeal brulee (steel-cut oats, golden raisins, and maple cream.)

Now that you're suitably fed, it's time to walk off some of those calories. **Cincinnati Nature Center** in Milford, just minutes from downtown, covers more than 1,700 acres, forests, fields, streams and ponds with almost 20 miles of trails. Wear comfortable walking shoes and enjoy spring wildflowers or autumn foliage, depending on the season.

If you're on a budget and fancy a free outing instead, mosey on over to **French Park** in Amberley Village, where a series of trails are hidden behind French House, a 1900s brick mansion set majestically on the hill. There are four trailheads that lead out of the parking lot. The outermost trail is about three miles long and is an intermediate trail, not for novice hikers.

For lunch, head to **Senate,** which serves gourmet hot dogs in Cincy's hip Over-the-Rhine neighborhood. The space is rustic and sleek and the dogs are creative and tasty. Try the Shia LaBeouf with goat cheese, caramelized onions, bacon, arugula, and balsamic vinegar. For healthier fare, hightail it over to Trio and order one of its specialty salads. The Scottish Salmon Salad with field greens is a local favorite.

This afternoon, sit back, relax, and enjoy a sightseeing cruise on the Ohio River. **BB Riverboats** offers a 90-minute sightseeing tour full of interesting tidbits from the captain. For example, did you know that one out of every four steamboats built in the United States came from Cincinnati?

Don your best duds for dinner at one of the most celebrated restaurants in Cincinnati, if not Ohio. **The Orchids at Palm Court** restaurant in the National Historic Landmark **Hilton Cincinnati Netherland Plaza** (where Churchill stayed), not only boasts towering ceilings and Romanesque murals, but also a French-influenced, 10-course tasting menu. Dishes change depending on what's in season, but might include squash blossoms with green tomato and soubise or seared scallops with lardo, dukkah, and sunflower seeds. End your evening with a tipple at the adjoining bar.

For a less formal affair, head to Over-the-Rhine and the casual **Forty Thieves,** a walk-up Middle Eastern street-food counter by the streetcar stop at Liberty and Race.

Before bedtime, make your way to the **Cincinnati Observatory,** open late on Saturday. It hosts a date-night-under-the-stars event where you and your main squeeze will be able to view astronomical objects through the observatory's giant telescope.

Day 3

On your last day, head to **Findlay Market,** Cincinnati's oldest covered public market, selling unique foods at its many stalls. Occasionally there's even live music. Enjoy breakfast on-the-go with a pastry from **Blue Oven** or a Honey Puff Donut from **Cherbourg Cyprus** (their T-shirts make a great Cincy souvenir). People-watch and shop for everything from artisan goods to specialty food items to homemade dog biscuits for your canine.

Spend the rest of the morning walking across the John A. Roebling Suspension Bridge, named for the civil engineer who designed it and offering some of the most beautiful views of the Cincy skyline. When the Roebling opened in 1867, its 1,057-foot span made it the longest suspension bridge in the world. It remained so until 1883 when Roebling's even more famous project, the Brooklyn Bridge, opened.

For lunch head to **Commonwealth Bistro** for modern American fare and reward yourself for your walk with a craft beer at the restaurant's midcentury modern-style rooftop bar, **Yonder,** Or choose **Frida 602** just up the road for a la carte tacos and other Mexican dishes in a stylish setting inspired by artist Frida Kahlo.

Head back over the bridge to the **Underground Railroad Freedom Center.** On the banks of the Ohio River, the center displays relics from the era such as a shackle-filled pen that once held slaves going to auction. The museum features a Rosa Parks virtual-reality exhibit whereby visitors don a headset to experience how the civil rights pioneer refused to give up her seat on a bus.

Before hitting the road, grab a pulled pork sandwich from **Eli's BBQ** or the Reuben at **Izzy's.** Both are Cincy favorites.

Recommendations

Sights

Cincinnati Nature Center. ⊠ 4949 Tealtown Rd., Milford, OH ☎ 513/831–1711 ⊕ www.cincynature.org ⌚ $9.

Cincinnati Observatory. ⊠ 3489 Observatory Pl., Cincinnati, OH ☎ 513/321–5186 ⊕ www.cincinnatiobservatory.org ⌚ $5.

Contemporary Arts Center. ⊠ 44 E. 6th St., Cincinnati, OH ☎ 513/345–8400 ⊕ www. contemporaryartscenter.org ⌚ Free ⊙ Closed Mon. and Tues.

French Park. ⊠ 3012 Section Rd., Cincinnati, OH ☎ 513/357–2604 ⊕ www. cincinnatiparks.com ⌚ Free.

National Underground Railroad Freedom Center. ⊠ 50 E. Freedom Way, Cincinnati, OH ☎ 513/333–7739 ⊕ www. freedomcenter.org ⌚ $15 ⊙ Closed Mon.

Weston Art Gallery ⊠ 650 Walnut St., Cincinnati, OH ☎ 513/621–2787 ⊕ www. cincinnatiarts.org ⌚ Free ⊙ Closed Mon.

⦿ Restaurants

Cheapside Café. Ⓢ Average main: $9 ⊠ 326 E. 8th St., Cincinnati, OH ☎ 513/345–6618 ⊕ www.facebook.com/ cheapsidecincinnati ⊙ No dinner.

Commonwealth Bistro. Ⓢ Average main: $25 ⊠ 621 Main St., Covington, KY ☎ 859/916–6719 ⊕ commonwealthbistro. com ⊙ Closed Mon. and Tues. No lunch Wed.–Fri.

Eli's BBQ. Ⓢ Average main: $21 ⊠ 133 W. Elder St., Cincinnati, OH ☎ 513/533–1957 ⊕ www.elisbarbeque.com.

Fausto. Ⓢ Average main: $25 ⊠ Contemporary Arts Center,44 E. 6th St., Cincinnati, OH ☎ 513/345–2979 ⊕ www. faustoatthecac.com ⊙ No dinner Mon.

Forty Thieves. Ⓢ Average main: $10 ⊠ 1538 Race St., Cincinnati, OH ☎ 513/818–9020 ⊕ fortythievesgang.com ⊙ Closed Mon. No lunch Tues.–Thurs.

Frida 602. Ⓢ Average main: $10 ⊠ 602 Main St., Covington, KY ☎ 859/815–8736 ⊕ www.fridaonmain.com ⊙ Closed Mon.

Izzy's. Ⓢ Average main: $10 ⊠ 800 Elm St., Cincinnati, OH ☎ 513/721–4241 ⊕ izzys.com.

Maplewood Kitchen & Bar. Ⓢ Average main: $15 ⊠ 525 Race St., Cincinnati, OH ☎ 513/421–2100 ⊕ www.maplewoodkitchenandbar.com.

Nada. Ⓢ Average main: $19 ⊠ 600 Walnut St., Cincinnati, OH ☎ 513/721–6232 ⊕ www.eatdrinknada.com.

Orchids at Palm Court. Ⓢ Average main: $44 ⊠ Hilton Cincinnati Netherland Plaza, 35 W. 5th St., Cincinnati, OH

☎ 513/564–6465 🌐 www.orchidsatpalm-court.com ⏰ Closed Mon.

Senate. [$] *Average main: $18* ✉ *1212 Vine St., Cincinnati, OH* ☎ *513/421–2020* 🌐 *senatepub.com* ⏰ *Closed Sun.–Wed.*

Sotto. [$] *Average main: $35* ✉ *118 E. 6th St., Cincinnati, OH* ☎ *513/977–6886* 🌐 *www.sottocincinnati.com* ⏰ *No lunch.*

Trio Bistro. [$] *Average main: $28* ✉ *7565 Kenwood Rd., Cincinnati, OH* ☎ *513/984–1905* 🌐 *www.triobistro.com.*

Coffee and Quick Bites

Blue Oven. [$] *Average main: $6* ✉ *125 W. Elder St., Cincinnati, OH* ☎ *513/421–9100* 🌐 *www.blueovenbakery.com* ⏰ *Closed Mon. No dinner.*

Cherbourg Cyprus. [$] *Average main: $5* ✉ *1804 Race St., Cincinnati, OH* ☎ *513/827–9767* 🌐 *cherbourgcyprus.com* ⏰ *Closed Mon. No dinner.*

Deeper Roots Coffee. [$] *Average main: $5* ✉ *2108 Colerain Ave., Cincinnati, OH* ☎ *513/655–6535* 🌐 *www.deeper-rootscoffee.com* ⏰ *No dinner.*

Hotels

Hilton Cincinnati Netherland Plaza. [$] *Rooms from: $141* ✉ *35 W. 5th St., Cincinnati, OH* ☎ *513/421–9100* 🌐 *www.hilton.com* 🍴 *No meals.*

Hotel Covington. [$] *Rooms from: $199* ✉ *638 Madison Ave., Covington, KY* ☎ *859/905–6600* 🌐 *hotelcovington.com* 🍴 *No meals.*

Six Acres Bed & Breakfast. [$] *Rooms from: $146* ✉ *5350 Hamilton Ave., Cincinnati, OH* ☎ *513/541–0873* 🌐 *sixacresbb.com* 🍴 *Free breakfast.*

21C Museum Hotel. [$] *Rooms from: $216* ✉ *609 Walnut St., Cincinnati, OH* ☎ *513/578–6600* 🌐 *www.21cmuseumhotels.com* 🍴 *No meals.*

Nightlife

Night Drop. ✉ *1535 Madison Rd., Cincinnati, OH* ☎ *513/221–2702* 🌐 *www.drinkatdrop.com.*

Yonder. ✉ *Commonwealth Bistro, 621 Main St., Covington, KY* ☎ *859/916–6719* 🌐 *commonwealthbistro.com.*

Shopping

Findlay Market. ✉ *19 W. Elder St., Cincinnati, OH* ☎ *513/665–4839* 🌐 *www.findlaymarket.org* ⏰ *Closed Mon.*

Activities

BB Riverboats. ✉ *101 Riverboat Row, Newport, KY* ☎ *800/261–8586* 🌐 *bbriverboats.com* 🎫 *Cruises from $23.*

Cleveland, OH

Cleveland is 345 miles (approx. 5 hours) from Chicago.

It's common knowledge that LeBron James led the Cleveland Cavaliers to their first NBA championship in his hometown in 2016, and that disc jockey Alan Freed coined the term "rock and roll" on his Cleveland radio show in 1951. But did you know that this former steel town is also a wilderness mecca with countless opportunities for outdoor recreation? Founded by Moses Cleaveland on July 22, 1796, C-town was originally called the "Forest City," a moniker derived from the high density of trees within the city limits. More recently, it's been dubbed "The Emerald Necklace" because from above, Cleveland's plethora of parks, nature preserves, golf courses, and hiking trails resemble a green necklace wrapped around the city. In fact, Cleveland's Metroparks System is one of the most extensive city park systems in the country, encompassing more than 23,000 acres of parkland. And

An easy hiking trail takes you to Quarry Rock Falls in Cleveland's South Chagrin Reservation.

the 100-mile long Cuyahoga River, which famously caught fire in 1969, has cleaned up its act and became an official Ohio Water Trail in 2019, making it a better, safer place to play.

Planning

GETTING THERE AND BACK
To get to Cleveland, drive five hours east on I–90 from Chicago.

WHEN TO GO
Cleveland is a year-round destination, although temperatures dip into the low 20s from December to February, when cold-water surfers have been known to brave the waves on Lake Erie. Enjoy hiking and biking in spring, boating in summer, and fall foliage in autumn.

WHERE TO STAY
The National Register of Historic Places–ranked 60-room **Glidden House** in University Circle is surrounded by gardens and offers "vintage suites" in a 1910 French Gothic mansion and newer rooms in a

contemporary addition. Glidden House is within minutes of the Cleveland Museum of Art, The Cleveland Botanical Gardens, The Museum of Contemporary Art, and The Cleveland Cultural Gardens, a three-mile path created in the 1920s as a tribute to the diverse ethnic groups who contributed to the city's heritage.

Architecture buffs will swoon over a getaway at the **Louis Penfield House,** one of nine Usonian homes in Ohio built by Frank Lloyd Wright in 1955. This three-bedroom design masterpiece sits on a rise overlooking the Chagrin River in the Cleveland suburb of Willoughby Hills.

Day 1

Leave Chicago early morning and arrive in Cleveland for a late lunch at **Brassica,** a casual Lebanese restaurant in the Market Hall of Shaker Heights' Van Aken District. Something akin to a Mediterranean-style Chipotle, this buzzing eatery is known for its pita sandwiches and salads filled with brassica vegetables, falafel, chicken, brisket, or glazed-lamb bacon. Order a side of seasoned fries and you'll be fortified for an afternoon of outdoor fun. If you crave Italian, walk a few feet across the marketplace to **Scorpacciata Pasta Co.**

Head 20 minutes north up Chagrin Boulevard to **South Chagrin Reservation,** one of 18 protected wilderness preserves in the Cleveland Metroparks where hemlock-lined hiking trails and sandstone ledges straddle the scenic Chagrin River. Visit the massive sculpture known as Henry Church Rock, chiseled from a sandstone boulder by Cleveland blacksmith Henry Church in 1885. Be on the lookout for nesting forest birds in this Audubon-designated "important bird area."

After communing with your inner naturalist, choose from a menu of a dozen thin-crust wood-fired oven pies at **Vero Pizza** in Cleveland Heights. These unfussy though tasty pizzas are best when accompanied by Vero's Caesar salad. If you're in the mood for tacos instead, snag a seat on the patio at **Barrio** just across the street.

For a festive end to your first evening, pop into **Nighttown** next door for a cocktail and an earful of jazz. Nighttown draws some of the best jazz talent in the country and a diverse, upscale crowd (expect a cover charge for live bands).

Day 2

Start the day with breakfast at **Luna Bakery & Café** (get herb scrambled eggs or avocado toast). Luna's friendly baristas will make you something to sip long after you've eaten, so you can ease into your day at an outdoor table with some of the best people watching on Cleveland's east side. If diner food is more your thing, **Tommy's Restaurant** is just up the road.

It's an easy drive along Fairmount Boulevard past stately Rockefeller-era mansions to the **Nature Center at Shaker Lakes.** Once there, hop on the elevated (and ADA-accessible) boardwalk, which runs along the All People's Trail. You'll see marshes, ravines, streams and woodlands, rife with native blooms in summer. Stroll across the street to Lower Shaker Lake, home to mallard families and great blue herons.

A few minutes from here you'll find **The Stone Oven,** where you can enjoy a farm-to-table lunch of soup, salad, and iced tea. Try the dill tuna salad sandwich on Stone Oven's famous crusty bread with a bowl of gazpacho. **Boss Dog Brewing** up the road serves sandwiches and local craft beer on tap.

While it may sound strange to spend time in a cemetery while on vacation, ask anyone who's ever been to **Cleveland's Lake View Cemetery** and they'll put your mind at ease. This 284-acre scenic park on a hill at the edge of Cleveland Heights is covered in hundreds of daffodils, earning it the name Daffodil Hill. Benches are peppered throughout, as well as unique grave markers for notables such as industrialist John D Rockefeller, former President James Garfield, and prohibition agent Elliot Ness. Don't miss the stained-glass windows inside Lake View's Wade Memorial Chapel designed by Louis Comfort Tiffany.

The perfect Saturday night dinner spot is **L'Albatros,** a French brasserie inside an old carriage house with an excellent wine list and one of the loveliest outdoor patios in Cleveland. After dinner, hightail it to Hingetown and gallery hop from **SPACES** to **Transformer Station,** both showing newly commissioned contemporary work. Wind down your evening at **Jukebox,** a bar with a rotating jukebox selection that highlights bands coming to town for shows.

Day 3

On your last day, head to the **West Side Market,** an indoor/outdoor market and Cleveland institution. Browse more than 100 food stalls and get to know the locals with a crepe in hand from **Crepes de Luxe.** For a sit-down brunch, head to **Flying Fig** and order the breakfast sandwich on brioche.

Spend the rest of the morning exploring funky Ohio City. Browse through boutiques like **Wild Cactus** and **Salty Not Sweet,** or get your groove on at **The Stone Oven** record shop. The **Glass Bubble Project** sells blown-glass tableware and lighting pendants by local artisans.

Drive across the Hope Memorial Bridge for lunch at **Downtown Heinen's,** an upscale grocery store with a dining area inside the refurbished Cleveland Trust Bank. This architectural gem has been compared to the Pantheon in Rome and food writer Michael Ruhlman sings the store's praises in his critically acclaimed book, *Grocery.* If you prefer a more formal atmosphere, **Parker's Downtown** is just across the street.

After lunch, make a jaunt to the East 9th Street Pier for a peak at the *William G. Mather* Steamship. This restored Great Lakes freighter has been called "The Ship that Built Cleveland" on account of its many voyages to Cleveland's steel mills.

Before hitting the road, grab a corned beef on rye at **Slyman's,** a longtime Cleveland favorite. For something on the lighter side, go to **Dave's Cosmic Subs** and order the vegetarian Haight Ashbury Sub with vinaigrette.

Recommendations

Sights

Lake View Cemetery. ⊠ *12316 Euclid Ave., Cleveland, OH* ☎ *216/421–2665* ⊕ *lakeviewcemetery.com* ⌦ *$14.*

Nature Center at Shaker Lakes. ⊠ *2600 S. Park Blvd. Cleveland, OH* ☎ *216/421– 2665* ⊕ *shakerlakes.org* ⌦ *Free.*

South Chagrin Reservation. ⊠ *Hawthorn Hwy., Cleveland, OH* ☎ *440/248–5919* ⊕ *www.clevelandmetroparks.com* ⌦ *Free.*

Steamship *William G. Mather* **Museum.** ⊠ *601 Erieside Ave., Cleveland, OH* ☎ *216/694–2000* ⊕ *greatscience.com/ explore/exhibits/william-g-mather-steamship* ⌦ *$9.*

Restaurants

Barrio. Ⓢ *Average main: $10* ⊠ *2466 Fairmount Blvd., Cleveland Heights, OH* ☎ *216/862–3498* ⊕ *barrio-tacos.com* ☾ *No lunch Mon.–Thurs.*

Boss Dog Brewing. Ⓢ *Average main: $16* ⊠ *2179 Lee Rd., Cleveland Heights, OH* ☎ *216/321–2337* ⊕ *bossdogbrewing.com* ☾ *No lunch weekdays.*

Brassica. Ⓢ *Average main: $10* ⊠ *20301 Meade Rd., Shaker Heights, OH* ☎ *216/848–0450* ⊕ *brassicas.com.*

Crepes de Luxe. Ⓢ *Average main: $8* ⊠ *1979 W. 25th St., Cleveland, OH* ☎ *216/241–2479* ⊕ *www.crepesdeluxe. com.*

Dave's Cosmic Subs. Ⓢ *Average main: $11* ⊠ *1918 E. 6th St., Cleveland, OH* ☎ *216/861–4199* ⊕ *www.davescosmicsubs.com.*

Flying Fig. Ⓢ *Average main: $18* ⊠ *2523 Market Ave., Cleveland, OH* ☎ *216/241– 4243* ⊕ *www.theflyingfig.com* ☾ *No lunch weekdays.*

Heinen's of Downtown Cleveland. $
Average main: $12 ✉ *900 Euclid Ave.,
Cleveland, OH* ☎ *216/302–3020* ⊕ *www.
heinens.com.*

L'Albatros. $ *Average main: $24*
✉ *11401 Bellflower Rd., Cleveland, OH*
☎ *216/791–5555* ⊕ *albatrosbrasserie.
com.*

Luna Bakery & Café. $ *Average main:
$10* ✉ *2482 Fairmount Blvd., Cleveland
Heights, OH* ☎ *216/791–5555* ⊕ *ww.
lunabakerycafe.com* ⊗ *No dinner.*

Parker's Downtown. $ *Average main:
$28* ✉ *2000 E. 9th St., Cleveland, OH*
☎ *216/357–2680* ⊕ *www.parkersdown-
town.com.*

Scorpacciata Pasta Co. $ *Average main:
$12* ✉ *3441 Tuttle Rd., Shaker Heights,
OH* ☎ *216/513–9822* ⊕ *www.scorpacciat-
apastaco.com* ⊗ *No dinner Sun.*

Slyman's Restaurant and Deli. $ *Average
main: $16* ✉ *3106 St. Clair Ave. NE,
Cleveland, OH* ☎ *216/621–3760* ⊕ *www.
slymans.com* ⊗ *No dinner.*

The Stone Oven Bakery. $ *Average main:
$8* ✉ *2267 Lee Rd. Cleveland, OH*
☎ *216/932–3003* ⊕ *stone-oven.com.*

Tommy's Restaurant. $ *Average main: $10*
✉ *1824 Coventry Rd., Cleveland Heights,
OH* ☎ *216/321–7757* ⊕ *tommyscoventry.
com.*

Vero Pizza Napoletana. $ *Average main:
$18* ✉ *12421 Cedar Rd., Cleveland
Heights, OH* ☎ *216/229–8383* ⊕ *vero-
cleveland.com* ⊗ *Closed Sun. and Mon.*

 Hotels

Glidden House. $ *Rooms from: $163*
✉ *1901 Ford Dr., Cleveland, OH*
☎ *216/800–9467* ⊕ *www.gliddenhouse.
com* ⦿ *Free breakfast.*

Louis Penfield House. $ *Rooms from:
$300* ✉ *32203 River Rd., Willoughby
Hills, OH* ☎ *440/867–6667* ⊕ *www.pen-
fieldhouse.com* ⦿ *No meals.*

 Nightlife

Jukebox. ✉ *1404 W. 29th St., Cleveland,
OH* ☎ *216/206–7699* ⊕ *www.jukeboxcle.
com.*

Nighttown. ✉ *12387 Cedar Rd., Cleveland, OH* ☎ *216/795–0550* ⊕ *www.
nighttowncleveland.com.*

 Shopping

The Glass Bubble Project. ✉ *2421 Bridge
Ave., Cleveland, OH* ☎ *216/696–7043*
⊕ *glassbubbleproject.com.*

Salty Not Sweet. ✉ *2074 W. 25th St.,
Cleveland, OH* ☎ *330/690–6810* ⊕ *sa-
ltynotsweetcraft.wordpress.com.*

SPACES. ✉ *2900 Detroit Ave., Cleveland,
OH* ☎ *216/621–2314* ⊕ *www.spacescle.
org.*

Transformer Station. ✉ *1460 W. 29th St.,
Cleveland, OH* ☎ *216/938–5429* ⊕ *trans-
formerstation.org.*

West Side Market. ✉ *1979 W. 25th St.,
Cleveland, OH* ☎ *216/664–3387* ⊕ *west-
sidemarket.org.*

Wild Cactus. ✉ *2138 W. 25th St., Cleveland, OH* ☎ *216/970–4537* ⊕ *wildcactus-
company.com.*

Columbus, IN

*Columbus, IN is 189 miles (approx. 3
hours) from Columbus, OH, and 228
miles (approx. 3½ hours) from Chicago.*

Although it's surrounded by much larger
cities like Indianapolis, Cincinnati, and
Louisville, the modestly sized Midwestern community of Columbus draws
architect buffs from around the world.
It is home to the country's largest concentration of Modernist buildings, with
celebrated architects like I. M. Pei, Eero
Saarinen, Harry Weese, and Richard Mai-
er contributing some of their best work.
Even the local hangout for skateboarding

enthusiasts, Jolie Crider Memorial Skate Park, is a gem, designed by renowned Finnish designer Janne Saario.

But Columbus is also a magnet for craft brewery connoisseurs, art lovers (look for the striking installations by glass artist Dale Chihuly), and outdoors lovers (there are more than 27 miles of biking and hiking trails).

Planning

GETTING THERE AND BACK
To get here from Chicago, drive three hours and 45 minutes south on I-65. From Columbus, OH, take I-71 W, then skirt around the edge of Indianapolis and head south on I-65.

INSPIRATION
See the film *Columbus* starring Parker Posey and John Cho, a touching story about how relationships are affected by the buildings around us.

WHEN TO GO
The best time to visit is from May to September. Temperatures are pleasant and there's usually very little rain. January and December are the least comfortable months for a visit as temperatures fall into the 20s and snow is frequent.

WHERE TO STAY
A stately 1910 mansion, **The Inn at Irwin Gardens** is set on 2 acres in the heart of downtown Columbus. It's filled with original Edwardian furnishings and surrounded by sunken gardens designed to resemble Pompei. Breakfast at this impressive lodging includes freshly-baked breads among other homemade treats.

Day 1

Leave Chicago after breakfast and arrive in Columbus for lunch at **The Savory Swine,** a butcher shop and wine store with a lunch menu that serves sandwiches, salads, and charcuterie accompanied by a selection of fine vintages. Want to stretch your legs in the sun after the drive? Hit **Joe Willy's Burger Bar** and grab a seat at a table outside in this favorite local spot for American pub fare set in a 19th-century house with a patio.

Given Columbus' design cred, the first thing on your to-do list should be an architectural tour. The city offers a self-guided tour that covers more than 70 buildings. Though it's part of the tour, it's worth visiting the 1957 **Miller House and Garden** on your own. Designed by renowned architect Eero Saarinen, it's been ranked alongside Frank Lloyd Wright's Fallingwater, Mies van der Rohe's Farnsworth House, and Philip Johnson's Glass House as a perfect example of Modernism. Look for the interesting conversation pit, cylindrical fireplace, and grid pattern of skylights.

Enjoy dinner at **Flavors of India,** a stylish Indian restaurant serving authentic fare from Southern Asia. Knowledgeable servers and an extensive menu with vegetarian options have quickly made this a popular spot with locals. For something less formal, head to the **4th Street Bar and Grill,** where you'll find elevated pub grub like burgers with kimchi. There's often live music while you dine.

Day 2

Start the day with a stroll to the **Columbus Farmer's Market,** which takes place Saturday morning in downtown. Vendors from the area include farmers with fresh produce and local merchants with baked goods, coffee, and more. Grab a cup a joe at Dancing Goat Coffee and a pastry from Geri Girl Bakery, then share a pint of raspberries or basket of peaches from any number of vendors for a full-on market meal.

This morning, head just a few miles southeast of Columbus to the 11-acre lake at **Ceraland** and take a relaxing ride

Three-story-high windows surround the indoor playground at The Commons.

around the water in one of the four-seat paddle boats. Considered by many to be the city's best-kept secret, this once-private park is an oasis in the midst of the suburban sprawl. The park has a host of other outdoor activities, including miniature golf, horseshoes, and even cricket.

Prolong the green theme and go to **Fresh Take Kitchen** for lunch, where you can dine outside on a Green Goddess Salad (or another made-to-order treat). For a destination lunch, head to the 1903 **Columbus Pump House,** a former power station turned craft brewery. Nurse a local brew and feast on a pulled pork sandwich, then take a stroll around this Harrison Albright–designed landmark building.

After lunch, make your way to **The Commons,** a glass-enclosed community space that includes a playground with a gigantic children's climbing structure. Have teenagers in tow? Hightail it to the **Jolie Crider Memorial Skatepark,** designed by former professional skater Janne Saario. The 2,500 square foot park is as

beautiful to look at as it is challenging for board fanatics.

For dinner, treat yourselves to the hip **Henry Social Club,** a New American eatery in downtown Columbus serving everything from salt cod beignets to New York Strip steak. If you want to ditch fine dining and go casual, check out **ZwanzigZ** for gourmet pizza and beer.

After dinner, head to **Brown County Music Center,** just 20 minutes west of downtown. This 200-seat live music venue on the banks of Salt Creek hosts artists playing everything from jazz to rock to country. If you want to go rogue and brave the amateurs, visit the **Cozy Lounge** where craft cocktails, conversation, and karaoke comingle with mixed results.

Day 3

For breakfast, grab a booth at **Jill's Diner,** a local favorite with friendly service, hot coffee, and reliable diner fare. If you just want a quick bite, go to **Gramz Bakery** instead, where you can choose between a cinnamon roll or a pecan sticky bun to accompany your coffee.

After breakfast, rent a bike and explore the city. (The city's "People and Bike Trails" map is invaluable) You're likely to see swaths of wildflowers and several small creeks as you pass some of the city's striking modern architecture.

For lunch, head to **Ramen Alley** or **Tacolumbus,** then hit the road so you can be home at a reasonable hour.

Recommendations

Sights

Ceraland. ✉ *3989 S. 525 E, Columbus, IN* ☎ *812/377–5849* 🌐 *www.ceraland.org* 🎟 *$5.*

The Commons. ✉ *300 Washington St., Columbus, IN* ☎ *812/376–2681* 🌐 *thecommonscolumbus.com* 🎟 *Free.*

Jolie Crider Memorial Skatepark. ✉ *Clifty Park, Indiana Ave., Columbus, IN* ☎ *812/378–2622* 🌐 *columbus.in.us/crider-skatepark* 🎟 *Free.*

Miller House and Garden. ✉ *506 5th St., Columbus, IN* ☎ *800/468–6564* 🌐 *columbus.in.us/miller-house-and-garden-tour* 🎟 *$25* 🕑 *Closed Sun.–Thurs.*

Restaurants

Columbus Pump House. [$] *Average main: $14* ✉ *48 Lindsey St., Columbus, IN* ☎ *812/799–3587* 🌐 *www.uplandbeer.com/locations/columbus-pump-house* 🕑 *Closed Mon.*

Flavors of India. [$] *Average main: $12* ✉ *217 Washington St., Columbus, IN* ☎ *812/799–0050* 🌐 *flavorsofindia.co.*

4th Street Bar and Grill. [$] *Average main: $11* ✉ *433 4th St., Columbus, IN* ☎ *812/376–7063* 🌐 *www.4thstreetbar.com* 🕑 *Closed Sun.*

Fresh Take Kitchen. [$] *Average main: $7* ✉ *424 Washington St., Columbus, IN* ☎ *812/799–1097* 🌐 *www.freshtakekitchen.com.*

Henry Social Club. [$] *Average main: $32* ✉ *423 Washington St., Columbus, IN* ☎ *812/799–1371* 🌐 *henrysocialclub.com* 🕑 *Closed Sun. and Mon.*

Jill's Diner. [$] *Average main: $7* ✉ *421 7th St., Columbus, IN* ☎ *812/418–8970.*

Joe Willy's Burger Bar. [$] *Average main: $11* ✉ *1034 Washington St., Columbus, IN* ☎ *812/379–4559* 🌐 *www.joewillysburgers.com.*

The Savory Swine. [$] *Average main: $8* ✉ *410 Washington St., Columbus, IN* ☎ *812/657–7752* 🌐 *thesavoryswine.com* 🕑 *No dinner Sun.*

Tacolumbus. [$] *Average main: $7* ✉ *1637 N. National Rd., Columbus, IN* ☎ *812/393–1423.*

ZwanzigZ. [$] *Average main: $16* ✉ *1038 Lafayette Ave., Columbus, IN* ☎ *812/376–0200* 🌐 *www.zwanzigz.com.*

Coffee and Quick Bites

Gramz Bakery. [$] *Average main: $5* ✉ *409 Washington St., Columbus, IN* ☎ *812/378–9728* 🌐 *www.facebook.com/gramzbakery* 🕑 *Closed Sun. No dinner.*

Hotels

The Inn at Irwin Gardens. [$] *Rooms from: $236* ✉ *608 5th St., Columbus, IN* ☎ *812/376–3663* 🌐 *www.irwingardens.com* 🍴 *Free breakfast.*

Nightlife

Cozy Lounge. ✉ *3870 E. 25th St., Columbus, IN* ☎ *812/372–3165.*

🎭 Performing Arts

Brown County Music Center. ✉ *200 Maple Leaf Blvd., Nashville, IN* ☎ *812/988–5323* ⊕ *www.browncountymusiccenter.com* ✉ *Prices vary.*

Shopping

Columbus Farmer's Market. ✉ *123 Washington St., Columbus, IN* ☎ *812/371–1876* ⊕ *columbusfarmersmarket.org.*

Dubuque, IA

Dubuque is 180 miles (approx. 3½ hours) from Chicago.

Iowa's oldest city, Dubuque is in the middle of an exciting renaissance. A longtime farming and manufacturing town, Dubuque is seeing many of its gorgeously intact Industrial warehouses and Italianate commercial structures being transformed by an influx of new residents into thriving restaurants, bars, and hotels in the bustling Millwork District. Dubuque's culinary scene has recently created some buzz with spots like Brazen Open Kitchen, First and Main, and 7 Hills Brewing. Outdoor adventures include hiking at Mines of Spain and ziplining through the forests of Union Park.

Planning

GETTING THERE AND BACK
To get to Dubuque, head west on I–90 and U.S. Highway 20.

WHEN TO GO
The best time to visit Dubuque is from May to September. Temperatures then are pleasant, and there's little rain to keep you inside. The city is also popular for winter sports.

WHERE TO STAY
The 1839-built **Hotel Julien** has hosted Abraham Lincoln, Mark Twain, and the notorious mafia boss Al Capone, after whom the hotel named a suite. Back in the day, Capone was rumored to have reserved the entire eighth floor, stationing guards at all entrances and elevators for protection. Hotel Julien is considered Dubuque's grand dame, with an indoor pool, full-service spa, and highly regarded restaurant and bar.

On the National Register of Historic Places, the 1891 **Hancock House Bed & Breakfast Inn** has a sweeping outdoor terrace and garden. And **Drake House** is in a historic red brick home in the flourishing Millwork District, within walking distance to several local restaurants, breweries, and shops.

Day 1

Leave Chicago after breakfast and arrive in Dubuque for lunch at **1st and Main,** an industrial-chic telegraph-office-turned-restaurant in the heart of Dubuque's Millwork District. While you feast on bourbon-glazed Atlantic salmon or a gourmet burger, enjoy sunshine pouring in through the restaurant's fancy Frank Lloyd Wright windows, specially designed to disperse light upward rather than onto the floor. In the mood for Mexican? Hit up the casual, counter serve **Adobos Mexican Grill** where you can build your own burrito.

After lunch, make your way to **Mines of Spain Recreation Area,** a 1,437-acre swath of prairie and woodlands, which serve as a backdrop for hiking, biking, and cross-country ski trails. You'll encounter limestone canyons, a bird-and-butterfly garden, woodland flower gardens, a historic farm site, and a monument marking Julien Dubuque's final resting place at the confluence of Catfish Creek and the Mississippi River. Hike Horseshoe Bluff trail and enjoy stunning views of the Mississippi River below.

The 60-acre Dubuque Arboretum and Botanical Gardens has been called a "museum of trees."

After an afternoon in the Iowa wilderness, settle in for dinner at Dubuque's **Brazen Open Kitchen,** which has created a stir in epicurean circles. Native son Kevin Scharpf offers creative dishes such as duck tacos, coriander-crusted pork chop, and carrot and turmeric soup. Reservations are recommended. If you're craving a burger, head to local hangout **Dubuque Mining Company** instead.

Before turning in, enjoy a craft cocktail or local Iowa brew on the roof at **Smokestack,** a renovated warehouse in the Millwork District and now something of a Dubuque cultural center with two rooftops, a gallery and an outdoor garden. It frequently hosts live bands and even has an in-house recording studio.

Day 2

Start the day with breakfast at **Sunshine Family Restaurant,** a diner-style eatery with great pancakes and friendly locals. If you just want to grab a quick coffee and

pastry, pop into **Charlotte's Coffee** in the Millwork District.

Head to Cable Car Square and browse its two-dozen shops and galleries including **Nash Gallery, Gotta Have It, Fig Leaf,** and **Potpourri.** Then hop on Dubuque's newly rebuilt **Fenelon Place Elevator,** the world's shortest and steepest railway. In 1882, a wealthy citizen built the railway along the bluffs in Dubuque as a way to speedily reach his home. Three fires and countless owners later, the quirky attraction still exists. The 296-foot elevator ends at a bluff top overlooking the city.

For lunch, mosey on over to **7 Hills Brewing** for a hearty lunch and a local craft brew. Choose from a huge menu that includes slow-smoked pulled pork, brisket, artisan salads, sandwiches, and more. The crafty brewers here reuse their bourbon barrels as décor and make dog treats out of spent grain. If you're prepared to wait for a table, have lunch at local favorite **Copper Kettle** for everything from fish and chips to mac and cheese to scallops.

After lunch, take a scenic drive out to Dyersville, 30 miles west of Dubuque, to visit the **Field of Dreams Movie Site,** where the 1989 hit was filmed. Tourists still come to the century-old farm to hit a few balls, play catch, and run the bases. A few Sundays throughout the summer, the ghosts return from the surrounding cornfields to play games with visitors.

Head back to town and call upon the quirky **National Farm Toy Museum,** where displays thousands of tiny vehicles and exhibits provide an interesting overview of farm life. Afterwards, stop by **Betty Jane's Homemade Candies,** an old-fashioned candy store where you can sample the Gremlin, a mound of nuts and caramel drenched in chocolate.

For dinner, head to **Caroline's Restaurant** in the Hotel Julien. This elegant restaurant with stained-glass windows and parquet wood details is a popular choice for regional dishes including catfish cakes and Cajun chicken and shrimp. About five minutes from here you'll find **Pepper Sprout,** another upscale Dubuque eatery serving excellent Midwestern cuisine.

After dinner, step outside Caroline's and into the **Riverboat Lounge** to converse over cocktails and watch the mighty Mississippi roll by. If you're lucky, there may even be live music.

Day 3

Go to **Inspire Café** for breakfast on your last day. The café serves a selection of breakfast sandwiches with vegetarian and vegan options and a long list of coffee and tea drinks. For a quick drive-through breakfast, swing by the fair trade-focused **Jumble Coffee Company.**

After breakfast, take a leisurely walk along the Riverwalk that winds along the Port of Dubuque. Every summer, the City of Dubuque selects 10 works of public art to temporarily display. Make your way next over to the **Dubuque Arboretum and Botanical Gardens** for a look at one of the largest hosta gardens in the country. The Japanese Garden is an ideal spot for reflection with its serene setting.

For lunch, head to the hills in northern Dubuque to **Stone Cliff Winery** and order a few of the restaurant's flatbread pizzas paired with a featured wine. If you prefer lunch downtown, descend upon **L May Eatery** on Main Street, which offers a range of dishes from bratwurst to scallops to salads. There's an outdoor patio, too.

Recommendations

 ## Sights

Dubuque Arboretum and Botanical Gardens. ✉ *3800 Arboretum Dr., Dubuque, IA* ☏ *563/556–2100* ⊕ *dubuquearboretum. net* 🎟 *Free.*

Fenelon Place Elevator. ✉ *512 Fenelon Pl., Dubuque, IA* ☏ *563/582–6496* ⊕ *www. fenelonplaceelevator.com* 🎟 *$3* ⊘ *Closed Dec.–Mar.*

Field of Dreams Movie Site. ✉ *28995 Lansing Rd., Dyersville, IA* ☏ *888/875–8404* ⊕ *www.fieldofdreamsmoviesite.com* 🎟 *Free* ⊘ *Closed Dec.–Mar. Closed weekdays in Nov.*

Mines of Spain Recreation Area. ✉ *8991 Bellevue Heights Rd., Dubuque, IA* ☏ *563/556–0620* ⊕ *www.minesofspain. org* 🎟 *Free.*

National Farm Toy Museum. ✉ *1110 16th Ave. SE, Dyersville, IA* ☏ *563/875–2727* ⊕ *www.nationalfarmtoymuseum.com* 🎟 *$7.*

Restaurants

Adobos Mexican Grill. $ *Average main: $7* ✉ *756 Main St., Dubuque, IA* ☏ *563/556–4407* ⊕ *www.adobosmexicangrill.com* ⊘ *Closed Sun.*

Brazen Open Kitchen. [$] *Average main: $25* ✉ *Schmid Innovation Center, 955 Washington St., Dubuque, IA* ☎ *563/587–8899* 🌐 *www.brazenopenkitchen.com* 🕒 *Closed Sun. and Mon.*

Caroline's Restaurant. [$] *Average main: $20* ✉ *Hotel Julien Dubuque, 200 Main St., Dubuque, IA* ☎ *563/588–5595* 🌐 *hoteljuliendubuque.com.*

Copper Kettle. [$] *Average main: $20* ✉ *2987 Jackson St., Dubuque, IA* ☎ *563/845–0567* 🌐 *www.copperkettledbq.com.*

Dubuque Mining Company. [$] *Average main: $13* ✉ *Kennedy Mall, 555 John F. Kennedy Rd., Dubuque, IA* ☎ *563/557–1729* 🌐 *dubuqueminingcompany.com* 🕒 *Closed Mon. and Tues.*

1st & Main. [$] *Average main: $13* ✉ *101 Main St., Dubuque, IA* ☎ *563/587–8152* 🌐 *www.1standmaindbq.com.*

Inspire Café. [$] *Average main: $8* ✉ *Schmid Innovation Center, 955 Washington St., Dubuque, IA* ☎ *563/583–8338* 🌐 *www.inspire-cafe.com* 🕒 *No dinner.*

L May Eatery. [$] *Average main: $22* ✉ *1072 Main St., Dubuque, IA* ☎ *563/556–0505* 🌐 *www.lmayeatery.com* 🕒 *Closed Mon. and Tues.*

Pepper Sprout. [$] *Average main: $22* ✉ *378 Main St., Dubuque, IA* ☎ *563/556–2167* 🌐 *peppersprout.com* 🕒 *Closed Mon. and Tues.*

7 Hills Brewing. [$] *Average main: $17* ✉ *1085 Washington St., Dubuque, IA* ☎ *563/587–8306* 🌐 *www.7hillsbrew.com.*

Stone Cliff Winery. [$] *Average main: $9* ✉ *600 Star Brewery Dr., Dubuque, IA* ☎ *563/583–6100* 🌐 *www.stonecliffwinery.com* 🕒 *No dinner.*

Sunshine Family Restaurant. [$] *Average main: $7* ✉ *401 Central Ave., Dubuque, IA* ☎ *563/582–3090* 🕒 *Closed Sun. and Mon. No dinner.*

Coffee and Quick Bites

Charlotte's Coffee. [$] *Average main: $8* ✉ *1104 White St., Dubuque, IA* ☎ *563/231–3716* 🌐 *www.charlottescoffeehouse.com* 🕒 *No dinner.*

Jumble Coffee Company. [$] *Average main: $5* ✉ *820 Wacker Dr., Dubuque, IA* ☎ *563/564–3870* 🌐 *www.jumblecoffee.com* 🕒 *No dinner.*

Hotels

Drake House. [$] *Rooms from: $159* ✉ *1118 White St., Dubuque, IA* ☎ *563/599–8807* 🌐 *www.drakehousestay.com* 🍴 *No meals.*

Hancock House Bed & Breakfast. [$] *Rooms from: $190* ✉ *1105 Grove Terr., Dubuque, IA* ☎ *563/235–0000* 🌐 *thehancockhouse.com* 🍴 *Free breakfast.*

Hotel Julien. [$] *Rooms from: $120* ✉ *200 Main St., Dubuque, IA* ☎ *563/556–4200* 🌐 *hoteljuliendubuque.com* 🍴 *No meals.*

Nightlife

Riverboat Lounge. ✉ *Hotel Julien, 200 Main St., Dubuque, IA* ☎ *563/556–4200* 🌐 *hoteljuliendubuque.com.*

Smokestack. ✉ *62 E. 7th St., Dubuque, IA* ☎ *No phone* 🌐 *www.smokestackdbq.com.*

Shopping

Betty Jane's Homemade Candies. ✉ *3049 Asbury Rd., Dubuque, IA* ☎ *563/582–4668* 🌐 *www.bettyjanecandies.com.*

Fig Leaf. ✉ *345 Bluff St., Dubuque, IA* ☎ *563/588–3160.*

Gotta Have It. ✉ *315 Bluff St., Dubuque, IA* ☎ *563/588–3956.*

Nash Gallery. ✉ *371 Bluff St., Dubuque, IA* ☎ *563/580–4029.*

Potpourri. ⊠ *474 Bluff St., Dubuque, IA* ☎ *563/581–5845.*

Activities

YMCA Union Park Camp. ⊠ *11764 John F. Kennedy Rd., Dubuque, IA* ☎ *563/484–4248* ⊕ *www.skytourszipline.com* ✉ *From $65.*

Duluth, MN

155 miles (approx. 2½ hours) from Minneapolis.

This port town along Lake Superior is most closely associated with blues-folk musician Bob Dylan, but also boasts a gorgeous lakefront and the country's only all-freshwater aquarium. With just 86,000 residents, you'll find lots of culture here, along with a vibrant food scene and plenty of outdoor activities.

Planning

GETTING THERE AND BACK
The 155-mile drive between Minneapolis and Duluth travels along I–35 N.

PIT STOPS
Pine City's **Snake River Fur Post,** run by the Minnesota Historical Society, tells the story of the state's fur traders.

WHEN TO GO
Temperatures drop significantly in the winter, but spring and fall can also be chilly. Pack extra layers and you should be fine. A summer weekend can be quite lovely, with longer days and warmer temperatures. Fall is a favorite time because of the changing foliage. If you like cross-country skiing, ice fishing, or snowshoeing, winter is prime time.

WHERE TO STAY
There's a mix of historic accommodations in Duluth, from your very own log cabin perched high above Lake Superior

at **Dodges Log Lodges** to a cozy room in a 19th-century inn at **Fitger's.** Here you'll find three eateries, a microbrewery, and a spa.

Day 1

If you arrive in Duluth with enough time to spare, visit **Tweed Museum of Art,** an intriguing mix of permanent and temporary exhibits on the University of Minnesota campus. Or tour the 39-room, 20,000-square-foot **Glensheen Mansion,** a showplace dating back to 1908.

Kick back with a Guinness and some filling fare at **Sir Benedict's Tavern on the Lake.** This cozy pub along East Superior Street offers live Irish-style music (you'll probably hear a banjo and fiddle) on Friday night.

Day 2

Your first full day in Duluth will probably require some caffeine: fuel up at **Duluth Coffee Company,** which sources beans directly from farmers whenever possible. Most locals prefer the newer location, inside a historic building in Canal Park.

Great Lakes Aquarium, on the downtown waterfront, is devoted to the freshwater environments like Lake Superior. More than a dozen exhibits document fish, wildlife, and plants from as far away as the Amazon.

A late lunch at **Va Bene Caffé**—owned by an Italian couple and specializing in modern Italian fare—includes a lake view. With dishes like salmon and mascarpone crostini, you won't leave hungry. There are even vegan and gluten-free options.

If everyone in your group has a different idea about how to spend Saturday night, **Zeitgeist** is the perfect solution, with a café, cinema, and theater all under one roof. Dinner, which includes entrees like

Dating back more than a century, the Glensheen Mansion is Duluth's grandest estate.

Lake Superior trout, is served until quite late. The menu also satisfies vegans, vegetarians, and those on a gluten-free diet.

Day 3

After a hearty brunch (everything from biscuits with chorizo gravy to vegan bibimbap) at **Sara's Table Chester Creek Café** in Chester Park, pack some fruit pie slices to-go and rent bikes from **Wheel Fun Rentals** in Canal Park, just north of the Aerial Lift Bridge. It's a blast to explore the shoreline stretching to Park Point Recreation Area. This is 10 miles round trip.

Drop off the bikes and enjoy a cold beer or root-beer float on the patio at nearby **Canal Park Brewing Company.** The food will please even picky palates (from pork nachos to a protein bowl).

Recommendations

Sights

Glensheen Mansion. ✉ *3300 London Rd., Duluth, MN* ☎ *888/454–4536* 🌐 *www.glensheen.org* 🎫 *$18.*

Great Lakes Aquarium. ✉ *353 Harbor Dr., Duluth, MN* ☎ *218/740–3474* 🌐 *www.glaquarium.org* 🎫 *$14.*

Snake River Fur Post. ✉ *12551 Voyageur La., Pine City, MN* ☎ *320/629–6356* 🌐 *www.mnhs.org* 🎫 *$10* 🕒 *Closed Tues. and Wed.*

Tweed Museum of Art. ✉ *1201 Ordean Ct., Duluth, MN* ☎ *218/726–8222* 🌐 *www.d.umn.edu* 🎫 *Free* 🕒 *Closed Mon.*

Restaurants

Sara's Table Chester Creek Café. [$] *Average main: $15* ✉ *1902 E. 8th St., Duluth, MN* ☎ *218/724–6811* 🌐 *www.astccc.net.*

Sir Benedict's Tavern on the Lake. $ *Average main: $8 ⌧ 805 E. Superior St., Duluth, MN ☎ 218/728–1192 ⊕ www.sirbens.com.*

Va Bene Caffé. $ *Average main: $15 ⌧ 734 E. Superior St., Duluth, MN ☎ 218/722–1518 ⊕ www.vabenecaffe.com.*

Coffee and Quick Bites

Duluth Coffee Company. $ *Average main: $5 ⌧ 105 E. Superior St., Duluth, MN ☎ 218/221–6643 ⊕ www.duluthcoffeecompany.com.*

Hotels

Dodges Log Lodges. $ *Rooms from: $238 ⌧ 5852 N. Shore Dr., Duluth, MN ☎ 218/525–4088 ⊕ www.dodgeslog.com ❍❘ No meals.*

Fitger's. $ *Rooms from: $159 ⌧ 600 E. Superior St., Duluth, MN ☎ 218/722–8826 ⊕ www.fitgers.com ❍❘ Free breakfast.*

☗ Nightlife

Zeitgeist. ⌧ *22 E. Superior St., Duluth, MN ☎ 218/722–7300 ⊕ www.zeitgeistarts.com.*

Activities

Wheel Fun Rentals. ⌧ *365 S. Lake Ave., Duluth, MN ☎ 218/464–7292 ⊕ www.wheelfunrentals.com 🖘 Rentals from $27.*

Grand Marais and Isle Royale National Park

Grand Marais is 264 miles (approx. 4¼ hours) from Minneapolis.

Many outdoors lovers have ticked popular national parks like Acadia, Yellowstone, and Yosemite off their list. But very few have visited Isle Royale National Park, located near the Canadian border on the largest island in Lake Superior. Home to majestic moose, grey wolves, and red foxes, this gem attracts only about 25,000 visitors per year. That means you can easily find places to be alone with nature. Although many visitors choose to backpack their way through the park over at least five days, day hikes are also rewarding.

Planning

GETTING THERE AND BACK
From Minneapolis, take I–35 N and MN 61 N to Grand Marais. From there, make the final leg of the trip to Isle Royale National Park by ferries departing from Grand Portage (a 40-minute drive from Grand Marais) or a seaplane from Grand Marais. Cars are not allowed in the park or on the ferries.

PIT STOPS
Along the northern shore of Lake Superior, **Black Beach Park,** in Silver Bay, Minnesota, has an unusual black-sand shoreline. This is along the route to Grand Marais, an hour south of town.

WHEN TO GO
Isle Royale National Park is only accessible between mid-April and late October. June, July and August have longer days and, of course, warmer weather, but also more people on the trails. Book your ferry trips and overnight accommodations as far ahead as possible for these months. Late summer tends to attract fewer visitors, which means few people on the trails and more affordable hotel rates.

WHERE TO STAY
Overnight in Grand Marais, a convenient gateway to Isle Royale National Park. Right on the water is the loft-like **Mayhew Inn,** the town's most boutique-y property. Fire pits on the lakefront deck

Fronting on Lake Superior, Grand Portage National Monument is home to historic Fort Charlotte.

are surrounded by plush sofas, adding a sophisticated feel.

Isle Royale National Park's only accommodation, **Rock Harbor Lodge,** is in Copper Harbor, which is not where most people arrive when coming from Minnesota. However, the lodge offers two one-room cabins on the southwestern part of the island in Windigo, making them convenient for Minnesota arrivals. There is no indoor plumbing, and cooking is not allowed in the cabins. However, a picnic table and grill are just outside. The park also offers 36 wilderness campgrounds accessible only by foot or by water.

Day 1

Once you get out of the Twin Cities, the drive up the coast of Lake Superior is easy and peaceful. Grand Marais (population 1,350) is an arts-oriented community along a harbor. It's near the million-acre **Boundary Waters Canoe Area Wilderness Area,** part of the Superior National Forest, where many outfitters set up their businesses.

Take a stroll to Grand Marais Light, which has been in operation since 1922. Drop by the **Cook County Historical Society Museum,** tucked into the original lighthouse keeper's house.

Shopping in this compact community is surprisingly cool and eclectic, including **The Big Lake** (locally made pottery and other crafts), **Gunflight Mercantile** (fudge made on the premises), and **Drury Lane Books** (a great selection of books about the region).

Break for dinner at **Wunderbar,** serving interesting fare like portobello mushroom tacos and open until midnight. There's live music, a game room, and a popular patio. There's even five vintage campers and two tents if you like it so much you want to stay the night.

Day 2

Wake early and load up on 30 different types of doughnuts from **World's Best Donuts** before heading out by seaplane or ferry to **Isle Royale National Park.** Keep in mind that you might need enough doughnuts for Sunday morning breakfast, too.

Once in Windigo, orient yourself at the Windigo Visitor Center and plot your day hike with the helpful staff. There's an easy nature walk for beginners, along with a short hike along Feldtmann Lake Trail to Grace Creek Overlook. More challenging treks take you into the backcountry. The Windigo Store sells sandwiches, so you can enjoy a quick lunch on the patio or pack a picnic lunch. To cool off, don your swimsuit for a chilly dip at Windigo's Washington Harbor.

Dinner is far from fine dining, but still one to remember. In addition to sandwiches, the Windigo Store sells groceries, along with beer and wine, to help you cobble together a feast. Just don't wait too late, as it often closes by 6 pm.

Day 3

To explore the area by kayak or canoe, rent your chosen watercraft at the marina for half-day or full-day rentals. This is no quiet lake or lazy river—it's one of the Great Lakes, so the water can be choppy. It's recommended that you wear a life jacket, carry an extra paddle, and bring along a portable radio if you go out too far from land.

On your way home, stop by the tiny town of Grand Portage. For your last meal, head the Grand Portage Lodge & Casino's **Island View** restaurant. It definitely focuses on meat and potatoes, although you can also feast on locally caught walleye or trout. You can also sample poutine, a cheese curd and gravy dish popular over the border in Canada.

Before driving back to the Twin Cities, drop by the 710-acre **Grand Portage National Monument,** a living-history museum along the famed fur route that seeks to educate about indigenous Anishinaabe and Ojibwe culture, art, and history.

Recommendations

Sights

Black Beach Park. ✉ E. Lakeview Dr., Silver Bay, MN ☎ 218/226–4214 ⊕ www.silverbay.com ⌲ Free.

Boundary Waters Canoe Area Wilderness Area. ✉ Superior National Forest, Lake County, MN ☎ 218/626–4395 ⊕ www.exploreminnesota.com/iconic-destinations/boundary-waters ⌲ $16.

Cook County Historical Society Museum. ✉ 8 S. Broadway Ave., Grand Marais, MN ☎ 218/387–2883 ⊕ www.cookcountyhistory.org.

Grand Portage National Monument. ✉ Heritage Visitors Center, 170 Mile Creek Rd., Grand Portage, MN ☎ 218/475–0123 ⊕ www.nps.gov/grpo ⌲ Free.

Isle Royale National Park. ✉ Windigo Visitor Center, southwestern end of Isle Royale National Park ☎ 906/482–0984 ⊕ www.nps.gov/isro ⌲ Free ⊙ Closed late Oct.–mid-Apr.

Restaurants

Island View. $ Average main: $16 ✉ Grand Portage Lodge and Casino, 70 Casino Dr., Grand Portage ☎ 800/543–1384 ⊕ www.grandportage.com.

Wunderbar. $ Average main: $14 ✉ 1615 W. Hwy. 61, Grand Marais, MN ☎ 218/877–7655 ⊕ wunderbarmn.com ⊙ Closed Mon.–Wed.

Coffee and Quick Bites

World's Best Donuts. $ *Average main: $5* ✉ *10 Wisconsin St., Grand Marais, MN* ☎ *218/387–1345* ⊕ *www.worldsbestdonutsmn.com.*

Hotels

Mayhew Inn. $ *Rooms from: $175* ✉ *107 W. Wisconsin St., Grand Marais, MN* ☎ *612/386–3096* ⊕ *www.themayhewinn.com* ❘◎❘ *No meals.*

Rock Harbor Lodge Cabins. $ *Rooms from: $52* ✉ *Washington Harbor, southwestern end of Isle Royale National Park* ☎ *906/337–4993* ⊕ *www.rockharborlodge.com/index.php/windigo-camper-cabins* ❘◎❘ *No meals* ⊗ *Closed mid-Sept.–mid-June.*

Shopping

The Big Lake. ✉ *12 1st Ave. W, Grand Marais, MN* ☎ *No phone* ⊕ *thebiglakelife.com* ⊗ *Closed Sun. and Mon.*

Drury Lane Books. ✉ *12 E. Wisconsin St., Grand Marais, MN* ☎ *No phone* ⊕ *drurylanebooks.indielite.org.*

Gunflight Mercantile. ✉ *12 1st Ave. W, Grand Marais, MN* ☎ *218/387–9228* ⊕ *www.gunflintmercantile.com.*

Windago Store. ✉ *Washington Harbor, southwestern end of Isle Royale* ☎ *906/337–4993* ⊕ *www.rockharborlodge.com/windigo-store* ⊗ *Closed mid-Sept.–mid-June.*

Green Bay and Door County, WI

244 miles (approx. 3¾ miles) from Chicago and 320 miles (approx. 5 hours) from Minneapolis.

A straight shot north of Chicago, and following the Lake Michigan shoreline, yields an itinerary packed with hiking at state parks and beaches, artisan cheese, locally grown cherries, the state's Swedish side and the Midwest's version of Cape Cod. Yet there are also little luxuries, such as massages at The American Club in the company town of Kohler and gawking at Outsider art at John Michael Kohler Arts Center, one of the Midwest's best art museums (totally free to enter).

Planning

GETTING THERE AND BACK
From Chicago, drive north on I–94 toward Wisconsin. Take the scenic route by exiting I–94 at U.S. 51 N/Calumet Avenue in Manitowoc, taking Route 42 north all the way north into Door County.

INSPIRATION
Sheboygan is often dubbed "the Malibu of the Midwest," in large part due to its surfing culture each summer and into early fall. Watch *Step Into Liquid,* a documentary, to learn more.

PIT STOPS
Door County is home to five state parks and 19 county parks. Stretch your legs and hike a bit—both on trails and along the beach on the Lake Michigan side—at **Whitefish Dunes State Park,** in the southern part of "the Door." Another great pit stop further north is the century-old **Wilson's Restaurant & Ice Cream** in Ephraim (just look for the red-and-white striped awning). Enjoy your ice cream in the park across the street, along Green Bay.

WHEN TO GO
Since this is among the most northern points of the country, summer-like weather starts late (the second week of June) and ends early (the second week of September), but choosing to go at those times might mean amazing hotel deals and smaller crowds. Avoid Fourth of July and Labor Day weekends in Door County, as that's when Chicagoans flee to their vacation homes. And check into pro-golf

Football fans shouldn't pass up a tour of Lambeau Field, home of the Green Bay Packers.

events at Kohler if you plan to play the courses or you may be locked out.

WHERE TO STAY

The **American Club's** lavishness—tucked into the company town of Kohler, near Sheboygan—might make you think you can't afford a night here but, guess what, you can. The **Inn at Woodlake** is the most affordable option, with a substantial breakfast buffet included in rates. In Door County, **Double S Lodge** in the Swedish-settled town of Sister Bay is one of the most boutique-y accommodations.

Day 1

Set out early on Friday—with coffee and granola bars or muffins on hand—because this is the longest stretch of the drive: about four hours to Sturgeon Bay, the gateway to Door County. It's another hour north to Gills Rock, on the peninsula's northernmost tip. And because you can't leave Door County without taking the car ferry to Washington Island, do that first. Once on island, pop into a cool indie bookstore (**Fair Isle Books & Gifts,** attached to **Red Cup Coffee House,** which serves more than coffee on weekends; try a sausage cheddar scramble or the chorizo breakfast burrito) and walk along the smooth stones on School House Beach. **Fragrant Isle,** on the island, is among the Midwest's largest lavender farms, also retailing lavender products in its store.

Back on the peninsula, Sister Bay is a great place to base camp with **Door County Creamery's** deli, boutique, creamery, and herd of goats split between its "in town" locale and farmstead a mile away. Even if you can't squeeze in yoga with the goats or a farm tour, the sandwiches—folding in the creamery's cheese—are yummy. Enjoy yours at the adjacent Sister Bay Beach, hugging Green Bay, and save room for goat's-milk gelato.

Check out the "quieter side" of the peninsula in Bailey's Harbor, home to a super-cute farm stand called **Koepsel's Farm Market** that's been in business since 1958 (pick up the yummy cherry-amaretto pie filling); a coffee shop in a tiny house called **Bearded Heart Coffee,** and one of the county's best restaurants. **Chives,** with farm-to-fork fine dining and Lake Michigan views from its elevated dining room, is open for dinner only. Want something more casual? **Door County Brewing Co.,** just down the block, often has food trucks, including one from Chives, in its outdoor beer garden; and live music, too.

Day 2

Kick start the day with thin Swedish-style pancakes at **Al Johnson's Swedish Restaurant & Butik,** where goats literally roam the grass roof and sweaters and jars of lingonberries imported from Sweden, along with Swedish snacks, are sold in the gift shop.

Head to Green Bay early for a tour of **Lambeau Field,** the Green Bay Packers' home turf. Even if you're not a sports fan—or your favorite team is a Packers rival—the team's history will wow you. It's the fifth-largest NFL stadium and the only community-owned team in the league. Lunch at the nearby **Hinterland Restaurant and Brewery,** with its outdoor patio and wood-fired pizzas. A favorite destination for a select few Packers players, you may even spot a few at the bar.

By the time you pull into Sheboygan and Kohler (two adjacent towns: the first rims Lake Michigan while the second is a company town for the high-end plumbing manufacturer), you may be pooped. If you're into the finest of meals, book a reservation ahead of time at **The Immigrant Restaurant.** You won't be sorry, as most Midwestern foodies consider this a rite of passage. And the pizzas at **Il Ritrovo** are baked in the state's first pizza oven imported from Naples, under the tutelage of local chef Stefano Viglietti.

Day 3

Today is the most artsy day of the weekend. After breakfast, or maybe a 7:45 am Vinyasa class at **Yoga on the Lake,** experience the **Kohler Design Center,** where the "wall of china"—spoiler alert: it's a bunch of toilets—is a hoot. There's also a museum about the company's history on the lower level and, on the top level, vignettes of kitchens and baths curated by celeb designers.

Most people come to Kohler for the world-class spa or golf courses, but its top-par dining is lesser-known. Fuel up on sandwiches or salads and grab some house-made chocolates that resemble works of art for the drive home at **Craverie Chocolatier Cafe.**

About 10 minutes away is Sheboygan, an up-and-coming community hugging the lakeshore. The **Kohler Art Preserve** is the first gallery dedicated to artist-built environments but, in the meantime, wander immersive installations by some of the country's best Outsider artists at the **John Michael Kohler Arts Center.**

Recommendations

Sights

Fragrant Isle Lavender Farm. ✉ *1350 Airport Rd., Washington Island, WI* ☎ *920/847–2950* ⊕ *www.fragrantisle.com* 🎟 *$5* ⏱ *Closed Mon.*

John Michael Kohler Arts Center. ✉ *608 New York Ave., Sheboygan, WI* ☎ *920/458–6144* ⊕ *www.jmkac.org* 🎟 *Free.*

Kohler Arts Preserve. ✉ *3636 Lower Falls Rd., Sheboygan, WI* ☎ *920/458–6144* ⊕ *www.jmkac.org/artpreserve.html* 🎟 *Free.*

Kohler Design Center. ✉ *101 Upper Rd., Kohler, WI* ☎ *920/457–3699* ⊕ *www. us.kohler.com* 🎫 *Free* ⊘ *Closed Sun.*

Lambeau Field. ✉ *1265 Lombardi Ave., Green Bay, WI* ☎ *920/569–7512* ⊕ *www. packershofandtours.com/explore/stadium-tours* 🎫 *$15.*

Whitefish Dunes State Park. ✉ *Clarks Lake Rd., Sturgeon Bay, WI* ☎ *920/746–9539* ⊕ *dnr.wi.gov/topic/parks/name/whitefish* 🎫 *$8 per car.*

Restaurants

Al Johnson's Swedish Restaurant & Butik. $ *Average main: $12* ✉ *10698 N. Bay Shore Dr., Sister Bay, WI* ☎ *920/854–2626* ⊕ *www.aljohnsons.com* ⊘ *No dinner.*

Chives. $ *Average main: $25* ✉ *1749 Riverside Dr., Suamico, WI* ☎ *920/434–6441* ⊕ *www.chivesdining.com* ⊘ *Closed Sun. and Mon.*

Hinterland Restaurant and Brewery. $ *Average main: $25* ✉ *1001 Lombardi Access Rd., Ashwaubenon, WI* ☎ *920/438–8050* ⊕ *www.hinterlandbeer.com.*

Il Ritrovo. $ *Average main: $16* ✉ *515 S. 8th St., Sheboygan, WI* ☎ *920/803–7516* ⊕ *www.ilritrovopizza.com* ⊘ *Closed Sun.*

The Immigrant Restaurant. $ *Average main: $52* ✉ *The American Club, 419 Highland Dr., Kohler, WI* ☎ *800/344–2838* ⊕ *www.americanclubresort.com.*

☕ Coffee and Quick Bites

Bearded Hearty Coffee. $ *Average main: $8* ✉ *8093 WI 57, Baileys Harbor, WI* ☎ *920/839–9111* ⊕ *www.beardedheartcoffee.com* ⊘ *No dinner.*

Red Cup Coffee House. $ *Average main: $9* ✉ *1885 Detroit Harbor Rd., Washington Island, WI* ☎ *920/847–3304* ⊕ *www. redcupkillercoffee.com* ⊘ *No dinner.*

Hotels

The American Club. $ *Rooms from: $424* ✉ *The American Club, 419 Highland Dr., Kohler, WI* ☎ *800/344–2838* ⊕ *www. americanclubresort.com* ⦿ *No meals.*

Double S Lodge. $ *Rooms from: $295* ✉ *11086 WI 42, Sister Bay, WI* ☎ *920/854–3253* ⊕ *www.doubleslodge. com* ⦿ *Free breakfast.*

Inn at Woodlake. $ *Rooms from: $275* ✉ *705 Woodlake Rd., Kohler, WI* ☎ *800/344–2838* ⊕ *www.americanclubresort.com* ⦿ *Free breakfast.*

Nightlife

Door County Brewing Co. ✉ *8099 WI 57, Baileys Harbor, WI* ☎ *920/839–1515* ⊕ *www.doorcountybrewingco.com.*

🛍 Shopping

Craverie Chocolatier Café. ✉ *The Shops at Woodlake Kohler, 725 Woodlake Rd., Kohler, WI* ☎ *920/208–4933* ⊕ *www. americanclubresort.com.*

Door County Creamery. ✉ *10653 N. Bay Shore Dr., Sister Bay, WI* ☎ *920/854–3388* ⊕ *www.doorcountycreamery.com.*

Fair Isle Books & Gifts. ✉ *1885 Detroit Harbor Rd., Washington Island, WI* ☎ *920/847–2565* ⊕ *www.fairisleshop. com.*

Koepsel's Farm Market. ✉ *9669 WI 57, Baileys Harbor, WI* ☎ *920/854–2433* ⊕ *www. koepsels.com.*

Activities

Yoga on the Lake. ✉ *725 Woodlake Rd., Kohler, WI* ☎ *920/453–2817* ⊕ *www. yogaonthelake.com* 🎫 *Classes from $20.*

Kansas City, MO

248 miles (approx. 3¾ hours) from St. Louis.

You might be tempted to compare Kansas City to other towns, but the truth is, it's one of a kind. "KCMO"—that is, Kansas City, Missouri—is locked right in the middle of America. (And shouldn't be confused with smaller "KCK," or Kansas City, Kansas, right across the Kansas River.)

Just as the city's central coordinates suggest, Kansas City is a hub for everything from agriculture and transportation, to gastronomy, arts, and culture. It's surprisingly diverse and progressive, yet it's proud to be a heartland city sprung from old-west traditions.

Planning

GETTING THERE AND BACK
By car, enjoy a four-hour road trip westward from St. Louis across the state via I–70, or choose the more leisurely U.S. 50. You can also fly from St. Louis to Kansas City in under an hour. Amtrak also operates the Missouri River Runner train across the Show-Me State, it takes about 5½ hours.

INSPIRATION
Queue up a Charlie Parker jazz mix or playlist of 20th-century jazz greats to get you in the mood for KC's musical legacy. You can also channel the town's harmonic heritage listening to literally dozens of songs by major artists about and named for Kansas City—most famously, Wilbert Harrison's 1959 smash hit "Kansas City," inviting you to sing "Kansas City here I come" on your way in.

PIT STOPS
Taking the less-traveled U.S. 50 lets you swing through capitol Jefferson City for a scoop of its famous **Central Dairy** ice-cream shop, and to check out the Lewis

and Clark Monument next to the Missouri State Capitol. (The duo launched their famous expedition just outside of St. Louis.)

WHEN TO GO
Prime times to visit Kansas City are fall and spring, to avoid the very coldest winter and hottest summer months. Festival season kicks off around April, starting with the 18th and Vine Jazz Festival, through Kansas City Pridefest, and KC Riverfest for July 4th. The city's biggest festival, American Royal, runs August through December with a bevy of events from rodeo to food. The good news is that good music, art, and barbeque are dreamy all year long.

WHERE TO STAY
No, you can't stay with the guys from Netflix's *Queer Eye* while you're in Kansas City. But downtown's **Hotel Phillips Kansas City** is a stylish spot in a good location, with handsome decor, a subterranean speakeasy, and an inviting lobby lounge with a shuffleboard table. The **Ambassador Kansas City** is a charming art deco showplace inside a 1906 bank building, serving sophistication in its accommodations and Reserve restaurant.

Day 1

Whether you arrive by air or land, you'll likely hit Kansas City ready for a bite, and you may as well grab a local brew too. **Grünauer** is an unexpectedly fun first stop, where you can sample some of the Midwest's best, authentic Austrian food. It's a roomy gasthaus with indoor and outdoor beer-garden seating, serving up traditional dishes like stelze and wiener schnitzel, and of course, a hearty selection of European and local beers (plus wine and creative cocktails).

Just across the boulevard from Grünauer is historic **Union Station.** Opened in 1914 and restored in 1999, the active train station now is home to restaurants, a live

Kansas City pays tribute to sports pioneers at the Negro Leagues Baseball Museum.

theater, shops, a popular (and free) model railroad, the **Arvin Gottlieb Planetarium,** and **Science City.** Stop by **Parisi Coffee's** flagship location in the great hall to sip an artisan coffee and marvel at the beaux arts architecture.

Exit Union Station to the south, then head uphill into Penn Valley Park. Across its 176 acres you'll find statues, a lake, lawns, fitness areas, and landmarks, including the soaring Liberty Memorial marking the **National World War I Museum.** It's a rare U.S. landmark dedicated to the Great War, and well worth a visit. Afterward, climb atop the museum's hilltop plaza for the best view of Kansas City, including Union Station, the Federal Reserve, and the city's iconic 73-foot-tall "Western Auto" sign.

Day 2

Start your day with house-made biscuits and gravy or perhaps a tofu hash at **Happy Gillis** in Columbus Park, an easygoing spot loved by locals for breakfast and lunch. You'll be near the Kansas River, so afterwards, consider a stroll along the **Berkley Riverfront** promenade over to the historic River Market area. Or head into Kessler Park to check out the Colonnade, a local landmark. Nearby in the Garment District, explore local history at the mansion that's home to the Kansas City Museum.

Kansas City is home to incredible African-American history, much of it rooted in the neighborhood simply called 18th and Vine, the city's jazz district. To celebrate local musical heritage, the **American Jazz Museum** has exhibits and artifacts tied to legends including Duke Ellington, Ella Fitzgerald, Louis Armstrong, and of course Charlie "Bird" Parker—a KC native who's commemorated by the 18-foot-tall Bird Lives brass sculpture, anchoring his namesake plaza. There's also a live jazz venue inside, so check the museum calendar for upcoming shows.

In the same building, swing into the **Negro Leagues Baseball Museum** to view memorabilia, browse rare and autographed items, and learn all about this unique 20th-century sports league. You'll be wise to top off quality time in 18th and Vine at **Arthur Bryant's Barbeque,** the no-frills joint serving the original Kansas City, slow-cook, dry-rub ribs for more than a century now.

Of course, there are plenty of choices when it comes to Kansas City barbeque. If you want to compare tastes, consider the playful zestiness of **Char Bar,** the sophisticated sauces of **Q39,** or the old-time casual style of local chain Gates Bar-B-Q.

Arts and culture are cornerstones of this city, sometimes called "Paris of the Plains." So the world-class **Nelson-Atkins Museum of Art** fits right in by showcasing an encyclopedic collection of artworks from around the globe. Its surrounding sculpture park features the museum's most iconic mega pieces, "Shuttlecocks," installed by husband-and-wife artist team Claes Oldenburg and Coosje van Bruggen in 1994. Nearby, the **Kemper Museum of Contemporary Art** is a free, compact institution exhibiting thought-provoking works. It's home to the excellent **Café Sebastienne,** serving contemporary cuisine within the museum.

Artsy time continues at the Crossroads Arts District, an enclave of shops, bars, restaurants, studios, and galleries. The neighborhood is always busy and a good place to walk around, and on every first Friday of the month, it's flooded with locals who come to view art, hear bands, and join pop-up events and eateries.

Don't miss a stop at **Mission Taco Joint** on East 18th Street for fresh Mexican fare and tangy margaritas. Just down the way, try local pints of everything from IPAs to seasonal ales to stouts at **Border Brewing Co.,** and compare theirs with the brews at **Strange Days Brewing Co.** in River Market.

Cap off your night the old-fashioned way, with tipples and tunes at the **Green Lady Lounge,** hosting all the great Kansas City jazz musicians. Or slip into the romantic, historic 1930s speakeasy **P.S.,** under downtown's Hotel Phillips.

Day 3

Hopefully you've saved some of your wherewithal to make it to the city's unforgettable drag brunch at **Hamburger Mary's.** Shows feature a talented lineup of buxom, bawdy queens—remember to bring plenty of dollar bills to tip the performers. (If drag shows are your jam, catch nightly revues at one of the local LGBTQ community's favorite clubs, **Missie B's.**) Chase Mary's laughs with a sweet treat from retro-styled **Donutology** on Westport Road.

Some of the city's best souvenirs await at **Made in Kansas City,** a local chain selling only locally made goods. Their products also are sold at **The Bunker** clothing and accessory store in Old Westport. It's a cute neighborhood for a walkabout, and for tasty Japanese fare at **Komatsu Ramen.**

Between the Chiefs and the Royals, Kansas City is a huge sports town. If you're in town for a game, head downtown to the Power and Light District, where big games often turn the neighborhood into a makeshift block party. The area also hosts street fairs, music and beer festivals, wine walks, and lots more monthly and seasonal events. Better still, you can take the local RideKC Streetcar to and from the district—its arrival is trackable online, and rides are always free.

Recommendations

Sights

American Jazz Museum. ✉ *1616 E. 18th St., Kansas City, MO* ☎ *816/474–8463* ⊕ *www.americanjazzmuseum.org* ✉ *$10* ⊗ *Closed Mon.*

Arvin Gottlieb Planetarium. ✉ *Union Station, W. Pershing Rd., Kansas City, MO* ☎ *816/460–2020* 🌐 *www.unionstation.org/sciencecity/planetarium* 🎟 *$8* 🕒 *Closed Mon. and Tues.*

Kansas City Museum. ✉ *3218 Gladstone Blvd., Kansas City, MO* ☎ *816/513–0720* 🌐 *www.kansascitymuseum.org* 🎟 *$9* 🕒 *Closed Sun.–Tues.*

Kemper Museum of Contemporary Art. ✉ *4420 Warwick Blvd., Kansas City, MO* ☎ *816/753–5784* 🌐 *www.kemperart.org* 🎟 *Free* 🕒 *Closed Mon.*

National World War I Museum. ✉ *2 Memorial Dr., Kansas City, MO* ☎ *816/888–8100* 🌐 *www.theworldwar.org* 🎟 *$18* 🕒 *Closed Mon.*

Negro Leagues Baseball Museum. ✉ *1616 E. 18th St., Kansas City, MO* ☎ *816/221–1920* 🌐 *www.nlbm.com* 🎟 *$10* 🕒 *Closed Mon.*

Nelson-Atkins Museum of Art. ✉ *4525 Oak St., Kansas City, MO* ☎ *816/751–1278* 🌐 *www.nelson-atkins.org* 🎟 *Free* 🕒 *Closed Tues.*

Penn Valley Park. ✉ *Broadway Blvd., Kansas City, MO* ☎ *816/513–7500* 🌐 *www.kcparks.org* 🎟 *Free.*

Science City. ✉ *Union Station, 30 W. Pershing Rd., Kansas City, MO* ☎ *816/460–2020* 🌐 *www.unionstation.org* 🎟 *$14* 🕒 *Closed Mon. and Tues.*

Union Station. ✉ *30 W. Pershing Rd., Kansas City, MO* ☎ *816/460–2020* 🌐 *www.unionstation.org* 🎟 *Free.*

🍴 Restaurants

Arthur Bryant's Barbeque. [$] *Average main: $10* ✉ *1727 Brooklyn Ave., Kansas City, MO* ☎ *816/231–1123* 🌐 *www.arthurbryantsbbq.com.*

Café Sebastienne. [$] *Average main: $18* ✉ *Kemper Museum of Contemporary Art, 4420 Warwick Blvd., Kansas City, MO* ☎ *816/561–7740* 🌐 *www.kemperart.org* 🕒 *Closed Mon.*

Char Bar. [$] *Average main: $11* ✉ *4050 Pennsylvania Ave., Kansas City, MO* ☎ *816/389–8600* 🌐 *www.charbarkc.com* 🕒 *Closed Mon. No lunch weekdays.*

Gates Bar-B-Q. [$] *Average main: $15* ✉ *3205 Main St., Kansas City, MO* ☎ *816/531–7522* 🌐 *www.gatesbbq.com.*

Grünauer. [$] *Average main: $11* ✉ *101 W. 22nd St., Kansas City, MO* ☎ *816/283–3234* 🌐 *www.grunauerkc.com* 🕒 *Closed Mon. and Tues.*

Hamburger Mary's. [$] *Average main: $12* ✉ *3700 Broadway Blvd., Kansas City, MO* ☎ *816/842–1919* 🌐 *www.hamburgermarys.com* 🕒 *Closed Mon.*

Happy Gillis. [$] *Average main: $10* ✉ *549 Gillis St., Kansas City, MO* ☎ *816/471–3663* 🌐 *www.happygillis.com* 🕒 *Closed Mon.*

Komatsu Ramen. [$] *Average main: $9* ✉ *3951 Broadway Blvd., Kansas City, MO* ☎ *816/469–5336* 🌐 *www.komatsuramen.co.*

Mission Taco Joint. [$] *Average main: $9* ✉ *5060 Main St., Kansas City, MO* ☎ *816/326–2706* 🌐 *www.missiontacojoint.com.*

Q39. [$] *Average main: $20* ✉ *1000 W. 39th St., Kansas City, MO* ☎ *816/255–3753* 🌐 *www.q39kc.com.*

☕ Coffee and Quick Bites

Central Dairy. [$] *Average main: $5* ✉ *610 Madison St., Jefferson City, MO* ☎ *573/635–6148* 🌐 *www.centraldairy.biz.*

Donutology. [$] *Average main: $3* ✉ *1009 Westport Rd., Kansas City, MO* ☎ *816/298–5222* 🌐 *www.donutology.com* 🕒 *No dinner.*

Parisi Coffee. [$] *Average main: $3* ✉ *Union Station, 30 W. Pershing Rd., Kansas*

222

City, MO ☎ 816/569–2399 ⊕ parisicoffee. com/parisi-union-station.

Hotels

Ambassador Kansas City. $ *Rooms from: $254 ✉ 1111 Grand Blvd., Kansas City, MO ☎ 816/298–7700 ⊕ www.ambassadorkcmo.com ⦾ No meals.*

Hotel Phillips Kansas City. $ *Rooms from: $136 ✉ 106 W. 12th St., Kansas City, MO ☎ 816/221–7000 ⊕ www.hilton.com/en/hotels/mkccuqq-hotel-phillips-kansas-city ⦾ No meals.*

Nightlife

Border Brewing Co. *✉ 406 E. 18th St., Kansas City, MO ☎ 816/315–6807 ⊕ www.borderbrewco.com.*

Green Lady Lounge. *✉ 1809 Grand Blvd., Kansas City, MO ☎ 816/215–2954 ⊕ www.greenladylounge.com.*

Missie B's. *✉ 805 W. 39th St., Kansas City, MO ☎ 816/561–0625 ⊕ www.missiebs.com.*

P.S. *✉ Hotel Phillips Kansas City, 106 W. 12th St., Kansas City, MO ☎ 816/346–4432 ⊕ www.hilton.com/en/hotels/mkccuqq-hotel-phillips-kansas-city/dining.*

Strange Days Brewing Co. *✉ 316 Oak St., Kansas City, MO ☎ 816/469–5321 ⊕ www.strangedaysbrewing.com.*

Shopping

The Bunker. *✉ 4056 Broadway Blvd., Kansas City, MO ☎ 800/476–6513 ⊕ www.bunkeronline.com.*

Made in Kansas City. *✉ 4155 N Mulberry Dr., Kansas City, MO ☎ 816/349–9646 ⊕ www.madeinkc.co.*

Louisville and the Bourbon Trail, KY

206 miles (approx. 3¼ hours) from Columbus and 299 miles (approx. 5 hours) from Chicago.

Louisville is home to more than just the racetrack that most people associate with this cosmopolitan city in Northern Kentucky. Whether you're looking for great eats, a bourbon experience you can't get elsewhere, or a moment away from the hustle and bustle, this friendly city that brings Southern hospitality a little further North has something for everyone.

Planning

GETTING THERE AND BACK
It's a straight shot along I–71 from Columbus to Louisville. The drive from Chicago along I–65 is also relatively simple. You might hit traffic in Chicago or Indianapolis, but neither will add serious time to the trip.

PIT STOPS
From Chicago, Indianapolis is good stopping point (though it's definitely closer to Louisville than Chicago). You can check out the **Indiana State Capitol** or take a quick break to walk the downtown canal.

WHEN TO GO
Summer can be rainy and hot in Louisville, so try to plan your trip for the equally beautiful spring and fall seasons.

WHERE TO STAY
A boutique hotel with a restaurant and bar on the first floor, the **21c Museum Hotel Louisville** is absolutely expensive, but it's also remarkable. Wonder what it's like to stay inside a kaleidoscope? This hotel has the answer. The riverview **Galt House** and the historic **Brown Hotel** are also good options.

A strip of scrap yards and sand pits was transformed into the handsome walkways of Louisville Waterfront Park.

Day 1

One of the great things about Louisville is that it's a small city. When you're downtown, parking is a nonissue. Rather than heading to your hotel to park, you can start the day off right by heading straight to breakfast in the cool, east-of-downtown neighborhood of Nulu.

Biscuit Belly quickly became a hit for people living in the Kentuckiana area. It brings people from the city and those from across the bridge in Indiana who are looking to start their morning right—with a biscuit. Because of its popularity, expect a short wait. Another Nulu breakfast staple, **Toast on Market,** has a great selection for those looking for a slightly more traditional breakfast. Don't pass up on the hashbrown casserole—this side takes the prize. Even if you aren't a coffee person, head to **Please & Thank You.** Get a little caffeine to hold you over and grab a package of the magical cookies, that even hours later goo like they were just pulled from the oven.

While this neighborhood might be best known for its trendy restaurants, it also has a collection of interesting local shops. Some of the best include **Red Tree, Scout,** and **Revelry Gallery.** And if you find yourself in the city on the second weekend of the month, visit **Flea Off Market.** This outdoor market brings together local vendors, restaurateurs, and musicians.

If you're looking to enjoy the food Louisville loves, then a stop at **Royals Hot Chicken** is an absolute must. This counter-service stop offers hot chicken (though the different levels of heat cater to those with a more sensitive pallet), southern sides, and boozy slushies—it's a one-stop shop and the perfect place to get your grub on at lunch.

After lunch, head west to downtown to explore the city's museums. If you've got kids, they definitely won't be bored at the incredibly interactive **Kentucky Science Center.** Other great stops include the **Frazier History Museum,** the **Muhammad Ali Center,** and the **Kentucky Center for the**

Arts, which houses small- and large-scale plays and musicals.

While exploring downtown on foot, make a quick stop to check out the Belvedere, a part of **Louisville Waterfront Park,** for a great view of the river. It's not stunning in the winter, but is beautiful come summer.

To start the evening off right (with a cocktail), look for the giant, golden, seemingly out of place reproduction of Michelangelo's David. Behind it lies the **21c Louisville,** a boutique hotel with a restaurant and bar on the first floor.

Louisville's downtown has some great spots for dinner. **Sidebar** is a wonderful place to grab a gourmet burger, fries, and a chilled glass of the state's most famous beverage. If Italian food is what you're looking for, **Vincenzo's** will hit the spot. The portions are large, the atmosphere is sophisticated, and the food is delicious. And you can't visit a city and not try its signature dish. The **English Grill,** at The Brown Hotel, invented the rich, open-faced sandwich beloved by Louisville residents. For after-dinner drinks, **Fourth Street Live** is a Louisville-must. At night bars along the street open their doors and start pouring!

Day 2

We're kicking day two off in Louisville's Highland and Crescent Hill neighborhoods, the areas that are all about "Keeping Louisville Weird." On Bardstown Road in Highland, **Highland Morning** has a wide-ranging menu, so you'll find something for every eater. In Crescent Hills, you're sure to encounter a line at **Eggs Over Frankfort.** They do egg dishes right, but don't overlook the biscuits and gravy or cinnamon rolls. **Con Huevos** is the perfect breakfast spot if you're looking for something a little different—get your breakfast in taco form topped with hot sauce.

Both neighborhoods are great for strolling. Consider checking out **Carmichael's,** the city's oldest independent bookstore, with locations on both Bardstown Road and Frankfurt Avenue. In Crescent Hill you'll find **Cherokee Park,** the perfect place for an easy hike and taking in the stunning houses that surround the green space.

For lunch, **Bunz Burgers** is a great place for a cheap and easy meal in the Highlands. Every type of burger connoisseur (including pescatarians, vegetarians, and vegans) can find something on the menu. And please, for your sake, don't pass up on the fries. Across from Bunz, **Taco Luchador** offers a long list of Mexican fare. In Crescent Hill, **Irish Rover** has a large selection of brews and traditional Irish cuisine.

Bourbon is serious business in Kentucky, so leaving the city without getting a sip of its claim to fame would be a serious mistake. After lunch, spend your afternoon exploring Bourbon Trail. (Though the name suggests walkability, these distilleries are scattered about). Downtown distilleries include **Old Forrester, Kentucky Peerless,** and **Jim Beam Urban Stillhouse.** If you're looking to venture outside of downtown, head to the **Brown-Forman Distillery** or the **Stitzel-Weller Distillery.**

End the afternoon with a stop at a Louisville brewery. Consider checking out **Akasha Brewing Company** or **Goodwood Brewery** for a predinner drink (and game of cornhole). If you're just looking to sit in the sunshine, **Garage Bar** in Nulu offers wonderful drinks and an outdoor ping-pong table for those wanting to show off their skills.

If you're a real afficianado, then you may want to do a bit more ambitious exploring beyond Louisville itself. A mere hour to the east of Louisville in the state capital of Frankfort is **Buffalo Trace.** Though smaller than other distilleries along the Kentucky Bourbon Trail, Buffalo Traces makes up in quality what it lacks in size. Some of the country's finest brands—from Pappy Van Winkle to W.L. Weller—pour from the charred oak barrels here. From Buffalo Trace it's a quick half-hour drive to **Woodford Reserve.** Bourbon has been distilled on this site since the late 1700s, and there are many stunning historic buildings along the pastoral grounds. Tour reservations are encouraged. If you want to visit a larger, more commercial distillery, consider **Maker's Mark,** where you'll have the chance to seal a bottle of bourbon with the company's trademark red wax, and the gift shop is stocked with goodies. This is a busy distillery, so tours are best booked in advance.

Though Louisville may not be famed for barbecue in the way that Kansas City or Memphis are, there are some excellent local spots. In Nulu, **Feast BBQ** became one of the city's go-to spots for traditional Southern BBQ. This counter-service restaurant offers sandwiches, racks of ribs, and every comforting side you can think of. For a less trendy (but still totally delicious) option, head back towards Crescent Hills to **Frankfort Avenue Beer Depot.** With tons of outdoor seating, a small putt-putt course to keep the kids entertained, and pitchers of cheap beer, this dive is worth the short drive.

Your nightlife options include **Downs After Dark,** a chance to see Churchill Downs, place some bets, and hear live music. Most nights tend to have a theme, so dress accordingly. Even if you don't believe in ghosts, the whole family will enjoy some thrills and chills during the **Waverly Hills Sanatorium Ghost Tour.** The old hospital is considered one of the most haunted places on earth.

Day 3

Before breakfast, head to the **Big Four Walking Bridge.** A stroll across will put you in Jeffersonville, Indiana, a wonderful place to grab breakfast before heading back. Consider stopping at **Adrienne and Company** for a morning sweet, **Early Edition** or **Geraldine's Kitchen** for a classic American breakfast, or **Pearl Street Game & Coffee House** for those who prefer a coffee breakfast.

Downtown Jeffersonville also offers lots of local shopping (conveniently right off the bridge). If you're going to make a stop anywhere, it has to be at **Schimpff's Confectionery,** which has been around since 1891. This spot makes its own Cinnamon Red Hots, and you can watch the process from inside or through the front window (inside viewers get samples).

Across the bridge back in Louisville, head downtown to **Cunningham's Creekside,** a seafood restaurant has been around for ages. The fried fish sandwich is a local lunchtime staple. Or head to **Cottage Café,** well worth the drive for the fluffy homemade desserts. To get a look at famous Churchill Downs, the **Kentucky Derby Museum** is a must. For those seeking a thrill, head to **Kentucky Kingdom** for its huge waterpark and exciting roller-coasters.

Don't leave Louisville without dinner at **Vietnam Kitchen.** Despite a less-than-stunning location (it's in a strip mall), this restaurant is consistently voted one of the best in the city. The menu is incredibly expansive, which can be overwhelming, but rest-assured that there is no bad dish.

Recommendations

Sights

Big Four Walking Bridge. ✉ *1101 River Rd., Louisville, KY* ☎ *502/574–3768* 🎫 *Free.*

Buffalo Trace Distillery. ✉ *113 Great Buffalo Trace, Frankfort, KY* ☎ *502/696–5926* 🌐 *www.buffalotracedistillery.com* 🎫 *Free.*

Frazier History Museum. ⊠ *829 W. Main St., Louisville, KY* 🕾 *502/753–5663* ⊕ *www.fraziermuseum.org* 🎟 *$14* ⊙ *Closed Mon.–Wed.*

Indiana State Capitol. ⊠ *200 W. Washington St., Indianapolis, IN* 🕾 *317/233–5293* ⊕ *www.visitindy.com/indianapolis-indiana-state-capitol* 🎟 *Free* ⊙ *Closed Sun.*

Kentucky Derby Museum. ⊠ *704 Central Ave., Louisville, KY* 🕾 *502/637–1111* ⊕ *www.derbymuseum.org* 🎟 *$16* ⊙ *Closed Tues.*

Kentucky Kingdom. ⊠ *937 Phillips La., Louisville, KY* 🕾 *502/813–8200* ⊕ *www.kentuckykingdom.com* 🎟 *$59.*

Kentucky Science Center. ⊠ *727 W. Main St., Louisville, KY* 🕾 *502/561–6100* ⊕ *www.kysciencecenter.org* 🎟 *$17.*

Louisville Waterfront Park. ⊠ *401 River Rd., Louisville, KY* 🕾 *502/574–3768* ⊕ *www.louisvillewaterfront.com* 🎟 *Free.*

Maker's Mark. ⊠ *3350 Burks Spring Rd., Loretto, KY* ⊕ *www.makersmark.com* 🎟 *$9.*

Muhammed Ali Center. ⊠ *144 N. 6th St., Louisville, KY* 🕾 *502/584–9254* ⊕ *www.alicenter.org* 🎟 *$14* ⊙ *Closed Mon.*

Woodford Reserve. ⊠ *7785 McCracken Pike, Versailles, KY* 🕾 *859/879–1812* ⊕ *www.woodfordreserve.com* 🎟 *$20.*

🍴 Restaurants

Biscuit Belly. 💲 *Average main: $9* ⊠ *900 E. Main St., Louisville, KY* 🕾 *502/409–5729* ⊕ *www.biscuit-belly.com* ⊙ *No dinner.*

Bunz Burgers. 💲 *Average main: $7* ⊠ *969½ Baxter Ave., Louisville, KY* 🕾 *502/632–1132* ⊕ *www.orderbunzburgerz.com.*

Con Huevos. 💲 *Average main: $10* ⊠ *2339 Frankfort Ave., Louisville, KY* 🕾 *502/384–3027* ⊕ *www.conhuevos.com* ⊙ *No dinner.*

Cottage Café. 💲 *Average main: $9* ⊠ *11609 Main St., Middletown, KY* 🕾 *502/244–9497* ⊕ *www.facebook.com/cottagecafemiddletown* ⊙ *No dinner.*

Cunningham's Creekside. 💲 *Average main: $17* ⊠ *6301 River Rd., Prospect, KY* 🕾 *502/228–3625* ⊕ *www.facebook.com/cunninghamscreekside.*

Early Edition. 💲 *Average main: $9* ⊠ *149 Spring St., Jeffersonville, IN* 🕾 *812/590–1280* ⊙ *No dinner.*

Eggs Over Franfort. 💲 *Average main: $9* ⊠ *2712 Frankfort Ave., Louisville, KY* 🕾 *502/709–4452* ⊕ *www.facebook.com/eggsoverfrankfort* ⊙ *No dinner.*

English Grill. 💲 *Average main: $33* ⊠ *The Brown Hotel, 335 W. Broadway, Louisville, KY* 🕾 *502/583–1234* ⊕ *www.brownhotel.com/dining.*

Feast BBQ. 💲 *Average main: $14* ⊠ *909 E. Market St., Louisville, KY* 🕾 *502/749–9900* ⊕ *www.feastbbq.com.*

Frankfort Avenue Beer Depot. 💲 *Average main: $10* ⊠ *3204 Frankfort Ave., Louisville, KY* 🕾 *40206 502/895–3223* ⊕ *www.fabdsmokehouse.com.*

Geraldine's Kitchen. 💲 *Average main: $8* ⊠ *402 Wall St., Jeffersonville, IN* 🕾 *812/924–7707* ⊕ *www.geraldineskitchen.com* ⊙ *No dinner.*

Highland Morning. 💲 *Average main: $10* ⊠ *1416 Bardstown Rd., Louisville, KY* 🕾 *502/365–3900* ⊕ *www.highlandmorning.org* ⊙ *No dinner.*

Irish Rover. 💲 *Average main: $9* ⊠ *2319 Frankfort Ave., Louisville, KY* 🕾 *502/899–3544* ⊕ *www.theirishroverky.com* ⊙ *Closed Sun.*

Royals Hot Chicken. 💲 *Average main: $6* ⊠ *736 E. Market St., Louisville, KY* 🕾 *502/919–7068* ⊕ *www.royalshotchicken.com.*

Sidebar. 💲 *Average main: $9* ⊠ *129 N. 2nd St., Louisville, KY* 🕾 *502/384–1600*

⊕ www.sidebarlouisville.com ⊗ Closed Sun.

Taco Luchador. Ⓢ Average main: $6 ✉ 938 Baxter Ave., Louisville, KY ☎ 502/583–0440 ⊕ www.el-taco-luchador.com.

Toast on Market. Ⓢ Average main: $8 ✉ 620 E. Market St., Louisville, KY ☎ 502/50–0499 ⊕ www.toastonmarket.com ⊗ Closed Mon.

Vietnam Kitchen. Ⓢ Average main: $11 ✉ 5339 Mitscher Ave., Louisville, KY ☎ 502/363–7535 ⊕ www.vietnamkitchen.net ⊗ Closed Wed.

Vincenzo's. Ⓢ Average main: $12 ✉ 150 S. 5th St., Louisville, KY ☎ 502/580–1350 ⊕ www.vincenzositalianrestaurant.com ⊗ Closed Sun.

Coffee and Quick Bites

Adrienne and Company. Ⓢ Average main: $8 ✉ 129 W. Court Ave., Jeffersonville, IN ☎ 812/282–2665 ⊕ www.cakestoday.com ⊗ No dinner.

Pearl Street Game & Coffee House. Ⓢ Average main: $5 ✉ 405 Pearl St., Jeffersonville, IN ☎ 502/648–1663 ⊕ www.gameandcoffee.com.

Please & Thank You. Ⓢ Average main: $5 ✉ 800 E. Market St., Louisville, KY ☎ 502/553–0113 ⊕ www.pleaseandthankyoulouisville.com ⊗ No dinner.

🛏 Hotels

The Brown Hotel. Ⓢ Rooms from: $125 ✉ 335 W. Broadway, Louisville, KY ☎ 888/888–5252 ⊕ www.brownhotel.com ⑩ No meals.

Galt House. Ⓢ Rooms from: $171 ✉ 140 N. 4th St., Louisville, KY ☎ 502/589–5200 ⊕ www.galthouse.com ⑩ No meals.

21c Museum Hotel Louisville. Ⓢ Rooms from: $239 ✉ 700 W. Main St., Louisville, KY ☎ 502/217–6300 ⊕ www.21cmuseumhotels.com ⑩ No meals.

Nightlife

Akasha Brewing Company. ✉ 909 E. Market St., Louisville, KY ☎ 502/742–7770 ⊕ www.akashabrewing.com Closed Mon.

Brown-Forman Distillery. ✉ 2921 Dixie Hwy., Louisville, KY ☎ 502/778–1053 ⊕ www.brown-forman.com.

Downs After Dark. ✉ Churchill Downs, 700 Central Ave., Louisville, KY ☎ 502/636–4400 ⊕ www.churchilldowns.com.

Fourth Street Live. ✉ 411 S. 4th St., Louisville, KY ☎ 502/584–7170 ⊕ www.4thstlive.com.

Garage Bar. ✉ 700 E. Market St., Louisville, KY ☎ 520/749–7100 ⊕ www.garageonmarket.com.

Goodwood Brewery. ✉ 636 E. Main St., Louisville, KY ☎ 502/584–2739 ⊕ www.goodwood.beer/venue/goodwood-taproom ⊗ Closed Mon. and Tues.

Jim Beam Urban Stillhouse. ✉ 404 S. 4th St., Louisville, KY ☎ 502/855–8392 ⊕ www.jimbeam.com ⊗ Closed Sun.

Kentucky Peerless. ✉ 120 N. 10th St., Louisville, KY ☎ 502/566–4999 ⊕ www.kentuckypeerless.com.

Old Forester. ✉ 119 W. Main St., Louisville, KY ☎ 502/779–2222 ⊕ www.oldforester.com.

Stitzel-Weller Distillery. ✉ 3860 Fitzgerald Rd., Louisville, KY ☎ 502/810–3800 ⊕ www.bulleit.com ⊗ Closed Tues.

Performing Arts

Kentucky Center for the Arts. ✉ 501 W. Main St., Louisville, KY ☎ 502/584–7777 ⊕ www.kentuckyperformingarts.org.

🛍 Shopping

Carmichael's. ✉ 2720 Frankfort Ave., Louisville, KY ☎ 502/896–6950 ⊕ www.carmichaelsbookstore.com.

Flea Off Market. ✉ *1000 E. Market St., Louisville, KY* ☎ *502/552–0061* ⊕ *www. thefleaoffmarket.org.*

Red Tree. ✉ *701 E. Market St., Louisville, KY* ☎ *502/582–2555* ⊕ *www.redtreefurniture.com.*

Revelry Gallery. ✉ *742 E. Market St., Louisville, KY* ☎ *502/414–1278* ⊕ *www. revelrygallery.com.*

Scout. ✉ *720 E. Market St., Louisville, KY* ☎ *502/584–8989* ⊕ *www.scoutonmarket. com.*

 Activities

Waverly Hills Sanatorium Ghost Tour.
✉ *4400 Paralee Dr., Louisville, KY* ☎ *502/933–2142* ⊕ *www.therealwaverlyhills.com* ⌦ *Tours from $25.*

Madison and Baraboo, WI

147 miles (approx. 2½ hours) from Chicago

College towns are always compact cultural pockets—particularly when school's out of session (fewer folks at cafes and restaurants). Doubling as the home for the University of Wisconsin–Madison and the state's capital, Madison (pop. around 250,000) is filled with unique activities, like the country's largest producer-only farmers market, quirky shopping, and water fun (much of the city sits on an isthmus, snug between Lake Monona and Lake Mendota). Baraboo is a half-hour jaunt and a recreational paradise also home to many of the state's vineyards.

Planning

GETTING THERE AND BACK
Once Chicago's morning rush-hour traffic dies down, start the three-hour trip (190 miles) to Baraboo, traveling north along I-90 W/I-94 W. There's no bus or train service between the two cities, although you could take the Van Galder coach bus from downtown Chicago to Madison (and skip Baraboo) for a 3½-hour one-way trip.

PIT STOPS
For a quick stroll in nature just south of the Wisconsin border, visit **Rock Cut State Park,** off I-90 in Loves Park, near Rockford. This is about halfway to Baraboo. The 3,000-acre park features two lakes and 100 wildflower varieties when in bloom.

WHEN TO GO
Summer is lovely here, aside from the occasional humid day. There are festivals all season, so there's always something interesting to do. Fall is also a great time to visit, especially if you're a fan of college football. Winter can be harsh, and usually only attracts diehard winter sports aficionados.

WHERE TO STAY
For a low-key vibe, check into **Graduate Madison,** a block off State Street and a block in from Lake Mendota. There's a lovely rooftop lounge and restaurant. The **Edgewater** is Madison's most lavish stay, hugging Lake Mendota near downtown, State Street and the East Side near East Johnson Street. Without leaving the property you can receive a massage at the spa, experience three restaurants, and walk onto its docks.

Day 1

Devil's Lake State Park, in Baraboo, is among Wisconsin's most popular state parks, but Fridays are less crowded than Saturday and Sunday. Be sure to pack a picnic lunch (so many great areas to

The golden-roofed Thai Pavilion glitters in the sun at Madison's Olbrich Botanical Gardens.

spread out a blanket or use a picnic table), a swimsuit (for swimming in the lake or renting a stand-up paddleboard) and shoes that aren't flip-flops (those hills are rocky and steep). You may even spot rock climbers.

New Life Lavender and Cherry Farm is a newer addition to Baraboo, providing a Sonoma-like experience on its lavender farm. Its boutique retails all things lavender, from lavender lattes to lavender salsa. Is it five o'clock already? Pull into **Broken Bottle Winery** 's tasting room—also a year old—before checking in to your Madison hotel.

A bit off the beaten path—in other words, not downtown—is a mini restaurant district along Williamson Street and Atwood Avenue on the East side. Here, you'll find eclectic ethnic dining such as **Buraka** (Ethiopian) and **Lao Laan-Xang** (Laotian). Or, if you want to champion one of the country's original farm-to-table restaurant, book a table at **L'Etoile,** open since 1976 and now owned by James Beard Award–winning chef Tory Miller.

Day 2

Rise and shine for the **Dane County Farmers' Market,** the country's largest producer-only farmers market, held on the Capitol Square every Saturday morning. From Amish-made pastries to award-winning artisan Wisconsin cheese, you can create a breakfast on site. Check out stalls that meander onto State Street for locally made art and jewelry. Cheese fan? **Fromagination** is a darling little Parisian-style cheese shop right on Capital Square. Pick up some "cheese orphans" (small wedges) to whet your palate for more.

For lunch, any number of ethnic eateries on nearby State Street will do, but two options are **Himal Chuli** (Nepalese cuisine) and **Dubai Restaurant & Bar** (Mediterranean, with a Syrian owner who formerly cooked in Dubai). Poke into a few boutiques, such as—on the western section of State Street—**Rethreads** (you might score a Diane von Furstenberg wrap dress), **Little Luxuries** (gifts for all the amazing people in your life) and **Serrv** (fair trade goods made in communities around the world.) Coffee shops are in abundance because, you know, college town. Open since 1997 is **Michelangelo's Coffee House,** with its vintage-y black-and-white striped awning.

If you make it all the way west on State Street, reward yourself with a **Babcock Hall Dairy Plant** ice cream cone at Memorial Union Terrace that's crafted on campus. The raised terrace is open to nonstudents and rents out kayaks and stand-up paddleboards.

The state's most famous architect—Frank Lloyd Wright—grew up in nearby Spring Green and built his residence there (**Taliesin,** worth a visit to the 800-acre estate if you're a huge fan) but Madison is also home to many of his projects. One is **Monona Terrace,** a conference center a few blocks from the state capital building and based on Wright's design (although completed in 1997, long after his death). The open-air rooftop boasts a killer view of Lake Monona.

Fill out the day with another artsy excursion, to the admission-free galleries at **Overture Center for the Arts.** Look for the glass-enclosed building that juts out onto State Street. Exhibits rotate often.

Dinner should include beer—after all, this is Wisconsin—and be outdoors if possible. **Capital Brewery** in Middleton is a sure bet, with live music in its Bier Garten. Carry-in food is welcomed and there's live music some weekend nights.

Day 3

Brunch is a big deal in Madison, but you'd better get there quick. Experience a different part of town today by trekking to **Ancora Coffee** on University Avenue, on the near-West side, for fluffy omelets and indulgent pastries served in a colorful atmosphere.

On your way out of town, swing into **Olbrich Botanical Gardens** in Monona where a genuine Thai pavilion (or sala) is the resident darling, crafted by a crew from Thailand and a gift from the Thai government and the Thai chapter of the Wisconsin Alumni Association, in honor of the many Thai students at UW–Madison.

Recommendations

Sights

Broken Bottle Winery. ⊠ S2229 Timothy La., Wisconsin Dells, WI ☎ 608/432–3786 ⊕ www.brokenbottlewinery.net 🎫 Tastings $4.

Devil's Lake State Park. ⊠ Devil's Lake State Park Visitor Center, Park Rd., Baraboo, WI ☎ 608/356–8301 ⊕ dnr.wi.gov/topic/parks/name/devilslake 🎫 $8 per car.

New Life Lavender and Cherry Farm. ⊠ E10766 County Rd. W, Baraboo, WI ☎ 608/477–4023 ⊕ www.newlifelavender.com 🎫 Free ⊗ Closed Sun. and Mon.

Olbrich Botanical Gardens. ⊠ Olbrich Park Beach, 3330 Atwood Ave., Madison, WI ☎ 608/246–4550 ⊕ www.olbrich.org 🎫 Free.

Overture Center for the Arts. ⊠ 201 State St., Madison, WI ☎ 608/258–4141 ⊕ www.overture.org 🎫 Galleries free.

Rock Cut State Park. ⊠ 7318 Harlem Rd., Loves Park, IL ☎ 815/885–3311 ⊕ www2.illinois.gov/dnr/parks/pages/rockcut.aspx 🎫 Free.

Taliesin. ⊠ 5481 County Rd. C, Spring Green, WI ☎ 608/588–7900 ⊕ www.taliesinpreservation.org 🎫 Tours from $56 ⊗ Closed Tues. and Wed.

Restaurants

Ancora Coffee. $ *Average main: $12* ✉ *3318 University Ave., Madison, WI* ☎ *608/233–5287* ⊕ *www.ancoracafes. com* ⊘ *No dinner.*

Buraka. $ *Average main: $15* ✉ *1210 Williamson St., Madison, WI* ☎ *608/286– 1448* ⊕ *www.buraka-madison.com.*

Dubai. $ *Average main: $14* ✉ *419 State St., Madison, WI* ☎ *608/819–8222.*

Himal Chuli. $ *Average main: $18* ✉ *318 State St., Madison, WI* ☎ *608/251–9225* ⊕ *www.himalchulimadison.com.*

Lao Laan-Xang. $ *Average main: $15* ✉ *2098 Atwood Ave., Madison, WI* ☎ *608/819–0140* ⊕ *www.laan-xang.com* ⊘ *Closed Sun.*

L'Etoile. $ *Average main: $50* ✉ *U.S. Bank Plaza, 1 S. Pinckney St., Madison, WI* ☎ *608/251–0500* ⊕ *www.letoile-res- taurant.com* ⊘ *Closed Sun. and Mon. No lunch.*

☕ Coffee and Quick Bites

Babcock Hall Dairy Plant. $ *Average main: $4* ✉ *1605 Linden Dr., Madison, WI* ☎ *608/262–3045* ⊕ *www.babcockhall- dairystore.wisc.edu* ⊘ *Closed Sun. No dinner.*

Michelangelo's Coffee House. $ *Average main: $4* ✉ *114 State St., Madison, WI* ☎ *608/251–5299* ⊕ *www.michelangelo- scoffeehouse.com.*

🛏 Hotels

The Edgewater. $ *Rooms from: $449* ✉ *1001 Wisconsin Pl., Madison, WI* ☎ *608/535–8200* ⊕ *www.theedgewater. com* ⦿ *No meals.*

Graduate Madison. $ *Rooms from: $110* ✉ *601 Langdon St., Madison, WI* ☎ *608/257–4391* ⊕ *www.graduatehotels. com* ⦿ *Free breakfast.*

Nightlife

Capital Brewery. ✉ *7734 Terrace Ave., Middleton, WI* ☎ *608/836–7100* ⊕ *www. capitalbrewery.com.*

🛍 Shopping

Dane County Farmers' Market. ✉ *3241 Garver Green, Madison, WI* ☎ *608/455–1999* ⊕ *www.dcfm.org.*

Fromagination. ✉ *12 S. Carroll St., Madison, WI* ☎ *608/255–2430* ⊕ *www. fromagination.com.*

Little Luxuries. ✉ *230 State St., Madison, WI* ☎ *608/255–7372* ⊕ *www.littleluxu- riesmadison.com.*

Rethreads. ✉ *410 State St., Madison, WI* ☎ *608/257–1018* ⊕ *www.rethreadsfash- ion.com.*

Serrv. ✉ *224 State St., Madison, WI* ☎ *608/251–2370* ⊕ *www.serrv.org.*

Milwaukee and Lake Geneva, WI

Milwaukee is 92 miles (approx. 1½ hours) from Chicago and 337 miles (approx. 5 hours) from Minneapolis.

Craving a little bit of city and country? Great news: Wisconsin offers the best of both. Milwaukee's art and food scene continues to fly under the radar (this is a good thing: less crowds) while Lake Geneva, the "Newport of the Midwest," is still that tony town you remember as a kid. Bring your comfiest walking shoes and something to wear to a nice dinner.

One of the architectural treasures of the Midwest is the soaring Milwaukee Art Museum.

Planning

GETTING THERE AND BACK

The drive from Chicago couldn't be simpler: simply head north on I–94 to Milwaukee. Lake Geneva is an hour southwest of Milwaukee via I–43.

INSPIRATION

The Violent Femmes—Milwaukee's most famous indie band—released a new album in 2019 called *Hotel Last Resort.* The music video for their single "I'm Nothing" was filmed at Milwaukee's Black Cat Alley.

PIT STOPS

It's not a kitschy tourist attraction, promise. **Mars Cheese Castle**—just look for the castle turrets on the west side of I–94 in Kenosha County—actually retails 700-some varieties of Wisconsin artisan cheese, proving there's more to the Dairy State than curds, port-wine cheese spread, and wax-covered cheese shaped like a football helmet.

WHEN TO GO

Summer is the best time to visit Milwaukee. Several major outdoor events are held in July and August. The area's vegetation explodes with color in the spring.

WHERE TO STAY

The artsy **Iron Horse Hotel,** in Milwaukee's Walker's Point neighborhood, is perfect whether you ride a Hog (local-speak for Harley) or not. Rooms are spacious and flaunt high ceilings. **Brewhouse Inn & Suites,** just north of downtown, is at the former Pabst Brewery complex with some relics still intact, like six antique copper kettles once used to make beer.

In Lake Geneva, **Grand Geneva Resort & Spa** is a sprawling luxury resort (the former Playboy Club, in fact), with its sleek outdoor pool, on-site spa, golf course, and excellent dining (including Ristorante Brissago). **Maxwell Mansion,** dating back to 1856, has an Old Hollywood–style pool and a speakeasy.

Day 1

Get an early start with art. The **Milwaukee Art Museum's** Quadracci Pavilion, the work of Spanish architect Santiago Calatrava, has long been a local landmark. Of particular note are world-renowned collections of Haitian art and Outsider art, plus one of the largest collections of Georgia O'Keeffe paintings.

For lunch, skip Milwaukee Public Market, the city's original food hall, for one lesser known. Almost every café, business, and food stall at **Sherman Phoenix**—open since 2018 in Sherman Park—is black-owned, from Funky Fresh Spring Rolls to Shindig Coffee. Give your stomach a rest at **Black Cat Alley,** an installation of art murals on the East Side. Need a java jolt? Perfect. Milwaukee's first cat café, **Sip & Purr,** is around the corner, for cuddles with your caffeine.

Before checking into your hotel, pick up pastries for tomorrow's breakfast from **Glorioso's.** It's in the Italian-immigrant neighborhood along Brady Street. One more stop: cheese curds so fresh they squeak at **Clock Shadow Creamery** in Walker's Point, one of only two urban creameries in the United States (the other's at Pike Place Market in Seattle).

Whether you're staying at the nearby Iron Horse Hotel or not, raise a glass to the weekend at **The Yard,** the city's largest outdoor patio. Across the street, **MobCraft's** taproom is among the 20 or so craft breweries that have opened in the last five years. Walker's Point—particularly South 2nd Street—is akin to Chicago's Fulton Street Market in that historic buildings have now been transformed into hip eateries. **Crazy Water** is a cozy houselike atmosphere with an eclectic menu while farm-to-fork **Braise** just celebrated its ninth anniversary, with a culinary school in case you want to go deeper on your next Milwaukee trip. For a sip of old Milwaukee, the nearby **Bryant's Cocktail Lounge** makes a memorable Pink Squirrel and its lounge dates back to 1938.

Day 2

Yesterday was go-go-go but today is more chill. Sleep in and rent a **Bublr** (shared bicycle, named for what native Wisconsinites call a water fountain) to cycle on a paved path along Lincoln Memorial Drive, marveling at the lakefront. Bradford Beach's numerous volleyball nets and tiki bar with its thatched-hut roof could easily be mistaken for Malibu or Hawaii.

If you'd rather be on water, **Milwaukee Kayak Company** rents kayaks at its Harbor District location, just east of Walker's Point and along the mouth to Lake Michigan, where the Menomonee and Milwaukee rivers meet.

Grab lunch at another food hall—seriously, the city welcomes them warmly—via **Crossroads Collective** on the East Side, a few blocks off Lincoln Memorial Drive. Vendors include Heaven's Table BBQ and Juana Taco Co. But save room for dessert: on the drive to Lake Geneva, you'll want to pull off I–43 at the South 76th Street exit for a custard stop at **Kopp's.**

Once in Lake Geneva—the relaxing portion of your weekend—kick it poolside at your hotel, resting sore muscles. One of the town's finest-dining restaurants is **Sopra Bistro,** snug on Main Street, and you should try to get a reservation there. If not, **Pier 290**—on the other side of the lake, the quieter side, in Williams Bay—offers a chill vibe outside.

Day 3

Walking the 26-mile pedestrian path around Geneva Lake might sound ambitious (it's the length of a marathon), but it's fun to see how far you can go. You may get farther than you'd ever dreamed.

Start early before the hottest point of the day.

Reward yourself with lunch by straying from Chicago's deep dish to a thinner style at **Oakfire,** which pops Napoletana-style pies out of its wood-fired oven a block in from Geneva Lake. The city's public beach is here, too.

For a glimpse at mansions—built by some of Chicago's founding families, like the Sears and the Wrigleys—and what life was like here at the turn of last century, hop onto one of the narrated afternoon lake tours offered by **Lake Geneva Cruise Line.** The Geneva Bay Tour lasts one hour and covers the eastern half of the lake, while the two-hour Full Lake Tour covers more ground.

Before heading home, pop into Main Street's cute boutiques (even the Starbucks is in a converted gas station) and don't be a wine snob: **Studio Winery's** wines are among Wisconsin's best, with grapes grown nearby. An artist and musician own this winery and the tasting room reflects those interests (there's even a recording studio), with locally made art sold here and live music on weekends.

Recommendations

Sights

Black Cat Alley. ✉ *E. Ivanhoe Pl., Milwaukee, WI* ☎ *414/477–7282* 🌐 *blackcatmke.com* 🎫 *Free.*

Milwaukee Art Museum. ✉ *700 N. Art Museum Dr., Milwaukee, WI* ☎ *414/224–3200* 🌐 *mam.org* 🎫 *$19* ⏰ *Closed Mon.*

Restaurants

Braise. [$] *Average main: $26* ✉ *1101 S. 2nd St., Milwaukee, WI* ☎ *414/212–8843* 🌐 *www.braiselocalfood.com* ⏰ *Closed Sun. and Mon. No lunch.*

Crazy Water. [$] *Average main: $16* ✉ *839 S. 2nd St., Milwaukee, WI* ☎ *414/645–2606* 🌐 *www.crazywatermilwaukee.com* ⏰ *No lunch.*

Oakfire. [$] *Average main: $16* ✉ *831 Wrigley Dr., Lake Geneva, WI* ☎ *262/812–8007* 🌐 *www.oakfire.pizza.*

Pier 290. [$] *Average main: $30* ✉ *1 Liechty Dr., Williams Bay, WI* ☎ *262/245–2100* 🌐 *www.pier290.com* ⏰ *Closed Tues.*

Sopra Bistro. [$] *Average main: $38* ✉ *724 W. Main St., Lake Geneva, WI* ☎ *262/249–0800* 🌐 *soprabistro.com* ⏰ *No lunch.*

Coffee and Quick Bites

Glorioso's [$] *Average main: $6* ✉ *1011 E. Brady St., Milwaukee, WI* ☎ *414/272–0540* 🌐 *shop.gloriosos.com* ⏰ *Closed Mon.*

Kopp's. [$] *Average main: $6* ✉ *7631 W. Layton Ave., Greenfield, WI* ☎ *414/282–4312* 🌐 *www.kopps.com.*

Sip & Purr. [$] *Average main: $6* ✉ *2021 E. Ivanhoe Pl., Milwaukee, WI* ☎ *414/585–0707* 🌐 *www.sipandpurr.com* ⏰ *Closed Mon. and Tues.*

Hotels

Brewhouse Inn & Suites. [$] *Rooms from: $119* ✉ *1215 N. 10th St., Milwaukee, WI* ☎ *414/810–3350* 🌐 *www.brewhousesuites.com* 🍴 *No meals.*

Grand Geneva Resort & Spa. [$] *Rooms from: $158* ✉ *7036 Grand Geneva Way, Lake Geneva, WI* ☎ *262/248–8811* 🌐 *www.grandgeneva.com* 🍴 *No meals.*

Iron Horse Hotel. [$] *Rooms from: $159* ✉ *500 W. Florida St., Milwaukee, WI* ☎ *414/374–4766* 🌐 *theironhorsehotel.com* 🍴 *No meals.*

Maxwell Mansion. [$] *Rooms from: $194* ✉ *314 S. Wells St., Lake Geneva, WI*

☎ 262/248–9711 ⊕ www.maxwellmansion1856.com ﾟ◯ﾟ No meals.

Nightlife

Bryant's Cocktail Lounge. ✉ 1579 S. 9th St., Milwaukee, WI ☎ 414/383–2620 ⊕ www.bryantscocktaillounge.com.

MobCraft. ✉ 505 S. 5th St., Milwaukee, WI ☎ 414/488–2019 ⊕ www.mobcraftbeer.com.

Studio Winery. ✉ 401 E. Sheridan Springs Rd., Lake Geneva, WI ☎ 262/348–9100 ⊕ www.studiowinery.com.

The Yard. ✉ Iron Horse Hotel, 500 W. Florida St., Milwaukee, WI ☎ 414/374–4766 ⊕ theironhorsehotel.com/food-beverage.

Shopping

Clock Shadow Creamery. ✉ 138 W. Bruce St., Milwaukee, WI ☎ 414/273–9711 ⊕ www.clockshadowcreamery.com.

Crossroads Collective. ✉ 2238 N. Farwell Ave., Milwaukee, WI ☎ 414/763–9081 ⊕ www.crossroadscollectivemke.com.

Mars Cheese Castle. ✉ 2800 W. Frontage Rd., Kenosha, WI ☎ 855/352–6277 ⊕ www.marscheese.com.

Milwaukee Public Market ✉ 400 N. Water St., Milwaukee, WI ☎ 414/366–111 ⊕ milwaukeepublicmarket.org.

Sherman Phoenix. ✉ 3536 W. Fond Du Lac Ave., Milwaukee, WI ☎ 262/228–6021 ⊕ www.shermanphoenix.com.

Activities

Bublr. ✉ 275 W. Wisconsin Ave., Milwaukee, W ☎ 414/931–1121 ⊕ bublrbikes.org ⌷ Rentals from $26.

Lake Geneva Cruise Line. ✉ 812 Wrigley Dr., Lake Geneva, WI ☎ 262/248–6206 ⊕ www.cruiselakegeneva.com ⌷ Cruises from $34.

Milwaukee Kayak Company. ✉ 318 S. Water St., Milwaukee, WI ☎ 414/301–2240 ⊕ www.milwaukeekayak.com ⌷ Rentals from $35.

Omaha, NE

Omaha is 379 miles (approx. 5¾ hours) from Minneapolis.

Omaha's story goes back more than 250 years, beginning with the Omaha and Ponca Native American tribes, through the 1804 explorations of Lewis and Clark, and on to the industrial booms of the 19th- and 20th centuries. This heartland city was built on railroads and breweries, stockyards and agriculture.

These days, Omaha is famously home to billionaire Warren Buffet and a gaggle of Fortune 500 companies. Omaha's half-million residents are proud of their interesting art, delicious food, and yes, their history as the "Gateway to the West."

Planning

GETTING THERE AND BACK
For the drive from Minneapolis to Omaha, enjoy leisurely road-tripping via smaller highways (U.S. 169, MN 60, IA 60, U.S. 75), which takes more time but offers better scenery than Interstates 35 and 80.

PIT STOPS
Along U.S. 75, you'll ride Nebraska's section of the Lewis & Clark Scenic Byway, just west of the Missouri River. On your way, stop in the small town of Winnebago to visit the **Honoring-the-Clans Sculpture Garden and Cultural Plaza,** made up of 12 statues representing the Winnebago Tribe's clans. Then stretch your legs along a trail at the **DeSoto National Wildlife Refuge,** where you'll encounter migrating snow geese, bald eagles, and ducks.

On the National Register of Historic Places, Omaha's Joslyn Castle is crowned by a limestone turret.

WHEN TO GO

The Nebraska plains give way to bone-chilling low temperatures in winter, though the annual Holiday Lights Festival is a lovely reason to visit in December. Summer is prime time for a visit, yielding plenty of sunshine, with the usual bouts of high humidity and thunderstorms.

WHERE TO STAY

Stay at the **Cottonwood Hotel,** a contemporary property in the former Blackstone Hotel. Near the Old Market, the **Magnolia Omaha** offers chic accommodations in a restored 1923 building.

Day 1

Sweep into town and veer westward for your first stop, the understated **Crescent Moon** tavern. It's an award-winning craft-beer bar, but locals know that it's the best place in town for a Reuben sandwich, which was invented at Omaha's Blackstone Hotel. (They even say that the Crescent Moon makes Buffet's favorite Reuben.)

All aboard for your next stop, the **Durham Museum,** the former Union Station that's a gloriously preserved time capsule of art deco design. Today, you can tour the 1931 station—a National Historic Landmark since 2016—and explore the museum's lovingly preserved train cars, vintage photos, artworks, and history exhibits.

One of Omaha's more recent skyline additions opened to instant fanfare. The Bob Kerrey Pedestrian Bridge forms a foot and bicycling link across the Missouri River to Council Bluffs, Iowa. Named for Nebraska Senator Kerrey, the Bob's S-shape span sparkles at night, and invites you to go "Bobbing"—by standing in both Nebraska and Iowa simultaneously.

Catch another heightened view at **1912 Benson,** a lovely lounge and gastropub pouring potent cocktails in its historic building, as well as on the roomy rooftop. When you're ready for dinner, consider **Gorat's** steak house, a Nebraska institution since 1944. It's a low-key restaurant serving Italian specialties, salads, and all manner of strips and chops, not to mention being another favorite eatery of Mr. Buffet.

If you're seeking a meal that's hearty but far less meaty, head to **Modern Love** in Midtown for self-described "swanky vegan comfort food." Its decor is bright, its cocktails are creative, and its menus entice the taste buds with filling plant-based burgers, bowls, and curries. For a nightcap, pull up a rolling leather chair at **Pageturners Lounge,** an easygoing bar and music venue co-owned by Conor Oberst, pouring classic cocktails at sweet prices.

Day 2

Start your day with the difficult decision of which tasty brunch entrée to try at **Railcar,** one of Omaha's best American kitchens. It's known for its fried cheese curds, but lemon ricotta pancakes, eggs Florentine, and house-made sausage patties may prove worthwhile temptations.

Omaha was and is home to many successful entrepreneurs, and the Joslyn family was among the richest at the turn of the 20th century. That will explain the 35-room Gothic Revival–style **Joslyn Castle** in Midtown. And it will lead you to the **Joslyn Art Museum,** the city's premier institution and an art deco reliquary of international art, from ancient Greek pottery to Renaissance and baroque pieces to impressionist and modern-art masterpieces.

Grab a pick-me-up at **Muglife Coffee** on Harney Street, then head toward the river to explore the Old Market. This historic district is Omaha's culinary, shopping, gallery, and nightlife neighborhood, and the best place to ditch your car and wander on foot across the cobblestone streets. Browse clothing and accessories at **Flying Worm Vintage** and the **Lotus,** page through **Jackson Street Booksellers,** and pick up handcrafted sweets from **Chocolat Abeille.**

Don't miss a visit to **Hollywood Candy,** one of Omaha's most famous shops selling old-fashioned candies, fudge, ice cream, and more. The variety store also has a wall of vintage pinball machines and an old-school soda-fountain counter.

Break for a beer and bite at **Brickway Brewery & Distillery** on Jackson Street, a favorite outpost pouring a full lineup of craft beer and single-malt whiskies. (By the way, if you're a craft-ale buff, be sure to make time for a taproom visit to **Nebraska Brewing Company** on the far west side of town.)

In the Old Market, put a needle on the record at **Drastic Plastic Vinyl Lounge,** Omaha's first record store featuring a full bar and a large selection of records to buy, and naturally, all music here is played on vinyl. It's perched upstairs from the Monster Club, a horror-themed pub.

Reserve well in advance for an elegant dinner at the **Grey Plume,** one of Omaha's top white-tablecloth dining experiences. You can order à la carte from the ever-changing dinner menu, or opt for a four-, six-, or eight-course chef tasting menu (all surprisingly affordable) that is always seasonally driven and proudly built on the local-food movement.

Day 3

Weekend brunch time starts on the late side (10 or 11 am) at many favorite Omaha restaurants, like the **Twisted Fork Saloon,** where you'll fill up on biscuits and gravy, huevos rancheros, and various egg skillets. If you're less decisive, over in Aksarben–Elmwood Park is Inner Rail Food Hall, with 10 food vendors serving pizza, burgers, Vietnamese, Indian, and other tasty dishes.

Enjoy some waterfront scenery with a walk through downtown's **Heartland of America Park and Fountain,** part of the city's plan to transform 90 acres along the Missouri River. Construction is nearing completion, with a landscaped public green space outfitted with a performance pavilion, an urban beach, and sculpture garden.

Kick up the nature vibes with a visit to the **Henry Doorly Zoo and Aquarium,** considered one of the country's best zoos. It's on the south side of town in Deer Park and features an enormous dome with sprawling rain forest and desert ecosystems, plus an amazing variety of species dwelling in replicated natural habitats.

Before you leave town, there are two uniquely Nebraskan foods you may not know but must try. One is the runza, a simple-and-yummy sandwich baked with fillings like beef and cabbage (and other variations), sold at a local fast-food restaurant chain called **Runza.** Another local fave is the cheese frenchee, a grilled-cheese sandwich that's been battered and deep fried. You'll find its deliciousness at different restaurants, but **Don & Millie's** is one of the most famous fast-food stops for a cheese frenchee—so don't leave Nebraska without one.

Recommendations

Sights

DeSoto National Wildlife Refuge. ⊠ 1434 316th La., Missouri Valley, NE ☎ 712/388–4800 ⊕ www.fws.gov/refuge/desoto 🎫 $3 per vehicle ⊙ Closed mid-Oct.–mid-Apr.

Durham Museum. ⊠ 801 S. 10th St., Omaha, NE ☎ 402/444–5071 ⊕ durhammuseum.org 🎫 $11 ⊙ Closed Mon.

Heartland of America Park and Fountain. ⊠ 800 Douglas St., Omaha, NE ☎ 402/444–7762 ⊕ www.visitomaha.com/listings/heartland-of-america-park-and-fountain/56947 🎫 Free.

Henry Doorly Zoo and Aquarium. ⊠ 3701 S. 10th St., Omaha, NE ☎ 402/733–8401 ⊕ www.omahazoo.com 🎫 $21.

Honoring-the-Clans Sculpture Garden and Cultural Plaza. ⊠ 509 Ho-Chunk Plaza, N. Winnebago, NE ☎ 402/878–2192 ⊕ visitnebraska.com/winnebago/honoring-clans-sculpture-garden-and-cultural-plaza 🎫 Free.

Joslyn Art Museum. ⊠ 2200 Dodge St., Omaha, NE ☎ 402/342–3300 ⊕ www.joslyn.org 🎫 Free ⊙ Closed Mon.

Joslyn Castle. ⊠ 3902 Davenport St., Omaha, NE ☎ 402/595–2199 ⊕ joslyncastle.com 🎫 $10 ⊙ No tours Tues.–Sat.

🍴 Restaurants

Crescent Moon. 💲 Average main: $8 ⊠ 36th and Farnam, Omaha, NE ☎ 402/345–1708 ⊕ beercornerusa.com/crescentmoon.

Don & Millie's. 💲 Average main: $5 ⊠ 4430 Farnam St., Omaha, NE ☎ 402/558–9928 ⊕ donandmillies.com.

Gorat's. 💲 Average main: $32 ⊠ 4917 Center St., Omaha, NE ☎ 402/551–3733 ⊕ goratsomaha.com ⊙ Closed Sun.

Grey Plume. 💲 Average main: $36 ⊠ 220 S. 31st Ave., Omaha, NE ☎ 402/763–4447 ⊕ www.thegreyplume.com ⊙ Closed Tues. and Wed.

Modern Love. 💲 Average main: $12 ⊠ 3157 Farnam St., corner of Turner Blvd., Omaha, NE ☎ 402/614–6481 ⊕ modernloveomaha.com.

Railcar. 💲 Average main: $14 ⊠ 1814 N. 144th St., Omaha ☎ 402/493–4743 ⊕ www.railcaromaha.com.

Runza. 💲 Average main: $8 ⊠ 2952 Farnam St., Omaha, NE ☎ 402/346–8551 ⊕ www.runza.com ⊙ Closed Sun.

Twisted Fork Saloon. 💲 Average main: $18 ⊠ 1014 Howard St., Omaha, NE ☎ 402/932–9600 ⊕ twistedforksaloon.com.

Coffee and Quick Bites

Muglife. $ *Average main: $5* ⊠ 2452½ *Harney St., Omaha, NE* ☎ 402/637–5837 ⊕ *squareup.com/store/muglife* ◔ *Closed Mon.*

Hotels

Cottonwood Hotel. $ *Rooms from: $180* ⊠ 302 S. 36th St., Omaha, NE ☎ 402/810–9500 ⊕ *www.thecottonwood-hotel.com* ⦿ *No meals.*

Magnolia Omaha. $ *Rooms from: $98* ⊠ 1615 Howard St., Omaha, NE ☎ 402/341–2500 ⊕ *magnoliahotels.com/omaha* ⦿ *No meals.*

ⓨ Nightlife

Brickway Brewery & Distillery. ⊠ 1116 *Jackson St., Omaha, NE* ☎ 402/933–2613 ⊕ *www.drinkbrickway.com.*

Drastic Plastic Vinyl Lounge. ⊠ 1217 *Howard St., Omaha, NE* ☎ 402/346–8843 ⊕ *www.drasticplasticonline.com.*

Monster Club. ⊠ 1217 Howard St., Omaha, NE ☎ 402/346–8843 ⊕ *www.monster-clubomaha.com* ◔ *Closed Mon. and Tues.*

Nebraska Brewing Company. ⊠ 6950 S. 108th St., La Vista, NE ☎ 402/934–7988 ⊕ *nebraskabrewingco.com.*

1912 Benson. ⊠ 6201 Maple St., Omaha, NE ☎ 402/964–2900 ⊕ *1912benson.com.*

Pageturners Lounge. ⊠ 5004 Dodge St., Omaha, NE ☎ 402/933–3973.

Shopping

Chocolat Abeille. ⊠ 421 S. 11th St. Omaha, NE ☎ 402/315–9006 ⊕ *choco-latabeille.com.*

Flying Worm Vintage. ⊠ 1125 Jackson St., Omaha, NE ☎ 402/932–3229 ⊕ *www.omahavintage.com.*

Hollywood Candy. ⊠ 1209 Jackson St., Omaha, NE ☎ 402/346–9746 ⊕ *www.hollywoodcandy.com.*

Jackson Street Booksellers. ⊠ 1119 Jackson St., Omaha, NE ☎ 402/341–2664 ⊕ *jacksonstreetbooksellers.squarespace.com.*

The Lotus. ⊠ 1207 Howard St., Omaha ☎ 402/346–8080 ⊕ *oldmarket.com/omaha/business/the-lotus.*

The Ozarks, MO and AR

Eureka Springs is 295 miles (approx. 4¾ hours) from St. Louis, 328 miles (approx. 5½ hours) from Memphis.

Eureka Springs, Arkansas, is a quirky Victorian town with an active arts scene and more than 60 bubbling natural springs, not what you might expect from the Ozarks. Branson, on the other hand, has spent years building up its reputation as a family-friendly destination with a focus on country music, but it's the breathtaking panoramas and densely forested terrain surrounding this gem of the Ozarks that has outdoor enthusiasts buzzing lately. Mom-and-pop-shops dot the landscape, where sparkling lakes and craggy caves are found a stone's throw from freshly built luxury lodgings. A weekend in Eurkea Springs, Branson, and the surrounding areas is enough to quench an adventure traveler's spirit with the pure and raw charm of the Ozarks. Day trips can include scenic hikes through Dogwood Canyon Nature Park and Mark Twain National Forest to take in the fresh Ozark Mountain air.

Planning

GETTING THERE AND BACK

The quickest route from St. Louis to Eureka Springs is on I–44, but the longer journey via U.S. 54 has you passing by the gorgeous Lake of the Ozarks on

Just outside Eureka Springs, the light-filled Thorncrown Chapel takes advantage of its wooded setting.

the way. From Memphis, it's just under 5½ hours to Eureka Springs via I-40 and up Highway 23—considered one of the state's most scenic drives. Eureka Springs to Branson is less than 60 miles, by car but opt for Highway 23 to complete the "Pig Trail" before heading to Highway 86.

INSPIRATION

Author Harold Bell Wright's *Shepherd of the Hills* was the first novel to introduce Americans to the beauty of the Ozarks, and the audiobook introduces listeners to some colorful characters while painting a picture of what life was like in the frontier days in the Ozarks.

WHEN TO GO

Book early if you plan to arrive in fall, when the maple, oak, and hickory trees paint the hills with vibrant shades of red, yellow, and orange. Summers are ideal for swimming or boating in the cool mountain lakes, while the mild winters make sauntering through the festive streets a merry experience. Songs have been written about the spectacular "Ozark Mountain Springs," when festivals fill the calendar with pie cookoffs, film festivals, and the Bluegrass and BBQ Festival.

WHERE TO STAY

The 1886 **Crescent Hotel and Spa** in Eureka Springs has been called the most haunted hotel in America, but it's this upscale hotel's hauntingly romantic ambience that earned it the reputation as "The Grand Ol' Lady of the Ozarks." This property features 72 rooms with four luxury lodges and some of the best views of the surrounding area from its rooftop Sky Bar. The adults-only **Branson Hotel** is just a short walk from the Branson Landing, where each of the nine rooms are uniquely decorated and set within a 1903 historic building. The lakefront condos at **Still Waters Resort** are an affordable option for families looking to explore Branson's Table Rock Lake or sleep among the Technicolor foliage during Branson's fall changing of the leaves.

Day 1

Arrive hungry in Eureka Springs and head straight to **Sparky's Roadhouse Café** (just look for the bicycle on top of the retro marquee) and grab a seat on the climate-controlled patio to get your first taste of this funky town's laid-back vibe. You'll have to sign a waiver to try their Stupid Hott Burger with a homemade ghost chili salsa, but they have 99 beers on the menu to help you cool down after the meal.

Check in to the Crescent Hotel after lunch and make sure to book your tickets for the nightly ghost tour at the front desk to get a haunting tour through this hotel's twisted past. Drop off your bags and head back out to explore the hippie haven within the **Art Colony Eureka Springs,** where the artists are as colorful as the community itself. Chat with the studio artists as you wander through the treehouse-style workshop village to see glass being blown, chainsaws carving sculptures, and so much more. Dinner at **Ermilio's Italian Restaurant** is a must, where the sauces and pastas are made from scratch (just like Aunt Millie used to make) and the dining rooms trail throughout a renovated Victorian house.

One of the most-visited sights in the Ozarks is the monumental Christ of the Ozarks, more than 60 feet of molded concrete erected atop Magnetic Mountain in the mid-1960s; it's a local tourist magnet you may have seen in the movie *Elizabethtown* or Season 3 of the television series *True Detective*. In the summer, a version of *The Great Passion Play* is presented there. The surrounding park has, in addition to the amphitheater where the *Passion* is performed, several other religious-theme attractions. Of more architectural interest is the gorgeous Thorncrown Chapel, designed in the Prairie style by E. Fay Jones. It opened in a wooded area just west of Eureka Springs on Highway 62 in 1980.

Day 2

Check out early, and start your morning off with a quick trip to the **Eureka Springs Coffee House,** where they serve locally roasted coffee from Onyx Coffee Lab alongside freshly baked croissants from inside a 130-year-old building. From there, it's roughly an hour's drive to Branson on the interstate, but opt instead for the scenic route along Highway 23 N to Highway 86 E for the chance to drive an electric vehicle to the **Lost Canyon Cave and Nature Trail.** Soak in those authentic Ozark views from four levels of viewing balconies before grabbing a glass of John L's signature lemonade from the secret bar beneath the waterfall and continuing on toward Branson.

Once you arrive, take a stroll down Branson's historic Main Street and stop in **Dick's 5 & 10**—one of the last five and dimes in the country—or grab a burger with a side of fried green beans at **Clockers Café** for an old-school experience. Be sure to check the calendar during your visit to **Silver Dollar City** to see if there are any events or festivals going on, as this 1880s-style theme park celebrates each season with Ozarkian gusto when it's not thrilling visitors on the world's fastest and tallest spinning roller-coaster, the Time Traveler.

The **Shepherd of the Hills Adventure Park** sits on the very spot where Harold Bell Wright wrote his 1907 novel, *The Shepherd of the Hills* (the first American novel to sell more than one million copies). Inspiration Tower now sits on the lookout point where Wright wrote most of the novel, and today visitors can climb (or ride in a glass elevator) 230 feet to get panoramic views of the gorgeous Ozark Mountains. Climb back down or exit via zipline on the tower's Vigilante Extreme ZipRider to get back on the ground to see the live action reenactment of *The Shepherd of the Hills* (featuring 90 actors, 40 horses, and a herd of sheep).

Ozark barbecue has been smoking Kansas City– and Memphis-style joints in recent competitions, and Branson's **Gettin' Basted** and **Danna's BBQ and Burger Shop** offer up some of the best versions in town. The BBQ nachos at both restaurants won't disappoint, but the pork belly cheesy mac at Gettin' Basted is obscenely satisfying.

Day 3

No need to rush this morning, since breakfast is served all day at **Billy Gail's Café.** Do come hungry, because the house-made apple-cinnamon rolls weigh in at one pound, and the "Billion Dollar Bacon" is listed as an entrée all its own on the menu. Work off breakfast by booking a tee time at **Payne's Valley Golf Course**—where a select number of golfers can play a round at Tiger Woods' first and only public-access golf course each day—or head to **Dogwood Canyon Nature Park** to hike among 10,000 acres of pristine Ozark landscapes. A single-day ticket at Dogwood Canyon includes access to the entire park, including the original Treehouse Masters' treehouse that is lined in birdhouses and made from sustainable materials.

Stop by the **Farmhouse Restaurant** before heading back home to fill up on southern specialties like chicken fried steak, fried okra, red skinned mashed potatoes, and, of course, the famous blackberry cobbler.

Recommendations

👁 Sights

Art Colony Eureka Springs. ✉ *185 Mill Hollow Rd., Eureka Springs, AR* ☎ *479/981–2626* 🌐 *www.theartcolonyeurekasprings.com* 🎫 *Free.*

Christ of the Ozarks. ✉ *935 Passion Play Rd., Eureka Springs, AR* ☎ *479/253–9200* 🌐 *www.greatpassionplay.org* 🎫 *Free.*

Dogwood Canyon Nature Park. ✉ *2038 State Hwy. 86, Lampe, MO* ☎ *877/459–5687* 🌐 *www.dogwoodcanyon.org* 🎫 *$15.*

Lost Canyon Cave and Nature Trail. ✉ *150 Top of the Rock Rd., Ridgedale, MO* ☎ *417/339–5305* 🌐 *www.bigcedar.com/activity* 🎫 *$34.*

Shepherd of the Hills Adventure Park. ✉ *5586 W. 76 Country Blvd., Branson, MO* ☎ *417/334–4191* 🌐 *www.theshepherdofthehills.com* 🎫 *$12.*

Silver Dollar City. ✉ *399 Silver Dollar City Pkwy., Branson, MO* ☎ *800/888–7277* 🌐 *www.silverdollarcity.com* 🎫 *$39.*

Thorncrown Chapel. ✉ *State Hwy. 62, 1½ miles west of Eureka Springs, AR* ☎ *479/253–7401* 🌐 *thorncrown.com* 🎫 *Free.*

🍴 Restaurants

Billy Gail's Café. [$] *Average main: $7* ✉ *5291 State Hwy. 265, Branson, MO* ☎ *417/338–8883* 🕒 *No dinner.*

Clockers Café. [$] *Average main: $8* ✉ *103 S. Commercial St., Branson, MO* ☎ *417/335–2328* 🌐 *www.clockerscafe.com.*

Danna's BBQ and Burger Shop. [$] *Average main: $10* ✉ *963 MO 165, Branson, MO* ☎ *417/337–5527* 🌐 *www.dannasbbq.com* 🕒 *Closed Sun.*

Ermilio's Italian Restaurant. [$] *Average main: $16* ✉ *26 White St., Eureka Springs, AR* ☎ *479/253–8750* 🌐 *www.ermilios.com* 🕒 *Closed Mon. No dinner.*

Farmhouse Restaurant. [$] *Average main: $10* ✉ *119 W. Main St., Branson, MO*

☎ 417/334–9701 🌐 *www.farmhouserestaurantbranson.com.*

Gettin' Basted. [$] *Average main: $12* ✉ *2845 W. Hwy. 76, Branson, MO* ☎ *417/320–6357* 🌐 *www.gettinbasted.com.*

Sparky's Roadhouse Café. [$] *Average main: $17* ✉ *147 E. Van Buren, Eureka Springs, AR* ☎ *479/253–6001* 🌐 *www.sparkysroadhouse.com* ⏲ *Closed Sun. and Mon.*

Coffee and Quick Bites

Eureka Springs Coffee House. [$] *Average main: $3* ✉ *11 N. Main St., Eureka Springs, AR* ☎ *479/239–2010* 🌐 *www.eurekaspringscoffee.com.*

Hotels

Branson Hotel. [$] *Rooms from: $141* ✉ *214 W. Main St., Branson, MO* ☎ *417/544–9814* 🌐 *www.thebransonhotel.com* ⏲ *No meals.*

Crescent Hotel and Spa. [$] *Rooms from: $162* ✉ *75 Prospect Ave., Eureka Springs, AR* ☎ *855/725–5720* 🌐 *www.crescent-hotel.com* 🍴 *Free breakfast.*

Still Waters Resort. [$] *Rooms from: $260* ✉ *21 Stillwater Tr., Branson, MO* ☎ *800/777–2320* 🌐 *www.stillwatersresort.com* 🍴 *No meals.*

Shopping

Dick's 5 & 10. ✉ *103 W. Main St., Branson, MO* ☎ *417/334–2410* 🌐 *www.dicks5and10.com.*

Activities

Payne's Valley Golf Course. ✉ *1250 Golf Club Dr., Hollister, MO* ☎ *800/255–6343* 🌐 *www.bigcedar.com* 🎫 *Greens fees from $195.*

Pittsburgh and Fallingwater, PA

Pittsburgh is 186 miles (approx. 3 hours) from Columbus.

The Steel City has a soft side. A blue-collar town at first glance, one must only dig a little deeper to find that Pittsburgh is home to cutting-edge art, incredible eats, and plenty of outdoor adventures. The city is a master at rebirth, an expert at modernizing its industrial past with art galleries in old warehouses (The Mattress Factory) and restaurants built along rail lines and inside car dealerships (Eleven, Superior Motors). In terms of art, there are more than 8,000 works by local legend Andy Warhol at the Warhol Museum. And, of course, the original Mister Rogers' neighborhood is Pittsburgh's upscale Squirrel Hill, where Fred Rogers and his wife Joanne raised their two children while he started filming the award-winning television show. There's plenty for outdoor enthusiasts, too, with 24 miles of riverfront trails for walkers and cyclists alike.

Planning

GETTING THERE AND BACK

To get to Pittsburgh, drive three hours east on I–70 from Columbus.

INSPIRATION

Listen to "Positively Pittsburgh Live" or the "Pittsburgh City Paper" podcast for all the details on what's going down in Pittsburgh.

WHEN TO GO

Pittsburgh's weather is similar to that of New York City, only with more humidity. The weather is changeable, with heat waves in the summer and chilly temperatures in the winter and spring. Late spring and early fall are the best times for visiting Pittsburgh, weather-wise. If you are planning to tour Fallingwater, you'll no doubt plan your trip around when you get that tour reservation; summer is the busiest season.

WHERE TO STAY

Once the home of industrialist Henry Clary Frick's lawyer, Willis McCook, the 20,000 square-foot **Mansions on Fifth** were designed in the Tudor and Elizabethan Revivalist styles on "Millionaire's Row" in Pittsburgh's posh Shadyside neighborhood. Return to the Gilded Age at this impeccably-restored hotel from 1906 (a main house and smaller, adjoining home), which offers 22 individually decorated guest rooms, a dining room, pub, chapel, library, and wine cellar with butlers on call seven days a week.

Centrally located and dog friendly, the boutique **Shadyside Inn All Suites Hotel** has studio, one-bedroom, or two-bedroom suites, each with a clean, contemporary look. Amenities include kitchenettes, a complimentary local shuttle, and the hotel's own dog park. Fido will feel positively pampered. A former Benedictine monastery on Pittsburgh's North Shore in the historic Deutschtown neighborhood, **The Priory** has a parlor scattered with Edwardian antiques and a cozy fireplace. Rooms are spacious with high ceilings, and the miniscule Monk's Bar is just off the lobby. There's a highway nearby, so request a room facing the inner courtyard, where a burbling fountain provides white noise.

Day 1

Leave Columbus late morning and arrive in Pittsburgh midafternoon for a late lunch at **Federal Gallery,** a pared down food hall on the North Side where you can choose from burgers and banh mi at Provision PGH; tacos and tortas at El Lugar; pizza at Michigan and Trumbull; or farm-to-table seasonal eats at Supper. Order lunch and a local craft brew then grab a seat on the outdoor patio in summer.

After lunch, take a short stroll to the **Mattress Factory,** a four-story Stearns & Foster warehouse that became an art installation space in 1977. Walk through James Turrell's light sculptures or immerse yourself in a sea of Japanese artist Yoyoi Kusama's red dots.

Top off your afternoon with a visit to **The Andy Warhol Museum,** a short walk away. Seven floors of works by the Prince of Pop Art are on display here, in the artist's hometown, including drawings, prints, paintings, sculptures, videos, and films. If you're lucky, there might be a Sound Series concert taking place in the museum's theater. These live performances from bands around the world were inspired by Warhol's role as a record producer and manager of the Velvet Underground.

Once you've had your fill of culture, call a cab from the museum and cross over the Allegheny River by way of the Andy Warhol Bridge to arrive at **Eleven,** an elegant farm-to-table restaurant in a rehabilitated warehouse along the old Pennsylvania Railroad lines. Entrées include Elysian Fields Farm lamb loin with cherry-almond salsa and Gerber Farms chicken with thyme jus. For a more casual dinner, head to **Tako,** a gourmet Mexican street food spot that's garnering buzz with its unique preparations like grilled octopus tacos.

Day 2

How you structure your second day will depend on whether you plan on touring one or more of the area's Frank Lloyd Wright sights. If you are an architecture enthusiast, you will not want to miss a trip to see the architect's most famous house, **Fallingwater,** about 90 minutes southeast of Pittsburgh. Advance reservations are required, and you'll want to

On every architecture buff's bucket list is Frank Lloyd Wright's Fallingwater, southeast of Pittsburgh.

allow at least two hours for your visit. If you still have some time, nearby is **Wright at Polymath Park,** a collection of three other homes you can see on a one-hour tour; tour tickets are booked through the Fallingwater website.

Start your day with a hearty breakfast at **Pamela's,** a retro diner in the Strip District serving hearty basics. It's a favorite of Barack Obama, who shared an order of pancakes here with Michelle during his presidential campaign. For an on-the-go breakfast, grab a coffee and pastry at **Allegro Hearth Bakery** instead.

If you are not venturing out to Fallingwater (or if your reservation isn't until the afternoon), make your way on foot to **Phipps Conservatory and Botanical Gardens** and absorb the blossoming eye candy: tropical bonsai, desert plants, ferns, orchids, and palms. Opened in 1893, the conservatory was a gift to the city from philanthropist Henry W. Phipps and makes an excellent year-round excursion, especially for kids.

Leave the confines of the conservatory and explore **Schenley Park** itself. Listed on the National Register of Historic Places as a historic district, the 456-acre wooded park in Pittsburgh's Oakland community offers hiking trails, a swimming pool, a disc golf course, ice skating, and even film screenings. The main trails that run through the park are in Panther Hollow.

For a healthy lunch, no need to go far since **Café Phipps** has been ranked one of the "Best Museum Restaurants in the U.S." The light, airy café at the entrance to the conservatory serves dishes like organic Waldorf salad and grilled tempeh Rueben. If you're hankering for something more filling, head to **The Porch at Schenley** where you can sit on the patio and enjoy the famous burger on a brioche roll with giardiniera pickles.

Now that you've sampled Pittsburgh's culinary landscape, hop on a bicycle and burn it off. Rent bikes for a guided, 2½-hour tour of the Steel City with **Golden Triangle Bike Rentals.** The tour takes advantage of the city's 24 miles of riverfront trails.

For dinner, shift from two wheels to four as you descend upon Pittsburgh's most talked about restaurant of the decade, **Superior Motors,** opened in 2017 in an old Chevy dealership. The eclectic, seasonal fare here includes everything from beef tartar to gnocchi with Swiss chard and cashews to scallops with turnips, pomegranates, and kimchi. Or visit **Carmi Soul Food** for shrimp and grits in a 1900s Victorian Row House on the South Side.

After dinner, head to **Arcade Comedy Theatre** in downtown Pittsburgh, where they keep the laughs coming with the best local talents and national touring acts who perform stand-up, sketch, and improv on the theater's open stage. The theater offers children's comedy shows on a monthly basis.

Day 3

For breakfast, stop into **Bluebird Kitchen** in downtown Pittsburgh for the house-made granola served with Greek yogurt, honey, and fruit. Or, pop by **Geppetto's Café** for a savory crepe and a cup of the house coffee.

You can't visit Pittsburgh without paying tribute to Pittsburgh native Fred Rogers, whose critically acclaimed *Mister Roger's Neighborhood* ran for 33 years. At the **Heinz History Center** in the Strip District, you can visit the Land of Make-Believe by checking out the display of the original set and items from the show, including the entryway and living room where Mister Rogers would lace his sneakers, King Friday's Castle, and the Great Oak Tree where Henrietta Pussycat and X the Owl live.

For lunch, head to the achingly hip Ace Hotel in an old YMCA building in the East Liberty neighborhood and experience **Whitfield,** the hotel restaurant, run by James Beard Award–nominated chef Bethany Zozula. It serves food based on the culinary traditions of the region's Polish, German, Eastern European, Italian, and Jewish settlers. Lunch includes entrées like steak and eggs with fries and bearnaise and a trout niçoise with lemon caper vinaigrette. At the nearby **Fireside Public House,** craft beer and wood-grilled burgers are the specialty.

With a full stomach, explore the neighborhood on foot. Formerly scrappy Lawrenceville, along the Allegheny northeast of the Strip District, has become one of the city's hippest hangouts. Butler Street from 34th to 54th Streets is an eclectic strand of shops, galleries, bars, and eateries on every cool kid's radar. East of Allegheny Cemetery, you'll find the Garfield and Bloomfield neighborhoods, both Polish and Italian strongholds. Due east is the gentrified East Liberty enclave, now home to a Google office.

Recommendations

 ## Sights

The Andy Warhol Museum. ✉ 117 Sandusky St., Pittsburgh, PA ☎ 412/237–8300 ⊕ www.warhol.org ⬚ $20.

Fallingwater. ✉ 1491 Mill Run Rd., Mill Run, PA ☎ 724/329–8501 ⊕ fallingwater.org ⬚ $18 ⊗ Closed Wed.

Heinz History Center. ✉ 1212 Smallman St., Pittsburgh, PA ☎ 412/454–6000 ⊕ www.heinzhistorycenter.org ⬚ $18.

Mattress Factory. ✉ 500 Sampsonia Way, Pittsburgh, PA ☎ 412/231–3169 ⊕ www.mattress.org ⬚ $20 ⊗ Closed Mon.

Phipps Conservatory and Botanical Gardens. ✉ 1 Schenley Dr., Pittsburgh, PA ☎ 412/622–6914 ⊕ www.phipps.conservatory.org ⬚ $20.

Schenley Park. ✉ 45 S. 23rd St., Pittsburgh, PA ☎ 412/682–7275 ⊕ www.pittsburghparks.org/schenley-park ⬚ Free.

Wright at Polymath Park. ✉ *187 Evergreen La., Acme, PA* ☎ *877/833–7829, 724/329–8501 for tour reservations (the latter is the number for Fallingwater)* 🌐 *fallingwater.org* 🎫 *$26* 🕒 *Closed Wed.*

Restaurants

Bluebird Kitchen. $ *Average main: $9* ✉ *221 Forbes Ave., Pittsburgh, PA* ☎ *412/642–4414* 🌐 *www.bluebirdkitchen.com* 🕒 *No dinner.*

Café Phipps. $ *Average main: $10* ✉ *Phipps Conservatory and Botanical Gardens: Café Phipps, 1 Schenley Dr., Pittsburgh, PA* ☎ *412/622–6914* 🌐 *www.phipps.conservatory.org.*

Carmi Soul Food. $ *Average main: $18* ✉ *1825 E. Carson St., Pittsburgh, PA* ☎ *412/231–0100* 🌐 *carmirestaurant.com* 🕒 *Closed Mon.*

Eleven. $ *Average main: $36* ✉ *1150 Smallman St., Pittsburgh, PA* ☎ *412/201–5656* 🌐 *www.elevenck.com.*

Federal Gallery. $ *Average main: $20* ✉ *200 Children's Way, Pittsburgh, PA* ☎ *412/517–6400* 🌐 *www.federalgalley.org.*

Fire Side Public House. $ *Average main: $25* ✉ *6290 Broad St., Pittsburgh, PA* ☎ *412/381–5105* 🌐 *firesidepublichouse.com.*

Geppetto's Café. $ *Average main: $11* ✉ *4121 Butler St., Pittsburgh, PA* ☎ *412/709–6399* 🌐 *geppettocafe.com* 🕒 *No dinner.*

Pamela's Diner. $ *Average main: $8* ✉ *232 North Ave., Pittsburgh, PA* ☎ *412/821–4655* 🌐 *www.pamelasdiner.com* 🕒 *No dinner.*

The Porch at Schenley. $ *Average main: $20* ✉ *221 Schenley Dr., Pittsburgh, PA* ☎ *412/687–6724* 🌐 *www.dineattheporch.com.*

Superior Motors. $ *Average main: $26* ✉ *1211 Braddock Ave., Braddock, PA* ☎ *412/271–1022* 🌐 *superiormotors15104.com* 🕒 *Closed Mon. and Tues.*

Tako. $ *Average main: $16* ✉ *214 6th St., Pittsburgh, PA* ☎ *412/471–8256* 🌐 *takopgh.com* 🕒 *Closed Mon.*

Whitfield. $ *Average main: $30* ✉ *Ace Hotel, 120 S. Whitfield St., Pittsburgh, PA* ☎ *412/626–3090* 🌐 *www.whitfieldpgh.com.*

Coffee and Quick Bites

Allegro Hearth Bakery. $ *Average main: $5* ✉ *2034 Murray Ave., Pittsburgh, PA* ☎ *412/422–5623* 🌐 *allegrohearth.com.*

Hotels

The Mansions On Fifth. $ *Rooms from: $193* ✉ *5105 5th Ave., Pittsburgh PA* ☎ *412/381–5105* 🌐 *mansionsonfifth.com* 🍽 *Free breakfast.*

The Priory Hotel. $ *Rooms from: $237* ✉ *614 Pressley St., Pittsburgh, PA* ☎ *412/231–3338* 🌐 *thepriory.com* 🍽 *Free breakfast.*

Shadyside Inn All Suites Hotel. $ *Rooms from: $278* ✉ *5405 5th Ave., Pittsburgh, PA* ☎ *412/441–4444* 🌐 *www.shadysideinn.com* 🍽 *No meals.*

Performing Arts

Arcade Comedy Theatre. ✉ *943 Liberty Ave., Pittsburgh, PA* ☎ *412/339–0608* 🌐 *www.arcadecomedytheater.com.*

Activities

Golden Triangle Bike Rentals. ✉ *600 1st Ave., Pittsburgh, PA* ☎ *412/600–0675* 🌐 *goldentrianglebike.com* 🎫 *Rentals from $20.*

Sioux Falls, SD

239 miles (approx. 4 hours) from Minneapolis.

The beautiful, namesake waterfalls here have been a natural attraction for more than 2,500 years. Prehistoric tribes inhabited the Sioux Falls area, followed by Lakota and Dakota Native American tribes, and, in recent centuries, by early American explorers, traders, and trappers. It was incorporated as a city within the Dakota Territory in 1876, 13 years before South Dakota's statehood.

Sioux Falls is the state's biggest city, home to memorable restaurants and breweries, leafy parks and bike trails, and plenty of ways to relax in nature—including in downtown Falls Park, watching the Big Sioux River rush over the falls. Here's how to enjoy a weekend in Sioux Falls, with a visit to nearby Mitchell for a taste of the famous Corn Palace.

Planning

GETTING THERE AND BACK
The nearly four-hour drive from Minneapolis is favored for its Midwestern scenery. The zippy option is I–35 to I–90, but you can take in small towns and even save a little time on a shortcut via U.S. 169 to MN 60.

INSPIRATION
Musicians have sung about South Dakota for decades, so you can curate a playlist expressly for your Sioux Falls getaway. Among the variety to run with: Johnny Cash's "Big Foot," Bright Eyes's "Four Winds," Stereophonics's "Dakota," Bruce Springsteen's "Badlands," the Bee Gees's "South Dakota Morning," and Dwight Yoakam's "Rapid City, South Dakota." Or queue up Spill Canvas, a rockin' indie band of Sioux Falls's natives.

PIT STOPS
In the Minnesota town of Blue Earth, about a mile south of I–90, Minnesota, check in with the Jolly Green Giant, a 55-foot-tall version of Green Giant's century-old mascot. Keep driving westward on I–90, then take the last exit before the South Dakota border onto County Highway 17 South. In about 10 minutes, you'll reach the Tri-State Iron Post Historical Marker, where in one spot you can stand in Minnesota, South Dakota, and Iowa at the same time.

WHEN TO GO
Sioux Falls has a true inland climate, so count on warm humid summers and cold, dry winters. Storms can blow through fast, especially those summer thunderstorms, but the warmer months are still ideal for travelers who love sunshine.

WHERE TO STAY
Big-brand hotels offer many lodging choices for Sioux Falls visitors. But the **Hotel on Phillips** offers a boutique experience with individually styled rooms in a converted 1918 bank building. The **ClubHouse Hotel & Suites Sioux Falls** has a modern hunting-lodge feel, with handsome furnishings and plenty of beautifully finished wood. It has a big sunny terrace, complimentary bike rentals, and an indoor children's water playland.

Day 1

Sweeping into Sioux Falls, in South Dakota's southeast corner, you'll soon find a slower pace that invites low-key explorations. The historic downtown is a perfect starting point. Park your car and check out many of the city's big sights, cute boutiques, and one-of-a-kind bars and eateries.

Make your first stop a delicious meal at **M.B. Haskett Delicatessen** on Phillips Avenue, making tasty crepes, sandwiches, and other daily specials. Follow lunch

The 123-acre Falls Park surrounds a picturesque section of the Big Sioux River.

with a choice of treats, be it a daring flavor from **Parlour Ice Cream House,** or a tasting flight at the airy downtown tap-room of local **Fernson Brewing Company.**

You'll notice that downtown is dotted with colorful public art, thanks to Sculp-tureWalk, the annual exhibit of outdoor sculptures. Enjoy them with a walk along Phillips and Main avenues (or hop on the free Downtown Trolley, operating June through August). Phillips continues north to 123-acre **Falls Park,** an enchanting spot along the Big Sioux River. Follow the pedestrian trails for photo ops on both sides of the falls, as well as from the observation tower in the visitor center.

Then head down river to **Fawick Park** for another unforgettable piece of art, a full-size bronze reproduction of Michel-angelo's David, among the few castings ever made. It was donated to the city by millionaire musician and inventor Thomas Fawick, a Sioux-Falls native who designed the world's first four-door car, along with hundreds of other patented inventions.

Before dinner, sip finely made cocktails at **The Treasury,** a deco-styled lounge located inside a former bank vault within the Hotel on Phillips. From libations, walk to a refined dinner at **Minerva's,** serving hearty entrées from steak to salmon, along with chislic, a traditional South Dakotan dish of cubed, grilled meat (simi-lar to Middle Eastern shashlik).

Day 2

Start your day at the **Phillips Avenue Diner,** a classic American eatery housed inside a vintage Airstream trailer, serving all the best diner dishes (plus poutine and "crazy" shakes in flavors like strawberry swirl cheesecake).

Whether you've longed to see it in person or only just discovered it, today is your big day to visit the **World's Only Corn Palace,** located an hour away in Mitchell. Attracting half a million visitors a year, this unique attraction was built more than a century ago to prove that South Dakota was an agricultural powerhouse.

You can tour the landmark to see its famous corn-clad décor. If you're here in August, check out the annual Corn Palace Festival.

History lovers shouldn't miss Mitchell's **Prehistoric Indian Village and Archeodome,** the only archaeological dig in South Dakota that's open to the public. The 6-acre site holds dual status as a National Register and National Historic Landmark site and is home to a museum and active excavations inside the "archeodome."

Get into the ranch-country spirit with a hearty lunch at **Cattleman's Club,** serving up serious steaks, burgers, and other filling meals at insider's prices. Or if you're ready for some of South Dakota's best Mexican fare, **Corona Village** serves classic Mexican dishes like carne asada and taquitos rancheros.

On your return trip, leave time to explore **Porter Sculpture Park** in Montrose, where a small admission fee supports artist Wayne Porter and his impressive works—most notably the 60-foot-tall Bull's Head, visible from miles away. If you love vintage souvenirs, duck into **Ace's ShopWise** thrift store in Salem for new and used treasures. Just outside of Sioux Falls in Hartford, break for a taste at **Buffalo Ridge Brewing Project,** considered one of the state's best craft-beer breweries.

Back in the metropolis, polish up for a fine cocktail, wine, and bar bite in the atmospheric **Carpenter Bar.** For dinner, dare to dine differently at family-owned **Hagere,** with a casual vibe and authentic Ethiopian cuisine. Or return to zesty classics at **Squealer's Smoke Shack** on the south side of town, serving up pulled pork, ribs, and lots of other smoked meats, all of which can be added to the salad.

Day 3

Rise and shine with a tasty breakfast wrap and fresh fruit smoothie at **Camille's Sidewalk Café.** It's on the south side of town near both Yankton Trail Park and Tomar Park, where you can walk and bike along the Big Sioux River. Then take a 10-minute jaunt down to Tea to browse the handmade wares and jewelry of local artisans at **Stacey's Vintage Art Boutique.**

Sioux Falls is home to many beautiful green spaces, but few compare to the Asian-inspired landscapes of **Shoto Tien Japanese Gardens** in Terrace Park, in the North End West neighborhood. Beyond its entrance arbor, you'll find exotic flowers, quartzite-stone pagodas, lanterns, and blooming trees across two acres with lovely Covell Lake views.

Wind down your weekend visit by stocking up on French-style macarons and other delicate pastries at downtown's award-winning **CH Patisserie.** Then head up to **Falls Overlook Café** at the north end of Falls Park, where you can enjoy a grilled Dakota Cuban and homemade ice cream from the local Stensland family farm. It's a perfect spot for a last look at the rushing river before you get on the road.

Recommendations

Sights

Falls Park. ⊠ 131 E. Falls Park Dr., Sioux Falls, SD ☎ 605/367–7430 ⊕ www.sioux-falls.org ⌨ Free.

Fawick Park. ⊠ 200 S. 2nd Ave., Sioux Falls, SD ☎ 605/367–8222 ⊕ www.sioux-falls.org ⌨ Free.

Porter Sculpture Park. ⊠ 45160 257th St., Montrose, SD ☎ 605/204–0370 ⊕ portersculpturepark.com ⌨ $10.

Prehistoric Indian Village and Archeodome. ✉ 3200 Indian Village Rd., Mitchell, SD ☎ 605/996–5473 ⊕ www.mitchellindian-village.org ⊠ $6 � Closed Sun. Apr. and Oct.–Nov.

Shoto-Tiene Japanese Gardens. ✉ Terrace Park, 1001 W. Madison St., Sioux Falls, SD ☎ 605/367–8222 ⊕ www.siouxfalls.org/parks/parks/locations/terrace ⊠ Free.

World's Only Corn Palace. ✉ 604 N. Main St., Mitchell, SD ☎ 605/995–8430 ⊕ cornpalace.com ⊠ Free ☉ Closed Sun. Dec.–Apr.

 Restaurants

Camille's Sidewalk Café. ⓢ Average main: $8 ✉ 1216 W. 41st St., Sioux Falls, SD ☎ 605/333–9727 ⊕ www.camillessiouxfalls.com ☉ No dinner Sun.

Cattleman's Club. ⓢ Average main: $18 ✉ 601 E. Norway Ave., Mitchell, SD ☎ 605/990–2222 ⊕ cattlemansclub.com.

Corona Village Mexican Restaurant. ⓢ Average main: $14 ✉ 1101 S. Burr St., Mitchell, SD ☎ 605/996–9391.

Falls Overlook Café. ⓢ Average main: $8 ✉ Falls Park, 825 N. Weber Ave., Sioux Falls, SD ☎ 605/367–4885 ⊕ fallsoverlook.com.

Hagere. ⓢ Average main: $11 ✉ Southway Shopping Center, 2113 S. Minnesota Ave., Sioux Falls, SD ☎ 605/271–1084 ⊕ hagereethiopianrestaurant.business.site ☉ Closed Tues.

M.B. Haskett Delicatessen. ⓢ Average main: $9 ✉ 324 S. Phillips Ave., Sioux Falls, SD ☎ 605/367–1100 ⊕ mbhaskett.com ☉ Closed Mon. and Tues. No dinner.

Minerva's. ⓢ Average main: $15 ✉ 301 S. Phillips Ave., Sioux Falls, SD ☎ 605/334–0386 ⊕ www.minervas.net ☉ Closed Sun.

Phillips Avenue Diner. ⓢ Average main: $10 ✉ 121 S. Phillips Ave., Sioux Falls, SD ☎ 605/335–4977 ⊕ www.phillipsavenuediner.com ☉ No dinner Sun.

Squealer's Smoke Shack. ⓢ Average main: $15 ✉ 840 Gateway La., Tea, SD ☎ 605/679–7675 ⊕ www.squealerssmokeshack.com.

 Coffee and Quick Bites

CH Patisserie. ⓢ Average main: $5 ✉ 309 S. Phillips Ave., Sioux Falls, SD ☎ 605/275–0090 ⊕ chpastries.com ☉ No dinner.

Parlor Ice Cream House. ⓢ Average main: $5 ✉ Washington Sq., 340 S. Main Ave., Sioux Falls, SD ☎ 605/271–0734 ⊕ www.parlouricecreamhouse.com.

🛏 Hotels

ClubHouse Hotel and Suites Sioux Falls. ⓢ Rooms from: $169 ✉ 2320 S. Louise Ave., Sioux Falls, SD ☎ 605/361–8700 ⊕ siouxfalls.clubhouseinn.com ❗⃝ Free breakfast.

Hotel on Phillips. ⓢ Rooms from: $159 ✉ 100 N. Phillips Ave., Sioux Falls, SD ☎ 605/274–7445 ⊕ www.hotelonphillips.com ❗⃝ No meals.

🍸 Nightlife

Buffalo Ridge Brewing Project. ✉ 102 N. Main Ave., Hartford, SD ☎ 605/528–2739 ☉ Closed Sun.–Wed.

Carpenter Bar. ✉ 215 S. Phillips Ave., Sioux Falls, SD ☎ 605/271–0983 ⊕ thecarpenterbar.com.

Fernson Brewing Company. ✉ 1400 E. Robur Dr., Sioux Falls, SD ☎ 605/789–3822 ⊕ www.fernson.com.

🛍 Shopping

Ace's ShopWise. ✉ 222 N. Main St., Salem, SD ☎ 605/425–3008 ☉ Closed Sun.–Wed.

Stacey's Vintage Art Boutique.
✉ *27102 Albers Ave., Sioux Falls, SD*
☎ *605/213–0045* ⊕ *www.facebook.com/
staceysstore.*

Springfield, IL

*97 miles (approx. 90 min.) north of St.
Louis, 203 miles (approx. 3 hours) from
Chicago.*

If you grew up in Illinois, chances are you
learned all about the state's most famous
resident: Abraham Lincoln. He was born
in Kentucky, but spent so much of his
life in this capital city that it rightly holds
claim to his legacy. There's lots to see
here pertaining to the 16th president, but
Springfield also has interesting architecture, fascinating museums, and a burgeoning restaurant scene. A weekend in
this small city will likely leave you feeling
refreshed and rejuvenated.

Planning

GETTING THERE AND BACK
It's a straight shot up I–55 N from St.
Louis to Springfield, and the drive takes
less than two hours even if you encounter some traffic in St. Louis. Driving here
from Chicago is equally a breeze: just
take I–55 S all the way. Traveling between
Chicago and Springfield on Amtrak
takes roughly the same amount of time,
making it a viable option for exploring the
walkable city.

PIT STOPS
If you're driving from Chicago, pull off
I–55 in Bloomington-Normal—home to
Illinois State University and the University of Illinois—for a late breakfast or
early lunch. The **Coffeehouse & Deli** in
Normal's Uptown, a local favorite, serves
vegetarian (and some vegan) diner food
alongside coffee and espresso drinks.

WHEN TO GO
Southern Illinois's climate tends to be
warmer than Chicago, which means
you aren't resigned to a slim window
of travel, but that also could also mean
humidity and high temperatures in summer. Spring, early summer, and fall tend
to attract fewer crowds and provide more
pleasant weather.

WHERE TO STAY
Springfield's boutique-hotel scene might
pale in comparison to Chicago's, but you
only need one option, right? Check into
the 125-room **State House Inn** downtown,
tucked into a landmark and a short walk
to historical attractions. For a more intimate or romantic stay, **Inn at 835 Boutique
Hotel**—also walking distance to many
sites—offers 19 rooms and whips up a
hearty breakfast each morning.

Day 1

Even if you stopped for a bite in Normal,
your stomach is probably growling or you
need a second cup of coffee. Fuel up
at **Café Moxo** downtown with its all-day
breakfast (check out the "breakfast fondue" for two, with Belgian waffles and
bacon-cheddar biscuits), individual pot
pies, and sandwiches.

For a small town, Springfield is home to
a lot of public art. Get the lay of the land
on a self-guided stroll. Some of the most
interesting works include "Acts of Intoler-
ance" (6th and Madison, commemorating a 1908 race riot); "The Rail Splitter" (a
statue of Lincoln at 801 Sangamon Avenue); and a memorial to Martin Luther
King Jr. (401 South 2nd Street). "Here I
Have Lived," which includes 40 exhibits
on Lincoln's life in Springfield, is another
fun way to experience downtown.

Happy hour at **Anvil & Forge Brewing and
Distilling,** with its outdoor seating and
long line of beers on tap, is a favorite
with locals. Get here early if you want to
try its delicious pour-over coffee.

Abraham Lincoln lived in this handsome clapboard house before being elected President.

Before turning in for the night, head to **Cozy Dog,** a drive-in restaurant that's been on Old Route 66 since 1949. It's signature hot dog is stuck on a stick, dipped in batter, and deep-fried. Burgers, chili dogs, and picnic-y sides like cole slaw are also on the menu.

Day 2

Today you'll brush up on history before a night out on the town. In the shadow of the State Capitol Building, the **Old Capitol Farmers Market** is the best place to start the day. Learn more about Honest Abe at the **Abraham Lincoln Presidential Library and Museum.** Among the items on display are dioramas of his childhood home and the box at Ford's Theatre where he was shot, as well as Mary Todd Lincoln's wedding dress.

Break for sandwiches at the venerable **Wm. Van's,** in a lovingly restored home from the 1850s. It's across the street from Lincoln's former digs at the **Lincoln Home National Historic Site.** The Greek Revival house with green shutters is where Lincoln lived with his wife for 17 years.

In the afternoon, tour the **Illinois State Museum,** which spans 500 million years of the state's history with three floors of exhibits.

American Harvest Eatery is one of Springfield's most trending dinner spots. This farm-to-table eatery features entrees like udon spaghetti with maitake mushrooms and Szechuan pork ragu. This place shares the same owners as **Augie's Front Burner,** another modern restaurant that wows locals.

Springfield is home to a rare drive-in featuring first-run films. Screenings at the **Route 66 Twin Drive-In** typically begin around dusk.

Day 3

After a lavender latte at **Free Press Coffee House,** enjoy a short hike at the 40-acre **Adams Wildlife Sanctuary,** a pretty and peaceful downtown spot operated by the Illinois Audubon Society.

Before heading back to Chicago, tour the Frank Lloyd Wright–designed **Dana-Thomas House.** Commissioned by socialite Susan Lawrence Dana, the home was designed in Wright's signature Prairie style and unveiled in 1904.

Recommendations

Sights

Abraham Lincoln Presidential Library and Museum. ✉ *500 E. Madison St., Suite 200, Springfield, IL* ☎ *217/557–6251* 🌐 *www.alplm.org* 🎫 *$15.*

Adams Wildlife Sanctuary. ✉ *2315 Clear Lake Ave., Springfield, IL* ☎ *217/544–2473* 🌐 *www.illinoisaudubon.org* 🎫 *Free.*

Dana-Thomas House. ✉ *301 E. Lawrence Ave. Springfield, IL* ☎ *217/782–6776* 🌐 *www.dana-thomas.org* 🎫 *$10.*

Illinois State Museum. ✉ *502 S. Spring St., Springfield, IL* ☎ *217/782–7386* 🌐 *www.illinoisstatemuseum.org* 🎫 *$5.*

Lincoln Home National Historic Site. ✉ *413 S. 8th St., Springfield, IL* ☎ *217/492–4241* 🌐 *www.nps.gov/liho* 🎫 *Free.*

Route 66 Twin Drive-In. ✉ *1700 Knights Recreation Dr., Springfield, IL* ☎ *217/698–0066* 🌐 *www.route66-drivein.com* 🎫 *$8.*

Restaurants

American Harvest Eatery. [$] *Average main: $12* ✉ *3241 W. Iles Ave., Springfield, IL* ☎ *217/546–8300* 🕒 *Closed Mon.*

Augie's Front Burner. [$] *Average main: $28* ✉ *109 S. 5th St., Springfield, IL* ☎ *217/544–6979* 🌐 *www.augiesfrontburner.com* 🕒 *Closed Sun.*

Café Moxo. [$] *Average main: $9* ✉ *411 E. Adams St., Springfield, IL* ☎ *217/788–8084* 🌐 *www.cafemoxo.digitallhost.com* 🕒 *Closed Sun.*

The Coffeehouse & Deli. [$] *Average main: $6* ✉ *114 E. Beaufort St., Normal, IL* ☎ *309/452–6774* 🌐 *www.thecoffeehouse-normal.com* 🕒 *Closed Sun.*

Cozy Dog. [$] *Average main: $4* ✉ *2935 S. 6th St., Springfield, IL* ☎ *217/525–1992* 🌐 *www.cozydogdrivein.com* 🕒 *Closed Sun.*

Coffee and Quick Bites

Free Press Coffee House. [$] *Average main: $5* ✉ *916 S. Grand Ave. W, Springfield, IL* ☎ *217/679–1866* 🌐 *www.freepress-coffeehouse.com* 🕒 *Closed Sun. and Mon. No dinner.*

Wm. Van's. [$] *Average main: $9* ✉ *503 S. 7th St., Springfield, IL* ☎ *217/679–4726* 🌐 *www.connshg.com/wm-vans-coffee-house* 🕒 *No dinner.*

Hotels

Inn at 835 Boutique Hotel. [$] *Rooms from: $104* ✉ *835 S. 2nd St., Springfield, IL* ☎ *217/523–4466* 🌐 *www.connshg.com/Inn-at-835* 🍴 *Free breakfast.*

State House Inn. [$] *Rooms from: $85* ✉ *101 E. Adams St., Springfield, IL* ☎ *217/528–5100* 🌐 *www.state-houseinnspringfield.com* 🍴 *Free breakfast.*

Nightlife

Anvil & Forge Brewing and Distilling. ✉ *619 E. Washington St., Springfield, IL* ☎ *217/679–1195* 🌐 *www.anvilandforge.com.*

🛍 Shopping

Old Capitol Farmers Market. ✉ *Adams St., between 3rd and 5th Sts., Springfield, IL* ☏ *217/544–1723* ⊕ *www.downtownspringfield.org.*

Traverse City and Michigan Wine Country

320 miles (approx. 5 hours) from Chicago.

With only 16,000 residents and a charming "Main Street" (actually called Front Street), the official cherry capital of the country is—pardon the pun—also a sweet little getaway. Hugging the shores of Grand Traverse Bay, which flows into Lake Michigan, it's also a wine region winning accolades from Chicago sommeliers and placing high at national wine competitions. Also, it's worth noting that Madonna's family owns and manages a vineyard and winery here (Ciccone Vineyard and Winery) while Trading Spaces star Carter Oosterhouse (a Traverse City native) and his brother Todd founded Bonobo Winery on Old Mission Peninsula.

Planning

GETTING THERE AND BACK

The easiest way to reach Traverse City is by car, especially because you'll need transportation between tasting rooms. From downtown Chicago, the 320-mile trip takes about five hours. A combination of Indian Trails and Greyhound bus lines yields a grueling 10-hour ride, and you'll still need to rent a car or invest in hefty Uber or Lyft fares upon arrival.

INSPIRATION

Listen to Emily St. John Mandel's dystopian novel *Station Eleven,* set in Traverse City and about a group of actors in a postapocalyptic world.

WHEN TO GO

Like most Upper Midwest destinations, summer is when crowds converge for the year's warmest temps, cherry season (early July through early August) and true beach weather. But shoulder seasons—spring and fall—are when you can chat with winemakers and, come fall, experience harvest. Avoid the National Cherry Festival in early July, when hotel rooms are booked solid.

WHERE TO STAY

There are more boutique inns, guest houses and Airbnbs than chains in Traverse City. Sleep near the vines at **Brys Estate Vineyard & Winery's** former barn turned luxe farmhouse on the winery's 111-acre estate—reservations include a cheese and charcuterie board, bottle of wine, and glass of wine for each guest—or "in town" at **Bayshore Resort,** which hugs the beach and is a short walk to East Front Street.

Day 1

After the five-hour drive from Chicago (plus setting your watch one hour forward to EST), you'll need that first glass of wine, right? Take a short walk on **West End Beach,** then sit down for an early drink at **Left Foot Charley,** a wine- and hard-cider producer with a chic (think modern-industrial aesthetic) tasting room. Tasting flights are a quick tour of the portfolio. Next, slip into **The Cooks' House** downtown for dinner, run by two Michelin-star chefs who moved home to Traverse City and where farm-to-table and foraged dishes include Michigan artisan cheeses plate or a walleye roasted in butter with foie gras cream and sunflower sprouts.

Climb the tower at Grand Traverse Lighthouse, located at the tip of the Leelanau Peninsula.

Day 2

Hit up tasting rooms early so you can space out your sips and also catch morning's golden light for perfect photos. Just like Napa and Sonoma, most are open from 10 or 11 to 5 or 6. Wineries lie in one of two American Viticultural Areas: Old Mission Peninsula AVA and Leelanau Peninsula AVA.

Kickstart a full day of wine tasting with a hearty breakfast of an egg-biscuit sandwich or French-style omelet at **Benedict,** then buckle up for some wine tasting. The key here to is to work your way south. Start at the far northern tip of the Leelanau Peninsula, home to the **Grand Traverse Lighthouse** and **Leelanau State Park** (both are along Grand Traverse Bay, for photo-taking ops, then roll into your first tasting room. **Green Bird Organic Cellars** in Northport is about more than wine. Wines (from Gewürztraminer to Pinot Gris) are organically certified, they make hard ciders, too, and you can try

both in this 67-acre farm setting, which is also a popular wedding venue. For your designated driver, cherry soda—plus a meat and cheese board—is also served here.

Sample a regional specialty—smoked whitefish pâté, whitefish taco, garlic parmesan whitefish, or items with cherry-chicken flavor, capping off with a slice of cherry pie—at the no-frills **The Cove** in Leland (don't leave without checking out the lower-level Rick's Café). If you feel like you're in a fishing cabin, that's the whole idea.

Work off all that food with an easy stroll at **Sleeping Bear Dunes National Lakeshore,** where dunes overlook Lake Michigan and 65 miles of shoreline will make you believe in the healing powers of the Great Lakes.

Curl south to your next winery along Lake Michigan, on M–22. Just two miles in from the Lake Michigan coast, family-owned **Good Harbor Vineyards** has quietly been making wine from its own vines since 1980. Try six of its wines for $5, seated on the tasting room's patio.

Head to the region's second AVA (home to fewer wineries) for a quick tour by tasting at **Bonobo Winery.** Wines range from familiar (Chardonnay) to a Rose crafted from eight grape varieties, including lesser-known varietals like Auxerrois and Ariana.

Nap back at the hotel or change clothes for a night "out on the town" Traverse City style (read: comfy but chic). **The Filling Station Microbrewery**—within a former train depot—is one of the region's hottest dinner spots (featuring salads and wood-fired pizzas)—and super casual. If you're tired of wine, you'll love the craft beers brewed on site. Treat yourself to a patio seat and lake view and, if available, live music.

Day 3

Need a morning jolt or just want to check out the local café scene? **Morsels** on East Front Street is a darling brick-exterior café touting an outdoor patio, espresso and coffee drinks crafted from Intelligentsia beans, and its signature "morsels" (doughy cookies with dollops of frosting). Browse three nearby indie bookstores (the wellness-oriented **Higher Self Bookstore, Horizon Books,** and **Brilliant Books**) for reads to dive into back home.

The tasting room at the 160-acre **Black Star Farms**—its bubbly can be found at fine establishments in Chicago—is the kind of winery you'll want to spend all day at. After a stroll through the grounds, which includes an inn, hiking trails, café and equestrian facility, indulge in the premium wine and cheese tasting at noon or 2 (reservations required the day prior). Want to do a comparison tasting? Nearby **Mawby Vineyards and Winery** is another sparkling-wine producer and

open to visitors, sourcing grapes from its own vineyards as well as from across the United States.

Before heading home, swing by **Cherry Republic** in downtown Traverse City and scoop up some dark-chocolate-covered cherries, and slices of cherry pie, for the ride back to Chicago. Even the wines this brand makes are crafted with cherry (try them in the store).

Recommendations

Sights

Black Star Farms. ⊠ *360 McKinley Rd. E, Traverse City, MI* ☎ *231/944–1300* ⊕ *www.blackstarfarms.com* 🍷 *Tastings $10.*

Bonobo Winery. ⊠ *12011 Center Rd., Traverse City, MI* ☎ *231/282–9463* ⊕ *www.bonobowinery.com* 🍷 *Tastings $10.*

Ciccone Vineyards and Winery. ⊠ *10343 E. Hilltop Rd., Suttons Bay, MI* ☎ *231/271–5553* ⊕ *cicconevineyard.com* 🍷 *Tastings $10.*

Good Harbor Vineyards. ⊠ *34 S. Manitou Tr., Lake Leelanau, MI* ☎ *231/256–7165* ⊕ *www.goodharbor.com* 🍷 *Tastings $6.*

Grand Traverse Lighthouse. ⊠ *N. Lighthouse Pond Rd., Leelanau Township, MI* ☎ *231/386–9145* ⊕ *www.grandtraverselighthouse.com* 🍷 *$5.*

Green Bird Organic Cellars. ⊠ *9825 E. Engles Rd., Northport, MI* ☎ *231/386–5636* ⊕ *www.greenbirdcellars.com* 🍷 *Tastings $5.*

Leelanau State Park. ⊠ *15310 N. Lighthouse Point Rd., Northport MI* ☎ *231/386–5422* ⊕ *www.michigan.org/property/leelanau-state-park* 🍷 *$16 per vehicle.*

Mawby Vineyards and Winery. ⊠ *4519 Elm Valley Rd., Suttons Bay, MI* ☎ *231/271–3522* ⊕ *mawby.wine* 🍷 *Tastings $9.*

Sleeping Bear Dunes National Lakeshore.
⊠ 9922 Front St., Empire, MI ☎ 231/326–
4700 ⊕ www.nps.gov/slbe ⊠ $15.

West End Beach. ⊠ 716 W. Grandview
Pkwy., Traverse City, MI ☎ 231/922–4900
⊠ Free.

🍴 Restaurants

Benedict. $ Average main: $10 ⊠ 405 S.
Union St., Traverse City, MI ☎ 231/421–
1000 ⊕ www.benedicttc.com ⊙ Closed
Mon. No dinner.

The Cooks' House. $ Average main: $32
⊠ 115 Wellington St., Traverse City, MI
☎ 231/946–8700 ⊕ www.cookshousetc.
com ⊙ Closed Mon.

The Cove. $ Average main: $20 ⊠ 111
River St., Leland, MI ☎ 231/256–9834
⊕ cordwoodbbq.com.

The Filling Station. $ Average main: $14
⊠ 642 Railroad Pl., Traverse City, MI
☎ 231/946–8168 ⊕ thefillingstationmicro-
brewery.com.

Morsels. $ Average main: $5 ⊠ 321 E.
Front St., Traverse City, MI ☎ 231/421–
1353 ⊕ www.morselsbakery.com ⊙ No
dinner.

🛏 Hotels

Bayshore Resort. $ Rooms from: $124
⊠ 833 E. Front St., Traverse City, MI
☎ 800/634–4401 ⊕ www.bayshore-re-
sort.com ⦿ Free breakfast.

Brys Estate Vineyard & Winery. $ Rooms
from: $325 ⊠ 3309 Blue Water Rd., Trav-
erse City, MI ☎ 231/223–9303 ⊕ www.
brysestate.com ⦿ No meals.

🍸 Nightlife

Left Foot Charley. ⊠ 806 Red Dr., Traverse
City, MI ☎ 231/995–0500 ⊕ www.left-
footcharley.com.

🛍 Shopping

Brilliant Books. ⊠ 118 E. Front St., Traverse City, MI ☎ 231/946–2665 ⊕ www.
brilliant-books.net.

Cherry Republic. ⊠ 154 E. Front St., Traverse City, MI ☎ 231/932–9205 ⊕ cher-
ryrepublic.com.

Higher Self Bookstore. ⊠ 313 E. Front
St., Traverse City, MI ☎ 231/941–5805
⊕ www.higherselfbookstore.com.

Horizon Books. ⊠ 243 E. Front St., Traverse City, MI ☎ 231/946–7290 ⊕ www.
horizonbooks.com.

Chapter 4

SOUTHEAST

WELCOME TO SOUTHEAST

TOP REASONS TO GO

★ **Shore Excursions:** Find solitude in Cape Hatteras, luxury in Hilton Head, or family fun in Myrtle Beach.

★ **Regional Fare:** Enjoy Lowcountry cuisine in the Carolinas or seafood along the Gulf of Mexico.

★ **History Lessons:** Climb the ramparts at St. Augustine's Castillo de San Marcos, dating from 1695.

★ **Underwater Adventures:** Dip below the surface with the snorkeling trail on the Palm Beach Coast.

★ **Pamper Yourself:** Stay in a historic hotel in Hot Springs, known for a century as "Spa City."

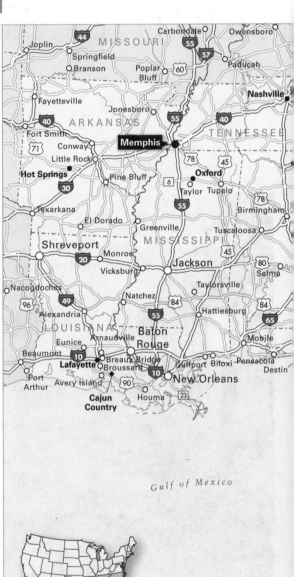

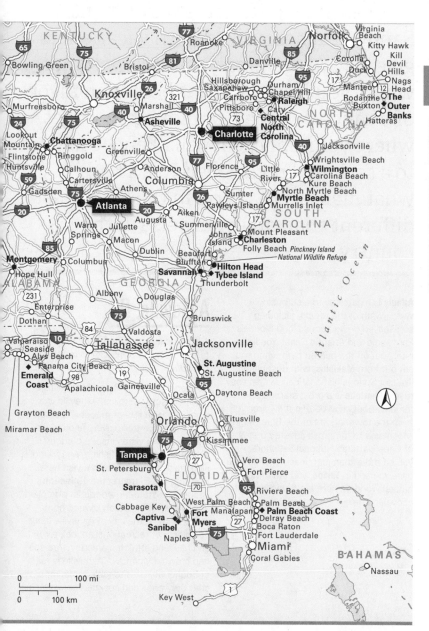

In the Southeast, you can drive a hundred miles in any direction and be in an entirely different environment. Sandy beaches packed with vacationers give way to seemingly endless wetlands where you leave your car behind in favor of a canoe or kayak, or mountain ridges where your only goal will likely be hiking to a secluded rocky overlook. That's what makes a road trip in the Southeast different than anywhere else in the country.

Atlanta is a gateway to a surprisingly wide swath of the region, including sun-soaked destinations along Florida's Panhandle and Atlantic Coast. You'll definitely get off the beaten path when you set out from **Memphis,** with destinations like Hot Springs National Park within easy reach. **Charlotte** is a great starting point for just about anywhere in the Carolinas, from the towering firs of the Blue Ridge Mountains to the grass-covered dunes of Cape Hatteras National Seashore. And you hit more than just beaches when you base yourself in **Tampa,** and the intriguing natural wonders here are found both above and below the water line.

Asheville, NC

198 miles (approx. 3½ hours) from Atlanta, 131 miles (approx. 2½ hours) from Charlotte.

Nestled in the Blue Ridge Mountains of Western North Carolina, Asheville is a small city with lots of mountain personality. Gorgeous trails, rivers and creeks, and sweeping vistas inspire outdoor activities like rafting, fishing, and hiking, all certainly main draws to a visit here. Home to the Biltmore, the 19th-century Vanderbilt estate-turned-tourist attraction and the largest privately owned home in the country, the city of Asheville itself has plenty of recreational appeal, too, and has long attracted an artsy, free-spirited crowd. Downtown Asheville is full of boutiques, farm-to-table restaurants, craft breweries and cocktails bars; you'll

You could easily imagine getting lost in the 250 rooms of Asheville's Biltmore Estate.

find hip cafés, art galleries, and more in outskirting neighborhoods like West Asheville and the River Arts District.

Planning

GETTING THERE AND BACK

Asheville is less than three hours from Charlotte by car, via I–85, U.S. 321, and I-40. The last stretch on I–40 is especially scenic.

Several major airlines offer hour-long direct flights from Atlanta to Asheville's small regional airport; but, given that you'll probably want a car when you're here, driving can be a better option. Once you've escaped Atlanta traffic, it's a pleasant three-plus-hour drive to Asheville, much of it through the Nantahala National Forest and Smoky Mountains.

WHEN TO GO

Spring means the various shrubbery and trees of the Blue Ridge Mountains—and impressive gardens at the Biltmore—are in full bloom, though temperatures can remain brisk through May. By July, it gets quite hot in Asheville; this is the most popular time to hit the river and trails, and rafting companies and other outdoor outfitters are in full swing (some continue through early fall for a shoulder season). Winter can be a snowy wonderland (especially in late January and February), but occasional storms mean that mountain roads (and outdoor activities) are harder to access.

WHERE TO STAY

If you want to be right downtown, the **Foundry Hotel** offers value, location, and character. Part of Hilton's Curio Collection, the hotel makes use of a historical steel foundry and warehouse, is close to many attractions, and home to Benne on Eagle, an excellent Southern- and Caribbean-inspired restaurant that pays homage to Asheville's African American history. Elsewhere in town, you can stay at the **Biltmore Estate** itself (there is both a luxury and somewhat budgeted option), or the **Omni Grove Park Inn** offers a more remote (but very refined) resort stay with great mountain views.

Day 1

Plan to arrive hungry and drive straight to the River Arts District and **12 Bones Smokehouse**: this Asheville institution is only open on weekday afternoons, so it's imperative you get your fix while you can. Known for their ribs and sauces (and for nods from celebs like Barack Obama), you can't really go wrong with anything on the menu here—and it's best to try a few things.

The River Arts District, a neighborhood that runs along the French Broad River and is mostly made up of old factories and warehouses, adorned with colorful murals and converted into artists studios, galleries, restaurants, and cafés. You can float along these placid sections of the river in a tube or canoe, and enjoy riverside refreshments at great bars like **The Wedge Brewing Co.** Head here if you're ready for a beer and some parking lot lawn games after lunch. Otherwise, walk along the river and Lyman and Foundy streets, and explore the various art studios and galleries. Asheville has long been known as a haven for artists; glass blowing and ceramic work are especially popular mediums.

Head to the **Biltmore Estate** for a few hours exploring. Tickets may seem a bit steep (around $60 for an adult), but between the vast 8,000 acre grounds and 250-room house there is plenty to explore, and a wine tasting at the **Biltmore Estate Winery** is included in the price. Extra activities are up to you, and the choices are pretty endless: spa treatments, falconry, bike and kayak rentals, and shopping are among the options.

Since lunch was meaty, opt for the lighter, more sophisticated side of Asheville cuisine for dinner tonight. At **Rhubarb,**

in downtown Asheville, you'll snack on house pickles and smoked fish before indulging in a seasonal menu based on local ingredients. Though you'll be up early tomorrow for an action-packed day, it's worth getting one nightcap at the swanky **Times Bar.** If you absolutely can't go to bed yet, catch a DJ set at the happening **Imperial Life.**

Day 2

About 30 minutes northwest of Asheville, the French Broad River winds through the mountains and becomes whitewater, with sections of class II and III rapids. Book a half day rafting trip at **Blue Heron Whitewater** for a few perfect, adventure-filled hours and a great front seat to see the Blue Ridge's beauty. Plan to leave around 8:15 to get there at 9; you can grab a quick bagel sandwich at **Button Bagel Co.** on your way out of town.

A half day on the river includes a simple lunch—sandwiches or burgers—but having a riverside picnic (set up by the staff) is special. On your way home, stop in Marshall, North Carolina, a little town along the river that's known for its folksy small town charm. There are art galleries, gift shops, and a small brewery here; across from the courthouse on Main Street, **Zuma Coffee** serves cookies and milk shakes that make a great afternoon treat.

After you've made it home for a shower and rest, it's about time for an ice cold craft beer. Early to the microbrew craze, there are something like 60 breweries in the region, and almost 30 in Asheville alone. Tasting rooms at craft operations like **Burial Beer Co., Catawba Brewing Co., Thirsty Monk Pub & Brewery,** and **Asheville Brewing Company** are all in a small downtown Asheville radius, so you can go around on foot and easily taste from a few. These Asheville institutions generally do a good job of catering to nonbeer enthusiasts with nonalcoholic ciders and kombucha. If a member of your party loses interests, just point them towards Patton Avenue for Asheville's best boutiques (**From Afar** has gorgeous textiles from India and Mexico) or let them wander into the bar at **Cúrate** for on-tap vermouth and a charcuterie plate with freshly shaved jamon iberico.

For dinner, it's back to the river. Dine outside at **Smoky Park Supper Club,** a hip young spot created out of shipping containers in the River Arts District. Affordable dishes utilize a wood-burning oven and smoker, and highlight favorite ingredients like local trout and ramps. After dinner, it's a good night to check out Asheville's live music scene either at **The Orange Peel** or **The Grey Eagle** before calling it a day.

Day 3

If you're feeling spry, wake early to get in a short hike before breakfast. The **Warren Wilson River Trail** is an easy 10- to 15-minute drive from downtown, and is a perfect opportunity for some fresh air and exercise when you don't have time for an all-day trek. The mostly flat, 5-mile trail runs along the river near the Warren Wilson College campus. Take a swimsuit with you in warmer months; there are places to dip in along the way.

Whether you've opted to hike or to sleep, plan for brunch around 11 am. This is a meal Asheville does especially well. For a more local experience, head to **Sunny Point Cafe** on Haywood Road, the main stretch in West Asheville's business district and home to an eclectic mix of community-owned small businesses—as well as some higher-end boutiques and restaurants, harbingers of this neighborhood's ongoing gentrification. Egg dishes at Sunny Point are excellent, served with plenty of West Asheville personality and fresh vegetables from their garden. After brunch, browse **Firestorm Books & Coffee** on the opposite corner. This small bookstore and community aide center has a great selection—everything from bestselling fiction to anarchist manifestos—and is an important neighborhood resource.

After brunch, pack up for the drive home with plans to make a few detours on your way south, out of the city. First stop is the **WNC Farmers Market,** a year-round covered market specializing in regional treats like chow chow, barbeque sauce, jams, and jellies.

Next, take 26 E toward Brevard to drive the southern section of the Blue Ridge Parkway, and stop for a hike at Looking Glass Rock. This is a 5½-mile round-trip trek with sweeping views of the Blue Ridge. About a mile from the Looking Glass Overlook, you'll find Skinny Dip Falls, a series of waterfalls and popular swimming area. Heading south out of Brevard, it's about an hour of scenic driving through mountains, national forest, and stops for scenic overlooks and waterfalls—before meeting back up with I–85 and heading home.

Recommendations

Sights

Biltmore Estate. ✉ *1 Lodge St., Asheville, NC* ☎ *800/411–3812* 🌐 *www.biltmore.com* 🎫 *$50.*

Biltmore Estate Winery. ✉ *1 Lodge St., Asheville, NC* ☎ *800/211–9803* 🌐 *www.biltmore.com/tour/behind-the-scenes-winery-tour-tasting* 🎫 *Tours from $10.*

Warren Wilson River Trail. ✉ *749 Warren Wilson Rd., Asheville, NC* ☎ *828/785–1503* 🎫 *Free.*

Restaurants

Rhubarb. [$] *Average main: $25* ✉ *7 S.W. Pack Sq., Asheville, NC* ☎ *828/785–1503* 🌐 *rhubarbasheville.com* 🕓 *Closed Mon. No lunch.*

Smoky Park Supper Club. $ *Average main: $28* ✉ *350 Riverside Dr., Asheville, NC* ☎ *828/350–0315* ⊕ *www.smokypark.com* ⊙ *Closed Mon.*

Sunny Point Cafe. $ *Average main: $20* ✉ *626 Haywood Rd., Asheville, NC* ☎ *828/630–0330* ⊕ *sunnypointcafe.com.*

12 Bones Smokehouse. $ *Average main: $14* ✉ *5 Foundy St., Asheville, NC* ☎ *828/630–0330* ⊕ *www.12bones.com.*

Coffee and Quick Bites

Button & Co. Bagels. $ *Average main: $5* ✉ *32 S. Lexington Ave., Asheville, NC* ☎ *828/630–0330* ⊕ *katiebuttonrestaurants.com* ⊙ *Closed Mon. No dinner.*

Zuma Coffee. $ *Average main: $12* ✉ *7 N. Main St., Marshall, NC* ☎ *828/649–1617* ⊕ *www.zumascoffee.com* ⊙ *Closed Sun. No dinner.*

🛏 Hotels

Biltmore Estate. $ *Rooms from: $389* ✉ *1 Lodge St., Asheville, NC* ☎ *800/411–3812* ⊕ *www.biltmore.com* ⫠ *No meals.*

Foundry Hotel. $ *Rooms from: $250* ✉ *51 S. Market St., Asheville, NC* ☎ *828/255–4077* ⊕ *foundryasheville.com* ⫠ *No meals.*

Omni Grove Park Inn. $ *Rooms from: $389* ✉ *290 Macon Ave., Asheville, NC* ☎ *828/255–4077* ⊕ *www.omnihotels.com* ⫠ *No meals.*

🍸 Nightlife

Asheville Brewing Company. ✉ *77 Coxe Ave., Asheville, NC* ☎ *828/255–4077* ⊕ *www.ashevillebrewing.com.*

Burial Beer Co. ✉ *40 Collier Ave., Asheville, NC* ☎ *828/552–3934* ⊕ *burialbeer.com.*

Catawba Brewing Co. ✉ *32 Banks Ave., Asheville, NC* ⊕ *catawbabrewing.com.*

Cúrate. ✉ *13 Biltmore Ave., Asheville, NC* ☎ *828/239–2946* ⊕ *katiebuttonrestaurants.com/curate.*

The Grey Eagle. ✉ *185 Clingman Ave., Asheville, NC* ☎ *828/232–5800* ⊕ *www.thegreyeagle.com.*

Imperial Life. ✉ *48 College St., Asheville, NC* ☎ *828/254–8980* ⊕ *imperialbarasheville.com.*

The Orange Peel. ✉ *101 Biltmore Ave., Asheville, NC* ☎ *828/398–1837* ⊕ *theorangepeel.net.*

Thirsty Monk Brewery. ✉ *2 Town Square Blvd., Asheville, NC* ☎ *828/687–3873* ⊕ *thirsty-monk-brewery.square.site.*

Times Bar. ✉ *56 Patton Ave., Asheville, NC* ☎ *828/774–5028* ⊕ *www.thetimesbarasheville.com.*

The Wedge Brewing Co. ✉ *37 Paynes Way, Asheville, NC* ☎ *828/505–2792* ⊕ *www.wedgebrewing.com.*

🛍 Shopping

Firestorm Books & Coffee. ✉ *610 Haywood Rd., Asheville, NC* ☎ *828/255–8115* ⊕ *www.firestorm.coop.*

From Afar. ✉ *36 Battery Park Ave., Asheville, NC* ☎ *828/251–7992* ⊕ *from-afar.business.site.*

WNC Farmers Market. ✉ *570 Brevard Rd., Asheville, NC* ☎ *828/253–1691* ⊕ *www.ncagr.gov/markets/facilities/markets/asheville.*

🏃 Activities

Blue Heron Whitewater. ✉ *35 Little Pine Rd., Marshall, NC* ☎ *828/255–8115* ⊕ *www.blueheronwhitewater.com* ✉ *Rafting from $50 per person.*

Charleston, SC

305 miles (approx. 5 hours) from Atlanta, 208 miles (approx. 3½ hours) from Charlotte.

In Charleston, history is as deep and rich as a serving of homemade perlou. And just like the famous Lowcountry rice dish, the city's flavors get more interesting with every bite. Charleston has long drawn travelers to its balmy terrain along the mid-Atlantic coast. In fact, it drew some of the very first cross-Atlantic travelers—English colonists, who established "Charles Town" back in 1670. The roots of their influences remain, as do traditions of African Americans, whose Gullah culture is distinct in the region, and infused into local food, farming, crafts, and music.

These days, Charleston is a favorite for weekend getaways, often prompted by hankerings for coastal seafood, barbeque, biscuits, and other South Carolina staples. Between meals, though, await discoveries of Charleston's enduring, complex history; its contemporary arts; its parks and beaches; and its timeworn architecture and secret alleyways.

Planning

GETTING THERE AND BACK

It's just short of a five-hour drive from Atlanta into downtown Charleston, half of it along I–20 and half on I–26. Route 52, Route 78, and Route 17 (also known as the Savannah Highway) are smaller highways that all lead into town, too.

Charlotte is even closer to Charleston, and it's a straight shot via I–77 and I–26. The drive usually takes no more than 3½ hours.

PIT STOPS

If you're hungry on your way into Charleston from Atlanta, consider an introductory pit stop along the Savannah

Highway at the **Early Bird Diner.** Friendly and affordable, the diner serves breakfast all day, including some of the best local fried chicken and waffles.

WHEN TO GO

Let's face it, South Carolina runs hot and humid almost all year. Nevertheless, summer is fun for annual festivals like June's Blessing of the Fleet and Seafood Festival and September's Party in the Park, Flowertown Festival, and Restaurant Week. Late May through mid-June is the big Spoleto Festival of art, music, and theater. Bivalve lovers should mark calendars for January's Lowcountry Oyster Festival and August's Seafood Beer and Wine Festival.

WHERE TO STAY

There are a good number of lovely lodgings in downtown Charleston. The **Belmond Charleston Place** is a grand choice with a spa and rooftop pool, while **The Restoration** is a similar but hipper option. There are a handful of boutique accommodations inside actual historic buildings, like the **Andrew Pinckney Inn** and the **Fulton Lane Inn.**

Day 1

Heading into downtown Charleston may feel less like you're entering South Carolina's largest city and more like a secret metropolis. The city occupies several islands across the "Lowcountry," the marshy territory along the Atlantic coast. But visitors usually think of the downtown peninsula as Charleston, since it's where the city began and is home to most of the action. Head there for central accommodations, and leave your car parked while you explore by foot or via the free DASH trolley that traverses downtown.

Get a great city introduction with **Bulldog Tours** 's history, food, or ghost tour. You'll learn about some of Charleston's layers, its Revolutionary War history, and get the

Rainbow Row is a favorite photo op in the colorful city of Charleston.

lay of the land, including eyes on East Bay Street's famous **Rainbow Row**, 13 pastel row houses built between 1748 and 1845.

For tours focused on the African-American experience, check out **Gullah Geechee Tours, Sights and Insights Tours,** or browse the helpful Explore Charleston's roundup of best black-history tours. The city also hosts a cool virtual museum called "Voices: Stories of Change," exploring African-American culture and diaspora in Charleston since pre-Colonial times.

Once the sun begins to set, it's cocktail hour. If the weather is right, visit the **Rooftop Bar at The Vendue** waterfront hotel for a local craft beer, or specialty cocktail or mocktail while you look over Charleston Harbor, Waterfront Park, and modern Ravenel Bridge across the Cooper River.

Or head to **Prohibition** on busy King Street for a refined libation in a romantic atmosphere—if timing is right, arrive during weekday happy hours for drinks,

snacks, and inexpensive oysters on the half shell. You can enjoy dinner there, too, or consider a stroll to **Magnolias** for classic Carolina fare, or **The Grocery** for Southern dishes with Asian and Italian twists.

Day 2

Some cities enjoy brunch, but in Charleston, brunch is a way of life. Many restaurants open early on weekends to serve up faves like crab-cake eggs Benedict and sweet-potato pancakes. Spots like the posh **Charleston Grill** and **High Cotton** each put on a "gospel brunch" with live music. More casual brunching awaits at **Poogan's Porch,** a Queen Street institution inside a restored Victorian house. Reserve in advance for a shady courtyard table, and be ready to sample she-crab soup, pimiento cheese fritters, and fried green tomatoes.

Speaking of choices, are you in the mood for art or activity today? Let's do both! Around the corner from Poogan's Porch is the **Gibbes Museum of Art,** downtown Charleston's only visual-arts museum dating to 1905. Its first-floor galleries are free, but it's worth the $12 to head to floors two and three, where you'll find paintings, sculptures, decorative arts, drawings, and miniature portraits by American artists. Stroll Meeting Street and its cross streets down to Broad to explore private galleries and maybe pick up a treasure to bring home.

Once you're ready to burn off some biscuits, consider checking out wheels from **Holy Spokes,** the Charleston bike-share system, to explore the ever-expanding bike-route network in the "Holy City." Tool around town and—if the season's right—breathe in blooming magnolia, wisteria, and jasmine. Don't miss a spin (or walkabout) in **White Point Garden** at the peninsula's southern tip, where you'll find The Battery, wartime monuments, marvelous mansions, and a waterfront promenade.

On hot days, the **Charleston Water Taxi** is a fun way to cool off. Board at Waterfront Park or the Charleston Maritime Center for a one-hour harbor sightseeing cruise, or apply your $12 all-day pass to travel across the Cooper River to visit the **Patriots Point Naval and Maritime Museum,** home to the U.S.S. *Yorktown* and other decommissioned vessels and airplanes.

Once suppertime rolls around, head to **Melvin's Legendary BBQ**—across the river in Mt. Pleasant, open since 1939—for ribs, brisket, chicken, and "Charleston's original" chopped BBQ pork.

Top off your evening with a fine pour from **Graft Wine Shop** on King Street, a hot spot for chill conversation, music, and general oenophilia. For a local's go-to bar with plenty of beer and a back patio, duck into **Local 616** for craft ales, classic cocktails and a half-dozen different "mules," including a Buenos Aires Mule made with Fernet Branca and bitters.

Day 3

By Day 3, you may still be feeling full from the past two days. But make room in your belly—because no trip here is complete without a pickup from the counter of **Callie's Hot Little Biscuit,** with locations on Upper King Street, and inside **Historic Charleston City Market.** Try the sausage, egg, and pimiento cheese; or build your own; or try a gluten-free biscuit.

The history in Charleston seems to be everywhere, but nowhere is it better encapsulated than at the **Charleston Museum.** It's America's first museum, founded in 1773, with exhibits and artifacts on display from the Revolutionary War, as well as galleries of natural history and African-American stories. You can also check out historic houses that are part of the museum, and on the way, stroll some of downtown's hidden alleyways.

For your final few hours in town, adventure farther afield with a drive to sandy Folly Beach. Nature fans won't want to miss seeing the magnificent **Angel Oak** on nearby St. John's Island. It's a massive oak tree estimated to be 400 to 500 years old, producing shade that covers 17,200 square feet. There are plantations all around the region, and **Magnolia Plantation and Gardens** is a good one for visitors interested in learning about how slavery contributed to Charleston's development, agriculture, and culture.

If there's time, as you head home, take the Savannah Highway and grab one last meal at **Swig & Swine,** a roadside barbeque joint that's mastered the Lowcountry art of smoked meats. And don't worry if you're in a hurry—they pack to-go, too.

4

Southeast CHARLESTON, SC

Recommendations

Sights

Angel Oak. ✉ *3688 Angel Oak Rd., Johns Island, SC* ☎ *843/559–3496* 🌐 *angeloaktree.com* 🎟 *Free.*

Charleston Museum. ✉ *360 Meeting St., Charleston, SC* ☎ *843/722–2996* 🌐 *www.charlestonmuseum.org* 🎟 *$12.*

Folly Beach. ✉ *E. Ashley Ave., Folly Beach, SC* ☎ *No phone* 🌐 *www.follybeach.com* 🎟 *Free.*

Gibbes Museum of Art. ✉ *135 Meeting St., Charleston, SC* ☎ *843/722–2706* 🌐 *www.gibbesmuseum.org* 🎟 *$10.*

Historic Charleston Market. ✉ *188 Meeting St., Charleston, SC* ☎ *843/937–0920* 🌐 *www.thecharlestoncitymarket.com* 🎟 *Free.*

Magnolia Plantation and Gardens. ✉ *3550 Ashley River Rd., Charleston, SC* ☎ *843/571–1266* 🌐 *www.magnoliaplantation.com* 🎟 *$20.*

Patriots Point Naval and Maritime Museum. ✉ *40 Patriots Point Rd., Mt. Pleasant, SC* ☎ *843/884–2727* 🌐 *www.patriotspoint.org* 🎟 *$24.*

Rainbow Row. ✉ *83 E. Bay St., Charleston, SC* ☎ *803/528–8317* 🌐 *rainbowrowcharlestonsc.com* 🎟 *Free.*

White Point Garden. ✉ *2 Murray Blvd., Charleston, SC* ☎ *No phone* 🌐 *www.charlestonparksconservancy.org/park/white-point-garden* 🎟 *Free.*

Restaurants

Callie's Hot Little Biscuit. [$] *Average main: $6* ✉ *476½ King St., Charleston, SC* ☎ *843/737–5159* 🌐 *calliesbiscuits.com/pages/hlb-upper-king* 🕒 *Closed Tues.*

Charleston Grill. [$] *Average main: $18* ✉ *224 King St., Charleston, SC* ☎ *843/577–4522* 🌐 *www.charlestongrill.com* 🕒 *Closed Tues.*

Early Bird Diner. [$] *Average main: $14* ✉ *1644 Savannah Hwy., Charleston, SC* ☎ *843/277–2353* 🌐 *earlybirddiner.com.*

The Grocery. [$] *Average main: $7* ✉ *4 Cannon St., Charleston, SC* ☎ *843/302–8825* 🌐 *www.thegrocerycharleston.com* 🕒 *Closed Mon.*

High Cotton. [$] *Average main: $10* ✉ *199 E. Bay St., Charleston, SC* ☎ *843/724–3815* 🌐 *www.highcottoncharleston.com.*

Magnolia's. [$] *Average main: $12* ✉ *185 E. Bay St., Charleston, SC* ☎ *843/321–9333* 🌐 *www.magnoliascharleston.com.*

Melvin's Legendary BBQ. [$] *Average main: $14* ✉ *925 Houston Northcutt Blvd., Mt Pleasant, SC* ☎ *843/881–0549* 🌐 *www.melvinsbbq.com* 🕒 *Closed Sun.*

Poogan's Porch. [$] *Average main: $11* ✉ *72 Queen St., Charleston, SC* ☎ *843/577–2337* 🌐 *www.pooganssporch.com.*

Swig & Swine. [$] *Average main: $25* ✉ *1990 Old Trolley Rd., Summerville, SC* ☎ *843/974–8688* 🌐 *swigandswinebbq.com.*

Hotels

Andrew Pinckney Inn. [$] *Rooms from: $349* ✉ *40 Pinckney St., Charleston, SC* ☎ *843/937–8800* 🌐 *www.andrewpinckneyinn.com* 🍴 *Free breakfast.*

Belmond Charleston Place. [$] *Rooms from: $452* ✉ *205 Meeting St., Charleston, SC* ☎ *843/722–4900* 🌐 *www.belmond.com* 🍴 *No meals.*

Fulton Lane Inn. [$] *Rooms from: $269* ✉ *202 King St., Charleston, SC* ☎ *843/720–2600* 🌐 *www.fultonlaneinn.com* 🍴 *Free breakfast.*

The Restoration. [$] *Rooms from: $428* ✉ *75 Wentworth St., Charleston, SC* ☎ *843/518–5100* 🌐 *www.*

therestorationhotel.com ‍⏲ Free breakfast.

Nightlife

Local 616. ✉ 616 Meeting St., Charleston, SC ☎ 843/414–7850 ⊕ local616.com.

Prohibition. ✉ 547 King St., Charleston, SC ☎ 843/793–2964 ⊕ prohibition-charleston.com.

Rooftop Bar at the Vendue. ✉ The Vendue, 19 Vendue Range, Charleston, SC ☎ 843/577–7970 ⊕ www.thevendue.com/charleston-dining/the-rooftop.

Shopping

Graft Wine Shop. ✉ 700B King St., Charleston, SC ☎ 843/718–3359 ⊕ www.graftchs.com.

Activities

Bulldog Tours. ✉ 18 Anson St., Charleston, SC ☎ 843/722–8687 ⊕ www.bulldog-tours.com ☞ Tours from $29.

Charleston Water Taxi. ✉ 103 St. Philip S., Charleston, SC 29403 ☎ 843/727–6800 ⊕ www.charlestonwater.com ☞ Rides from $12.

Gullah Geechee Tours. ✉ 375 Meeting St., Charleston, SC ☎ 843/478–0000 ⊕ www.gullahgeecheetours.com ☞ Tours from $27.

Holy Spokes. ✉ 7 Radcliffe St., Charleston, SC ☎ 843/480–9859 ⊕ www.charleston-bikeshare.com ☞ Rentals from $8.

Sights and Insights Tours. ✉ 1220 Folly Rd., Charleston, SC ☎ 843/552–9995 ⊕ www.sitesandinsightstours.com ☞ Tours from $15.

Chattanooga, TN

337 miles (approx. 5 hours) from Memphis, 118 miles (approx. 2 hours) from Atlanta.

Frequently touted as one of the country's best outdoors towns, Chattanooga, Tennessee has a unique vibe that is totally different from Nashville, its much-praised neighbor to the north. Set in the shadow of Lookout Mountain, it was the site of a major Civil War battle at Chickamauga and was later made famous by the Glenn Miller Orchestra's rollicking "Chattanooga Choo Choo." The city has nearby rock climbing, hiking trails, and kayaking on the Tennessee River. But foodies can also enjoy award-winning restaurants without the waitlists of bigger cities.

Planning

GETTING THERE AND BACK

Most travelers will be using I–75 N via Atlanta. State Roads 27 and 193 are alternatives when traffic backs up at the state line.

If you are coming from Memphis, take I–40 and I–26 via Franklin and Murfeesboro. It's a seemingly indirect but speedy route across the state.

PIT STOPS

Taking I–75 allows for detours like the **Booth Museum of Western Art** in Cartersville, the **New Echota State Historic Site** in Calhoun, and the **Georgia Winery** in Ringgold.

INSPIRATION

Download old-school tunes like "Chattanooga Choo Choo" by Glenn Miller, "Chattanooga City Limit Sign" by Johnny Cash, and "Downhearted Blues" by Chattanooga native Bessie Smith.

WHEN TO GO

The experience of visiting Chattanooga is similar year-round, but spring and summer bring added travelers and the

Coolidge Park is a quick stroll across the Walnut Street Pedestrian Bridge from downtown Chattanooga.

famous humidity. Expect crowds at the Tennessee Aquarium during school breaks. The fall months are comfortable and still allow travelers to get outside. There's always a festival or event going on, but the Riverbend Music Festival, held annually in May, is the city's largest, drawing more than 600,000 people to the riverfront. The nearly 40-year tradition has brought big-name acts as well as local musicians. Don't miss the Chattanooga Market, a seasonal farmers market with live music and artisan goods.

WHERE TO STAY

While Chattanooga is touted as an outdoorsy town, that doesn't mean there aren't luxurious accommodations. The **Dwell Hotel** is a funky, midcentury-inspired boutique hotel near the Warehouse Row shopping and dining complex. Each room is styled differently and has perks like claw-foot bathtubs and balconies. The **Chattanooga Choo Choo** is one of the few places where you can stay in converted train cars. The lobby is where passengers previously boarded trains. There are also rooms in the former rail company's offices.

For budget travelers, **Crash Pad** is a trendy Southside hostel popular with the rock climbing crowd. It has private rooms and daily breakfast. Adventurous types will love **Treetop Hideaways**, just across the Georgia line. There are two stylish treehouses, including one built by Pete Nelson of Treehouse Masters. Both have unrivaled views of the forest.

Day 1

Since Chattanooga is around two hours from several major cities, visitors can easily arrive by lunchtime. You probably won't be able to check in yet, so grab a bite to eat at one of the restaurants in St. Elmo, the neighborhood at the base of Lookout Mountain. **Mojo Burrito** is a funky local spot known for overstuffed burritos, tacos, and Tex-Mex favorites. Order your drinks at the bright blue counter and choose the fillings for your burrito.

Sit inside under the disco ball or on the patio.

Once you're fueled up, hit up the Lookout Mountain area attractions. Start at the **Incline Railway,** which is just across the street from Mojo. It climbs to the top at a heart-stopping incline of 72 degrees. At the top, you can see Point Park, which encompasses Lookout Mountain Civil War Battlefield.

Back on street level, drive a few blocks north to the entrance to **Ruby Falls,** the nation's tallest and deepest underground waterfall open to the public. It was discovered in 1928 and has been welcoming visitors into its caverns ever since.

Just across the Georgia state line is **Rock City,** a technicolor wonderland of kitsch. Wander through the rock formations or "See Seven States" from an overlook. The Fairyland Caverns and Mother Goose Village are inspired by your favorite storybook characters.

Depending on the time, check into your hotel and get ready for dinner. Return to St. Elmo for an evening at the **1885 Grill,** known for its Southern coastal fare. Try the award-winning wings or creamy shrimp and grits.

Day 2

Start your day early to pack in as much sightseeing as possible, beginning in the funky Northshore, just across the Walnut Street Pedestrian Bridge from downtown. Here you can explore Coolidge Park's skyline views or visit the shops lining Frazier Avenue.

Hop back in the car to have breakfast in a more residential part of the city. In a charming old house, **Aretha Frankenstein's** almost always has a wait for its offbeat decor and massive pancakes, served from early morning to late into the night. The plentiful portions make it a tourist favorite, but locals enjoy it as well.

Head back downtown to the **Tennessee Aquarium,** the city's most popular attraction. Set along the Tennessee River, the aquarium is split between two buildings, River Journey and Ocean Journey. Catch a glimpse of massive catfish, jellyfish, and the always-popular otters. It's easy to spend a few hours here, especially if you take advantage of the IMAX Theater.

For lunch, walk across the street to **The Blue Plate,** a modern diner on the river. Enjoy the views while you chow down on the double-stack burger on a local Niedlov's bun or the buttermilk fried chicken. From here, climb the hill to the Bluff River Arts District, set on the namesake bluffs overlooking the river and the Northshore. The **Hunter Museum of American Art** is in several buildings, including a historic mansion. The collection spans every period of American art from colonial to the present.

Head back to your hotel to freshen up before dinner at **Easy Bistro,** run by James Beard nominee Chef Erik Niel. The menu features creative cocktails like the Scenic City (their local take on the Old Fashioned) alongside house-made pasta dishes and savory moules frites.

Day 3

On your final morning, head to the Southside neighborhood, easily accessible via the free electric downtown shuttles or the bike-share program. Head to breakfast at **Niedlov's,** a bakery that supplies most restaurants with their bread and pastries. Grab a flaky sausage biscuit and a cup of Velo Coffee, a roaster located down the street.

The famous **Chattanooga Choo Choo** has been revitalized in past years, transforming the former train station and rail cars to an entertainment complex that includes a live music venue called the **Songbirds Guitar Museum.** Across the street, those looking to imbibe can tour the **Chattanooga Whiskey Distillery,** the first distillery in town since Prohibition—make a reservation, as space is limited. If you can't get a spot, you can always buy a bottle as a souvenir.

The Southside also has a number of craft breweries, including **Hutton & Smith** and **OddStory,** both in the Martin Luther King Jr. District. Visit the **Bessie Smith Cultural Center and African American Museum,** also in this corridor, which honors the singer and Chattanooga native.

Before leaving town, enjoy one last meal at **Kenny's Southside Sandwiches,** which has tasty sandwiches for breakfast and lunch. Try the decadent Croque Madam, or keep it simple with avocado toast. On the way to the highway, make a quick detour to the **Sculpture Fields at Montague Park,** a 33-acre park and outdoor art gallery. The colorful large scale installations on the site of a former dump are free to visit.

Recommendations

Sights

Bessie Smith Cultural Center and African American Museum. ✉ *200 E. Martin Luther King Blvd., Chattanooga, TN* ☎ *423/266–8658* 🌐 *www.bessiesmithcc.org* 🎟 *$7* 🕒 *Closed Sun.*

Booth Museum of Western Art. ✉ *501 N. Museum Dr., Cartersville, GA* ☎ *770/387–1300* 🌐 *www.boothmuseum.org* 🎟 *$12* 🕒 *Closed Mon.*

Chattanooga Whiskey Distillery. ✉ *1439 Market St., Chattanooga, TN* ☎ *423/760–4333* 🌐 *www.chattanoogawhiskey.com* 🎟 *Tours $12.*

Georgia Winery. ✉ *6469 Battlefield Pkwy., Ringgold, GA* ☎ *706/937–9463* 🌐 *www.georgiawines.com* 🎟 *Tastings $3.*

Hunter Museum of Art. ✉ *10 Bluff View Ave., Chattanooga, TN* ☎ *423/267–0968* 🌐 *www.huntermuseum.org* 🎟 *$20.*

Incline Railway. ✉ *3917 St. Elmo Ave., Chattanooga, TN* ☎ *423/821–4224* 🌐 *www.ridetheincline.com* 🎟 *$15 round-trip.*

New Echota State Historical Park. ✉ *1211 GA 225, Calhoun, GA* ☎ *706/624–1321* 🌐 *www.gastateparks.org* 🎟 *$7.*

Rock City. ✉ *1400 Patten Rd., Lookout Mountain, GA* ☎ *706/820–2531* 🌐 *www.seerockcity.com* 🎟 *$22.*

Ruby Falls. ✉ *Scenic Hwy.* ☎ *423/821–2544* 🌐 *www.rubyfalls.com* 🎟 *$23.*

Sculpture Fields at Montague Park. ✉ *1800 Polk St., Chattanooga, TN* ☎ *423/266–7288* 🎟 *Free.*

Tennessee Aquarium. ✉ *1 Broad St., Chattanooga, TN* ☎ *423/265–0695* 🌐 *www.tnaqua.org* 🎟 *$35.*

Restaurants

The Blue Plate. [$] *Average main: $15.* ✉ *191 Chestnut St., Chattanooga, TN* ☎ *423/648–6767* 🌐 *www.theblueplate.info* 🕒 *Closed Mon.*

1885 Grill. [$] *Average main: $9* ✉ *3914 St. Elmo Ave., Chattanooga, TN* ☎ *423/485–3050* 🌐 *www.1885grill.com.*

Kenny's Southside Sandwiches. [$] *Average main: $12* ✉ *1251 Market St., Chattanooga, TN* ☎ *423/498–5888* 🌐 *www.kennys-sandwiches.com* 🕒 *Closed Mon.*

Mojo Burrito. [$] *Average main: $8* ✉ *1800 Dayton Blvd., Chattanooga, TN* ☎ *423/870–6656* 🌐 *www.mojoburrito.com.*

Niedlov's. [$] *Average main: $7* ✉ *215 E. Main St., Chattanooga, TN* ☎ *423/756–0303* 🌐 *www.mojoburrito.com* 🕒 *Closed Sun.*

🛏 Hotels

Chattanooga Choo Choo Hotel. $ *Rooms from: $159* ✉ *1400 Market St., Chattanooga, TN* ☎ *423/266–5000* ⊕ *www.choochoo.com* ⦿ *No meals.*

Crash Pad. $ *Rooms from: $250* ✉ *29 Johnson St., Chattanooga, TN* ☎ *423/648–8393* ⊕ *www.crashpadchattanooga.com* ⦿ *Free breakfast.*

Dwell Hotel. $ *Rooms from: $225* ✉ *120 E. 10th St., Chattanooga, TN* ☎ *423/267–7866* ⊕ *www.thedwellhotel.com* ⦿ *No meals.*

Treetop Hideaways. $ *Rooms from: $250* ✉ *576 Chattanooga Valley Rd., Flintstone, GA* ☎ *423/377–6476* ⊕ *www.treetophideaways.com* ⦿ *No meals.*

🍸 Nightlife

Hutton & Smith. ✉ *431 E. Martin Luther King Blvd., Chattanooga, TN* ☎ *423/760–3600* ⊕ *www.huttonandsmithbrewing.com.*

Oddstory. ✉ *336 E. Martin Luther King Blvd., Chattanooga, TN* ☎ *423/682–7690* ⊕ *www.oddstorybrewing.co* ⊗ *Closed Sun. and Mon.*

Songbirds Guitar Museum. ✉ *35 Station St., Chattanooga, TN* ☎ *423/531–2473* ⊕ *www.songbirds.rocks.*

Emerald Coast, FL

Destin is 331 miles (approx. 5 hours) from Atlanta.

Weekends are better at the beach. That's especially true if the beach is Florida's Emerald Coast, where the water is jewel-hue and the sand is as white and fine as powder. From Atlanta, all it takes is a five-hour drive to sun-kissed bliss. And since you drove all this way, you can nix a lazy, sit-on-the-beach and never-leave-the-chair kind of trip. No, you're going to do

and see it all. Think of it as a sampler of the Gulf's subcultures—the posh, manicured set of South Walton, the honky tonk, family-friendly vibes of Panama City Beach, and everything in between. This, my friends, is how to pack your weekends at Florida's prettiest beaches like you've never done before.

Planning

GETTING THERE AND BACK
Take the five-hour drive from Atlanta, Georgia to Destin, Florida on I–85 S. Note that Destin is Central Time Zone so you will gain an hour heading here and lose an hour leaving. When leaving from Panama City Beach, you can take I–85 N, or via U.S. 231 N and U.S. 431 N (the latter is usually the fastest route, via Columbus, Georgia.

INSPIRATION
For your drive, pick up an audio book or two: *Florida* by Lauren Groff or *The Yearling* by Marjorie Kinnan Rawlings.

PIT STOPS
Montgomery, Alabama is a good halfway point on your drive from Atlanta to Destin; see the **National Memorial for Peace and Justice** and the **Legacy Museum**. On the way home, stop in Columbus, Georgia for some **Country's Barbecue** if you decide to take U.S. 431 N.

WHEN TO GO
You can visit year-round, but May and October have mild temperatures and fewer crowds. Unlike South Florida, summer is high season here, with temperatures reaching the 90s. Winter is quiet but chilly, with the temperature hovering around 40°F–60°F. Note that hurricane season runs from June to November; September is usually the most active month. Otherwise, it's a sunny paradise. And as always in Florida, if you don't like the weather, wait five minutes.

Palm-lined Front Beach Road runs the length of Panama City Beach.

WHERE TO STAY

Base yourself in Destin at **Emerald Grande at HarborWalk Village** (aside from its pool and spa, the harborfront hotel is right next to a shopping, restaurant, and entertainment center for built-in fun), or choose the **Henderson Beach Resort & Spa** for a more luxurious stay. You can also choose to move to a South Walton hotel on Saturday night, such as the quaint, European-style **Rosemary Beach Inn.** Alternatively, in nearby WaterColor, the **WaterColor Inn,** has sweeping views of the beach (even from your shower).

Day 1

To maximize your day and arrive at the beach by early afternoon, get on the road by 8 am. You should reach your first Emerald Coast beach town, Destin, or the "world's luckiest fishing village" by lunch. Spend it at **Marina Café,** with its sunny harbor views, and tuck into a Gulf specialty: pan-seared grouper, or at **Another Broken Egg Café,** a casual brunch

and lunch spot with great biscuit beignets and omelets

After checking into the hotel that will be your base for this trip, such as **Henderson Beach Resort & Spa** or **Emerald Grande at HarborWalk Village,** your first order of business is to relax on the fine Florida sand you came for at **Henderson Beach State Park.** Admire the 30-foot tall sand dunes. Walk or bike off lunch. Soak up the rays, dip in the warm Gulf waters, and do absolutely nothing. You deserve it.

Getting active is also an option—arrange a stand up paddleboard yoga class at the location of your choice with **Emerald Coast Paddleboard,** or book a one-hour rental and lessons from **GUSU Paddleboards.** You can also do as the locals do and arrange a boat excursion to **Crab Island,** a sandbar where you can drop anchor and mingle with a beer in hand.

When you work up an appetite again, head to family-run, local favorite **Harbor Docks** for sunset views and seafood with a Southern slant. It's this region's specialty (think: Gulf shrimp and grits, fried green tomatoes, seafood gumbo). The **Back Porch** has similar fare.

And since this is northwest Florida, the party doesn't stop after dinner. Take a 15-minute walk down the beach to **AJ's Seafood & Oyster Bar** to drink beer and sway to live Southern rock and country music. You'll be singing "Sweet Home Alabama" to sleep, in the best way. You can keep the night going by bar hopping to the handful of hot spots in this area, including **1835 Porch Bar,** just a two-minute walk away. Sipping one of their craft cocktails on the breezy patio is the perfect way to end a night.

Day 2

On Saturday, explore a whole different side of the Panhandle: South Walton (or 30-A, as it's known locally). Its 16 beach towns strung along Scenic Highway 30-A have unique personalities, community-centric, walkable layouts, and are known to be the most upscale beach towns in the area.

Wake up early and pick up North Florida's classic on the go breakfast—doughnuts and coffee—from **Donut Hole Bakery Café** on your way from Destin to Seaside. (**Maple Street Biscuit Co.** on the way out of town in Miramar is also a good choice for those who aren't afraid of oversize biscuits stacked with gravy and fixings). The drive is only about 40 minutes, but you'll see how drastically the area changes. Tall beach condos and commercialized shopping complexes turn into perfectly manicured lawns, pastel beach homes, and perfectly planned communities with families biking to and fro. No wonder it was the setting for the film *The Truman Show.*

Explore Seaside's quaint shops, pick up an ice cream, and then meander by foot or bike to neighboring South Walton community, WaterColor, to see something

you can only see a handful of places in the world: coastal dune lakes. Head to **The Boat House,** where you can rent paddleboards or kayaks to explore Western Lake. You'll float among lily pads, tall pine trees, and those tall sand dunes.

Escape from the sun and grab lunch at **Fish Out of Water,** where you can eat Gulf oysters, pimento cheese dip, and stare out to the crashing waves from your seats on the patio. Or, grab a bite to-go at **The Shrimp Shack.**

After you're done with lunch, head to **Grayton Beach State Park,** where you can spend an hour hiking through beautiful sea oat-covered sand dunes that line salt marshes. Afterward, lie on the beach, or go for a dive at the 60-foot-deep **Underwater Museum of Art,** a collection of submerged sculptures off the coast of the park. If you're not a diver, you can snorkel at **Turtle Reef,** a man-made reef that's crafted into the shape of a sea turtle and attracts plenty of sea life.

You should be done by 4 pm or so, enough time to head back to the hotel for a shower and a change. (If you left the hotel in Destin for good, now is the time to check into your South Walton hotel—**WaterColor Inn** is a good, central choice with ocean views.) Choose your "in case of nice dinner" outfit and drive 10 minutes (and a world away) to Alys Beach—the poshest neighborhood in these parts. Its striking, stark-white geometric buildings are worth a wander for a photo shoot at golden hour.

When you're done snapping photos, head to sophisticated cocktail bar **Neat** for predinner drinks and charcuterie on the patio or in the tasting room. Dinner is right across the street at the place to see and be seen in town, **George's at Alys Beach,** where you can treat yourself to steak or red snapper alfresco. Another good choice in Alys is the chic poolside scene at **Caliza.**

Linger at George's or Caliza's bar for a few drinks, or snap out of the socialite life and head back into Seaside for some casual live music and local 30-A beer on the laid-back rooftop of **Bud and Alley's.**

Day 3

Wake up early on Sunday and drive to Grayton Beach to pick up iced coffee and a pastry at **Black Bear Bread Co.** before driving an hour over to Panama City Beach, your final stop before heading home. If you prefer to sit down for breakfast, go to **Great Southern Café** and order hearty grits before hitting the road.

When you get to Panama City Beach, choose your own adventure: do you want to relax on one last beach? Head to **St. Andrews State Park** for the calmest, most pristine beaches in PCB; the $8 entry fee keeps it so. Or do you want to take in more North Florida nature? Bike on one of the 12 trails in **Conservation Park.**

There's a different crowd in PCB, surely, but this isn't crazy Spring Break–central of which you've heard legends; in fact, it's got more family-friendly activities than ever, including multiple water parks. Of course, you can find the party scene too at beach bars along the water, if that's what you're looking for. Whatever you choose, you'll notice a laid-back, Southern kind of town with the same beautiful stretch of emerald water and white sand beach as the rest of the coast.

Grab one last lunch at **Capt. Anderson's,** a waterside classic where you can order stuffed grouper while watching the boats dock and unload their catch of the day. **Schooners** is another popular joint for a Southern coastal lunch, and it's right on the beach. Stay and listen to live music until the sun sets, if you like—it's the perfect way to say goodbye to the Emerald Coast.

Recommendations

Sights

Conservation Park. ✉ *100 Conservation Dr., Panama City Beach, FL* ☎ *850/233–5045* 🌐 *www.panamacitybeachparksandrecreation.com/conservation-park.html* 🎟 *Free.*

Crab Island. ✉ *Henderson Park Beach State Park. 17000 Emerald Coast Pkwy., Destin, FL* 🎟 *Free.*

Grayton Beach State Park. ✉ *357 Main Park Rd., off Rte. 30A, Grayton Beach, FL* ☎ *850/26–8300* 🌐 *www.floridastateparks.org/graytonbeach* 🎟 *$5 per vehicle.*

Henderson Park Beach State Park. ✉ *17000 Emerald Coast Pkwy., Destin, FL* ☎ *850/837–7550* 🌐 *www.floridastateparks.org/parks-and-trails/henderson-beach-state-park* 🎟 *$6 per vehicle.*

St. Andrews State Park. ✉ *4607 State Park La., Panama City Beach, FL* ☎ *850/708–6100* 🌐 *www.floridastateparks.org/parks-and-trails/st-andrews-state-park* 🎟 *$8 per vehicle.*

Underwater Museum of Art. ✉ *Grayton Beach State Park, 357 Main Park Rd., off Rte. 30A, Grayton Beach, FL* ☎ *850/622–5970* 🌐 *umafl.org* 🎟 *$6 per vehicle for park entrance.*

Restaurants

Another Broken Egg Café. [$] *Average main: $9* ✉ *979 Harbor Blvd., Destin, FL* ☎ *850/650–0499* 🌐 *anotherbrokenegg.com* 🕒 *Closed Mon. No dinner.*

The Back Porch. [$] *Average main: $30* ✉ *16220 Front Beach Rd., Panama City Beach, FL* ☎ *850/233–1750* 🌐 *www.theback-porch.com.*

Caliza. [$] *Average main: $35* ✉ *23 Nonesuch Way, Alys Beach, FL*

☎ 850/213–5700 🌐 www.calizarestaurant.com ⏲ Closed Mon. No lunch.

Capt. Anderson's. [$] *Average main: $30 ✉ 5551 N. Lagoon Dr., Panama City Beach, FL ☎ 850/650–0499 🌐 www.captainandersons.com.*

Fish Out Of Water. [$] *Average main: $22 ✉ 34 Goldenrod Cir., 2nd fl., Santa Rosa Beach ☎ 850/534–5050 🌐 www.foow30a.com.*

George's at Alys Beach. [$] *Average main: $33 ✉ 30 Castle Harbour Dr., Alys Beach, FL ☎ 850/641–0017 🌐 www.georgesatalysbeach.com.*

Great Southern Cafe. [$] *Average main: $9 ✉ 83 Central Sq., Seaside, FL ☎ 850/231–7327 🌐 www.thegreatsoutherncafe.com.*

Harbor Docks. [$] *Average main: $23 ✉ 538 Harbor Blvd., Destin, FL ☎ 850/837–2506 🌐 www.harbordocks.com.*

Marina Café. [$] *Average main: $17 ✉ 404 Harbor Blvd., Destin, FL ☎ 850/837–7960 🌐 www.marinacafe.com.*

Schooners. [$] *Average main: $21 ✉ 5121 Gulf Dr., Panama City Beach, FL ☎ 850/235–3555 🌐 www.schooners.com.*

The Shrimp Shack. [$] *Average main: $15 ✉ 2236 Hwy. 30A, Seaside, FL ☎ 850/279–6358 🌐 www.sweetwilliamsltd.com/shrimp_shack.asp.*

Coffee and Quick Bites

Black Bear Bread Co. [$] *Average main: $13 ✉ 26 Logan La., Santa Rosa Beach, FL ☎ 850/588–2086 🌐 www.blackbearbreadco.com ⏲ No dinner.*

Donut Hole Bakery Café. [$] *Average main: $10 ✉ 635 Harbor Blvd., Destin, FL ☎ 850/837–8824 🌐 www.sweetwilliamsltd.com/shrimp_shack.asp.*

Maple Street Biscuit Co. [$] *Average main: $10 ✉ 9375 Emerald Coast Pkwy., Miramar Beach, FL ☎ 850/231–3799 🌐 www.maplestreetbiscuits.com ⏲ No dinner.*

Hotels

Emerald Grande at HarborWalk Village. [$] *Rooms from: $205 ✉ 10 Harbor Blvd., Destin, FL ☎ 850/676–0091 🌐 www.emeraldgrande.com 🍴 No meals.*

The Henderson Beach Resort & Spa. [$] *Rooms from: $179 ✉ 200 Henderson Resort Way, Destin ☎ 850/741–2777 🌐 www.hendersonbeachresort.com 🍴 No meals.*

Rosemary Beach Inn. [$] *Rooms from: $300 ✉ 78 Main St., Rosemary Beach, FL ☎ 866/348–8952 🌐 www.therosemarybeachinn.com 🍴 Free breakfast.*

WaterColor Inn and Resort. [$] *Rooms from: $325 ✉ 34 Goldenrod Circle, Santa Rosa Beach, FL ☎ 850/534–5000 🌐 www.watercolorresort.com 🍴 No meals.*

Nightlife

AJ's Seafood & Oyster Bar. *✉ 116 U.S. 98 E, Destin, FL ☎ 850/837–1913 🌐 www.ajsdestin.com.*

Bud & Alley's. *✉ 2236 E. Rte. 30A, Seaside, FL ☎ 850/231–5900 🌐 www.budandalleys.com.*

1835 Porch Bar. *✉ 200 Harbor Blvd., Destin, FL ☎ No phone 🌐 www.1835porchbar.com.*

Neat. *✉ 11 N. Castle Harbour Dr., Alys Beach, FL ☎ 850/213–5711 🌐 alysbeach.com/neat.*

Activities

The Boat House. *✉ WaterColor Inn, 34 Goldenrod Circle, WaterColor, FL ☎ 850/419–6188 🌐 www.watercolorresort.com/amenities/recreation 🎫 Rentals from $24.*

Emerald Coast Paddleboard. ✉ *Twin Cities Park, N. John Sims Pkwy., Valparaiso, FL* ☎ *850/376–3966* ⊕ *emeraldcoastpaddleboard.com* 🛶 *Yoga classes from $10.*

GUSU Paddlesports. ✉ *219 Mountain Dr., Destin, FL* ☎ *850/460–7300* ⊕ *www.gusupaddlesports.com* 🛶 *Rentals from $30.*

Fort Myers, Sanibel, and Captiva, FL

125 miles (approx. 2 hours) from Tampa.

The barrier islands off the coast of Fort Myers are a glimpse at Florida's low-key side. Narrow roads—many unpaved, by design—are engulfed by towering tropical palms and jungle-like foliage and rimmed by sandy beaches. Artist Robert Rauschenberg snapped up a beach house in Captiva in the 1970s (now an artists' residency) and in-the-know travelers have vacationed on Sanibel for decades. Combined, these two islands are home to only 7,000 or so residents. Fort Myers (pop. 82,000)—the gateway to these two islands—is an often-over-looked cultural mecca.

Planning

GETTING THERE AND BACK
From Tampa, wait until morning rush hour dies down, then hop onto I–75 S for the two-hour, 125-mile trip to Fort Myers. You will definitely need a car to explore Sanibel and Captiva islands.

INSPIRATION
Sanibel Island resident Randy Wayne White—owner of **Doc Ford's Sanibel Rum Bar & Grille**—pens crime fiction based in Florida and Cuba, through the eyes of retired NSA agent now marine biologist Doc Ford. Listen to *Sanibel Flats* or *Captiva* on audio while you drive.

WHEN TO GO
Summers can be hot here—although not as steamy as Miami—but a cool spot in the shade or by the pool make it bearable. The shoulder seasons of spring and fall mean fewer crowds once the kids are back in school. Avoid holiday weekends, which is when residents retreat to their vacation pads and clog up the region's restaurants and beaches.

WHERE TO STAY
Fort Myers's **Pink Shell Beach Resort & Marina** hugs a sandy shoreline and the marina, while flaunting three restaurants, three pools, a spa, and yoga classes. Or dial down the luxe at **Hotel Indigo** in the River District, which boasts a rooftop pool and vibrant mural. **South Seas Island Resort,** on Captiva Island, is a sprawling 330-acre resort with surprisingly low rates. It has everything from a private beach (with beach club), pools, water sports equipment, and a trio of casual bars and cafés. For a more intimate stay, check into a no-fuss (but still stylish) one-bedroom cottage at **The Parrot Nest,** on Sanibel's quieter eastern end.

Day 1

If it's the third Friday evening of the month, you're lucky: this is when Music Walk, sponsored by the River District Alliance, brings the latest tunes to the Fort Myers River District. A festive Art Walk takes place in the same neighborhood on the first Friday of each month.

Once you arrive in Fort Myers, sink into a booth at the 1950s-theme **Mel's Diner.** With 300-some items on the menu, options range from biscuits and gravy and chicken and waffles to an untraditional (but delicious) quinoa bowl. Also, mimosas are always nicely priced.

Pop into a gallery on the Lee County Campus of Florida SouthWestern State College that's dedicated to the region's most famous artist: Robert

Sanibel Island Lighthouse is a local landmark along this stretch of the Gulf Coast.

Rauschenberg. At the **Bob Rauschenberg Gallery**—on the campus since 1979—there's always something interesting going on.

Inspired by the art, take a painting class at **Vino's Picasso,** which hosts guided painting sessions paired with wine every Friday afternoon. (Make sure to sign up in advance.) You're not only creating a vacation memory—you'll have something to hang on the wall back home.

Southwest Florida is no exception when it comes to the current obsession with craft beer. **Point Ybel Brewing Company's** taproom likes to experiment with small-batch beers—such as a smoked porter and sour IPA—and also hosts live music on Friday nights. And over at **Millennial Brewing Company's** industrial-chic taproom, you can sample everything from a farmhouse-style ale to hard seltzers and sour beers. Wash it all down with international dishes from the cluster of food trucks parked outside.

Day 2

Before you make the journey to Captiva Island—an hour from Fort Myers—be sure to fuel up on coffee and donuts from **Bennett's Fresh Roast,** three blocks from the river and just south of the Fort Myers River District. Get your sea legs and your geographical bearings with a half-day **Captiva Cruises** ferry ride to the private island of Cabbage Key, departing from Captiva's South Seas Island Resort. You're almost certain to pass through pods of dolphins en route. The lone restaurant on the island is an open-air eatery seemingly inspired by Jimmy Buffet's "Cheeseburger in Paradise." At **Cabbage Key Restaurant,** thousands of dollar bills dangle from the ceilings while you dine on just-caught stone-crab claws, black beans and rice, and frozen key-lime pie. Get an even better view by climbing the water tower (not for the faint of heart, however).

After some sun-lounging or strolling Captiva's 2½-mile beach—or maybe you prefer to cool off with ice cream from the South Seas Island Resort's 1950s-style **Scoops and Slices** eatery—head into Captiva proper for dinner at the flamboyant, rainbow-stripe **Bubble Room.** Tucked into each room are quirky curiosities and antiquities. Don't leave without a slice of old-school cake—think Orange Crunch or Red Velvet—for dessert. And if there's a wait for your table, that's a good thing: the Bubble Room's boutique across the street is filled with everything from gag gifts and home decor items.

Day 3

Enjoy an indulgent brunch—How does a loaded seafood omelet or pigs-in-a-blanket pancakes sound?—at **The Island Cow** in Sanibel. (Get here early if you want to beat the line.) Start your day in earnest with some adrenaline. Rent a bikes and explore Sanibel's **J.N. "Ding" Darling National Wildlife Refuge,** a 5,200-acre mangrove forest that's home to river otters, alligators, and birds galore. Brush up on local flora, fauna and wildlife at the free visitor and education center. Pine Island National Wildlife Refuge is folded into this park's acreage, too.

Next, you need to try shelling. Sanibel—with its more than 400 shell varieties—ranks as one of the world's best spots for shelling, as it's in the sweet spot where the Caribbean Sea and Gulf of Mexico converge. Any beach should do. The **Bailey-Matthews National Shell Museum,** on Sanibel, has 30 exhibits, daily tank talks, and guided beach walks.

Cantinas and beach shacks are mainstays of the island dining scene. Close out the weekend with dinner at Casa Ybel Resort's **Thistle Lodge,** where legends like Henry Ford and Thomas Edison once dined. From cedar-smoked grilled octopus to Basque-style chicken with Andouille sausage, the menu is a fusion of Asian, European, and Floridian influences.

Recommendations

Sights

Bailey-Matthews National Shell Museum. ⊠ *3075 Sanibel Captiva Rd., Sanibel, FL* ☎ *239/395–2233* ⊕ *www.shellmuseum. org* 🎫 *$24.*

Bob Rauschenberg Gallery. ⊠ *8099 College Pkwy., Fort Myers, FL* ☎ *239/489–9313* ⊕ *www.rauschenberggallery.com* 🎫 *Free.*

J.N. "Ding" Darling National Wildlife Refuge. ⊠ *1 Wildlife Dr., Sanibel, FL* ☎ *239/472–1100* ⊕ *www.fws.gov* 🎫 *$5 per car.*

 Restaurants

Bennett's Fresh Roast. $ *Average main: $12* ⊠ *2011 Bayside Pkwy., Fort Myers, FL* ☎ *239/332–0077* ⊕ *www.bennettsfreshroast.com* ☉ *No dinner.*

Bubble Room. $ *Average main: $24* ⊠ *15001 Captiva Dr., Captiva FL* ☎ *239/472–5558* ⊕ *www.bubbleroomrestaurant.com.*

Cabbage Key Restaurant. $ *Average main: $32* ⊠ *Waterfront Dr., Cabbage Key, FL* ☎ *239/283–2278* ⊕ *www.cabbagekey. com.*

The Island Cow. $ *Average main: $20* ⊠ *2163 Periwinkle Way, Sanibel Island, FL* ☎ *239/472–0606* ⊕ *www.sanibelislandcow.com.*

Mel's Diner. $ *Average main: $16* ⊠ *4820 Cleveland Ave., Fort Myers, FL* ☎ *239/275–7850* ⊕ *www.melsdiners. com.*

Scoops and Slices. $ *Average main: $24* ⊠ *South Seas Island Resort, 5400 Plantation Rd., Captiva Island, FL* ☎ *239/472–5111* ⊕ *www.southseas.com.*

Thistle Lodge. $ *Average main: $40* ⊠ *Casa Ybel Resort, 2255 West Gulf Dr., Sanibel, FL* ☎ *239/472–3145* ⊕ *www. casaybelresort.com.*

Hotels

Hotel Indigo. $ *Rooms from: $123* ✉ *520 Broadway, Fort Myers, FL* ☎ *239/337–3446* ⊕ *www.ihg.com* ⦶ *No meals.*

The Parrot Nest. $ *Rooms from: $99* ✉ *1237 Anhinga La., Sanibel, FL* ☎ *800/247–0448* ⊕ *www.parrotnest.com* ⦶ *No meals.*

Pink Shell Beach Resort & Marina. $ *Rooms from: $210* ✉ *275 Estero Blvd., Fort Myers Beach, FL* ☎ *888/222–7465* ⊕ *www.pinkshell.com* ⦶ *Free breakfast.*

South Seas Island Resort. $ *Rooms from: $259* ✉ *5400 Plantation Rd., Captiva, FL* ☎ *239/472–5111* ⊕ *www.southseas.com* ⦶ *No meals.*

ⓨ Nightlife

Doc Ford's Sanibel Rum Bar & Grille. ✉ *708 Fishermans Wharf, Ft. Myers Beach, FL* ☎ *239/765–9660* ⊕ *www.docfords.com.*

Millennial Brewing Company. ✉ *1811 Royal Palm Ave., Fort Myers, FL* ☎ *239/271–2255* ⊕ *www.millennialbrewing.com.*

Point Ybel Brewing Company. ✉ *16120 San Carlos Blvd., Fort Myers, FL* ☎ *239/603–6535* ⊕ *www.pointybelbrew.com.*

Activities

Captiva Cruises. ✉ *11401 Andy Rosse La., Captiva Island, FL* ☎ *239/472–5300* ⊕ *www.captivacruises.com* 🛥 *Cruises from $30.*

Hilton Head, SC

280 miles (approx. 4¼ hours) from Atlanta, 247 miles (approx. 4 hours) from Charlotte.

Sometimes all you need is a beach getaway, and there's no better place to escape than Hilton Head—far from the crowds off the South Carolina coast. We have General Joseph Fraser to thank for the balanced mix of development and nature here. As plantation lands were sold at auction in the 1800s, he and his son bought them up, developing the island's various communities. So today, as the nation's first eco-planned destination, there are beautiful places to stay, with all of the requisite amenities, amid some of the South's most stunning Lowcountry beauty.

You could spend all day simply soaking up the Vitamin D and splashing in the waves at the 12 miles of beaches, but there are plenty of water sports to enjoy as well, along with après-sun activities: golf, fine dining, nature walks, kayaking, and the list goes on. Come here for romance, a friends' getaway, or family vacation—it literally has something for everyone.

Planning

GETTING THERE AND BACK

Hilton Head is a four-hour drive (280 miles) from Atlanta via I–75 and I–16. You could also take Amtrak to Savannah, Georgia, which is 45 minutes from Hilton Head, or Yemassee, South Carolina, which is an hour from Hilton Head, and then transfer by taxi or shuttle.

From Charlotte, it's a little faster on the route straight south via I–77, I–26, and I–95. Once there, it's easiest to drive around the small island, but public transportation and cabs are available.

WHEN TO GO

Hilton Head is a year-round destination. The shoulder seasons—April and May as well as September and October—are the best times to visit, with warm weather but fewer crowds and lower lodging rates. Summer is prime, with great beach weather but lots of people. In winter, watersport companies and some restaurants close. But, with temps rarely

Sleek sailboats are a common sight at Hilton Head Island's Harbour Town Marina.

dipping below 64°F, there are still things going on, including world-class golf.

WHERE TO STAY

The lion's share of accommodation options are rental homes and villas, from oversize oceanfront homes to quaint villas with a lagoon view to cozy condos next to putting greens. There are resort options as well. The **Omni Hilton Head Oceanfront Resort,** for example, has oceanfront accommodations and all the accoutrements, including tennis courts, fitness center, swimming pools, and restaurants. There's also the **Sonesta Resort Hilton Head Island,** with private balconies or patios, swimming pools, restaurants, and proximity to Shelter Cove Marina.

Day 1

You should arrive at Hilton Head around noon, just in time for lunch at the **Salty Dog Cafe,** an island institution. Sitting on the waterfront, watching pelicans gliding above, you know you have arrived in the Lowcountry. Sit back and enjoy a

hyperlocal seafood experience, including she-crab soup, shrimp and grits, hush puppies, and perhaps an ice-cold beer.

Then, first things first: the beach. All of the beaches are public, but many of the beach accesses are limited to hotel guests or otherwise private. You'll find access at Coligny Beach Park, Burkes Beach, Driessen Beach Park, and Folly Field Beach Park, among others. Coligny Beach Park has a wooden boardwalk and swings—a favorite with families.

If you prefer golf over the beach, you are in for a treat. With more than 40 courses, including 24 championship golf courses, you can be swinging the club all weekend. Two have oceanfront views: the famed Robert Trent Jones course at **Palmetto Dunes Oceanfront Resort** and the Atlantic Dunes course by Davis Love III at the **Sea Pines Resort.**

One of the most popular things to do, and an ideal predinner activity, is to pedal around the island. The island prides itself on more than 60 miles of paved pathways—not to mention, the beach's wide, hard-packed sand makes for a perfect ride. A favorite place to bike is Sea Pines Plantation. You can't bike in—you'll have to drive them in or rent inside—but 17 miles of gorgeous trails winding through wetlands and shady woods. Here, too, is the iconic candy-cane-stripe lighthouse.

Hopefully you like seafood, because you'll find one of the best dinners around at **Hudson's Seafood House on the Docks,** built over Port Royal Sound. The seafood is locally sourced and super fresh, and they even cultivate their own oysters and soft shell crabs. Don't leave without ordering the bread pudding; Ms. Bessie has been making their desserts for more than 35 years. As you watch dolphins frolic as the sun sets, you know you have entered Lowcountry paradise.

Day 2

Get up early and enjoy a morning nature walk at **Pinckney Island National Wildlife Refuge,** which has 14 miles of trails and an abundance of birds: bald eagles, wood storks, raptors, white ibis, herons, egrets, and more. The hike to Ibis Pond is a short and sweet—don't forget your camera. Grab breakfast at **Palmetto Bay Sunrise Café,** a local favorite serving breakfast all day; they're known for their Bloody Mary's.

Then hop aboard a boat tour with **Mermaid Encounter Boat Tour** to go in search of dolphins. Hilton Head is one of only two places in the world to see dolphins stand feeding—where they form a group to create a wave, pushing fish up onto mud banks.

The rest of the day could easily be spent sprawled on the beach. One of the island's prettiest—and most isolated—beaches is accessed from Fish Haul Creek Park. It's not really a swimming beach, meaning you'll find plenty of sand without all the beach umbrellas and chairs. Another option is Driessen Beach for a secluded feel.

But if you can be convinced to break away from the sun, there are more options. Kayak or stand-up paddleboard the island's estuaries, where you'll see shorebirds, dolphins, and the occasional river otter and bald eagle; Broad Creek is a popular spot. Small individual "cat boat" excursions—two-person catamaran boats—are popular as well. Water-sports rentals and guided tours are available at **Shelter Cove Harbour.**

Break up the day with a visit to the interactive **Coastal Discovery Museum,** which showcases Lowcountry culture, ecosystems, and history. It's a great place to take a stroll around the 68-acre property, taking in gardens, marshes, and Spanish-moss-dripping live oaks. There's also a butterfly enclosure beloved by kids.

And when you get hungry, **A Lowcountry Backyard Restaurant** is a great pause for lunch. Regional specialties, including potato-chip meat loaf, fried green tomato BLT, and a Lowcountry boil (shrimp, sausage, corn, fried potatoes, and crab) are served in a homey backyard garden, often serenaded by live music. Its shrimp and grits are considered among the best in the state.

A day like this deserves a umbrella drink, and the **Tiki Hut** is the perfect place to sip a killer Tiki Hut Punch on the beach. If you're there before 4, enjoy beach volleyball and live music.

Toast the sunset (BYOB) with a cruise aboard **Cheers,** a sailboat that takes you on a 2½ hour ride through Port Royal Sound and the Intracoastal Waterway. You'll see dolphins up close, listen to the captain share tales about the island, and watch the spectacle as the sun descends, casting brilliant colors across the sky.

Then seek out **Lucky Rooster Kitchen and Bar** for an unexpected place for dinner. Owned by Chef Clayton Rollison, who grew up on the island but earned his chops in New York, it's the place to go for Southern with a flair: pan-roasted scallops with heirloom carrots, almonds, apricots, and lemon-herb yogurt; baked smoke pork ragout; and blackened catfish with tasso, butter beans, boiled peanuts, and tomato jam are just a few of its striking creations. The craft cocktails are second to none.

Day 3

Rise early and go to the beach to watch the sun peak over the horizon. If it's low tide, be on the lookout for sand dollars. You'll likely see dolphins cavorting in the waves.

Then find breakfast at **Bad Biscuit,** which has every possible configuration of biscuits and gravy on the planet, mixing in such crazy ingredients as pimento cheese, bacon (stacks of it), grilled jalapenos, wild mushrooms, even local honey. If you'd rather linger over brunch, another option is the **Skull Creek Boathouse,** right on the water. They offer a Southern-style brunch on Sunday, including jambalaya, shrimp and grits, and French toast casserole. You won't need lunch, and even dinner, after this foodie extravaganza.

Get one last hurrah on the beach, or enjoy more water sports before heading home. And when you finally do decide to pack up and leave, consider stopping by the historic river town of Bluffton, located just over the bridge from Hilton Head. Perched on the May River, it effuses Southern history, with a past rooted in rice and cotton plantations, then canning and fishing. **Bluffton Oyster Company,** established in 1899, is the last working oyster factory in South Carolina, where you can pick up fresh shrimp, oysters, scallops, fish filets, and live blue crabs to take home, or enjoy a meal on the spot at the sit-down restaurant. You can tour the antebellum **Heyward House,** built by enslaved people in 1841. And the historic **Garvin-Garvey House** in Oyster Factory Park is a great example of the freedmen's cottages that dotted the May River once slavery ended. Calhoun Street is walkable, with mom-and-pop shops and funky galleries. At its end, the wooden Gothic **Church of the Cross** rises along the banks of the May River. Take your time, breathing in the area's fresh ocean air, before heading back home to Atlanta.

Recommendations

◉ Sights

Church of the Cross. ✉ 110 Calhoun St., Bluffton, SC ☎ 843/757–2661 ⊕ www.thechurchofthecross.net ⌖ Free.

Coastal Discovery Museum. ✉ 70 Honey Horn Dr., Hilton Head Island, SC ☎ 843/689–6767 ⊕ www.coastaldiscovery.org ⌖ $10.

Garvin-Garvey House. ✉ Oyster Factory Park, Bluffton, SC ☎ 843/757–6293 ⊕ www.townofbluffton.sc.gov ⌖ $5☉ Closed Wed. and Fri.–Mon.

Heyward House. ✉ 70 Boundary St., Bluffton, SC ☎ 843/757–6293 ⊕ www.heywardhouse.org ⌖ $10 ☉ Closed Sun.

Pinckney Island National Wildlife Refuge. ✉ Beaufort County, SC ☎ 843/784–2468 ⊕ www.fws.gov/refuge/pinckney_island ⌖ Free.

Restaurants

Bad Biscuit. $ Average main: $10 ✉ 19 Dunnagans Alley, Hilton Head Island, SC ☎ 843/785–2323 ⊕ www.bad-biscuit.com ☉ No dinner.

Hudson's Seafood House on the Docks. $
Average main: $25 ⊠ *1 Hudson Rd.,
Hilton Head Island, SC* ☎ *843/681–2772*
⊕ *www.hudsonsonthedocks.com.*

A Lowcountry Backyard Restaurant. $ *Average main: $22* ⊠ *The Village Exchange,
32 Palmetto Bay Rd., Hilton Head Island,
SC* ☎ *843/785–9273* ⊕ *www.hhbackyard.
com* ☾ *No dinner Sun.*

Lucky Rooster Kitchen and Bar. $ *Average
main: $30* ⊠ *841 William Hilton Pkwy.,
Hilton Head Island, SC* ☎ *843/681–3474*
⊕ *www.luckyroosterhhi.com* ☾ *Closed
Mon. No dinner Sun.*

Salty Dog Cafe. $ *Average main: $30*
⊠ *South Beach Marina, 232 S. Sea Pines
Dr., Hilton Head Island, SC* ☎ *843/671–
2233* ⊕ *www.saltydog.com.*

Skull Creek Boathouse. $ *Average main:
$25* ⊠ *397 Squire Pope Rd., Hilton Head
Island, SC* ☎ *843/681–3663* ⊕ *www.
skullcreekboathouse.com.*

Hotels

Omni Hilton Head Oceanfront Resort. $
Rooms from: $152 ⊠ *23 Ocean La.,
Hilton Head Island, SC* ☎ *843/842–8000*
⊕ *www.omnihotels.com* ⦿ *No meals.*

Sonesta Resort Hilton Head Island. $
Rooms from: $269 ⊠ *130 Shipyard Dr.,
Hilton Head Island, SC* ☎ *843/842–2400*
⊕ *www.sonesta.com* ⦿ *No meals.*

Nightlife

Tiki Hut. ⊠ *1 S. Forest Beach Dr., Hilton
Head Island, SC* ☎ *843/785–5126*
⊕ *www.tikihuthhi.com.*

Shopping

Bluffton Oyster Company. ⊠ *63 Wharf St.,
Bluffton, SC* ☎ *843/757–4010* ⊕ *www.
blufftonoyster.com.*

Activities

Cheers. ⊠ *18 Simmons Rd., Hilton Head
Island, SC* ☎ *843/671–1800* ⊕ *www.
cheerscharters.com* ☷ *Cruises from $35.*

Palmetto Dunes Oceanfront Resort. ⊠ *4
Queens Folly Rd., Hilton Head Island, SC*
☎ *843/776–2995* ⊕ *www.palmettodunes.
com* ☷ *Greens fees from $109.*

Sea Pines Resort. ⊠ *32 Greenwood Dr.,
Hilton Head Island, SC* ☎ *843/785–3333*
⊕ *www.seapines.com* ☷ *Greens fees
from $179.*

Shelter Cove Harbour. ⊠ *1 Shelter Cove
La., Hilton Head Island, SC* ☎ *866/661–
3822* ⊕ *www.sheltercovehiltonhead.com*
☷ *Cruises from $35.*

Hot Springs, AR

*189 miles (approx. 3 hours) from Memphis, 294 miles (approx. 4½ hours) from
Dallas.*

Tucked away in the Ouachita Mountains of Central Arkansas—earning its name from the gallons of 143-degree thermal waters that flow from the ground each day—Hot Springs has long been a haven for natural immersions and relaxing escapes. Native Americans once referred to it as "the Valley of the Vapors," but it wasn't until a row of Victorian bathhouses were built that Hot Springs began to attract vacationers. In the late 1880s baseball fans flocked to the town to see one of the first spring training fields that would later host Jackie Robinson and Babe Ruth, and in the 1930s, "Spa City" became inundated with mobsters taking respite in the discrete mountain town's loose gambling laws, lively bars, and rejuvenating spas. (It's said Al Capone rented out entire floors at hotels for him and his bodyguards.) Today, people come to soak up Hot Springs' historic sites and natural marvels.

Planning

GETTING THERE AND BACK
Interstate 30 is an almost direct shot between Dallas and Hot Springs, the journey clocking in at less than 4½ hours. It's a three-hour drive from Memphis to Hot Springs via I–40 W, where the route passes through Arkansas' capital city of Little Rock.

INSPIRATION
Native Arkansan David Hill's *The Vapors,* an incredibly true tale of the original capital of vice, is a great audiobook on Audible.

PIT STOP
You'll add just 40 minutes of driving time from Dallas if you follow TX 24 N for the chance to pass through Paris, Texas—the "second largest Paris in the world"—and see the 65-foot Eiffel Tower topped with a red cowboy hat.

WHEN TO GO
Spring and fall are busy seasons in Hot Springs, when bathers can take to the warm waters and still head out into nature without so much as a chill. Summers are festive, with the Hot Springs Music Festival and the famed Running of the Tubs occurring in early June. The World's Shortest St. Patrick's Day Parade happens every March along Bridge Street, and wintry strolls through the Garvan Woodland Gardens around the holidays are nothing short of magical.

WHERE TO STAY
The **Hotel Hale** was one of the original bathhouses in Hot Springs. Built in 1892, the hotel has been remodeled into a boutique hotel where each of the nine rooms feature exposed brick walls and luxurious soaking tubs fed by the thermal spring waters below. The **Arlington Hotel** is one of the city's most impressive landmarks, where its two domed towers rise above Bathhouse Row. Presidents, celebrities, and gangsters have stayed at this almost 500-room hotel, where Al

Capone's favored room was 443 because it allowed him to keep an eye on the goings-on at the Southern Club (now the Wax Museum) across the street.

Day 1

After a long drive in from either Memphis or Dallas, head straight to the **Quapaw Bathhouse** for your inaugural mid-afternoon soak in Hot Springs' famous healing waters. Travelers have been immersing themselves in the thermal waters at this spa since it opened in 1922, where it now includes thermal pools, private baths, massages, and even a steam cave powered directly by the natural thermal spring below.

Stop in at the **Bathhouse Row Emporium,** inside the former Lamar Bathhouse, to buy locally made spa products and a glass water bottle to fill with the mineral-rich spring water flowing from fountains throughout the city before heading to the **Gangster Museum of America** to learn more about the town's nefarious past. For dinner, simply stroll down the road to the **Superior Bathhouse Brewery.** Housed inside Al Capone's allegedly favored former bathhouse, this brewpub uses the 144-degree thermal water from **Hot Springs National Park** in all their beers, including the Superior Pale Ale, also known as SPA beer.

Day 2

Breakfast is served all day at **Kollective Coffee and Tea,** a third-wave coffee shop where everything is either organic or local … and often fair-trade, too. It's hard to pick a favorite drink—a French lemon ginger rooibos tea, an Onyx Coffee Lab nitro cold brew, and a coconut lavender latte are only three of the hundreds of drink options—but the vegan frijoles ranchero served on freshly baked naan is an easy winner on the breakfast menu.

Constructed between 1892 and 1923, the elegant spas of Bathhouse Row face the Grand Promenade.

Hot Springs was rated as a bronze-level ride center by the International Mountain Biking Association, and the Northwood Trails around the city range from joy ride to grueling, including the 33-mile IMBA Epic Ride at Womble Trail and the 108-mile Ouachita National Recreational Trail. Whether you're into mountain biking or if you just want a leisurely ride through the city, **Spa City Cycling** has you covered for any rental needs or bike repairs.

After working up an appetite on the trails, grab a seat at the 1950s-style bar inside local-favorite **BubbaLu's Bodacious Burgers and Classy Dogs.** These award-winning, no-frills burgers are hand-pressed fresh each morning and are best served with an ice-cold beer or frosty malt. After lunch, test your luck at **Oaklawn Racing Casino Resort** (a favorite horse betting venue of Al Capone and his men) or head to the **Garvan Woodland Gardens** near Lake Hamilton. There's an adventure garden for kids and tons of walking trails, but the showstopper of this botanical garden is the Bob and Sunny Evans Treehouse.

The four-level treehouse is an Instagram story waiting to happen, where it floats and bends among the pine trees and oak trees.

Stick nearby for dinner at **Fisherman's Wharf,** a steak and seafood restaurant located on the banks of Lake Hamilton, or sample some of the best Ark-Mex in the state at **Diablos.** It pairs more than 50 different mezcals and tequilas with everything from al pastor tacos to salmon ceviche and Spanish-style tapas. Don't make the mistake by calling the cheese dip "queso." There's a long-standing battle between Texas and Arkansas on who invented the dip first, but this version is one of the best. For late night drinks, head to the **Ohio Club.** This former speakeasy was once the heart of the mobster action back in Al Capone's day, when gambling and bootlegged liquor kept the precarious patrons happy through the night.

Day 3

Only in Hot Springs would an authentic French creperie owned by a Ukrainian family who learned the art of crepe making while living in Brussels be right at home in an unassuming strip mall. **Alexa's Creperie** opened shortly after the Plyakov family immigrated to the United States in 2013, when they began hand-making everything on-site. They specialize in "crepes for all tastes," but their Swiss cheese, scrambled egg, fresh spinach breakfast crepe with Arkansas Petit Jean ham is a local favorite.

After breakfast, grab your phone and head back to Bathhouse Row in the **Hot Springs National Park**. This national park is unlike any other in the country in that it is actually located within the limits of downtown Hot Springs, surrounded by shops and restaurants. Guided tours are available, but cell phone tour signs are located throughout the park for you to simply call in to get more info on the history of each marked area. There are more than 26 miles of hiking trails throughout the park though, so bring your water bottle and fill up at either of the two (filtered) cold water springs within the park before heading toward the 1.1-mile-long Goat Rock Trail starting at the overlook on North Mountain. A well-worn path winds through switchbacks as it climbs up to a scenic overlook rising 40 feet above the Indian Mountain and east Hot Springs.

Spend your last moments in Hot Springs soaking in the views without worrying about rushing back in time for lunch before leaving town, because **Café 1217** offers gourmet boxed lunches to go. Chef Diana Bratton's Black and Blue Sliders with shaved rib-eye, caramelized onions, and blue cheese on a toasted brioche bun may require a pit stop to be able to fully enjoy, but her house-made garlic pepper potato chips make for mess-free and delicious snacking while driving.

Recommendations

👁 Sights

Gangster Museum of America. ✉ *510 Central Ave., Hot Springs, AR* ☎ *501/318–1717* 🌐 *www.tgmoa.com* 🎟 *$15.*

Garvan Woodland Gardens. ✉ *550 Arkridge Rd., Hot Springs, AR* ☎ *501/262–9300* 🌐 *www.garvangardens.org* 🎟 *$15.*

Hot Springs National Park. ✉ *101 Reserve St., Hot Springs, AR* ☎ *501/620–6715* 🌐 *www.nps.gov/hosp/index.htm* 🎟 *Free.*

Oaklawn Racing Casino Resort. ✉ *2705 Central Ave., Hot Springs, AR* ☎ *800/625–5586* 🌐 *www.oaklawn.com* 🎟 *Free.*

Quapaw Bathhouse. ✉ *413 Central Ave., Hot Springs, AR* ☎ *501/609–9822* 🌐 *www.quapawbaths.com* 🎟 *Spa services from $50* 🕒 *Closed Mon.–Wed.*

🍴 Restaurants

Alexa's Creperie. [$] *Average main: $12* ✉ *238 Cornerstone Blvd., Hot Springs, AR* ☎ *501/760–4799* 🌐 *www.alexascreperie.com* 🕒 *Closed Sun. and Mon.*

BubbaLu's Bodacious Burgers and Classy Dogs. [$] *Average main: $6* ✉ *408 Central Ave., Hot Springs, AR* ☎ *501/321–0101* 🕒 *Closed Wed.*

Café 1217. [$] *Average main: $10* ✉ *1217 Malvern Ave., Hot Springs, AR* ☎ *501/318–1094* 🌐 *www.cafe1217.net* 🕒 *Closed Sun. No dinner Sat.*

Diablos. [$] *Average main: $12* ✉ *528 Central Ave., Hot Springs, AR* ☎ *501/701–4327* 🌐 *www.diablostacosandmezcal.com.*

Fisherman's Wharf. [$] *Average main: $17* ✉ *5101 Central Ave., Hot Springs, AR* ☎ *501/525–7437.*

Superior Bathhouse Brewery. [$] *Average main: $10* ✉ *329 Central Ave., Hot*

Springs, AR ☎ 501/624–2337 ⊕ www.superiorbathhouse.com.

☕ Coffee and Quick Bites

Kollective Coffee and Tea. Ⓢ *Average main: $4* ⊠ *110 Central Ave., Hot Springs, AR* ☎ *501/701–4000* ⊕ *www.kollectivecoffeetea.com.*

🛏 Hotels

Arlington House. Ⓢ *Rooms from: $153* ⊠ *239 Central Ave., Hot Springs, AR* ☎ *800/643–1502* ⊕ *www.arlingtonhotel.com* ℉ *No meals.*

Hotel Hale. Ⓢ *Rooms from: $185* ⊠ *341 Central Ave., Hot Springs, AK* ☎ *501/760–9010* ⊕ *www.hotelhale.com* ℉ *Free breakfast.*

🍸 Nightlife

Ohio Club. ⊠ *336 Central Ave., Hot Springs, AR* ☎ *501/627–0702* ⊕ *www.theohioclub.com.*

👜 Shopping

Bathhouse Row Emporium. ⊠ *515 Central Ave., Hot Springs, AR* ☎ *501/620–6740* ⊕ *www.hotsprings.org.*

🏃 Activities

Spa City Cycling. ⊠ *873 Park Ave., Hot Springs, AR* ☎ *501/463–9364* ⊕ *www.spacitycycling.com* 🎫 *From $48.*

Lafayette and Cajun Country, LA

217 miles (approx. 3¼ hours) from Houston.

Lafayette and the surrounding area are rooted in Cajun culture, dating back to the 18th century when French-Canadian settlers made a life here among the bayous, lakes, and swamps. That way of life, combined with African, Creole, Spanish, Italian, and Native American cultures, makes Cajun country what it is today, seen especially in its unique food and music.

Planning

GETTING THERE AND BACK
It makes the most sense to drive from Houston to Lafayette; it takes a little over three hours on I–10, and you'll want a car here to explore the countryside. There are, however, a few nonstop flights that fly into Lafayette Airport.

INSPIRATION
The young pop/rock ensemble of Sweet Crude brings Cajun music into the present with lively instrumentals and bilingual lyrics celebrating the band's Southern Louisiana roots.

PIT STOPS
Some of the best places to purchase boudin (sausage stuffed with rice and seasoning), cracklins (fried pork rinds), and other indulgent Cajun country treats are at humble roadside stands dotting I–10.

WHEN TO GO
In springtime, Cajun country comes to life with cultural festivals like Cajun Mardi Gras, Festival International de Louisiane, and Black Pot Festival. These coincide with crawfish season (which usually runs into the summer), adding to the festive experience. After some of the heat burns off in late September, the fall also makes a lovely time to visit.

WHERE TO STAY
Looking at Lafayette today, you get the feeling it's only a matter of time before there's a hip boutique hotel here. For the time being, choices are basically limited to budget chains and B&Bs around the city's outskirts like **T'Frere's House.** The

In southern Louisiana, Atchafalaya National Heritage Area includes more wetlands than the Everglades.

charming **Juliet Hotel** is a nice in-between option downtown.

Day 1

Arriving midmorning, take some time to explore the natural beauty of this region. Drive through the **Atchafalaya National Heritage Area,** just northeast of Lafayette. This is the largest wetland area in the country—larger than the Florida Everglades—and is home to bald eagles, alligators, black bears, and the tens of millions of pounds of crawfish that the country (mostly Louisiana) eats every year. You can kayak through parts of the Atchafalaya with the outfitter **Pack and Paddle.**

Drive back toward Lafayette to explore **Acadian Village,** a remote and well-kept historical re-creation of an Acadian Settlers' village from the 1800s. It takes about an hour to explore here, leaving you plenty of time after to check in to your hotel before heading to downtown Lafayette.

While small towns of Acadian charm are certainly main appeals to a Cajun Country trip, in recent years, Lafayette itself has picked up a young and vibrant energy, and its hipster "city life" is a nice juxtaposition to more traditional rustic surroundings. Dig into Lafayette's history first, with a quick look at the **Hilliard Art Museum,** a walk by the picturesque Cathedral of St. John the Evangelist, or a stroll around the Vermilionville Historic Village.

Dine at **The French Press,** a hip café with a James Beard nod and some elevated, delicious Cajun comfort food. From dinner it's a short walk to the **Blue Moon Saloon,** just one of the many Cajun dance halls surrounding Lafayette.

Day 2

Have a casual, fun breakfast at **Johnson's Boucaniere,** where breakfast bowls and biscuits incorporate plenty of Cajun sausage. You'll probably want to return here at some point for an extra sandwich or two. After breakfast, pack up for a day of exploring Cajun country.

Your first stop is Avery Island, about 40 minutes southeast of downtown Lafayette. Here, it's time to marvel at yet another geological wonder: the island is actually a solid salt dome, rising above its flat coastal marsh surroundings and covering more than 2,000 acres. Most geologists accredit its creation to salt deposits left over from an ancient seabed. The island has been privately owned for almost 200 years by the Avery-McIlhenny family, the creators of Tabasco hot sauce. A good excuse to visit here is a tour of the **Tabasco Factory.** Aside from a fun tour of the factory, you visit Avery Island for the flora and fauna, which have been well preserved in their natural and wild habitat. Walk through the botanical gardens, learn about the salt dome's geology and Tabasco's pepper plantings, and marvel at the natural wonderland of Bird City—a sanctuary created for the snowy egret.

For lunch, stop in Broussard for a country diner experience at **Ton's Drive In.** Ton's is known for the homemade burgers and massive lunch platters of fried seafood. Lafayette and Cajun Country are full of treasure troves in the form of roadside antique malls that are part junk shop, part treasure trove. Head north into Lafayette, passing **Rooster's Antique Market, Lafayette Antique Market,** and more, and then continue to the small town of Breaux Bridge. Here, you can park downtown and hit up a few excellent antique malls in a small radius.

Tonight it's back to the down-home roots of Cajun country at **Rocky's Cajun Kitchen** in Eunice. If you're lucky enough to come in season, get a tray of boiled crawfish. Otherwise there's plenty of etouffee, jambalaya, and fried seafood platters year-round—and live Cajun music and dancing on weekends.

Day 3

Head back to the town of Breaux Bridge for Zydeco Breakfast at **Buck and Johnny's.** This is eggs with a big side of entertainment: biscuits and beignets are piled with crawfish etouffee, and lively zydeco music—and even dancing—begins around 8 am. This town runs right along Bayou Teche so take a stroll before driving to **Bayou Teche Brewery.** This little family-run operation makes good beer and offers free tours of their rustic bayou-side facility.

Recommendations

Sights

Acadian Village. ✉ *200 Greenleaf Dr., Lafayette, LA* ☎ *337/981–2364* 🌐 *www.acadianvillage.org* 🎟 *$11* 🕒 *Closed Sun.*

Atchafalaya National Heritage Area. ✉ *2022 Atchafalaya River Hwy., Breaux Bridge, LA* ☎ *225/228–1094* 🌐 *www.nps.gov/attr* 🎟 *Free.*

Bayou Teche Brewing. ✉ *1094 Bushville Hwy., Arnaudville, LA* ☎ *337/754–5122* 🌐 *bayoutechebrewing.com* 🎟 *Free* 🕒 *Closed Mon.–Wed.*

Hilliard Art Museum. ✉ *710 East St. Mary Blvd., Lafayette, LA* ☎ *337/482–2278* 🌐 *www.hilliardmuseum.org* 🎟 *$5* 🕒 *Closed Sun.*

Tabasco Factory. ✉ *Hwy. 329, Avery Island, LA* ☎ *337/373–6139* 🌐 *www.tabasco.com/visit-avery-island/tabasco-tour* 🎟 *Free.*

Restaurants

Buck and Johnny's. [$] *Average main: $18* ✉ *100 Berard St., Breaux Bridge, LA* ☎ *337/442–6630* 🌐 *buckandjohnnys.com* 🕒 *No dinner Sun. and Mon.*

The French Press. [$] *Average main: $32* ✉ *214 E. Vermilion St., Lafayette, LA*

☎ *337/233–9449* 🌐 *www.thefrenchpress-lafayette.com.*

Johnson's Boucaniere. [$] *Average main: $9* ✉ *1111 St. John St., Lafayette, LA* ☎ *337/269–8878* 🌐 *www.johnsonsboucaniere.com* 🕒 *Closed Sun. and Mon.*

Rocky's Cajun Kitchen. [$] *Average main: $10* ✉ *1415 E. Laurel Ave., Eunice, LA* ☎ *337/457–6699* 🕒 *No dinner Sun.*

Ton's Drive In. [$] *Average main: $10* ✉ *101 W. Main St., Broussard, LA* ☎ *337/837–6684* 🌐 *tonsdrivein.com* 🕒 *Closed Sun. No dinner.*

Hotels

Juliet Hotel. [$] *Rooms from: $80* ✉ *800 Jefferson St., Lafayette, LA* ☎ *337/261–2225* 🌐 *www.juliethotels.com* 🍴 *Free breakfast.*

T'Frere's House. [$] *Rooms from: $148* ✉ *1905 Verot School Rd., Lafayette, LA* ☎ *337/984–9347* 🌐 *www.tfrereshouse.com* 🍴 *Free breakfast.*

Nightlife

Blue Moon Saloon. ✉ *215 E. Convent St., Lafayette, LA* ☎ *337/234–2422* 🌐 *bluemoonpresents.com.*

Shopping

Lafayette Antique Market. ✉ *3108 Johnston St., Lafayette, LA* ☎ *337/981–9884.*

Rooster's Antique Market. ✉ *3209 Kaliste Saloom Rd., Lafayette, LA* ☎ *337/216–0513.*

Activities

Pack and Paddle. ✉ *601 E. Pinhook Rd., Lafayette, LA* ☎ *337/232–5854* 🌐 *packpaddle.com/recreational-kayaking* 🎟 *Rentals from $49.*

Montgomery, AL

160 miles (2½ hours) southwest of Atlanta, 334 miles (5 hours) southeast of Memphis.

You must work a bit to get to Alabama's capital. Although it's about halfway between Atlanta and Mobile (via I–85), it's not really on the way to anywhere else. However, it's well worth your time to make this trek, which has become a pilgrimage of sorts for those interested in The National Memorial for Peace and Justice and the Legacy Museum, which have brought some 400,000 visitors to Montgomery in their first year. Once you arrive, you'll find a city that hasn't exactly reached its pinnacle, but is certainly becoming a destination to be reckoned with.. Few cities have done a better job of laying out the stakes of the Civil Rights movement than Montgomery, which is both acknowledging and reckoning with its role in both the slave trade and what followed. After all, this is where the Civil Rights movement was born, where Martin Luther King Jr. preached, and where the Equal Justice Initiative, one of the country's most successful legal aid organizations, is currently seeing much success. With good food, fun bars, and plenty of other activities, you'll be able to occupy yourself easily for three very packed days.

Planning

GETTING THERE AND BACK

Atlanta is 160 miles northeast of Montgomery, a fairly brisk 2½-hour drive via I–85 South. If you leave fairly early, you'll be in Montgomery in time for an early lunch.

It's a longer, five-hour drive from Memphis to Montgomery via I–22.

The fight against slavery is recounted at Montgomery's National Memorial for Peace and Justice.

PIT STOPS

History buffs may want to take the short detour to Warm Springs to visit Franklin Roosevelt's **Little White House,** where he found comfort after his bout with polio; the side trip will add about 45 minutes to your drive time in either direction. If you go to Warm Springs, make the effort to stop for lunch at **Dinner's Ready by Chad** for some great down-home Southern cooking.

Travelers from Memphis will almost certainly want to stop. If you wait until you make it to Birmingham, consider a late lunch at **Bottega Cafe,** where you can enjoy the culinary delights of executive chef Frank Stitt and add a slice of coconut cake from revered pastry chef Dolester Miles; or you can just skip the lunch and dig right into the cake.

INSPIRATION

A playlist of the greatest hits of Montgomery native son Hank Williams may put you in the mood for your trip. But *Just Mercy,* narrated by the author and founder of the Equal Justice Initiative

Bryan Stevenson, will give you both inspiration and context for your visit.

WHEN TO GO

Montgomery has viciously hot summers, so keep that head in mind when planning a trip, though Alabama can have nice winters, with mostly cold nights and cool days. To maximize your time and opportunities for good food, remember that some of the city's best local breakfast and lunch spots are closed on Saturday.

WHERE TO STAY

Downtown Montgomery has several good hotels, and this is the easiest place to base yourself for a long or short stay. If you're looking for modern comforts, you can choose from a **DoubleTree, Hampton Inn & Suites,** and **Renaissance.** Several other hotels are in development. If you are looking for atmosphere, look no further than the **Scott & Zelda Fitzgerald Museum** in the Cottage Hill neighborhood, which operates two AirBnB units upstairs.

Day 1

If you are planning a long weekend, try to arrive early enough on Friday or Saturday to do a little touring, ideally by late morning. A fitting place to begin your Montgomery visit is the **King Memorial Baptist Church** on Dexter Avenue, where Martin Luther King Jr. was pastor during the Montgomery bus boycott. The church is within easy walking distance of all the downtown hotels. You can tour the church and also the **Dexter Parsonage Museum** on South Jackson Avenue, a few blocks away, where the King family lived during their time in Montgomery. If you are short on time, book a timed tour in advance (the last Friday tour is at 3 pm), but walk-ins are accommodated if they have room; allow an hour for the church, two if you visit the parsonage. Nearby, on Washington Avenue, is the Maya Lin–designed **Civil Rights Memorial** that sits in front of the Civil Rights Memorial Center. If you have time, definitely go inside to see the exhibits, the Wall of Justice, and to watch the short film on the Civil Rights Movement. Set aside an hour for this visit.

By this time, you may be ready for a break. Take it at **Chris' Hot Dogs,** which has been selling hot dogs, hamburgers, chili, chicken salad, and a few other things since 1917 at its location on Dexter Avenue. You will not be disappointed if you get your dog with chili sauce. If coffee is more your thing, then you'll find **Prevail Union,** a modern coffee shop in the old Kress building, also on Dexter Avenue.

If you still have time and the literary inclinations, you may wish to make the pilgrimage to the Cottage Hill neighborhood to see the historic **Scott and Zelda Fitzgerald Museum.** Zelda was born in Montgomery in 1900 (her childhood friend Tallulah Bankhead was born there in 1902), and she and Scott came back to Montgomery to live for about six months from 1931 to 1932 in this house, when he was writing *Tender Is the Night* and Zelda began work on her only published novel, *Save Me the Waltz.* On display are some of Zelda's paintings, Scott's books, and various possessions and even clothing. Plan on an hour for this museum.

If you aren't a fan of the Fitzgeralds, then you may prefer spending some time strolling shopping in Cloverdale, which is home to several locally owned shops, galleries, restaurants, and other businesses along East Fairview Avenue. But the area's large, historic homes may be familiar to you if you've seen the movie *Big Fish,* which was filmed here in 2003. You can also take a break at **Cafe Louisa,** a bakery that also serves great coffee.

Downtown Montgomery doesn't roll up the sidewalks at night. In fact, downtown is home to many popular bars and restaurants, including Montgomery's only production brewery, **Common Bond**. You can have a pint or a flight, and if you're hungry bring over something from **Bibb Street Pizza Company**, next door. If you're looking for a more formal dinner, downtown has many other choices, including **Wintzell's Oyster House**, a branch of the Mobile original, and **Central**, one of the city's most popular upscale restaurants, which specializes in steaks, chicken, and fish from its wood-fired oven. If you're not ready to call it a night, **Aviator Bar**, also downtown, is a local favorite.

Day 2

You'll want to set aside a day for Montgomery's two signature attractions (**The Legacy Museum** and the **National Memorial for Peace and Justice**), which you can visit in either order. The museum is busy enough that you'll need a timed ticket, and you may want to go early because it can be very busy, especially on weekends, but you'll have a fulfilling experience regardless of the order of your visits. The museum, housed in a former slave warehouse, covers lynching, racial segregation ("Jim Crow") laws, and mass incarceration, the three primary successors to slavery in the United States. It takes a while to digest all there is to see and read here, and it's well worth every moment you spend.

After the museum, you'll need a break to decompress and unwind. You can sit in the adjacent cafe, which shares space with a wonderful bookstore, or you can head out to lunch somewhere like **Martin's** (if you are looking for delicious fried chicken, this is definitely your spot). Unfortunately, it's not open on Saturday. If you have a car and don't mind driving a bit, **Southern Comfort** in Hull (out near the airport) is a popular spot for barbecue and other southern comfort foods (including its own pretty good fried chicken), and it's open every day.

When you're ready, head back downtown and visit the National Memorial for Peace and Justice, which documents and memorializes the thousands of lynchings that occurred since the Civil War. The memorial, set on six acres, demands a slow pace, which is fitting for the subject matter. A slow walk through the memorial takes at least 60 to 90 minutes.

Have dinner at **Vintage Year** in the Cloverdale neighborhood, a favorite special-occasion spot in Montgomery that began as a wine shop. The wine list has won awards, while the restaurant's food has been recognized by the James Beard Society. You'll need reservations. After dinner, if you aren't ready for bed, head over to **Leroy,** also in Cloverdale. It may look like a dive, but you'll find a surprisingly long list of craft cocktails and 18 beers on tap. If you are looking for a little Williamsburg, Brooklyn atmosphere in Montgomery, you'll find it here.

Day 3

You aren't done with Montgomery yet. Your final day can go in any number of directions, but especially if it's Sunday, you won't want to miss the chance to have a good southern breakfast. If you can manage to get up early (and even if you can't), head over to **Cahawba House** to fortify yourself for the day. If you're looking for some delicious biscuits and gravy, grits, cinnamon beignets, locally made jams and jellies, or Conecuh sausages, you may find yourself standing in a long line to order at the counter. It's definitely worth the wait.

Just around the corner is the **New-South Bookstore,** an excellent source for anything related to Southern history or literature. They will also be happy to give you advice on what to see and do.

The final don't-miss attraction in Montgomery is the **Rosa Parks Museum**, which offers a look at the beginning of the Civil Rights era. The museum is not just about Ms. Parks but rather all the people and events associated with the year-long Montgomery bus boycott that lasted from December 1955 to December 1956. If you have time, it's a short walk over to the **Freedom Rides Museum,** in Montgomery's former Greyhound bus station. These museums are worth at least an hour, perhaps more.

If your interests are primarily in the Civil Rights era, once you have hit the Montgomery highlights of the Civil Rights Trail, you may want to explore further. Selma is about an hour west of Montgomery. The **National Voting Rights Museum and Institute** is here, as is the infamous Edmund Pettus Bridge, named after the Confederate general and grand wizard of the Ku Klux Klan.

If you are interested in Alabama history, you are in luck. There's the **Museum of Alabama,** which covers the history of the state in some detail. It's near the **Alabama State Capitol** (the building is open weekdays and Saturdays, and there are regularly scheduled guided tours on Saturday). You may especially want to visit the **Goat Hill Museum Store** inside the Capitol building.

Are you are a baseball fan? If you are visiting between April and August, there's a pretty good chance the Montgomery Biscuits will be playing during your visit. The games are held in the Montgomery Riverwalk Stadium. How about Hank Williams? The native son is memorialized in the **Hank Williams Museum** in downtown Montgomery.

And if you are looking for culture, the **Alabama Shakespeare Festival** offers live theater performances, both locally developed and touring productions, year-round (Shakespeare performances are usually in March and April) in a theater in Wynton M. Blount Cultural Park.

Whatever you do, try to find time to get out to **Capitol Oyster Bar**. It's decidedly off the beaten path but has a scenic, riverfront location and is a wonderful destination for fresh fried seafood at lunch and dinner, open Wednesday through Sunday. On Sundays, you'll almost always find some kind of blues performance around 5 pm, which typically has a cover charge (though you can eat inside without paying the cover).

Recommendations

Sights

Alabama State Capitol. ⊠ *600 Dexter Ave., Montgomery, AL* ☎ *334/242–3935* ⊕ *ahc. alabama.gov/alabama-state-capitol.aspx* 🖼 *Free.*

Civil Rights Memorial. ⊠ *400 Washington Ave., Montgomery, AL* ☎ *334/956–8200* ⊕ *www.splcenter.org* 🖼 *$2* ⊙ *Closed Sun.*

Dexter Parsonage Museum. ⊠ *309 S. Jackson St. Montgomery, AL* ☎ *334/261–3270* ⊕ *www.dexterkingmemorial.org* 🖼 *$8* ⊙ *Closed Sun.*

Freedom Rides Museum. ⊠ *210 S. Court St., Montgomery, AL* ☎ *334/414–8647* ⊕ *ahc.alabama.gov/properties/freedom-rides/freedomrides.aspx* 🖼 *$5.*

Hank Williams Museum. ⊠ *118 Commerce St., Montgomery, AL* ☎ *334/262–3600* ⊕ *www.thehankwilliamsmuseum.net* 🖼 *$10.*

King Memorial Baptist Church. ⊠ *454 Dexter Ave., Montgomery, AL* ☎ *334/263–3970* ⊕ *www.dexterkingmemorial.org* 🖼 *Free* ⊙ *Closed Sun.*

The Legacy Museum. ⊠ *115 Coosa St., Montgomery, AL* ☎ *334/386–9100* ⊕ *museumandmemorial.eji.org/museum* 🖼 *$8* ⊙ *Closed Tues.*

Little White House. ⊠ *401 Little White House Rd., Warm Springs, GA* ☎ *706/655–5870* ⊕ *gastateparks.org/littlewhitehouse* 🖼 *$12.*

Museum of Alabama. ⊠ *624 Washington Ave., Montgomery, AL* ☎ *334/242–4435* ⊕ *www.museum.alabama.gov* 🖼 *Free* ⊙ *Closed Sun.*

National Memorial for Peace and Justice. ⊠ *417 Caroline St., Montgomery, AL* ☎ *334/386–9100* ⊕ *www.museumand-memorial.eji.org* 🖼 *$5* ⊙ *Closed Tues.*

National Voting Rights Museum and Institute. ⊠ *6 U.S. Hwy. 80 E, Selma, AL* ☎ *334/526–4340* ⊕ *www.nvrmi.com* 🖼 *$7.*

Rosa Parks Museum. ⊠ *252 Montgomery St., Montgomery, AL* ☎ *334/241–8615* ⊕ *www.troy.edu* 🖼 *$8* ⊙ *Closed Sun.*

Scott and Zelda Fitzgerald Museum. ⊠ *919 Felder Ave., Montgomery, AL* ☎ *334/264–4222* ⊕ *www.thefitzgeraldmuseum.org* 🖼 *$10* ⊙ *Closed Mon. and Tues.*

🍴 Restaurants

Bibb Street Pizza Company. $ *Average main: $19* ✉ *424 Bibb St., Montgomery, AL* ☎ *334/593–7080* ⊕ *www.bibbstpizza-co.com.*

Bottega Cafe. $ *Average main: $18* ✉ *2240 Highland Ave. S, Birmingham, AL* ☎ *205/939–1000* ⊕ *bottegarestaurant.com.*

Cahawba House. $ *Average main: $18* ✉ *31 S. Court St., Montgomery, AL* ☎ *334/356–1877* ⊕ *www.cahawbahouse.com* ⊘ *Closed weekends.*

Central. $ *Average main: $29* ✉ *129 Coosa St., Montgomery, AL* ☎ *334/517–1155* ⊕ *www.central129coosa.com* ⊘ *Closed Sun.*

Chris' Hot Dogs. $ *Average main: $8* ✉ *138 Dexter Ave., Montgomery, AL* ☎ *334/265–6850* ⊕ *www.chrishotdogs.com* ⊘ *Closed Sun.*

Dinner's Ready by Chad. $ *Average main: $7* ✉ *5928 Spring St., Warm Springs, GA* ☎ *706/655–2066* ⊕ *www.dinnersreadyby-chad.com* ⊘ *Closed Sun.*

Martin's. $ *Average main: $10* ✉ *1796 Carter Hill Rd., Montgomery, AL* ☎ *334/265–1767* ⊘ *Closed Sat.*

Southern Comfort. $ *Average main: $12* ✉ *210 Wasden Rd., Hope Hull, AL* ☎ *334/280–0012* ⊘ *No dinner Sun.*

Vintage Year. $ *Average main: $30* ✉ *405 Cloverdale Rd. Montgomery, AL* ☎ *334/819–7215* ⊕ *www.vymgm.com* ⊘ *Closed Sun and Mon.*

Wintzell's Oyster House. $ *Average main: $18* ✉ *105 Commerce St., Montgomery, AL* ☎ *334/262–4257* ⊕ *www.wintzell-soysterhouse.com.*

☕ Coffee and Quick Bites

Cafe Louisa. $ *Average main: $5* ✉ *503 Cloverdale Rd., Montgomery AL* ☎ *334/356–1212* ⊕ *www.cafelouisa.com.*

Prevail Union. $ *Average main: $5* ✉ *39 Dexter Ave., Montgomery, AL* ☎ *334/416–8399* ⊕ *www.prevailunion-mgm.com* ⊘ *No dinner Sun.*

🛏 Hotels

DoubleTree. $ *Rooms from: $122* ✉ *Madison Ave., Montgomery, AL* ☎ *334/245–2320* ⊕ *www.hilton.com* ⦿ *No meals.*

Hampton Inn & Suites. $ *Rooms from: $141* ✉ *100 Commerce St., Montgomery, AL* ☎ *334/265–1010* ⊕ *www.hilton.com* ⦿ *Free breakfast.*

Renaissance. $ *Rooms from: $190* ✉ *201 Tallapoosa St., Montgomery, AL* ☎ *334/481–5000* ⊕ *www.marriott.com* ⦿ *No meals.*

🍸 Nightlife

Aviator Bar. ✉ *166 Commerce St., Montgomery, AL* ☎ *334/284–2867.*

Common Bond. ✉ *424 Bibb St., Montgomery, AL* ☎ *334/676–2287* ⊕ *www.commonbondbrewers.com.*

Leroy. ✉ *2752 Boultier St., Montgomery, AL* ☎ *334/356–7127* ⊕ *www.leroylounge.com.*

🎭 Performing Arts

Alabama Shakespeare Festival. ✉ *1 Festival Dr., Montgomery, AL* ☎ *334/271–5353* ⊕ *www.asf.net.*

🛍 Shopping

NewSouth Bookstore. ✉ *105 S. Court St., Montgomery, AL* ☎ *334/834–3556* ⊕ *www.newsouthbooks.com.*

Myrtle Beach, SC

Myrtle Beach is 175 miles (approx. 3½ hours) from Charlotte.

It's no big city, but Myrtle Beach has bright lights aplenty. The Grand Strand boasts 60 miles of beaches, but just as many people visit for the golf, go-karts and generous buffets. Behind the glitz, there's deep culture and wild nature to explore. This is where shag dancing began, and you can still cut a rug with the old-timers at the clubs along Main Street in North Myrtle Beach. Several piers offer productive fishing, and Huntington Beach State Park is home to dozens of alligators that lie around lazily in the sun. Hungry diners choose from platters of Calabash-style fried seafood, piled high, and an endless array of pancake houses. Myrtle Beach is a beachside Gatlinburg, or Las Vegas sans the sin. The best approach? Relax and embrace this vacation-oriented stretch of coast in all its gaudy glory.

Planning

GETTING THERE AND BACK

There's no interstate to Myrtle Beach, so sit back and enjoy the scenery through the backroads of the Carolina Sandhills and Pee Dee regions. Cue up The Tams and Chairmen of the Board for a classic beach music playlist as you drive southeast, roughly paralleling the North and South Carolina border. Head out of Charlotte on U.S.74 E to Monroe, then stay on 74 to Wadesboro, crossing the border to Cheraw, or drop onto Route 601 to drive through the heart of the Pee Dee (and pass directly alongside the Darlington Raceway NASCAR track). Driving time is the same, so make the trip part of the adventure and try one route for each direction. The diverging roads meet in Marion, South Carolina. From there, it's a straight shot down Highway 501 to the heart of Myrtle Beach.

WHEN TO GO

The Grand Strand comes alive in the summer, when families descend from across the Eastern Seaboard. Although many attractions close or limit hours in the winter, you'll find significantly reduced hotel prices, restaurant wait times, golf green fees, and beach crowds between October and March (and daytime temps are generally more comfortable than during the sweltering peak season of midsummer).

WHERE TO STAY

The majority of Myrtle Beach hotels are oceanfront high rises, of varying levels of swank. Many tend to be jam packed with families during the summer months. For an adult getaway, **Ocean 22** features modern decor, suites with balconies overlooking the Atlantic and a classy covered beachfront pool area. If you have kids in tow, **Caravelle Resort** is an affordably priced classic that features a waterpark, lazy river, and multiple pools.

Day 1

Leave Charlotte after an early breakfast to arrive hungry, and head straight to **Rockefeller's Raw Bar.** Grab a seat in a distinctive captain's chair barstool. The no-reservations joint has lines out the door at dinnertime for its steamed scallops, clams, and mussels, so revel in your leisurely lunch. If you're running behind or don't eat seafood, **Dagwood's Deli** builds a mean loaded sub.

Spend the rest of the afternoon soaking up the sun on the beach or at your hotel's pool, unless you're ready to explore. **Helicopter Adventures** offers 2-mile aerial tours for $20 that help you get your bearings. Directly next door is **Broadway Grand Prix,** where seven go-kart tracks let you channel your inner Dale Earnhardt.

In the evening, take a sunset drive to **Murrells Inlet Marsh Walk,** where diners take their pick from seven waterfront

More than 60 miles of beaches make up the Grand Strand at Myrtle Beach.

restaurants. Enjoy the stroll across the salt marsh and the outdoor live music, but then head two minutes further south to your reservation at **Costa,** a cozy Italian spot bathed in cool blue hues. Costa's kitchen impresses with its focus on local seafood, paired with an excellent wine list. For a more casual option, head to the **Hot Fish Club,** a creekfront institution where live bands play the sun to sleep over the marsh.

Cap the night with a ride on the **Myrtle Beach SkyWheel,** taking in views across the boardwalk and ocean from 200 feet in the air, or go dancing at the **Spanish Galleon,** where the music appeals to everyone by varying from modern EDM to Carolina Beach music from the 1970s.

Day 2

Migrate from your oceanfront hotel room to an oceanfront table. Order a crab and shrimp Seafarer's Omelet at **Sea Captain's House,** a classic joint in a beachside

mansion now dwarfed by high rises on either side.

If you're a golfer, save Sea Captain's House for lunch and beat the heat with an early tee time at **Pine Lakes Country Club,** the granddaddy of Myrtle Beach links and the place where *Sports Illustrated* magazine was born. Otherwise, sleep off breakfast with a lazy morning on the beach, or cast a line from the **Cherry Grove Pier**—fishing rods, tackle and bait are all available for rent on-site.

Head to Broadway at the Beach for lunch, where options include sushi and local beer at **The Grumpy Monk** and pulled pork BBQ platters at **Sweet Carolina's.**

With satiated bellies, catch a dive show at **Ripley's Aquarium,** or get your adrenaline pumping with a high-speed ride at **Beach Rider Jet Boats.** Then it's time for more beach/pool R&R before a big night out. Make reservations at **The Parson's Table,** a chef-owned, historic church-turned-restaurant where a farm-to-table ethos drives the surf-and-turf menu.

When the sun goes down, head to Main Street in North Myrtle Beach for a night of club hopping that's distinctly South Carolina. **Fat Harold's Beach Club** is home base, where the decor and dance floor feel like stepping back in time to a simpler age when teenagers and old-timers all shagged to the same familiar tunes (they still do that here). Hop across the street to **Duck's Beach Club,** where live cover bands keep hips moving, before dropping into **OD Arcade & Lounge** for more shag dancing or a game of pool.

Day 3

Shag late and sleep in later. When you finally emerge, head straight to the **House of Blues** at Barefoot Landing, where the "Gospel Brunch" on Sunday reinvigorates the spirit with Southern gospel singing and an all-you-can-eat buffet.

Today is recovery day—no need to push it. Play 18 leisurely holes at **Hawaiian Rumble Minigolf,** lorded over by a 40-foot volcano and home to the annual Masters tournament of minigolf.

Round out your trip with a visit to **Huntington Beach State Park** and Atalaya, the ruins of a sprawling early-20th-century estate, and gawk at the alligators that laze around the freshwater lake. Take a last dip in the ocean before swinging through the **Hammock Shops Village** in Pawley's Island for a souvenir rope hammock. Before hitting the road, work yourself into a food coma at **Hog Heaven,** where the buffet tempts you to go way overboard with both fried shrimp and pulled pork. You're navigating back roads to get home, so leave yourself some daylight for the scenic drive. Eat a salad for dinner—or what the heck, scarf down that leftover barbecue—before collapsing into bed.

Recommendations

Sights

Cherry Grove Pier. ✉ *3500 N. Ocean Blvd., North Myrtle Beach, SC* ☎ *843/249–1625* ⊕ *www.cherrygrovepier.com.*

Hawaiian Rumble Minigolf. ✉ *3210 Hwy. 17 S, North Myrtle Beach, SC* ☎ *843/272–7812* ⊕ *www.hawaiianrumbleminigolf. com* 💲 *$14.*

Huntington Beach State Park. ✉ *16148 Ocean Hwy., Murrells Inlet, SC* ☎ *843/237–4440* ⊕ *southcarolinaparks. com/huntington-beach* 💲 *$8.*

Myrtle Beach SkyWheel. ✉ *1110 N. Ocean Blvd., Myrtle Beach, SC* ☎ *843/839–9200* ⊕ *www.skywheelmb.com* 💲 *$14.*

Ripley's Aquarium. ✉ *1110 Celebrity Circle, Myrtle Beach, SC* ☎ *843/916–0888* ⊕ *www.ripleyaquariums.com* 💲 *$14.*

Restaurants

Costa. 💲 *Average main: $13* ✉ *4606 U.S. 17 BUS, Murrells Inlet, SC* ☎ *843/299–1970* ⊕ *www.costamyrtlebeach.com* ⊙ *No lunch.*

Dagwood's Deli. 💲 *Average main: $9* ✉ *400 Mr. Joe White Ave, Myrtle Beach, SC* ☎ *843/448–0100* ⊕ *www.dagwoods-deli.com* ⊙ *Closed Sun.*

The Grumpy Monk. 💲 *Average main: $7* ✉ *4545 U.S. 501, Myrtle Beach, SC* ☎ *843/236–5888* ⊕ *www.grumpymonk-myrtlebeach.com.*

Hog Heaven. 💲 *Average main: $9* ✉ *7147 Ocean Hwy., Pawleys Island, SC* ☎ *843/237–7444* ⊕ *www.hogheaveninc. com.*

Hot Fish Club. 💲 *Average main: $11* ✉ *4911 U.S. 17 BUS, Murrells Inlet, SC* ☎ *843/357–9175* ⊕ *www.hotfishclub.com* ⊙ *Closed Mon.*

House of Blues. $ *Average main: $18* ✉ *4640 Hwy. 17 S, North Myrtle Beach, SC* ☎ *843/272–3000* ⊕ *www.houseofblues.com* ☾ *No lunch.*

The Parson's Table. $ *Average main: $12* ✉ *4305 State Rd. S-26-850, Little River, SC* ☎ *843/249–3702* ⊕ *www.parsonstable.com* ☾ *Closed Sun.*

Rockefeller's Raw Bar. $ *Average main: $14* ✉ *3613 Hwy. 17 S, North Myrtle Beach, SC* ☎ *843/361–9677* ⊕ *www.rockefellersrawbar.com.*

Sea Captain's House. $ *Average main: $14* ✉ *3002 N. Ocean Blvd., Myrtle Beach, SC* ☎ *843/448–8082* ⊕ *www.seacaptains.com* ☾ *Closed Sun.*

Sweet Carolina's. $ *Average main: $14* ✉ *Broadway at the Beach, 1207 Celebrity Circle, Myrtle Beach, SC* ☎ *843/444–5522* ⊕ *www.broadwayatthebeach.com.*

Hotels

Caravelle Resort. $ *Rooms from: $69* ✉ *6900 N. Ocean Blvd., Myrtle Beach, SC* ☎ *843/310–3420* ⊕ *www.thecaravelle.com* ❢⃝❘ *No meals.*

Ocean View 22. $ *Rooms from: $163* ✉ *2200 N. Ocean Blvd., Myrtle Beach, SC* ☎ *843/848–0022* ⊕ *www3.hilton.com* ❢⃝❘ *No meals.*

Nightlife

Duck's Beach Club. ✉ *231 Main St., North Myrtle Beach, SC* ☎ *843/663–3858* ⊕ *www.ducksatoceandrive.com.*

Fat Harold's Beach Club. ✉ *212 Main St., North Myrtle Beach, SC* ☎ *843/249–5779* ⊕ *www.fatharolds.com.*

OD Arcade & Lounge. ✉ *100 S. Ocean Blvd., North Myrtle Beach, SC* ☎ *843/249–6460* ⊕ *www.odarcade.com.*

Spanish Galleon. ✉ *98 N. Ocean Blvd., North Myrtle Beach, SC* ☎ *843/249–1048* ⊕ *www.spanishgalleonbeachclub.com.*

Shopping

Barefoot Landing. ✉ *4898 Hwy. 17 S, North Myrtle Beach, SC* ☎ *843/272–8349* ⊕ *www.bflanding.com.*

Broadway at the Beach. ✉ *1325 Celebrity Circle, Myrtle Beach, SC* ☎ *843/444–3200* ⊕ *www.broadwayatthebeach.com.*

Hammock Shops Village. ✉ *10880 Ocean Hwy., Pawleys Island, SC* ☎ *843/350–2220* ⊕ *www.thehammockshops.com.*

Murrells Inlet Marsh Walk. ✉ *4025 Hwy. 17 Business, Murrells Inlet, SC* ☎ *No phone* ⊕ *www.marshwalk.com.*

Activities

Beach Rider Jet Boats. ✉ *1325 Celebrity Circle, Myrtle Beach, SC* ☎ *843/839–2883* ⊕ *beachrideramusement.com* ✇ *Rentals from $20.*

Broadway Gran Prix. ✉ *1820 21st Ave. N, Myrtle Beach, SC* ☎ *843/839–4080* ⊕ *broadwaygrandprix.com* ✇ *Rides from $20.*

Helicopter Adventures. ✉ *1860 21st Ave. N, Myrtle Beach, SC* ☎ *800/359–4386* ⊕ *www.helicopteradventures.com* ✇ *Rides from $20.*

Pine Lakes Country Club. ✉ *5603 Granddaddy Dr., Myrtle Beach, SC* ☎ *843/315–7700* ⊕ *pinelakes.com* ✇ *Greens fees from $60.*

Nashville, TN

248 miles (approx. 3¾ hours) from Atlanta, 212 miles (approx. 3½ hours) from Memphis.

Tennessee's largest city, Nashville evokes ornate and flashy honky tonks and neon cowboy boot insignias, but it's also known for its classy speakeasies and craft cocktail bars. Go casual in smaller neighborhoods like Germantown and East Nashville, where you'll find dive

Nashville's offerings range from rough-and-ready honky-tonks to classy craft cocktail bars.

bars, record stores, and thrift shops. Like any southern city, expect charming residents, hot summers, and homestyle cooking. Teeming with musical and civil rights history, visitors can easily get lost in Nashville culture. By all means reserve a table at the upscale chef-driven joints, but try the hot chicken that locals swear by.

Planning

GETTING THERE AND BACK
From Atlanta, take I–75 N to I–24 W. The drive is just under four hours.

It's similarly and easy and directly shot on I–40 from Memphis to Nashville via I–40.

INSPIRATION
If you aren't cranking up some country music, then you aren't adequately preparing yourself for your arrival in Nashville. Might we suggest a couple of the great female voices to put you in the mood. Perhaps Dolly Parton's first solo master album, *Coat of Many Colors,* or The

Definitive Colleciton by Patsy Cline. For something completely differently, there's *Modern Sounds in Country and Western Music* by Ray Charles (yes, that Ray Charles). If you are looking for something more contemporary, then try *Taking the Long Road* from The Chicks (formerly the Dixie Chicks) or *Carnival Ride* from Carrie Underwood. Even if you get stuck in traffic, you'll still be entertained.

PIT STOPS
About halfway between Atlanta and Nashville is Chattanooga, Tennessee, where you can break for a quick bite downtown, or to take in the Tennessee river from the waterfront.

WHEN TO GO
Winter is the off-season, but spring is less crowded and more affordable than summer, and has the best weather. Nashville is a popular stopover in mid-June on the way to Bonnaroo Music & Arts Festival in Manchester, Tennessee.

WHERE TO STAY

With locations in Brooklyn and the Catskills in addition to Nashville, the Southwestern-inspired **Urban Cowboy** in a Victorian mansion is a trusted place to stay. Claw-foot tubs and A-frame ceilings, plus bold patterns and stunning natural light, complete the understated luxury of each unique suite. The **Fairlane Hotel** is another great option, especially for a view of the city from one of the many stories in this landmark midcentury building. **Noelle** downtown, part of the Tribute Portfolio, is a minimalist's paradise, and boasts the rooftop bar Rare Bird, plus an in-house coffee shop, Drug Store Coffee, and their Trade Room bar.

Day 1

After a long drive from Atlanta, embrace the chance to indulge in this lively southern city. Pull up in time for lunch at **Prince's Hot Chicken.** Though it may not get the same amount of press as **Hattie B's,** locals argue that it is superior. Plus, the lines aren't as long. Why not try both and decide for yourself?

Next head to Lower Broad to experience the honky tonks you've heard all about. **Tootsie's Orchid Lounge,** notable for famous past performers like Willie Nelson, is a great place to get a moonshine buzz in the afternoon and listen to some country covers. You won't know the local performers by name, but they're musical deftness will blow you away.

Class it up for a dinner at **Husk,** an absolute Southern staple with locations in Savannah and Charleston. Located downtown in an historic mansion, dining here is an experience in itself. Expect classic southern dishes with a contemporary twist. Don't forget to order cornbread for the table. If there's no room, head to **Hermitage Cafe.**

For a nightcap, have a craft cocktail at the meticulously designed **Pinewood Social,** a modern industrial-chic joint, or on the rooftop at **Rare Bird.**

Day 2

Wake up with biscuits and coffee at **Biscuit Love** (they have a few locations throughout the city). You'd be remiss not to try their bacon and grits. For a quick bite to go, **Frothy Monkey** coffee shop is a great option (multiple locations).

Take a quick 15-minute day trip to Music Valley, home to the **Grand Ole Opry.** Shop for antiques and mid-century furniture, and wander through the gardens of **Gaylord Opryland Resort.** Dance to live music at The **Nashville Palace,** then feast on some delicious barbecue at **Caney Fork River Valley Grille** (they also have live music). You also can't go wrong at **Cock of the Walk.**

Keep the music alive by brushing up on a country star at the **Johnny Cash Museum** and **Patsy Cline Museum** (though they share a building, the museums are separate and each charges its own admission). They're a little pricey, you won't regret a peek into the lives of either of these Nashville legends.

Brace yourself for a mouthwatering dinner at **Rolf & Daughters,** which serves shared plates from a daily changing menu. The ambience almost rivals the food, but the innovative creations, including homemade pastas and sorbet, are the number one draw. A good backup: the highly lauded **Catbird Seat.**

Tonight is your night to go out on the town. Start with a specialty cocktail at the exclusive, limited-capacity **The Patterson House** speakeasy, followed by a night in Downtown Nashville. See live music at **3rd and Lindsley,** then explore the many floors of **Acme Feed and Seed.**

4

Southeast NASHVILLE, TN

Day 3

Replenish yourself after a night out at **Dose Cafe and Dram Bar** in East Nashville, which serves specialty coffee and teas, and baked goods. Another great option is **Five Daughters Bakery.**

Next get some fresh air strolling **Centennial Park,** where you can check out the **Parthenon,** a replica of the Grecian monument. Have a healthy lunch at **Butcher and Bee,** which emphasizes local ingredients. You can also sample fresh-from-the-smoker favorites at **Edley's BBQ.**

Head to East Nashville to peruse record shops and thrift stores. Stop in at the Jack White–owned **Third Man Records,** where you can shop for vinyl or record your own. Even if you don't buy anything (they mostly sell music merch) the building itself is interesting to explore and a great photo-op.

Before hitting the road, get a giant, New York–style slice and cannoli at **Five Points Pizza.**

Recommendations

👁 Sights

Centennial Park. ✉ *2500 West End Ave., Nashville, TN* ☎ *615/862–8400* 🌐 *www.nashville.gov/Parks-and-Recreation/Parks/Centennial-Park.aspx* 🎟 *Free.*

Johnny Cash Museum. ✉ *119 3rd Ave. S, Nashville, TN* ☎ *615/645–6358* 🌐 *www.johnnycashmuseum.com* 🎟 *$17.*

Parthenon. ✉ *2500 West End Ave., Nashville, TN* ☎ *615/862–8431* 🌐 *www.nashville.gov/Parks-and-Recreation/Parthenon.aspx* 🎟 *$6* 🕒 *Closed Mon.*

Patsy Cline Museum. ✉ *119 3rd Ave. S, Nashville, TN* ☎ *615/454–4722* 🌐 *www.patsymuseum.com* 🎟 *$19.*

🍴 Restaurants

Biscuit Love. [$] *Average main: $11* ✉ *316 11th Ave. S, Nashville, TN* ☎ *615/490–9584* 🌐 *biscuitlove.com* 🕒 *No dinner.*

Butcher and Bee. [$] *Average main: $12* ✉ *902 Main St., Nashville, TN* ☎ *615/226–3322* 🌐 *www.butcherandbee.com/nashville* 🕒 *Closed Tues. and Wed. No lunch Mon. and Thurs.–Sat.*

Caney Fork River Valley Grille. [$] *Average main: $11* ✉ *2400 Music Valley Dr., Nashville, TN* ☎ *615/724–1200* 🌐 *www.caneyforkrestaurant.com* 🕒 *No lunch Mon.–Thurs.*

Catbird Seat. [$] *Average main: $15* ✉ *1711 Division St., Nashville, TN* ☎ *615/810–8200* 🌐 *www.thecatbirdseatrestaurant.com* 🕒 *Closed Sun.–Tues. No lunch.*

Cock of the Walk. [$] *Average main: $25* ✉ *2624 Music Valley Dr., Nashville, TN* ☎ *615/889–1930* 🌐 *www.cockofthewalkrestaurant.com* 🕒 *No lunch Mon.–Thurs.*

Edley's BBQ. [$] *Average main: $12* ✉ *4500 Murphy Rd., Nashville, TN* ☎ *615/873–4085* 🌐 *www.edleysbbq.com.*

Five Points Pizza. [$] *Average main: $7* ✉ *1012 Woodland St., Nashville, TN* ☎ *615/915–4174* 🌐 *fivepointspizza.com.*

Hattie B's. [$] *Average main: $12* ✉ *112 19th Ave. S, Nashville, TN* ☎ *615/678–4794* 🌐 *hattieb.com* 🕒 *No dinner Sun.*

Hermitage Cafe. [$] *Average main: $10* ✉ *71 Hermitage Ave., Nashville, TN* ☎ *615/254–8871* 🌐 *hermitage-cafe.com.*

Husk. [$] *Average main: $32* ✉ *37 Rutledge St.* ☎ *615/256–6565* 🌐 *husknashville.com.*

The Pharmacy. [$] *Average main: $7* ✉ *731 Mcferrin Ave., Nashville, TN* ☎ *615/712–9517* 🌐 *thepharmacynashville.com.*

Prince's Hot Chicken. [$] *Average main: $13* ✉ *5814 Nolensville Pike, Nashville,*

TN ☎ 615/810–9388 🌐 www.princeshotchicken.com 🕑 Closed Sun.

Rolf & Daughters. [$] *Average main: $16* ✉ *700 Taylor St., Nashville, TN* ☎ *615/866–9897* 🌐 *www.rolfanddaughters.com.*

Coffee and Quick Bites

Dose Cafe and Dram Bar. [$] *Average main: $5* ✉ *1400 McGavock Pk, Nashville, TN* ☎ *615/730–8625* 🌐 *dosenashville.com* 🕑 *No dinner.*

Five Daughters Bakery. [$] *Average main: $7* ✉ *1110 Caruthers Ave., Nashville, TN* ☎ *615/490–6554* 🌐 *fivedaughtersbakery.com.*

Frothy Monkey. [$] *Average main: $6* ✉ *12th Ave. S, Nashville, TN* ☎ *615/600–4756* 🌐 *frothymonkey.com.*

Hotels

Fairlane Hotel. [$] *Rooms from: $369* ✉ *401 Union St., Nashville, TN* ☎ *615/988–8511* 🌐 *www.fairlanehotel.com* 🍴 *No meals.*

Gaylord Opryland Resort. [$] *Rooms from: $229* ✉ *2800 Opryland Dr., Nashville, TN* ☎ *615/889–1000* 🌐 *www.marriott.com/hotels/travel/bnago-gaylord-opryland-resort-and-convention-center* 🍴 *No meals.*

Noelle. [$] *Rooms from: $409* ✉ *200 4th Ave. N, Nashville, TN* ☎ *615/649–5000* 🌐 *www.marriott.com/hotels/travel/bnatx-noelle-nashville-a-tribute-portfolio-hotel* 🍴 *No meals.*

Urban Cowboy. [$] *Rooms from: $295* ✉ *1603 Woodland St., Nashville, TN* ☎ *347/840–0525* 🌐 *urbancowboy.com* 🍴 *Free breakfast.*

Nightlife

Acme Feed and Seed. ✉ *101 Broadway, Nashville, TN* ☎ *615/915–0888* 🌐 *www.acmefeedandseed.com.*

Nashville Palace. ✉ *2611 McGavock Pk., Nashville, TN* ☎ *615/889–1541* 🌐 *www.nashville-palace.com.*

The Patterson House. ✉ *1711 Division St., Nashville, TN* ☎ *615/636–7724* 🌐 *www.thepattersonnashville.com.*

Pinewood Social. ✉ *33 Peabody St., Nashville, TN* ☎ *615/751–8111* 🌐 *www.pinewoodsocial.com.*

Rare Bird. ✉ *Noelle Hotel, 200 4th Ave. N, Nashville, TN* ☎ *615/649–5000* 🌐 *www.noelle-nashville.com/dine-drink/rare-bird-rooftop-bar.*

3rd and Lindsley. ✉ *818 3rd Ave. S, Nashville, TN* ☎ *615/259–9891* 🌐 *www.3rdandlindsley.com.*

Tootsie's Orchid Lounge. ✉ *422 Broadway, Nashville, TN* ☎ *615/726–0463* 🌐 *www.tootsies.net.*

Performing Arts

Grand Ole Opry. ✉ *2804 Opryland Dr., Nashville, TN* ☎ *615/871–6779* 🌐 *www.opry.com* 🎟 *$55.*

Shopping

Third Man Records. ✉ *623 7th Ave. S, Nashville, TN* ☎ *615/891–4393* 🌐 *www.thirdmanrecords.com.*

The Outer Banks, NC

363 miles (approx. 5½ hours) from Charlotte.

Take a drive through the thin chain of barrier islands that make up the Outer Banks and it's easy to see why this area is such a coveted vacation spot. Charming towns, historic lighthouses, and well-preserved coastlines—full of pristine beaches, wild terrain, and unique flora and fauna—make the Outer Banks a special place. The extent of development varies from town to town, and many

Bodie Island Lighthouse has illuminated Cape Hatteras National Seashore since 1872.

corners of the Outer Banks—from the protected beaches of Cape Hatteras National Seashore, to the wild mustang sanctuaries of Corolla—feel completely untouched. And it's not just nature here: the barrier islands are dotted with lively seafood shacks, funky boutiques, and historic memorials that tell of colorful coastal legends.

Planning

GETTING THERE AND BACK

Heading east on I-85, you'll reach U.S. 64 E, which will connect you to Nags Head via Roanoke Island. Travelling within the Outer Banks themselves, the only main road is U.S. 12.

PIT STOP

About halfway to Nags Head, you can stop in Chapel Hill and check out the restaurants, shops, and museums along Franklin Street, the bustling main drag of this popular college town.

WHEN TO GO

Many businesses in the Outer Banks—especially on the north and south ends—shut down for the off season, which usually includes parts of January and February (but can extend from November to March). The height of summer comes with crowds at the beaches, inflated lodging prices and creating congestion on U.S. 12, so it's best to aim for a sweet spot in between.

WHERE TO STAY

The historic **Sanderling Resort** rules the northern end of the islands, and provides a peaceful stay with a bird sanctuary, kayak expeditions, and some luxury touches at its pool, spa, and restaurants. To the south, The **Inn on Pamlico Sound** is smaller but very elegant and close to the wild beaches of Cape Hatteras National Seashore. The **First Colony Inn** is a more centrally located choice, in Nags Head, with lots of colonial hotel charm. Other good options in the OBX are motels like the **Surfside Hotel.**

Day 1

Arriving from Charlotte on U.S. 64, the first beach town you'll reach is Nags Head. Have lunch at the **Blue Moon Beach Grill,** great for fried seafood and Southern comforts, and a lively, colorful spot that is sure to get you in the vacation mood.

While in Nags Head, take a minute to orient yourself. U.S. 12 is the only main road in the Outer Banks, connecting the beaches, towns, and islands of the Outer Banks from north to south. To the north, you'll find small communities like Kitty Hawk, Duck, and Corolla; to the south, Rodanthe, Avon, Buxton, and Hatteras Island (connected by bridge), and finally Ocracoke Island, the southernmost inhabited island of the OBX that can only be reached by boat or plane.

Take today to explore the northern beaches and towns. Just before Kitty Hawk, in the community of Kill Devil Hills, you'll see the memorial to the Wrights Brothers and their first flight, launched here. The **Wright Brothers National Memorial** visitor center contains original artifacts and exhibits on the flying brothers and their planes.

Continue on U.S. 12 to Corolla, where wild horses roam freely. These Colonial Spanish Mustangs, once "stranded" here by early settlers, are federally protected and thrive in the isolated environments of the northern beaches. Get a closer look (but not too close: it is illegal and dangerous to touch the feral horses) with **Wild Horse Adventure Tours,** an off-road vehicle tour through the Mustang sanctuaries.

Heading south again, you'll pass the red-bricked Currituck Beach Lighthouse (OBX is famous for its historic lighthouses), where you can climb all 220 steps inside. The small resort town of Duck is the best place to stop for dinner. Slightly more elegant than most Outer Banks' choices, a farm-to-table dinner at **The Blue Point** comes with views of Currituck Sound

and exciting dishes of scallops, shrimp, and other fresh caught seafood.

Day 2

Grab a breakfast burrito at **Ten O Six**—or doughnuts and coffee from the original **Duck's Donuts**—before heading out for a long day exploring OBX's southern communities.

The southern reaches of the Outer Banks include some of the most pristine and wild coastline, evident as you approach the end of U.S. 12 and the Cape Hatteras National Seashore and **Pea Island National Wildlife Refuge.** Take some time here (before or after heading to Ocracoke) to watch for birds over the marshes, kayak the sound, or just walk the beach. At **Bodie Island Light Station,** you can climb yet another towering historic lighthouse.

Take the ferry (from Hatteras Village) to the small community of Ocracoke Island for wild ponies, the Ocracoke Lighthouse, and truly beautiful beaches. Before boarding the ferry, you can have lunch in Hatteras Village, at fun, casual seafood joints like **The Wreck** (by the ferry terminal) or **Dinky's Waterfront** (at the marina).

For dinner tonight, deviate from a more formal dinner for a shake and burger at **John's Drive In,** a real local treasure. John's is known for its hot dogs and burgers, as well as fresh fish sandwiches. If you have an extra sweet tooth, head to **Big Buck's** for homemade ice cream sundaes later.

Day 3

Since you have a long drive ahead of you today, avoid spending any time traveling U.S. 12, and explore Nag's Head and Roanoke Island instead. Have a relaxing morning in Nag's Head, hanging out on the beach or taking a catamaran cruise for dolphin sightings. Check out Jennette's Pier, stroll the nature trails and boardwalks, and visit the large dunes of **Jockey's Ridge State Park.** You can grab a breakfast sandwich at **Sam and Omie's,** a popular prefishing breakfast stop since 1937. Later, have lunch at laid-back **Tortuga's Lie,** for conch fritters, steamed seafood baskets, and burgers.

On your way back to the mainland, stop in Roanoke island. Sights in Roanoke focus on the island's history as the 1587 site of the first English settlement; a few years later, these settlers mysteriously vanished, and are referred to now as "The Lost Colony." Today, the site where they landed is the **Fort Raleigh National Historic Site,** and during summer evenings, the award-winning dramatic performance of "The Lost Colony" is held at the outdoor Waterside Theatre here. Other Roanoke attractions include the **North Carolina Aquarium on Roanoke Island, National Wildlife Refuges Visitor Center,** and a re-created **Elizabethan Gardens.** Stop at the **Lost Colony Brewery and Cafe** for one last local refreshment before heading home.

Recommendations

Sights

Bodie Island Light Station. ✉ *8210 Bodie Island Lighthouse Rd., Nags Head, NC* ☎ *252/441–5711* 🌐 *www.nps.gov/caha/planyourvisit/bils.htm* 🎟 *$10.*

Elizabethan Gardens. ✉ *1411 National Park Dr., Manteo, NC* ☎ *252/473–3234* 🌐 *www.elizabethangardens.org* 🎟 *$10.*

Fort Raleigh National Historic Site ✉ *1401 National Park Dr., Manteo, NC* ☎ *252/473–2111* 🌐 *www.nps.gov/fora/index.htm* 🎟 *Free.*

Jockey's Ridge State Park. ✉ *300 W. Carolista Dr., Nags Head, NC* ☎ *252/441–7132* 🌐 *www.ncparks.gov/jockeys-ridge-state-park* 🎟 *Free.*

National Wildlife Refuges Visitor Center. ✉ *100 Conservation Way, Manteo, NC* ☎ *252/473–1131* 🌐 *www.fws.gov/ncgatewayvc* 🎟 *Free.*

North Carolina Aquarium on Roanoke Island. ✉ *374 Airport Rd., Manteo, NC* ☎ *252/475–2300* 🌐 *www.ncaquariums.com/roanoke-island* 🎟 *$13.*

Pea Island National Wildlife Refuge. ✉ *14500 NC 12, Rodanthe, NC* ☎ *252/987–2394* 🌐 *www.fws.gov/refuge/pea_island* 🎟 *Free.*

Wright Brothers National Memorial. ✉ *1000 N. Croatan Hwy., Kill Devil Hills, NC* ☎ *252/473–2111* 🌐 *www.nps.gov/wrbr/index.htm* 🎟 *$10.*

Restaurants

Blue Moon Beach Grill. [$] *Average main: $12* ✉ *4104 S. Virginia Dare Trail, Nags Head, NC* ☎ *252/261–2583* 🌐 *www.bluemoonbeachgrill.com.*

The Blue Point. [$] *Average main: $16* ✉ *1240 Duck Rd., Duck, NC* ☎ *252/261–8090* 🌐 *thebluepoint.com.*

Dinky's Waterfront Restaurant. [$] *Average main: $18* ✉ *Village Marina Hotel, 57980 NC 12, Hatteras, NC* ☎ *252/986–2020* 🌐 *www.villagemarinahatteras.com* 🕒 *No lunch.*

John's Drive In. [$] *Average main: $6* ✉ *3716 N. Virginia Dare Trail, Kitty Hawk, NC* ☎ *252/261–6227* 🌐 *johnsdrivein.com* 🕒 *Closede Mon.–Wed.*

Lost Colony Brewery and Cafe. [$] *Average main: $18* ✉ *208 Queen Elizabeth St., Manteo, NC* ☎ *252/473–6666* 🌐 *lostcolonybrewery.com* 🕒 *Closed Mon.*

Sam & Omie's Restaurant. [$] *Average main: $16* ✉ *7228 S. Virginia Dare Trail, Nags Head, NC* ☎ *252/441–7366* 🌐 *www.samandomies.net* 🕒 *No dinner Sun.*

Ten O Six. [$] *Average main: $9* ✉ *1006 S. Virginia Dare Trail, Kill Devil Hills, NC*

☎ 252/441–9607 ⊕ www.tenosixobx.com ⊗ No dinner.

Tortuga's Lie. Ⓢ Average main: $20 ✉ 3016 S. Virginia Dare Trail, Nags Head, NC ☎ 252/441–7299 ⊕ www.tortugaslie. com.

The Wreck. Ⓢ Average main: $12 ✉ 58848 Marina Way, Hatteras Island, NC ☎ 252/996–0162 ⊕ thewreckobx.com ⊗ Closed Sun. No dinner.

Coffee and Quick Bites

Big Buck's Homemade Ice Cream. Ⓢ Average main: $4 ✉ Timbuck 11 Shopping Center, 785 Sunset Blvd., Corolla, NC ☎ 252/453–3188 ⊕ www.bigbucksice-cream.com ⊗ No lunch.

Duck's Donuts. Ⓢ Average main: $10 ✉ 5000 S. Croatan Hwy., Nags Head, NC ☎ 252/255–5730 ⊕ www.duckdonuts. com ⊗ Closed Tues. and Wed. No dinner.

🛏 Hotels

First Colony Inn. Ⓢ Rooms from: $175 ✉ 6715 S. Croatan Hwy., Nags Head, NC ☎ 855/207–2262 ⊕ www.firstcolonyinn. com ❶◎❶ Free breakfast.

The Inn on Pamlico Sound. Ⓢ Rooms from: $237 ✉ 49684 NC 12, Buxton, NC ☎ 866/726–5426 ⊕ www.innonpamlico-sound.com ❶◎❶ Free breakfast.

Sanderling Resort. Ⓢ Rooms from: $390 ✉ 1461 Duck Rd., Duck, NC ☎ 866/860–3979 ⊕ www.sanderling-resort.com ❶◎❶ No meals.

Surfside Hotel. Ⓢ Rooms from: $181 ✉ 6701 Virginia Dare Trail, Nags Head, NC ☎ 252/441–2105 ⊕ www.surfsideobx. com ❶◎❶ Free breakfast.

🏃 Activities

Wild Horse Adventure Tours. ✉ 610 Currituck Clubhouse Dr., Corolla, NC ☎ 252/489–2020 ⊕ wildhorsetour.com 🎟 Rides from $49.

Oxford, MS

86 miles (approx. 1½ hours) from Memphis.

Oxford, Mississippi is the quintessential college town, home to the University of Mississippi, nicknamed "Ole Miss." The campus has dramatically curving oak trees and handsome brick buildings clustered around a quad. But it's more than just football and frat parties. It was also the home of literary lion William Faulkner, has a culinary scene that rivals big cities, and draws stolling couples to its charming downtown. Less than two hours from Memphis, it's a delightful weekend getaway year-round, whether you're a student or just curious to learn more.

Planning

GETTING THERE AND BACK
For most travelers, the easiest way to get to Oxford is to drive from Memphis via I-55 to TN 278. You can also drive from the west through Clarksdale, the "blues capital of the world," all the way TN 278. Or enter Oxford from the east, passing through Tupelo, birthplace of Elvis Presley.

INSPIRATION
On your drive, listen to an audiobook of *Absalom, Absalom,* one of Faulkner's best books set in a fictional version of Oxford. You can also listen to the "Thacker Mountain Radio Hour," a weekly radio variety show recorded live in town and broadcast on Mississippi Public Broadcasting.

WHEN TO GO

Fall is the most popular time to visit Oxford, so choose a weekend when the team is away or risk big crowds. But there's no better time in terms of weather. The Double Decker Arts Festival is a favorite at the end of summer, featuring live music and an artists market. In May, the Oxford Blues Fest showcases the music Mississippi is known for. March's Oxford Film Festival showcases more than 200 films from around the world.

WHERE TO STAY

Graduate Oxford was the first boutique hotel in town, and features Ole Miss colors and the a painting of The Grove. Guests can visit the rooftop bar and restaurant or relax in the downstairs coffee shop. Bikes are available for exploring the town. **Chancellor's House** is a luxury hotel that offers visiting parents and discerning tourists an upscale experience. It serves afternoon tea at its restaurant.

Set across multiple historic homes, The **Z Bed and Breakfast** features perks like a daily Southern-style breakfast and afternoon wine receptions. The rooms include stylish furnishings. Outside of town, **Taylor Inn** is an 1890s farmhouse with five unique rooms and a family of chickens that roams the grounds.

Day 1

Plan on arriving in Oxford by midday to see as much as possible. Begin your culinary adventure with a stop at **Oxford Canteen.** It started as an outpost in a downtown alley, but now is in a former gas station. Stop here for breakfast tacos, avocado toast, and iced Vietnamese coffee.

From here, drive to **Rowan Oak,** a plantation that Faulkner purchased in 1930. He lived here for much of his career and it now serves as a museum devoted to his life. Artifacts include early copies of his work. Then make the short drive to **Oxford**

Memorial Cemetery to pay your respects at Faulkner's grave. Fans bring bottles of Jack Daniels, his drink of choice, to leave on the headstone. Pick one up at Safari Wine & Spirits, a theme liquor store nearby.

After freshening up at your hotel, head to **Snackbar,** led by James Beard award winner Vishwesh Bhatt. The menu incorporates Southern and French dishes with ingredients from the chef's native India. Dine on curry lamb and grits or sweet tea-brined fried chicken.

Day 2

Get an early start at **Big Bad Breakfast,** another in the City Grocery empire, as it gets busy on weekends. Grab a seat at the counter and dig into house-cured bacon, French toast, or a heaping cathead biscuit. Then it's time to get a glimpse of the Ole Miss campus. Start at The Grove, which is ground zero for tailgating. Stop by the **Civil Rights Memorial** that honors James Meredith, the first African-American student to enroll at the university.

Next, check out the university-run museums, starting with the **University of Mississippi Museum.** It contains an eclectic collection of scientific instruments, Greek and Roman antiquities, and artworks. The Buie-Skipwith collection includes Civil War artifacts and decorative arts.

Take a break from the arts and culture with lunch at Chef John Currence's **City Grocery,** one of the town's three James Beard award winners. As the name implies, it's set in a former grocery store on a historic square. Dine on Southern favorites like fried catfish and grits. It's next door to Faulkner Alley, named for the town's most famous resident, novelist William Faulkner. It was here that a drugstore once stood that offered a lending library where he would borrow books.

Learn about the region's African American history at the **Burns-Belfry Museum**

A statue honoring James Meredith, the first African American student to attend Oxford's University of Mississippi

and Multicultural Center. It's set in a church founded by freed African Americans after the Civil War and has exhibits from the slave trade to the present.

After some downtime at your hotel, head to Taylor, a rural community south of Oxford. Start at **Wonderbird Spirits,** the United States' only gin distillery to use rice as its neutral grain. The Japanese-style gin is made using rice grown in the fertile Mississippi Delta. They offer tastings of their spirits and tours of the facility.

Then head to **Taylor Grocery,** a rustic former grocery store that has a reputation for the best catfish around. Only open Thursday to Sunday, bring your own wine and make sure your entire party is together before getting a table. Start with a sausage and cheese plate as the band plays and don't leave without signing your name on the wall.

Day 3

Grab breakfast at **Bottletree Bakery,** a favorite of students since 1995, right off the Oxford Square. Grab a table and enjoy freshly baked pastries like the apple muffins and ham and egg croissant, along with the all-important coffee.

Once you've had your fill, check out the downtown shops, centered around the historic Lafayette County Courthouse. The National Register-listed building was first constructed in 1872 and was featured in many Faulkner stories.

Square Books—along with Off Square Books, and Square Books Jr.—is an incredible independent bookstore covering every genre. They also host a weekly radio show. **Neilson's** is one of the town's original department stores, in operation since 1839. **Cicada** has funky women's clothing.

Before heading home, have a lavish lunch at **Saint Leo,** another James Beard nominee. Split a wood-fired pizza like the nduja and kale or indulge in the pork ragu with house made pappardelle.

Recommendations

Sights

Burns-Belfry Museum and Multicultural Center. ✉ 710 Jackson Ave. E, Oxford, MS 🕾 662/801–4590 ⊕ www.burns-belfry.com 💺 Free ⊙ Closed Mon., Tues., and Sat.

Civil Rights Memorial. ✉ University of Mississippi, University Circle, Oxford, MS 🕾 662/232–2477 ⊕ www.visitoxfordms.com 💺 Free.

Oxford Memorial Cemetery. ✉ Jefferson Ave. and N. 16th St., Oxford, MS 🕾 662/232–2477 ⊕ www.visitoxfordms.com 💺 Free ⊙ Closed Mon.

Rowan Oak. ✉ 916 Old Taylor Rd., Oxford, MS 🕾 662/234–3284 ⊕ www.rowanoak.com 💺 $5.

University of Mississippi Museum. ✉ University of Mississippi, University Ave. and S. 5th St., Oxford 🕾 662/915–7073 ⊕ www.museum.olemiss.edu 💺 Free ⊙ Closed Sat. and Mon.

Wonderbird Spirits. ✉ 618 County Rd. 303, Taylor, MS 🕾 662/205–0779 ⊕ www.wonderbirdspirits.com 💺 Free ⊙ Closed Sun.–Tues.

 Restaurants

Big Bad Breakfast. $ Average main: $10 ✉ 719 N. Lamar Blvd., Oxford, MS 🕾 662/236–2666 ⊕ www.bigbadbreakfast.com ⊙ No dinner.

Bottletree Bakery. $ Average main: $7 ✉ 923 Van Buren Ave., Oxford, MS 🕾 662/236–5000 ⊙ Closed Mon.

City Grocery. $ Average main: $23 ✉ 152 Courthouse Sq., Oxford, MS 🕾 662/232–8080 ⊕ www.citygroceryonline.com ⊙ No dinner Sun.

Oxford Canteen. $ Average main: $16 ✉ 1101 E. Jackson Ave, Oxford, MS 🕾 662/380–5141 ⊕ www.eatsaintleo.com ⊙ Closed Tues.

Snackbar. $ Average main: $9 ✉ 721 N. Lamar Blvd., Oxford, MS 🕾 662/236–6363 ⊕ www.citygroceryonline.com ⊙ No dinner Sun.

Taylor Grocery. $ Average main: $11 ✉ 4 1st St., Taylor, MS 🕾 662/236–1716 ⊕ www.taylorgrocery.com ⊙ Closed Mon.–Wed.

Hotels

Chancellor's House. $ Rooms from: $111 ✉ 425 S. Lamar Blvd., Oxford, MS 🕾 662/371–1400 ⊕ www.chancellorshouse.com ⊙⊙ No meals.

Graduate Oxford. $ Rooms from: $135 ✉ 400 N. Lamar Blvd., Oxford, MS 🕾 662/234–3031 ⊕ www.graduatehotels.com ⊙⊙ No meals.

Taylor Inn. $ Rooms from: $290 ✉ 736 Old Taylor Rd., Taylor, MS 🕾 662/715–0799 ⊕ www.taylor-inn.com ⊙⊙ Free breakfast.

The Z Bed and Breakfast. $ Rooms from: $238 ✉ 1405 Pierce Ave., Oxford, MS 🕾 281/804–8022 ⊕ www.thez-oxford.com ⊙⊙ Free breakfast.

Shopping

Cicada. ✉ 307 S. Lamar Blvd., Oxford, MS 🕾 662/281–0541 ⊕ www.shopcicada.com.

Neilson's. ✉ 119 Courthouse Sq., Oxford, MS 🕾 662/234–1161 ⊕ www.neilsonsdepartmentstore.com.

Safari Wine & Spirits. ✉ 407 S. 11th St., Oxford, MS 🕾 662/234–2679.

Square Books. ✉ 160 Courthouse Sq., Oxford, MS 🕾 662/236–2262 ⊕ www.squarebooks.com.

Palm Beach Coast, FL

204 miles (approx. 3½ hours) from Tampa.

While the exclusive barrier island of Palm Beach (one of the wealthiest enclaves in the United States) is the most famous address in the Palm Beaches, there's much more to this stretch of Florida's Gold Coast than most visitors know. Palm Beach County covers some 47 miles of Florida's Atlantic Coast, from Jupiter in the north to Boca Raton down south. Whether you plan to just kick back in the sand at a grand dame beach resort or are feeling more intrepid—after all, you can snorkel an incredible underwater trail here to spot sea horses and explore formal Japanese gardens, too—you'll be surprised at all you can pack into a weekend in the Palm Beaches.

Planning

GETTING THERE AND BACK
From Tampa, it takes roughly 3½ hours to drive east across the belly of the state and south to get to the Palm Beaches.

PIT STOPS
Once you hit the East Coast and before continuing south, detour from the highway in Vero Beach to refresh with an orange slushy at **Countryside Citrus**, which has great you-pick strawberry fields and luscious Indian River grapefruit for sale in season, too.

WHEN TO GO
The summer months—June through September—are hot and humid, even with the sea breeze. They bring regular patterns of afternoon thunderstorms (this is also the heart of hurricane season, but also some enticing deals at hotels). Palm Beach's social season coincides with high season—and, generally, the most pleasant weather, too—and runs from December to April.

WHERE TO STAY
Florida's most famous grand dame hotel—**The Breakers Palm Beach**—occupies a class all its own as well as prime oceanfront real estate right in Palm Beach. Spa-lovers should book in at **Eau Palm Beach Resort & Spa,** another worthy splurge with a fun-loving spa on the oceanfront in Manalapan, to the south. On the cheap(er) and cheerful side of the spectrum, **Hotel Biba** is a boutique inn on the National Register of Historic Places in West Palm Beach, with an outdoor pool and some great extras like free parking, Wi-Fi, and breakfast.

Day 1

On arrival, set your sights on Palm Beach for your first lunch in the area—but give stuffy (if gorgeous) Worth Avenue a pass in favor of the more fun vibe at The Royal Poinciana Plaza, where you can settle in at the bistro called **Sant Ambroeus** for food every bit as delicious as in Italy. If you order just one thing, make it the charcuterie platter.

A fun way to get the lay of the land in Palm Beach while doing some mansion and yacht-spotting is by renting a bike at the **Palm Beach Bicycle Trail Shop** to pedal the island's roughly 5-mile-long Lake Trail. It skirts the Intracoastal Waterway (referred to as "the lake," or Lake Worth Lagoon, in these parts) and wends all the way south to Worth Avenue. You can either turn in your bike after or pedal across the Flagler Memorial Bridge to neighboring West Palm Beach, where you've likely earned a sweet reward at **Sloan's,** a whimsical ice cream parlor that's been around forever and packs the house for fun flavors like Ginger Snappy and Almond Joy.

Finish the day by letting someone else do the driving with a sunset cruise aboard **Hakuna Matata Catamaran Cruises,** during which you'll nearly be able to peer into the windows of incredible waterfront mansions and super yachts while waiting for the sun to set over the Intracoastal Waterway.

Back on dry land, there are tons of restaurants around nearby Clematis Street, including a cozy little Spanish tapas joint called **Tapeo Tapas,** where a tabla mixta appetizer includes Serrano ham, chorizo, and olives.

Day 2

Depending on the tidal chart, start the day as soon as the sun's up with one of Florida's best snorkeling excursions at the underwater snorkel trail at **Phil Foster Park.** You can just rent snorkeling gear or hire a guide at **Pura Vida Divers.** An hour before high tide is when conditions are best for entering the water under the Blue Heron Bridge. In the shallow waters of the Intracoastal Waterway (they turn crystal clear at the tide change) you might spot eagle rays, sea horses, and sea turtles along a marked underwater path.

Towel off and hop in the car to drive south to the chilled-out beach town of Lake Worth for a brunch that attracts locals and out-of-towners in equal measure at **Benny's on the Beach.** Avocado toast, acai bowls, and shrimp and grits round out the menu, and if you're feeling ready for a cocktail (and someone else is driving), enjoy the festive feel of sipping a piña colada from a hollowed-out pineapple within earshot of the surf.

Your next stop takes you inland a tad, with a jaunt to the **Morikami Museum and Japanese Gardens** in Delray, where a former pineapple plantation started by a Japanese immigrant has morphed into exquisite gardens with groves of bamboo, koi ponds, and a traditional tea house. At **Cornell Cafe** here you can enjoy a bento box, gyoza dumplings, or wakame salad for a healthy lunch overlooking the gardens.

Next, head back east for some beach time in Boca Raton. But first, stop at the **Gumbo Limbo Nature Center,** where you can observe rescued sea turtles being rehabilitated for eventual release into the wild and stroll along a boardwalk trail through the surrounding hardwood hammock. Ready for a swim? Right across the street is **Red Reed Park,** where 67 acres of pristine coastal terrain give you a taste of how this stretch of shoreline has always looked. Get cleaned up for dinner along happening Atlantic Avenue in Delray Beach at **Deck 84,** a waterfront restaurant with outdoor seating and killer fish tacos (stuffed with flash-fried Florida mahimahi) on the menu.

Day 3

Start your day with breakfast at one of Palm Beach's most unassuming and laid-back greasy spoons, **Green's Pharmacy,** where billionaires perusing the New York Times dine alongside landscaping crews on diner-style staples like omelets and steak and eggs. Cross the Intracoastal to West Palm Beach for a visit to the **Norton Museum of Art,** which looks stunning following a $100 million upgrade that included newly redesigned gardens. Before you head home, pretend you're at a Parisian sidewalk cafe in Paris at Pistache French Bistro on Clematis Street.

Recommendations

Sights

Gumbo Limbo Nature Center. ✉ 1801 N. Ocean Blvd., Boca Raton, FL ☎ 561/544–8605 ⊕ www.gumbolimbo.org ⌨ $5.

Morikami Museum and Japanese Gardens. ✉ 4000 Morikami Park Rd., Delray Beach, FL ☎ 561/495–0233 ⊕ www.morikami.org ⌨ $15 ☉ Closed Mon.

Norton Museum of Art. ✉ 1450 S. Dixie Hwy., West Palm Beach, FL

☎ 561/832–5196 🌐 www.norton.org 🎟 $18 🕓 Closed Mon.

Phil Foster Park ✉ 900 E. Blue Heron Blvd., Riviera Beach, FL ☎ 561/966–6600 🌐 www.pbcgov.org 🎟 Free.

Red Reef Park. ✉ 1400 N. Ocean Blvd., Boca Raton, FL ☎ 561/393–7815 🌐 www.myboca.us 🎟 Free.

Restaurants

Benny's on the Beach. $ *Average main: $15* ✉ 10 S. Ocean Blvd., Lake Worth Beach, FL ☎ 561/582–9001 🌐 www.bennysonthebeach.com.

Cornell Cafe. $ *Average main: $11* ✉ Morikami Museum and Japanese Gardens, 4000 Morikami Park Rd., Delray Beach, FL ☎ 561/233–1366 🌐 www.morikami.org 🕓 Closed Mon.

Deck 84. $ *Average main: $15* ✉ 840 E. Atlantic Ave., Delray Beach, FL ☎ 561/665–8484 🌐 www.deck84.com.

Green's Pharmacy. $ *Average main: $11* ✉ 151 N. County Rd., Palm Beach, FL ☎ 561/832–4443 🌐 www.greenspb.com 🕓 Closed Sun.

Pistache French Bistro. $ *Average main: $34* ✉ 101 N. Clematis St., West Palm Beach, FL ☎ 561/833–5090 🌐 www.pistachewpb.com.

Sant Ambroeus. $ *Average main: $25* ✉ Royal Poinciana Plaza, 340 Royal Poinciana Way, Palm Beach FL ☎ 561/285–7990 🌐 www.santambroeus.com.

Tapeo Tapas. $ *Average main: $30* ✉ 118 Clematis St., West Palm Beach, FL ☎ 561/514–0811 🌐 www.tapeotapas.com 🕓 Closed Mon.

Coffee and Quick Bites

Sloan's $ *Average main: $5* ✉ 700 S. Rosemary Ave., West Palm Beach, FL ☎ 561/833–4303 🌐 www.sloansicecream.com.

Hotels

The Breakers Palm Beach. $ *Rooms from: $395* ✉ 1 S. County Rd., Palm Beach, FL ☎ 877/724–3188 🌐 www.thebreakers.com 🍴 No meals.

Eau Palm Beach Resort & Spa. $ *Rooms from: $419* ✉ 100 S. Ocean Blvd., Manalapan, FL ☎ 561/533–6000 🌐 www.eaupalmbeach.com 🍴 No meals.

Hotel Biba. $ *Rooms from: $79* ✉ 320 Belvedere Rd., West Palm Beach, FL ☎ 561/832–0094 🌐 www.hotelbiba.com 🍴 Free breakfast.

Shopping

Countryside Citrus. ✉ 6325 81st St., Vero Beach, FL ☎ 772/581–0999 🌐 www.countrysidecitrus.com.

Activities

Hakuna Matata Catamaran Cruises. ✉ 100 N. Clematis St., West Palm Beach, FL ☎ 561/881–9757 🌐 www.visitpalmbeach.com/catamaran-adventures 🎟 From $30.

Palm Beach Bicycle Trail Shop. ✉ 50 Cocoanut Row, Palm Beach, FL ☎ 561/659–4583 🌐 www.palmbeachbicycle.com 🎟 Rentals from $20.

Pura Vida Divers. ✉ 2513 Beach Ct., Singer Island, FL ☎ 561/840–8750 🌐 www.puravidadivers.com 🎟 Dives from $60.

Raleigh and Central North Carolina, NC

Raleigh is 166 miles (approx. 2½ hours) from Charlotte.

Most people traveling to North Carolina head straight for the mountains or the Outer Banks, both justly popular destinations. But if you're looking for a less touristy getaway, or have a few days to spare en route to one side of the state

On the Duke University campus, Durham's Sarah P. Duke Gardens is a great spot to cool off on a warm afternoon.

or the other, North Carolina's Piedmont offers plenty of urban and rural charms. Numerous parks appeal to outdoor enthusiasts, and gently rolling farmland supplies ingredients to more James Beard–recognized chefs than any other region of the country. Arts enthusiasts will delight in the area's museums and galleries, while music lovers will have a hard time choosing among venues ranging from classical concert halls to shadowy underground punk clubs.

Planning

GETTING THERE AND BACK

Charlotte Douglas International Airport is the largest flight hub in the state, and is well served by direct flights from all major cities in the United States. From Charlotte, the "Research Triangle"— Raleigh, Durham, and Chapel Hill—is about 150 miles northeast, or about a two- to three-hour drive. Most people make the trip along I-85 N/I-40 E, but traveling along U.S. Route 64 East takes about the same amount of time and carries you through more scenic small-town territory.

WHEN TO GO

North Carolina is at its best in spring, when everything is in bloom but temperatures are still mild. Autumn is also beautiful, as the elevation is just high enough for the area's forests to put on a vibrant show of colorful foliage. Spring and fall are also the busiest times, between university commencements, football or basketball games, and popular annual events like Durham's Full Frame Documentary Film Festival (early April) or Raleigh's Hopscotch Music Festival (mid-September).

WHERE TO STAY

Central North Carolina is home to numerous universities (UNC–Chapel Hill, Duke University, and North Carolina State University being the largest) as well as numerous corporate and tech headquarters, so all the chain hotels are well represented. But all the downtown areas and surrounding towns have plenty of independent lodgings ranging from the quaint **Inn at Teardrops** in Hillsborough, to the elegant **Carolina Inn** or **Fearrington House Inn** in Chapel Hill, to hip downtown digs at Durham's **21C Museum Hotel** and the **Durham Hotel,** or the resort-like accommodations at Raleigh's **Umstead Hotel and Spa.**

Day 1

A late-morning start from Charlotte will get you to one of the state's best and most unusual lunch spots by midday. Exit I–85/I–40 at Graham and follow NC 54 east toward Chapel Hill, before turning south and following Saxapahaw-Beth-lehem Church Road for about 4 more miles. The road delivers you to the heart of tiny Saxapahaw, a former cotton mill town that has reinvented itself as an artsy farming community and regional destination for locavore cuisine. Anchoring the village is the **Saxapahaw General Store,** which bills itself as "your local five-star gas station." They do indeed sell gas, but once inside, visitors will find a cheerful chaos of groceries, local crafts, and a kitchen turning out diverse and sophisticated farm-focused plates. If you can't score a seat at one of the communal tables, visit the equally excellent **Eddy Pub** next door, which similarly prides itself on a menu built from the bounty of surrounding farms. Enjoy lunch from a seat on their dining deck overlooking the Haw River, where you can watch herons and otters browsing in the shallows.

After lunch, a 25-minute back-road drive northeast will bring you to the charming historic town of Hillsborough, whose main street is lined with art galleries, antiques shops, and boutiques. Serious antiques shoppers will want to head a mile or two south of downtown town to the sprawling **Hillsborough Antique Mall,** where you can easily spend the entire afternoon browsing its labyrinthine stalls. For dinner, if you're in the mood

for elegance, book a table at the highly lauded **Panciuto.** More casual fare (much of it from their own farm) is on offer at the **Wooden Nickel Pub** or the **Hillsborough BBQ Company.** For an after-dinner drink and some music, check out **Volume Hillsborough** or **Nash Street Tavern.**

Day 2

Before leaving Hillsborough, grab coffee and a hearty pastry downtown at **Cup A Joe.** It's a good thing that Chapel Hill and Durham (both about a 15-minute drive from Hillsborough) are next-door neighbors, as both cities are so packed with cultural, culinary, outdoors, and family-friendly attractions that it's hard to choose between them. Each city has a distinct flavor—Chapel Hill, home to the state's flagship university, has a laid-back feel, with most attractions centered around the campus. Carrboro, a small town just west of Chapel Hill, is best known as the epicenter of music and the arts in the region. Durham is more urban, with a tight downtown core of high-rises surrounded by the Duke University campus and tree-shaded historic neighborhoods.

Nature lovers will find plenty to do in both cities. If you start out with Chapel Hill, spend the morning strolling through the **North Carolina Botanical Garden** and **Coker Arboretum** on the UNC-Chapel Hill campus. For lunch, stop in at **Mama Dip's** for classic Southern soul food or **Mediterranean Deli** for lighter fare. If Durham is the first stop, the **Sarah P. Duke Gardens** on the Duke University campus combine breathtaking formal gardens with wild native plantings. Favorite area lunch spots near the garden include **Grub Durham** and **Guglhupf,** both with hearty, homemade sandwiches and airy dining terraces. For a longer afternoon excursion, visitors can hike nearly 30 miles of trails at **Eno River State Park** or go fishing and swimming at **West Point on the Eno.**

Those looking for art will find plenty to please the eye as well. UNC's **Ackland Art Museum** and Duke's **Nasher Museum of Art** both house well-curated collections ranging from antiquities to contemporary art. For more avant-garde (and 24-hour) browsing, visit the 21C Museum Hotel in downtown Durham, which features rotating exhibitions of contemporary art installations.

If you're traveling with kids, Durham's **Museum of Life and Science** will delight young people with a butterfly house, animal exhibits, interactive science stations, and a prototype of the Apollo 15 Lunar Lander. The **Duke Lemur Center** provides close encounters and educational exhibits on the beloved (and critically endangered) primates. In spring and summer, take in a home game with the beloved local minor-league baseball team, the **Durham Bulls.**

Come evening, excellent dining options abound in both Durham and Chapel Hill. In Durham, popular spots include **Mateo, Mothers & Sons, Pizzeria Toro,** or **M Sushi** downtown. In Chapel Hill and Carrboro, **Crook's Corner, Acme Food & Beverage Company,** and **Lantern** have devoted followings. Reservations are highly recommended at all places on weekends.

Both cities provide rich nightlife options, as well. Durham clubs **Motorco Music Hall** and **The Pinhook** host local and national touring acts nearly every night of the week, and craft beer aficionados can sample local brews at **Durty Bull, Fullsteam,** and **Ponysaurus** breweries. For 50 years, Carrboro's **Cat's Cradle** has ruled the area's music scene, often showcasing bands on the roster of local indie label Merge Records. Nearby venues **Local 506** or **The Cave** host up-and-coming or more experimental acts. A pre- or postshow drink at the **Orange County Social Club** will likely find you clinking glasses with at least one of the musicians playing in town that evening.

Day 3

Even if you were up until the wee hours at local clubs, get an early start to maximize your day in the state capital before heading home. Luckily, a great cup of coffee and a quick breakfast is easy to find; try **Rise Biscuits** (with locations in Chapel Hill, Durham, and Raleigh) or **Cocoa Cinnamon** (three locations in Durham).

Hop on I–40 E for the 30-minute drive to Raleigh; just before the downtown exits begin, turn off and spend the morning wandering the galleries of the **North Carolina Museum of Art,** which boasts impressive collections ranging from ancient artifacts to contemporary multimedia installations. Take some time to walk through the extensive sculpture park surrounding the museum as well.

After the museum, fuel up with a hearty brunch at **Mandolin** (chef Sean Fowler supplies many ingredients from his own farm, of course), in the tony Cameron Village neighborhood, or downtown at **Beasley's Chicken + Honey,** helmed by Ashley Christensen, who was crowned America's best chef in 2019 by the James Beard Foundation. For lighter bites, try a poké bowl and fresh juice at **Raleigh Raw.**

If your credit card needs a workout after lunch, downtown Raleigh has numerous boutiques showcasing local designers' wares. **Deco** has a variety of NC-made gifts and accessories (pick up a bag by Holly Aiken to stash your purchases), or you can get fitted for the perfect pair of jeans at **Raleigh Denim Workshop.** Pick up treats for the drive home at **Videri Chocolate Factory** or at the vast **State Farmers' Market.**

Recommendations

Sights

Ackland Art Museum.. ✉ *101 S. Columbia St., Chapel Hill, NC* ☎ *919/966–5736* 🌐 *ackland.org* 🎫 *Free.*

Duke Lemur Center. ✉ *3705 Erwin Rd., Durham, NC* ☎ *919/401–7240* 🌐 *lemur.duke.edu* 🎫 *$14.*

Eno River State Park. ✉ *6101 Cole Mill Rd., Durham, NC* ☎ *919/707–9300* 🌐 *www.ncparks.gov/eno-river-state-park/home* 🎫 *Free.*

Museum of Life and Science. ✉ *433 W. Murray Ave., Durham, NC* ☎ *919/220–5429* 🌐 *lifeandscience.org* 🎫 *$21.*

Nasher Museum of Art. ✉ *2001 Campus Dr., Durham, NC* ☎ *919/684–5135* 🌐 *nasher.duke.edu* 🎫 *$7.*

North Carolina Botanical Garden and Coker Arboretum. ✉ *100 Old Mason Farm Rd., Chapel Hill, NC* ☎ *919/962–0522* 🌐 *ncbg.unc.edu* 🎫 *Free.*

North Carolina Museum of Art. ✉ *2110 Blue Ridge Rd., Raleigh, NC* ☎ *919/839–6262* 🌐 *ncartmuseum.org* 🎫 *Free.*

Sarah P. Duke Gardens. ✉ *420 Anderson St., Durham, NC* ☎ *919/684–3698* 🌐 *gardens.duke.edu* 🎫 *Free.*

West Point on the Eno. ✉ *5101 N. Roxboro St., Durham, NC* ☎ *919/471–1623* 🌐 *www.enoriver.org/what-we-protect/parks/west-point-on-the-eno* 🎫 *Free.*

Restaurants

Acme Food & Beverage Company. [$] *Average main: $18* ✉ *110 E. Main St., Carrboro, NC* ☎ *919/929–2263* 🌐 *acme-carrboro.com.*

Beasley's Chicken + Honey. [$] *Average main: $10* ✉ *237 S. Wilmington St., Raleigh, NC* ☎ *919/322–0127* 🌐 *ac-restaurants.com/beasleys.*

Crook's Corner. [$] *Average main: $23* ✉ *610 W. Franklin St., Chapel Hill, NC* ☎ *919/929–7643* 🌐 *crookscorner.com.*

The Eddy Pub. [$] *Average main: $13* ✉ *1715 Saxapahaw-Bethlehem Church Rd., Saxapahaw, NC* ☎ *336/525–2010* 🌐 *theeddypub.com.*

Grub. [$] *Average main: $9* ✉ *1200 W. Chapel Hill St., Durham, NC* ☎ *919/973–3636* 🌐 *grubdurham.com.*

Guglhupf. [$] *Average main: $12* ✉ *2706 Durham-Chapel Hill Blvd., Durham, NC* ☎ *919/401–2600* 🌐 *guglhupf.com.*

Hillsborough BBQ. [$] *Average main: $10* ✉ *236 S. Nash St., Hillsborough, NC* ☎ *919/732–4647* 🌐 *hillsboroughbbq.com* 🕓 *Closed Mon.*

Lantern. [$] *Average main: $22* ✉ *423 W. Franklin St., Chapel Hill, NC* ☎ *919/969–8846* 🌐 *lanternrestaurant.com* 🕓 *Closed Sun. No lunch.*

M Sushi. [$] *Average main: $14* ✉ *311 Holland St., Durham, NC* ☎ *919/908–9266* 🌐 *www.m-restaurants.com/m-sushi.*

Mama Dip's. [$] *Average main: $14* ✉ *408 W. Rosemary St., Chapel Hill, NC* ☎ *919/942–5837* 🌐 *mamadips.com* 🕓 *Closed Mon. and Tues.*

Mandolin. [$] *Average main: $17* ✉ *2519 Fairview Rd., Raleigh, NC* ☎ *919/322–0365* 🌐 *mandolinraleigh.com* 🕓 *No lunch weekdays.*

Mateo. [$] *Average main: $12* ✉ *109 W. Chapel Hill St., Durham, NC* ☎ *919/530–8700* 🌐 *mateotapas.com* 🕓 *Closed Mon.*

Mediterranean Deli. [$] *Average main: $10* ✉ *410 W. Franklin St., Chapel Hill, NC* ☎ *919/967–2666* 🌐 *mediterraneandeli.com.*

Mothers and Sons. [$] *Average main: $24* ✉ *107 W. Chapel Hill St., Durham, NC* ☎ *919/294–8247* 🕓 *No lunch.*

Panciuto. [$] *Average main: $30* ✉ *110 S. Churton St., Hillsborough, NC*

☎ *919/732-626* 🌐 *panciuto.com* 🕐 *Closed Sun.–Tues.*

Pizzeria Toro. [$] *Average main: $15* ✉ *105 E. Chapel Hill St., Durham, NC* ☎ *919/908-6936* 🌐 *pizzeriatoro.com* 🕐 *No lunch.*

Raleigh Raw. [$] *Average main: $9* ✉ *7 W. Hargrett St., Raleigh, NC* ☎ *919/400-0944* 🌐 *raleighraw.com.*

Saxapahaw General Store. [$] *Average main: $12* ✉ *1735 Saxapahaw-Bethlehem Church Rd., Saxapahaw. NC* ☎ *336/376-5332* 🌐 *saxgenstore.com.*

Wooden Nickel. [$] *Average main: $12* ✉ *113 N. Churton St., Hillsborough, NC* ☎ *919/643-2223* 🌐 *thewnp.com.*

Coffee and Quick Bites

Cocoa Cinnamon. [$] *Average main: $5* ✉ *420 W. Geer St., Durham, NC* ☎ *No phone* 🌐 *littlewaves.coffee.*

Cup A Joe. [$] *Average main: $5* ✉ *112 W. King St., Hillsborough, NC* ☎ *919/732-2008.*

Rise. [$] *Average main: $5* ✉ *401 Foster St., Durham, NC* ☎ *984/439-2220* 🌐 *rise-biscuitschicken.com.*

Hotels

Carolina Inn. [$] *Rooms from: $169* ✉ *211 Pittsboro St., Chapel Hill, NC* ☎ *800/962-8519* 🌐 *www.destinationhotels.com/carolina-inn* 🍴 *No meals.*

The Durham Hotel. [$] *Rooms from: $179* ✉ *31 E. Chapel Hill St., Durham, NC* ☎ *919/768-8830* 🌐 *thedurham.com* 🍴 *No meals.*

Fearrington House Inn [$] *Rooms from: $375* ✉ *2000 Fearrington Village Center, Pittsboro, NC* ☎ *919/542-2121* 🌐 *fearrington.com/inn* 🍴 *Free breakfast.*

The Inn at Teardrops. [$] *Rooms from: $165* ✉ *175 W. King St., Hillsborough, NC* ☎ *919/732-1120* 🌐 *innatteardrops.com* 🍴 *Free breakfast.*

Origin Hotel. [$] *Rooms from: $* ✉ *603 W. Morgan St., Raleigh, NC* ☎ *984/275-2220* 🌐 *originhotel.com/raleigh* 🍴 *No meals.*

21C Museum Hotel. [$] *Rooms from: $170* ✉ *111 N. Corcoran St., Durham, NC* ☎ *919/956-6700* 🌐 *www.21cmuseumhotels.com/durham* 🍴 *No meals.*

Umstead Hotel and Spa. [$] *Rooms from: $339* ✉ *100 Woodland Pond Drive, Cary, NC* ☎ *919/447-4000* 🌐 *theumstead.com* 🍴 *No meals.*

Nightlife

Cat's Cradle. ✉ *300 E. Main St., Carrboro, NC* ☎ *919/967-9053* 🌐 *catscradle.com.*

The Cave. ✉ *452½ W. Franklin St., Chapel Hill, NC* ☎ *984/234-0293* 🌐 *caverntavern.com.*

Durty Bull Brewery. ✉ *206 Broadway St., Durham, NC* ☎ *919/688-2337* 🌐 *durty-bull.com.*

Fullsteam Brewery. ✉ *726 Rigsbee Ave., Durham, NC* ☎ *919/682-2337* 🌐 *full-steam.ag.*

Local 506. ✉ *506 W. Franklin St., Chapel Hill, NC* ☎ *919/942-5506* 🌐 *local506.com.*

Motorco Music Hall. ✉ *723 Rigsbee Ave., Durham, NC* ☎ *919/901-0875* 🌐 *motorco-music.com.*

Nash Street Tavern. ✉ *250 S. Nash St., Hillsborough, NC* ☎ *919/245-1956.*

Orange County Social Club. ✉ *108 E. Main St., Carrboro, NC* ☎ *919/933-0669.*

The Pinhook. ✉ *117 W. Main St., Durham, NC* ☎ *984/244-7243* 🌐 *thepinhook.com.*

Ponysaurus Brewing. ✉ *219 Hood St., Durham, NC* ☎ *919/584-4265* 🌐 *pony-saurusbrewing.com.*

Volume Hillsborough. ✉ *226 S. Churton St., Hillsborough, NC* ☎ *919/643-2303* 🌐 *volumehillsborough.com.*

● Shopping

Deco. ✉ 207 S. Salisbury St., Raleigh, NC ☎ 919/828–5484 ⊕ decoraleigh.com.

Raleigh Denim Workshop. ✉ 319 W. Martin St., Raleigh, NC ☎ 919/917–8969 ⊕ raleighdenimworkshop.com.

State Farmers' Market ✉ 1201 Agriculture St., Raleigh, NC ☎ 919/733–7417 ⊕ www.ncagr.gov/markets/facilities/markets/raleigh/index.htm.

Videri Chocolate Factory. ✉ 327 W. Davie St., Raleigh, NC ☎ 919/755–5053 ⊕ viderichocolatefactory.com.

St. Augustine, FL

384 miles (approx. 5½ hours) from Atlanta, 181 miles (approx. 3 hours) from Tampa.

Take the weekend to escape the hot and humid Atlanta sun by heading south. While it might not be any cooler in Florida, the ability to be in the ocean at a moment's notice is a welcomed change. So pack your bags and don't forget a towel and bathing suit, because we're heading to the charming and historic beach town of St. Augustine for the weekend.

Planning

GETTING THERE AND BACK

I–75 S is the quickest route from Atlanta to St. Augustine. Head east on I–10 after you cross the Florida border, then south again on I–95.

If you are coming from Tampa, you'll take I–75 the entire way.

INSPIRATION

Start your journey by listening to Doug Alderson's audio book *The Ghostly Ghost Tour of St. Augustine and Other Tales from Florida*. Along with getting you acquainted with the history of the city, the book uncovers its supernatural side. After a spooky listen, mellow out with a little Jimmy Buffett. Nothing puts you in the sun-and-sand mood quite like "Margaritaville."

WHEN TO GO

In winter the weather is pleasant, but temperatures sometimes dips below freezing for a day or two. Summer temperatures hover around 90, but the humidity makes it seem hotter, and late-afternoon thunderstorms are frequent. April and May are good months to visit, because the ocean is beginning to warm up and the beaches aren't yet packed.

WHERE TO STAY

There are a number of bed-and-breakfasts to choose from in the historic downtown area, including the gorgeous **St. George Inn.** For those in search of a taste of the way Florida used to be, **Casa Monica** is a late-1800s masterpiece with turrets, towers, and wrought-iron balconies.

Day 1

We're headed to the beach, but not without a little sustenance. Stopping at **Stir It Up,** a beachside eatery with plenty of outdoor seating, lets you fuel up for your day in the surf and sun. Whether you opt for a vegetarian wrap, a loaded burrito, a protein-packed smoothie, or a little bit of all everything, you won't be disappointed. For those who need a little more than juice to get them going, **The Kookaburra,** a local coffee shop with some tasty breakfast and lunch pies, is across the street.

A little path next to Stir It Up that leads you right to the white beaches of St. Augustine. Spend the day soaking in the sun. Looking for a little more adventure? Stop by **Pit Surf Shop** (also next to Stir It Up) to rent a board. And for those dipping their toes into the choppy waves for the first time, lessons are available. While you probably won't become a certified Johnny Tsunami, you're likely to have a few successful surfs under their belt.

After spending a day at the beach, we're taking our sun-kissed skin to the historic downtown area for dinner and a drink. Put your name in at **Harry's,** a Creole restaurant beloved for dishes like shrimp and grits and she-crab soup, and while you wait (it's a pretty popular destination), head next door to **Tradewinds Lounge** for an air-conditioned wait and a glass of sangria.

For the rest of the night, stick to downtown area and enjoy bar hopping around the country's oldest city. For something a little rowdier you might head to the **Bar With No Name,** which boasts live music on the weekend. For something a little more refined, consider **Casa De Vino 57** for local wines and late-night charcuterie.

Day 2

Today we'll start where last night ended: downtown. It's a completely different experience in the daytime, with a huge selection of local shops waiting to be explored. Start the morning at **Maple Street Biscuit Company** where you can get just about any type of biscuit—sweet, savory, or smothered in gravy.

This popular breakfast spot is a short walk from the impressive **Flagler College,** the former Ponce de León Hotel. The college offers tours of the grounds and buildings for architecture enthusiasts, but if you just want a quick glimpse at the beautiful buildings, simply walking around the outskirts can be breathtaking.

The rest of the morning should be spent exploring the downtown area and its unique shops, including **Red Pineapple,** a small boutique store for women's clothing and jewelry, **Claude's Chocolate,** the perfect stop for a prelunch treat, and the **Coat of Arms Shoppe,** a must-see for the history buff in your family.

Everyone in the family can enjoy the history lesson at **Castillo de San Marcos,** the oldest masonry fort in the United States. On the weekends, it showcases the still-functioning canons every hour. A tour here can set the scene of an early St. Augustine, giving you insight into America's oldest town.

Catch 27 is a great weekend lunch spot, especially if you love fresh seafood. Save some room for dessert—this Spanish city does deserts exceptionally well. Head to **Café del Hidalgo,** a gelato stop serving up some seriously good sweets. Sample everything and mix-and-match your cone with whatever flavors are most tempting—there's no going wrong here.

A great excursion on a sunny afternoon is a visit to **Fort Matanzas,** a historic war fort that can only be reached by ferry. This national monument gives you the chance to see a different side of this beach town as you ride along the Matanzas River to reach your off-the-beaten-path destination. If you got too many UV rays yesterday, you might prefer the **Ripley's Believe It or Not Museum.** This place is interactive and trippy, so while it might be geared at kids, it's still a blast for adults.

To end the afternoon, we're heading to the edge of the marshes. **Salt Water Cowboys** is a quaint restaurant (the oldest in St. Augustine) serving southern classics from fried fish to barbecue pork. While the food is delicious and homey, the view is what makes it spectacular. From the patio you can watch the sun go down over the seemingly endless expanse of green and the clouds turn pink. Is there a better dinner view than that?

Taking a trip to St. Augustine without a ghost tour would be like a visit to Paris without seeing the Eiffel Tower. Besides being entertaining, these tours fill you in about the lesser-known history of the city. Our favorite is the **Ghosts and Gravestones Tour.** The **Dark of the Moon Ghost**

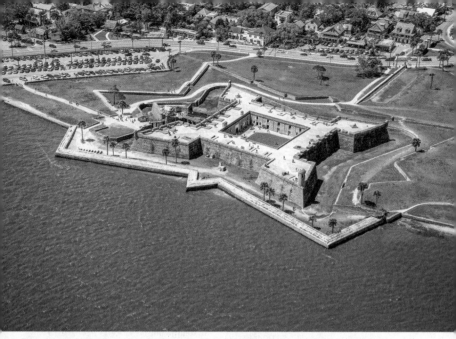

The country's oldest masonry fort, Castillo de San Marcos is the perfect introduction to learn about the history of St. Augustine.

Tour even takes you to the city's haunted lighthouse.

Day 3

To start the morning right, grab a quick bite at **Anastasia Kitchen.** This place offers a classic breakfast at a great price, making it the perfect place to fill up before a morning of activity. If you didn't take a haunted lighthouse tour last night, this is the perfect time to explore the giant candy-stripe tower. You can climb to the top for an aerial view of the town.

If you want something a little more adventurous, you're a three-minute walk from **Kayak and Stand Up Paddle Board St. Augustine.** This company lets you rent the equipment and explore the waters alone, or join a group tour. You'll likely get the chance to see sea life, with dolphin and manatee sightings being common.

Enjoy a super-simple lunch at **The Tin Pickle,** also near the lighthouse. This place might not be fancy, but the hot dogs are excellent. For the afternoon, there are a few options, including a hike in **Anastasia State Park,** or visit the kid-approved **Alligator Farm.** Besides alligators, there are sloths and other animals your kids will go crazy for.

And that brings us to our last meal in this historic city. For dinner, consider **The Conch House,** located right on the beach. Another great option is **Beachcomber,** with patio seating so you can watch the waves crash as the sun sets, making it the perfect conclusion to the weekend.

Recommendations

Sights

Anastasia State Park. ✉ *300 Anastasia Park Rd., St. Augustine, FL* ☎ *904/461–2033* ⊕ *www.floridastateparks.org/anastasia* ✎ *$8 per vehicle.*

Castillo de San Marcos National Monument. ✉ *1 S. Castillo Dr., St. Augustine, FL*

☎ 904/829–6506 ⊕ www.nps.gov/casa
✉ $15.

Flagler College. ⊠ 74 King St., St. Augustine, FL ☎ 800/304–4208 ⊕ www.flagler.edu ✉ Free.

Fort Manzanas National Monument. ⊠ 8635 A1A S, St. Augustine, FL ☎ 904/471–0116 ⊕ www.nps.gov/foma ✉ Free.

Ripley's Believe It or Not Museum. ⊠ 19 San Marco Ave., St. Augustine, FL ☎ 904/824–1606 ⊕ www.ripleys.com ✉ $15.

🍴 Restaurants

Anastasia Kitchen. $ Average main: $7 ⊠ 900 Anastasia Blvd., St. Augustine, FL ☎ 904/808–1585 ⊙ Closed Tues.

Beachcomber. $ Average main: $13 ⊠ 2 A St., St Augustine Beach, FL ☎ 904/471–3744 ⊕ www.beachcomberstaugustine.com.

Catch 27. $ Average main: $18 ⊠ 40 Charlotte St., St. Augustine, FL ☎ 904/217–3542 ⊕ www.catchtwenty-seven.com ⊙ No lunch Mon.–Thurs.

The Conch House. $ Average main: $14 ⊠ 57 Comares Ave., St. Augustine, FL ☎ 904/829–8646 ⊕ www.conch-house.com.

Harry's. $ Average main: $12 ⊠ 46 Ave. Menendez, St. Augustine, FL ☎ 970/824–7765 ⊕ www.hookedonharrys.com.

Maple Street Biscuit Company. $ Average main: $12 ⊠ 39 Cordova St., St. Augustine, FL ☎ 904/398–1004 ⊕ www.maplestreetbiscuits.com ⊙ No dinner.

Saltwater Cowboys. $ Average main: $15 ⊠ 299 Dondanville Rd., St. Augustine, FL ☎ 904/471–2332 ⊕ www.saltwatercowboys.com ⊙ Closed Mon. and Tues. No lunch.

Stir It Up. $ Average main: $15 ⊠ 18 A St., St. Augustine, FL ☎ 904/461–4552 ⊕ stiritupstaugustine.com.

☕ Coffee and Quick Bites

Café del Hidalgo. $ Average main: $5 ⊠ 35 Hypolita St., St. Augustine, FL ☎ 904/823–1196.

The Kookaburra. $ Average main: $6 ⊠ 24 Cathedral Pl., St. Augustine, FL ☎ 904/209–9391 ⊕ www.thekookaburra-coffee.com.

The Tin Pickle. $ Average main: $4 ⊠ 100 Red Cox Dr., St. Augustine, FL ☎ 904/829–0745.

🛏 Hotels

Casa Monica. $ Rooms from: $195 ⊠ 95 Cordova St., St. Augustine, FL ☎ 904/827–1888 ⊕ www.casamonica.com ⫿⊙⫿ No meals.

St. George Inn. $ Rooms from: $215 ⊠ 4 St. George St., St. Augustine, FL ☎ 888/827–5740 ⊕ www.stgeorgeinn.com ⫿⊙⫿ Free breakfast.

🍸 Nightlife

Bar With No Name. ⊠ 16 S. Castillo Dr., St. Augustine, FL ☎ 904/826–1837 ⊕ www.nonamepub.com.

Casa de Vino 57. ⊠ 57 Treasury St., St. Augustine, FL ☎ 904/217–4546 ⊕ www.casadevino57.com.

Tradewinds Lounge. ⊠ 124 Charlotte St., St. Augustine, FL ☎ 904/826–1590 ⊕ www.tradewindslounge.com.

🛍 Shopping

Claude's Chocolate. ⊠ 6 Granada St., St. Augustine, FL ☎ 904/808–8395 ⊕ www.claudeschocolate.com.

Coat of Arms Shoppe. ⊠ 113 St. George St., St. Augustine, FL ☎ 904/810–5877.

Pit Surf Shop. ⊠ 18 A St., St. Augustine, FL ☎ 904/471–4700 ⊕ www.thepitsurf-shop.com.

Red Pineapple. ✉ *120 St. George St., St. Augustine, FL* ☎ *904/342–0875.*

Activities

Dark of the Moon Ghost Tour. ✉ *100 Red Cox Rd., Augustine, FL* ☎ *904/829–0745* ⊕ *www.staugustinelighthouse.org* ✉ *$25.*

Ghosts and Gravestones. ✉ *Old Town Trolley Welcome Center, 27 San Marco Ave., St. Augustine, FL* ☎ *866/955–6101* ⊕ *www. ghostsandgravestones.com/st-augustine* ✉ *$21.*

Kayak St. Augustine. ✉ *442 Ocean Vista Ave., St. Augustine, FL* ☎ *904/315–8442* ⊕ *www.kayakingstaugustine.com* ✉ *Rentals from $40.*

Sarasota, FL

60 miles (approx. 1 hour) from Tampa.

If you think Sarasota is a sleepy snow-bird town, you're not even close. The city and its eight islands are definitely warm, beachy, and half-full of transplants in search of a more carefree lifestyle, but they're not the listless, lollygagging type. This is a town of culture, art, and innovation, with a dazzling history as the legendary home of the American circus tradition and the birthplace of the Sarasota School of Architecture (that's a style, not a classroom), and Florida's West Coast gem has never let go of its performative prowess.

Planning

GETTING THERE AND BACK
The route from Tampa to Sarasota is simple and quick, clocking in at just about an hour (60 miles) via I–75 S to FL 780 W. It's possible to take a two-hour bus trip from Tampa, but you'll need to transfer at Cattlemen Transfer Station before the last

half-hour-leg or grab a cab from there for a 15-minute ride to the downtown area.

INSPIRATION
Get in the circus spirit by listening to *The Greatest Showman* soundtrack on the way (P. T. Barnum ultimately sold out to Ringling Brothers).

WHEN TO GO
Sarasota is visually beautiful year-round, but most will want to avoid a summertime visit when the sun can be extreme, the temperatures daunting, and several attractions either closed or operating under considerably reduced hours. If you're looking for a secluded escape with can't-beat prices, then summer is a solid option. If you want to do anything in town (or in the parks or at the beach), consider June, July, and August off limits for an action-packed getaway.

WHERE TO STAY
If you're coming to town for the quirkier side of Sarasota, hang your hat in one of the colorful casas at **Tiny House Siesta.** This village of teeny-tiny homes offers accommodations from one to three beds with pet-friendly houses available, too. It's located just across the bridge from the famous beach of Siesta Key. Over-packers might be tempted to look elsewhere, but you'd be surprised how much can fit into these cleverly designed digs.

For the fine arts crowd, **Art Ovation** is one of the city's most exciting luxury hotels, boasting its own local art collection (free tours included), art studio (lessons are available), sketching supplies in each room, and even a free musical instrument library program that delivers the likes of cellos and drums to your room on-demand. The rooftop pool bar, vibrant lobby bar with live music, and Overture Restaurant are all worth experiencing.

A quiet moment at Bayfront Park, on a crescent of sand that juts into Sarasota Bay.

Day 1

Arrive in Sarasota by noon and drop your bags at your accommodation early enough to squeeze an extra lunch into your itinerary. With all the fantastic food in town, especially superfresh seafood, you'll want as many meals as possible here. Start with lunch at **Duval's** on Main Street for an instant taste of both the city's charming downtown hub and its favorite restaurant. The selection is considerable, but you won't want to miss the famous shrimp po'boy, voted by locals as the best sandwich in town, also available with chicken or oyster.

After lunch, spend an hour or so sightseeing and shopping in the downtown area, and be sure to check out the **Sarasota Opera House** before taking a quick drive to the **Marie Selby Botanical Gardens.** It's a walkable distance (about 15 minutes), but you may want to save your energy for exploring the gorgeous grounds, where you'll likely spend more

than two hours on the trails and in the galleries of the former Selby house.

By now your home away from home will be ready for check-in, so head back to settle in and freshen up before dinner. Head to the Towles Court district for a memorable meal at **Indigenous Restaurant,** where market-fresh, sustainable seafood is the star of the seasonal American menu. Start with the Parmesan beignets and, if you're not down for the daily market specials, rely on favorites like baked scallops or short rib radiatori with a black garlic Caesar salad.

Day 2

Start with an early breakfast at **Blue Dolphin Café.** This daytime-only breakfast and lunch spot in the historic circle of Saint Armands Key serves all the typical morning fare with a large omelet menu, plenty of waffles, and a trove of essential sides, but pay particular attention to the griddle menu, offering sweet pancakes ranging from apple cinnamon to pumpkin. Walk off a few of your morning calories checking out the picturesque circle outside, then drive five minutes to City Island for a morning at the **Mote Marine Laboratory & Aquarium.** Home to more than 100 species of marine animals, including sharks, manatees, and sea turtles, the center is also the site of a renowned research lab and animal hospital. You'll easily spend a few hours here.

By early afternoon you'll be ready for lunch at **Lila,** back in the downtown area just 10 minutes away by car. Take a break from fish and enjoy the creative vegan-friendly vibe of this buzzy restaurant making waves in Sarasota. Most dishes are vegetable-centric and avoid all animal products, but there is some organic, locally sourced meat on the menu (cooked on separate surfaces) for those who just can't abstain. Order from the shared plates menu for the best variety.

No visit to Sarasota is complete without an afternoon spent at **The Ringling,** learning about the city's deep circus roots and appreciating the inspiring collections of John and Mable Ringling, whose impact on the city's development was considerable. You'll pass the rest of the afternoon here touring the palatial, pink Museum of Art with its collection of more than 28,000 works (including one of the world's best Rubens galleries), the wildly entertaining Circus Museum with try-it-yourself exhibits and a 44,000-piece miniature panorama, and epically fanciful Ca' d'Zan, the 36,000-square-foot Venetian-style palazzo on Sarasota Bay once home to the Ringlings and now restored to its Roaring Twenties glitz and glory.

By now you should be properly inspired by Sarasota's tradition of creativity, so check out one of the city's most innovative and vibrant restaurants for dinner. The seasonal dishes at **MéLange** blend international ingredients from the chef's travels with trending industry techniques on an attention-grabbing menu of small plates categorized by origin: From the Garden, From the Woods, and From the Sea. Look for treats like mushroom strudel with artichoke, rabbit tacos with curry, and blue crab soup with sherry flan and ginger caviar. The craft cocktail menu is stellar here, and each dish comes with a pairing suggestion.

Day 3

Feel free to sleep in a bit before heading to the best brunch in Sarasota at **M.A.D.E.** (Modern. American. Delicious. Eats.). There are plenty of hearty entrées on offer, but don't overlook the Benedicts menu if you're in the mood for morning decadence. Feel free to pack it in; you'll be walking it all off.

After brunch, drive 10 minutes to Lido Shores, park, and stroll the scenic neighborhood where the Sarasota School of Architecture took flight. This neighborhood was designed to draw savvy buyers to Lido Key with fabulously modern homes, the style of which had never been seen before, and many of its original stunners remain. You don't need to have a clue what you're looking for—you'll see it on every block—but keep a eye out for the Umbrella House on Westway Drive to catch a glimpse at the most famous of the bunch.

Grab a final meal at **Nancy's Bar-B-Q** for an unexpected treat. While most don't consider Florida part of the cultural South, you'll instantly sense that unmistakable charm and salivate over the traditional Southern barbecue dished out here. The house specialty is Carolina-style pulled pork, but don't forget to go overboard on sides like red-skinned potato salad, mac and cheese, and baked beans.

You just can't leave Sarasota without trying its beaches, so head to Siesta Key to experience the best of the best. Enjoy warm, shallow waters and fine, powdery sand made from 99% quartz crystal (so it stays cool on your feet) for as long you can stand the sun. Everyone should bring sunscreen, and pros will come prepared with an umbrella. It's only an hour back to Tampa, so there's no hurry.

Recommendations

Sights

Marie Selby Botanical Gardens. ✉ *900 S. Palm Ave., Sarasota, FL* ☎ *941/366–5731* 🌐 *www.selby.org* 🎫 *$15.*

Mote Marine Laboratory & Aquarium. ✉ *1600 Ken Thompson Pkwy., Sarasota, FL* ☎ *941/388–4441* 🌐 *www.mote.org* 🎫 *$24.*

The Ringling. ✉ *5401 Bay Shore Rd., Sarasota, FL* ☎ *941/359–5700* 🌐 *www.ringling.org* 🎫 *$20.*

Restaurants

Blue Dolphin Café. [$] *Average main: $11* ✉ *470 John Ringling Blvd., Sarasota, FL* ☎ *941/388–3566* 🌐 *www.bluedolphincafe.com* 🕒 *No dinner.*

Duval's. [$] *Average main: $11* ✉ *1435 Main St., Sarasota, FL* ☎ *941/312–4001* 🌐 *www.duvalsfreshlocalseafood.com.*

Indigenous Restaurant. [$] *Average main: $14* ✉ *239 S. Links Ave., Sarasota, FL* ☎ *941/706–4740* 🌐 *www.indigenoussarasota.com* 🕒 *Closed Sun. and Mon.*

Lila. [$] *Average main: $23* ✉ *1576 Main St., Sarasota , FL* ☎ *941/296–1042* 🌐 *www.lilasrq.com* 🕒 *Closed Sun.*

M.A.D.E. [$] *Average main: $15* ✉ *1990 Main St., Sarasota, FL* ☎ *941/953–2900* 🌐 *www.maderestaurant.com* 🕒 *Closed Mon.*

MéLange. [$] *Average main: $16* ✉ *1568 Main St., Sarasota, FL* ☎ *941/953–7111* 🌐 *www.melangesarasota.com* 🕒 *Closed Sun.*

Nancy's Bar-B-Q. [$] *Average main: $15* ✉ *301 S. Pineapple Ave., Sarasota, FL* ☎ *941/366–2271* 🌐 *www.nancysbarbq.com* 🕒 *Closed Sun.*

Hotels

Art Ovation. [$] *Rooms from: $156* ✉ *1255 N. Palm Ave., Sarasota, FL* ☎ *941/316–0808* 🌐 *www.artovationhotel.com* 🍴 *No meals.*

Tiny House Siesta. [$] *Rooms from: $177* ✉ *6600 Ave. A, Sarasota, FL* ☎ *941/474–3782* 🌐 *www.tinyhousesiesta.com* 🍴 *No meals.*

Performing Arts

Sarasota Opera House. ✉ *61 N. Pineapple Ave., Sarasota, FL* ☎ *941/328–1300* 🌐 *www.sarasotaopera.org* 🎫 *Performances from $20.*

Savannah and Tybee Island, SC

248 miles (approx. 3¾ hours) from Atlanta, 253 miles (approx. 4 hours) from Charlotte.

Dripping with Southern charm, Savannah beckons with stately architecture, rich history, and a culinary scene that spans classic down-home cooking to James Beard–Award nominees. This is the place to come to soak up the age-old romance of bygone days, people-watch in flower-filled squares, and appreciate art in lauded museums. Get ready to stroll a lot, because that's the best way to see, feel, and smell its luxuriant essence. Never fear, plenty of benches promise a properly Southern pace (just ask Forrest Gump). But it's not all elegance and sophistication here. You also have Tybee Beach, a quirky, fun-in-the-sun, relaxing place to spend an afternoon—or all

Spanish moss hangs from the canopy of oak trees surrounding Savannah's Forsyth Park.

day, with all of its accompanying water sports.

Planning

GETTING THERE AND BACK

Savannah is about 250 miles east of Atlanta. The drive, via I–75 and I–16, takes close to four hours. There's also bus service between Atlanta and Savannah, with a journey on Greyhound taking about six hours. It's almost the same distance due south from Charlotte.

WHEN TO GO

Consider a fall or spring to visit Savannah, when the tourists are gone, the humidity is manageable, and the room rates are lower. Spring has the additional perk of blooming flowers.

WHERE TO STAY

Savannah offers a wide assortment of accommodations, ranging from historic inns and B&Bs, to vacation rentals to comfortable hotels and motels. **Perry Lane Hotel,** just steps from Forsyth Park,

is an award-winning luxury hotel with a chic rooftop bar. And the **Andaz Savannah,** located on the corner of the famous City Market, is modern and spacious.

Day 1

Leaving Atlanta at a decent hour, you'll pull into Savannah in time for lunch. At **B. Matthew's Eatery,** a casual bistro in the heart of the historic district, you can't go wrong with a fried fish wrap or fried green tomato and pimento cheese sandwich.

Fortified, it's time to explore Savannah's famous Historic District. Laid out in a neat grid by General James Oglethorpe in 1733, its 20 blocks overflow with antebellum mansions, flower-filled gardens, live-oak-shaded parks, and historic churches. You'll find 22 historic squares here, each with its own personality; Chippewa is the one made famous by Forrest Gump, and while his exact bench isn't there, plenty of others provide places to relax. The French-Gothic

Cathedral of St. John the Baptist, founded in 1799, has dazzling stained glass and rich murals, and there are several art and history museums to check out, including **Telfair Academy, Jepson Center for the Arts,** and the **Owens Thomas House and Slave Quarters.** Simply stroll the quarter on your own, or join any number of specialty tours, including trolley tours, horse-drawn carriages, ghost tours, foodie tours, pub tours, and the list goes on.

Three miles east of downtown on the Wilmington River, **Bonaventure Cemetery** is known to anyone who has read *Midnight in the Garden of Good and Evil* (or seen the movie). The historic section, very Victorian, has curving pathways and marble carvings—and benches.

Now head for River Street, a 200-year-old cobblestone street edged with more than 75 galleries, art studios, restaurants, and pubs occupying old-world cotton warehouses. Pop into the boutiques, watch the cargo ships float past, or simply take in live open-air music. From here, board a four-deck paddlewheeler with **Savannah Riverboat Cruises** for a sunset cruise, complete with live entertainment, an à la carte specialty menu, and breathtaking views.

Vic's on the River, also on River Street, is an excellent dinner choice, offering sophisticated takes on southern dishes: wild Georgia shrimp and smoked-cheddar grits, shellfish mélange, and braised short ribs, for starters. The setting on the outside patio beneath swaying live oaks makes the experience pure magic.

Day 2

Get up early to take a stroll through **Forsyth Park,** 30 acres of paths and shady spaces draped in Spanish moss. The main walkway passes the famous Forsyth Park Fountain, dating from 1858. Enjoy coffee on a bench, sniff the fragrant garden, and peruse the Saturday farmer's market.

Linger over breakfast at **The Grey Market,** a cross between a New York–style bodega and a Southern lunch counter. You'll find egg creams and bagels here, along with melts and biscuits and gravy of the day.

Staying in the relax mode, head for Tybee Island, a 20-minute drive from downtown, where locals have been vacationing since the late 1800s. There's the beach, of course, where you can plop down and spend all day. But there are plenty of water activities as well: kayaking, standup paddle boarding, and dolphin cruises with **Captain Mike's Dolphin Tours** or **Captain Derek's Dolphin Adventure Tours.** The quaint town features antique shops, art galleries, seaside eateries, and quirky beach shops—you'll find everything from locally made jewelry to pottery to photography, and more. **The Shoppes at 1207** on Tybrisa Street is all owned by local artisans. Civil War buffs should seek out **Fort Pulaski National Monument,** which also has trails and picnic spots.

For those really wanting to ditch the world, the paddle from Tybee Island to the uninhabited barrier island of Little Tybee is the perfect remedy. The only beings you'll see are egrets, ibis, osprey, Atlantic bottlenose dolphins, and maybe a manatee or two along the way.

Break for a lunch at your leisure at one of Tybee's buzzy outdoor dining venues—wild Georgia shrimp and oysters, anyone? It's hard to beat the huge patio overlooking bird-filled marshlands at the casual **Crab Shack,** with a diverse menu featuring seafood plates, barbecue platters, and sandwiches.

When you're done with the sun, head back into Savannah. If you still have energy, the Starland District is an emerging neighborhood of artists and local businesses—a really fun place to stroll. You'll find numerous galleries and studio spaces, vintage clothing stores, and much more. Take a breather at **Starland Cafe & Gallery** or **Back in the Day Bakery.** Here, too, you can join a workshop to make your own scrub or clay mask at **Salacia Salt Studio.** Your skin will thank you.

Then, soak in the balmy Savannah night on the semi-covered patio of a 1900s mansion at **Elizabeth on 37th.** Amid chirping crickets and flickering candlelight, you'll enjoy exquisite southern coastal cuisine: spicy Savannah red rice with Georgia shrimp; local blue crab two ways; roasted chicken breast with local wild mushrooms. Sip a mint julep, which they have perfected, and call it a day.

Day 3

Linger over breakfast at **22 Square,** offering fresh spins on southern favorites, with an all-out effort to support local producers. Specials include swine and fowl Benedict, bistro filet hash, and shrimp and grits, complete with pork belly, leeks, and maple-smoked cheddar.

Then pack up but, before leaving for home, make a detour 20 miles south to **Wormsloe Historic Site** on the Isle of Hope. The 1½-mile-long entranceway itself is worth the drive: an avenue of towering live oaks on either side festooned with Spanish moss. Wormsloe, dating from the 1700s and now in ruins, is Savannah's oldest structure. Walking trails wander through a maritime forest, and there's also a small museum with artifacts unearthed here.

Before leaving the Savannah area for good, it's not too late for one last hurrah at the beach. You'll pass the turnoff as you leave Wormsloe. When you do finally head back to Atlanta, consider stopping at the **Whistle Stop Café** in Juliette. Yes, this is where *Fried Green Tomatoes* took place—and was filmed for the 1991 movie.

Recommendations

⦿ Sights

Bonaventure Cemetery. ⊠ *330 Bonaventure Rd., Thunderbolt, GA* ☎ *912/651–6843* ⊕ *www.bonaventurehistorical.org* 🖃 *Free.*

Cathedral of St. John the Baptist. ⊠ *222 E. Harris St., Savannah, GA* ☎ *912/233–4709* ⊕ *www.savannahcathedral.org* 🖃 *Free* ⊙ *Closed Sun.*

Forsyth Park. ⊠ *2 W. Gaston St., Savannah, GA* ☎ *912/351–3841* ⊕ *www.savannah.com* 🖃 *Free.*

Fort Pulaski National Monument. ⊠ *U.S. 80, Savannah, GA* ☎ *912/786–8182* ⊕ *www.nps.gov/fopu* 🖃 *$10.*

Jepson Center for the Arts. ⊠ *207 W. York St., Savannah, GA* ☎ *912/790–8800* ⊕ *www.telfair.org* 🖃 *$20, includes Owens-Thomas House and Slave Quarters and Telfair Academy.*

Owens Thomas House and Slave Quarters. ⊠ *124 Abercorn St., Savannah, GA* ☎ *912/790–8889* ⊕ *www.telfair.org* 🖃 *$20, includes Jepson Center for the Arts and Telfair Academy.*

Telfair Academy. ⊠ *121 Barnard St., Savannah, GA* ☎ *912/790–8800* ⊕ *www.telfair.org* 🖃 *$20, includes Jepson Center for the Arts and Owens Thomas House and Slave Quarters.*

Wormsloe Historic Site. ⊠ *7601 Skidaway Rd., Savannah, GA* ☎ *912/353–3023* ⊕ *gastateparks.org/wormsloe* 🖃 *$10.*

🍴 Restaurants

B. Matthew's Eatery. $ *Average main: $12* ⊠ *325 E. Bay St., Savannah, GA* ☎ *912/233–1319* ⊕ *www.bmatthewseatery.com* ⊙ *No dinner Sun.*

Crab Shack. $ *Average main: $25* ⊠ *40 Estill Hammock Rd., Tybee Island, GA* ☎ *912/786–9857* ⊕ *thecrabshack.com.*

Elizabeth on 37th. $ *Average main: $35* ⊠ *105 E. 37th St., Savannah, GA* ☎ *912/236–5547* ⊕ *www.elizabethon37th.net* ⊘ *No lunch.*

The Grey Market. $ *Average main: $24* ⊠ *109 Jefferson St., Savannah, GA* ☎ *912/201–3924* ⊕ *www.thegreymkt.com* ⊘ *Closed Mon.–Wed.*

22 Square. $ *Average main: $31* ⊠ *14 Barnard St., Savannah, GA* ☎ *912/233–2116* ⊕ *www.hyatt.com/en-US/hotel/georgia/andaz-savannah/savrd/dining.*

Vic's on the River. $ *Average main: $28* ⊠ *26 E. Bay St., Savannah, GA* ☎ *912/721–1000* ⊕ *www.vicsontheriver.com.*

Whistle Stop Café. $ *Average main: $19* ⊠ *443 McCrackin St., Juliette, GA* ☎ *478/992–8886* ⊕ *www.thewhistlestopcafe.com* ⊘ *No dinner.*

Coffee and Quick Bites

Back in the Day Bakery. $ *Average main: $5* ⊠ *2401–2403, Bull St., Savannah, GA* ☎ *912/495–9292* ⊕ *www.backinthedaybakery.com.*

Starland Cafe & Gallery. $ *Average main: $11* ⊠ *11 E. 41st St., Savannah, GA* ☎ *912/443–9355* ⊕ *www.thestarlandcafe.com* ⊘ *Closed Sun.*

Hotels

Andaz Savannah. $ *Rooms from: $175* ⊠ *14 Barnard St., Savannah, GA* ☎ *912/233–2116* ⊕ *www.hyatt.com/en-US/hotel/georgia/andaz-savannah/savrd* ⊘ *No meals.*

Perry Lane Hotel. $ *Rooms from: $269* ⊠ *256 E. Perry St., Savannah, GA* ☎ *912/415–9000* ⊕ *www.perrylanehotel.com* ⊘ *No meals.*

Shopping

Salacia Salt Studio. ⊠ *208B W. Hall St., Savannah, GA* ☎ *478/561–0181* ⊕ *www.salaciasalts.com.*

The Shoppes at 1207. ⊠ *1207 U.S. Hwy. 80 E, Tybee Island, GA* ☎ *912/660–7298* ⊕ *www.visittybee.com.*

Activities

Captain Derek's Dolphin Adventure Tours. ⊠ *3 Old U.S. Hwy. 80, Tybee Island, GA* ☎ *912/658–2322* ⊕ *www.tybeedolphinadventure.com* ⊠ *Sightseeing tours from $18.*

Captain Mike's Dolphin Tours. ⊠ *1 Old U.S. Hwy. 80, Tybee Island, GA* ☎ *912/786–5848* ⊕ *www.tybeedolphins.com* ⊠ *Tours from $15 per person.*

Savannah Riverboat Cruises. ⊠ *9 E. River St., Savannah, GA* ☎ *912/232–6404* ⊕ *www.savannahriverboat.com* ⊠ *Sightseeing cruises from $28.*

Wilmington, NC

200 miles (approx. 3 hours) from Charlotte.

The port city of Wilmington and its surrounding beaches make for a perfect weekend trip: it's perfectly doable to fit in the right amounts of culture, cuisine, surf, and sun the area has to offer in just three days. Wilmington's coastline— made up of small beach communities like Wrightsville, Carolina, and Kure Beaches— is known for its natural beauty and for its great surfing, fishing, and scuba potential—especially diving among the historic sunken shipwrecks of the "Graveyard of the Atlantic." The picturesque Wilmington Riverwalk, and a recent influx of hip restaurants, cocktail bars, and breweries, give Downtown Wilmington recreational appeal; the Cameron Art Museum, with its modern interactive exhibits, is definitely worth an afternoon. The Battleship North Carolina, permanently parked on the Cape Fear River, tells the story of the North Carolina Coast's involvement in WWII.

Planning

GETTING THERE AND BACK
To reach Wilmington, head east out of Charlotte on I–74 for about three hours (200 miles).

INSPIRATION
Get a taste for Carolina beach music by listening to bands like The Embers, The Entertainers, and Band of Oz on your drive to Wilmington. These R&B-pop hybrid sounds are the soundtrack of "shag," a swing-type 1950s and 1960s dance craze claimed by both the North and South Carolina coasts.

PIT STOPS
As you drive toward the coast, look out for rustic (and often handwritten) signs advertising fresh fruit and vegetables, as well as boiled peanuts. Brown bags of this regional treat—fresh (not roasted), chewy peanuts boiled in saltwater—are sold hot at small roadside stands throughout Eastern North Carolina.

WHEN TO GO
Summer is peak season for Wilmington and its beaches, though it's best to keep an eye on the weather when planning a trip during hurricane season (technically June through November). High temps continue here until early October, making fall a good time to enjoy the beach while avoiding summer vacation crowds. Expect many beachside businesses to shutter during winter months.

WHERE TO STAY
You'll find all the standard chain hotels in Wilmington (the city hosts frequent conventions and events), but only in recent years have there been more interesting choices available like **Hotel Ballast,** a large riverfront hotel with boardwalk access

and a poolside lounge. The newest addition, **ARRIVE Wilmington,** is a hip, boutique-style hotel with excellent bar and dining outlets. The historic **Blockade Runner Resort,** renovated in a chic-retro style to celebrate its 1960s charm, is the best stay at Wrightsville Beach: there's an oceanside pool and patio, a few bars and restaurants, and lots of activities and tours.

Day 1

Plan to head to the beach pretty soon after arriving in Wilmington. This section of Atlantic coastline is highly underrated, and much less populated and developed than areas to the north or south. Here you'll find miles and miles of powder-like sand beaches, pristine and left untouched, aside from the occasional fishing pier or boardwalk.

Wrightsville Beach is the closest beach access from Wilmington, and is a local favorite, laid-back surf spot. On the way you'll pass **Arlie Gardens,** a nice place to stop first for a stroll to admire the coastal flowers, live oaks, and many species of birds.

Before crossing the bridge from Wilmington into Wrightsville, look out for the small colorful building belonging to **Ceviche's,** the place to stop for your first taste of fresh coastal fare—and margaritas—with Latin American and Caribbean flair.

Next, you can head for a quick peek at the **Wrightsville Beach Museum of History,** an exploration of the beach town throughout the decades, before parking near the beach. You can take a scenic boat tour, cast a line off of Johnny Mercer's Fishing Pier, or rent surf and stand-up paddle boards at **Aussie Island Surf Shop.** Wrightsville's small downtown is full of seafood shacks, clothing and swimwear boutiques, and relaxed bars and cafés.

Head back to Wilmington, where you can visit the shops and restaurants of the Downtown Riverwalk before having a cocktail in the chic courtyard at **Dram Yard** (at the ARRIVE hotel).

Dine in downtown Wilmington at **PinPoint Restaurant.** The chef here does wonders with oysters and other local produce, and the modern Southern menu is both comforting and sophisticated. Afterward, if you're still feeling festive, head to the **Blind Elephant,** a happening 1920s speakeasy (tucked into an alley downtown) known for their Moscow Mules.

Day 2

Grab a sweet treat and coffee at **Wake N Bake Donuts** (or **Port City Java**) before heading out to explore Wilmington and its farther beaches, Carolina and Kure. It's a quick detour to **Cameron Art Museum** on your drive southeast to the beaches, so stop here first to explore for an hour or two before hitting the coast. The museum hosts a well-curated permanent collection by North Carolina artists, local and international exhibits on photography and different fine arts, as well as interactive, technology-fueled experiences.

Today is a good day for a more involved beach activity, like a boat tour or renting a fishing boat. Otherwise, you can leisurely explore Kure Beach Oceanfront Park and Fishing Pier, visit the **North Carolina Aquarium at Fort Fisher,** and tour **Fort Fisher,** an Civil War Confederate fort.

Carolina Beach's most sophisticated spot is **Surf House Oyster Bar and Surf Camp,** great for lunch, an early dinner, or just a dozen on the half shell and a glass of wine. As you head back into Wilmington, spend time exploring the breweries of downtown. New-wave craft breweries like **New Anthem Beer Project, Ironclad Brewery,** and **Flytrap Brewing** are all within walking distance in Downtown Wilmington. Then continue your stroll, or opt for a horse-drawn carriage ride with **Horse-drawn Tours.**

Dinner can be casual tonight, with burgers piled in pimento cheese and other fixings at hipster **Rebellion,** or fish-and-chips at **Copper Penny** pub. There's plenty of time for a nightcap at **Tails Piano Bar,** a unique and entertaining venue.

Day 3

Go for brunch at **Spoonfed Kitchen,** a bright café where breakfast and lunch plates are piled high with seasonal vegetables and house-made ingredients like sausages and baked goods.

Next, head back to the Downtown Riverwalk to board a **Wilmington Water Tour.** The 50-minute Eagle Island cruise is a casual, guided tour through the Cape Fear River and the history and natural beauty of Wilmington's waterways. A quick drive from the cruise's dock will take you across the Cape Fear to the **Battleship North Carolina.** The permanently docked museum-ship has nine levels to explore (decks and interior rooms) and teaches you all about the Navy's involvement in WWII's Pacific Theater.

There's a few options for your last lunch in Wilmington. **The Foxes Boxes** is a cute (and affordable) way to take gourmet salads and sandwiches on the road; **Beer Barrio** offers casual, modern Mexican dishes; and **Indochine,** with Vietnamese and Thai-fusion lunch specials in a lively setting—complete with East Asian decor, pavilions, and gazebos—is a local favorite.

Recommendations

Sights

Arlie Gardens. ⊠ *300 Airlie Rd., Wilmington, NC* ☎ *910/798–7700* ⊕ *airliegardens. org* 🖾 *$9.*

Battleship North Carolina. ✉ 1 Battleship Rd., Wilmington, NC ☎ 910/399–9100 ⊕ www.battleshipnc.com ⊡ $10.

Cameron Art Museum. ✉ 3201 S. 17th St., Wilmington, NC ☎ 910/395–5999 ⊕ cameronartmuseum.org ⊡ $10 ⊗ Closed Mon.

Fort Fisher State Historic Site. ✉ 1610 Ft. Fisher Blvd. S, Kure Beach, NC ☎ 910/251–7340 ⊕ historicsites.nc.gov/all-sites/fort-fisher ⊡ Free ⊗ Closed Sun. and Mon.

North Carolina Aquarium at Fort Fisher. ✉ 900 Loggerhead Rd., Kure Beach, NC ☎ 910/772–0500 ⊕ www.ncaquariums.com/fort-fisher ⊡ $10.

Wrightsville Beach. ✉ 505 Nutt St., Wilmington, NC ☎ 877/406–2356 ⊕ www.wilmingtonandbeaches.com ⊡ Free.

Wrightsville Beach Museum of History. ✉ 303 W. Salisbury St., Wrightsville Beach, NC ☎ 910/256–2569 ⊕ wbmuseumofhistory.com ⊡ Free ⊗ Closed Mon.

🍴 Restaurants

Beer Barrio. $ Average main: $12 ✉ 34 N. Front St., Wilmington, NC ☎ 910/769–5452 ⊕ beerbarrionc.com.

Ceviche's. $ Average main: $22 ✉ 7210 Wrightsville Ave., Wilmington, NC ☎ 910/762–5282 ⊕ www.wbceviche.com ⊗ Closed Sun.

Copper Penny. $ Average main: $14 ✉ 109 Chestnut St., Wilmington, NC ☎ 910/762–1373 ⊕ www.copperpennync.com.

Foxes Boxes. $ Average main: $10 ✉ 622 N. 4th St., Wilmington, NC ☎ 910/769–0125 ⊕ thefoxesboxes.com ⊗ Closed Mon.

Indochine Restaurant. $ Average main: $10 ✉ 7 Wayne Dr., Wilmington, NC ☎ 910/251–9229 ⊕ www.indochinewilmington.com ⊗ No lunch Sun. and Mon.

PinPoint Restaurant. $ Average main: $28 ✉ 114 Market St., Wilmington, NC ☎ 910/769–2972 ⊕ pinpointrestaurant.com ⊗ No lunch Mon.–Sat.

Rebellion. $ Average main: $10 ✉ 15 S. Front St., Wilmington, NC ☎ 910/399–1162 ⊕ rebellionnc.com ⊗ Closed Mon.

Spoonfed Kitchen. $ Average main: $14 ✉ 1930 Eastwood Rd.. Wilmington, NC ☎ 910/679–8881 ⊕ spoonfedkitchen.com ⊗ Closed Mon. No dinner.

Surf House Oyster Bar and Surf Camp. $ Average main: $28 ✉ 604 N. Lake Park Blvd., Carolina Beach, NC ☎ 910/707–0422 ⊕ www.surfhousenc.com ⊗ No lunch.

Coffee and Quick Bites

Port City Java. $ Average main: $5 ✉ 21A N. Front St. Wilmington, NC ☎ 910/762–5282 ⊕ www.portcityjava.com ⊗ No dinner.

Wake N Bake Donuts. $ Average main: $4 ✉ 114 Princess St., Wilmington, NC ☎ 910/470–4348 ⊕ wakenbakedonuts.square.site ⊗ No dinner.

🛏 Hotels

ARRIVE Wilmington. $ Rooms from: $189 ✉ 101 S. 2nd St., Wilmington, NC ☎ 910/447–4704 ⊕ arrivehotels.com ⋈ No meals.

Blockade Runner Beach Resort. $ Rooms from: $135 ✉ 275 Waynick Blvd., Wrightsville Beach, NC ☎ 877/684–8009 ⊕ blockade-runner.com ⋈ No meals.

Hotel Ballast Wilmington. $ Rooms from: $189 ✉ 301 N. Water St., Wilmington, NC ☎ 910/763–5900 ⊕ www.hilton.com/en/hotels/ilmwrup-hotel-ballast-wilmington ⋈ No meals.

Nightlife

Blind Elephant. ✉ *21 N. Front St., Wilmington, NC* ☎ *910/256–5454* ⊕ *www. blindelephantspeakeasy.com.*

Dram Yard. ✉ *101 S. 2nd St., Wilmington, NC* ☎ *910/782–2400* ⊕ *www.dramyard. com.*

Flytrap Berewing. ✉ *319 Walnut St., Wilmington, NC* ☎ *910/769–2881* ⊕ *www. flytrapbrewing.com.*

Ironclad Brewery. ✉ *115 N. 2nd St., Wilmington, NC* ☎ *910/769–2881* ⊕ *www. ironcladbrewery.com.*

New Anthem Beer Project. ✉ *116 Dock St., Wilmington, NC* ☎ *910/399–4683* ⊕ *newanthembeer.com.*

Tails Piano Bar. ✉ *115 S. Front St., Wilmington, NC* ☎ *910/399–6428* ⊕ *www. tailspianobar.com.*

Shopping

Aussie Island Surf Shop. ✉ *5101 Dunlea Ct., Wilmington, NC* ☎ *910/256–5454* ⊕ *www.aussieisland.com.* .

🏃 Activities

Horsedrawn Tours. ✉ *16 Market St., Wilmington, NC* ☎ *910/251–8889* ⊕ *www. horsedrawntours.com* 🎫 *From $14.*

Wilmington Water Tours. ✉ *212 S. Water St., Wilmington, NC* ☎ *910/256–5454* ⊕ *wilmingtonwatertours.net* 🎫 *Cruises from $15.*

Chapter 5

NORTHEAST AND MID-ATLANTIC

WELCOME TO
NORTHEAST AND MID-ATLANTIC

TOP REASONS TO GO

★ **Coastal Excursions:**
From grass-covered dunes in Cape Cod to rocky shorelines around Acadia.

★ **Just-Caught Seafood:**
Choose your lobster right from the tank at area seafood shacks.

★ **Leaf Peeping:** The best fall foliage is in the Berkshires, the Catskills, and the White Mountains.

★ **Stately Mansions:**
Tour the "summer cottages" of Newport or the historic houses of the Hudson Valley.

★ **Island Getaways:**
Join locals who flock to exclusive Nantucket and Martha's Vineyard.

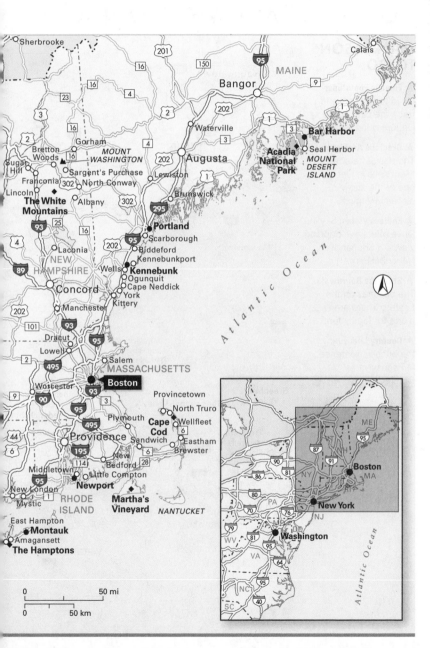

WELCOME TO
NORTHEAST AND MID-ATLANTIC

TOP REASONS
TO GO

★ **Famous Footsteps:**
Head to Anappolis to
trace the path of the
Underground Railroad.

★ **Gracious Architecture:**
Thomas Jefferson's
Monticello is just
one of the show-
places in Virginia.

★ **Endless Vistas:** Skyline
Drive offers eye-popping
views of Shenandoah
Nationbal Park.

★ **Stroll the Boardwalk:**
The beaches on the
Eastern Shore are
made for family fun.

★ **Country Life:** Enjoy
the bucolic existence
in Pennsylvania
Dutch Country.

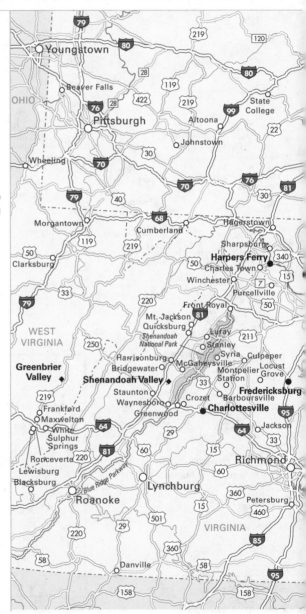

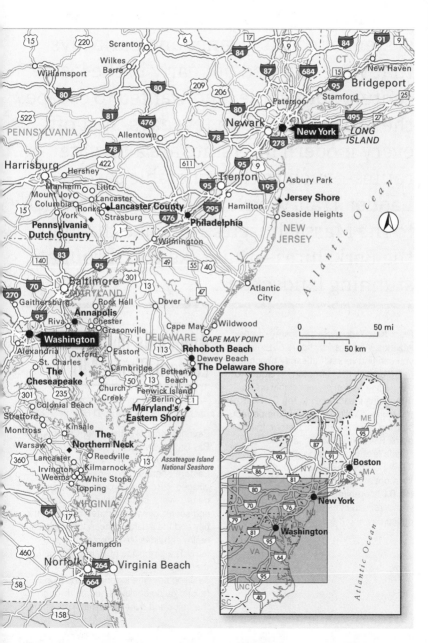

The country's Northeast and Mid-Atlantic regions were designed with road trips in mind. We're talking about the system of country lanes and parkways that were mapped out early in the last century for people who wanted to escape the urban areas for a few days. Just off every modern interstate are alternate routes—such as the venerable Jacob's Ladder Trail, which runs roughly parallel to the Massachusetts Turnpike through the Berkshires—that take you through stunning landscapes.

From **New York,** there are plenty of possibilities. Within a few hours of the city you can find yourself at sandy beaches (head east to the Hamptons or south to the Jersey Shore) or impossibly green mountains (head north to the Catskills or the Hudson Valley). **Boston** is the perfect starting point for trips to historic towns (think Bar Harbor, Maine, and Newport, Rhode Island) and gorgeous scenery (New Hampshire's White Mountains or Vermont's Made River Valley). **Washington, D.C.,** combines history and natural wonders in destinations like the Chesapeake Bay and the Shenandoah Valley.

Annapolis and the Eastern Shore, MD

Annapolis is 37 miles (approx. 45 minutes) from Washington, D.C.

Beyond Annapolis, the great Chesapeake Bay Bridge sweeps you across the nation's largest estuary into the pastoral Eastern Shore. A domain of waterfront villages, corn and soybean fields, meandering rivers, crab shacks, farm stands, and scenic byways perched between the bay and the Atlantic Ocean, this magical realm entwines life between bay and farm. The birthplace of Harriet Tubman, there are Underground Railroad stories detailing how the legendary abolitionist helped guide enslaved people through the fields and river-laced marshes—much of which remain the same today. And while the region is quiet, an urbane artsy and culinary scene reigns in its towns, notably Easton, Oxford, and St. Michaels. The gateway is the small city of Annapolis, with the famous U.S. Naval Academy, a historic harbor front, and tons of little shops and restaurants in historic buildings. If you enjoy small-town browsing, blue-crab eating, country-lane biking, bird-watching, and simply breathing in the fresh, bay-scented outdoors, this weekend getaway is for you.

Planning

GETTING THERE AND BACK

You'll need a car to explore the Eastern Shore. On the first day, take U.S. 50 E from Washington, D.C., over the Chesapeake Bay Bridge. Kent Island awaits just 5 miles beyond, about an hour from D.C. From here, head to Chestertown via U.S. 301, about 50 minutes; Rock Hall is about 20 minutes beyond Chestertown via MD 20. Now backtrack, heading south to Easton via U.S. 50, about 50 minutes. On the next day, Cambridge to Annapolis takes about an hour, backtracking the way you came. From there, home awaits less than an hour away (depending on traffic—it can get bad on U.S. 50, especially on Sunday evening, when everyone is heading back from the beach).

WHEN TO GO

The Eastern Shore is a year-round destination, with summer being the busiest. It's hot and humid, then, cooled by bay breezes. The shoulder seasons are lovely—May and September—when temperatures are comfortable and migrating birds are winging their way through. Winter is pleasant, too, and while you won't be partaking in watery activities, you can enjoy plenty of other goings-on, including regional festivals and holiday celebrations.

WHERE TO STAY

Charming, elegant, yet relaxed is how you'll find most of the accommodations on the Eastern Shore, ranging from stately inns and hotels to charming B&Bs, with many occupying historic buildings. Be aware that many require a minimum of two-night stays on weekends and other busy times. The historic **Tidewater Inn,** anchoring downtown Easton, is a go-to, with its elegant guest rooms and alfresco lobby. The romantic, seven-room **Oxford Inn** in Oxford, perched on one of the nation's oldest streets, occupies a charming 19th-century house overlooking a creek; enjoy a cup of coffee on the breezy porch and you will never want to leave. In downtown Annapolis, the 215-room **Graduate Annapolis Hotel** mixes bayside style, Navy pomp, and campus lore. History pervades the three properties belonging to the Historic Inns of Annapolis, dating back to the late 1700s: the **Governor Calvert House,** the **Robert Johnson House,** and the Maryland Inn.

Day 1

Head across the Chesapeake Bay Bridge onto the Eastern Shore. People normally zip across Kent Island, just 5 miles east of the bridge, but this time slow down. Stop by the **Chesapeake Heritage & Visitor Center** to see exhibits about the area; it also accesses **Ferry Point Park,** where a 530-foot marshland boardwalk leads to a sandy beach area. Alternatively, hop aboard a kayak at the **Chesapeake Bay Environmental Center** in Grasonville to spot bald eagles, ospreys, and herons. Get your first taste of delectable Chesapeake seafood—out-of-this-world crab cakes, fried oyster Caesar salad, sautéed little neck clams, served dockside, of course—at **The Narrows Restaurant** on Kent Narrows Waterfront.

Continuing on, opt for a quick detour north to the adorable little town of Chestertown on the Chester River, with

Annapolis Harbor is a popular weekend destination for residents of Baltimore and Washington, D.C.

its red-brick sidewalks, artist studios, and the state's greatest concentration of 18th- and 19th-century buildings outside Annapolis. The nearby **Eastern Neck National Wildlife Refuge** is another place to spot birds, including nesting bald eagles; while the adorable little fishing village of Rock Hall has a museum devoted to the region's watermen.

Now head south to Easton, figuring you'll arrive in the late afternoon, just in time for a predinner stroll. As storybook as it is with its historic buildings, flowery gardens, and tree-lined streets, this bustling place is considered the mini-metropolis of the region, notable for its world-class theater, internationally acclaimed art galleries, and lauded restaurants. Treat yourself to **Bas Rouge,** a classic, white-tablecloth French establishment where everything from service to decor is jewel-box exquisite. A three-course prix-fixe menu might feature wagyu tatki, Chesapeake Bay rockfish, and chocolate mousse cake. And there's no better

way to end this glorious day than with a Scotch at the next-door **Stewart.**

Day 2

You are in the heart of the Eastern Shore here, with the entire day to soak it up. But first things first—linger over a homestyle breakfast at the cozy **Breakfast in Easton.** If you're into scrapple (slabs of pork meat scraps boiled with spices and cornmeal), this is the place to try it.

Then, you're in for a fabulous morning pedaling some of the region's meandering byways, on the 30-mile Easton/St. Michaels/Oxford loop. (Driving is great, too.) From Easton, go south to Oxford, a white-picket-fence, lost-in-time town with front-porched homes, the historic **Robert Morris Inn** (where James Michener outlined Chesapeake), and handcrafted ice cream at **Scottish Highland Creamery.** Hop aboard the **Oxford-Bellevue Ferry**— the nation's oldest privately run ferry service, since 1683—across the Tred Avon River, and head up to St. Michaels.

Perched on the Miles River, this historic waterfront town has antique shops, boutiques, and (more) homemade ice cream. The **Chesapeake Bay Maritime Museum** has all-things-Chesapeake, including a lighthouse built in 1879, a small boat shed filled with Chesapeake watercraft (including a Native American fishing and oystering canoe), and a re-created crabber's shanty. From here, Easton is 10 miles away.

Back in Easton, grab a late lunch at **Sunflowers & Greens,** a small, charming café offering divine salads, seasonal soups, and gourmet sandwiches, then head south to Cambridge. You have a couple of good options here. To see more wildlife, head for **Blackwater National Wildlife Refuge,** where the Blackwater River moseys through tidal flats, past tree-clad islands, before joining the Chesapeake Bay. The refuge's extensive marshes make prime habitat for migratory birds—Canada geese, great cormorants, pied-bill grebes, yellowlegs, and more. Wildlife Drive opens up this natural world to hikers and drivers.

Another option is to explore Harriet Tubman history. The legendary abolitionist escaped from slavery on a nearby plantation, returning many times to transport enslaved friends and family to freedom along the Underground Railroad. The **Harriet Tubman Underground Railroad Visitor Center**'s four state-of-the-art buildings provide insight. From here, you can drive the self-guided **Harriet Tubman Byway** that connects other related sites, all the way to the Delaware border. For today, stick to the sites around Cambridge, including **Bucktown Village Store,** where Tubman received a blow to the head when she was 13 or 14 for speaking up against authority to protect another child; the store is now a museum.

When you're ready, make the push back to Annapolis, about an hour north. Serving as Maryland's colonial capital, then state capital, its capitol building reigns

as the nation's oldest in continuous use, since 1772. With that history comes one of the nation's greatest concentrations of 18th-century buildings. Yes, it's cute. Very cute.

Okay, you must be tired and hungry by now. Annapolis has more than its fair share of outstanding restaurants, though for something totally Annapolis, try **Mike's Crab House**, an authentic, open-air crab shack with butcher paper picnic tables and piles and piles of Old-Bay–doused blue crabs. And, if you haven't had enough ice cream already today, top it off with a scoop—or three—of homemade ice cream from the **Annapolis Ice Cream Company** on Main Street.

Day 3

Start off the day at **Iron Rooster,** which serves breakfast all day. Hope you're hungry, because the extensive menu includes the likes of Angry Pig Omelet (several different kinds of pork with chopped jalapeños), crab hash, and chicken and pancakes.

From here, explore the city's cobbled streets. The main artery, Main Street, is lively with shops and restaurants, ending at City Dock, the heart and soul of Annapolis. Find a spot along the seawall and watch the parade of people and big boats float along Ego Alley.

Explore the quaint alleyways that are part and parcel of the baroque street plan laid out in the late 1600s—possessing charms of their own. Chancery Lane, for example, provides photogenic views of the **Maryland State House.** And Wayman Alley shortcuts to Prince George Street, home of the historic **William Paca House and Garden.**

From here, head to the **U.S. Naval Academy** for a tour of the "Yard," the 300-acre undergraduate college of the U.S. Navy, established in 1845. If you take the full-on tour, which leaves from the

Armel-Leftwich Visitor Center, you'll visit the world's third largest dormitory and see the crypt of Revolutionary War–era naval hero John Paul Jones. You can also just wander around on your own. Be sure to stop by the **Naval Academy Museum** for perspective.

For a late lunch, walk or catch a water taxi from City Dock for a five-minute ride to garden-filled Eastport. Here, the **Boatyard Bar and Grill** is known for its crab cakes, raw bar, smoked fish of the day, and, in season, soft-shell crab sandwiches. Nearby, the **Annapolis Maritime Museum and Park** has permanent exhibits about life on the Chesapeake, plus a refurbished skipjack (a traditional Chesapeake fishing boat) open for tours.

As you wind up the weekend, there's no need to rush back home. Leaving Annapolis, take a detour to **Quiet Waters Park,** located between the South River and Harness Creek just outside town. Here, trails wind through forests and grassy fields of a 340-acre oasis, providing one last gulp of fresh bay air.

Recommendations

 Sights

Annapolis Maritime Museum and Park. ✉ 723 2nd St., Annapolis, MD ☎ 410/295–0104 ⊕ www.amaritime.org 🖭 $35.

Armel-Leftwich Visitor Center. ✉ 52 King George St., Annapolis, MD ☎ 410/293–8687 ⊕ www.usnabsd.com 🖭 $12 ⊙ Closed Sun.

Blackwater National Wildlife Refuge. ✉ 2145 Key Wallace Dr., Cambridge, MD ☎ 410/228–2677 ⊕ www.fws.gov 🖭 $3 per vehicle.

Bucktown Village Store. ✉ 4303 Bucktown Rd., Cambridge, MD ☎ 410/901–9255 ⊕ www.bucktownstore.com 🖭 Free ⊙ Closed Sun.

Chesapeake Bay Environmental Center. ✉ 6 Herndon Ave., Annapolis, MD ☎ 410/268–8816 ⊕ www.bayrestoration. org 🖭 $35.

Chesapeake Bay Maritime Museum. ✉ 723 2nd St., Annapolis, MD ☎ 410/295–0104 ⊕ www.cbmm.org 🖭 $5.

Chesapeake Heritage & Visitor Center. ✉ 425 Piney Narrows Rd., Chester, MD ☎ 410/604–2100 ⊕ www.findyourchesapeake.com 🖭 Free.

Eastern Neck National Wildlife Refuge. ✉ 1730 Eastern Neck Rd., Rock Hall, MD ☎ 410/639–7056 ⊕ www.fws.gov 🖭 Free.

Ferry Point Park. ✉ 425 Piney Narrows Rd., Chester, MD ☎ 410/778–4430 ⊕ www.alltrails.com 🖭 Free.

Harriet Tubman Byway. ✉ 4068 Golden Hill Rd., Church Creek, MD ☎ 410/221–2290 ⊕ www.harriettubmanbyway.org 🖭 Free.

Harriet Tubman Underground Railroad Visitor Center. ✉ 4068 Golden Hill Rd., Church Creek, MD ☎ 410/221–2290 ⊕ www.nps. gov 🖭 Free.

Maryland State House. ✉ 100 State Cir., Annapolis, MD ☎ 410/946–5000 ⊕ www. msa.maryland.gov 🖭 Free.

Naval Academy Museum. ✉ 118 Maryland Ave., Annapolis, MD ☎ 410/293–2108 ⊕ www.usna.edu 🖭 Free.

Quiet Waters Park. ✉ 600 Quiet Waters Park Rd., Annapolis, MD ☎ 410/222–1777 ⊕ www.aacounty.org 🖭 $6 per vehicle.

U.S. Naval Academy. ✉ 118 Maryland Ave., Annapolis, MD ☎ 410/293–2108 ⊕ www. usna.edu 🖭 Free.

William Paca House and Garden. ✉ 186 Prince George St., Annapolis, MD ☎ 410/990–4543 ⊕ www.annapolis.org 🖭 $10.

🍴 Restaurants

Bas Rouge. $ _Average main: $23_ ⊠ _19 Federal St., Easton, MD_ ☎ _410/822–1637_ ⊕ _www.basrougeeaston.com_ ⊗ _Closed Mon.–Wed._

Boatyard Bar and Grill. $ _Average main: $16_ ⊠ _400 4th St., Annapolis, MD_ ☎ _410/216–6206_ ⊕ _www.boatyardbarand-grill.com._

Breakfast in Easton. $ _Average main: $5_ ⊠ _28-A S. Washington St., Easton, MD_ ☎ _410/820–4057_ ⊗ _Closed Mon._

Iron Rooster. $ _Average main: $16_ ⊠ _12 Market Space, Annapolis, MD_ ☎ _410/990–1600_ ⊕ _www.ironroosterall-day.com._

Mike's Crab House. $ _Average main: $13_ ⊠ _3030 Riva Rd., Riva, MD_ ☎ _410/956–2784_ ⊕ _www.mikescrabhouse.com._

The Narrows Restaurant. $ _Average main: $19_ ⊠ _3023 Kent Narrow Way S, Gra-sonville, MD_ ☎ _410/827–8113_ ⊕ _www.thenarrowsrestaurant.com._

Sunflowers & Greens. $ _Average main: $12_ ⊠ _11 Federal St., Easton, MD_ ☎ _410/882–7972_ ⊕ _www.sunflowersand-greens.com_ ⊗ _Closed Sun._

☕ Coffee and Quick Bites

Annapolis Ice Cream Company. $ _Average main: $4_ ⊠ _196 Main St., Annapolis, MD_ ☎ _443/714–8674_ ⊕ _www.annapolisice-cream.com_ ⊗ _Closed Tues.–Thurs._

Scottish Highland Creamery. $ _Average main: $6_ ⊠ _314 Tilghman St., Oxford, MD_ ☎ _410/924–6298_ ⊕ _www.scottishhigh-landcreamery.com_ ⊗ _Closed Tues. and Wed._

🛏 Hotels

Governor Calvert House. $ _Rooms from: $89_ ⊠ _23 State Cir., Annapolis, MD_ ☎ _410/263–2641_ ⊕ _www.historicinnso-fannapolis.com_ �ⓞ _No meals._

Graduate Annapolis Hotel. $ _Rooms from: $97_ ⊠ _126 West St., Annapolis, MD_ ☎ _410/263–7777_ ⊕ _www.graduatehotels.com_ ⓞ _No meals._

Maryland Inn. $ _Rooms from: $79_ ⊠ _16 Church Cir., Annapolis, MD_ ☎ _410/263–2641_ ⊕ _www.historicinnsofannapolis.com/stay/maryland-inn_ ⓞ _No meals._

Oxford Inn. $ _Rooms from: $132_ ⊠ _504 S. Morris St., Oxford, MD_ ☎ _410/226–5220_ ⊕ _www.oxfordinn.net_ ⓞ _Free breakfast._

Robert Johnson House. $ _Rooms from: $129_ ⊠ _23 State Cir., Annapolis, MD_ ☎ _410/263–2641_ ⊕ _www.historicinnso-fannapolis.com_ ⓞ _No meals._

Robert Morris Inn. $ _Rooms from: $175_ ⊠ _314 N. Morris St., Oxford, MD_ ☎ _410/226–5111_ ⊕ _www.robertmorrisinn.com_ ⓞ _Free breakfast._

Tidewater Inn. $ _Rooms from: $135_ ⊠ _101 E. Dover St., Easton, MD_ ☎ _410/822–1300_ ⊕ _www.tidewaterinn.com_ ⓞ _No meals._

🍸 Nightlife

Stewart. ⊠ _3 Federal St., Easton, MD_ ☎ _410/793–4128_ ⊕ _www.thestewart.com._

🏃 Activities

Oxford-Bellevue Ferry. ⊠ _27456 Oxford Rd., Oxford, MD_ ☎ _410/745–9023_ ⊕ _www.oxfordferry.com_ ⊠ _$22._

Bar Harbor and Acadia National Park, ME

285 miles (approx. 5 hours) from Boston.

Mount Desert Island was once the summer home of America's wealthiest families, including the Rockefellers, Van-derbilts, and Astors. While its Gilded Age heyday has passed, this "Downeast"

The craggy coastline of Acadia National Park makes it one of the most visually stunning road trips in the Northeast.

island off the coast of Maine is still a laid-back yet sophisticated hideaway. The pleasures here are simple: a stroll through the main town of **Bar Harbor,** a boat ride along Frenchman Bay, and consuming as much fresh-off-the-boat lobster as humanly possible.

But what separates Mount Desert (pronounced dessert) from other postcard-perfect New England getaways is the fact that it's home to **Acadia National Park.** This 47,000-acre wonderland of seaside cliffs, forested mountains, and pristine beaches is one of the East Coast's most jaw-droppingly scenic spots, attracting nature lovers from all over the world.

Planning

GETTING THERE AND BACK
From Boston take 1–95 N to Bangor, MA, then pick up Route 1A to Ellsworth and follow Route 3 to Bar Harbor. The trip takes about five hours.

PIT STOPS
Portland, at the approximate halfway point between Boston and Bar Harbor, is a perfect place for a pit stop. Stroll the Old Port District overlooking Casco Bay and slurp some oysters at **Eventide.** If you have time, check out the Winslow Homer collection at the I. M. Pei–designed **Portland Museum of Art.**

WHEN TO GO
Peak season is May through September, when all the shops and restaurants are buzzing. Fall is an especially beautiful time to visit, with (slightly) smaller crowds coming to see the spectacular fall foliage in Acadia National Park. Events-wise, the Art in the Park art show takes place in June and the Bar Harbor Music festival is held throughout the month of July.

WHERE TO STAY
For such a small island, Bar Harbor has several full-scale resorts. The **Bar Harbor Inn** sits right on Frenchman Bay and is home to the elegant Reading Room restaurant and the more casual Terrace

Grille. The **Harborside Hotel, Spa & Marina** is also on the waterfront (the same owners also run **Stewman's Lobster Pound** next door). In town, its sister property is the boutique-style **West Street Hotel,** featuring a pub with outdoor seating and a rooftop swimming pool.

Day 1

Once you cross the causeway from the mainland and travel east on Route 3, you won't have to wait long to encounter traditional lobster shacks. At **Rose Eden Lobster,** lunch on steamed lobster and corn-on-the-cob at one of the outdoor picnic tables. Once in Bar Harbor—after a quick hotel check-in and change—head down to the pier for a sunset cruise on Frenchman Bay.

Aboard the four-masted schooner *Margaret Todd,* you can help hoist the sails if you're so inclined, or simply sit back as the cooling bay breezes blow and take in the idyllic scenes of lobstermen hauling in their traps and puffins perched on rocky coastlines as the sun starts to cast its magical glow.

For satisfying pub grub and a few beers (say yes to locally brewed blueberry ale), head to the **Thirsty Whale Tavern,** affectionately known by locals as the Whale. A bowl of clam chowder to start is a must, followed by comfort dishes like haddock fish and chips or a blackened blue cheese burger. Make it an early night, because you'll want to be in top form for your day exploring Acadia.

Day 2

After fortifying yourself with a tall stack of wild blueberry pancakes at **Jennie's Great Maine Breakfast,** head over to **Acadia National Park** (it's just a few minutes' drive from town). First-timers often get the lay of the land by taking a leisurely drive along the 27-mile Park Loop Road.

Pull over when the mood strikes, but must-sees include crescent-shape Sand Beach (dip your toes in the frigid water if you dare); Thunder Hole, to hear the thunderous clap of the surf crashing against coastal rocks; and the summit of 1,528-foot Cadillac Mountain, with eye-popping panoramas of island-dotted Frenchman Bay.

Another popular pastime in the park is to have tea and popovers on the lawn at **Jordan Pond House,** the only restaurant in the park (lunch is available in season). While it certainly can get crowded (it's wise to make a reservation), the stellar views of glacial Jordan Pond framed by a twin-peaked mountain dubbed Bubbles really shouldn't be missed. From there, you can access the park's famous Carriage Roads, 45 miles of scenic paths built between 1913 and 1940 by John D. Rockefeller that attract hikers, bikers, and horseback riders.

Back in town, immerse yourself in a little of that Gilded Age glamour by dining at the fancy **Reading Room** in the Bar Harbor Inn. Book a bay-facing table and order classics like lobster bisque and filet mignon with a Cabernet demi-glace, and don't skimp on dessert—the blueberry pie a la mode is legendary. Cap off your night with a few beers at **Leary's Landing,** a centrally located Irish-style pub that attracts both locals and travelers. It has craft beers and more than 50 whiskeys. And while Bar Harbor isn't exactly known for its nightlife scene, you'll find DJs and dancing at **Carmen Verandah.**

Day 3

Spend your last morning poking around Bar Harbor—after a breakfast at **Jordan's,** that is. The three-egg omelet is the thing to get here (we're partial to the Western or the feta, spinach, and tomato). At the **Abbe Museum,** learn about Maine's Native American community, collectively known as the Wabanaki. Browse among the state's largest collection of basketry and artifacts discovered in the Frenchman Bay area.

The **Rock and Art Shop** is a cool little spot selling crystals, terrariums, and scented candles, and **Cool as a Moose** is where you can stock up on souvenirs like T-shirts, jewelry, and jars of wild blueberry jam. Take a break on the Village Green, preferably with a cone from **Mt. Desert Island Ice Cream.**

Finally, you can't leave Bar Harbor without stopping by the **Side Street Cafe.** This local staple has a great atmosphere, especially during happy hour where you can order a pitcher of margaritas and nosh on lobster mac and cheese and pan-fried peekytoe crab cakes.

Recommendations

Sights

Abbe Museum. ✉ *26 Mt. Desert St., Bar Harbor, ME* ☎ *207/288–3519* 🌐 *www.abbemuseum.org* 🎟 *$10* 🕓 *Closed Jan.*

Acadia National Park. ✉ *Hulls Cove Visitor Center, Rte. 3, Bar Harbor, ME* ☎ *207/288–3338* 🌐 *www.nps.gov/acad/index* 🎟 *$30 per vehicle.*

Margaret Todd. ✉ *Bar Harbor Inn Pier, Newport Dr., Bar Harbor, ME* ☎ *207/288–4585* 🌐 *downeastwindjammer.com* 🎟 *$42.*

Restaurants

Jennie's Great Maine Breakfast. [$] *Average main: $12* ✉ *15 Cottage St., Bar Harbor, ME* ☎ *207/288–4166.*

Jordan Pond House. [$] *Average main: $21* ✉ *2928 Park Loop Rd., Seal Harbor, ME* ☎ *207/276–3610* 🌐 *www.jordanpondhouse.com.*

Jordan's. [$] *Average main: $12* ✉ *80 Cottage St., Bar Harbor, ME* ☎ *207/288–3586* 🌐 *www.jordansbarharbor.com.*

Reading Room. [$] *Average main: $30* ✉ *1 Newport Dr., Bar Harbor, ME* ☎ *844/814–1668* 🌐 *barharborinn.com/dining/reading-room.*

Rose Eden Lobster. [$] *Average main: $32* ✉ *864 Hwy. 3, Bar Harbor, ME* ☎ *207/610–3060* 🌐 *www.roseeden.com.*

Stewman's Lobster Pound. [$] *Average main: $20* ✉ *35 West St., Bar Harbor, ME* ☎ *207/288–0346* 🌐 *www.stewmanslobsterpound.com.*

Thirsty Whale Tavern. [$] *Average main: $12* ✉ *40 Cottage St., Bar Harbor, ME* ☎ *207/288–9335* 🌐 *www.thirstywhaletavern.com.*

Coffee and Quick Bites

Mt. Desert Island Ice Cream. [$] *Average main: $5* ✉ *7 Firefly La., Bar Harbor, ME* ☎ *207/801–4006* 🌐 *www.mdiic.com.*

Hotels

Bar Harbor Inn. [$] *Rooms from: $318* ✉ *1 Newport Dr., Bar Harbor, ME* ☎ *844/814–1668* 🌐 *barharborinn.com.*

Harborside Hotel, Spa & Marina. [$] *Rooms from: $190* ✉ *55 West St., Bar Harbor, ME* ☎ *207/288–5033* 🌐 *www.theharborsidehotel.com.*

West Street Hotel. [$] *Rooms from: $240* ✉ *50 West St., Bar Harbor, ME* ☎ *207/288–0825* 🌐 *www.theweststreethotel.com.*

Nightlife

Carmen Verandah. ✉ *119 Main St., Bar Harbor, ME* ☎ *207/288–2886* 🌐 *www.eatfishmaine.com/carmen-verandah.*

Leary's Landing. ✉ *156 Main St., Bar Harbor, ME* ☎ *207/664–3919* 🌐 *www.learyslanding.com* 🕓 *Closed Sun.*

👜 Shopping

Cool as a Moose. ✉ 118 Main St., Bar Harbor, ME ☎ 207/288–3904 ⊕ www.coolasamoose.com.

Rock and Art Shop. ✉ 23 Cottage St., Bar Harbor, ME ☎ 207/288–4800 ⊕ www.therockandartshop.com ⊘ Closed Dec.–Apr.

The Berkshires, MA

Great Barrington is 135 miles (approx. 3 hours) from New York City, 137 miles (approximately 2¾ hours) from Boston.

Three hours north of New York City (and almost equidistant from Boston) is Berkshire County in Western Massachusetts, an area flanked by mountains that display piercing hues in fall. Made up of some of America's best small towns, mention the Berkshires to anyone on the East Coast and you'll notice a glimmer of recognition and awe in their eyes. New Yorkers keep second homes here, and celebrities inhabit Victorian houses tucked away on hillsides, though it's rare to see them emerge. Summers are about picnics on the lawn at Tanglewood in Lenox and perusing Main Street in Great Barrington with an ice cream cone in hand. In winter, snowbirds flock to the slopes; fall means breathing in crisp mountain air on hikes or drives to see the changing leaves.

Planning

GETTING THERE AND BACK

Driving is the best option, as you'll need a car to get around. The Taconic State Parkway is the most direct route from New York City. If you don't wish to drive, you can take the Peter Pan bus from New York City's Port Authority to the center of Great Barrington. Metro North's Harlem line goes from Grand Central Station to Wassaic Station in Amenia, New York, and from there you can take a pre-arranged taxi to the Berkshires (less than an hour), but this can be expensive.

From Boston, the Massachusetts Turnpike is the best and fastest route. Amtrak has one train daily from Boston to Pittsfield, about 21 miles from Great Barrington. Buses connect Boston to Williamstown, 41 miles from Great Barrington. However, public transportation within the Berkshires is extremely limited, so driving is almost always the best option.

WHEN TO GO

As James Taylor once sang, "the Berkshires seemed dream-like on account of that frosting." It's true: the Berkshires in winter are stunning, but also in spring, summer, and fall. Summer is the most crowded with tourists, but also means concerts at Tanglewood and Mass MoCa. Fall beckons leaf-peepers to the chagrin of locals, but who can blame them? The myriad hues are stunning on the Berkshire mountains.

WHERE TO STAY

There are a variety of lodging options in the Berkshires. Our favorites include the brand-new **Williams Inn** in Williamstown, with 64 rooms and a farm-to-table eatery on-site. The three story building was built from the ground up but inspired by classic New England farmhouse architecture. **Hotel on North** in Pittsfield is another recent addition to the Berkshires, melding historic and modern in a more urban setting than the aforementioned options. The boutique property features a cocktail bar in a birdcage elevator and an excellent on-site restaurant, Eat on North, and 45 unique guestrooms. For something a little more central, try bed and breakfast **The Barrington** right on Main Street in Great Barrington, or the upscale **Wyndhurst Manor and Club in Lenox.**

Day 1

Leave the city no later than mid-morning to avoid hitting Friday afternoon traffic. Take a break at **Taste NY** on the Taconic Parkway for a cone, coffee, or some organic road trip snacks. The market is open year-round daily (except Tuesday) and has a farmers market in the parking lot during summer.

Spend the first day in the town of Great Barrington, where you should arrive in time for lunch at **Marketplace Kitchen Table.** Spacious with friendly service, they serve healthy sandwiches, wraps, and salads, beef and vegetarian burgers (quinoa, black bean) hand-cut fries, and beer and wine. In the summer there is limited outdoor seating. Or, try the no-frills, no-fail **Great Barrington Bagel Company** for classic deli sandwiches on bagels baked fresh daily.

Next, take a short drive to **Beartown State Forest** for any and all outdoor activities, like hiking, biking, camping, fishing, or swimming. The gaze over Benedict Pond is a quintessential Berkshire view. Parking is $15 per vehicle for non-Massachusetts residents. If the outdoors aren't your thing, consider the **Norman Rockwell Museum** in Stockbridge, which has the biggest collection of the artist and illustrator's work, including the famous *Four Freedoms*. Before dinner, head to Main Street in Great Barrington to peruse clothing shops like **Karen Allen Fiber Arts** (the same Karen Allen of Indiana Jones fame), eclectic trinkets and gifts at **Out of Hand,** a cook shop, used bookstore and more. Get some ice cream at **Soco Creamery** or espresso drinks at **Rubi's** (the storefront also offers wine and cheese tastings on select days). At the end of Main Street is **Griffin** for gifts and clothes, and streetwear and skateboard wheels and decks at the brand-new **Library Skate Shop.**

You'll end up right across the street from your dinner destination, **Prairie Whale** (reservations essential), whose chef-owner of Marlow and Sons brought Brooklyn to the Berkshires. The rustic farm-to-table eatery pairs locally sourced meat and veggies with drinks from a full bar. Cozy up to the fireplace in winter; in summer kids can play cornhole on the lawn between courses. It's worth a trip for the ambience alone. As an alternative, **Baba Louie's** brick oven pizza serves pies on homemade spelt or wheat crust in their new location on Railroad Street. Move to the bar for a nightcap, or head to the newly-opened **Moon Cloud** on Railroad Street for an impressive cocktail program in an intimate space. If it's packed, you might catch some live music at **No. 10,** one street over on Castle Street, next to the Mahaiwe Theater (but they tend to call last call fairly early).

Day 2

Start your day with breakfast at the local diner, **GB Eats,** where you can expect all kinds of classic egg dishes and sides, or **Fuel** coffee shop across the street for something to-go on your way out of town. Take a drive (about an hour) to **Mass MoCa**; though it's a bit of a hike, it's a must when visiting the Berkshires, and there is plenty to explore once you get there. The 16-acre complex of 19th century mill factory buildings was converted into the Massachusetts Museum of Contemporary Art in the 1980s. The space itself is fascinating to explore, with interlocking passageways and bridges that take you from building to building. Massive and drenched in sunlight due to floor to ceiling windows, the industrial space is filled with state of the art exhibitions. There's a permanent installation by Sol Lewitt, and artists like James Turrell and Annie Lennox have also displayed their works here. Admission is $20 for adults. In March, Mass MoCa hosts the High Mud Comedy festival with comedic

The brilliant colors of Berkshires make it one of the Northeast's top destinations for fall foliage.

talent like Mike Birbiglia and John Early, and in June, indie band Wilco hosts their annual Solid Sound music festival on the museum grounds.

Take a 12-minute walk or a 2-minute drive from Mass MoCa to **Korean Garden** for lunch. This casual Asian-fusion eatery is something of a hidden gem, perfecting classics like bibimbap and sushi. After lunch, take an easy hike along the river through the Cascade Trail or a somewhat steeper climb to Sunset Rock via the Hoosac Range Trail, then grab a beer just outside the museum at **Bright Ideas Brewing.**

For dinner, North Adams has a host of options, including **Public,** which has elevated pub food, plus their own spin on Morrocan, Mediterranean, and Thai dishes. If you're unable to get a table, another option is **Grazie,** an Italian restaurant serving cocktails.

At night, if you're staying in the North Adams area, have a drink at **Tourists,** a bohemian chic boutique hotel in an 1813

farmhouse. You can sink into soft leather loungers next to the fireplace while sipping cocktails and craft beer. Each suite is unique and minimal, constructed from and furnished with organic materials.

Day 3

Head from North Adams toward Lenox in the morning for breakfast at **Haven,** a casual but bustling counter-service breakfast and brunch spot and bakery. If they're too packed, try **Bagel and Brew** around the corner for a quick bagel and coffee. You have several options for how to spend your last day in town. Year-round, you can visit Edith Wharton's turn-of-the-century home, **The Mount,** which she designed herself in 1902. Explore the gardens and estate set on 113 acres. They offer tours of the property, including a ghost tour. If you've come to the Berkshires in winter to ski, you can head to **Bosquet Mountain** in Pittsfield, which has 24 trails across 200 acres. Have lunch either at the Tamarack

Lounge at Bosquet, or head to West Stockbridge and enjoy a delicious meal at **No. Six Depot Roastery & Cafe.** As the name implies they roast their own coffee; the space is filled with light, and they have comforting yet healthy lunch options.

In the summer, **Tanglewood** in Lenox hosts concerts by everyone from the Boston Symphony Orchestra to James Taylor and special guests. Locals and visitors flock to the grounds to picnic on the lawn during a concert. You can also sit under the shed, but if you are able to pack picnic gear, sitting on the lawn is preferable and more of an experience. If you're craving live music and the weather demands you stay indoors, **The Barn** at the Egremont Inn features local musicians.

Saving the best for last, dinner on your last day in town should be special. Make a reservation at **Cantina 229,** a farm-to-table restaurant on an actual farm. On your way inside you'll walk past lush vegetation, live chickens, and scenic surrounds. The restaurant itself is just as stunning, constructed from repurposed, weathered materials. The interior features exposed beams and natural wood, with tasteful cowhide upholstery used sparingly. As an alternative, dine at **Frankie's** in Lenox for upscale comfort food.

Recommendations

Sights

Beartown State Forest. ✉ 69 Blue Hill Rd., Monterey, MA ☎ 413/528–0904 ⊕ www.mass.gov/locations/beartown-state-forest ⊡ $15 per car.

Bosquet Mountain. ✉ 101 Dan Fox Dr., Pittsfield, MA ☎ 413/442–8316 ⊕ www.bousquets.com ⊡ $20.

Cascade Trail. ✉ 200 Marion Ave., North Adams, MA ☎ 413/398–4084 ⊕ www.explorenorthadams.com/item/the-cascades.

Hoosac Range Trail. ✉ 2441 Mohawk Trail, North Adams, MA ☎ No phone ⊕ www.bnrc.org/trails-and-maps/top-berkshire-trails/hoosac-range/hoosac-range.

Mass MoCa. ✉ 1040 Mass MoCa Way, North Adams, MA ☎ 413/662–2111 ⊕ www.massmoca.org ⊡ $20.

The Mount. ✉ 2 Plunkett St., Lenox, MA ☎ 413/551–5111 ⊕ www.edithwharton.org ⊡ $5.

Norman Rockwell Museum. ✉ 9 Glendale Rd. (Rte 183), Stockbridge, MA ☎ 413/298–4100 ⊕ www.nrm.org ⊡ $20.

🍴 Restaurants

Baba Louie's. ⓢ Average main: $15 ✉ 42 Railroad St., Great Barrington, MA ☎ 413/528–8100 ⊕ www.babalouiespizza.com.

Bagel and Brew. ⓢ Average main: $15 ✉ 18 Franklin St., Lenox, MA ☎ 413/637–0055 ⊕ www.bagelsandbrew.com.

The Barn. ⓢ Average main: $12 ✉ 17 Main St., Egremont, MA ☎ 413/528–1570 ⊕ www.theegremontbarn.com.

Cantina 229. ⓢ Average main: $12 ✉ 229 Hartsville-New Marlborough Rd., New Marlborough, MA ☎ 413/229–3276 ⊕ www.cantina229.com ⊗ Closed Tues.

Frankie's. ⓢ Average main: $18 ✉ 80 Main St., Lenox, MA ☎ 413/551–7474 ⊕ www.frankiesitaliano.com.

Fuel. ⓢ Average main: $14 ✉ 293 Main St., Great Barrington, MA ☎ 413/528–5505 ⊕ www.fuelgreatbarrington.com.

GB Eats. ⓢ Average main: $12 ✉ 282 Main St., Great Barrington, MA ☎ 413/528–8226.

Grazie Italian Restaurant. ⓢ Average main: $18 ✉ 80 Meadow Creek Dr., Dracu, MA ☎ 978/455–0054 ⊕ www.grazie.restaurant ⊗ Closed Mon.

Great Barrington Bagel Company. $ *Average main: $5* ✉ *777 S. Main St., Great Barrington, MA* ☎ *413/528–9055* ⊕ *www.gbbagel.com.*

Haven. $ *Average main: $17* ✉ *8 Franklin St., Lenox, MA* ☎ *413/637–8948* ⊕ *www.havencafebakery.com.*

Korean Garden. $ *Average main: $16* ✉ *139 Ashland St., North Adams, MA* ☎ *413/346–4097* ☉ *Closed Mon.*

Marketplace Kitchen Table. $ *Average main: $10* ✉ *240 Stockbridge Rd., Great Barrington, MA* ☎ *413/528–2233* ⊕ *www.marketplacekitchen.com.*

No. Six Depot Roastery & Café. $ *Average main: $12* ✉ *6 Depot St., West Stockbridge, MA* ☎ *413/232–0205* ⊕ *www.sixdepot.com.*

No. 10. $ *Average main: $16* ✉ *10 Castle St., Great Barrington, MA* ☎ *413/528–5244* ⊕ *www.numbertengb.com* ☉ *Closed Tues.*

Prairie Whale. $ *Average main: $16* ✉ *178 Main St., Great Barrington, MA* ☎ *413/528–5050* ⊕ *www.prairiewhale.com.*

Public. $ *Average main: $14* ✉ *34 Holden St., North Adams, MA* ☎ *413/664–4444* ⊕ *www.publiceatanddrink.com*

Rubi's $ *Average main: $8* ✉ *264 Main St., Great Barrington, MA* ☎ *413/528–0488* ⊕ *www.rubiners.com.*

Taste NY. $ *Average main: $8* ✉ *4640 Taconic State Pkwy., Lagrangeville, NY* ☎ *845/849–0247* ⊕ *www.ccedutchess.org/taste-ny-at-todd-hill.*

Coffee and Quick Bites

Soco Creamery. $ *Average main: $4* ✉ *5 Railroad St., Great Barrington, MA* ☎ *413/644–9866* ⊕ *www.www.sococreamery.com.*

Hotels

The Barrington. $ *Rooms from: $301* ✉ *281 Main St., Great Barrington, MA* ☎ *413/528–6159* ⊕ *www.thebarringtongb.com.*

Hotel on North. $ *Rooms from: $244* ✉ *297 North St., Pittsfield, MA* ☎ *413/358–4741* ⊕ *www.hotelonnorth.com.*

Tourists. $ *Rooms from: $368* ✉ *915 State Rd., North Adams, MA* ☎ *413/346–4933* ⊕ *www.touristswelcome.com.*

Williams Inn. $ *Rooms from: $370* ✉ *101 Spring St., Williamstown, MA* ☎ *413/458–9371* ⊕ *www.williamsinn.com.*

Wyndhurst Manor and Club. $ *Rooms from: $441* ✉ *55 Lee Rd., Lenox, MA* ☎ *402/501–9899* ⊕ *www.wyndhurstmanorandclub.com.*

Nightlife

Bright Ideas Brewing. ✉ *111 Mass MoCA Way, North Adams, MA* ☎ *413/346–4460* ⊕ *www.brightideasbrewing.com.*

Moon Cloud. ✉ *47 Railroad St., Great Barrington, MA* ☎ *413/429–1101* ⊕ *www.mooncloudgb.com* ☉ *Closed Mon. and Tues.*

Performing Arts

Tanglewood. ✉ *297 West St., Lenox, MA* ☎ *413/637–5180* ⊕ *www.bso.org/brands/tanglewood-music-center/explore-the-tanglewood-music-center.aspx.*

🛍 Shopping

Griffin. ✉ *47 Railroad St., Great Barrington, MA* ☎ *413/528–5000* ⊕ *www.griffingiroux.com.*

Karen Allen Fiber Arts. ✉ *8 Railroad St., Great Barrington, MA* ☎ *413/528–8555* ⊕ *karenallen-fiberarts.com.*

Library Skate Shop. ✉ *177 Main St., Great Barrington, MA* ☎ *413/717–4100* ⊕ *www.libraryskateshop.com.*

Out of Hand. ✉ *81 Main St., Great Barrington, MA* ☎ *413/528–3791* ⊗ *Closed Wed.*

Cape Cod, MA

Wellfleet is 102 miles (approx. 2 hours) from Boston.

If you love the sun, surf, and seafood, then Cape Cod's 560 miles of pristine coastline, and everything in between, is your dream destination. It has been said that the Cape is "sand dunes and salty air, quaint little villages here and there." Here you'll find the calm waters of Cape Cod Bay's beaches that juxtapose with the crashing waves of the Cape Cod National Seashore, a 40-mile stretch of unspoiled sandy beach that faces the Atlantic Ocean.

You'll find seafood shacks, breakfast places, ice-cream shops, and "fine" dining spots. You'll find 18-hole golf courses and minigolf courses, arcades and bowling alleys, the 22-mile trail Rail to Trail bike path and hiking paths, souvenir shops and clothing boutiques, and the theater … oh, the theater. Summer stock on the Cape is some of the best theater around.

Planning

GETTING THERE AND BACK

Driving is the best way to get to, and explore, all the Cape has to offer. From Boston, take I–93 S to Route 3 S over the Sagamore Bridge. From there, take Route 6 E for about an hour to Wellfleet. The total trip should be about two hours.

However, if driving's not your thing, you can take the CapeFLYER—a weekend passenger train that runs from late-June to Labor Day—from Boston's South Station to Hyannis and then an Uber to Wellfleet (and you'll need to Uber around). Another option is the 90-minute Provincetown Ferry that leaves from Boston's Long Wharf.

PIT STOPS

About 20 minutes before you cross the Sagamore Bridge and enter Cape Cod, stop at **Plimoth Plantation** to get some history and stretch your legs—most of the reenactments are outside. The **Plentiful Cafe** is a great place to grab a snack and the visitor center's well-stocked gift shop is the perfect place to pick up a few souvenirs.

As of this writing, Plimoth Plantation has not announced their official, more inclusive name, which will debut in late 2020.

INSPIRATION

Created by *Cape Cod Times* staffers Eric Williams and Gregory Bryant, "The Cape Cod Fun Show" podcast, launched in 2018, provides year-round insight into what's fun to do on the Cape. They cover everything from the best bakeries and the best meat loaf to great places to hike as well as local happenings and whether thick or thin chowder is best.

WHEN TO GO

Cape Cod teems with activity from late June to Labor Day, but with perfect beach weather comes large crowds and high costs, so keep that in mind. For many, fall (September through early November) is the optimal time to visit because the crowds have gone, the weather is still lovely (low 60s to low 70s), the scenery is still remarkable, and many restaurants, shops, and hotels are still open.

WHERE TO STAY

The lodging options on Cape Cod are endless and include everything from charming inns and B&Bs, to converted sea captains houses, retro motels, and seaside resorts. It's hard to pick just one, or even three, to recommend but if you want to be conveniently located between Wellfleet and Provincetown, the

Plimoth Plantation recreates the original settlement of the Pilgrims.

family-friendly **Even'tide** is just off Route 6 in South Wellfleet. There's a 60-foot indoor pool as well as direct access to the Cape Cod Rail Trail and Wellfleet's beaches are close by. If you want to be in the heart of Provincetown and close to the beach, the retro-style **Harbor Hotel Provincetown** is the perfect spot to roll out of bed and enjoy the sun and the surf in no time. If a resort, and all the amenities that go with it, is more your cup of tea, **Ocean Edge Resort** in Brewster is your home away from home. You'll feel very Cape Cod pulling up the drive to the grand old estate, and it's one of the few lodging options open year round.

Day 1

Your destination is Wellfleet, a tranquil artist community that's world-renowned for its succulent namesake oysters. Less than 2 miles wide, it's one of the most charming Cape towns, with great restaurants, historic houses, art galleries, and a good old Main Street. If you leave Boston

in the early morning, you should arrive in time for lunch—so head straight to **Moby Dick's** for the Nantucket Bucket—a pound of whole-belly Monomoy steamers, a pound of native mussels, and corn on the cob. If you're craving those famous oysters, you can order them from the raw bar by the half dozen or dozen. Lines can be long, so kill some time browsing Moby's Cargo, the bustling gift shop next door. Or opt for **Box Lunch,** known for its famous "rollwich"—homemade pita bread rolled around every filling (including lobster) imaginable.

Once you've filled your bellies, hit the beach. Part of the **Cape Cod National Seashore, Marconi Beach** is accessed via a series of staircases that lead down to the beach, which is flanked by the Atlantic Ocean—waves can be a bit rough so take note for little ones. In season there are lifeguards, showers, and toilets. Daily parking is $20, but the annual seashore pass ($60) grants access to all six national park beaches (including the ones in Provincetown) and costs the same as three days of parking. And if you're lacking any beach paraphernalia, there are plenty of places along Route 6 to get chairs, beach toys, umbrellas, and so on.

Leave the beach around 4 so you can stop at the **Truro Vineyards of Cape Cod** for some wine tasting before dinner; there's plenty of room for the kids to play. Open until 5, the vineyard makes several notable reds and whites, as well as a cranberry-flavor red table wine that comes in a lighthouse-shape bottle. It makes for a cute container for all the found shells, rocks, and so on, you're bound to collect.

Since this is the Cape, we're assuming you're still in the mood for seafood, and **Mac's on the Pier,** right at Wellfleet Harbor, serves some of the freshest seafood around. The menu features a variety of local fish dishes, plus more adventurous fare like sushi, grilled-scallop burritos, and linguica sausage sandwiches. And, there's the great water views. **Wicked Oyster,** on Wellfleet's Main Street, has that in abundance plus a great burger and braised short ribs. Housed in an 18th-century clapboard house, try the oyster stew or the buttermilk fried oysters (you can get them on the half shell, too).

Day 2

About 13 miles northwest of Wellfleet, Provincetown is a summer playground for families, artists, seafaring folk, and the LGBTQ community. It's the perfect place to spend the chunk of your time as it's a great microcosm for everything that Cape has to offer. Commercial Street is the town's main drag—pun-intended as there's some great drag shows to catch if you're so inclined—and it's where you'll find most of the restaurants, shops, bars, and so on. It's also where most of the traffic is—driving the 3 miles of this downtown thoroughfare in season could take forever, so avoid it if possible. Parking is not one of Provincetown's better

amenities, so plan to get here as early as possible to grab a spot in one of two large, paid central parking lots.

Your first stop on your way to P'town should be **The Flying Fish** in Wellfleet to pick up some grab-and-go egg sandwiches—you can substitute a bagel or croissant and add bacon, sausage, ham, or linguica (Portuguese sausage)—and Beanstock coffee or an iced chai. Healthier options include smoothies and housemade granola. Or try **Savory & the Sweet Escape** in Truro, where the display cases are stocked with croissants, scones, cinnabuns, and doughnuts.

After you're fortified, head to **Province Lands Visitor Center.** Part of the Cape Cod National Seashore, the visitor center has short films on local geology and exhibits on the life of the dunes and the shore. More than 7 miles of bike and walking trails surround the center and you can pick up information on guided walks, birding trips, lectures, and other programs; don't miss the awe-inspiring panoramic view of the dunes and the surrounding ocean from the center's observation deck. After you've gotten your fill of the educational stuff, head to **Race Point Beach** (**Herring Cove Beach** is another option) to enjoy the wide swath of sand that stretches far off into the distance around the point and Coast Guard station; in season there are lifeguards, showers, and toilets. And, because the beach faces north, you can expect sun all day long.

Whale-watching is definitely a Cape thing, so if that's on your "to-do" list you're in luck. Whales—humpback, finback, minke, right, and pilot—can usually be seen in the Provincetown area from early spring to October and there are numerous operators including the **Center for Coastal Studies** and **SeaSalt Charter.**

Lunch at the always entertaining **Bayside Betty's** comes with great views of P'town Harbor from their deck and great food that ranges from salads and burgers to chicken parmigiana and braised short ribs. If you're looking for lighter fare, grab a seat at the bar (or on the deck—did we mention that yet?) and order some of P'town's best clam chowder or the mac n' cheese bombs. Sometimes a great sandwich and a sweet treat is just what you need to quell the lunch hanger pains. At **Relish** on the west end of Commercial Street, you can't go wrong with The Ptownie (turkey, Swiss, and cranberry-sage mayo) or the Italian (Genoa salami, hot capicola, provolone, and balsamic, and sweet heat sauce) followed by freshly baked cookies, gluten-free macaroons, or mini–fruit pies. It's also a great spot for breakfast sandwiches and pastries.

After lunch, take a stroll along Commercial Street; the Provincetown Historical Society offers a walking-tour pamphlet ($1) available at many shops. You'll find the crowds and the best people-watching in the center of town, especially if you grab a spot on a bench in front of the beautiful Town Hall. The East End has a number of nationally renowned galleries; the West End has a number of small inns with neat lawns and elaborate gardens. Keep an eye out for the Bob Gasoi Memorial Art Alley, next to **Shop Therapy,** and the **Penney Patch** candy shop, which brings out the kid in everyone with its nostalgic collection of treats.

Strolling and window shopping can work up quite an appetite (or is that just us?), which means it's time for dinner at **The Mews.** Expect picture-perfect harbor views and a culturally diverse menu that focuses on seafood and grilled meats, plus a lighter bistro menu. The bar is a perfect spot for a romantic cocktail before or after dinner. Inside the beautifully restored Crowne Pointe Inn, **The Pointe** occupies the parlor and sunroom of a grand sea captain's mansion. The kitchen serves modern American food,

and there's an extensive wine list to accompany it.

Provincetown's Commercial Street is the epicenter of Cape Cod's nightlife and there's a place for every taste and mood. But, if you're looking for a classic spot to enjoy a cocktail or an ice cold beer with live music and beach front views, the legendary **Beachcomber** in Wellfleet is where it's at. If your tastes are a little more low key, the **Wellfleet Drive-In** near the Eastham town line shows first-run films starting at dusk (May–September); there's also an indoor theater, minigolf, and a snack stand. And, if theater is more your thing, there are plenty of options in Provincetown and Wellfleet like the **Provincetown Theater** and the **Wellfleet Harbor Actors Theater.**

Day 3

To enjoy the most of your last day, rise and shine bright and early and head to the **Hole In One Bakery & Coffee Shop** in Eastham (there's a location in Orleans as well that does sit down breakfast) for freshly brewed coffee and hand-cut doughnuts made every morning. You'll have your pick of more than 15 options (especially if you go early) that include sour cream, honey dipped, glazed cruellers, and jelly donuts. There's also homemade muffins and pastries, and yummy things called stuffed croissants—spinach and feta, swiss and ham, and bacon (or sausage), egg, and cheese.

You've seen the Cape Cod National Seashore from the beach, but the only way to actually experience the dunes is with **Art's Dune Tours,** which has been offering the experience since 1946. The hour-long rides are offered four times a day in large SUVs (so everyone can enjoy the experience) that transport you through the Peaked Hill Bars Historic District Sand Dunes past surreal sandy vistas and the infamous Dune Shacks, which are now registered historic landmarks.

One last stop before you go, and we have one question for you: Do you like Cape Cod Potato Chips? Who doesn't, right? Well, the lighthouse on the bag is real and you can visit it; it's also the lighthouse you see on many Massachusetts license plates. When you're done with your dunes tour, head to the iconic, red and white **Nauset Lighthouse.** The restored beacon dates from 1838 and it's open for seasonal tours that allow visitors to climb the light, visit the lookout room, and learn about its history.

If you haven't had the opportunity to partake in the Cape's most beloved summer pastime of mini-golf, now's your chance. The **Wellfleet Dairy Bar & Mini-Golf,** at the same place as the Wellfleet Drive-In, is located on Route 6 and it's the ideal spot to stop for one last hurrah of ice cream and minigolf. On your way off Cape, stop by **Arnold's Lobster & Clam Bar** to grab your final meal of the weekend. There's plenty of to-go options like fried seafood platters, lobster rolls, and delish raw bar.

Recommendations

Sights

Cape Cod National Seashore. ✉ *99 Marconi Site Rd., Wellfleet, MA* ☎ *508/255–3421* 🌐 *www.nps.gov/caco/index.htm* 🎟 *$20 per vehicle.*

Herring Cove Beach. ✉ *Race Point Rd., Provincetown, MA* ☎ *508/487–1256* 🎟 *$20 per vehicle.*

Marconi Beach. ✉ *99 Marconi Site Rd., Wellfleet, MA* ☎ *508/255–3421* 🌐 *www.nps.gov/caco/planyourvisit/marconi-beach.htm* 🎟 *$20 per vehicle.*

Nauset Lighthouse. ✉ *120 Nauset Light Beach Rd., Eastham, MA* ☎ *508/240–2612* 🌐 *www.nausetlight.org* 🎟 *Free.*

Plimoth Plantation. ✉ *137 Warren Ave., Plymouth, MA* ☎ *508/746–1622* 🌐 *www.plimoth.org* 🎟 *$35.*

Province Lands Visitor Center. ✉ *171 Race Point Rd., Provincetown, MA* ☎ *508/487–1256* 🌐 *www.nps.gov/caco/index.htm* 🎟 *Free.*

Race Point Beach. ✉ *Race Point Rd., Provincetown, MA* ☎ *508/487–1256* 🎟 *$20 per vehicle.*

Truro Vineyards of Cape Cod. ✉ *11 Shore Rd., North Truro, MA* ☎ *508/487–6200* 🌐 *trurovineyardsofcapecod.com.*

Wellfleet Cinemas. ✉ *51 U.S. 6, Wellfleet, MA* ☎ *508/349–7176* 🌐 *www.wellfleet-cinemas.com* 🎟 *$13.*

Restaurants

Arnold's Lobster & Clam Bar. [$] *Average main: $20* ✉ *3580 U.S. 6, Eastham, MA* ☎ *508/255–2575* 🌐 *www.arnoldsrestaurant.com* 🕒 *Closed Tues.–Thurs.*

Bayside Betsy's Restaurant. [$] *Average main: $14* ✉ *177 Commercial St., Provincetown, MA* ☎ *508/487–6566* 🌐 *baysidebetsys.com*

Box Lunch. [$] *Average main: $10* ✉ *50 Briar La., Wellfleet, MA* ☎ *508/349–2178* 🌐 *www.boxlunchcapecod.com* 🕒 *No dinner.*

Flying Fish Café. [$] *Average main: $12* ✉ *29 Briar La., Wellfleet* ☎ *508/349–7292* 🌐 *www.flyingfishwellfleet.com.*

Hole In One Bakery & Coffee Shop. [$] *Average main: $12* ✉ *4295 U.S. 6, Eastham* ☎ *508/255–9446* 🌐 *www.theholecapecod.com* 🕒 *No dinner.*

Mac's on the Pier. [$] *Average main: $15* ✉ *265 Commercial St., Wellfleet* ☎ *508/349–9611* 🌐 *www.macsseafood.com.*

The Mews. [$] *Average main: $22* ✉ *429 Commercial St., Provincetown, MA* ☎ *508/487–1500* 🌐 *www.mewsptown.com.*

Moby Dick's. [$] *Average main: $16* ✉ *3225 Rt. 6, Wellfleet, MA*

☎ 508/349–9795 🌐 www.mobys.com 🕑 No lunch Mon.–Thurs.

The Pointe Restaurant. [$] *Average main: $16* ✉ *82 Bradford St., Provincetown, MA* ☎ *508/487–2365* 🌐 *www.provincetown-restaurant.com* 🕑 *Closed Tues. and Wed. No lunch.*

6A Café. [$] *Average main: $10* ✉ *415 MA 6A, Sandwich, MA* ☎ *508/888–5220* 🌐 *www.sixacafe.wpengine.com* 🕑 *Closed Tues. and Wed.*

The Wicked Oyster. [$] *Average main: $20* ✉ *50 Main St., Wellfleet, MA* ☎ *508/349–3455* 🌐 *www.thewickedo.com* 🕑 *Closed Sun.–Tues.*

Coffee and Quick Bites

Relish. [$] *Average main: $12* ✉ *93 Commercial St., Provincetown, MA* ☎ *508/487–8077* 🌐 *www.ptownrelish.com* 🕑 *No dinner.*

Savory & the Sweet Escape. [$] *Average main: $10* ✉ *316 U.S. 6, Truro, MA* ☎ *508/487–2225*

Hotels

Even'tide Motel & Cottages. [$] *Rooms from: $133* ✉ *650 U.S. 6, Wellfleet, MA* ☎ *508/349–3410* 🌐 *www.eventidemotel.com* 🍴 *No meals.*

Harbor Hotel Provincetown. [$] *Rooms from: $196* ✉ *698 Commercial St., Provincetown, MA* ☎ *508/487–1711* 🌐 *www.harborhotelptown.com* 🍴 *No meals.*

Ocean Edge Resort. [$] *Rooms from: $278* ✉ *2907 Main St., Brewster, MA* ☎ *508/896–9000* 🌐 *www.oceanedge.com* 🍴 *No meals.*

Nightlife

The Beachcomber. ✉ *1120 Cahoon Hollow Rd., Wellfleet, MA* ☎ *508/349–6055* 🌐 *www.thebeachcomber.com.*

The Provincetown Theater. ✉ *238 Bradford St., Provincetown, MA* ☎ *508/487–7487* 🌐 *www.provincetowntheater.org.*

Wellfleet Harbor Actors Theater. ✉ *2357 Old Rte. 6, Wellfleet, MA* ☎ *508/349–9428* 🌐 *www.what.org.*

Shopping

Penney Patch Candies. ✉ *281 Commercial St., Provincetown, MA* ☎ *508/487–2766* 🌐 *www.penneypatch.com.*

Shop Therapy. ✉ *286 Commercial St., Provincetown, MA* ☎ *508/487–0372* 🌐 *www.shoptherapy.com.*

Activities

Art's Dune Tours. ✉ *4 Standish St., Provincetown, MA* ☎ *508/487–1950* 🌐 *www.artsdunetours.com* 🎟 *$28.*

Center for Coastal Studies. ✉ *5 Holway Ave., Provincetown, MA* ☎ *508/487–3622* 🌐 *www.coastalstudies.org.*

SeaSalt Charters. ✉ *19 Ryder St. E, Provincetown, MA* ☎ *508/444–2732* 🌐 *www.seasaltcharters.com* 🎟 *Private charter $550.*

Wellfleet Dairy Bar & Mini-Golf. ✉ *51 U.S. 6, Wellfleet, MA* ☎ *508/349–0278* 🌐 *www.wellfleetcinemas.com/dairy-bar-mini-golf* 🎟 *$5.*

The Catskills, NY

Woodstock is 101 miles (approx. 2 hours) from New York City.

Northwest of Manhattan, the series of tiny hamlets that makes up the Catskills is a place of untamed wilderness and historical intrigue. The Catskills Park and Forest Preserve incorporates 700,000 acres, and more than 200,000 acres of that are protected land, kept forever wild. In the mid-19th century, artists came here to capture the area's rural beauty, drawing

In the heart of the Catskills, numerous hiking trails fan out from around the iconic Kaaterskills Falls.

New Yorkers out of their urban dwellings to the pine-covered, fairytale-like mountain range. Home to the Borscht Belt in the 1920s until the 1970s, a series of now-abandoned resorts where comedians like Joan Rivers came to perform, the area has long been a welcoming place for visitors of all backgrounds and cultures. Today it's a haven for skiers and artists, and anyone with a sense of adventure and a need for respite from city life.

Planning

GETTING THERE AND BACK

Woodstock is just over two hours north on I–87 from New York City.

WHEN TO GO

The Catskills are truly a year-round destination. Many escape here in the winter for skiing or cozying up in the lodge. Take in views while hiking or biking here in the fall, or relive the summers of decades past.

WHERE TO STAY

You're spoiled for choice when it comes to lodging in the Catskills. Some of our favorites include **The Arnold House** in Livingston Manor, an inn with just 10 guestrooms plus a two-bedroom lake house. The casual-chic property on Shandelee Mountain has a spa on-site and a tavern with live entertainment in the summer. The **Eastwind Hotel** is a new addition to Windham; the former hunting and fishing lodge has a small spa, bar and lounge, and A-frame cabins so you can wake up to gorgeous mountain views. The retro **Kate's Lazy Meadow** (owned by Kate Pierson of the B-52s) is a 1950s motel; rooms have vintage kitchens, and outside there is a communal fire pit.

Day 1

Leave New York City midmorning to arrive in Woodstock for lunch at **Shindig**, a sunny spot serving organic comfort food, craft beer, cider, and wine. Ingredients are sourced from local purveyors, and breakfast, including delectable baked goods, is served until 3 pm. Or, try the all-vegan **Garden Cafe.**

Once you've fueled up, head to **Belleayre** Mountain, with ski trails for all skill levels. Belleayre hosts a festival in fall, and in the summer you can swim at Belleayre Beach, take a gondola ride, or go for a hike. Après ski (or hike, or swim) dine at **Peekamoose Restaurant and Tap Room** in Phoenicia, a converted farmhouse with exposed beams and a patio with a firepit where you can have cocktails and toast marshmallows. Hearty meat dishes are their specialty. As an alternative, try **Ze Windham Wine Bar.**

Enjoy a craft cocktail, beer, or wine, at the intimate but fully stocked bar at the boutique **Eastwind Hotel.** Though seating around the bar is minimal, there is plenty of room to relax in the lounge area, including around a fireplace or in front of a chessboard. Down the road you'll find the casual **Mulligan's Pub** at the Windham Country Club.

Day 2

Start the day with breakfast at **Robin Hood Diner** in the town of Livingston Manor, a classic diner with home-cooked breakfast. In the nearby hamlet of Roscoe is the wonderful **Roscoe Diner.**

There are more than 300 miles of trails to hike in **Catskill Park,** with summits and fire towers offering unparalleled views of the region in every season. The vast wilderness includes wetlands, lakes, forest, and meadows. Mongaup Pond is an easily accessible introduction. For your posthike lunch, **Main Street Farm** in Livingston Manor is a rustic café with an emphasis on local ingredients. Menu items include inventive sandwiches, salads, and soups. **Upward Brewing Company** nearby also serves lunch.

Enjoy a boozy afternoon at the **Prohibition Distillery.** The restored 1920s firehouse now produces small batches of gin, vodka, and whiskey. Tours are also offered, or you can just hang out in the tasting room.

Have dinner (served Thursday through Sunday) at **Northern Farmhouse Pasta** in Roscoe, whose pasta dishes are made with 100% New York grown wheat. Vegetables are fresh and seasonal, and the ravioli is their signature dish. You can also dine outdoors at gourmet pizza spot, **The Kaatskeller.**

Liven up the evening by heading to **The Arnold House** in Livingston Manor, whose tavern hosts karaoke and occasional live music and bonfires. They also have a popular pool table and a jukebox.

Day 3

For breakfast on your last day, your best bet is the highly rated yet simple breakfast at the **Phoenicia Diner.** Specialties include corned beef hash and chicken and waffles.

Take an easy jaunt to Kaaterskill Falls, the subject of paintings and folklore, or get a massage at the luxurious **Windham Spa** before returning to fast-paced city life.

For lunch, try the quaint **Bear and Fox Provisions** for something tasty in their coffee shop/grocery store. The charming spot in Tannersville has rotating dishes like soups, avocado toast, and creative lattes. Or, dine at **Phoenicia Market and Deli.**

Spend the afternoon perusing art, collectibles, and housewares you can only find in the Catskills. Your choices include the vintage wonderland, **Mystery Spot,** in Phoenicia, with records, costume jewelry, and other fun finds, and **Nest** in Livingston Manor, filled with eclectic wares; among many other shops. Art galleries and museums include the **Woodstock Artists Association & Museum**; the **Center for Photography at Woodstock** where Janis Joplin, Joan Baez, and Bob Dylan performed when it was a coffee house; the enormous **Emerson Kaleidoscope** housed in a grain silo; and so much more.

Before you hit the road, stop in for a burger or fondue at **Last Chance Cheese and Antiques Cafe.** Browse or buy something from their vintage candy selection as a souvenir before heading home. Or hold out for Eggs McMaggie at **Maggie's Krooked Cafe.**

Recommendations

Sights

Belleayre. ✉ *181 Galli Curci Rd., Highmount, NY* ☎ *845/254–5600* 🌐 *www.belleayre.com* 🎟 *Free.*

Catskill Park. ✉ *Mongaup Pond, 231 Mongaup Pond Rd., Livingston Manor, NY* ☎ *518/678–9729* 🌐 *www.stateparks.com/catskill_state_park_in_new_york* 🎟 *Free.*

Center for Photography at Woodstock. ✉ *59 Tinker St., Woodstock, NY* ☎ *845/679–9957* 🌐 *www.cpw.org* 🎟 *Free.*

Emerson Kaleidoscope. ✉ *5340 NY 28, Mt. Tremper, NY* ☎ *845/688–5800* 🌐 *emersonresort.com* 🎟 *Free.*

Woodstock Artists Association & Museum. ✉ *28 Tinker St., Woodstock, NY* ☎ *845/679–2940* 🌐 *www.woodstockart.org* 🎟 *www.woodstockart.org.*

Restaurants

The Arnold House. [$] *Average main: $15* ✉ *839 Shandelee Rd., Livingston Manor, NY* ☎ *845/439–5070* 🌐 *www.thearnoldhouse.com.*

Garden Cafe. [$] *Average main: $12* ✉ *6 Old Forge Rd., Woodstock, NY* ☎ *845/679–3600* 🌐 *thegardencafewoodstock.com.*

The Kaatskeller. [$] *Average main: $12* ✉ *39 Main St., Livingston Manor, NY* ☎ *845/439–4339* 🌐 *www.thekaatskeller.com* 🕒 *Closed Wed.*

Last Chance Cheese and Antiques Cafe. [$] *Average main: $9* ✉ *6009 Main St., Tannersville, NY* ☎ *518/589–6424* 🌐 *www.lastchanceonline.com.*

Maggie's Krooked Cafe. [$] *Average main: $12* ✉ *6000 Main St., Tannersville, NY* ☎ *518/589–6101* 🌐 *maggieskrookedcafe.com.*

Main Street Farm. [$] *Average main: $8* ✉ *36 Main St., Livingston Manor, NY* ☎ *845/439–4309* 🌐 *www.mainstreetfarm.com.*

Northern Farmhouse Pasta. [$] *Average main: $18* ✉ *65 Rockland Rd., Roscoe, NY* ☎ *607/290–4064* 🌐 *www.northernfarmhousepasta.com* 🕒 *Closed Tues.*

Peekamoose Restaurant and Tap Room. [$] *Average Main $28* ✉ *8373 NY 28, Big Indian, NY* ☎ *845/254–6500* 🌐 *www.peekamooserestaurant.com* 🕒 *Closed Mon.*

Phoenicia Diner. [$] *Average main: $15* ✉ *5681 NY 28, Phoenicia, NY* ☎ *845/688–9957* 🌐 *www.phoeniciadiner.com* 🕒 *Closed Wed.*

Phoenicia Market and Deli. [$] *Average main: $12* ✉ *46 Main St., Phoenicia, NY* ☎ *845/688–5125* 🌐 *www.phoeniciany.com* 🕒 *Closed Sun. and Mon.*

Roscoe Diner. [$] *Average main: $10* ✉ *1908 Old Rte. 17, Roscoe, NY* ☎ *607/498–4405* 🌐 *www.theroscoediner.com.*

Shindig. [$] *Average main: $12* ✉ *1 Tinker St., Woodstock, NY* ☎ *772/684–7091* 🌐 *www.woodstockshindig.com.*

Upward Brewing Company. [$] *Average main: $12* ✉ *171 Main St., Livingston Manor, NY* ☎ *845/439–1382* 🌐 *www.upwardbrewing.com.*

Ze Windham Wine Bar. $ *Average main: $18* ⊠ *5369 Main St., Windham, NY* ☏ *518/734–9200* ⊕ *www.zewinebar.com*

Coffee and Quick Bites

Bear and Fox Provisions. $ *Average main: $8* ⊠ *5932 Main St., Tannersville, NY* ☏ *518/589–4004* ⊕ *www.bearandfoxprovisions.com* ☉ *Closed Wed. and Thurs.*

🛏 Hotels

Arnold House. $ *Rooms from: $249* ⊠ *839 Shandelee Rd., Livingston Manor, NY* ☏ *845/439–5070* ⊕ *www.thearnoldhouse.com* ⏺ *Free breakfast.*

Eastwind. $ *Rooms from: $129* ⊠ *5088 NY 23, Windham, NY* ☏ *518/734–0553* ⊕ *www.eastwindny.com* ⏺ *Free breakfast.*

Kate's Lazy Meadow. $ *Rooms from: $189* ⊠ *5191 NY 28, Mt. Tremper, NY* ☏ *845/688–7200* ⊕ *www.lazymeadow.com* ⏺ *No meals.*

🍸 Nightlife

Mulligan's Pub. ⊠ *36 South St., Windham, NY* ☏ *518/ 734–5200* ⊕ *www.windhammountain.com/dining/mulligans-pub-2.*

Prohibition Distillery. ⊠ *10 Union St., Roscoe, NY* ☏ *607/498–4511* ⊕ *www.prohibitiondistillery.com.*

🛍 Shopping

Mystery Spot. ⊠ *72 Main St., Phoenicia, NY* ☏ *845/688–7868* ⊕ *lauralevine.com.*

Nest. ⊠ *34 Main St., Livingston Manor, NY* ☏ *845/588–5316* ⊕ *nestcatskills.com.*

Windham Spa. ⊠ *16 Mitchell Hollow Rd., Windham, NY* ☏ *518/734–9617* ⊕ *www.thewindhamspa.com.*

Charlottesville, VA

116 miles (approx 2¼ hours) from Washington, D.C.

A genteel escape less than three hours from D.C., Charlottesville is Thomas Jefferson's town. His invention-filled home (better known as Monticello) is here, as is his neoclassical University of Virginia, both of which provide fascinating insights into the original neo-Renaissance man. But even without Jefferson, Charlottesville is a standout destination with lauded regional cuisine, a noteworthy music scene, hiking in the nearby Blue Ridge, and local vineyards that rate among Virginia's best. Top this off with the fact that it's a splendid scenic drive to get here, through Virginia's hilly green countryscape, with tree lines and grazing horses behind fences and farms that seem to go on for miles. If you need a countryside diversion with a dash of culture and history, this is the getaway for you.

Planning

GETTING THERE AND BACK
A car is the best option for this weekend getaway. From Washington, D.C., follow I–66 W and U.S. 29 S for about three hours. You can also take a train (2½ hours) or bus (about three hours), though will miss out on some of the excursions.

WHEN TO GO
Charlottesville is a year-round destination, but May through July is the best time to visit, when the students are gone and flowers are in full bloom. Fall is prime for leaf-peeping hiking and harvest wine festivals, although it can be crowded. Winters are mild, and hotel rates will be lower. Be sure to plan around the city's academic calendar—if the Cavaliers are playing, or it's graduation weekend, you will not find a room for miles.

WHERE TO STAY

Charlottesville offers a wide variety of accommodations for all tastes and budgets, from luxury suites to historic B&Bs to budget-friendly rooms. **Oakhurst Inn** is a beautiful, contemporary boutique hotel near the University of Virginia—with an awesome breakfast. **The Townsman,** located on the Downtown Mall, is referred to as an "unhotel," because all operations for its four rooms take place online—there is no on-site staff. It's a great option for multigenerational families and girlfriend getaways.

Day 1

Leaving D.C. behind, U.S. 29 eases you into the relaxed pace of the Virginia countryside. Arriving in Charlottesville, stop by the colonialesque **Michie Tavern,** where servers in period garb serve southern staples including hickory-smoked pulled pork and stewed tomatoes—though, honestly, its homestyle fried chicken is the major draw. Dating back to the 1780s, its grounds host a gathering of old-style shops.

Then, head just up the hill for **Monticello,** Thomas Jefferson's pet project. The super-talented third president spent four decades (1769–1809) "pulling up and pulling down" his neoclassical plantation house, drawing on ancient and modern architectural writings to create a markedly American style. What's really cool are his inventions, from the folding doors to the dumbwaiters to the duplicate-writing machine. Guided tours take in the house, showcasing his books, furnishings, and collections in 43 rooms, then explore the expansive gardens, where you'll learn about Jefferson's agricultural prowess as well.

When you're ready, head back into Charlottesville for a predinner stroll through the historic **Downtown Mall,** an open-air urban park, really, featuring eight buzzy blocks with more than 120 shops, bookstores, restaurants, and cafés—many of which have outdoor dining spaces beneath shade-giving old oak trees. There are always fun events going on here, including concerts, art exhibits, and street mimes.

Continue on to the **University of Virginia,** Jefferson's proudest academic achievement. Founded in 1819, its must-see centerpiece is the main Lawn, edged with architecturally masterful dorm rooms for lucky seniors and headed by the Roman-style Rotunda (free one-hour tours are offered).

After that trip through time, settle into an outdoor table at the fun and festive **Red Pump Kitchen** back in the Downtown Mall area and enjoy Tuscan-style fare: gourmet pizzas fresh from the wood-burning oven, seafood, and homemade pastas. Jefferson would have ended the evening with a glass of sherry—why not join him? The Downtown Mall has plenty of options to partake.

Day 2

Pick up oven-hot bagels at **Bodo's Bagels,** an absolute must. Then kick off the morning with a refreshing hike along the **Humpback Rocks Trail** on the Blue Ridge Parkway, just 35 minutes away. It's early enough, so you should beat the crowds. This short, steep trek brings you to a breathtaking view of misty hills, the Shenandoah and Rockfish Valleys far below. For real go-getters, the view is especially breathtaking at sunrise. If you want to extend the hike, the Appalachian Trail adds on as many miles as you wish.

On the short drive back, you're in for a treat at the landmark **Crozet Pizza,** a family-owned pizzeria since 1977 in the small town of Crozet. Don't let the strip mall or its dive-bar vibe turn you away, for here you'll find an astounding array of specialty pizzas, made with the perfect hand-tossed crust with just the right

Reminiscent of Monticello, the University of Virginia is Thomas Jefferson's proudest architectural achievement.

amount of char. Great Balls of Fire is a crazy hot pizza with homemade tomato sauce, mozzarella, sliced meatballs, julienned red peppers, and basil chiffonade. You'll dream about it for days.

As this is wine country, your afternoon is devoted, naturally, to wine-tasting. While Jefferson dabbled in wine way back when, he failed miserably. Virginia really didn't get into the wine groove until recently—but these days they're winning accolades right and left. Several wineries offer tastings in spectacular, Blue-Ridge-shadowed settings near Crozet, including **King Family Vineyards, Pollak Vineyards,** and **White Hall Vineyards.** They're all part of the Monticello Wine Trail, which includes 40 different wineries in the area.

And if beer's more your thing, you're in the right place. Hop vines love the climate here, so you'll find plenty of small-batch breweries making innovative ales. The Brew Ridge Trail features several local breweries, including **Starr Hill Brewery** right near Crozet.

You might want to spruce up for dinner, because tonight is something special. **Barboursville Vineyards,** about 30 minutes north of Charlottesville, is a renowned wine estate centering on a historic house designed in the early 1800s by Thomas Jefferson. After being devastated by fire 1884, only ruins remain, which you can visit. Feel free to do another wine-tasting, then head for the **Palladio Restaurant.** Here, in a cozy but elegant Italianesque setting, you're in for an extraordinary Northern Italian farm-to-table experience, with several courses and the option of wine pairing (which, of course, you should do).

Back in Charlottesville, if you're not ready to call it a night, check out the unassuming **Miller's Downtown,** a three-story restaurant-bar with a breezy outdoor patio and music seven days a week. Musician Dave Matthews got his start in 1991 when he worked here as a bartender (he owns **Blenheim Vineyards,** by the way).

Day 3

Linger over breakfast, served all day, at **The Nook** on the Downtown Mall. A vintage diner with outdoor seating, its breakfast menu offers country fried steak, four-egg omelets, "the" chicken and waffles, and more, all perfectly paired with a peach bellini (because, why not?).

Charlottesville is located near the James River, ideal for a lazy, socially distant float. **James River Reeling and Rafting,** in the small river town of Scottsville south of Charlottesville, offers equipment and rides to a put-in spot. From there, take a leisurely 7-mile paddle along calm flatwater, enjoying a couple stretches of Class I and II rapids thrown in for good measure. This hardwood-shaded realm is a haven for wildlife, including deer, bald eagles, osprey, and herons.

And now, it's time to pack up and head home—though the weekend is not over yet. Take your time meandering country roads back north, with several stops along the way. Near the historic town of Orange (worth taking a stroll), visit another forefather's house at **Montpelier,** the lifelong resident of James Madison, the nation's fourth president. There's an education center, a walking tour including a stop at the cemetery holding James and his wife, Dolley, and a lovely path that wanders through old-growth forest.

Next stop: Culpeper. This is a hip, historic little town, with fun, funky shops to browse along East Davis Street. If you're not wined-out yet, there are wineries here, too, including **Old House Vineyards,** which has a sweet southern-style veranda.

Recommendations

Sights

Barboursville Vineyards. ✉ 17655 Winery Rd., Barboursville, VA ☎ 540/832–3824 ⊕ www.bbvwine.com 🍷 Tastings $7.

Blenheim Vineyards. ✉ 31 Blenheim Farm, Charlottesville, VA ☎ 434/293–5366 ⊕ www.blenheimvineyards.com 🍷 Tastings $10.

Downtown Mall. ✉ E. Main St., Charlottesville, VA ☎ 434/295–9073 ⊕ www.downtowncharlottesville.com 🍷 Free.

King Family Vineyards. ✉ 6550 Roseland Farm, Crozet, VA ☎ 434/823–7800 ⊕ kingfamilyvineyards.com 🍷 Tastings $10.

Monticello. ✉ 931 Thomas Jefferson Pkwy., Charlottesville, VA ☎ 434/984–9800 ⊕ www.monticello.org 🍷 $29.

Montpelier. ✉ 11350 Constitution Hwy., Montpelier Station, VA ☎ 540/672–2728 ⊕ www.montpelier.org 🍷 $20 ⊙ Closed Tues. and Wed.

Old House Vineyards. ✉ 18351 Corkys La., Culpeper, VA ☎ 540/423–1032 ⊕ www.oldhousevineyards.com 🍷 Tastings $8 ⊙ Closed Tues.

Pollak Vineyards. ✉ 330 Newtown Rd., Greenwood, VA ☎ 540/456–8844 ⊕ www.pollakvineyards.com 🍷 Tastings $11 ⊙ Closed Mon. and Tues.

University of Virginia. ✉ Charlottesville, VA ☎ 434/924–0311 ⊕ www.virginia.edu 🍷 Free.

White Hall Vineyards. ✉ 5282 Sugar Ridge Rd., Crozet, VA ☎ 434/823–8615 ⊕ whitehallvineyards.com 🍷 Tastings $10 ⊙ Closed Mon. and Tues.

Restaurants

Crozet Pizza. $ *Average main: $10*
✉ *5794 Three Notched Rd., Crozet, VA*
☎ *434/823-2132* ⊕ *www.crozetpizza.com*
⊘ *Closed Tues.*

Michi Tavern. $ *Average main: $19* ✉ *683 Thomas Jefferson Pkwy., Charlottesville, VA* ☎ *434/977-1234* ⊕ *www.michietavern.com.*

The Nook. $ *Average main: $14* ✉ *415 E. Main St., Charlottesville, VA* ☎ *434/295-6665* ⊕ *www.thenookcville.com.*

Palladio Restaurant. $ *Average main: $15*
✉ *17655 Winery Rd., Barboursville, VA*
☎ *540/832-7848* ⊕ *www.bbvwine.com*
⊘ *Closed Mon. and Tues.*

Red Pump Kitchen. $ *Average main: $12*
✉ *401 E. Main St., Charlottesville, VA*
☎ *434/202-6040* ⊕ *www.redpumpkitchen.com.*

☕ Coffee and Quick Bites

Bodo's Bagels. $ *Average main: $5*
✉ *505 Preston Ave., Charlottesville, VA*
☎ *434/293-5224* ⊕ *www.bodosbagels.com.*

🛏 Hotels

Oakhurst Inn. $ *Rooms from: $199*
✉ *122 Oakhurst Cir., Charlottesville, VA*
☎ *434/872-0100* ⊕ *oakhurstinn.com* ¶Ol
No meals.

The Townsman. $ *Rooms from: $225*
✉ *211 W. Main St., Charlottesville, VA*
☎ *434/260-7145* ⊕ *www.thetownsmanhotel.com* ¶Ol *Free breakfast*

🍸 Nightlife

Miller's Downtown. ✉ *109 W. Main St., Charlottesville, VA* ☎ *434/971-8511*
⊕ *www.millersdowntown.com.*

Starr Hill Brewery. ✉ *5391 Three Notched Rd., Crozet, VA* ☎ *434/823-5671* ⊕ *starrhill.com.*

Activities

James River Reeling and Rafting. ✉ *265 Ferry St., Scottsville, VA* ☎ *434/286-4386* ⊕ *www.reelingandrafting.com* 🎫 *From $25.*

Fredericksburg and the Northern Neck, VA

Fredericksburg is 51 miles (approx. 1 hour) from Washington, D.C.

Tucked between the Potomac and Rappahannock Rivers, Virginia's Northern Neck protrudes into the Chesapeake Bay east of Fredericksburg, an under-the-radar, historic realm cooled by briny bay breezes. Scenic byways meander to historic villages, passing wineries, grazing cows, trail-laced parks, sweet little beaches, tobacco fields, and historic sites, including the birthplaces of three of the first five U.S. presidents. Watermen here have earned a living off oysters, rockfish, and blue crabs for centuries—and they still do, stocking local restaurants, food shops, farm stands with their fresh, hand-harvested fare.

The gateway is Fredericksburg, its historic downtown appearing straight out of colonial days. During the Civil War, the Battle of Fredericksburg exploded within city limits—followed by three more now-famous battles on its outskirts. Fredericksburg and Spotsylvania National Military Park offers driving tours, walks, museums, and insights into these critical battles, where you can linger until it's time to head back home.

Of the grand country estates around Fredericksburg, Historic Kenmore is one of the most genteel.

Planning

GETTING THERE AND BACK

Fredericksburg, the gateway to the Northern Neck, is about an hour's drive from D.C. via I–95. From there, it's another two hours or so on scenic byways to Irvington, your base for the first night. You'll need a car for this weekend getaway. However, if you want to take the train, Fredericksburg is on the Amtrak route. You won't be able to visit the Northern Neck, but Fredericksburg has sufficient offerings to stand alone as a weekend getaway.

WHEN TO GO

The Northern Neck and Fredericksburg are a year-round destination, though there's nothing like experiencing it during the warm summer months, when you can hang out outside, taking advantage of the cool Chesapeake breezes. The shoulder seasons of May and June and September and October are pleasant, too. In winter, when the temperatures are cooler, the outside activities aren't available, though you can still visit museums and other indoor activities. Oyster season is October to May, when you'll find the freshest oysters around. The Northern Neck Wine and Oyster Fair takes place in May.

WHERE TO STAY

The Northern Neck has loads of locally owned accommodations. In Irvington, the **Tides Inn and Resort** has been a family favorite for generations, offering all kinds of activities, including paddle boarding, canoeing, kayaking, golf—plus a little beach and swimming pool to simply relax. The upscale **Hope & Glory Inn,** also in Irvington, has cute little bungalows and a haute-cuisine menu in its Dining Hall. In Fredericksburg's old town, the **Richard Johnston Inn** and the **1890 Caroline House** are beautifully restored historic townhouses.

Day 1

Your destination for the day is the bayside village of Irvington, but don't rocket straight there. Hiking is divine at **Westmoreland State Park,** about two hours from D.C., where a trail leads to a beach where you can find ancient shark teeth and other fossils. This is bald eagle habitat, so keep your eyes peeled for the national bird. **George Washington Birthplace National Monument** and **Stratford Hall Plantation,** the birthplace of Robert E. Lee, are two nearby properties with more options for scenic grounds-strolling.

Heading south on VA 3, dubbed the History Land Highway, pick up fresh hot sandwiches or made-to-order salads at **The Daily** in Warsaw. Making your way farther south through bucolic fields and pockets of trees, you'll arrive in Irvington. Founded as a steamboat town at the turn of the 20th century, the town fell into oblivion after a fire in 1917, only to be revived thanks largely to the opening of the Tides Inn and Resort in 1947—which remains a local institution. The petite downtown has one-of-a-kind shops, galleries, and eateries, perfect for an afternoon stroll. Or go wine-tasting at the **Dog and Oyster Vineyard,** whose four varietals pair perfectly with local oysters. Recently, the number of wineries in the area has grown, falling within the Northern Neck George Washington Birthplace American Viticultural Area.

For sunset cocktails and dinner, head out to **Rappahannock Oyster Co.,** across the Route 3 Bridge in Topping. Although this brothers-run enterprise ships out more than 180,000 oysters a week—all harvested here—the place has a mom-and-pop feel. You can check out the oyster-sorting shed, then enjoy cocktails at **Merroir** on the Rappahannock River, followed by a meal centered on the freshest seafood around: oyster po boys, red pepper crab soup, and shrimp salad roll, for example. Or stay in Irvington for dinner at **Dredge,** famous for its fried oyster tacos and Chesapeake conch chowder.

Day 2

Even if you're not an early riser, consider setting the alarm to take advantage of the neck's calm morning vibe. There's nothing more relaxing than going hiking or kayaking at **Belle Isle State Park,** not far from the waterfront historic district of Morattico.

Grab breakfast in Irvington—**The Local** is a morning coffee hot spot, with yummy hyperlocal dishes including crab muffins (local crabmeat on a warm English muffin half); and the ham scram jam sam (ham, egg, cheese, local berry jam on a cinnamon raisin bagel)—be sure to ask about the daily specials. Then head out to explore a string of the Northern Neck's quiet, off-the-beaten-path historic waterfront villages, which evoke life a century ago, with Fredericksburg your evening destination.

In the nearby hamlet of White Stone, the **Allure Art Center** features Chesapeake-inspired artwork and a unique artisan shop where you can buy your own forged steel oyster knife. The **Kilmarnock Museum** in Kilmarnock occupies the village's oldest house, and the nearby **Historic Christ Church and Museum,** dating from 1735, has oyster shells mixed into its mortar and plaster. In Reedville, the **Reedville Fishermen's Museum** delves into the watermen's history. Even if it's not open, its historic ships berthed along the living shoreline garden can be viewed. And Kinsale is an old fishing village with a charming historic district. Pick up supplies at a town deli and picnic on the **Kinsale Museum's** scenic grounds. Another option for picnicking is **Rivah Vineyards at the Grove,** sitting on a patchwork of farm, woods, and riverfront. And while you're there, why not do some wine-tasting, too?

Catpoint Creek borders the **Rappahannock River Valley National Wildlife Refuge,** a critical habitat for bald eagles 4 miles outside Warsaw. Here, the Wilna Unit is open for walking, fishing, paddling (with your own craft)—and bird-watching, with possible sightings including red-bellied woodpeckers, eastern wood-pewees, and Acadian flycatchers.

As you meander north, another possible detour is Colonial Beach, where a boardwalk edges the Potomac River (and is great for biking). **Colonial Beach Brewing** offers an excuse for a midafternoon beer tasting.

At your leisure, pull into Fredericksburg's brick-paved old town, filled with antique shops, art galleries, and specialty boutiques in restored 18th- and 19th-century buildings. And as much as history pervades these hallowed grounds, the town is also noted for its sophisticated art and culinary scene. A roster of exquisite restaurants for dinner, for example, includes **Foode.** Here, farm-to-table dishes tap into California and southern traditions, all decidedly modern: Rosie's fried chicken on a rosemary-cheddar waffle, open-faced cauliflower melt, and shrimp and grits mixed with crumbled sausage. (P.S.: Don't forget dessert.) The building itself, by the way, is full of history—President Lincoln addressed Union troops on one side of the building, and Jefferson Davis addressed Confederate troops on the other. That's just the sort of town the 'Burg is.

Day 3

Start off the day with a leisurely breakfast at **Eileen's Café,** where out-of-this-world crepes and breakfast sandwiches are best enjoyed on the sunny courtyard. Or, if you're hoping for something a little fancier, the **Kenmore Inn** outdoes itself with an extensive brunch menu (French toast bread pudding or crab cake Benedict).

Then head out to explore the historic downtown, popping into historic sites including several related to none other than George Washington, who grew up across the river at **Ferry Farm.** These include the **Mary Washington House,** which he bought for his mother; **Historic Kenmore,** the genteel home of his sister; and the **Rising Sun Tavern,** built by his youngest brother around 1760. There's also the **James Monroe Museum and Memorial Library,** showcasing personal items such as the musket the fifth president took to war and the desk on which he wrote the Monroe Document; and the **Hugh Mercer Apothecary Shop,** looking every bit like it did in colonial times.

If that's not enough history for you, Fredericksburg also was at the heart of a decisive Civil War Battle in 1862. Check out the Fredericksburg Battlefield Visitor Center for an overview, then stroll along Stone Wall and Sunken Road, where much of the fighting took place. The restored Chatham Manor, overlooking the Rappahannock River, served as Union headquarters, hospital, and soup kitchen.

And if that's not enough history, three more Civil War battlefields await nearby: Spotsylvania Court House, Chancellorsville, and the Wilderness. All units of the **Fredericksburg and Spotsylvania National Military Park,** they each have self-guided driving routes with numbered stops. And here's an odd fact: Thomas J. "Stonewall" Jackson died from pneumonia after being shot by friendly fire in the Battle of Chancellorsville; his arm had to be amputated, which was buried separate from him, at **Ellwood Plantation.** You can visit the marker today. When you wrap up, home is about an hour away.

Recommendations

Sights

Bell Isle State Park. ✉ *1632 Belle Isle Rd., Lancaster, VA* ☎ *804/462–5030* ⊕ *www.dcr.virginia.gov* 🖾 *Free.*

Chatham Manor. ✉ *120 Chatham La., Fredericksburg, VA* ☎ *540/693–3200* ⊕ *www.nps.gov* 🖾 *Free.*

Dog and Oyster Vineyard. ✉ *170 White Fences Dr., Irvington, VA* ☎ *800/438–9463* ⊕ *hopeandglory.com/the-dog-oyster-vineyard* 🖾 *Tastings $12.*

Ellwood Plantation. ✉ *36380 Constitution Hwy., Locust Grove, VA* ☎ *540/ 693–3200* ⊕ *www.nps.gov* 🖾 *Free.*

Ferry Farm. ✉ *268 Kings Hwy., Fredericksburg, VA* ☎ *540/370–0732* ⊕ *www.ferryfarm.org* 🖾 *$12.*

Fredericksburg and Spotsylvania National Military Park. ✉ *Fredericksburg Battlefield Visitor Center, 1013 Lafayette Blvd., Fredericksburg, VA 540/693–3200* ⊕ *www.nps.gov* 🖾 *Free.*

George Washington Birthplace National Monument. ✉ *268 Kings Hwy., Fredericksburg, VA* ☎ *540/370–0732* ⊕ *www.kenmore.org* 🖾 *$12.*

Historic Christ Church and Museum. ✉ *420 Christ Church Rd, Weems, VA* ☎ *804/438–6855* ⊕ *www.christchurch1735.org* 🖾 *$5.*

Historic Kenmore. ✉ *1201 Washington Ave., Fredericksburg, VA* ☎ *540/373–3381* ⊕ *www.kenmore.org* 🖾 *$12.*

Hugh Mercer Apothecary Shop. ✉ *1020 Caroline St., Fredericksburg, VA* ☎ *540/373–3362* ⊕ *www.washingtonheritagemuseums.org* 🖾 *$7.*

James Monroe Museum and Memorial Library. ✉ *908 Charles St., Fredericksburg, VA* ☎ *540/654–1043* ⊕ *www.jamesmonroemuseum.umw.edu* 🖾 *Free.*

Kilmarnock Museum. ✉ *76 N. Main St., Kilmarnock, VA* ☎ *804/436–9100* ⊕ *www.virginiasriverrealm.com* 🖾 *Free.*

Kinsale Museum. ✉ *449 Kinsale Rd., Kinsale, VA* ☎ *804/472–3001* ⊕ *www.kinsalefoundation.org* 🖾 *Free* ⊗ *Closed Sun.–Thurs.*

Mary Washington House. ✉ *1200 Charles St., Fredericksburg, VA* ☎ *540/373–1569* ⊕ *www.washingtonheritagemuseums.org* 🖾 *$7.*

Rappahannock River Valley National Wildlife Refuge. ✉ *Wilna Rd., Warsaw, VA* ☎ *804/333–1470* ⊕ *www.fws.gov* 🖾 *Free.*

Reedville Fishermen's Museum. ✉ *504 Main St., Reedville, VA* ☎ *804/453–6529* ⊕ *www.rfmuseum.org* 🖾 *Free* ⊗ *Closed weekdays.*

Rising Sun Tavern. ✉ *1304 Caroline St., Fredericksburg, VA* ☎ *540/371–1494* ⊕ *www.washingtonheritagemuseums.org* 🖾 *$7.*

Rivah Vineyards at the Grove. ✉ *671 Kinsale Bridge Rd., Kinsale, VA* ☎ *757/621–0618* ⊕ *www.rivahvineyards.com* 🖾 *Tastings $8* ⊗ *Closed Tues.–Thurs.*

Stratford Hall Plantation. ✉ *483 Great House Rd., Stratford, VA* ☎ *804/493–8038* ⊕ *www.stratfordhall.org* 🖾 *$15.*

Westmoreland State Park. ✉ *145 Cliff Rd., Montross, VA* ☎ *804/493–8821* ⊕ *www.dcr.virginia.gov* 🖾 *Free.*

🍴 Restaurants

The Daily. 💲 *Average main: $16* ✉ *130 Court Cir., Warsaw, VA* ☎ *804/333–3455*

Eileen's Cafe. 💲 *Average main: $20* ✉ *1115 Caroline St., Fredericksburg, VA* ☎ *540/372–4030* ⊕ *www.eileensbakeryandcafe.com* ⊗ *Closed Mon.*

Foode. 💲 *Average main: $15* ✉ *900 Princess Anne St., Fredericksburg, VA*

☎ 540/479–1370 🌐 www.foodefredericksburg.com.

The Kenmore Inn. [$] *Average main: $21 ✉ 1200 Princess Anne St., Fredericksburg, VA ☎ 540/371–7622 🌐 www.thekenmorebar.com*

The Local. [$] *Average main: $10 ✉ 824 Hinton Ave., Charlottesville, VA ☎ 434/984–9749 🌐 www.thelocal-cville.com.*

Rappahannock Oyster Co. [$] *Average main: $22 ✉ 784 Locklies Creek Rd., Topping, VA ☎ 804/204–1709 🌐 www.rroysters.com.*

Hotels

1890 Caroline House. [$] *Rooms from: $175 ✉ 528 Caroline St., Fredericksburg, VA ☎ 540/899–7606 🌐 www.thecaroline-house.com 🍴 Free breakfast.*

Hope & Glory Inn. [$] *Rooms from: $265 ✉ 65 Tavern Rd., Irvington, VA ☎ 804/438–6053 🌐 www.hopeandglory.com 🍴 Free breakfast.*

Richard Johnston Inn. [$] *Rooms from: $175 ✉ 711 Caroline St., Fredericksburg, VA ☎ 540/899–7606 🌐 www.therichard-johnstoninn.com 🍴 Free breakfast.*

Tides Inn& Resort. [$] *Rooms from: $395 ✉ 480 King Carter Dr., Irvington, VA ☎ 844/244–9486 🌐 www.tidesinn.com 🍴 No meals.*

Nightlife

Colonial Beach Brewing. *✉ 215C Washington Ave., Colonial Beach, VA ☎ 540/760–5661 🌐 www.colonial-beach-virginia-attractions.com 🕒 Closed Tues.*

Merroir. *✉ 784 Locklies Creek Rd., Topping, VA ☎ 804/758–2871 🌐 www.rroysters.com.*

Shopping

Allure Art Center. *✉ 419 Rappahannock Dr., White Stone, VA ☎ 804/323–3169 🌐 www.allureartcenter.com 🕒 Closed Mon.–Thurs.*

Greenbrier Valley, WV

249 miles (approx. 4 hours) from Washington, D.C.

Country roads, take me home to Greenbrier Valley. This spot in West Virginia has a lot to offer both those just passing through and those who are looking to cozy up in a bed-and-breakfast for a few days and immerse themselves in the area's local arts scene and picturesque scenery.

Planning

GETTING THERE AND BACK

Take I–66 W, to I–81 S to I–64 W. The average drive time is just over four hours.

PIT STOPS

Stop and stretch your legs in Harrisonburg, Virginia, just off the 81. Seek out the **Edith J. Carrier Arboretum** on the James Madison University campus.

INSPIRATION

Please listen to "Country Roads" by John Denver at some point. It's sort of a West Virginia thing. Additionally, tune into the long-running "The Mountain Stage" podcast hosted by Larry Groce to hear a variety of tunes—from synth pop to country—recorded in front of a live audience.

WHEN TO GO

There's not a bad time to visit Greenbrier Valley. If you're planning a summer trip, any time between June and August (especially if you plan on doing outdoor activities) will do just fine, but expect it to be humid as heck. It's much crisper in October and the landscapes are stunning

West Virginia's sprawling Greenbrier Resort has been welcoming guests since 1778.

(so there's plenty of leaf-peeping to be had).

WHERE TO STAY

If you love bed-and-breakfasts, you came to the right place. **The James Wylie House Bed & Breakfast Inn** was built in 1819, so a stay there is like stepping (comfortably) back in time. **The Greenbrier Resort** is the reason why a lot of people come to town—it's stunning, stately, and there's a ton to do on the property. The charming, atmospheric **Edgarton Inn B&B** is a Victorian home lover's dream.

Day 1

Plan on leaving Washington, D.C., at around 7 am (early, yes, but you'll have more time for activities) and expect to get there around noon. We recommend lunching at **The Wild Bean,** a quaint little deli with a variety of vegetarian options and fresh, organic coffee from local roasters to help you jazz-up your arrival.

A majestic sight for tourists young and old, the wonder that is **The Lost Caverns** was discovered in 1942 and features, 120 feet beneath the surface, a series of rock formations that must be seen to be believed. We're talking a 30-pound stalactite called The Snow Chandelier and a 28-foot stalagmite called the War Club. The general admission half-mile tour is self-guided, but there is a more in-depth tour (literally) where you'll go a little further and get a little muddier. If you're looking for a more refined activity on your first day in town, experience a tour and a tasting at **Smooth Ambler Spirits** where you'll see how local whiskeys go from barrel to delicious, classic cocktails.

Now, it's time to fill that belly with something more than just alcohol. A French-style bistro with an eclectic twist and a substantial wine list, **The French Goat** in the heart of Lewisburg, might just knock you off your feet with its charm—it's located in a home originally built in the 1800s.

Speaking of being knocked off your feet, tonight you'll be indulging in libations at **The Asylum** where, on any given night, there's live music on the heated rooftop.

Day 2

Start off your morning right (and early) in a booth at **Cook's Country Kitchen** with an omelet, blueberry pancakes, or cinnamon roll. It will likely be a filling breakfast, but that's ideal, as you'll be fairly active today so you'll need the energy.

You'll need a sturdy pair of hiking boots for where you're going next: the **Greenbrier River Trail.** The 78-mile trail (you don't have to hike the whole stretch) was a former railroad that crosses 35 bridges and snakes through multiple towns. It's open year-round and we recommend starting (and finishing) in Lewisburg, where you'll likely be staying for the duration of your weekend getaway.

Afterward, warm up your tummy with a delicious pizza at **The Humble Tomato,** which has specials nearly every day. It might not be a bad idea to grab your pie to go and plop down on a nearby picnic table for a breezy, outdoor lunch.

Now, it's time to truly treat yourself— you're headed to get pampered at The Greenbrier Resort. While the spa services offered here are on the pricier side, they are decadent to say the least. For example, the 80-minute Sweet Tea Simplicity begins with a soak in the property's famous sulphur water and ends with a shea butter body massage.

Following your afternoon activities, The Greenbrier Resort has more than a few dining options, and you don't need to stay here to enjoy them. The Main Dining Room is particularly elegant, with its chandeliers and dress code (no denim, jacket and tie required for men, and dresses or evening suits for women). Additionally, there's live music every night.

Day 3

You'll start the next day at one of the state's most well-known franchises: **Tudor's Biscuit World.** Grab a Mary B (a bacon, egg, and cheese biscuit) and a large coffee, and you'll feel right as rain going into Day 3. Today, you'll be antiquing at some of the area's most interesting boutiques, including **Robert's Antiques,** which also carries wine and stocks more than 700 labels from around the world; **Brick House Antiques,** housed in a pre–Civil War home where each room is a different theme—and **Tattered & Worn,** where you'll find plenty of fine furniture and intriguing decor. Around lunchtime, head to **The Local** where you can munch on soup, salad, or a panini on the deck. You can also purchase local produce from here if you decide to swing by on your way out of town to pick something up for your own kitchen.

Getting a peek at the Greenbrier River is a must (and sort of unavoidable) while you're in town, so why not go big before you go home and choose to explore it on kayak? The river is the longest undammed in the entire country and it has no shortage of serene pockets: If you're visiting in the winter months—getting on the river isn't ideal then, obviously—swing back around to The Greenbrier for a cozy sleigh ride.

Recommendations

Sights

Edith J. Carrier Arboretum. ⊠ *780 University Blvd., Harrisonburg, VA* ☏ *540/568–3194* ⊕ *www.jmu.edu* ✉ *Free.*

Greenbrier River Trail. ⊠ *Greenbrier River Trail, Frankford, WV* ☏ *304/799–4087* ⊕ *www.wvstateparks.com* ✉ *Free.*

The Lost Caverns. ⊠ *907 Lost World Rd., Lewisburg, WV* ☏ *304/645–6677* ⊕ *www. lostworldcaverns.com* ✉ *$12.*

Restaurants

Cook's Country Kitchen. $ *Average main: $5* ✉ *38154 Midland Trail, White Sulphur Springs, WV* ☎ *304/536–9227* ⊕ *www.cookscountrykit.com* ⊙ *No dinner Sun.*

Del Sol Cantina. $ *Average main: $10* ✉ *206 Washington St., Lewisburg, WV* ☎ *304/645–1717* ⊕ *www.delsolcantina.com* ⊙ *Closed Sun.*

The French Goat. $ *Average main: $14* ✉ *290 Lafayette St., Lewisburg, WV* ☎ *304/647–1052* ⊕ *www.thefrenchgoat.com* ⊙ *Closed Mon. and Tues.*

The Humble Tomato. $ *Average main: $9* ✉ *855 Washington St. W, Lewisburg, WV* ☎ *681/318–3788* ⊕ *www.thehumbletomato* ⊙ *Closed Tues.*

The Local. $ *Average main: $15* ✉ *824 Hinton Ave., Charlottesville, VA* ☎ *434/984–9749* ⊕ *www.thelocal-cville.com* ⊙ *No lunch.*

Tudor's Biscuit World. $ *Average main: $11* ✉ *1083 Main St., Elkview, WV* ☎ *304/965–7769* ⊕ *www.tudorsbiscuitworld.com.*

The Wild Bean. $ *Average main: $9* ✉ *1056 E. Washington St., Lewisburg, WV* ☎ *304/645–3738* ⊕ *www.thewildbrew.com* ⊙ *No dinner.*

Hotels

Edgarton Inn B&B. $ *Rooms from: $100* ✉ *305 Walnut St., Ronceverte, WV* ☎ *304/645–1588* ⊕ *www.edgartoninn.com* ⦿ *Free breakfast.*

The Greenbrier Resort. $ *Rooms from: $297* ✉ *101 W. Main St., White Sulphur Springs, WV* ☎ *844/837–2466* ⊕ *www.greenbrier.com* ⦿ *No meals.*

The James Wylie House Bed & Breakfast Inn. $ *Rooms from: $130* ✉ *208 Main St. E, White Sulphur Springs, WV* ☎ *304/536–9444* ⊕ *www.jameswylie.com* ⦿ *Free breakfast.*

Nightlife

The Asylum. ✉ *393 E. Randolph St., Lewisburg, WV* ☎ *304/667–2213* ⊕ *thehotelescape.com.*

Smooth Ambler Spirits. ✉ *745 Industrial Park Rd., Maxwelton, WV* ☎ *304/497–3123* ⊕ *www.smoothambler.com.*

Shopping

Brick House Antiques. ✉ *1066 E. Washington St., Lewisburg, WV* ☎ *304/645–4082* ⊕ *www.greenbrierwv.com.*

Robert's Antiques. ✉ *26 E. Mellen St., Hampton, VA* ☎ *757/722–0222* ⊕ *www.robertsantiquesphoebus.com.*

Tattered & Worn. ✉ *1717 N. Jefferson St., Lewisburg, WV 24901* ☎ *304/845–3977* ⊕ *www.tatteredandwornantiques.com.*

The Hamptons and Montauk, NY

Southampton is 92 miles (approx. 2 hours) from New York City.

The Hamptons is the quintessential weekend destination for New Yorkers. Beautiful beaches, cozy hotels, posh restaurants, and raucous bars lure city dwellers to this playground of the rich and famous. Although the Hamptons shines brightest in the summer, it's so much more than just a beach destination, thanks to the artists that call this place home—galleries and museums abound, while star-studded events fill the calendar. And while the Hamptons has a reputation for luxury, it's not all champagne and caviar delivered by a butler—some of the best meals can be found at seafood shacks and dive bars.

The Hamptons isn't just one town, it's a series of towns on the South Fork of Long Island, including Southampton, Bridgehampton, East Hampton, Sag

At the tip of Long Island, Montauk Lighthouse commands a spot on a rocky beach.

Harbor, Amagansett, and Montauk. Each town is worthy of a trip on its own, but here's how to experience the best of what this little slice of paradise has to offer.

Planning

GETTING THERE AND BACK

Without traffic, the Hamptons is an easy two-hour drive from New York City, taking the Long Island Expressway east until you reach Manorville and continuing east on Highway 27 via Highway 111 to Southampton. If you're without a car, the Long Island Railroad is an efficient way to travel, with multiple daily departures in the summer from Penn Station and Jamaica Station that will get you to Southampton in about 2½ hours. If you've got cash to burn, there's also seaplane service and helicopter ridesharing with Blade.

INSPIRATION

Colson Whiteau's *Sag Harbor* is an autobiographical novel about spending summers in the area. Many of the chapters can standalone as essays or short stories, so don't feel like you have to listen to the whole thing before you arrive.

PIT STOPS

The glamorous **Oheka Castle** looks like a French Chateau straight out of a movie. In reality, it's a gilded-age mansion that's been converted into a (possibly haunted) three-star hotel. Make a reservation to stop by and explore the grounds or have a drink or snack at the bar.

WHEN TO GO

The Hamptons and Montauk come alive in the summer, when harried New Yorkers flock to the beach to escape the oppressive heat of the city. It's the time of year with the best weather, the wildest parties, and the worst traffic. In the winter, a visit to the Hamptons is completely different, with brisk beach walks and cozy meals at the bars and restaurants that remain open year-round. But the most magical time to visit the Hamptons is in September, when the weather is still delightful but the crowds have gone back to the city.

WHERE TO STAY

Encompassing a handful of towns miles apart, choosing your home base for the weekend can play a big role in how much driving you have to do. If you're visiting in the summer, Montauk has the most accommodation options, from the grownup summer camp vibes at **Ruschmeyers** to the exclusive resort amenities at **Gurney's Montauk.** In East Hampton, the **Maidstone** is a stylish and cozy boutique hideaway walking distance from town and with easy access to the beach.

Day 1

Plan to arrive in Southampton by mid-morning to make a stop at **Tate's Bake Shop.** Tate's cookies are now available in bougie supermarkets throughout the country, but this is where it all began. Here, you'll get the freshly baked version of your thin, crispy, and buttery chocolate chip cookie, but you'll also find cookie varieties and other baked goods like pies and brownies that are only available in the Hamptons and in select New York City grocery stores. Sample everything and make sure to buy extra for souvenirs.

Coast on your sugar high to Watermill to the **Parrish Art Museum,** a small but impressive art collection that highlights the beauty of the East End as seen through the eyes of some of the area's most famous resident artists, like Fairfield Porter and William Merritt Chase. In addition to the permanent collection, there are rotating exhibitions. Even if you're not a huge fan of art, the building itself—a modern barn-esque behemoth—is a sight to behold.

Once you've worked up an appetite, continue on to Bridgehampton for a luxurious lunch at **Pierre's,** a Hamptons institution that's open for breakfast, lunch, and dinner seven days a week and 365 days a year, a rarity in this seasonal enclave. The menu is French with a focus on seafood classics—treat yourself to moules frites, bouillabaisse, or a whole Branzino with herbes de provence.

After lunch, take a stroll down Main Street to browse for designer clothes and high-end home goods. If you need a good-old-fashioned ice cream sundae to top off lunch, **Candy Kitchen** has you covered. The 100-plus year-old soda shop has soft serve and all the toppings you could ever want.

While the beach beckons, it's worth exploring the lesser-visited outdoor spaces on the South Fork. The Napeague Dunes, part of **Hither Hills State Park** between Amagansett and Montauk, is the perfect place for a sunset stroll. The sandy trail weaves through sand dunes, which are harder to climb than you might think. Wear appropriate footwear and keep in mind that you might have to stop to empty the sand out of your shoes a few times. Don't worry, the views in here are worth it.

Once the sun goes down, it's time for dinner back in Amagansett. Settle into a table at **Wolffer Kitchen,** a restaurant by the Wolffer Estate Vineyard team. The restaurant serves homey-yet-healthy comfort food made with farm fresh local ingredients paired with Wolffer Wine.

After dinner, put on your dancing shoes for a night out at one of the most famous (and infamous) bars in the Hamptons. **Stephen Talkhouse** is a sprawling indoor/outdoor bar and venue that hosts everyone from rock and roll legends to local karaoke stars. The cover charge can be steep and the lines can stretch around the block, but it's a fun place to dance the night away.

Day 2

Start your day the Hamptons way with a bagel from **Goldberg's.** There are multiple locations throughout the Hamptons, so no matter where you're staying, you're never very far from a delicious bagel (or better yet, a flagel) with scallion cream cheese. Goldberg's has drip coffee, but if you're in need of something a little fancier, you can stop by **Jack's** for green juice and a cappuccino.

Once you've had breakfast, it's time to finally hit the beach at Georgica Beach in East Hampton. Many hotels and rentals in the area will provide you with umbrellas, chairs, and towels, but if not, make sure to bring a towel and some shade or plenty of sunscreen since there's nowhere to rent chairs here. If you're lucky, there might be a food truck parked on-site, but be sure to bring snacks and drinks anyway because there are few facilities.

If you're not looking to post up and get a sunburn, it's still worth a visit to the beach just for a walk down the shore to gawk at the beautiful mansions and plan which one you'd buy if you won the lottery. The ocean is frigid but swimmable from late spring to early fall, so plan accordingly.

Next, it's time to explore the town of Sag Harbor. Sag Harbor is probably the liveliest town in the Hamptons, especially in the off-season. Stroll down Main Street, stopping into shops and galleries (don't miss **Sag Harbor Books**) before popping into **Sag Pizza** for lunch. Casual and fun, this pizza place is the best Neapolitan-style pie in the Hamptons, using local ingredients like fresh clams and cheese from Mecox Bay Dairy.

After lunch, spend an hour or two rambling through the **Longhouse Reserve,** an outdoor sculpture park with works by artists like Yoko Ono and Buckminster Fuller. It's whimsical and fun, with plenty of surprises hidden throughout the 16-acre compound.

Tonight, you're off to Montauk for dinner and drinks. This sleepy fishing town has exploded in popularity in the past decade, with seasonal hipster hotels and nightlife hotspots that cater to a young, stylish, and affluent crowd. It can be overwhelmed with visitors during July and August, but year-round it's a beautiful and pleasant place to visit.

The **Crow's Nest** is arguably the most romantic restaurant in the Hamptons. During the summer, the backyard is filled with cozy dining tables and lounge chairs illuminated in the glow of string lights. The menu focuses on veggie-forward shareable small plates, making this the ideal date night spot.

After dinner, it's time to hit the town. For a night out in Montauk, there's a plethora of options, ranging from the celeb-studded **Surf Lodge** (where you might be charged $28 for a watered down mojito and the chance to spot a celeb) to **Shagwong Tavern,** an old-school pub where you can swap stores with local fishermen and surfers.

Day 3

After a long night of partying, you need some nutrients to put you back on track. Visit **Joni's Kitchen** for healthy juices and smoothies along with vegan- and vegetarian-friendly breakfast items.

Montauk is a surfer's town, and it's a great place to try and learn. Make a reservation for surf lesson through your hotel or with **Coreyswave.** They'll be able to set you up with a wetsuit and a board that's right for your ability.

After a morning of surfing (or just a walk on the beach if that's more your speed), take a drive to the **Montauk Lighthouse** for a walk around the postcard-perfect windswept and rocky beach.

On your way back to the city in the afternoon, stop for a late lunch or early dinner at the **Clam Bar** (or its across the street neighbor, the **Lobster Roll**) on Highway 27 between Montauk and Amangansett. The outdoor shack serves divine clam chowder as well as fried clams and lobster rolls—the cherry on top of a perfect weekend at the beach.

Recommendations

Sights

Hither Hills State Park. ⊠ 164 Old Montauk Hwy., Montauk, NY ☎ 631/668–2554 ⊕ www.parks.ny.gov/parks/hitherhills/details.aspx 💲 $8.

Longhouse Reserve. ⊠ 133 Hands Creek Rd., East Hampton, NY ☎ 631/329–3568 ⊕ www.longhouse.org 💲 $15 ⊙ Closed Sun.

Montauk Lighthouse. ⊠ 2000 Montauk Hwy., Montauk, NY ☎ 631/668–2544 ⊕ montauklighthouse.com 💲 $12.

Oheka Castle. ⊠ 135 W. Gate Dr., Huntington ☎ 631/659–1400 ⊕ www.oheka.com 💲 Free.

Parrish Art Museum. ⊠ 279 Montauk Hwy., Water Mill, NY ☎ 631/283–2118 ⊕ www.parrishart.org 💲 $12.

🍴 Restaurants

Clam Bar. 💲 Average main: $20 ⊠ 2025 Montauk Hwy., Amagansett, NY ☎ 631/267–6348 ⊕ www.clambarhamptons.com ⊙ No dinner weekdays.

The Crow's Nest. 💲 Average main: $20 ⊠ 4 Old West Lake Dr., Montauk, NY ☎ 631/668–2077 ⊕ www.crowsnestmtk.com.

Goldberg's. 💲 Average main: $10 ⊠ 28 S. Etna Ave., Montauk, NY ☎ 631/238–5976 ⊕ www.theoriginalgoldbergsbagels.com ⊙ No dinner.

Jack's. 💲 Average main: $10 ⊠ 146 Montauk Hwy., Amagansett, NY ☎ 631/267–5555 ⊕ www.jacksstirbrew.com/amagansett ⊙ No dinner.

Joni's Kitchen. 💲 Average main: $12 ⊠ 28 S. Etna Ave., Montauk, NY ☎ 631/668–3663 ⊕ www.jonismontauk.com ⊙ No dinner.

Lobster Roll. 💲 Average main: $20 ⊠ 1980 Montauk Hwy., Amagansett, NY ☎ 631/267–3740 ⊕ www.lobsterroll.com ⊙ Closed Tues.

Pierre's. 💲 Average main: $20 ⊠ 2468 Main St., Bridgehampton, NY ☎ 631/537–5110 ⊕ www.pierresbridgehampton.com.

Sag Pizza. 💲 Average main: $16 ⊠ 103 Main St., Sag Harbor, NY ☎ 631/725–3167 ⊕ www.sagpizza.com.

Wolffer Kitchen. 💲 Average main: $32 ⊠ 4 Amagansett Square Dr., Amagansett, NY ☎ 631/267–2764 ⊕ www.wollferkitchen.com ⊙ No lunch.

☕ Coffee and Quick Bites

Candy Kitchen. 💲 Average main: $12 ⊠ Montauk Hwy., Bridgehampton, NY ☎ 631/537–9885.

Tate's Bake Shop. 💲 Average main: $10 ⊠ 43 N. Sea Rd., Southampton, NY ☎ 631/283–9830 ⊕ www.tatesbakeshop.com.

🛏 Hotels

Gurney's Montauk. 💲 Rooms from: $413 ⊠ 290 Old Montauk Hwy., Montauk, NY ☎ 631/668–6500 ⊕ www.gurneysresorts.com/montauk ⑩ No meals.

The Maidstone. 💲 Rooms from: $695 ⊠ 207 Main St., East Hampton, NY ☎ 631/324–5006 ⊕ www.themaidstone.com ⑩ Free breakfast.

Ruschmeyers. $ *Rooms from: $225* ✉ *161 2nd House Rd., Montauk, NY* ☎ *631/668–2877* ⊕ *www.ruschmeyers. com* ⦿ *Free breakfast.*

Nightlife

Shagwong Tavern. ✉ *774 Montauk Hwy., Montauk, NY* ☎ *631/668–3050* ⊕ *www. shagwongtavern.com.*

Stephen Talkhouse. ✉ *161 Main St., Amagansett, NY* ☎ *631/267–3117* ⊕ *www. stephentalkhouse.com.*

Surf Lodge. ✉ *183 Edgemere St., Montauk, NY* ☎ *631/483–5041* ⊕ *www. thesurflodge.com.*

Shopping

Sag Harbor Books. ✉ *7 Main St., Sag Harbor, NY* ☎ *631/725–8425* ⊕ *www. southamptonsagharborbooks.com.*

Activities

Coreywave. ☎ *516/639–4879* ⊕ *www. coreyswave.com.*

Harpers Ferry, WV

67 miles (approx. 1½ hours) from Washington, D.C.

From meditative retreats to heart-pounding outdoor adventures, West Virginia, known as the Mountain State, has a lot of spots for travelers to consider road-tripping to. An excellent example is Harpers Ferry, a town not even 90 minutes from Washington, D.C., that has rich history and beguiling wildlife in equal measure, just waiting to be photographed and explored. The town is especially appealing to historians, as it's best known for abolitionist John Brown's raid in 1859, in which Brown used Harpers Ferry a base for a revolt against slavery. A visit will help you gain insight into a pivotal time in history and also give you a moment to breathe and appreciate scenery that you just can't get in the nation's capital.

Planning

GETTING THERE AND BACK

If you're driving, take the George Washington Memorial Parkway to I–495 to I–270 to U.S. 340. You can also hop aboard an Amtrak train and avoid the traffic. Either option should take you around 1 hour and 20 minutes.

INSPIRATION

Listen to "Country Roads" by John Denver, of course. In terms of podcasts, NPR's "Inside Appalachia" gives stories and insights into the area's culture.

PIT STOPS

If you're really taking your time on this trip, stop in Gaithersburg, Maryland (off I–270). Get out, stretch your legs, and have a gander in the **Gaithersburg Community Museum,** located in the old train station.

WHEN TO GO

An escape to this mountain town can (and should) be considered any weekend, but June to August is the best time to visit if you are planning outdoor activities (especially if they're water-related). But there's no leaf-peeping quite like West Virginia leaf-peeping when fall rolls around. The landscape in October is stunning.

WHERE TO STAY

You'd truly be missing out if you didn't stay in one of the area's B&Bs. **The Town's Inn** is incredibly close to trails, the train station, the shops, restaurants, and more. The **Ledge House Bed and Breakfast** has a charming garden and sun terrace. **The Lily Garden Inn** offers a hearty breakfast daily.

Harpers Ferry is best known for abolitionist John Brown's historic raid in 1859.

Day 1

If you're leaving Washington, D.C., Friday morning at 10 am, expect to arrive in Harpers Ferry around 11:20 am (give or take, due to infamous traffic). Stop for lunch at the quaint, plant-based **Kelley Farm Kitchen** (vegans, take note!), which prides itself on its fresh produce; you can also purchase local soaps and candles from its market, as well. If seating is limited, check out the **Cannonball Deli,** which offers subs and hand-dipped ice cream. As mentioned above, get acquainted with the town's rich history with a tour of **Harpers Ferry Historical National Park,** which, technically, houses the town of Harpers Ferry itself. See the **John Brown Fort,** the **John Brown Wax Museum,** and snag some stunning photos on the CSX railroad bridge that crosses the Potomac River. The **Harpers Ferry Park Association** offers certified guided tours for those looking to delve even further into the area's history.

Following your outdoor excursions, cool off (or warm up) with a beverage at **The Rabbit Hole.** As for dinner, feel free to stay there or finish up dinner at the **Anvil Restaurant,** a cozy seafood eatery known for its crab cakes.

Day 2

Get up early for some French Toast and a cup of joe from **Battle Grounds Bakery and Coffee.** Pick up a jar of one of their handmade jams while you're there. While it's about 10 minutes outside of town, **Mountain View Diner** has fresh baked biscuits daily.

Now that you have fueled for the day, grab your running shoes, because you can't go to West Virginia—especially a beautiful place like Harpers Ferry—and not expect to explore the outdoors. One hike in particular—Split Rock Overlook via the Loudoun Heights Trail—is about 6 miles and is accessible year-round. Your reward for all those steps is stunning views of the town and the Potomac and Shenandoah rivers. Another trail to consider (that's also open year-round) is the Maryland Heights Loop—a 5-mile trek that gazes down upon Harpers Ferry. Dogs are welcome on both trails, but must be leashed.

If you didn't pack sandwiches, head to the casual **Canal House Café.** The menu—complete with locally sourced ingredients and gluten-free options—includes create-your-own salads and freshly caught seafood.

If you're a history lover, **Antietam National Battlefield** is a must-visit about 20 minutes outside of Harpers Ferry. The Battle of Antietam saw Robert E. Lee's army pitted against Union General George McClellan in what would become the bloodiest single-day battle in American history and ultimately resulted in what is widely considered a win for the Union.

For dinner, head to the intimate, rather decadent **Hamilton's Tavern 1840**, whose menu contains offerings that are inspired by dishes around the globe. Reservations are recommended.

Day 3

Rise and shine with an omelet and coffee at **The Country Café.** If the weather permits, **Harpers Ferry Adventure Center** is the outfitter for tubing or whitewater rafting. Lunch is usually included in the packages, but if not you should be able to pack your own. Otherwise, grab a sandwich at **Almost Heaven Pub** when you're back on the streets.

After you've had a minute to breathe, get some final snapshots of the town's memorable architecture. St. Peter's Roman Catholic Church is one of the most beautiful churches in the region, and the Hilltop House Hotel will look great on Instagram. If you decide to indulge in dinner on your way home, make it a memorable one: upscale **Glendale Vintner's Table** is on

a working farm, which means your meal is pasture-to-table fresh.

Recommendations

Sights

Antietam National Battlefield. ⊠ *302 E. Main St., Sharpsburg, MD* ☏ *301/432–5124* ⊕ *www.nps.gov/anti/index.htm* ⊒ *Free.*

Gaithersburg Community Museum. ⊠ *9 S. Summit Ave. Gaithersburg, MD* ☏ *301/258–6160* ⊕ *www.gaithersburg-md.gov* ⊒ *$5* ⊘ *Closed Mon.*

Harpers Ferry National Historical Park. ⊠ *171 Shoreline Dr., Harpers Ferry, WV* ☏ *304/535–6029* ⊕ *www.nps.gov/hafe* ⊒ *$20.*

John Brown's Fort. ⊠ *Henandoah St. and Potomac St., Harpers Ferry, WV* ☏ *304/535–6029* ⊕ *www.nps.gov/hafe/learn/historyculture/john-brown-fort.htm* ⊒ *Free.*

John Brown Wax Museum. ⊠ *168 High St., Harpers Ferry, WV* ☏ *304/535–6342* ⊕ *www.johnbrownwaxmuseum.com* ⊒ *$7.*

🍴 Restaurants

Almost Heaven Bar & Grill. Ⓢ *Average main: $10* ⊠ *374 High St., Morgantown, WV* ☏ *304/943–7377* ⊕ *www.almostheavenbarandgrill.com* ⊘ *Closed Sun.*

The Anvil Restaurant. Ⓢ *Average main: $14* ⊠ *1290 W. Washington St., Harpers Ferry, WV* ☏ *304/535–2582* ⊕ *www.anvil-restaurant.com* ⊘ *Closed Thurs.*

The Canal House Café. Ⓢ *Average main: $14* ⊠ *226 W. Washington St., Harpers Ferry, WV* ☏ *304/535–8551* ⊕ *www.thecanalhousecafe.com* ⊘ *Closed Tues. and Wed.*

Cannonball Deli. $ *Average main: $10* ✉ *148 High St., Harpers Ferry, WV* ☎ *304/535–1762* ⊕ *www.cannonball-deli.hub.biz* ☾ *No dinner.*

The Country Café. $ *Average main: $10* ✉ *1723 W. Washington St., Harpers Ferry, WV* ☎ *304/535–2327* ⊕ *www.country-cafe.com* ☾ *Closed Mon. No dinner.*

Grandale Vintner's Table. $ *Average main: $21* ✉ *14001 Harpers Ferry Rd., Purcellville, VA* ☎ *540/668–6000* ⊕ *www.grandalerestaurant.com.*

Hamilton's Tavern 1840. $ *Average main: $16* ✉ *179 High St., Harpers Ferry, WV* ☎ *304/535–1860* ⊕ *www.hamiltonstavern1840.com* ☾ *Closed Tues. and Wed.*

Kelley Farm Kitchen. $ *Average main: $14* ✉ *1112 W. Washington St., Harpers Ferry, WV* ☎ *304/535–9976* ⊕ *www.kelleyfarmkitchen.com.*

Mountain View Diner. $ *Average main: $17* ✉ *903 E. Washington St., Charles Town, WV* ☎ *304/728–8522* ⊕ *www.mountainviewdiner.com/welcome-back.*

The Rabbit Hole. $ *Average main: $15* ✉ *186 High St., Harpers Ferry, WV* ☎ *304/535–8818* ☾ *Closed Tues. and Wed.*

☕ Coffee and Quick Bites

Battle Grounds Bakery and Coffee. $ *Average main: $10* ✉ *180 High St., Harpers Ferry, WV* ☎ *304/535–8583* ☾ *No dinner.*

🛏 Hotels

Ledge House Bed and Breakfast. $ *Rooms from: $201* ✉ *280 Henry Clay St., Harpers Ferry, WV* ☎ *877/468–4236* ⊕ *www.theledgehouse.com* ⦿❘ *Free breakfast.*

Lily Garden Inn. $ *Rooms from: $159* ✉ *701 Washington St., Harpers Ferry, WV* ☎ *304/535–2657* ⊕ *www.lilygardenbnb.com* ⦿❘ *Free breakfast.*

The Town's Inn. $ *Rooms from: $120* ✉ *179 High St., Harpers Ferry, WV* ☎ *304/932–0677* ⊕ *www.thetownsinn.com* ⦿❘ *No meals.*

Activities

Harpers Ferry Adventure Center. ✉ *37410 Adventure Center La., Purcellville, VA* ☎ *540/668–900* ⊕ *www.harpersferryadventurecenter.com* 🎟 *Activities from $30.*

Harpers Ferry Park Association. ✉ *723 Shenandoah St., Harpers Ferry, WV* ☎ *304/535–6881* ⊕ *www.harpersferryhistory.org* 🎟 *$10 per vehicle.*

Hudson Valley, NY

Kingston is 101 miles (approx. 2 hours) from New York City.

New York City is great, but it has a serious lack of nature (no offense, Central Park). And for the past few decades, wilderness-hungry New Yorkers have escaped the five boroughs for a peaceful enclave just a few hours north of the city: the Hudson Valley. Now a slew of farm-to-table restaurants, hipster bars, boutique hotels, and quaint shops have turned the region into an all-seasons destination filled with breweries, art galleries, historical stops, and plenty of fresh air. It's the perfect weekend getaway for anyone who wants great food, trendy bars, and wide-open spaces.

Planning

GETTING THERE AND BACK

The Hudson Valley is easily accessible via Metro-North and Amtrak, but getting between the different sites without a car might be tricky. Metro-North trains run regularly from NYC to Beacon (1 hour, 30 minutes), but you'll have to opt for the more expensive Amtrak trains to get

This massive sculpture by Alexander Liberman is a highlight of Storm King.

from Beacon to Kingston or Rhinebeck (1 hour, 20 minutes) and from Kingston/Rhinebeck to Hudson (30 minutes). To get to Hyde Park, you'll need to take an Amtrak from Hudson to Poughkeepsie (40 minutes), then a car service to Hyde Park. Then from Poughkeepsie, you can take the Metro-North to Tarrytown for dinner (1 hour) and then the Metro-North home from there to NYC (1 hour).

INSPIRATION

There's no shortage of Hudson Valley–adjacent podcasts to accompany you on this trip. Before you leave, download "Cidiot," a collection of 10-minute episodes about moving to the Hudson Valley and what it means to be a transplant here. You can also try "Hudson Valley Legends," a spooky podcast exploring the many ghost stories and legends in the area, from Sleepy Hollow to abandoned asylums (perfect for any October trips). You can also give a listen to "Welcome to the Nightvale," a popular podcast that takes the form of a radio show for a fictional desert town filled with conspiracy

theories; one of the creators lives in the Hudson Valley.

WHEN TO GO

The Hudson Valley is definitely a year-round destination with charms for each season, but fall is your best bet. There's incredible foliage (viewable from both a car or train) and lots of cute farms and shops who get into the season selling pumpkins, apples, cider, and more.

WHERE TO STAY

For your first night, you can stay in either young and fun Kingston or elegant and sophisticated Rhinebeck. If you choose Kingston, stay at the homey and affordable B&B **The Forsyth,** located within a historic home with modern touches (it's the city's first true boutique property). If you want to splurge, go with the **Beekman Arms** in Rhinebeck. It's one of the oldest hotels in America (it predates the Revolutionary War) and continues to offer understated luxury surrounded by history. In Hudson, **Wm. Farmers and Sons** is an eclectic, intimate option with the perfect blend of hipness and luxury. Or check out the laid-back yet fashionable **Rivertown Lodge** located in a restored movie theater on Hudson's main strip.

Day 1

Depart from New York City on Friday morning so you can get to the Beacon area early. Once an industrial center of the Hudson Valley, Beacon has reinvented itself in recent years as a bustling arts community, thanks to two very popular art projects. Your first stop is just south of Beacon, at the 500-acre outdoor sculpture park known as **Storm King** (get there right when it opens to maximize your time there). Take a tour or just stroll the Instagram-worthy collection of sculptures from the likes of Alexander Calder, Isamu Noguchi, and Sol LeWitt. Once you start getting hungry, head into town for lunch and your first taste of the Hudson Valley at **Homespun Foods,** serving seasonal, vegetarian-friendly eats; enjoy the region's top-notch produce through the menu's salads, soups, and sandwiches (the desserts are excellent, too). **Beacon Pantry,** which offers a long list of sandwiches featuring the region's top-notch produce, meats, and cheeses, is a good alternate.

After lunch, get ready to spend a few hours at **DIA Beacon,** the art museum that put Beacon on the map as a haven for artists and writers who were priced out of NYC. Located in a former Nabisco box factory, the space is a moody love letter to the Hudson Valley art scene with contemporary work from the 1960s on, including experimental work pieces from Andy Warhol, Louise Lawler, and Max Neuhaus.

On your way north from Beacon, you'll find the **Culinary Institute of America,** one of the country's most acclaimed culinary schools. While there are no one-day classes, there are several options for lunch or dinner that give you the chance to experience some of the country's most talented up-and-coming chefs.

There's the French-centric **Bocuse Restaurant** (named after celebrated French chef Paul Bocuse) and farm-to-table **American Bounty.** Even if you're not coming for food, there's a fun gift shop filled with culinary goodies and supplies.

Afterward, make the drive up to the charming bedroom community of Rhinebeck for a classy dinner at the **Amsterdam,** located within an 18th-century farmhouse and serving farm-to-table dishes like butter-poached salmon and roasted duck breast; be sure to dine in the back patio if there's space and don't forget to check out the wine list.

For the rest of the night, cross the river to the other side of the Hudson to check out up-and-coming Kingston, a historic city (it was New York State's first capital) with an artistic bent and family-friendly atmosphere. Drink the night away at spots like **Keegan Ales,** one of the Hudson Valley's many breweries. There's also live music haven, **BSP,** which regularly hosts local and established artists and DJs while serving craft brews and cocktails in a funky industrial theater setting.

Day 2

Spend the morning strolling Kingston's Saturday Farmer's Market and stop for breakfast before or afterward at **Outdated Cafe,** a quirky café set within an antique shop and serving coffee, breakfast sandwiches, and pastries made from scratch. (Back-up: stop for brunch before or afterward at **Duo Bistro,** a trendy eatery serving classic brunch dishes with a Hudson Valley twist like bread pudding French toast and a chickpea burger with beet hummus.) Be sure to eat up so you have the energy for an afternoon hiking through the Hudson Valley's many trails. Options include the **Poet's Walk** in nearby Red Hook, an easy 2.2-mile trail that is quite romantic, with several swoon-worthy stopping points at rivers, scenic overlooks, and even a gazebo. There's also the **High Falls Conservation Area** about 40 minutes north of Red Hook; it's a very easy 1.2-mile trail that ends with a gorgeous waterfall. If you plan your afternoon well enough, you should be able to do both.

Once you've worked up an appetite, you're only 15 minutes away from the industrial turned artistic (are you seeing a pattern here?) town of Hudson. Lunch is at the retro diner **Grazin'**, home to perhaps the best burgers in the Upper Hudson Valley. Spend the rest of your evening perusing the multitude of art galleries found on and around Hudson's main street, Warren Street; you'll also find a collection of boutique shops selling furniture and antiques that are basically art galleries themselves. Be sure to also stop for a tour of **Ole York Farm** distillery, a female-owned family distillery that uses Hudson Valley products to create their bourbons, whiskeys, and brandies; the on-site tasting room offers cocktails, cider, beer, wine, and local cheeses. If you are interested in the Hudson River School of Painters, you may be interested in a short detour to see Frederic Church's home, **Olana,** which is right outside of Hudson; it's now a museum. Once you feel hungry again, grab a late dinner at kitschy **Lil Deb's Oasis,** a colorful space serving Latin-inspired comfort food like sweet plantains, fried yucca, and ceviche; there's a great craft beer selection too. Afterward, bar-hop your heart out along Warren Street, but be sure to stop by the speakeasy-esque **Back Bar,** located in the back of an antique shop, and its Malayay-ian-inspired slushy cocktails.

Day 3

Start your morning in Hudson with an early breakfast at **MOTO Coffee Machine,** a motorcycle repair shop–slash–café that serves local coffee and a variety of breakfast items (including tasty waffles). **Cafe La Perche,** a French bakery and bistro

known for its decadent baked goods and hearty brunches, is also a good choice. Then head 50 minutes south to Hyde Park, a small town famous as the birth-place of President Franklin D. Roosevelt. Get to the **FDR Presidential Library and Museum** right when it opens to spend the morning exploring the Roosevelt family estate and the official records of FDR. Break for Sunday brunch at the **Hyde Park Brewing Company,** where you can enjoy craft brews alongside pub fare, or opt for a light lunch at **Eveready Diner,** which serves comfort food diner favorites in a retro setting.

Afterward, if you're interested in more history, take a guided tour of **Eleanor Roosevelt Historic Site,** commemorating the life of one of America's most accom-plished first ladies, or visit the **Vanderbilt Mansion National Historic Site,** one of the Hudson Valley's oldest houses. It was owned by Fredrick Vanderbilt and has since become a museum dedicated to the history and architecture of traditional English country houses. Or if you're over history lessons, go for a hike in **Mohonk Preserve,** located just across the river from Hyde Park.

Just south of Hyde Park is the Hudson Valley's biggest city, Poughkeepsie. It's worth a stop to take a quick stroll on the **Walkway Over the Hudson,** a scenic bridge (the world's longest elevated pedestrian bridge at 1.28 miles) that takes walkers over the Hudson River.

Recommendations

Sights

Culinary Institute of America. ⊠ *1946 Cam-pus Dr., Hyde Park, NY* ☎ *845/452–9600* ⊕ *www.ciachef.edu* ⌦ *Free.*

DIA Beacon. ⊠ *3 Beekman St., Beacon, NY* ☎ *845/440–0100* ⊕ *www.diaart.org/visit/visit-our-locations-sites/main/beacon* ⌦ *Free.*

Eleanor Roosevelt Historic Site. ✉ *106 Valkill Park Rd., Hyde Park, NY* ☎ *845/229–9422* 🌐 *www.nps.gov/elro/index* 🎫 *Free.*

FDR Presidential Library and Museum. ✉ *4079 Albany Post Rd., Hyde Park, NY* ☎ *845/486–7770* 🌐 *www.fdrlibrary.org* 🎫 *$20 (includes both the museum and the Roosevelt home).*

Mohonk Preserve. ✉ *197 Rte. 44 55, Gardiner, NY* ☎ *845/255–0919* 🌐 *www.mohonkpreserve.org* 🎫 *Free.*

Olana State Historic Site. ✉ *5720 State Rte. 9G, Hudson, NY* ☎ *518/751–0344* 🌐 *www.olana.org* 🎫 *$15.*

Storm King. ✉ *1 Museum Rd., New Windsor, NY* ☎ *845/534–3115* 🌐 *stormking.org* 🎫 *$18.*

Vanderbilt Mansion National Historic Site. ✉ *119 Vanderbilt Park Rd., Hyde Park, NY* ☎ *845/229–9115* 🌐 *www.nps.gov/vama/index* 🎫 *$10.*

Walkway Over the Hudson. ✉ *61 Parker Ave., Poughkeepsie, NY* ☎ *845/834–2867* 🌐 *walkway.org* 🎫 *Free.*

🍴 Restaurants

American Bounty. [$] *Average main: $26* ✉ *Culinary Institute of America, 1946 Campus Dr., Hyde Park, NY* ☎ *845/451–1011* 🌐 *www.americanbountyrestaurant.com.*

The Amsterdam. [$] *Average main: $30* ✉ *6380 Mill St., Rhinebeck, NY* ☎ *845/516–5033* 🌐 *www.lovetheamsterdam.com.*

Bocuse Restaurant. [$] *Average main: $32* ✉ *Culinary Institute of America, 1946 Campus Dr., Hyde Park, NY* ☎ *845/451–1012* 🌐 *www.bocuserestaurant.com.*

Blue Hill at Stone Barns. [$] *Average main: $95* ✉ *630 Bedford Rd., Tarrytown, NY* ☎ *914/366–9600* 🌐 *www.bluehillfarm.com.*

Cafe La Perche. [$] *Average main: $22* ✉ *230 Warren St., Hudson, NY* ☎ *518/822–1850* 🌐 *www.leperchehudson.com* 🕒 *Closed Wed.*

Equus Restaurant. [$] *Average main: $40* ✉ *Castle Hotel and Spa, 400 Benedict Ave., Tarrytown, NY* ☎ *914/631–3646* 🌐 *castlehotelandspa.com/attraction/equus-restaurant-menu* 🕒 *Closed Sun.*

Eveready Diner. [$] *Average main: $10* ✉ *4184 Albany Post Rd., Hyde Park, NY* ☎ *845/229–8100* 🌐 *www.evereadydiner.com.*

Homespun Foods. [$] *Average main: $9* ✉ *232 Main St., Beacon, NY* ☎ *845/831–5096* 🌐 *www.homespunfoods.com.*

Hyde Park Brewing Company. [$] *Average main: $12* ✉ *4076 Albany Post Rd., Hyde Park, NY* ☎ *845/229–8277* 🌐 *www.hydeparkbrewing.com.*

MOTO Coffee Machine. [$] *Average main: $12* ✉ *357 Warren St., Hudson, NY* ☎ *518/822–8232* 🌐 *www.motocoffeemachine.com.*

🛏 Hotels

Beekman Arms. [$] *Rooms from: $309* ✉ *6387 Mill St., Rhinebeck, NY* ☎ *845/876–7077* 🌐 *www.beekmandelamaterinn.com* 🍽 *No meals.*

The Forsyth. [$] *Rooms from: $229* ✉ *85 Abeel St., Kingston, NY* ☎ *845/481–9148* 🌐 *theforsythkingston.com* 🍽 *Free breakfast.*

Wm. Farmers and Sons. [$] *Rooms from: $279* ✉ *20 S. Front St., Hudson, NY* ☎ *518/828–1635* 🌐 *www.wmfarmerandsons.com* 🍽 *No meals.*

🍸 Nightlife

BSP. 323. ✉ *Wall St., Kingston, NY* ☎ *845/481–5158* 🌐 *www.bspkingston.com.*

Keegan Ales. ✉ *20 St. James St., Kingston, NY* ☎ *845/331–2739* ⊕ *www. keeganales.com.*

Jersey Shore, NJ

Asbury Park is 56 miles (approx. 1 hour) from New York City.

Lovers of the Jersey Shore tend to fall into one of two categories: there are die-hard Jerseyans who grew up spending summers on the shore and who will defend the area with their dying breath, or they are fans of a little reality television show called *Jersey Shore,* who come here expecting nothing less than the trashy, drunken fun immortalized by the MTV hit. The reality of the Jersey Shore lies somewhere in-between. It's a gorgeous 141-mile stretch of coastline that comes with family-friendly beaches, old-school boardwalks, and eateries ranging from the classically nostalgic to the modernly hip. Only a few hours drive from New York, our long weekend will take you to the best parts of the Jersey Shore on an itinerary that we hope makes both Bruce Springsteen and Snooki proud.

Planning

GETTING THERE AND BACK
You can take a New Jersey Transit train from Penn Station to Asbury Park (2 hours, 30 minutes), but there's no train service to Seaside Heights or Cape May, so a car is your best bet. It's about an hour drive from New York to Asbury Park with no traffic, then another 40 minutes from Asbury to Seaside Heights. Cape May is another 90 minutes from there. On your ride home, be ready for a 2½-hour drive back to NYC.

Keep in mind these times are all with minimal traffic; if you're traveling in the summer, the Garden State Parkway (the main artery that connects towns on the Jersey Shore) can get very jammed, especially on Saturday, which is when most of the weekly rentals change hands. Avoid traffic by leaving during the day Friday and returning home late Sunday night.

INSPIRATION
Come on now, your soundtrack for this trip has to be the Boss. Get a playlist together highlighting the best of Bruce Springsteen's long and storied career or just play "Born to Run" 20 times in a row. Whichever you choose, you'll get into the New Jersey spirit in no time.

PIT STOPS
While Atlantic City can make for a fun night out, the city's heyday is honestly long behind it. An hour south of Seaside Heights, it's still a fun detour to stroll the historic boardwalk (one of the oldest in the country) and relive its glory days. Or stop at the Wildwoods about 20 minutes north of Cape May. Another Jersey Shore summer mainstay, the resort town has another historic boardwalk, doo-wop architecture, and a popular amusement park, **Morley's Piers,** which includes two waterparks.

WHEN TO GO
Naturally, the Jersey Shore is a summer destination; June through August are the prime times for beachgoing, sports rentals, and crowds. Fall and spring are equally charming, but with way fewer people. The weather won't be as beach-friendly, however. Many businesses shut down for the winter, but you'll still be able to find some hotels and restaurants open while strolling along the charmingly deserted boardwalks.

WHERE TO STAY
Asbury Park has seen a slew of fashionable boutique hotels open in recent years, but the best is **The Asbury,** located in a restored 1950s brick building just minutes from the boardwalk. The rooftop pool and bar are where all the cool kids hang out while the chic rooms are worth

every penny. For a more affordable option, try **The Empress,** a family resort from the 1960s (Bruce Springsteen once worked here) that reopened in 2004 and is popular with the LGBTQ crowd.

In Cape May, the best place to stay is **Congress Hall,** one of the town's most architecturally stunning Victorian buildings. It's pricey, but worth it for the old-school glamour. If you don't want to splurge, there are dozens of B&Bs lining the streets that surround the Mall. The **Queen Victoria Bed & Breakfast,** located in a traditional 1876 house, is one of the best, with its wraparound porch, quaint interiors, and an excellent afternoon tea.

Day 1

On your first day head to Asbury Park, the Jersey Shore's answer to whether or not being from Jersey can be cool. A popular resort destination for New Yorkers in the 1920s and 1930s, it gained national acclaim beginning in the late 1970s as the breeding ground for music legends like Bruce Springsteen and Bon Jovi. The 2010s brought forth a slew of restaurants, bars, and hotels that have turned it once again into a popular weekend destination for city-dwellers. The nearby beach and blossoming art scene don't hurt, either. If you leave NYC by late morning, you can make it in time for brunch at the charm-filled **Cardinal Provisions.** Try the Nashville hot chicken or the chicken and waffles (the coffee is local, too). And if you're more in the mood for a hearty sandwich, you can make it in time to grab a sandwich for lunch at the aptly named **Vintage Subs Asbury Park.** Try the Carousel with roast beef, turkey, American cheese, and banana peppers.

After lunch, hit **Asbury Park Beach** for a few hours of sun and sand (if you need some shade and snacks, check out the **Beach Bar,** which serves beachside cocktails and bar food all day long). Afterward, stroll the historic boardwalk, where you

should be on the look out for stunning buildings like the gorgeously restored Paramount Theater and the street art decorating many of the other Beaux Arts buildings. You can also shop among the many trendy boutiques.

Once you've worked up an appetite, head to **Talula's Pizza** for dinner to find out why so many people say that the best New York pizza is actually in New Jersey. The organic sourdough pizza includes options like the Beekeeper's Lament, with tomato sauce, hot calabrian soppressata, mozzarella, and local honey. Or consider **Modine** for its delightful menu of Southern favorites like fried chicken skin and homemade biscuits. Afterward, spend the rest of your night at the Jersey Shore institution that is the **Stone Pony,** the legendary music spot where the Boss himself first got his start; there are still regular live music performances. And if you aren't totally exhausted, you can follow it up with a visit to **Asbury Park Distilling Co.,** the city's only distillery, where you can sample cocktails using the house-made bourbon, gin, and vodka.

Day 2

Start your day with a meal at breakfast haven **Toast,** where if you arrive early enough, you'll beat the crowds nursing their hangovers to enjoy an Irish eggs Benedict or a classic Californian scramble. Or consider trying a New Jersey staple: pork roll, egg, and cheese at **Frank's Deli.** Then make the drive to Seaside Heights, another classic seaside town with a boardwalk that rose to infamy in the early 2010s as the setting for MTV's Jersey Shore. The town has tried to lose its moniker as party-central in recent years, so instead of hitting up the many clubs and bars, spend your afternoon taking in the boardwalk entertainment. Spend a few hours on the beach, and then ride the various roller coasters at **Lucky Leo's** for some nostalgic arcade games. And for fans of the show, the house where the cast spent many a summer is a quick walk from the boardwalk; the Italian flag is still painted on the garage for a fun photo opp. For lunch, stop at boardwalk favorite the **Sawmill,** which serves classic beachside bar bites, decent burgers, and jumbo slices of pizza. And for those tired of pizza, there's **Park Seafood Bar,** which serves excellent clam chowder, crab legs, and lobster rolls.

Make sure you leave Seaside Heights in time to catch the sunset in Cape May, an 1½ hour drive. Dotted with Victorian mansions and lined with a family-friendly boardwalk, Cape May is the southernmost point of the Shore and one of the country's oldest seaside resorts. Once you get to town, rent a bike and cycle down the streets admiring the ornate architecture. Ride your bike to **Cape May Point State Park** and the 1859 **Cape May Lighthouse,** and then to Sunset Beach for one of New Jersey's best sunset vistas. For dinner, get a table at the **Ebbitt Room,** an upscale tavern serving farm-to-table cuisine. If available, try the heritage · chicken or the local fluke Francaise. And if it's full for the night, look for a table at the **Washington Inn,** another upscale restaurant serving dishes like seafood cioppino and grilled filet mignon. There's also an excellent wine list. After dinner, stroll the Washington Street Mall, the main avenue of the town lined with boutique shops, art galleries, and ice cream shops. End your night with a drink at the sophisticated **Brown Room** in Congress Hall, Cape May's landmark hotel, and if you're up for it, keep the party going in the **Boiler Room** nightclub downstairs.

Day 3

For breakfast, wake up early or be prepared to wait in line at the **Mad Batter,** a Cape May breakfast institution. You can't go wrong with the buttermilk or oatmeal pancakes. And if that pancake joint is packed, try **Uncle Bill's Pancake House,** pancakes are an obvious choice, but the stuffed French Toast is equally delicious.

When you get your fill of pancakes, get ready for an afternoon on any of the beaches lining the boardwalk; these are widely considered the best beaches on the Jersey Shore thanks to the impressive waves and family-friendly atmosphere. Be sure to take a break with lunch at the **Rusty Nail,** a low-key beach bar that has excellent burgers, fried seafood, and sandwiches.

Once you're all sunned out, take a detour to either **Cape May Winery** or **Cape May Brewing Company** for fantastic local wine and beer; tasting flights are available at both (just make sure someone is the designated driver since you'll be driving home tonight). If you're not a big drinker, try a house tour of the historic **Emlem Physick Estate,** one of Cape May's traditional Victorian homes that offers guided tours all year-round.

Before you depart on your 2½-hour drive back to New York, enjoy a farewell dinner at the **Lobster House,** a waterfront mainstay offering freshly caught seafood, including Jersey clams, Cape May scallops, and lobster. Or for one last taste of quality Italian food (and dessert), there's **Sapore Italiano,** a classic red-sauce Italian restaurant offering fresh seafood pasta, risottos, and other classic Italian dishes (it's also BYOB, so be sure to stock up beforehand, maybe with a purchase from the Cape May Winery).

Topped with turrets and ringed by gingerbread, handsome Victorian houses line the streets of Cape May.

Recommendations

Sights

Asbury Park Beach. ✉ *Boardwalk at 1st Ave., Asbury Park, NJ* ☎ *732/502–8863* 🌐 *www.cityofasburypark.com/185/Asbury-Park-Beach* 🎟 *$5.*

Cape May Lighthouse. ✉ *1048 Washington St., Cape May, NJ* ☎ *609/884–5404* 🌐 *capemaymac.org* 🎟 *Tours from $35.*

Cape May Point State Park. ✉ *Lighthouse Rd., Cape May Point, NJ* ☎ *609/884–2159* 🌐 *www.state.nj.us/dep/parksandforests/parks/capemay.html* 🎟 *Free.*

Cape May Winery. ✉ *711 Town Bank Rd., Cape May, NJ* ☎ *609/884–1169* 🌐 *capemaywinery.com* 🎟 *Tastings $12.*

Emlen Physick Estate. ✉ *1048 Washington St., Cape May, NJ* ☎ *609/884–5404* 🌐 *capemaymac.org/experience/emlen-physick-estate* 🎟 *$15.*

Lucky Leo's. ✉ *315 Boardwalk, Seaside Heights, NJ* ☎ *732/793–1323* 🌐 *luckyleos.com* 🎟 *Closed Wed. and Thurs.*

Morey's Piers & Beachfront Water Parks. ✉ *3501 Boardwalk, Wildwood, NJ* ☎ *609/729–3700* 🌐 *www.moreyspiers.com* 🎟 *$50.*

Paramount Theatre. ✉ *1300 Ocean Ave., Asbury Park, NJ* ☎ *732/897–6500* 🌐 *apboardwalk.com/portfolio/paramount-theatre* 🎟 *Free.*

Sunset Beach. ✉ *502 Sunset Blvd., Cape May, NJ* ☎ *609/884–7079* 🌐 *sunsetbeachnj.com* 🎟 *Free.*

Restaurants

Cardinal Provisions. [$] *Average main: $10* ✉ *513 Bangs Ave., Asbury Park, NJ* ☎ *732/898–7194* 🌐 *www.crdnal.com* 🕒 *Closed Tues. and Wed.*

Ebbitt Room. [$] *Average main: $38* ✉ *25 Jackson St., Cape May, NJ*

☎ 609/884–5700 🌐 www.caperesorts.com/virginia-hotel/ebbittroom.

Frank's Deli & Restaurant. $ *Average main: $8* ✉ *1406 Main St., Asbury Park, NJ* ☎ *732/775–6682* 🌐 *franksdelinj.com.*

Lobster House. $ *Average main: $22* ✉ *Fisherman's Wharf, Cape May, NJ* ☎ *609/884–8296* 🌐 *thelobsterhouse.com.*

Mad Batter. $ *Average main: $12* ✉ *19 Jackson St., Cape May, NJ* ☎ *609/884–5970* 🌐 *www.madbatter.com* ⏲ *Closed Tues.*

Modine. $ *Average main: $24* ✉ *601 Mattison Ave., Asbury Park, NJ* ☎ *732/893–5300* 🌐 *www.modineasbury.com.*

Park Seafood Bar & Restaurant. $ *Average main: $22* ✉ *901 Boardwalk, Seaside Heights, NJ* ☎ *732/250–4646.*

Rusty Nail. $ *Average main: $20* ✉ *205 Beach Ave., Cape May, NJ* ☎ *609/884–0017* 🌐 *www.caperesorts.com/capemay/rusty-nail.*

Sapore Italiano. $ *Average main: $16* ✉ *416 S. Broadway, West Cape May, NJ* ☎ *609/600–1422* 🌐 *saporeitalianorestaurant.com.*

The Sawmill. $ *Average main: $18.* ✉ *1807 Boardwalk, Seaside Park, NJ* ☎ *732/793–1990* 🌐 *sawmillcafe.com.*

Talula's Pizza. $ *Average main: $16* ✉ *550 Cookman Ave., Asbury Park, NJ* ☎ *732/455–300* 🌐 *talulaspizza.com.*

Toast. $ *Average main: $11* ✉ *516 Cookman Ave., Asbury Park, NJ* ☎ *732/776–5900* 🌐 *montclair.toastcitydiner.com* ⏲ *No dinner.*

Uncle Bill's Pancake House. $ *Average main: $8* ✉ *261 Beach Ave., Cape May, NJ* ☎ *609/884–7199* 🌐 *www.unclebillspancakehouse.com.*

Vintage Subs Asbury Park. $ *Average main: $12* ✉ *729 Bangs Ave., Asbury Park, NJ* ☎ *732/361–5839* 🌐 *vintagesubsasburypark.com.*

Washington Inn. $ *Average main: $40* ✉ *801 Washington St., Cape May, NJ* ☎ *609/884–5697* 🌐 *washingtoninn.com.*

Hotels

The Asbury Hotel. $ *Rooms from: $334* ✉ *210 5th Ave., Asbury Park, NJ* ☎ *732/774–7100* 🌐 *www.theasburyhotel.com* 🍽 *No meals.*

Congress Hall. $ *Rooms from: $332* ✉ *200 Congress Pl., Cape May, NJ* ☎ *888/944–1816* 🌐 *www.caperesorts.com/congress-hall* 🍽 *No meals.*

The Empress Hotel. $ *Rooms from: $249* ✉ *101 Asbury Ave., Asbury Park, NJ* ☎ *732/774–0100* 🌐 *asburyempress.com* 🍽 *Free breakfast.*

The Queen Victoria. $ *Rooms from: $321* ✉ *102 Ocean St., Cape May, NJ* ☎ *609/884–8702* 🌐 *www.queenvictoria.com* 🍽 *Free breakfast.*

Nightlife

Asbury Park Brewing Co. ✉ *810 Sewall Ave., Asbury Park, NJ* ☎ *732/455–5571* 🌐 *www.asburyparkbrewery.com.*

Beach Bar. ✉ *1300 Ocean Ave., Asbury Park, NJ* ☎ *732/361–0990* 🌐 *apbeachbar.com.*

Boiler Room. ✉ *Congress Hall, 200 Congress Pl., Cape May, NJ* ☎ *609/884–6507* 🌐 *www.caperesorts.com/capemay/brown-room.*

Brown Room. ✉ *Congress Hall, 200 Congress Pl., Cape May, NJ* ☎ *609/884–8421* 🌐 *www.caperesorts.com/capemay/boiler-room.*

Cape May Brewing Company. ✉ *409 Breakwater Rd., Cape May, NJ* ☎ *609/849–9933* 🌐 *www.capemaybrewery.com.*

The Stone Pony. ✉ *913 Ocean Ave., Asbury Park, NJ* ☎ *732/502–0600* 🌐 *www.stoneponyonline.com.*

Lancaster County and Pennsylvania Dutch Country, PA

90 miles (approx. 2½ hours) from Washington, D.C.

Rolling green hills and patchworks of farmland, pocket woods and bubbling streams. It's hard to imagine such an idyllic place exists anywhere near the nation's capital. But that it does, in Pennsylvania's Lancaster County, less than two hours away from Washington, D.C. We have the Amish to thank for much of that, who have tilled these fields since they first arrived in the 1700s, using age-old methods apart from the modern world. Here you'll slide into the slow pace of country life, exploring Amish villages, pastoral farms, and farmer's markets. It's also prime territory for long bike rides, scenic drives, kayaking, wine-tasting, and hot-air ballooning.

The anchor is Lancaster, a vibrant city with a fabulous weekend market and a walkable downtown. And if that hasn't convinced you of the merits of this supreme weekend getaway, you'll also find here Hershey's legacy, a whole town built on chocolate.

Planning

GETTING THERE AND BACK

Lancaster is about 90 miles or 2½ hours from Washington, D.C. You can go the quick route, via I–83 from Baltimore. Or go the bucolic route, following I–270 to U.S. 15 to U.S. 30, which adds on about half an hour—but quickly gets you in the mood for a quiet weekend getaway. U.S. 30 is the main artery through Amish country—which can become clogged with traffic, especially in summer.

PIT STOPS

On the scenic route to Lancaster is the town of Gettysburg, a charming, historic town with plenty of shops, restaurants, and museums to explore.

WHEN TO GO

Lancaster County is a four-season destination. Midsummer to September can be crowded, but it's a great time to explore the back roads and enjoy freshly harvested produce, jams, and homemade baked goods, Fall brings specular foliage, and more crowds. Both of these seasons you should aim to get off the beaten path as soon as possible. Winter is quiet and picturesque when snow falls. Spring is beautiful, with blooming flowers and the Amish mud sales—auctions where everything from horses to quilts are sold. Lodging is least expensive in winter and spring.

WHERE TO STAY

Lancaster County offers a plethora of bed-and-breakfasts, working farms, plush resorts, and stately hotels. **Lancaster Arts Hotel,** occupying a former tobacco warehouse in Lancaster, has an art gallery and organic fine-dining restaurant. North of the city in Lititz, **Hotel Rock Lititz** captures the local art and technology scene with decor repurposed from concert tours. West of the city in Mount Joy, **Rocky Acre Farm Bed and Breakfast** is located on a dairy farm. **Bird-in-Hand Family Inn,** east of Lancaster, is a great spot for families, with three pools, a game room, and an on-site smorgasbord.

Day 1

If you've opted for the slow route to Lancaster County, the drive from D.C. wanders through gorgeous rolling hills, setting the mood for the weekend ahead. Head for Strasburg, a historic little town with a quintessential Main Street lined with hip boutiques and antique shops. It's also ground zero for train lovers, starting off with **Strasburg Rail Road,** the nation's oldest short line. Hop aboard a vintage steam train for a chug through farm country. Here, too, are the **Railroad Museum of Pennsylvania,** the **Choo-Choo Barn** (a 1,700-square-foot custom model train display), and the **National Toy Train Museum.**

Get lunch at the **Speckled Hen** on Main Street, which partners with local farmers and purveyors to ensure the freshest ingredients. This is the place for gourmet sandwiches, scratch-made soups, seasonal salads, and more.

Then explore some of the surrounding pastoral backroads. Intercourse, named for the colonial term for intersection, is a hub of Amish life. It's fun just to stroll its streets, peeking into shops and seeing what's going on. Don't miss the landmark **Old Country Store,** where you'll find handcrafted quilts, folk art, and other items made by local Amish and Mennonites.

Meander your way to Leola, where dinner at the **Log Cabin** is sublime. Originally a log cabin dating from 1929, it operated as a speakeasy during Prohibition. Today, the restaurant specializes in local farm-to-table fare amid the log-cabin ambiance. On a nice evening, enjoy romantic dining on the patio.

Day 2

Today you need to set the alarm clock, but it'll be worth it, because you're going on a hot-air balloon ride with the **U.S. Hot Air Balloon Team.** Drift with the wind as you look down on the patchwork of farms, in the morning's early light. On clear days, you can see as far as the Chesapeake.

Then head for the Romanesque **Central Market** in Lancaster, where you can gather breakfast items fresh from the farm. Starting in the 1730s as open-air stalls, the market was granted permanent status in 1742 by none other than King George II. Today, more than 60

market stands purvey locally grown fruits and vegetables, homemade breads, cheeses, meats, flowers … and coffee. Note it's open only on Tuesday, Friday, and Saturday.

Lancaster's historic downtown is emerging as a hip sort of place, and it's definitely worth a saunter. It's home to several breweries, including **Lancaster Brewing,** producing heavy stouts, and the **Wacker Brewing Company,** the vestige of 19th-century German immigrants.

Before leaving Lancaster, find lunch at **Pressroom,** occupying a historic working microbrewery, near Penn Square. The open-air Park Bar seating is divine in the warmer months.

The Susquehanna River flows nearby, offering a restful afternoon floating on glittering waters. **Chiques Rock Outfitters** at the Columbia Crossing River Trails Center in Columbia, about 15 miles or 20 minutes from Lancaster, will hook you up with all you need. If you prefer biking or walking, the 14-mile Northwest Lancaster County River Trail kicks off from here as well, following the old route of the historic Pennsylvania Mainline Canal, alongside the Susquehanna River.

Or go wine-tasting. Grapevines thrive in Lancaster County, producing a variety of different wines. See for yourself at several wineries west of Lancaster, toward the river: **Nissley** in Bainbridge, **Waltz** in Manheim, and **Grandview** in Mount Joy.

Find dinner tonight in Lancaster, at **Horse Inn,** featuring innovative dishes based on the seasonal fare from local farms. The chalkboard menu changes daily, depending on what's available. Possibilities might include: Horse fries (with house-made sausage, Parmesan, provolone, and garlic heavy cream), asparagus and Carolina gold rice salad, and a hot chicken sandwich (with Nashville-style rub, blue cheese cole slaw, and a sesame potato roll).

A horse-drawn carriage makes its way through the countryside near Lancaster.

Day 3

Take a morning walk at **Lancaster County Central Park,** just south of Lancaster. Its network of trails moseys through fields and woods, across quiet creeks. There's also the Garden of Five Senses here, overlooking the Conestoga River.

Linger over a lovely gourmet brunch at **Citronelle** in Lancaster. You'll find seasonal, globally inspired dishes such as local leek and cheese soufflé, poached eggs à la Florentine, and pain de mie French toast.

Then, chocoholics should head north to Hershey, aka Chocolate Town USA. Milton S. Hershey established his company in Hershey in 1903, surrounding it with a model town for his employees, including homes, a public transportation system, and recreational and cultural activities. The town still thrives on his legacy, and it's a pleasant place to spend a few hours—even if you're not a chocolate lover.

Today, streetlights are shaped like foil-wrapped candies, and avenues are named Chocolate and Cocoa. There are two main sites here: **Hersheypark,** a theme park with rides, originally built by Hershey in 1906 so his employees would have a place to picnic and boat; and **Hershey's Chocolate World,** where you can learn how chocolate is made and test chocolatey drinks and treats. If that's not your thing, perhaps a chocolate spa might be. **MeltSpa by Hershey** offers treatments such as dark chocolate sugar scrub and body wraps, and cocoa massages and facials.

Part of Hershey's plan was to build an elegant hotel on a hill overlooking his chocolate factory. Today, the Hotel Hershey is a magnificent historic resort—and, if you're not otherwise engaged at Hersheypark, the perfect place for lunch. It has several restaurants, but **Harvest** is a standout for its devotion to salads, sandwiches, and entrées using local ingredients. When you're ready, ramble your way back to D.C.

Recommendations

Sights

Choo-Choo Barn. ✉ 226 Gap Rd., Strasburg, PA ☎ 717/687–7911 ⊕ www.choochoobarn.com ⌨ $9.

Hersheypark. ✉ 100 W. Hersheypark Dr., Hershey, PA ☎ 717/534–3900 ⊕ www.hersheypark.com ⌨ $50.

Lancaster County Central Park. ✉ 1050 Rockford Rd., Lancaster, PA ☎ 717/299–8215 ⊕ www.co.lancaster.pa.us/244/Lancaster-County-Central-Park ⌨ Free.

National Toy Train Museum. ✉ 300 Paradise La., Ronks, PA ☎ 717/687–8976 ⊕ www.nttmuseum.org ⌨ $8.

Railroad Museum of Pennsylvania. ✉ 300 Gap Rd., Strasburg, PA ☎ 717/687–8628 ⊕ www.rrmuseumpa.org ⌨ $10.

Strasburg Rail Road. ✉ 301 Gap Rd., Ronks, PA ☎ 866/725–9666 ⊕ www.strasburgrailroad.com ⌨ $19.

Restaurants

Citronelle. $ Average main: $28 ✉ 110 W. Orange St., Lancaster, PA ☎ 717/208–6697 ⊕ Closed Mon. and Tues. ⊗ Closed Mon. and Tues.

Harvest. $ Average main: $22 ✉ 1573 Fruitville Pike, Lancaster, PA ☎ 717/740–5282 ⊕ www.harvestseasonalgrill.com.

Horse Inn. $ Average main: $15 ✉ 540 E. Fulton St., Lancaster, PA ☎ 717/392–5528 ⊕ www.horseinnlancaster.com ⊗ No lunch. Closed Sun.–Tues.

The Log Cabin. $ Average main: $25 ✉ 11 Lehoy Forest Dr., Leola, PA ☎ 717/626–9999 ⊕ lancasterlogcabins.com ⊗ Closed Mon.

Speckled Hen Coffee. $ Average main: $10 ✉ 141 E Main St., Strasburg, PA ☎ 717/288–3139 ⊕ www.speckledhencoffee.com.

Hotels

Bird-in-Hand Family Inn. $ Rooms from: $124 ✉ 2760 Old Philadelphia Pike, Bird-in-Hand, PA ☎ 717/455–3322 ⊕ www.bird-in-hand.com ⦿ No meals.

Hotel Rock Lititz. $ Rooms from: $171 ✉ 50 Rock Lititz Blvd., Lititz, PA ☎ 717/925–7625 ⊕ www.hotelrocklititz.com ⦿ No meals.

Lancaster Arts Hotel. $ Rooms from: $166 ✉ 300 Harrisburg Ave., Lancaster, PA ☎ 717/299–3000 ⊕ www.lancasterartshotel.com ⦿ Free breakfast.

Rocky Acre Farm Bed and Breakfast. $ Rooms from: $236 ✉ 1020 Pinkerton Rd., Mount Joy, PA ☎ 717/453–4449 ⊕ www.rockyacre.com ⦿ Free breakfast.

Nightlife

Grandview Vineyard. ✉ 1489 Grandview Rd., Mount Joy, PA ☎ 717/653–4825 ⊕ www.grandviewwines.com.

Lancaster Brewing Company. ✉ 302 N. Plum St., Lancaster, PA ☎ 717/391–6258 ⊕ www.lancasterbrewing.com.

Nissley Vineyards. ✉ 481 Park City Center, Lancaster, PA ☎ 717/392–6055 ⊕ nissleywine.com.

Wacker Brewing Company. ✉ 25 S. Queen St., Lancaster, PA ☎ 717/617–2711 ⊕ www.wackerbrewing.com.

Waltz Vineyard Estates Winery. ✉ 1599 Old Line Rd., Manheim, PA ☎ 717/664–9463 ⊕ www.waltzvineyards.com.

Shopping

Hershey's Chocolate World. ✉ 101 Chocolate World Way, Hershey, PA ☎ 717/534–4900 ⊕ www.hersheys.com.

Lancaster Central Market. ✉ 23 N. Market St., Lancaster, PA ☎ 717/735–6890 ⊕ www.centralmarketlancaster.com.

Meltspa by Hershey ✉ *11 E. Chocolate Ave., Hershey, PA* ☎ *855/500–2366* ⊕ *www.meltspa.com.*

Old Country Store. ✉ *3510 Old Philadelphia Pike, Intercourse, PA* ☎ *717/768–7101* ⊕ *www.theoldcountrystore.com.*

Activities

Chiques Rock Outfitters. ✉ *41 Walnut St., Columbia, PA* ☎ *717/475–6196* ⊕ *www.chiquesrockoutfitters.net* ⊠ *Kayaking from $16.*

The United States Hot Air Balloon Team. ✉ *2727 Old Philadelphia Pike, Bird-in-Hand, PA* ☎ *800/763–5987* ⊕ *www.ushotairballoon.com* ⊠ *From $250 per person.*

Martha's Vineyard, MA

90 miles (approx. 2½ hours) from Boston.

A triangular island just seven miles south of Cape Cod in Massachusetts, Martha's Vineyard is the weekend getaway of your preppy, summer-camp dreams. Think: pristine beaches and pastoral farm fields; candy-color gingerbread Victorians and whaling captains' houses; scenic bike rides; and the iconic Jaws Bridge. And if your dreams involve lobster—lobster brunches, lobster rolls, lobster bakes, and lobster ice cream, too—this is the place.

While it has a reputation as the summer retreat of Hollywood stars and presidential families (Jackie O, Oprah, and the Obamas, to name a few O's), "The Vineyard" is not at all scene-y. The vibe (and dress code) is "relaxed New England"—casual, laid-back, and a lot less popped-collar than its sister island, Nantucket. The island has six towns: the rural and wild Chilmark, West Tisbury, and Aquinnah are referred to as Up-Island, while the more densely populated and lively towns of Oak Bluffs, Edgartown,

and Vineyard Haven are known as Down-Island. The only other directions you need involve getting from Off-Island to On-Island, which includes advance ferry reservations and a salty sea breeze.

Planning

GETTING THERE AND BACK

Ferries to Martha's Vineyard leave from several locations along Cape Cod, as well as from New Bedford, Massachusetts, and Kingston, Rhode Island. (By taking the ferry from Rhode Island, you can avoid the Cape Cod traffic on a busy weekend.) The ride only takes about 35 minutes. In addition, there is a SeaStreak ferry from New York City that takes five hours. Flights to Martha's Vineyard depart from big-city hubs as far south as Washington, D.C.

Allow sufficient time for traffic in summer months from Boston or New York, especially on Route 24 or Route 3 (south from Boston) and near the Bourne or Sagamore Bridges crossing the Cape Cod Canal. Driving time from Boston to Woods Hole is usually about 90 minutes, but can double during the summer. Driving time from New York to Woods Hole is generally around 4 hours, in the summer, five to seven hours is possible.

INSPIRATION

Listen to James Taylor at 22, the age when he bought 175 acres of woods in Lambert's Cove with the proceeds of his first record deal. Listen to his self-titled first record, *James Taylor,* as you make your way to the Vineyard. Then listen to Carly Simon's hits, "You're So Vain," "Anticipation," "The Right Thing to Do," "That's the Way I've Always Heard it Should Be," "Nobody Does it Better" and the theme song to the 1977 James Bond movie, *The Spy Who Loved Me.* Simon first moved here after marrying Taylor in 1972 (and stayed after they divorced in 1983), and she is still one of Martha's

The Cape Poge Lighthouse sits on the northeast tip of Chappaquiddick Island.

Vineyard's most popular year-round residents.

PIT STOPS

Mystic Connecticut, about 2½ hours from New York, is the perfect maritime mood setter on the way to Martha's Vineyard. It was a shipbuilding and whaling hub from the 17th to 19th centuries and is a lively and engaging stop for lunch (get your cheesiest Julia-Roberts smile on as you eat a slice of **Mystic Pizza**). If you have time to linger on the banks of the Mystic River, visit the **Mystic Seaport Museum** to climb aboard the *Charles W. Morgan* whaling ship; if you have kids, you may end up spending the weekend in the **Mystic Aquarium** research and rescue center instead.

WHEN TO GO

Peak season begins on Memorial Day weekend and ends on Labor Day weekend. There is a reason the island is so busy in summer: the weather is perfect (warm but rarely uncomfortably hot); the water is less frigid (but rarely comfortably warm), and the weather is ideal for hiking, biking, beaching, and sailing. If you're planning to stay overnight on a summer weekend, be sure to make reservations well in advance; spring (as in, *last* spring) is not too early. Avoid July Fourth and Labor Day weekends as they are the busiest and most expensive weekends on the island. Things stay busy for September and October weekends, a favorite time for weddings, but begin to slow down soon after. Inns and hotels offer discounted rates in the spring, fall, and winter months, and many island restaurants, shops, and bars are open year-round.

WHERE TO STAY

Stay Down-Island if you want to be close to nightlife and restaurants and Up-Island if you want the opposite. The charming and luxurious **Hob Knob** boutique hotel and spa in Edgartown is close to the summer scene but far enough away to be peaceful. The hotel provides guests with beach cruiser bikes, gourmet picnic lunches, beach chairs, and umbrellas. The elegant **Harbor View Hotel** has one of the most iconic views on the Vineyard (enjoy Edgartown Lighthouse views from the expansive wraparound porch) and is just a 10-minute walk from Edgartown's historic mansions. The **Beach Plum Inn** in rural Chilmark is located on seven acres of land overlooking Menemsha Harbor.

Day 1

Fresh off the ferry (before noon if you hit the road early) and clean out of snacks thanks to the seagulls, you'll want to refuel and gear up for the weekend with a stop at the harborfront **Black Dog Tavern.** It's a bit of a tourist-trap but also a local institution (in business since 1971), so line up for lobster eggs benedict or chowder and smile your best smile when asking for a seat on the patio. After, walk two minutes to the **Black Dog General Store** to gear up with T-shirts, sweatshirts, caps, water bottles, and coffee mugs emblazoned with the silhouette of a black Labrador. The Black Dog logo is a signal to everyone On-Island that you are a visitor and to everyone Off-Island that you've got great taste in weekend destinations.

Shake off the early-morning-car-ride-cobwebs by swapping four wheels for two at **Martha's Vineyard Bike Rentals.** Most bike rental companies on the island offer free island-wide drop-off and pick up of bikes, so arrange to have yours waiting for you at your hotel. The island is home to 44 miles of bike trails but a one-hour ride along the coastline from Oak Bluffs to remote Chappaquiddick Island—aka "Chappy"—provides a great Day 1 intro to the island's appeal. Stop at the Jaws Bridge (between Oak Bluffs and Edgartown along Beach Road) for the obligatory photo of you jumping into waters that once hosted a movie shark attack.

On Chappy, bike to the island's most remote lighthouse, relax on windswept beaches, bird-watch in **Cape Poge Wildlife Refuge,** and visit Mytoi's

Japanese-inspired gardens before heading back to town. The total ride is about 18 miles (9 miles each way), with a two-minute ferry to cross the water.

Keep up your Vineyard-Classics roll by heading to **Nancy's** for a classic lobster roll and an iconic Dirty Banana cocktail. In fact, have two, you're letting someone else take the wheel for the evening.

Sail into the sunset with **Farm Field Sea** on a two-hour, BYOB sunset sail to a working oyster farm, complete with shucking demos, tastings, and stunning views of the Vineyard Sound. Back on dry land, head to the **Lookout Tavern** for brews with killer views. If all that salty air is still keeping you buoyant, hit **Offshore Ale Co.** for a nightcap.

Day 2

Kick start your first full day with the best breakfast spot on the island, **Art Cliff Diner.** This beloved diner has been around since 1943, and you cannot go wrong with its time-tested breakfast menu, especially if you include a side of buttery biscuits.

Today, you should head Up-Island (which now that you're practically a salty local, you know means head west) to experience the breathtaking natural beauty of Martha's Vineyard with its storybook fishing villages, dense woods, and abundance of fisheries and farms. Stock up on cheeses, salads, fruits, juices, bread, and—you deserve this—pie at **Morning Glory Farm** en route, a family-run farm in business since 1975. These pies and other supplies will fuel your morning exploring **Long Point Wildlife Refuge,** a spectacular 600-acre reservation with woodland hiking trails, salt- and freshwater ponds, windswept dunes, and beautiful beaches. You can rent kayaks and stand-up paddleboards at Long Cove Pond in summer and bird-watch in the off-season here.

Spend the afternoon enjoying the charms of Up-Island's quaint fishing villages. Wander the picturesque 18th-century town of West Tisbury, where you will find **Alleys General Store** ("dealing in almost everything" since 1858) and the **West Tisbury Congregational Church** (dealing in all the rest since 1865). The **Field Gallery & Sculpture Garden** showcases a whimsical collection of sculptures and local art. Stop at **Larsen's Fish Market** in Menemsha fishing village to pick up stuffed scallops and fresh catch to enjoy on the village's tranquil beach. Wander around the shops here and then head to neighboring Chilmark, known for its rolling hills and meadows and its not-so-secret gem, **Chilmark General Store.** Then head to the remote town of Aquinnah in the westernmost tip of Martha's Vineyard, to take in its striking clay cliffs, natural dunes, the historic and active **Gay Head Lighthouse** (in operation since 1799), and Wampanoag Indian history and art. Follow a scenic trail to Moshup Beach for a quick sunset skinny dip if the mood so takes you. If you're not ready to retire yet, head to the **Great Rock Bight Preserve** for even more scenic hiking, views, beaches, and stunning scenery.

Cap off a nature-filled day with a special meal at West Tisbury's **State Road Restaurant** (reservations essential). You'll find a creative menu filled with local organic produce and served in a rustic-chic dining room with rough-hewn high beamed ceiling, a beautiful stone fireplace, and a shingle-sided porch. If you're here during the summer, mingle with the island's artists, writers, poets, and musicians at the Martha's Vineyard Summer Concert Series at the **Old Whaling Church** in Edgartown. Depending on your mood, cap the night with a drink at the island's legendary watering hole/dive bar and rock club, the **Ritz Café,** or at the more quirky cocktail lounge at the **Cardboard Box.**

Day 3

You may have noticed that there are no chain stores or restaurants on the island, which means that every mealtime, and every coffee and snack hankering, is an opportunity—nay, an excuse—to support a local purveyor and experience local deliciousness. Acknowledge Sunday morning on Martha's Vineyard in all its glory with sugar-and-cinnamon dusted, fresh-from-the-oven doughnuts and fritters from **Back Door Donuts.** Pick up a gourmet coffee to go at **Mocha Motts** and take a morning stroll in the most charming neighborhood in all of New England. The 34 acres of dollhouse-like Gingerbread Cottages at **Oak Bluffs Campground** are a wonder to wander. The more than 300 candy-colored Carpenter Gothic Victorian cottages with wedding trim were built in the 1860s and 1870s to replace tents on the site used to accommodate the groups of New England Methodists who gathered for retreats here. In summer, you can take guided tours and enjoy art shows, sing-alongs, and other performances. Be sure to visit the Cottage Museum to learn more about this National Historic Landmark.

If you are renting a property for the weekend, make your last day here special with a lunch delivery of a full clambake from **The Kitchen Porch.** If not, **The Net Result** fish market offers individual clambakes, steamed lobsters, and fried oyster plates that you can take to the beach for lunch; be sure to pick up some cold **Bad Martha** local brews to seal the experience. If the weather isn't cooperating, eat at **Raw 19 Oyster Bar** for their "shucking amazing" oysters along with other New England classics like clam chowder, smoked bluefish, and lobster.

After lunch, wander in and out of the cute shops in Edgartown's historic downtown area. Then, keep the history-appreciation going with a little background in the island's maritime history at the excellent **Martha's Vineyard Museum.** Hop on a bike for one last taste of island life and bike to **Edgartown Lighthouse** (about 40 minutes) and Lighthouse Beach. Martha's Vineyard has its share of lighthouses, but this one merits a visit for its stunning views and surroundings. Swing by **Mad Martha's** ice cream for an ice-cream sandwich made with homemade cookies or a Snickers ice cream before you make your way back to pack up your bags.

Recommendations

👁 Sights

Cape Poge Wildlife Refuge. ✉ *40 Rd. to the Gut, Edgartown, MA* ☎ *508/627–7689* 🌐 *www.thetrustees.org/places-to-visit/cape-cod-islands/cape-pogue.html* 🎟 *$5.*

Edgartown Lighthouse. ✉ *230 N. Water St., Edgartown, MA* ☎ *508/627–6145* 🌐 *mvmusmvmuseum.org/visit/edgartowneum.org* 🎟 *$5.*

Gay Head Lighthouse. ✉ *15 Aquinnah Circle, Aquinnah, MA* ☎ *508/645–2300* 🌐 *www.gayheadlight.org* 🎟 *$6.*

Great Rock Bight Preserve. ✉ *37 Brickyard Rd., Chilmark, MA* ☎ *508/627–7141* 🌐 *mvlandbank.com/34great.shtml* 🎟 *Free.*

Long Point Wildlife Refuge. ✉ *Scrubby Neck Rd., Vineyard Haven, MA* ☎ *508/693–7392* 🌐 *www.thetrustees.org/places-to-visit/cape-cod-islands/long-point.html* 🎟 *Free.*

Martha's Vineyard Museum. ✉ *151 Lagoon Pond Rd., Vineyard Haven, MA* ☎ *508/627–4441* 🌐 *www.mvmuseum.org* 🎟 *$18.*

Mystic Aquarium. ✉ *55 Coogan Blvd., Mystic, CT* ☎ *860/572–5955* 🌐 *www.mysticaquarium.org* 🎟 *$35.*

Mystic Seaport Museum. ✉ *75 Greenmanville Ave., Mystic, CT* ☎ *860/572–0711* 🌐 *www.mysticseaport.org* 🎟 *$15*

Old Whaling Church. ✉ *89 Main St., Edgartown, MA* ☎ *508/627–4442* 🌐 *vineyardtrust.org/property/old-whaling-church* 🎟 *Free.*

West Tisbury Congregational Church. ✉ *1051 State Rd., West Tisbury, MA* ☎ *508/693–2842* 🌐 *www.wtcongregationalchurch.org* 🎟 *Free.*

🍴 Restaurants

Art Cliff Diner. [$] *Average main: $11* ✉ *39 Beach Rd., Vineyard Haven, MA* ☎ *508/693–1224* 🌐 *artcliffdiner.com* 🕒 *Closed Wed.*

Black Dog Tavern. [$] *Average main: $18* ✉ *20 Beach St. Extension, Vineyard Haven, MA* ☎ *508/693–9223* 🌐 *www.theblackdog.com.*

Mystic Pizza. [$] *Average main: $14* ✉ *56 W. Main St., Mystic, CT* ☎ *860/536–3700* 🌐 *www.mysticpizza.com.*

Nancy's [$] *Average main: $13* ✉ *29 Lake Ave., Oak Bluffs, MA* ☎ *508/693–0006* 🌐 *www.nancysrestaurant.com.*

The Net Result. [$] *Average main: $12* ✉ *79 Beach Rd., Vineyard Haven, MA* ☎ *508/693–6071* 🌐 *www.mvseafood.com.*

State Road Restaurant. [$] *Average main: $30* ✉ *688 State Rd., West Tisbury, MA* ☎ *508/693–8582* 🌐 *www.stateroadrestaurant.com.*

☕ Coffee and Quick Bites

Back Door Donutes. [$] *Average main: $5* ✉ *1-11 Kennebec Ave., Oak Bluffs, MA* ☎ *508/693–3688* 🌐 *www.backdoordonuts.com* 🕒 *Closed Mon.–Thurs.*

Mad Martha's. [$] *Average main: $10* ✉ *51 Northern Blvd., Newbury, MA* ☎ *978/462–7707*

⊕ madmarthasislandcafe.com ⟳ Closed Mon.

Mocha Motts. $ Average main: $10 ⊠ 10 Circuit Ave., Oak Bluffs, MA ☎ 508/696–1922 ⊕ www.mochamotts.com.

 Hotels

The Beach Plum Inn. $ Rooms from: $250 ⊠ 50 Beach Plum La., Chilmark, MA ☎ 508/645–9454 ⊕ www.beachpluminn. com ◎ Free breakfast.

Harbor View Hotel. $ Rooms from: $300 ⊠ 131 N. Water St., Edgartown, MA ☎ 508/627–7000 ⊕ www.harborviewhotel.com ◎ No meals. ·

Hob Knob. $ Rooms from: $250 ⊠ 128 Main St., Edgartown, MA ☎ 508/627–9510 ⊕ www.hobknob.com ◎ Free breakfast.

 Nightlife

Bad Martha. ⊠ 270 Upper Main St., Edgartown, MA ☎ 508/939–4415 ⊕ www.badmarthabeer.com.

Cardboard Box. ⊠ 6 Circuit Ave., Oak Bluffs, MA ☎ 508/338–2621 ⊕ www.thecardboardbox.com.

Lookout Tavern. ⊠ 8 Seaview Ave., Oak Bluffs, MA ☎ 508/696–9844 ⊕ www.lookoutmv.com.

Offshore Ale Co. ⊠ 30 Kennebec Ave., Oak Bluffs, MA ☎ 508/693–2626 ⊕ www.offshoreale.com.

Raw 19 Oyster Bar. ⊠ 19 Church St., Edgartown, MA ☎ 774/224–0550 ⊕ 19rawoysterbar.com.

Ritz Café. ⊠ 4 Circuit Ave., Oak Bluffs, MA ☎ 508/693–9851 ⊕ www.theritzmv.com.

⊕ **Shopping**

Alley's General Store. ⊠ 1045 State Rd., West Tisbury, MA ☎ 508/693–0088 ⊕ vineyardtrust.org/property/alleys-general-store.

Black Dog General Store. ⊠ 11 Main St., Edgartown, MA ☎ 508/627–6412 ⊕ www.theblackdog.com.

Chilmark General Store. ⊠ 7 State Rd., Chilmark, MA ☎ 508/645–3739 ⊕ chilmarkgeneralstore.com.

Field Gallery & Sculpture Garden. ⊠ 1050 State Rd., West Tisbury, MA ☎ 508/693–5595 ⊕ www.fieldgallery.com.

The Kitchen Porch. ⊠ 14 A St., Edgartown, MA ☎ 508/645–5000 ⊕ www.kitchenporch.com.

Larsen's Fish Market. ⊠ 56 Basin Rd., Chilmark, MA ☎ 508/645–2680 ⊕ www.larsensfishmarket.com.

Morning Glory Farm. ⊠ 120 Meshacket Rd., Edgartown, MA ☎ 508/627–9003 ⊕ morninggloryfarm.com.

⊛ **Activities**

Farm Field Sea. ⊠ 11 Spring St., Vineyard Haven, MA ☎ 508/687–9012 ⊕ www.farmfieldsea.com ⊠ Tours from $135.

Martha's Vineyard Bike Rentals. ⊠ 1 Main St., Edgartown, MA ☎ 800/627–2763 ⊕ www.marthasvineyardbike.com ⊠ Bike rentals from $25.

Newport, RI

72 miles (approx 1½ hours) from Boston, 180 miles (approx. 3½ hours) from New York City.

The Gilded Age left its mark on Newport like nowhere else in America. There are mansions, yachts, and a polo club, not to mention St. Mary's Catholic Church, where Jacqueline Bouvier married then

One of Newport's massive "summer cottages" that were once home to famous families like the Astors and Vanderbilts.

Senator John F. Kennedy in 1953. Yet this coastal Rhode Island city has the everyday charm of a quintessential New England hamlet. Natural scenery is picture-perfect even in winter, and the summer sun makes the shoreline sparkle as it summons weekend visitors for seafood and local brews.

Across the Sakonnet River (really a tidal strait), Newport gives way to more nature in historic Little Compton. The town remains untouched by the past century's urban development, thanks to its isolated perch on Rhode Island's South Coast, where early colonists began settling in 1692, leaving relics for 21st-century explorers to visit.

Planning

GETTING THERE AND BACK
From New York City, Newport is a little more than a three-hour drive, mostly along I–95. It's faster from Boston, just more than an hour into downtown

Newport, the longest stretch on highway MA 24. Either drive will eventually lead to a pinch point as traffic narrows to the bridges onto Aquidneck Island, so avoid peak travel times to save time and make your arrival more enjoyable.

WHEN TO GO
Warm months are gorgeous in this pocket of coastal Rhode Island, where the ocean air cools even the hottest temperatures. Clambakes on the beach and open-air dining and drinking are irresistible. Peak-season visitors should reserve hotel rooms and restaurant tables in advance. You may consider joining a newportFILM Outdoors screening, a Newport Polo tailgate party, or August's famous Newport Jazz Festival. During winter, the 11 Newport Mansions doll up with holiday cheer, as does the rest of the sparkly city.

WHERE TO STAY
Hotels abound in Newport, where seasonal traffic peaks in summer, but still draws lots of travelers in fall, winter,

and spring. On Goat Island, **Gurney's Newport Resort & Marina** is a good choice for Narragansett Bay views, a spa, and good indoor/outdoor dining and drinking options. Regal lodging awaits at **Hotel Viking** and the **Vanderbilt,** both centrally located, and just as sophisticated as when they opened around a century ago. **The Wayfinder** is a cool, newer boutique hotel just north of downtown by Miantonomi Memorial Park.

Day 1

Newport fills out compact Aquidneck Island in Narragansett Bay, so visitors here can enjoy plenty of waterfront leisure time. The city's also been called the "Sailing Capital of the World," and hosted the America's Cup sailing regatta for 50 years, so sights of schooners, cruisers, and yachts here seem as common as cars.

For your first day in town, then, it seems fitting to find a lovely spot for a bite or a drink with a harbor view. Along the main drag that is America's Cup Avenue, settle into the **Mooring Seafood Kitchen & Bar** for a fine meal of chowder, stuffed clams, and Italian dishes, either indoors or on the covered terrace. If you're feeling casual, the **Lobster Shack** on the Long Wharf is the place to grab a lobster roll, fish and chips, and other straight-from-the-bay seafood to enjoy on dockside picnic tables.

As far back 1906, when the first Rolls Royce was introduced, wealthy Americans summering in Newport wanted to cruise its shores—and show off their fancy motor cars. Ocean Drive became the perfect 10-mile loop to do so while cooling off by the water. Today, you can rent your own vintage car or hire a car and driver from **Newport Classic Cars** to tour you along the loop. Or make the journey on two wheels with a bike rental from **Newport Bicycle,** and enjoy the bike lanes along the loop.

If you're feeling indoorsy, the **Newport Art Museum** is a treasure trove of American paintings, prints, drawings, and temporary exhibits. For a unique local history, visit **Touro Synagogue,** America's oldest synagogue, dating to the early 18th century.

By dinnertime, follow Gladys Carr Bollhouse Road across the bay to Goat Island, where you can dine on divine Italian and seafood dishes at indoor/outdoor **Scarpetta,** inside Gurney's Newport Resort. If you're curious about Newport's local craft brews paired with one of the best local raw bars, don't miss friendly **Midtown Oyster Bar,** with a big bar, expansive dining room, and harborside tables. Cap off your evening with a cocktail or glass of champagne at the posh **Roof Deck Bar** at the Vanderbilt, and take in one of the top vistas in town. (Side note: The Vanderbilt also hosts fun mixology classes for hotel guests.)

Day 2

Rise early if you want to catch Newport's brilliant Atlantic sunrise, and head to the Bellevue Historic District for breakfast at no-frills, local's-favorite diner **Annie's on Bellevue.** Fill up on breakfast any time of day, or go right to lunch with lobster mac and cheese, homemade bisque, and other tasty, affordable dishes.

Then set off down Bellevue Avenue on an ever-so-grand tour of **Newport Mansions,** a collection of 11 "summer cottages" built by Gilded Age magnates with names like Vanderbilt, Astor, and Belmont. **The Breakers** is the top draw, and its grounds alone are worth a peek, not to mention its 70-room, Italian Renaissance-style palatial interior. But each mansion has its own personality, and together they are part of the Bellevue Avenue Historic District, a designated National Historic Landmark.

From mansions to a fitting break for afternoon tea. At **One Bellevue** inside the Hotel Viking, chit chat over a proper Victorian tea service on weekends complete with sandwiches, scones, and truffles.

Newport's unique oceanside perch makes it a beachy destination, with access to Atlantic Beach and longer Easton Beach, both sandy havens facing Easton Bay. Bring a towel for sunbathing and swimming, or grab snacks and a pitcher of cold beer at **Flo's Clam Shack** on Wave Avenue.

Then head west for Newport's famous **Cliff Walk,** a 3.5-mile walking trail that begins beside the Chanler Hotel. The walk starts as a paved path flanked by the ocean on one side and mansions on the other. After a mile or so, the 40 Steps staircase invites a climb down to the shore, or just keep walking along the rocky trail for lovely, secluded sea views.

Emerge from the cliffs and return to the comfort of Newport's bay side, where you can head to **The Landing** on Bowens Wharf for open-air bar seating and a long drink menu with local beers and spirits. You can dine there, or zest up your dinner with barbeque at the **Smokehouse,** serving ribs and pulled pork, plus hearty salads and gluten-free dishes. For something different and delicious, duck into **Umi Asian Cuisine** for Newport's top sushi, hibachi, and Asian fusion.

Afterward, head to the speakeasy-style Boom Boom Room, a flirty dance club downstairs at the fancy **Clarke Cooke House.** Or get your groove going at the **Newport Blues Café,** the city's top live-music venue that hosts new and familiar musicians across all genres.

Day 3

Start your Sunday with brunch at **Stoneacre Brasserie,** where you'll find breakfast standards and more adventurous dishes, like braised pork chili verde, seasonal vegetable hash, and a lovely assortment of toasts (ricotta and orange with honey is delightful).

Hop into your car for a half-hour drive up and over the Sakonnet River to check out Little Compton. It doesn't have to be summer to enjoy a walk on South Shore Beach or Briggs Beach, where waves crashing on the rocky shore may send you into full zen mode. This village is all about history, though, so spend time exploring the Little Compton Town Common, a preserved site home to the **United Congregational Church** and Union Cemetery, where the oldest grave dates to 1692.

This isolated spot, believe it or not, has its very own winery. **Carolyn's Sakonnet Vineyard** opened in 1975 on 150 acres of land, and today has its own tasting room to sample award-winning whites, reds, and roses; plus a mercantile to pick up locally made souvenirs.

Recommendations

Sights

The Breakers. ✉ 44 Ochre Point Ave., Newport, RI ☎ 401/847–1000 ⊕ www.newportmansions.org 🎫 $24.

Carolyn's Sakonnet Vineyard. ✉ 162 W. Main Rd., Little Compton, RI ☎ 401/635–8486 ⊕ www.sakonnetwine.com ⊙ Closed Tues. and Wed.

Cliff Walk. ✉ Cliff Walk, Newport, RI ☎ 401/845–5802 ⊕ www.cliffwalk.com 🎫 Free.

Newport Art Museum. ✉ 76 Bellevue Ave., Newport, RI ☎ 401/848–8200 ⊕ www.newportartmuseum.org 🎫 $15 ⊙ Closed Mon.

Newport Mansions. ✉ 424 Bellevue Ave., Newport, RI ☎ 401/847–1000 ⊕ www.newportmansions.org 🎫 $35 combined ticket.

Touro Synagogue. ✉ *85 Touro St., Newport, RI* ☎ *401/847–4794* 🌐 *www.tourosynagogue.org* 🎟 *$12.*

United Congregational Church. ✉ *73 Pelham St., Newport, RI* ☎ *401/619–5109* 🌐 *www.lafargerestorationfund.org* 🎟 *Free.*

🍴 Restaurants

Annie's on Bellevue. [$] *Average main: $9* ✉ *176 Bellevue Ave., Newport, RI* ☎ *401/849–6731* 🌐 *www.anniesnewport.com* 🕒 *No dinner.*

Flo's Clam Shack. [$] *Average main: $20* ✉ *4 Wave Ave., Middletown, RI* ☎ *401/847–8141* 🌐 *www.flosclamshacks.com* 🕒 *Closed Mon.–Wed.*

The Landing. [$] *Average main: $22* ✉ *30 Bowens Wharf, Newport, RI* ☎ *401/847–4514* 🌐 *www.thelandingrestaurantnewport.com.*

Lobster Shack. [$] *Average main: $22* ✉ *150 Long Wharf, Newport, RI* ☎ *401/847–1700* 🌐 *www.newportlobstershack.com* 🕒 *Closed Mon.–Thurs. No dinner.*

Mooring Seafood Kitchen & Bar. [$] *Average main: $40* ✉ *1 Sayers Wharf, Newport, RI* ☎ *401/846–2260* 🌐 *www.mooringrestaurant.com.*

One Belleview. [$] *Average main: $35* ✉ *Hotel Viking, 1 Bellevue Ave., Newport, RI* ☎ *401/848–4824* 🌐 *www.hotelviking.com.*

Scarpetta. [$] *Average main: $35* ✉ *Gurney's Newport Resort & Marina, 1 Goat Island, Newport, RI* ☎ *401/851–3325* 🌐 *www.scarpettarestaurants.com.*

Smokehouse. [$] *Average main: $16* ✉ *31 Scott Wharf, Newport, RI* ☎ *401/848–9800* 🌐 *www.smokehousenewport.com.*

Stoneacre Brasserie. [$] *Average main: $16* ✉ *28 Washington Sq., Newport, RI* ☎ *401/619–7810* 🌐 *www.stoneacrebrasserie.com* 🕒 *No lunch weekdays.*

UMI Asian Cuisine. [$] *Average main: $30* ✉ *82 Broadway, Newport, RI* ☎ *401/846–2100* 🌐 *www.umiasiantogo.com.*

🛏 Hotels

Gurney's Newport Resort & Marina. [$] *Rooms from: $249* ✉ *Goat Island Marina, 1 Goat Island, Newport, RI* ☎ *401/849–2600* 🌐 *www.gurneysresorts.com* 🍽 *No meals.*

Hotel Viking. [$] *Rooms from: $180* ✉ *1 Bellevue Ave., Newport, RI* ☎ *401/847–3300* 🌐 *www.hotelviking.com* 🍽 *No meals.*

The Vanderbilt. [$] *Rooms from: $499* ✉ *41 Mary St., Newport, RI* ☎ *401/846–6200* 🌐 *www.aubergeresorts.com* 🍽 *No meals.*

The Wayfinder Hotel. [$] *Rooms from: $179* ✉ *151 Admiral Kalbfus Rd., Newport, RI* ☎ *401/849–9880* 🌐 *www.thewayfinderhotel.com* 🍽 *No meals.*

🍸 Nightlife

Clarke Cooke House. ✉ *24 Bannister's Wharf, Newport, RI* ☎ *401/849–2900* 🌐 *www.clarkecooke.com.*

Midtown Oyster Bar. ✉ *345 Thames St., Newport, RI* ☎ *401/619–4100* 🌐 *www.midtownoyster.com.*

Newport Blues Café. ✉ *286 Thames St., Newport, RI* ☎ *401/841–5510* 🌐 *www.newportblues.com.*

The Roof Deck. ✉ *The Vanderbilt, 41 Mary St., Newport, RI* ☎ *401/846–6200* 🌐 *www.aubergeresorts.com.*

Activities

Newport Bicycle. ✉ 130 Broadway, Newport, RI ☎ 401/846–0773 ⊕ www.newportbicycleri.com ✉ Bike rentals from $7.

Newport Classic Cars. ✉ 23 America's Cup Ave., Newport, RI ☎ 401/465–1246 ⊕ www.newportclassiccarsri.com ✉ Tours from $40.

Philadelphia, PA

95 miles (approx. 1¾ hours) from New York.

Without Philadelphia, there might not be a United States. The Declaration of Independence was signed here and the city was the young country's first capital. In fact, each year more than 4 million people visit Independence National Historical Park, home to the Liberty Bell, Independence Hall, and Congress Hall. And while history is everywhere in Philadelphia, there's much, much more to the City of Brotherly Love. There's great art like the museums along the Benjamin Franklin Parkway, great food from James Beard–nominated chefs, great cocktails and microbreweries, and great family options like the Franklin Institute and the Philadelphia Zoo.

Planning

GETTING THERE AND BACK
Philadelphia is an incredibly easy city to get to, especially from New York City. Driving will take you less than two hours via I–95 S, which you'll take across the Ben Franklin Bridge into the heart of the city. Parking can be difficult once you're here, so find a spot and leave it. The city is quite walkable, and taxis get you everywhere your feet can't.

INSPIRATION
"The Philly Blunt" is by Philly guys (Reef the Lost Cauze, Johnny Goodtimes, and Violations Greg) about Philly people, places, and things. They interview everyone from politicians and police detectives to restaurateurs and burlesque performers, and their love for, and passion about, the city is infectious.

PIT STOPS
Many people see New Jersey as a corridor between New York and Philly and rarely take the time to explore all the Garden State has to offer. We're going to let you in on a little secret—there's a hidden gem called **Grounds for Sculpture** not far from the NJ Turnpike in Hamilton. This 42-acre sculpture park, museum, and arboretum was founded by Seward Johnson on the site of the former New Jersey State Fairgrounds, and opened to the public in 1992. Johnson is famous for his extremely lifelike bronze sculptures including Portland, Oregon's beloved Umbrella Man (real name "Allow Me").

WHEN TO GO
There's really no bad time to visit Philadelphia, though summer can be hot and humid. To avoid the largest crowds and be assured that all seasonal attractions are open, visit in May–June or September–October. In the spring, the city's cherry blossoms bloom, rival those of Washington, D.C.

WHERE TO STAY
Across the street from City Hall, **The Notary** is located in the historic City Hall Annex. Part of Marriott's Autograph Collection, the brass, copper, and bronze details, as well as the lobby's ceiling and chandelier, are original from 1926. Reading Terminal Market is steps away, as is the historic Wanamaker Building (home to Macy's and the Wanamaker Organ, the world's largest musical instrument) and the iconic Love Park.

The **Philadelphia Marriott Old City** is in the heart of the historic district and it's within walking distance of the Independence Seaport Museum, Independence Hall, the Museum of the American Revolution, and Elfreth's Alley. The on-site Society Commons is the ideal place to unwind after a long day of sightseeing with a handcrafted cocktail.

AKA University City may be a bit removed from Center City, but it's perch across the Schuylkill gives the property awesome 360-degree views of the city in an uberluxury apartment-style setting. While it's just a 15-minute walk to Rittenhouse Square, a Tesla car and driver is available for guests (for a fee) and the property has Philadelphia's highest and largest indoor infinity-style pool.

Day 1

You're hungry to experience what the city has to offer. The best place to start your adventure is **Reading Terminal Market.** It can be a quick stop or long one based on your interest and time; there are 75-minute guided tours on Wednesday and Saturday at 10 am (preregistration required). There are restaurant and homegoods stalls, flowers and plants, international groceries, bakeries, and Pennsylvania Dutch vendors. The market is a great place to satiate your cheesesteak needs (either at **Carmen's** or **Spataro's**) without having to leave Center City, and an ice cream at **Bassetts** is a quintessential part of a market visit.

From the market, you're in a great position to turn your sights on Philly's Museum Mile, also known as the Parkway Museum District. It's here you'll find the **Philadelphia Museum of Art** (and its famous "Rocky Steps"), **Rodin Museum,** and the **Barnes Foundation,** as well as the iconic Boathouse Row (along the river north of the Philadelphia Museum of Art) and LOVE statue in John F. Kennedy Park. If you have kids in tow, the **Franklin**

Institute, Smith Memorial Playground and Playhouse, or **Please Touch Museum** will entertain for hours, and there's always the **Philadelphia Zoo.**

Catercorner to the Barnes Foundation, **Pizzeria Vetri** is helmed by noted Philly chef Marc Vetri. Wood-fired pizza is taken very seriously here, with personal and large pies available in traditional and more adventurous flavors.

There's nightlife options everywhere you look, but **XIX** on the 19th floor of The Bellevue Hotel in City Center West is a great spot for after-dinner drinks. For live music fans, **World Cafe Live** in University City is part of the radio station WXPN-FM, which specializes in contemporary acoustic, independent, and worldbeat sounds.

Day 2

You'll need to be up bright and early on your second day, because you're going to want to explore **Independence National Historical Park,** and an early start means you'll be able to adjust your schedule if one of the special events on the visitor center's daily schedule interests you. It's best if you do a grab and go situation for breakfast, and **High Street on Market,** near Independence Hall, is a great option. They've got breakfast pastries, bagels, and egg sandwiches.

Independence National Historical Park is home to more than 20 sites, including some of the country's most important historic places, so plan to spend an entire day here. Your first stop should be the Independence Visitor Center, where you can buy tickets for tours and pick up maps and brochures. From here you can easily explore the park on your own; in each building a park ranger can answer all your questions. Visitors are required to join a ranger-led tour to see **Independence Hall** (a UNESCO World Heritage site), **Congress Hall,** the **Todd House,** and the **Bishop White House.** Other highlights

A few blocks from the Liberty Bell, the African American Museum is a fresh look at the founding of the nation.

include the **Liberty Bell, Franklin Hall, Carpenters' Hall,** and **Christ Church.**

To save money, consider the **National Constitution Center's** discounted ticket packages bundled with sites outside the INHP's purview, such as the **Museum of the American Revolution** and the **African American Museum.**

When you're ready for a lunch break, Bourse Food Hall is located on Independence Mall. Built in 1895 as a stock exchange, the building now houses an internationally inspired food hall with more than 30 food and retail stalls. You can grab everything from a cup of coffee and a Korean Taco to a Philly cheesesteak or a bottle of bourbon.

Once you've done and seen all you can of Independence Hall National Park, head to **Mission Taqueria** in the Rittenhouse neighborhood. With its neon signs, colorful space, and games like shuffleboard, this is the cool kid on the block. The fresh tacos and margaritas (in numerous flavors) keep the crowds coming, as does happy hour.

Nightlife options are aplenty in Rittenhouse Square, but **The Franklin Bar** (also known as The Franklin Mortgage & Investment Co.) is a cool underground cocktail lounge that will have you feeling in the know while you sip elaborate cocktails. If there's a long wait, check out the more casual upstairs hangout. Nearby, **Chris' Jazz Café** just off of Broad Street, showcases top talent Monday through Saturday evening in an intimate setting.

Day 3

Located on the cobblestone streets of Headhouse Square, **Bloomsday Cafe** offers coffee, interesting egg dishes, and fresh-baked pastry. You can sit a while to enjoy breakfast, or grab your food and coffee to munch on while you walk along the Delaware River on your way to **Penn's Landing.** Here you'll find historic vessels like the world's largest four-masted tall ship, the *Moshulu,* which doubles as a restaurant, and the **Independence Seaport Museum,** which has nautical artifacts, figureheads, and model ships. There's also **Spruce Street Harbor Park** and farther north along the Landing, Race Street Pier and the mixed-use Cherry Street Pier, which all have places for snacking, sipping, and family-friendly recreation. If you make it all the way to Cherry Street Pier (it's about a 15-minute walk), try to see Elfreth's Alley. This cobblestone lane is the country's oldest continuously occupied street; it oozes charm.

When you're ready for lunch, grab a taxi to eat at **Middle Child.** Here you'll find great sandwiches, and if you haven't picked up on it yet, Philly is all about great sandwiches. The So Long Sal—with spicy lemon artichoke spread, Duke's mayo, meat, cheese, and arugula on a Sarcone's roll—is hugely popular, as is the vegan Phoagie.

The bohemian energy that made South Street famous is not as visible as it once was, but the section between Broad and Front Streets still hosts vintage stores, clothing boutiques, bookstores, and record sellers amid chain pharmacies and cell-phone stores. It's worth a look around before you enter **Philadelphia's Magic Gardens,** which features the work of mosaic muralist Isaiah Zagar. Consisting of two indoor galleries and an outdoor sculpture garden, you won't know where to look first in this impressive and immersive visual experience.

If you've worked up an appetite, **Bing Bing Dim Sum** in East Passyunk has funky, unorthodox dim sum like cheesesteak bao buns and corned beef ribs with beet barbecue sauce. There's definitely a "cool kids" vibe here but the food more than makes up for it. Or, on your way out of town, plan a detour to **John's Roast Pork** for a to-go roast pork sandwich; it's another must-do Philly food experience.

Recommendations

 Sights

African American Museum. ⊠ *701 Arch St., Philadelphia, PA* ☎ *215/574–0380* ⊕ *www.aampmuseum.org* ⊠ *$14* ⊙ *Closed Mon. and Tues.*

Barnes Foundation. ⊠ *2025 Benjamin Franklin Pkwy., Philadelphia, PA* ☎ *215/278–7000* ⊕ *www.barnesfoundation.org* ⊠ *$25* ⊙ *Closed Tues.*

Bishop White House. ⊠ *309 Walnut St., Philadelphia, PA* ☎ *215/278–7000* ⊕ *www.nps.gov/inde/planyourvisit/bishopwhitehouse.htm* ⊠ *Free* ⊙ *By tour only.*

Carpenters' Hall. ⊠ *320 Chestnut St., Philadelphia, PA* ☎ *215/925–0167* ⊕ *www.carpentershall.org* ⊠ *$2* ⊙ *Closed Mon.*

Christ Church. ⊠ *20 N. American St., Philadelphia, PA* ☎ *215/922–1695* ⊕ *www.christchurchphila.org.*

Congress Hall. ⊠ *Chestnut St. at 6th St., Philadelphia, PA* ☎ *215/278–7000* ⊕ *www.nps.gov/inde/planyourvisit/congresshall.htm* ⊠ *Free.*

Dolley Todd House. ⊠ *341 Walnut St., Philadelphia, PA* ☎ *215/965–2305* ⊕ *www.nps.gov/inde/planyourvisit/dolleytoddhouse.htm* ⊠ *Free* ⊙ *By tour only.*

Franklin Court. ⊠ *Between Market and Chestnut Sts., Philadelphia, PA* ☎ *215/965–2305* ⊕ *www.nps.gov/inde/planyourvisit/franklincourtcourtyard.htm* ⊠ *Free.*

Franklin Institute. ⊠ *222 N. 20th St., Philadelphia, PA* ☎ *215/448–1200* ⊕ *www.fi.edu* ⊠ *$23.*

Grounds for Sculpture. ⊠ *80 Sculptors Way, Hamilton Township, NJ* ☎ *609/586–0616* ⊕ *www.groundsforsculpture.org* ⊠ *$20.*

Independence Hall. ⊠ *520 Chestnut St., between 5th and 6th Sts., Philadelphia,*

PA ☎ 215/965–2305 ⊕ www.nps.gov/
inde/planyourvisit/independencehall.htm
⊠ Free.

Independence National Historical Park.
⊠ Philadelphia, PA ☎ 215/965–2305
⊕ www.nps.gov/inde/index.htm ⊠ Free.

Independence Seaport Museum. ⊠ 211
S. Christopher Columbus Blvd., Philadelphia, PA ☎ 215/413–8655 ⊕ www.
phillyseaport.org ⊠ $10.

Liberty Bell. ⊠ 526 Market St., Philadelphia, PA ☎ 215/413–8655 ⊕ www.nps.
gov/inde/learn/historyculture/stories-liber-
tybell.htm ⊠ Free.

Museum of the American Revolution. ⊠ 101
S. 3rd St., Philadelphia, PA ☎ 215/253–
6731 ⊕ www.amrevmuseum.org ⊠ $21.

National Constitution Center. ⊠ 525 Arch
St., Philadelphia, PA ☎ 215/409–6700
⊕ www.constitutioncenter.org ⊠ Free.

Philadelphia Museum of Art. ⊠ 2600
Benjamin Franklin Pkwy., Philadelphia, PA
☎ 215/763–8100 ⊕ www.philamuseum.
org ⊠ $25 ⊗ Closed Mon.

Philadelphia's Magic Gardens. ⊠ 1020
South St., Philadelphia, PA ☎ 215/763–
8100 ⊕ www.phillymagicgardens.org ⊠
$2 ⊗ Closed Tues.

Please Touch Museum. ⊠ Memorial
Hall, 4231 Ave. of the Republic, Philadelphia, PA ☎ 215/763–8100 ⊕ www.
pleasetouchmuseum.org ⊠ $20.

Rodin Museum. ⊠ 2151 Benjamin Franklin
Pkwy., Philadelphia, PA ☎ 215/685–7580
⊕ www.rodinmuseum.org ⊠ $12 ⊗
Closed Tues.

Smith Memorial Playground and Playhouse.
⊠ 3500 Reservoir Dr., Philadelphia, PA
☎ 215/76–4325 ⊕ www.smithplayground.
org ⊠ Free ⊗ Closed Mon.

Spruce Street Harbor Park. ⊠ 121 N.
Columbus Blvd., Philadelphia, PA
☎ 215/922–2386 ⊕ www.delawareriver-
waterfront.com ⊠ Free.

🍴 Restaurants

Bing Bing Dim Sum. $ Average main: $22
⊠ 1648 E. Passyunk Ave., Philadelphia,
PA ☎ 215/279–7702 ⊕ www.bingbing-
dimsum.com ⊗ Closed Mon. and Tues.
No lunch.

High Street on Market. $ Average main:
$16 ⊠ 308 Market St., Philadelphia, PA
☎ 215/625–0998 ⊕ www.highstreeton-
market.com.

John's Roast Pork. $ Average main:
$9 ⊠ 14 Snyder Ave., Philadelphia, PA
☎ 215/463–1951 ⊕ www.johnsroastpork.
com ⊗ Closed: Sun. and Mon.

Middle Child. $ Average main: $12 ⊠ 248
S. 11th St., Philadelphia, PA ☎ 267/930–
8344 ⊕ middlechildphilly.com ⊗ Closed
Mon. No dinner.

Mission Taqueria. $ Average main: $10
⊠ 1516 Sansom St., 2nd fl., Philadelphia,
PA ☎ 215/383–1200 ⊕ www.mission-
taqueria.com ⊗ Closed Sun. and Mon.

Pizzeria Vetri. $ Average main: $15
⊠ 1939 Callowhill St., Philadelphia PA
☎ 215/600–2629 ⊕ www.pizzeriavetri.
com.

☕ Coffee and Quick Bites

Bassetts. $ Average main: $6 ⊠ Reading
Terminal Market, 45 N. 12th St., Philadelphia, PA ☎ 215/864–2771 ⊕ www.
bassettsicecream.com.

Bloomsday Cafe. $ Average main: $12
⊠ 414 S. 2nd St., Philadelphia, PA
☎ 267/319–8018 ⊕ www.bloomsdaycafe.
com ⊗ Closed Mon.

Carmen's. $ Average main: $10 ⊠ Reading Terminal Market, 51 N. 12th St.,
Philadelphia, PA ☎ 215/592–7799 ⊕ read-
ingterminalmarket.org.

Spataro's. $ Average main: $6. ⊠ Reading Terminal Market, 51 N. 12th St.,
Philadelphia, PA ☎ 215/925–6833 ⊕ read-
ingterminalmarket.org.

Hotels

AKA University City. $ *Rooms from: $309* ⊠ *Cira Centre South, 2929 Walnut St., Philadelphia, PA* ☎ *215/372–9000* ⊕ *www.stayaka.com/aka-university-city* ⦾ *No meals.*

The Notary. $ *Rooms from: $232* ⊠ *21 N. Juniper St., Philadelphia, PA* ☎ *215/496–3200* ⊕ *www.marriott.com/hotels/travel/ phlak-the-notary-hotel-autograph-collection* ⦾ *No meals.*

Philadelphia Marriott Old City. $ *Rooms from: $186* ⊠ *1 Dock St., Philadelphia, PA* ☎ *215/238–6000* ⊕ *www.marriott.com/ hotels/travel/phlmo-philadelphia-marriott-old-city* ⦾ *No meals.*

Nightlife

Chris' Jazz Café. ⊠ *1421 Sansom St., Philadelphia PA* ☎ *215/922–2317* ⊕ *www. chrisjazzcafe.com.*

The Franklin Bar. ⊠ *112 S. 18th St., Philadelphia, PA* ☎ *267/467–3277* ⊕ *www. thefranklinbar.com.*

World Cafe Live. ⊠ *3025 Walnut St., Philadelphia, PA* ☎ *215/222–1400* ⊕ *www. worldcafelive.com.*

XIX. ⊠ *The Bellevue Hotel, 200 S. Broad St., 19th fl., Philadelphia, PA* ☎ *267/467–3277* ⊕ *www.nineteenrestaurant.com.*

Shopping

Bourse Food Hall. ⊠ *111 S. Independence Mall E, Philadelphia, PA* ⊕ *theboursephilly.com.*

Reading Terminal Market. ⊠ *Reading Terminal Market. 51 N. 12th St., Philadelphia, PA* ☎ *215/922–2317* ⊕ *readingterminalmarket.org.*

Portland and Kennebunk, ME

112 miles (approx. 2 hours) from Boston.

As you cross into Maine from New Hampshire, a sign greets you proudly declaring, "Maine, Welcome Home. The way life should be." That sentiment is hard to argue with if you've spent any time in the Pine Tree State. And we're pretty sure that after you've spent a weekend here, you'll agree.

One of the best places to visit is Maine's largest city: Portland. Though it may be considered small by national standards, its character, spirit, and appeal make it feel much larger. There's plenty to do to fill a few days, or even a week, even if you just spend your time visiting the restaurants, bakeries, craft cocktail bars, and microbreweries. But hey, there's art, culture, history, and outdoor adventures galore here, too.

South of Portland, the Kennebunks—and especially Kennebunkport—provide the complete Maine Coast experience: white-clapboard houses, rocky shorelines, sandy beaches, quaint downtowns, lobster boat-packed harbors, and seafood restaurants of every type.

Planning

GETTING THERE AND BACK

Driving is the best way to get to Portland and Kennebunk. Portland is about a two-hour drive north of Boston via I–495 N and I–95 N; and it's about 40 minutes from Kennebunkport to Portland. An alternate route is the much more scenic Route 1, which takes longer because of the traffic lights and local traffic, but the scenery is worth it.

WHEN TO GO

Visitors are welcome year-round, but note that some attractions and restaurants are open only in high season (Memorial Day to mid-October). Summer is hugely popular, so be sure to book accommodations a few months in advance; the same can be said for the fall when the leaf peepers arrive. Hotel rates drop significantly between Halloween and Thanksgiving when ski season begins.

WHERE TO STAY

Cliff House, between Portland and Kennebunk in the seaside town of Cape Neddick, is a grand old Maine resort that first welcomed guests in 1872. Today it's a modern escape complete with firepits, hiking trails, indoor and outdoor swimming pools, a beautiful luxury spa, and it's own seafood shack. The water views from every ocean facing window makes it feel like you're on a cruise ship.

Part of Marriott's Autograph Collection, the **Press Hotel** occupies the former Gannett Building, which housed the offices and printing plant of the Portland Press Herald, the state's largest newspaper. The property is adorned with nods to its past: a collection of typewriters over the registration, quotes from articles on the walls, Inkwell, the inhouse coffee shop and the fantastic Union restaurant.

Day 1

Today's destination is Kennebunkport and Kennebunk. Stop along the way at **Foster's Cafe,** where lobster plates, steamers, clam chowder, and lobster rolls will fill your bellies and curb your seafood cravings. Even the BBQ options—smoked chicken and ribs sandwiches and platters—will have you licking your fingers.

After lunch, it's time to explore **Nubble Lighthouse.** One of the world's most photographed lighthouses, Nubble sits on a small island just off the tip of the

Cape Neddick. While you can't actually access the lighthouse, there's a small park in front that has parking, informational plaques, benches, and a seasonal visitor center. Carry on to **Perkins Cove** to stretch your legs and breathe in some salty sea air. Do some window shopping at this lower part of Ogunquit village—sea-weathered buildings that were once part of an art school now house shops and restaurants—before you stroll the mile-long Marginal Way, a paved footpath that takes you around a rocky point.

Your final stop of the day (before you eat again—sea air makes you hungry) are the sister cities of Kennebunk and Kennebunkport. Known as the Hamptons of Maine, Kennebunkport has been a resort area since the 19th century and it's here that the Bush family summers. Its sister town, Kennebunk, has its own appeal with a lively shopping district, steepled churches, and fine examples of 18th- and 19th-century brick and clapboard homes. Plus there's plenty of space for walking, swimming, biking, and beaching at the lovely three-mile-long **Goose Rocks Beach.** There are no facilities at the beach, and you will need to pick up a $15 daily permit at the Kennebunkport Town Hall, but besides all that, this stretch of smooth sand is a great place to walk and play, and there are plenty of tidal pools for exploring.

As noted previously, sea air and a day at the beach have been known to spur the appetite, so make haste to the **Boathouse Restaurant** so you can grab a table on the outdoor wraparound deck; it's a great place to watch the sunset, cocktail in hand. The menu features contemporary takes on classic Maine fare as well as perfectly shucked local oysters and hearty clam and corn chowder.

The Casco Bay Bridge winds its way into downtown Portland.

Day 2

You've got a packed day ahead of you, so best to get an early start with a filling breakfast at the **Maine Diner** in Wells. We promise … one look at the 1953 exterior, and you'll start craving diner food. But, don't expect just a greasy spoon, as this place has an award-winning lobster pie, delicious seafood chowder, plenty of fried seafood, and all-day breakfast. Check out the adjacent gift shop, Remember the Maine.

There's so much to do and see in Portland that it's worth spending your one full day here. But first things first, head to the **Casco Bay Ferry Terminal** to buy tickets for the Mailboat Run. Casco Bay is what makes the city such a successful working waterfront, and this tour is a great way to see the bay and it's many islands as passengers, mail, and freight are shuttled to Little Diamond, Great Diamond, Long Island, Cliff Island, and Chebeague Island.

Lunch at **Gilbert's Chowder House** is a classic Maine dining experience with food—fried shrimp, haddock, clam strips, clam cakes—presented on paper places. At the very least get the clam chowder or lobster roll to go.

After lunch, take some time to explore the Old Port. Pop into the **Harbor Fish Market,** a Portland institution since 1968, to find the freshest-of-the-fresh seafood—bubbling lobster tanks and fish, clams, and other shellfish on ice—that can be shipped almost anywhere in the country. When you're done, wander to the right down Custom House Wharf to the **Sea Bags** flagship store. Started in 1999, this local, but nationally known company has been transforming old boat sails into nautical-theme totes and accessories.

Exchange Street, which heads west through the heart of the Old Port, is great for browsing. If you feel like snacking while you walk, **Gelato Fiasco,** just off Exchange on Fore Street, is the place to go for proper Italian gelato and sorbetto.

If your cravings lean more towards baked goods, **Holy Donut** on Exchange Sweet offers sweet and savory potato-based doughnuts that are glazed (maple, pomegranate, coffee brandy) or stuffed (fillings include Maine wild blueberries and bacon cheddar).

Portland Art Museum is home to sea and landscapes by Winslow Homer, Andrew Wyeth, and Edward Hopper. Along the way here you'll pass Monument Square, a lively part of the city that's great for people watching; **Longfellow House and Garden,** the childhood home of poet Henry Wadsworth Longfellow; **Maine College of Art,** whose window displays are always worth checking out; and **Reny's Department Store,** a Maine institution where you'll find things you needed, and didn't know you needed.

You'll need to get an Uber to get to dinner at **Fore Street.** Located in a renovated warehouse at the edge of the Old Port, the daily changing menu reflects the freshest ingredients received that day from Maine's farms and waters. You'll never go wrong with the Maine mussels oven roasted in garlic and almond butter, but plan to book two months in advance if you're coming in July and August; a third of the tables are reserved for walk-ins so you might get lucky.

Portland is a city, so there's plenty of nightlife options. You can grab a beer at **Gritty McDuff's,** Maine's original brewpub, or head to the **Portland Hunt and Alpine Club,** where Scandinavian-inspired small bites and serious craft cocktails are showcased in an intimate alpine-inspired setting. And then there's **Blyth and Burrows,** where the cocktail creations are taken to the next level with unusual ingredients like absinthe foam and blackstrap maple–chipotle syrup.

Day 3

We'd be remiss if we didn't suggest that you start your last day off with breakfast at **Becky's Diner.** The food is cheap, portions are good, and it has that satisfying, old-time-diner quality. Parking is easy, which makes up for the notoriously long lines, that is unless you get their super early or hit it on an off hour.

There are so, so many great places to eat in Portland that you can't possibly try them all in one weekend, but you can sample quite a few on a tour with **Maine Food for Thought Tours.** The carefully curated three-hour walking tour makes five stops in the Old Port visiting restaurants that work to connect the state's people, environment, and economy.

You're probably not hungry, but in case you are, **Highroller Lobster Co.** is worth the stop. Started as a food cart, this high-energy space serves lobster numerous ways—in a roll, on a stick, on a burger, over a salad, or even with your Bloody Mary. If you like condiments, be sure to try one of the sauces (lime mayo, curried ketchup, lobster ghee).

We know that this is your third tour, but with **Lucky Catch Lobster Tour** you get to experience the daily routine of an actual Maine lobsterman. The tour lasts about 1½ hours and any lobsters caught during your trip are available for purchase.

If there's any room left in your stomach, swing by **Micucci Grocery** on India Street on your way out of town for to-go Sicilian pizza slabs. If pizza isn't your thing, but 2020 James Beard Award–nominated chefs are, then hit up the **Palace Diner** in Biddeford on your way back to Boston. Try one of the deluxe sandwiches with applewood bacon, egg, jalapeño, and cheddar, or the fried-chicken sandwich with cabbage slaw and french fries.

Recommendations

Sights

Goose Rocks Beach. ✉ *Dyke Rd. Kennebunkport, ME* ☎ *207/967–3465* 🌐 *www.kporttrust.org/goose-rocks-beach* 🎫 *Free.*

Longfellow House and Garden. ✉ *489 Congress St., Portland, ME* ☎ *207/774–1822* 🌐 *www.mainehistory.org* 🎫 *$15.*

Maine College of Art. ✉ *522 Congress St., Portland, ME* ☎ *880/639–4808* 🌐 *www.meca.edu* 🎫 *Free.*

Nubble Lighthouse. ✉ *Sohier Park Rd., York, ME* ☎ *207/363–1040* 🌐 *www.nubblelight.org* 🎫 *Free.*

Perkins Cove. ✉ *Perkins Cove Rd., Ogunquit, ME* ☎ *No phone* 🎫 *Free.*

Portland Art Museum. ✉ *7 Congress St., Portland, ME* ☎ *207/775–6148* 🌐 *www.portlandmuseum.org* 🎫 *$18* 🕓 *Closed Tues.*

Restaurants

Becky's Diner. [$] *Average main: $8* ✉ *390 Commercial St., Portland, ME* ☎ *207/773–7070* 🌐 *www.beckysdiner.com.*

Boathouse Restaurant. [$] *Average main: $19* ✉ *21 Ocean Ave., Kennebunkport, ME* ☎ *207/967–8223* 🌐 *www.boathouseme.com.*

Fore Street. [$] *Average main: $25* ✉ *288 Fore St., Portland, ME* ☎ *207/775–2717* 🌐 *www.forestreet.biz.*

Foster's Cafe. [$] *Average main: $24* ✉ *5 Axholme Rd., York, ME* ☎ *207/363–3255* 🌐 *www.fostersclambake.com.*

Gilbert's Chowder House. [$] *Average main: 21* ✉ *92 Commercial St., Portland, ME* ☎ *207/871–5636* 🌐 *www.gilbertschowderhouse.com.*

Highroller Lobster Co. [$] *Average main: $21* ✉ *104 Exchange St., Portland, ME* ☎ *207/536–1623* 🌐 *www.highrollerlobster.com.*

Maine Diner. [$] *Average main: $13* ✉ *2265 Post Rd., Wells, ME* ☎ *207/646–4441* 🌐 *www.mainediner.com*

Micucci Grocery. [$] *Average main: $10* ✉ *45 India St., Portland, ME* ☎ *207/775–1854* 🌐 *www.micuccigrocery.com* 🕓 *Closed Sun.*

Palace Diner. [$] *Average main: $12* ✉ *18 Franklin St., Biddeford, ME* ☎ *207/284–0015* 🌐 *www.palacedinerme.com.*

Coffee and Quick Bites

Gelato Fiasco. [$] *Average main: $4* ✉ *74 Maine St., Brunswick, ME* ☎ *207/607–4262* 🌐 *www.gelatofiasco.com* 🕓 *Closed Mon.–Wed.*

Holy Donuts. [$] *Average main: $4* ✉ *398 US-1, Scarborough, ME* ☎ *207/303–0137* 🌐 *www.theholydonut.com.*

Hotels

Cliff House. [$] *Rooms from: $539* ✉ *591 Shore Rd., Cape Neddick, ME* ☎ *207/361–1000* 🌐 *www.cliffhousemaine.com* 🍴 *No meals.*

Press Hotel. [$] *Rooms from: $251* ✉ *119 Exchange St., Portland, ME* ☎ *207/808–8800* 🌐 *www.thepresshotel.com* 🍴 *No meals.*

Nightlife

Blyth and Burrows. ✉ *26 Exchange St., Portland, ME* ☎ *207/613–9070* 🌐 *www.blythandburrows.com.*

Gritty McDuff's. ✉ *396 Fore St., Portland, ME* ☎ *207/772–2739* 🌐 *www.grittys.com.*

Portland Hunt and Alpine Club. ✉ *75 Market St., Portland, ME* ☎ *207/747–4754* 🌐 *www.huntandalpineclub.com.*

Shopping

Harbor Fish Market. ☒ *9 Custom House Wharf, Portland, ME* ☎ *207/775–0251* ⊕ *www.harborfish.com.*

Kittery Outlets. ☒ *375 U.S. 1, Kittery, ME* ☎ *207/439–6548* ⊕ *www.thekitteryoutlets.com.*

Reny's Department Store. ☒ *540 Congress St., Portland, ME* ☎ *207/553–9061* ⊕ *www.renys.com.*

Sea Bags. ☒ *25 Custom House Wharf, Portland, ME* ☎ *207/780–0744* ⊕ *www.seabags.com.*

Activities

Casco Bay Ferry Terminal. ☒ *Maine State Pier, Portland ME* ☎ *207/774–7871* ⊕ *www.cascobaylines.com* ☒ *$7 per person.*

Lucky Catch Lobster Tour. ☒ *170 Commercial St., Portland, ME* ☎ *207/761–0941* ⊕ *www.luckycatch.com* ☒ *Tours from $35 per person.*

Maine Food for Thought Tours. ☒ *110 Marginal Way, Portland, ME* ☎ *207/619–2075* ⊕ *www.mainefoodforthought.com* ☒ *Tours from $80.*

Rehoboth Beach and the Delaware Shore, DE

121 miles (approx 2½ hours) from Washington, D.C.

Time seems to move a little slower when you reach the other side of the Chesapeake Bay Bridge. As you make your way across Maryland's Eastern Shore toward the nearby Delaware beach towns, afternoon seems to elongate to make room for all the crab cakes and beachgoing that are so vital to a no-frills, low-key, honest-to-goodness beach weekend getaway. Though each of the communities

has its own signature—Dewey is the party town, Bethany is family friendly, and Rehoboth is a popular LGBT destination—they all have the most important things in common: the water is sparkling, the beaches are inviting, and the vibes are indisputably good.

Planning

GETTING THERE AND BACK
From Washington, D.C., take U.S. 50 E toward Annapolis and cross the Chesapeake Bay Bridge. Around Wye Mills take MD 404 E and U.S. 113 S.

INSPIRATION
Allow Harry Nilsson's 1971 album *Nilsson Schmilsson* to set the laid-back tone of your beach road trip. You'll complement your preweekend positive energy with the peppy, reality-resetting tempo of "Gotta Get Up," test your lung capacity belting out the chorus of "Without You," and just generally get ready to "Let The Good Times Roll."

PIT STOPS
If you need to stretch your legs, the produce stands that line the roads to the shore make for a great way to grab some fresh strawberries to snack on.

WHERE TO STAY
The **Bellmoor Inn and Spa** creates a luxurious experience for its guests. Amenities here include a spa, pools, and (during the summer season) a shuttle that takes guests directly to the beach and beach chair and umbrella rentals. For a classic beach town charm outfitted with contemporary tastes in mind, try the beautifully renovated **Ocean Glass Inn.** In addition to its regular rooms, it also has cottages available.

If all you need is a homey, welcoming place to crash at night, check out the **Adam's Oceanfront Motel.** It's a charming spot where you'll be just steps from Dewey Beach and easy walking distance from restaurants, bars, and shops.

WHEN TO GO

The summer (Memorial Day through Labor Day) is the most popular time to visit. If you time your visit outside of the summer season, certain shops and restaurants may have limited hours or be closed altogether. The off season does have its charm, including smaller crowds and lower rates. In October, the area holds the annual Sea Witch Festival, featuring live entertainment, food vendors, scavenger hunt, and a costume parade.

Day 1

After white-knuckling it across the Chesapeake Bay Bridge, reward yourself with lunch at **The Narrows Restaurant.** Here you can enjoy a much more relaxing view of the water while dining on their award-winning crab cakes.

After lunch, start making your way toward **Assateague Island National Seashore.** This barrier island is famously home to the wild Assateague horses, though a related herd on the neighboring Chincoteague Island are called Chincoteague ponies because of their relatively diminutive stature. According to local legend, these feral equines are the descendants of horses that survived a shipwreck off the coast of the island. However they got here, seeing these incredible creatures frolicking in the surf is an experience that shouldn't be missed.

For dinner, stop by **Woody's** in Dewey Beach for some low-key comfort food. This beach-adjacent spot is also famous for the crab cakes, so if you missed them at The Narrows, this is your opportunity to sample this Mid-Atlantic staple.

Cap off your evening with some live music at **Bottle & Cork.** This rock and country music bar is a Dewey Beach institution. Over the years, everyone from cover bands to Blondie and Miranda Lambert have taken to the stage of this lively, open-air venue.

Day 2

Start your morning on a healthy note with breakfast at **Greenman Juice Bar & Bistro** in Rehoboth Beach, where you can enjoy your homemade quiche or coconut rice porridge with smashed berries with a fresh juice or smoothie from the comfort of their cozy patio.

Of course, what's a visit to a beach town without hitting the beach itself? It's time to finally sink your toes in the sand and enjoy. Lay back with a good book as the sound of the crashing waves washes over you (figuratively) or dive into the Atlantic and let the literal waves wash over you.

Pause for lunch at Rehoboth's **Back Porch Café,** which is known for its delightfully creative menu and dedication to detail. One of the perks of visiting in the off season is that **Henlopen City Oyster House** opens for lunch. The oysters (as you might expect from the name) are the star of the show here. Whether you like these mollusks fresh, steamed, or fried you're sure to be happy as a … well, you know.

It's time to stretch your legs on the famous Rehoboth Beach Boardwalk. The old-fashioned, wooden boardwalk stretches a mile long and is populated by all manner of shops, restaurants, and beach town classics like **Dolles** saltwater taffy. If you're lucky, you might be able to catch some live music at the Rehoboth Beach Bandstand.

You can still stroll along the boardwalk in the off season, though not as many as the quaint shops and eateries will be open. If you'd like to take a stroll back through time, however, head to the **Rehoboth Beach Museum,** where you can glimpse shipwreck artifacts, vintage swimwear, and an array of items that tell the story of this charming beach city.

It's time to mix things up with a mini getaway to the streets of Paris, courtesy

Wild horses roam the windswept barrier island at Assateague Island National Seashore.

of **La Fable,** a traditional French-style bistro in the heart of downtown Rehoboth. The menu features classic French dishes such as escargot, duck confit, and boeuf bourguignon, all served in an intimate, romantic setting.

Afterward, shift back into beach town mode with a couple of after dinner drinks at **Rehoboth Ale House,** where you'll find an impressive collection of rotating craft beers as well as a menu of delicious craft cocktails.

Day 3

Head to Bethany Beach for breakfast at **The Penguin.** This diner may look unassuming, but the philosophy is anything but. The food here is made with fresh, organic, and locally sourced ingredients. And while it is kiddie friendly, grown-ups still have three different Bloody Marys to choose from.

While the ocean takes center stage in this region, the Atlantic isn't the only game in town. The area is home to canals, ponds, and creeks, as well as the Indian River Bay. Rent a kayak or a stand up paddleboard and explore the bay on your own or sign up with an outfitter like **EcoBay Kayak & SUP** for a guided tour of the bay. If you're visiting when the water's a little too cold, opt for a leisurely hike on the Prickly Pear Trail, an easy 3.5 mile loop that offers views of pine trees, meadows, and the Indian River Bay.

Make the last meal of the weekend a special one and head to **Bluecoast Seafood Grill** for lunch. The seafood is fresh, the dishes are beautifully yet simply prepared, and the wine list has been expertly curated.

Before you start to make your way back across the bay bridge, check out the **DiscoverSea Shipwreck Museum** on Fenwick Island. There you'll be able to explore a collection of artifacts (such as coins, weapons, and a "mermaid") that were recovered from shipwrecks that occurred both in the Mid-Atlantic region and from around the world.

424

Recommendations

Sights

Assateague Island National Seashore.
⊠ 7206 National Seashore La., Berlin,
MD ☎ 410/641–1441 ⊕ www.assa-
teagueisland.com ▨ $30 per vehicle.

DiscoverSea Shipwreck Museum. ⊠ 708
Coastal Hwy., Fenwick Island, DE
☎ 302/539–9366 ⊕ www.discoversea.
com ▨ Free ⊘ Closed Wed.

Rehoboth Beach Museum. ⊠ 229 Rehoboth
Ave., Rehoboth Beach, DE ☎ 302/227–
7310 ⊕ www.rehobothbeachmuseum.
org ▨ $5.

 Restaurants

Back Porch Café. Ⓢ Average main: $38
⊠ 59 Rehoboth Ave., Rehoboth Beach,
DE ☎ 302/227–3674 ⊕ www.backporch-
cafe.com.

Bluecoast Seafood Grill. Ⓢ Average main:
$32 ⊠ 30115 Veterans Way, Rehoboth
Beach, DE ☎ 302/278–7395 ⊕ www.blue-
coastrehoboth.com.

Greenman Juice Bar & Bistro. Ⓢ Average main: $11 ⊠ 12 Wilmington Ave.,
Rehoboth Beach, DE ☎ 302/227–4909
⊕ www.greenmanjuicebar.com ⊘
Closed Mon.–Wed. No dinner.

Henlopen City Oyster House. Ⓢ Average main: $36 ⊠ 50 Wilmington Ave.,
Rehoboth Beach, DE ☎ 302/260–9193
⊕ www.hcoysterhouse.com.

La Fable. Ⓢ Average main: $32 ⊠ 26
Baltimore Ave., Rehoboth Beach, DE
☎ 302/227–8510 ⊕ www.bonjourfable.
com ⊘ Closed Mon.–Wed.

The Narrows Restaurant. Ⓢ Average main:
$32 ⊠ 3023 Kent Narrow Way S, Gra-
sonville, MD ☎ 410/827–8113 ⊕ www.
thenarrowsrestaurant.com.

The Penguin. Ⓢ Average main: $14 ⊠ 105
Garfield Pkwy. Bethany Beach, DE
☎ 302/541–8017 ⊕ www.thepenguin-
bethany.com ⊘ Closed Tues. and Wed.

Woody's. Ⓢ Average main: $21 ⊠ 1904
Coastal Hwy., Dewey Beach, DE
☎ 302/260–9945 ⊕ www.deweybeach-
bar.com.

Hotels

Adam's Oceanfront Motel. Ⓢ Rooms from:
$159 ⊠ 4 Read Ave., Dewey Beach, DE
☎ 302/227–3030 ⊕ www.adamsocean-
front.com ⑩ No meals.

Bellmoor Inn and Spa. Ⓢ Rooms from:
$299 ⊠ 6 Christian St., Rehoboth Beach,
DE ☎ 302/227–5800 ⊕ www.thebell-
moor.com ⑩ Free breakfast.

Ocean Glass Inn. Ⓢ Rooms from: $175
⊠ 37299 Rehoboth Ave., Rehoboth
Beach, DE ☎ 302/227–2844 ⊕ www.
oceanglassinn.com ⑩ Free breakfast.

Ⓨ Nightlife

Bottle & Cork. ⊠ 1807 Hwy. 1, Dewey
Beach, DE ☎ 302/227–7272 ⊕ www.
bottleandcork.com.

Rehoboth Ale House. ⊠ 15 Wilmington
Ave., Rehoboth Beach, DE ☎ 302/278–
7433 ⊕ www.rehobothalehouse.com.

⬠ Shopping

Dolles. ⊠ 1 Rehoboth Ave., Rehoboth
Beach, DE ☎ 302/227–0757 ⊕ www.
dolles-ibachs.com.

⬟ Activities

EcoBay Kayak & SUP. ⊠ 30048 Cedar Neck
Rd., Ocean View, DE ☎ 302/841–2722
⊕ www.ecobaykayak.com ▨ From $45.

Shenandoah Valley, VA

70 miles (approx. 1½ hours) from Washington, D.C.

A veritable paradise awaits just a 1½ hour drive from D.C., where the splendors of Shenandoah National Park embrace laurel-graced trails, rushing waterfalls, and leaf-framed vistas. Nearby, the mystical Shenandoah Valley, with the sinuous Shenandoah River winding through, is a plush, emerald landscape edged by rumpled peaks and sprinkled with historic towns, Civil War sites, apple orchards, wineries, and hiking trails. A Native American legend describes the creation of the Shenandoah Valley as a place where "the morning stars placed the brightest jewels from their crowns in the river." It couldn't be more aptly said.

If you're into hiking, kayaking, wine-tasting, admiring architecture, strolling small towns, and soaking up history, this getaway is for you.

Planning

GETTING THERE AND BACK

This getaway requires a car. Front Royal is about 70 miles west of Washington, D.C., a 1½ hour drive. Front Royal is the gateway town for Shenandoah National Park. You will travel south through the park, via 105-mile Skyline Drive, getting off at Rockfish Gap for Staunton. From there, you'll weave your way up the Shenandoah Valley, on and off I–81, the main artery through the valley. You'll loop back to Front Royal.

WHEN TO GO

Hiking is popular in the national park and kayaking and canoeing are favorite pastimes in the valley in the summer. Be aware that the weather can be hot and humid, however. Fall brings spectacular colors—and lots of people, and Skyline Drive becomes clogged. Spring is pretty, with blooming flowers everywhere. In winter, Skyline Drive can be closed due to snow, and the views aren't as breathtaking, but there will be fewer people.

WHERE TO STAY

The Shenandoah region offers a wide range of accommodations, from camping to luxury hotels. In Shenandoah National Park, your best bet is to camp. If that's not your thing, there are two park lodges, **Skyland** at milepost 41, and **Big Meadows** at milepost 51. Both offer both guestrooms and cabins, as well as dining rooms for meals. In Staunton, the **Stonewall Jackson Hotel** is an old-time favorite, dating from 1924 and beautifully renovated. And farther up the valley, **Massanutten Resort** is a four-season destination, with something for everyone: a bike park, spa, indoor/outdoor waterpark, two golf courses, and petting zoo.

Day 1

When you get to the gateway town of Front Royal, about an hour from the nation's capital, stock up on picnic supplies (if you haven't brought them from home). Feel free to stroll the historic town, perhaps grabbing some rib-sticking waffles, pancakes, or biscuits and sausage at **L'Dee's Pancake House**, a family-owned institution since 1989. Then it's time to hit the park.

Long and narrow, **Shenandoah National Park** essentially drapes over the Blue Ridge, with the 105-mile Skyline Drive teetering along the ridge. Turnouts provide chances to stop and take in classic views of the rolling green Piedmont to one side, the Shenandoah Valley to the other, with rumpled mountains marching off into the distance beyond. Along the way, trails of all lengths and difficulties meander across the landscape. Perennial favorites include the 1½-mile Stony Man Trail, near milepost 39, yielding magnificent views atop a rocky outcrop; and the

Skyline Drive offers one view after another as you make your way through Shenandoah National Park.

4½-mile round-trip White Oak Canyon Trail, at milepost 42.6, with its parade of five waterfalls rushing down the tree-shaded canyon.

Rapidan Camp is President Herbert Hoover's original Camp David, a gathering of rustic, buildings in the middle of the woods, including the president's cabin (known as the Brown House, to distinguish it from the White House). Here you can learn about the history of his Depression-era presidency. The 7½-mile moderate hike, accessed near milepost 53, takes in Big Rock Falls and plenty of spring wildflowers.

Day 2

Have breakfast at the lodge, or enjoy a breakfast-on-the-go if you've packed something from home. Then head out for one last hike, the short and sweet Dark Hollow Falls, at Big Meadows near milepost 50. It's a 1½-mile out and back trail leading to a pretty waterfall. It can

get crowded, but if you're early enough, you should be fine.

From here, it's a two-hour drive to Staunton. If you want to break up the drive with another short hike, the half-mile Blackrock Summit Trail, accessed near milepost 85, leads to a talus slope—a big field of boulders—at the summit, where a 360-degree view takes in a striking mountain-and-valley tableau.

As you come out of the national park, you will be entering the fabled Shenandoah Valley, cradled between the Alleghenies on one side and the Blue Ridge on the other. One of its most prominent communities, Staunton, has won tons of accolades for its small-town charm. Exquisite turn-of-the-20th-century architecture fills five historic neighborhoods, with **Cranberry's Grocery and Eatery** on South New Street dating back to 1830. Some 200 buildings are the handiwork of famed architect T. J. Collins and sons, designed in an eclectic mix of styles: Greek Revival, Queen Anne, Richardsonian, Romanesque, Stick, Tudor, and the list goes on. This once was a major economic and transportation hub, and of course the wealthy needed fashionable places to live. You can take a self-guided walking tour (start with the historic Beverley District in the center of downtown, or join a free tour on Saturday morning sponsored by the Historic Staunton Foundation. Be sure to keep looking up. The details on the rooftops and upper windows are stunning.

Have lunch at **Chicano Boy Taco,** tucked away in a small strip mall. The tacos and burritos are overstuffed with innovative combinations: chorizo and potato, squash with poblano peppers, and sweet potato and black bean.

You could easily spend more time in Staunton. Woodrow Wilson was born here, and the **Woodrow Wilson Presidential Library and Museum** delves into his life and times. An interactive exhibit gives a sense of what soldier life was like in World War I—one of Wilson's legacies. There's also the **Frontier Culture Museum,** providing an interesting look at rural life and culture. You could also admire some of the valley's most beautiful scenery by horse saddle. **Star B Stables,** near Staunton, offers leisurely rides for beginners and experts alike. Or follow the Beerwerks Trail, linking several craft breweries, including **Skipping Rock, Seven Arrows,** and **Queen City.**

Whatever you do, wrap up with dinner at **Blu Point**. You might not expect seafood so far from the coast, but this lauded restaurant blends the Chesapeake with New England, offering fresh takes on fried clam baskets, soft shell crabs, lobster rolls, and so much more.

Top off the evening with a lively play at the **American Shakespeare Center,** presented exactly as Shakespeare would have directed it (including audience participation). The building itself is the world's only replica of London's Blackfriars Playhouse.

Day 3

Kick off the day with a bagel and coffee at **The By & By.** Then take a slow meander up the valley, stopping at sweet little towns, historic sites, and hiking trails along the way. Serendipity is the best map, but here are a few places to consider.

Leaving Staunton, follow Route 42 and U.S. 250 to Harrisonburg. This hilly drive, with sweeping views of the Alleghenies, takes you through the picturesque towns of Bridgewater and Dayton. Stop at **Bluestone Vineyard** to taste at just one of the valley's many wineries; the valley views from here are breathtaking. In Dayton, the **Dayton Market** has local food and craft shops, many purveying Mennonite goods. This is a good place to stock up on picnic supplies.

Now is the perfect chance to get onto the water, with **Shenandoah River Adventures** near Harrisonburg. You'll get equipped with a kayak and paddle and in no time be floating on the Shenandoah River. You can rent canoes and tubes as well.

As you make your way farther up the valley, hop onto U.S. 11 at New Market. This is another scenic detour, passing through more historic towns: Mount Jackson, Edinburg, Woodstock. In Quicksburg, parade floats relive their glory days at the American Celebration on Parade, part of **Shenandoah Caverns.** You'll see a giant American flag made of 5,000 square yards of crushed silk; a mock-up of the U.S. Capitol; and a 20-foot-high banjo-playing pelican. In Mount Jackson watch potato chips being fried up at the **Route 11 Potato Chips Factory.** Near Woodstock, a tower affords fabulous views, including seven bends of the Shenandoah River.

Recommendations

Sights

Bluestone Vineyard. ⊠ *4828 Spring Creek Rd., Bridgewater, VA* ☎ *540/828–0099* ⊕ *www.bluestonevineyard.com* 🎫 *Tastings $9.*

Frontier Culture Museum. ⊠ *1290 Richmond Ave., Staunton, VA* ☎ *540/332–7850* ⊕ *www.frontiermuseum.org* 🎫 *$12.*

Rapidan Camp. ⊠ *Rapidan Fire Rd., Syria, VA* ☎ *540/999–3500* ⊕ *www.nps.gov/shen/learn/historyculture/rapidancamp.htm* 🎫 *$10.*

Route 11 Potato Chips Factory ⊠ *11 Edwards Way, Mt. Jackson, VA* ☎ *540/477–9664* ⊕ *www.rt11.com* 🎫 *Free* ☉ *Closed Sun.*

Shenandoah Caverns. ⊠ *261 Caverns Rd., Quicksburg, VA* ☎ *540/477–3115* ⊕ *www.shenandoahcaverns.com* 🎫 *$25.*

Shenandoah National Park. ⊠ *3655 U.S. 211, Luray, VA* ☎ *540/999–3500* ⊕ *www.nps.gov* 🎫 *$15.*

Woodrow Wilson Presidential Library and Museum. ⊠ *20 N. Coalter St., Staunton, VA* ☎ *540/885–0897* ⊕ *www.woodrow-wilson.org* 🎫 *$15.*

🍴 Restaurants

BLU Point Seafood Co. $ *Average main: $22* ⊠ *123 W. Beverley St., Staunton, VA* ☎ *540/712–0291* ⊕ *www.blupointseafoodco.com* ☉ *No breakfast.*

The By & By. $ *Average main: $6* ⊠ *140 E. Beverley St., Staunton, VA* ☎ *540/887–0041* ⊕ *www.thebyandby.us* ☉ *No dinner Sun.*

L'Dees Pancake House. $ *Average main: $7* ⊠ *522 E. Main St., Front Royal, VA* ☎ *540/635–379* ⊕ *www.ldeespancake-house.com* ☉ *Closed Tues.*

☕ Coffee and Quick Bites

Cranberry's Grocery and Eatery. $ *Average main: $10* ⊠ *7 S. New St., Staunton, VA* ☎ *540/885–4755* ⊕ *www.gocranberrys.com.*

🛏 Hotels

Big Meadows Lodge. $ *Rooms from: $125* ⊠ *Shenandoah National Park, Skyline Dr., Stanley, VA* ☎ *877/847–1919* ⊕ *www.goshenandoah.com* 🍽 *No meals.*

Massanutten Resort. $ *Rooms from: $98* ⊠ *1822 Resort Dr., McGaheysville, VA* ☎ *540/289–9441* ⊕ *www.massresort.com* 🍽 *No meals.*

Skyland. $ *Rooms from: $99* ⊠ *Skyland Upper Loop Mile 41, Luray, VA* ☎ *877/847–1919* ⊕ *www.goshenandoah.com* 🍽 *No meals.*

Stonewall Jackson Hotel. $ *Rooms from: $109* ⊠ *24 S. Market St., Staunton, VA* ☎ *540/885–4848* ⊕ *www.stonewalljacksonhotel.com* 🍽 *No meals.*

🍸 Nightlife

Queen City Brewing. ⊠ *834 Springhill Rd., Staunton, VA* ☎ *540/213–8014* ⊕ *www.qcbrewing.com.*

Seven Arrows. ⊠ *2508 Jefferson Hwy. 1, Waynesboro, VA* ☎ *540/221–6968* ⊕ *www.sevenarrowsbrewing.com.*

Skipping Rock. ⊠ *414 Parkersburg Turnpike, Staunton, VA* ☎ *540/466–5692* ⊕ *www.skippingrockbeer.com.*

🎭 Performing Arts

American Shakespeare Center. ⊠ *10 S. Market St,, Staunton, VA* ☎ *877/682–4236* ⊕ *www.americanshakespearecenter.com* 🎫 *Tours $7* ☉ *Closed Sun.*

Shopping

Dayton Market. ✉ *3105 John Wayland Hwy., Dayton, VA* ☎ *540/879–3801* ⊕ *www.thedaytonmarket.com.*

Activities

Shenandoah River Adventure. ✉ *415 Long Ave., Shenandoah, VA* ☎ *888/309–7222* ⊕ *www.shenandoahriveradventures.com* 🚣 *Canoe rental $25.*

Star B Stables. ✉ *2926 Barterbrook Rd., Staunton, VA* ☎ *540/885–8855* ⊕ *www.starbstables.com* 🐴 *$45 per person.*

Stowe and the Mad River Valley, VT

199 miles (approx. 3 hours) from Boston, 199 miles (approx. 4 hours) from New York City.

Rocky summits swan-dive to valley farms in the Green Mountains, drawing outdoors-lovers and foodies from around New England. Climbing the east flank of Mount Mansfield, which at 4,393 feet is Vermont's tallest peak, Stowe Mountain Resort is the starring attraction. Winter is all about skiing and riding, while summer means biking and hiking. If that doesn't appeal, Stowe is still a New England pinup of a mountain town, complete with a white-steeple church and browsable shops.

From craft beer to cider donuts, local food and drink are a big part of life here; bartenders sport encyclopedic knowledge of obscure breweries. Swimming holes beckon on sunny afternoons, trails spiderweb through the forest, and life is slow. You can get a taste of that Vermont good life on a daytrip to the valley village of Warren, where locals and visitors swap stories on the front porch of an old-fashioned general store.

Planning

GETTING THERE AND BACK

Drive to Stowe from New York City (4 hours), or Boston (3 hours), following I–89 N into the Green Mountains. Public transportation is limited in the area, making a car a necessity.

PIT STOPS

Stop in Vermont's capital city of Montpelier, the smallest state capital in the United States. You can use your cell phone for a self-guided tour of the pretty capitol building.

WHEN TO GO

This is a year-round destination. Summer means hiking, swimming, and boating, while autumn brings brilliant foliage and cool nights. Skiers and snowboarders come for snowy winters, when Mount Mansfield turns into a vertical playground. Spring, known locally as "mud season," is the quietest time of year. (It's muddy and cool enough to keep most visitors away, which means great spa deals in April.)

WHERE TO STAY

A long list of hotels line Mountain Road in Stowe. The **Hob Knob Inn** is a homey, budget-friendly option. (It also welcomes dogs.) For design-focused luxury, opt for **Edson Hill,** set on a property with trails great for hiking and cross-country skiing.

Day 1

Drop your bags and spend the afternoon on the **Stowe Recreation Path,** a mostly flat, 5-mile trail that winds back and forth across the West Branch of Little River. You can rent a bike or just walk, pausing along the way to explore a series of breweries, swim spots, and picnic areas

At the 2.5 mile mark, don't miss **Idletyme Brewing Company,** where a laid-back crowd sips house-brewed craft beers on a sunny deck. The refreshing Dunkel

Although it's a year-round destination, the Mad River Valley looks stunning in winter.

Lager is a perennial favorite, and the dry-hopped Doubletyme double IPA offers an aromatic introduction to Vermont's most celebrated beer style. (On Sunday, this is where the **Stowe Farmers Market** is held, as well.) If you make it all the way to the end of the path, you'll find a classic covered bridge just east of the final trailhead.

For dinner, check out the stylish **Doc Pond's Restaurant and Bar** on Stowe's Mountain Road, where the all-star draft list features some of the most sought-after beers in the state. (Including hard-to-find options from **Hill Farmstead Brewery.**) The gastropub is a favorite with the après-ski and-trail crowd, with a hearty menu whose highlights include confit potatoes, burgers made with local beef, and Vermont's ubiquitous kale salads. Bartenders keep it lively with a lineup of vintage tunes from Doc Pond's impressive record collection.

Day 2

Get an early start for a day of exploring the Mad River Valley. First, follow Route 100 to a sprawl of clapboard buildings in Waterbury Center, where you'll grab morning drinks to-go at **Vermont Artisan Coffee & Tea Company.** Next, continue to **Cold Hollow Cider Mill** 1 mile farther south. That's where breakfast is: the mill is famed for lightly sweet cider donuts made with a splash of the unfiltered juice that's pressed on-site. (In the autumn apple season, you can see the cider being made out back.)

From there, it's another 30 minutes to the historic town of Waitsfield, the rural Mad River Valley's biggest community. Pause to explore shops and galleries along Bridge Street, which leads to the 1833 **Great Eddy Covered Bridge,** one of the oldest covered bridges in Vermont. Underneath the bridge's wooden trusses, the Mad River curls by slow and quiet; when it's hot, the water under the bridge is a popular swim spot.

If you're ready for a hike, stock up on drinks and continue to Burnt Rock Mountain Trail, a 5-mile out-and-back hike along a portion of the Long Trail, the 272-mile footpath that runs the entire length of Vermont. It's steep, but hard work earns huge views from the summit, where the forested trail opens up onto bare rock.

When you make it back to the car, drive 15 minutes south to the dollhouse-sized village of Warren, just a general store, a few artist studios, and a gracious inn. You can pick up sandwiches made-to-order at **The Warren Store,** which also sells everything from maple syrup to mud boots. Take your meal to the front porch, where spandex-clad bikers, local farmers, and travelers mingle in the generous shade. Don't eat too much: the next stop is nearby **Warren Falls,** among the most famous swimming holes in the state, where the Mad River flows through a series of pools and boulders forming a natural playground.

Now, you've earned a leisurely afternoon of meandering back up Route 100 to Stowe. On your way back through Waitsfield, stop for a maple creemee at the **Canteen Creemee Company.** (Creemees are what Vermonters call soft-serve ice cream.) If you'd prefer Vermont apple brandy to maple ice cream, opt instead for the Waitsfield tasting room of **Mad River Distillers,** just across the street.

Dinner is in the bierhall at Austrian-style **Von Trapp Brewing,** part of a sprawling, forested property set high above the valley. Arrive before sunset to stroll the pretty gardens and trails on the property; it's still owned by the Austrian-American Von Trapp family from *The Sound of Music.* In the bierhall, Austrian fare meets Vermont products, and the beef, dairy, and some vegetables come from an on-site organic farm.

Day 3

Catch morning light as you head towards Smuggler's Notch, the narrow pass that winds over the shoulder of Mount Mansfield. The road is so steep and high that it's closed by snow all winter, when the Notch draws cross-country skiers and ice climbers. Pause for a coffee and croissant at **PK Coffee** on Mountain Road, before the route constricts into a narrow ribbon with granite boulders crowding the edges.

Park at the pass for the 2-mile, out-and-back hike to **Sterling Pond,** one of the gentler hikes starting in the steeply graded Notch. (It's justifiably popular, which is why this is a great trail if you started early.)

If you're feeling more ambitious, try tackling the almost-sheer Hell Brook Trail, which you can follow a sweaty 4 miles to the Long Trail and the summit of Mount Mansfield. By the time you make it back down from either hike, you'll be ready for a healthy lunch at the **Green Goddess Café,** which has a colorful selection of hippie-ish sandwiches, salads, and smoothies. (The soup is great on chilly days.)

If you can squeeze in one more outing before heading home, continue a few minutes south on Route 100 to **Waterbury Center State Park,** an access point for gorgeous Waterbury Reservoir. Here, you can rent a canoe, kayak, or stand-up paddleboard from **Umiak Outdoor Outfitters,** to paddle the long, winding arms of the man-made lake. Watch for black-and-white loons here; the reservoir is key habitat for the vulnerable bird species.

Recommendations

Sights

Cold Hollow Cider Mill. ⊠ *3600 Waterbury Stowe Rd., Waterbury Center, VT* ☏ *800/327–7537* ⊕ *www.coldhollow.com* ⊴ *Free.*

Great Eddy Covered Bridge. ⊠ *Bridge St., Waitsfield, VT* ☏ *No phone* ⊕ *www.nps.gov/nr/travel/centralvermont/cv6.htm* ⊴ *Free.*

Sterling Pond. ⊠ *Smugglers' Notch State Park, 6443 Mountain Rd., Burlington, VT* ☏ *802/253–4014* ⊕ *www.vtstateparks.com/smugglers.html* ⊴ *Free.*

Stowe Recreation Path. ⊠ *Main St., Stowe, VT* ☏ *802/253–6148* ⊕ *www.stowerec.org/parks-facilities/rec-paths/stowe-recreation-path* ⊴ *Free.*

Warren Falls. ⊠ *3919 VT 100, Warren, VT* ☏ *No phone* ⊴ *Free.*

Waterbury Center State Park. ⊠ *177 Reservoir Rd., Waterbury Center, VT* ☏ *802/244–1226* ⊕ *www.vtstateparks.com/waterbury.html* ⊴ *$4.*

🍴 Restaurants

Doc Pond's Restaurant and Bar $ *Average main: $18* ⊠ *294 Mountain Rd., Stowe, VT* ☏ *802/760–6066* ⊕ *www.docponds.com* ⊙ *No lunch Mon.–Thurs. No dinner Sun.*

Green Goddess Café. $ *Average main: $9* ⊠ *618 S. Main St., Stowe, VT* ☏ *802/253–525* ⊕ *www.greengoddessvt.com.*

Von Trapp Brewing. $ *Average main: $18* ⊠ *1333 Luce Hill Rd., Stowe, VT* ☏ *802/253–5750* ⊕ *www.vontrappbrewing.com.*

☕ Coffee and Quick Bites

Canteen Creemee Company. $ *Average main: $8* ⊠ *5123 Main St., Waitsfield, VT* ☏ *802/496–6003* ⊕ *www.canteencreemee.com* ⊙ *Closed Mon.–Wed.*

PK Coffee. $ *Average main: $4* ⊠ *1880 Mountain Rd., Stowe, VT* ☏ *802/760–6151.*

Vermont Artisan Coffee & Tea Company. $ *Average main: $4* ⊠ *11 Cabin La., Waterbury Center, VT* ☏ *802/244–8338* ⊕ *www.vtartisan.com* ⊙ *Closed Sun.*

🛏 Hotels

Edson Hill. $ *Rooms from: $300* ⊠ *1500 Edson Hill Rd., Stowe, VT* ☏ *802/253–7371* ⊕ *www.edsonhill.com* ⧌ *Free breakfast.*

Hoib Knob Inn. $ *Rooms from: $100* ⊠ *2364 Mountain Rd., Stowe, VT* ☏ *802/245–8540* ⊕ *www.hobknobinn.com* ⧌ *Free breakfast.*

🍸 Nightlife

Idletyme Brewing Company. ⊠ *1859 Mountain Rd., Stowe, VT* ☏ *802/253–4765* ⊕ *www.idletymebrewing.com.*

Mad River Distillery. ⊠ *89 Mad River, Green Waitsfield, VT* ☏ *802-496-3165* ⊕ *www.madrivertaste.com.*

🛍 Shopping

Hill Farmstead Brewery. ⊠ *403 Hill Rd., Greensboro Bend, VT* ☏ *802/533–7450* ⊕ *www.hillfarmstead.com.*

Stowe Farmers Market. ⊠ *1799 Mountain Rd., Stowe, VT* ☏ *No phone* ⊕ *www.stowefarmersmarket.com.*

The Warren Store. ⊠ *284 Main St., Warren, VT* ☏ *802/496–3864* ⊕ *www.warrenstore.com.*

☃ Activities

Umiak Outdoor Outfitters. ✉ *849 S. Main St., Stowe, VT* ☎ *802/253–2317* ⊕ *www. umiak.com* ⊠ *Tours from $59 per person.*

The White Mountains, NH

133 miles (approx. 2 hours) from Boston, 330 miles (approx. 5 hours) from New York.

Rocky summits stretch high above tree line in the White Mountains of New Hampshire, where outdoorsy visitors and locals chase year-round adventures among New England's most rugged terrain. From summer hiking to winter ski descents of Tuckerman's Ravine, the Whites are a compact mountain playground within driving distance of Boston and New York City. The 6,288-foot Mount Washington is the highest point and the crowning attraction, and clear days on its summit bring views that extend across three states.

The Appalachian Trail threads between Mount Washington and the surrounding peaks, passing remote cabins and lean-tos built by the 144-year-old Appalachian Mountain Club. Back on the valley floor, campgrounds and cozy lodges offer a taste of mountain life, with a small-town atmosphere that persists even through the buzzy—and often busy—summer months.

Planning

GETTING THERE AND BACK

Drive to the White Mountains from Boston (2 hours, 133 miles), following I–93 all the way to Franconia. From New York City (5 hours, 330 miles), take I–95 to I–91 through Vermont; the smaller routes 302 and 117 traverse east to Franconia. As public transportation within the White Mountains is limited, having your own car is essential.

PIT STOPS

On your way from Boston, add a stop at the cheerful tourist town of Laconia, New Hampshire. It's the starting point for cruises across Lake Winnipesaukee, or you can play your way through the **American Classic Arcade Museum,** which claims to be the largest collection of vintage arcade games in the world.

From New York, the Vermont town of Dummerston is home to **Scott Farm Orchard.** It grows more than 130 varieties of heirloom apples and other fruit on a property that once belonged to Rudyard Kipling. You can pick your own in the fall, when there's also cider doughnuts and fresh juice available for purchase.

WHEN TO GO

While summer sunshine draws the biggest crowds, the White Mountains are a year-round destination. Peak fall foliage generally lasts from late September through the second week of October, starting at the highest altitudes and moving downslope. In the winter, ski resorts, backcountry skiing, and ice climbing attract visitors ready to brave the cold.

WHERE TO STAY

About 10 minutes outside of North Conway, the cozy canvas tents of **Huttopia White Mountains** have fire pits, hot showers, and picnic tables at the edge of pretty Iona Lake. Run by the Appalachian Mountain Club, the rustic **Highland Center Lodge** at Crawford Notch offers basic rooms and great access to the high mountains; guests can even borrow from the extensive collection of loaner gear. If rustic isn't your thing, the **Omni Mount Washington Resort** is a grand dame with fascinating history, and staying overnight only betters your odds of seeing the resident royal ghost.

Day 1

Watch the mountains snap shut on the roadside as you approach **Franconia Notch State Park,** whose easily accessible trails are the perfect place to start exploring. Before you tie on the hiking boots, though, pick up lunch to go at **Franconia Coffee House,** choosing from hearty sandwiches named for area summits.

Next, set out on one of Franconia's many approachable walks. One favorite is the 2-mile Flume Gorge Trail, a family-friendly loop hike that squeezes between granite boulders, waterfalls, and mossy cliffs. To get the lay of the land, opt instead for the moderate Mount Pemigewasset Trail to Indian Head, where you'll gain 1,253 feet of elevation over a steep 1.5 miles of walking. The payoff is big: hopscotch across pretty streams and patches of wildflowers, then emerge to sweeping views across the valley.

Whichever hike you choose, cool off with a well-earned dip in nearby **Echo Lake,** whose clear water is framed by mountains on every side. There's a pretty man-made beach with a sheltered swimming area for kids, plus a general store with canoes, kayaks, and pedal boats available for rent. (In the winter, tackle the slopes at Franconia's **Cannon Mountain** ski area instead.)

Before the sun ducks below the skyline, start the 25-minute drive to the 1902 **Omni Mount Washington Resort,** the sole holdout among the grand hotels that used to dot the White Mountains. Staying in the historic rooms is a treat, but you don't have to be a guest to enjoy sunset cocktails or dinner on the gracious back porch, where you'll have unmatched views up Mount Washington's broad western flank.

Day 2

Start the day at **Polly's Pancake Parlor** in Franconia, which grinds flour for pancakes with a stone mill and makes maple syrup on-site. It's a hearty, New Hampshire breakfast fit for a day of exploring **Mount Washington.** Pack a picnic lunch and plenty of layers for your day in the mountains, as lower temperatures and windy conditions at high altitude mean very different weather than you'll find on the valley floor.

You can reach the top by rail, road, or hiking trail. The most unusual way to travel is the **Mount Washington Cog Railway,** a coal- and biodiesel-fired train built in 1869; it's an exciting ride in creaky old railcars, and in some places, the grade steepens to a harrowing 38%.

If you'd rather steer yourself, opt for the seasonal **Mount Washington Auto Road** that switchbacks up the mountain from the east. It's also incredibly steep, climbing 4,600 feet in just over 7 miles, with a GPS-enabled app to point out the key sights and history as you make your way up the narrow curves. (With admission to the private road, you'll also get a "This Car Climbed Mt. Washington" bumper sticker, a New England touchstone.)

The most strenuous way to the summit, of course, is walking. At roughly 9 miles round-trip, the Ammonoosuc Ravine Trail is the quickest way up, with gorgeous views of the summit and the Franconia Range to the west. After emerging above the tree line, the trail passes the Lakes of the Clouds Hut, an Appalachian Mountain Club hut surrounded by icy ponds and alpine flowers. It's possible to stay overnight here with advance reservations; bring cash if you want to buy soup and home-baked treats for lunch.

The fall foliage of the White Mountains dazzles visitors from late September to mid-October.

However, you reach the top, take some time while there to explore the **Mount Washington Observatory,** a weather station whose exhibits showcase the incredibly harsh weather that batters the summit throughout the winter months. (And sometimes in summer.)

When you make it back to the valley floor, continue towards the town of North Conway, which serves as a basecamp for year-round adventures in the surrounding peaks. Dinner is hearty fare on the patio at **May Kelly's Cottage,** an Irish pub where meals range from traditional corned beef and cabbage to quirky bar food. Irish nachos, anyone?

Day 3

Sunday breakfast at the **Stairway Café** in North Conway is a favorite here. If the weather is warm, grab a spot on the upstairs deck to watch the scene on the main road below.

That leaves the rest of the morning for a leisurely drive along the Kancamagus Highway, 35 miles of gorgeously switch-backed road linking the towns of Conway and Lincoln: Call it "the Kanc" for short. While you could rush through in an hour or so, it's worth lingering at a series of swimming, hiking, and photo stops along the way.

Six miles west of Conway, pause to walk the 3-mile Boulder Loop Trail, flanked by interpretive signs highlighting local plants, animals, and geology. Drive 1 mile farther and you'll see Lower Falls, where the Swift River plunges into a natural, rock-lined swimming hole. The highest point along the route is the 2,855 Kanca-magus Pass; from there you'll descend back to Lincoln for lunch at the quirky **Gypsy Café,** whose eclectic menu includes a pulled-duck grilled cheese sandwich and plenty of veggie-rich salads.

Recommendations

Sights

American Classic Arcade Museum. ✉ 579 Endicott St. N, Laconia, NH ☎ 603/393–7903 ⊕ www.classicarcademuseum.org 🎫 Free.

Echo Lake. ✉ 68 Echo Lake Rd., North Conway, NH ☎ 603/356–2672 ⊕ www.nhstateparks.org 🎫 $4.

Franconia Notch State Park. ✉ 260 Tramway Dr., Franconia, NH ☎ 603/823–8800 ⊕ www.nhstateparks.org 🎫 $4.

Mount Washington Auto Road. ✉ Rte. 16, Pinkham Notch, Gorham, NH ☎ 603/466–3988 ⊕ www.mt-washington.com 🎫 $35.

Mount Washington Cog Railway. ✉ 3168 Base Station Rd., Mount Washington, NH ☎ 800/922–8825 ⊕ www.thecog.com 🎫 $58.

Mount Washington Observatory. ✉ Mt. Washington State Park Sherman Adams Visitor Center, 1598 Mt. Washington Auto Rd., Sargent's Purchase, NH ☎ 603/356–2137 ⊕ www.mountwashington.org 🎫 $39.

Mount Washington State Park. ✉ Mt. Washington State Park Sherman Adams Visitor Center, 1598 Mt. Washington Auto Rd., Sargent's Purchase, NH ☎ 603/466–3347 ⊕ www.nhstateparks.org 🎫 $4.

Scott Farm Orchard. ✉ 707 Kipling Rd., Dummerston, VT ☎ 802/254–6868 ⊕ www.scottfarmvermont.com 🎫 $15.

🍴 Restaurants

Franconia Coffee House. 💲 Average main: $12 ✉ 334 Main St., Franconia, NH ☎ 603/823–2142 ⊕ www.franconiacoffeehouse.com ⊗ No dinner.

Gypsy Café. 💲 Average main: $20 ✉ 117 Main St., Lincoln, NH ☎ 603/745–4395 ⊕ www.gypsycaferestaurant.com.

May Kelly's Cottage. 💲 Average main: $18 ✉ 3002 White Mountain Hwy., North Conway, NH ☎ 603/356–7005 ⊕ www.maykellys.com ⊗ Closed Mon.–Wed. No lunch Thurs.

Polly's Pancake Parlor. 💲 Average main: $8 ✉ 672 Rte. 117, Sugar Hill, NH ☎ 603/823–5575 ⊕ www.pollyspancakeparlor.com ⊗ Closed Tues. and Wed. No dinner.

Stairway Café. 💲 Average main: $14 ✉ 2649 White Mountain Hwy. North Conway, NH ☎ 603/356–5200 ⊕ www.stairwaycafe.com ⊗ No dinner.

🛏 Hotels

Highland Center Lodge. 💲 Rooms from: $102 ✉ White Mountain National Forest, U.S. 302, Bretton Woods, NH ☎ 603/466–2822 ⊕ www.outdoors.org ⍾ No meals.

Huttopia White Mountains. 💲 Rooms from: $149 ✉ 57 Pine Knoll Rd., Albany, NH ☎ 603/466–2822 ⊕ www.canada-usa.huttopia.com/en/site/white-mountains ⍾ No meals.

Omni Mount Washington Resort. 💲 Rooms from: $278 ✉ 310 Mount Washington Hotel Rd., Bretton Woods, NH ☎ 603/278–1000 ⊕ www.omnihotels.com ⍾ No meals.

🏃 Activities

Cannon Mountain. ✉ 260 Tramway Dr., Franconia, NH ☎ 603/823–8800 ⊕ www.cannonmt.com 🎫 $4.

Index

Photo Credits

Fodor's BEST WEEKEND ROAD TRIPS

Publisher: Stephen Horowitz, *General Manager*

Editorial: Douglas Stallings, *Editorial Director*; Jill Fergus, Jacinta O'Halloran, Amanda Sadlowski, *Senior Editors*; Kayla Becker, Alexis Kelly, Rachael Roth, *Editors*

Design: Tina Malaney, *Director of Design and Production*; Jessica Gonzalez, *Graphic Designer*; Mariana Tabares, *Design and Production Intern*

Production: Jennifer DePrima, *Editorial Production Manager*; Elyse Rozelle, *Senior Production Editor*; Monica White, *Production Editor*

Maps: Rebecca Baer, *Senior Map Editor*; Mark Stroud (Moon Street Cartography), *Cartographer*

Photography: Viviane Teles, *Senior Photo Editor*; Namrata Aggarwal, Ashok Kumar, Carl Yu, *Photo Editors*; Rebecca Rimmer, *Photo Intern*

Business and Operations: Chuck Hoover, *Chief Marketing Officer*; Robert Ames, *Group General Manager*; Devin Duckworth, *Director of Print Publishing*; Victor Bernal, *Business Analyst*

Public Relations and Marketing: Joe Ewaskiw, *Senior Director Communications and Public Relations*

Fodors.com: Jeremy Tarr, *Editorial Director*; Rachael Levitt, *Managing Editor*

Technology: Jon Atkinson, *Director of Technology*; Rudresh Teotia, *Lead Developer*; Jacob Ashpis, *Content Operations Manager*

Editors: Doug Stallings, Mark Sullivan

Production Editors: Elyse Rozelle, Monica White

1st edition

ISBN 978–1–64097–420–3

ISSN 2692–4137

SPECIAL SALES

This book is available at special discounts for bulk purchases for sales promotions or premiums. For more information, e-mail SpecialMarkets@fodors.com.

PRINTED IN CANADA

10 9 8 7 6 5 4 3 2 1

About Our Writers

Kristy Alpert (Hot Springs, AK; Ozarks, MO)

Kayla Becker (Florida's Emerald Coast, FL; Olympic Peninsula, WA)

Kelsy Chauvin (Charleston, SC; Jackson and Yellowstone National Park, WY; Kansas City, MO; Oklahoma City, OK; Omaha, NE; Newport, RI; Sioux Falls, SD)

Cheryl Crabtree (Sequoia and Kings Canyon National Parks, CA)

Chantel Delulio (Santa Barbara, CA; Monterey Bay, CA; Napa Valley, CA; Rehoboth Beach and the Delaware Shore, DE; San Luis Obispo, CA)

Jennifer DePrima (Raleigh-Durham and Central North Carolina, NC)

Kaelin Dodge (Louisville and Bourbon Country, KY; St. Augustine, FL)

Caroline Eubanks (Oxford, MS; Chattanooga, TN)

Audrey Farnsworth (Las Vegas, NV; Palm Springs, CA; San Diego, CA)

Jill Fergus (Bar Harbor, ME)

Kristine Hansen (Ann Arbor and Grand Rapids, MI; Door County, WI; Duluth, MN; Galena, IL; Fort Myers, FL; Grand Marais and Isle Royale National Park, MN; Madison, WI; Milwaukee, WI; Springfield, IL; Traverse City and Michigan Wine Country, MI)

Alexis Kelly (Cape Cod, MA; Philadelphia, PA; Portland and Kennebunk, ME)

Barbara Noe Kennedy (Annapolis and the Eastern Shore, MD; Charlottesville, VA; Fredericksburg, VA; Humboldt County, CA; Lancaster and Pennsylvania Dutch Country, PA; Hilton Head, SC; Savannah and Tybee Island, GA; Shenandoah Valley, VA; Yosemite National Park, CA)

Stratton Lawrence (Myrtle Beach, SC)

Rachael Levitt (Austin, TX)

Laurie Lyons (San Antonio, TX; South Padre Island, TX; Texas Hill Country, TX)

Teddy Minford (The Hamptons and Montauk, NY; Mendocino, CA; Sun Valley, ID)

Lauren Monitz (Breckenridge, CO; Durango, CO; Estes Park and Rocky Mountain National Park, CO; Grand Junction, CO; Lake Tahoe, CA; Moab, UT; Santa Fe and Taos, NM)

Jacinta O'Halloran (Martha's Vineyard, MA)

Shoshi Parks (Carlsbad Canyons, NM)

Rachael Roth (The Berkshires, MA; The Catskills, NY; Nashville, TN)

Amanda Sadlowski (Hudson Valley, NY; Jersey Shore, NJ)

Kristan Schiller (Cincinnati, OH; Cleveland, OH; Columbus, IN; Dubuque, IA; Pittsburgh, PA)

Brandon Schultz (Rapid City, SD; Sarasota, FL)

Jenn Rose Smith (Bisbee and Tombstone, AZ; Grand Canyon, AZ; St. George and Zion National Park, UT; Sedona, AZ; Stowe and the Mad River Valley, VT; White Mountains, NH; White Sands, NM; Tucson, AZ)

Douglas Stallings (Montgomery, AL)

Jesse Tabit (Big Bear Lake, CA; Greenbrier Valley, WV; Harper's Ferry, WV)

Cameron Todd (Asheville, NC; Colorado Springs, CO; Lafayette and Cajun Country, LA; Outer Banks, NC; Wilmington, NC)

Naomi Tomky (Leavenworth, WA; Long Beach, WA to Cannon Beach, OR; Portland, OR; Walla Walla and Wine Country, WA; Whidbey and San Juan Islands, WA; Yakima Valley and Mount Rainier, WA)

Stefanie Waldek (Great Basin National Park, NV; Park City, UT; Waco, TX)

Terry Ward (Palm Beaches, FL)